P9-CIT-279

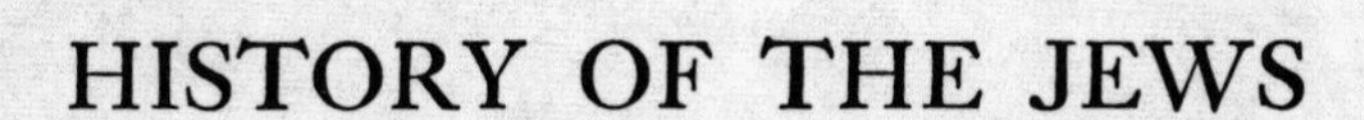

HISTORY OF THE JEWS

HISTORY OF THE JEWS

BY

HEINRICH GRAETZ

VOL. VI

CONTAINING A MEMOIR OF THE AUTHOR BY DR. PHILIP BLOCH
A CHRONOLOGICAL TABLE OF JEWISH HISTORY
AN INDEX TO THE WHOLE WORK

PHILADELPHIA
THE JEWISH PUBLICATION SOCIETY OF AMERICA
5717–1956

PRINTED IN THE UNITED STATES OF AMERICA

PREFACE TO THE INDEX VOLUME.

WITH the Index Volume, the *Jewish Publication Society of America* brings to a close the American edition of the "History of the Jews" by Professor H. Graetz. A glance at the title-page and the table of contents will show, that the celebrated historian cannot be held directly responsible for anything this volume contains. The History proper, as abridged under the direction of the author and translated into English from the eleven volume German edition, is complete in five volumes. In compiling this additional volume, the Publication Committee was prompted by the desire to render the work readily available for pedagogical purposes. To be of value to the general reader as well as to the scholar, a work containing upwards of three thousand pages needs to be equipped with indexes, tables, and helps of various kinds.

The importance of indexes can hardly be overestimated. The English jurist and writer who considered them so essential that he "proposed to bring a Bill into Parliament to deprive an author who publishes a book without an Index of the privilege of copyright" was not too emphatic. In books of facts, such as histories, indexes are indispensable. This has been fully recognized in

the Society's edition of Graetz's "History of the Jews." Each of the five volumes, as it appeared, was furnished with an adequate index. Yet there are two reasons justifying and even requiring the compilation of a general index to the whole work. The first is the reader's convenience. All who use books to any extent know the annoyance of taking volume after volume from the shelf to find the desired information only in the last. In fact, the separate indexes were compiled only because circumstances compelled the publication of the single volumes at rather long intervals. The other consideration is that Professor Graetz is the historiographer *par excellence* of the Jews. His work, at present the authority upon the subject of Jewish history, bids fair to hold its pre-eminent position for some time, perhaps decades. A comprehensive index to his work is, therefore, at the same time an index to the facts of Jewish history approximately as accepted by contemporary scholars—a sufficient reason for its existence.

To make it a worthy guide to Jewish history in general, the index necessarily had to be more than a mere compilation of the five separate indexes. In the matter of the names of persons and places, accordingly, the general index excels the others in the fullness and completeness of the references. But its chief title to superiority over them lies in its character as an Index of Subjects, illustrated by such captions as *Blood Accusation; Conversions, forced; Coins; Emancipation of the*

Jews; Bulls, Papal; Apostasy and *Apostates; Messiah* and *Messianic; Bible* under the headings *Law, Old Testament, Pentateuch, Scriptures, Septuagint, Translations,* and *Vulgate; Education* under the headings, *Colleges, Rabbinical* and *Talmudical, Law, Schools, Talmud,* and *Talmud Torah.* These summaries will be suggestive, it is hoped, to the teacher of Jewish history and to the student with sufficient devotion to the subject to pursue it topically and pragmatically as well as in its chronologic sequence. As an illustration of what use may be made of it, the compiler has prefixed to the index a guide to the study of Jewish history by means of the biographies of its great men, an apostolical succession, as it were. Under the class-names there given, the names of all persons of each class will be found grouped in the index. Again, if it is desirable to trace out a topic, as, for instance, the development of Hebrew grammar, or the cultivation of medicine among Jews, etc., the index is helpful by means of its lists of names of grammarians, physicians, astronomers, historians, poets, etc., under these and similar heads.

To facilitate its use, the student is urged to read the directions preceding the index. Great difficulties attach to the systematic arrangement of the names of persons connected with ancient and mediæval history of all kinds. In Jewish history, even down to recent times, these difficulties are largely increased by the comparatively late introduction among Jews of family names in the accepted

modern sense, and by their introduction among Spanish Jews earlier than among the others. The scheme adopted by Zedner, in his British Museum catalogue, has been followed as far as the peculiarities of our author and his subject, and its presentation in a modern language, permitted it. The arrangement is not ideal, but every effort has been made to minimize the difficulties.

In this preface, precedence has been given to the index, because, in spite of the consensus of opinions among connoisseurs, the importance of indexes and their usefulness are in some quarters still held to stand in need of vindication. In the book, however, the first place is occupied by a contribution whose value will be disputed by none, namely, the Memoir of the author, the greatest historian of the Jews. The Committee believes, not only that the public has a taste for biographical studies, but that in this instance it will be pleased with the choice of biographer, Dr. Philipp Bloch, rabbi of Posen, a disciple of Graetz and for more than a quarter of a century his intimate friend. Although not quite seven years have elapsed since Graetz passed away, and many that were closely associated with him are still among the living, it was not easy to find the man qualified for the task of writing his biography. Graetz was not inclined to be communicative about his early life or his emotional experiences. He had met with disappointments that emphasized the reticence of his nature. The venerable wife of the deceased historian was kind enough to put all her

husband's literary remains at the disposal of the biographer, who herewith acknowledges his deep obligation to her for the help thus afforded his work. The greater part of material of this kind, especially in the form of letters, Graetz burnt before his last change of residence. But his interesting diary was spared. It was kept with more or less regularity from 1832 to 1854, though for the latter part of this period it is hardly more than a bald summary of events, and the disappearance of loose leaves curtails the information that might have been gathered from it. The biographer's thanks are due also to the Board of Curators of the Fränkel Bequests for kindly putting at his service the documents in their archives bearing on Graetz's connection with the Breslau Jewish Theological Seminary, thus enabling him to verify facts long in his possession. Dr. Bloch furthermore availed himself of Dr. B. Rippner's interesting brochure, "Zum siebzigsten Geburtstage des Professors Dr. Heinrich Graetz," and of Professor Dr. David Kaufmann's eloquent eulogy of his teacher, "H. Graetz, der Historiograph des Judenthums." The Committee believes, that in securing the co-operation of Dr. Bloch it has been the instrument of eliciting an important original contribution to Jewish biographical literature.

The Chronological Table is another feature of the volume to which attention must be called. In the eighth volume of the German edition of the "History," Professor Graetz introduced a similar

table, reciting the succession of events from the Maccabæan struggle to the Expulsion of the Jews from Spain and Portugal. The present analysis includes the whole of Jewish history up to the year 1873 of this era. It assumes to be nothing more than a summary of the "History of the Jews" by Graetz. As no attempt has been made to indicate whether his conclusions are endorsed by the scholars of our day, it becomes a duty to refer to the vexed question of Biblical chronology. Since the time of Archbishop Ussher (1580–1656)—not to mention the Talmudic *Seder Olam Rabba*—it has been the subject of dispute, which is complicated by the various eras, the Seleucidæan, the Roman, and the Era of the World, in use among the Jews at different times. Even now the most diversified opinions are held by scholars, and no system has met with general acceptance. Graetz discusses the matter exhaustively in Note 19 of Vol. I of the German original of his "History." His researches led him to oppose the results of the historians Niebuhr, Ewald, and Movers, and of the Assyriologists Brandes, Smith, and Schrader. He inclines to the views of Oppert, who applied the information derived from the Assyrian inscriptions to the vindication of the Biblical chronology nearly as determined by Ussher. Since Graetz wrote his note (1873), almost amounting to a treatise, evidence for the one or the other opinion has been strengthened or invalidated by the more minute and extended study of the monuments, inscriptions, and other

records of Egypt, Babylonia, and Assyria. The reader interested in the subject is referred to the works of such scholars as Duncker, Oppert, Kamphausen, and Eduard Meyer.

Finally, it is hoped, that the four maps accompanying the Index Volume will meet with favor and frequent use. They have been inserted in a pocket and not bound with the book, so that they may be removed readily for reference in connection with any volume the student may be reading. The two maps of Palestine and that of the Semitic World are reproduced, with modifications, from Professor George Adam Smith's forthcoming Bible Atlas. The one of the Jewish-Mahometan World was made for the Society by Mr. J. G. Bartholomew of the Edinburgh Geographical Institute, the cartographer who drew the other three maps. The maps of the Jewish-Mahometan World and the Semitic World are general reference maps; the two of Palestine represent the political divisions of the land, the one at the time of the Judges, the other at the time of Herod the Great.

The Committee expresses the hope that this sixth volume, an epitome of Jewish history, may "manifest its treasures," "facilitate the knowledge of those who seek it, and invite them to make application thereof."

March, 1898.

records of Egypt, Babylonia, and Assyria. The reader interested in the subject is referred to the works of such scholars as Duncker, Oppert, Kampffmeyer, and Eduard Meyer.

Finally, it is hoped, that the four maps accompanying the Index Volume will meet with favor and frequent use. They have been inserted in a pocket and not bound with the book, so that they may be removed readily for reference in connection with any volume the student may be reading. The two maps of Palestine and that of the Semitic World are reproduced with modifications from Professor George Adam Smith's forthcoming Bible Atlas. The one of the Jewish-Mahometan World was made for the Society by Mr. J. G. Bartholomew of the Edinburgh Geographical Institute, the cartographer who drew the other three maps. The maps of the Jewish-Mahometan World and the Semitic World are general reference maps; the two of Palestine represent the political divisions of the land, the one at the time of the Judges, the other at the time of Herod the Great.

The Committee expresses the hope that this sixth volume, an epitome of Jewish history, may "manifest its treasures, facilitate the knowledge of those who seek it, and invite them to make application thereof."

CONTENTS.

MEMOIR OF HEINRICH GRAETZ 1

TABLES OF JEWISH HISTORY.

Chronological Table 89

Table of the Kings of Judah and Israel 127

Table of the High Priests (from the Captivity to the Dispersion) 128

Genealogical Table of the Hasmonæan Dynasty . 130

Genealogical Table of the Herodian Dynasty . . 134

INDEX.

Index to the whole work 139

CONTENTS

MEMOIR OF HEINRICH GRAETZ.

HISTORY OF THE JEWS.

MEMOIR OF HEINRICH GRAETZ.

I.

YOUTH.

The disruption and final partition of the Polish kingdom by its three neighboring states occurred in 1795. With its dissolution a new era began in the history of the numerous Jewish communities in that part of the Polish territory which passed under Prussian and Austrian sovereignty. The event that thus ushered them into the world of Western civilization may justly be considered as marking for them the transition from the middle ages to modern times. Prussia allowed no interval to elapse between the act of taking possession of her newly acquired domain and its organization. It was incorporated into the state as the provinces of South Prussia and New East Prussia. But after 1815 the Prussian crown remained in possession only of the Grand Duchy, or the Province, of Posen, the district that had constituted the kernel of Great Poland. This piece of land was of extreme importance to the Jews, being the home of the most numerous, the oldest, and the most respectable congregations. It was situated at only a short distance from the Prussian capital, to which it appeared to have been brought still nearer by the organic connection established with the older parts of the state. It was natural to expect that, in consequence of the political union, the economic rela-

tions with Berlin, always close, would become more intimate and more numerous, and would develop new business advantages. On the other hand, the capital was viewed with distrust as the home of the movement radiating from Mendelssohn and his school, which aimed at something beyond the one-sided Talmud study then prevalent, and strove to bring modern methods of education and modern science within reach of the younger generation.

The rigorous system of organization by which the Polish districts were placed upon a Prussian basis induced so radical a transformation of all the relations of life that the Jews experienced great difficulty in adjusting themselves to the new order of things. Opposition to the state authorities and the economic conditions was futile ; there was nothing for it but to try to adapt oneself without ado. By way of compensation, the efforts to keep religious practices and traditional customs pure, untouched by alien and suspicious influences, in the grooves worn by ancient habit, were all the more strenuous. Talmudic literature was to continue to be the center and aim of all study and science, and religious forms, or habits regarded as religious forms, were not to lose an iota of their rigidity and predominance. The urgent charge of the Prussian government to provide properly equipped schools to instruct and educate the young in a manner in keeping with the spirit of the times was evaded, now by subterfuges, now by promises. But in the long run the influences of the age could not fail to make themselves felt. Sparks from the hearth of the emancipation movement were carried into the Province, and burst into flame in one of the great congregations, that of the city of Posen, particularly proud and jealous of the Talmudic renown and the hoary piety of its Ghetto.

The position of rabbi in Posen had become vacant, and in 1802 it was proposed to fill it with

Samuel ben Moses Pinchas from distant Tarnopol, the brother of the deceased rabbi. He was the author of בית שמואל אחרון, and an arch-Talmudist of the old stamp. Under the shelter of assumed names, a number of the younger men ventured to send the government a protest against the choice of an "uncouth *Polack*." It was alleged that the mass of the people favored him on account of

"the Kabbalistic fable which constructs a genealogy for this Podolian that makes it appear that he belongs to the stock from which the Jewish Messiah is to spring, etc."

The government took the petition into consideration, and so informed the signers. On account of the fictitious names the answer went astray. Instead of reaching the petitioners, it fell into the hands of the directors of the congregation and into those of the deputy rabbis, the *B'ne Yeshiba*.

"They immediately assembled all so-called scholars and Talmud disciples after the manner of the ancient Synhedrin, and invited the parents, parents-in-law, and relatives of all persons suspected of harboring heterodox ideas. Then they summoned each of us singly, put him into the center of a terrifying circle of rough students, and upbraided him in the following words, accompanied by the most awful curses: 'Thou devilish soul that hast vowed thyself unto Satan! Thy appearance gives evidence of thy antipathy to our statutes; thy shaved beard, thy apparel (thy Jewish garb is only a sham), everything proves thee, thou impious one, a betrayer of Jewish mysteries to Christians. Thou readest German books. Instead of holy Talmud folios, thou keepest maps, journals, and other heathenish writings concealed in thy attic. Therefore, confess thy sin, that thou art one of the authors of the accursed memorial! Do penance as we shall direct. Deliver up to us thy unclean books immediately. Subscribe without delay to this sacred election of our rabbi; else, etc., etc.'"[1]

The hotly contested election of the rigidly Talmudic yet none the less gentle rabbi was carried, but no effort availed to check the spread of the new spirit. Steadily though slowly modern views gained the upper hand, and in 1816 a Jewish private school

[1] The above quotations are extracts from the original document: *Geheimes Staatsarchiv Berlin, General Direktorium Südpreussen, Ortschaften*, No. 964, Vol. II.

of somewhat advanced standing was successfully established in Posen. Now and again men of independent fortune mustered up courage to send their children to the *Gymnasium* or to the higher Christian schools, of which, to be sure, not a large number existed at the time. In 1824 the state interfered, and ordered the establishment of German elementary schools in all the Jewish communities of the Province giving evidence of vitality. The situation now assumed a peculiar aspect. General culture, acquaintance with the classic literature of Germany, France, and England, came to be esteemed an accomplishment and a personal charm; yet beyond the three R's the rising generation was not given the opportunity of acquiring a general education. On the contrary, the desire was to limit study to that of rabbinic and Hebrew writings. In the larger communities, like Posen and Lissa, the centers of Talmud study, a conscious effort was made to frighten off young people, especially Talmud disciples, from the acquisition of secular culture. It should be mentioned, however, that in many of the smaller communities the longing for education was encouraged as much as possible. So it came about that the highly endowed, ambitious spirits of that generation in the Province had to struggle most bitterly and painfully to make headway. But their hardships were counterbalanced by the advantages they derived from the conflict. Their intellectual energy and self-reliance came forth from the contest steeled. Impregnated as almost all of them were with the spirit of the Talmud, they had pierced to its essence, and, filled with enthusiasm for the rabbinical heroes, they had breathed in devotion to the ideals of Judaism.

This was the soil upon which Heinrich Graetz grew up, and such were the conditions and agencies moulding the development of a man destined to

create an historical work, at once monumental and popular; embracing thousands of years, the most widely separated regions, and the most diversified fields of human activity; retracing with all the resources of learning and ingenuity the magic, faded, illegible characters of the evolution of Judaism, and illuminating them with colors of fairy-like brilliance;—an historical work, which, by reason of the warmth of its narrative style, has come to be a book of edification, in the best sense of the word, unto the author's brethren-in-faith.

Heinrich Hirsch Graetz was born October 31 (Cheshwan 21), 1817, in Xions (pronounced Kshons), a wretched little village of 775 inhabitants in the eastern part of the Province of Posen. In a family of two brothers and one sister he was the first-born. His father, Jacob Graetz, was a man of tall stature, who, dying in 1876, reached an age of over ninety years. His mother, Vogel, of the family of Hirsch of Wollstein, was of average height and robust physique, with lustrous gray eyes. She died in 1848 only fifty odd years old. To her the son showed most resemblance, both spiritually and physically. A little butcher-shop yielded them an honest but paltry livelihood. In the hope of improving their material condition, the family removed to Zerkow, a few miles off, some years after Heinrich's birth. At the time the village contained not more than 800 inhabitants, among them a single person able to read, a real estate owner, to whom all letters were carried to be deciphered on the open street in solemn public assembly.[1] But the Jewish congregation consisted of one hundred members, and a remarkable increase in the population of the little town seemed to give fair promise of a prosperous future. It is worthy of mention, besides, that the scenery of Zerkow, wreathed round with

[1] Wuttke, *Städtebuch des Landes Posen,* p. 434.

hill and stream, forest and meadow, is not so flat and unattractive as that of most parts of the Province.

Here the boy received his first impressions, and here he enjoyed his first instruction in a school distinguishable from a genuine *Cheder* only inasmuch as it began in a measure to accommodate itself to the modest demands made by the government upon a Jewish primary school. He was taught reading, writing, ciphering, and the translation of the Bible. Great love of study and marked talent became apparent in him ; he was therefore introduced to a knowledge of Hebrew and the Talmud. When he was confirmed at thirteen, the age at which the boys of that period were in the habit of deciding definitely on their careers, his parents did not for a moment question the propriety of continuing their son's intellectual training. It would have been most natural to send him to Posen, where a popular Talmud school was flourishing under the direction of the highly esteemed Chief Rabbi Akiba Eger. But his parents' means were too slender to suffice for his maintenance, and shyness and pride prevented young Graetz from making his way after the fashion of beggar students. There was but one course, to send him to Wollstein, where his mother had sisters and other relatives. Though by no means possessed of great wealth, they were willing to give him assistance. The Wollstein sojourn proved eminently favorable to his development. The town, situated in the western part of the Province, was not destitute of natural charms, to which the boy's impressionable mind eagerly responded. The population, chiefly German, numbered 2258 persons, among them 841 Jews,[1] by no means an inconsiderable congregation. Besides, it was in fairly comfortable circumstances. It had always

[1] *Staatsarchiv* Posen, Wollstein C. 13.

taken pride in maintaining a Talmud school, which, at the time of Graetz's advent, was distinguished for the liberal, enlightened spirit pervading it and the active encouragement accorded its students in their desire for culture. Rumor had it that the rabbi, Samuel Samwel Munk, who had been called from Bojanowo to Wollstein at the beginning of the century, knew how to read and write German, and was in the habit of reading German books and even journals in the hours that are "neither day nor night." At all events, he did not put obstacles in their way, when his disciples, spurring each other on in the impetuous rivalry of youth for pre-eminence, sought to slake their thirst for secular knowledge.

Graetz arrived in Wollstein at the end of the summer of 1831, fourteen years old. At that youthful age, the *Bachur* had ventured to undertake, in a Hebrew far from perfect, it must be confessed, a work on the calendar entitled, "חשבון העתים, Jewish and German Chronology."[1] He was a zealous attendant upon the rabbi's Talmudic lectures, and derived great profit from them. His teacher conceived a lively and kind interest in him, as well as a high opinion of his ability, though he did not suspect his future eminence. Rabbinic studies did not occupy his mind to the exclusion of other pursuits. Inextinguishable thirst for knowledge had taken possession of him, and all books that fell in his way were read with avidity. Most of the available literature consisted of romances of chivalry, of the kind in vogue at that time. Among them "Raspo of Felseneck," now completely forgotten, made a particularly deep impression upon him. Reproved by one of his patrons, and provided with

[1] The booklet, copied out in a fair, neat hand, was found among the author's papers after his death. He states that he began it in Zerkow, on Wednesday, Ellul 27 (September 15), 1830, and finished it in Wollstein at about the age of fifteen.

more suitable books by him, he read with keen enjoyment Campe's narrative and moral writings. At the same time historical books began to attract him strongly. Though he had to confess to himself, somewhat crestfallen, that he did not understand the greater part of what he read in them, he studied Bredow's short compendium of universal history, Becker's large work on the same subject, and a biography of Napoleon. He soon realized the necessity of acquiring Latin and French. Without teacher, without guidance, without counsel other than that afforded by like-minded companions, he devoted himself to Meidinger's French grammar and later to Bröder's Latin grammar, until he had gotten all between their covers by heart. He was overjoyed when he could begin to read the classic writers of foreign countries in their own languages. In his zeal, he permitted himself to be governed by chance. Whatever fortune played into his hands, he grasped at with instantaneous ardor, and pursued with sporadic industry. He picks up a translation of Euclid, for instance. At once he devotes himself to it heart and soul, difficult though he finds it to gain a clear notion of geometric concepts and methods. An itinerant rabbi from Poland, offering his own commentary upon the Book of Job for sale, comes to Wollstein, and meets with appreciation and respect. Reason enough for the enthusiastic and ambitious Talmud disciple to take interest in nothing but Bible exegesis and Hebrew grammar for months thereafter. Keen, discriminating love of nature, to whose attractions he remained susceptible until his last days, develops in him. He spares no effort to acquaint himself with the flora of his native province and with the mysteries of the starry heavens. Success was a foregone conclusion with one whose equipment consisted of miraculously quick comprehension, a retentive memory, and industry oblivious of all but its object; coupled with

an iron constitution and indestructible working powers, not in the least impaired by lack of food and sleep.

Despite his modest demands, he constantly had to battle against want and distress. His nature was proud, self-reliant, and, it must be admitted, unpractical. An exaggerated sense of honor forbade his seeking help even when a petition would have been justified. He preferred to conceal his troubles. For example, he ate dry bread on many a Sabbath, a day on which it was considered a privilege to entertain Talmud disciples. Regardless of wind and weather, he would slip off into the country, a book in his pocket, in order not to reveal his helpless condition. Finally, in spite of his secretiveness, some friend or other discovered his plight, and found ways and means of relieving his distress. Of sanguine temperament, he sought and found consolation in books. Graetz managed to read and study an amazing quantity in the four years and a half of his Wollstein sojourn. His most determined efforts were applied to the acquisition of the French language and literature, his favorite studies, at that time ranking high in the scale of accomplishments. The more important works of Fénelon, Voltaire, Rousseau, and others, and the dramas of Racine and Victor Hugo he knew thoroughly. He had read Lessing, Mendelssohn, Schiller, and other classic writers of Germany, and was attracted particularly to Wieland, to whose works he devoted earnest attention. It is curious that the diary which he then kept does not contain a single reference to Goethe, as if by chance or for some reason he had remained in ignorance of the great poet's works. On the other hand, he became acquainted towards the end of the Wollstein period with the writings of Börne, Heine, and Saphir, which vivified the proneness to irony and satire dormant in him. The Latin authors gave him most trouble. Yet he mastered Cornelius Nepos,

Curtius, and several books of Ovid's Metamorphoses and of Virgil's Æneid. That he accomplished extensive reading of rabbinic literature at the same time, and did not neglect his Talmudic studies, is attested by the distinction with which Rabbi Munk honored Graetz, much to his surprise. At New Year 5595 (October, 1834), he was invested with the title *Chaber*, a degree conferred only upon most worthy and most rarely endowed Talmud disciples of his youthful age.

But now fermentation set in, and white flakes began to rise to the surface of the young wine. Wholly self-taught, he had devoted himself to reading without plan or method, following blind chance or humoring his whims. In this way he had laid up a store of knowledge, promiscuous as well as rich. A chaotic mixture of irreconcilable, disparate ideas and opinions surged through his head, and excited tumultuous commotion in his world of thought and feeling. In November, 1835, the following entry was written in his diary:

"By the various contradictory ideas that perplexed my brain—heathen, Jewish, and Christian, Epicurean, Kabbalistic, Maimonidian, and Platonic—my faith was made so insecure that, when a notion concerning God, eternity, time, or the like, assailed me, I wished myself into the abyss of the nether world."

Although his humor and his opinions were somewhat unsettled, he by no means had drifted from his moorings. The existence of God and the immortality of the soul were the fixed poles of his emotional world to which he clung. Another entry a little further on in his diary says:

"Like furies such thoughts tugged at my heart-strings, when, as often happened, they arose, suggested by my poverty as well as by certain classes of books. Only the clear, star-studded sky, upon which my eyes were wont to rest with delight on Saturday evenings after sundown, renewed the blessed comforting consciousness in me: Yes, there is a God beyond the starry canopy!"

On the other hand, he began to chafe against the daily religious practices of Judaism, which he had

always observed with scrupulous conscientiousness, as he had been taught to do. Even then he did not neglect them, but he was offended by the multiplicity of ceremonies and still more by the petty, poor-spirited, unæsthetic manner in which the people among whom he lived observed them. They no longer were religious observances; they were habits. Attributing the responsibility for these conditions to the Talmud, he bore it ill-will. His repugnance grew whenever he contrasted its style and method with those of the great works of literature with which he had recently become conversant. Comparisons of this kind did not serve to enhance the credit of the rabbinic collection with him. There was another cause for irritation. Up to that time he had lived, or rather studied, heedless of practical concerns. Now his parents and relatives were probably beginning to urge upon him the necessity of considering the choice of a vocation or of turning to professional studies. So just a demand he could not disregard, especially in the sensitive state of mind in which he then found himself. Often he brooded over the question, "What next?" and elaborated the most bizarre plans only to reject them. A seemingly slight incident occurred which quelled the commotion in his breast. His craft, helplessly driving among perilous crags, was guided into smooth waters by a little book appearing just then under the title, "אגרת צפון, Nineteen Letters on Judaism, published by Ben Usiel."[1]

The partisans of the reform movement, who proposed to remodel or set aside religious customs and traditional observances of historical Judaism as incompatible with modern life, had up to that time maintained the upper hand in the literary discussion of religious affairs. They were exerting constantly

[1] *Neunzehn Briefe über Judenthum, herausgegeben von Ben Usiel.*

increasing attraction upon the younger generation, and were growing bolder and more impetuous in their propaganda for the obliteration, as far as possible, of religious peculiarities. Bent upon the preservation of old faith and custom unimpaired, their opponents had at first refused to make any concession whatsoever to the modern demands, and had even failed to provide themselves with new weapons of defense. When the movement assumed threatening dimensions, the conservatives faced it unprepared and impotent. Bewildered strangers in the great world, habituated to the social forms of the Ghetto, enmeshed in the web of Talmudic ideas, they were wholly unable to put up an efficient leader or regenerator. Suddenly that which had long been painfully lacking seemed to incorporate itself in a young theologian. In the above-mentioned anonymous work, "Nineteen Letters," Samson Raphael Hirsch, rabbi at Oldenburg, championed the undiminished value of all religious usages with skill, eloquence, and intrepidity. His manner held out the hope that he would breathe a new spirit into the old forms. The boldness of the work in frankly presenting this point of view with all the consequences springing therefrom produced the effect of a sensational occurrence upon the Jewish public. Into the mind of Graetz, casting about for an anchor for his disturbed feelings, it fell like a flash of lightning, revealing the path to be followed in the search for his ideals. He reports:

"Often I spoke of it [religious doubt] to B. B., the only one to whom I could tell my thoughts on such subjects. Then he would allege the urgent necessity for reforms in view of the gradual decay of religion. But I realized, that reform, that is, the omission of a number of laws organically interwoven with the rest, would abrogate the whole Law. How delighted I therefore was with a new book, 'אגרת צפון, Nineteen Letters on Judaism, *anonymous*,' in which a view of Judaism I had never before heard or suspected was defended with convincing arguments. Judaism was represented as the best religion and as indispensable to the salvation of mankind. With avidity I devoured every word. Disloyal though I had been

to the Talmud, this book reconciled me with it. I returned to it as to a mistress deemed faithless and proved true, and determined to use my utmost effort to pierce to its depths, acquire a philosophical knowledge thereof, and, as many would have me believe that I might become a so-called 'rabbi-doctor of theology' (*studirter Rabbiner*), publicly demonstrate its truth and utility. I set about my task at once, beginning with the first folio ברכות and the first Book of Moses. I dwelt upon every point with pleasure, treating them not as remnants of antiquity, but as books containing divine help for mankind. My endeavor was materially advanced by the knowledge I had acquired here, among other things of theology, which only now I learned to esteem as a branch of science; of geometry—I had studied nearly the whole of the first three books of Euclid; and of history."

After that he could not content himself with life in Wollstein; the place had nothing more to offer him. The resolution to quit the town, which had grown into his heart as his second home, was facilitated by the removal of an uncle, depriving him of his strongest support; by the usual disappointment and revulsion of feeling following the usual extravagance of a youthful, fantastic love-affair; and by conflicts with companions and patrons, caused to some extent doubtless by the disharmonious state of his mind and aggravated by tittle-tattle. But whither was he to turn to satisfy the yearnings of his soul? He decided on Prague, the Mecca of the young Jewish theologians of the day, "a city most famous for learning, hospitality, and other virtues."

II.

THE APPRENTICE.

GRAETZ left Wollstein in April, 1836, and went to Zerkow to acquaint his parents with his intentions and consult with them. Letters of recommendation to families in Prague were obtained, and his parents and other relatives made up a small purse for him. Graetz secured a passport, packed his modest belongings in a handbag, and set out on his journey in high spirits. Partly afoot, partly by stage when the fare was not forbidding, he made

his way to Breslau, and thence through the Silesian mountains to the Austrian boundary, which he reached not far from Reinerz. Here, though he was fortified with a passport, the frontier inspector, like a cherub with a flaming sword, opposed his entrance into Austria. He was unable to produce ten florins ($5) cash, the possession of which had to be demonstrated by the traveler who would gain admission to the land of the double eagle, unless he came as a passenger in the mail-coach. Dismayed our young wanderer resorted to parleying, and appealed to his letters of recommendation. In vain; the official would hear of no compromise. Too proud and inflexible to have recourse to entreaty or trickery, Graetz grimly faced about, and much disheartened journeyed as he had come, over the same road, back to Zerkow. His parents were not a little astonished at his return, and equally rejoiced to have their son with them for some time longer. The adventure may be taken as typical of the curious mishaps that befell him in practical life, particularly at the beginning of his career. They often cut him to the quick, but never shook his belief in his lucky star. His originative and impressionable nature carried with it the power of discerning important points of view and valid aims, but he seems to have been too far-sighted and impetuous to lay due stress upon the means and levers necessary for the attainment of ends.

For the moment he sought to drown remembrance of his abortive journey in study. He became absorbed in Latin works; he read Livy, Cicero's *de natura deorum*, which compelled his reverential admiration, Virgil's Æneid, and the comedies of Terence. Besides, he busied himself with Schrökh's universal history and with his Wieland, whose "Sympathies," "Golden Mirror," and other works "delighted, refreshed, and fascinated" him "inexpressibly." The Talmud and Hebrew studies claimed no

less attention; he was especially zealous about the exegesis of the Earlier Prophets. Downcast by reason of the uncertainty of his future, and his scorn piqued by the pettiness and narrow-mindedness of his provincial surroundings, he found an outlet for his restlessness in all sorts of wanton pranks, such as high-spirited youths are apt to perpetrate in their "storm and stress" period. He ridiculed the rabbi, played tricks on the directors of the congregation, annoyed the burgomaster, always escaping unpunished, and even horrified his parents by accesses of latitudinarianism, such as the following. On the day before the eve of the Atonement Day, it is a well-known custom for men to swing a living rooster and for women to swing a living hen several times about their heads. At the same time a short prayer is recited, pleading that the punishment due for the sins committed by the petitioner be transferred to the devoted fowl. At the approach of the holy season, Graetz announced that he would certainly not comply with the *Kapores* custom, but his words were taken to be idle boastfulness. The fateful evening came, and the serio-comic celebration was long delayed by the non-appearance of the eldest son. The father's wrath was kindled, and he threatened to burn all books other than Hebrew found in the possession of his heretic offspring. The mother set out to search everywhere for her erring son. When she finally found him, he went home with her in affectionate obedience, but nothing could induce him to manipulate the rooster in the customary way. Unswung and uncursed the bird had to be carried to the butcher, and only on the following day a touching reconciliation was effected.

After the Fast, a bookdealer at Wollstein, a friend of his, who usually kept him informed about new books on Jewish subjects, sent Graetz the "Nineteen Letters by Ben Usiel," which he had

longed to possess. The book again electrified him, and he conceived the idea of offering himself as a disciple to its author, whose identity had meantime been revealed. Samson Raphael Hirsch appeared to him to be the ideal of a Jewish theologian of the time and of the confidence-inspiring teacher for whom he had yearned, to obtain from him guidance and, if possible, a solution of the manifold problems occupying his mind. Accordingly, Graetz wrote to the District Rabbi (*Landesrabbiner*) of Oldenburg. He did not conceal his views, but clearly and frankly laid bare the state of his feelings and the course of his intellectual development. He was successful. After a short time, Hirsch addressed the following letter to him :

"My dear young Friend:—With pleasure I am ready to fulfill, as far as in me lies, the wish expressed in your letter to me. You know the sentence of our sages, יותר משעגל רוצה לינק הפרה רוצה להניק,[1] and if, as I should gladly infer from your letter, the views therein expressed are more than an evanescent mood; if it is your resolute determination to study *Torah* for its own sake, you are most cordially welcome, and I shall expect to see you after פסח הבע״ל.[2] But I have one request to make. In the ardor of your feelings, you have conceived an ideal picture of the author of the 'Letters' by far exceeding the real man in size. Reduce the picture by half, by three-fourths, indeed, and ask yourself whether you are still attracted by it. Do not expect to find an accomplished master, but a student occupied with research. If your heart still says *yes*, then come. I should like to be informed as soon as possible, whether I may expect you after *Pessach*, as I shall have to modify another relation accordingly. Be kind enough, too, if you have no objection, to let me know how you expect to support yourself here. I trust that you will neither take umbrage at this question nor misconstrue it. It was put only because I wanted to express my willingness to assist you as much as I can during your stay here, if it should be necessary. Therefore, I beg you to be as frank and unreserved in your answer as I ventured to be in my question. With kindest regards, etc.

OLDENBURG, December 26, '36."

To this letter Graetz replied, that he did say "yes" from the bottom of his heart ; that it was

[1] *Pessachim* 112[a]: יותר ממה שהעגל רוצה לינק פרה רוצה להניק "More than the calf will suck, the cow desires to suckle."

[2] Next happy *Pessach*.

his dearest ambition to devote himself to genuine Judaism and its doctrines; that he especially desired to learn the methods of Talmud study, particularly of the *Halakha*, pursued by a man whom he admired profoundly; that as for his livelihood, the satisfaction of the most elementary needs sufficed for him; and that his parents would give him a small allowance.

In answer thereto, the formal invitation to come to Oldenburg was extended by Hirsch on February 1, 1837. He offered Graetz board and lodging in his own house, with the understanding that his parents would provide for other needs, and he expected his disciple after Passover (in May). Wishing to visit relatives on the way and see the sights of Berlin and Leipsic, Graetz set out as early as the beginning of April. In Berlin the museum and the picture-gallery made a deep impression upon him. That he was a remarkably sharp observer is shown in the following accurate characterization of the preacher Solomon Plessner, with whom he became acquainted in Berlin:

"This famous man I also visited, and I found attractive features indicative of acuteness, but a neglected exterior and careless, ungrammatical speech, not guiltless of the Jewish sing-song (*mauscheln*). This surprises me, for his language in his sermons is pure and choice. He is between forty and fifty years old, wears a beard, and seems to be honestly and genuinely religious. But his manner is excited; he speaks with rapid utterance, all the while running to and fro and arranging his books absent-mindedly."

In Leipsic he visited his countryman Fürst, concerning whom he reports:

"A little man whose face was familiar to me from my childhood days came towards me. I handed him the letter given me by his mother. He said indifferently: I shall write in a few days. But when I told him the goal and purpose of my journey, and showed him the letters [from Hirsch], his attitude changed, and he talked with me in a very friendly way. Finally, when he recognized that I was not an ignoramus, he confided several matters to me, told me about his scientific adversaries, and boasted that he had taught Gesenius, that he had become reconciled with Ewald, that the greatest scholars corresponded with him, etc. . . . Our conversation

grew more and more confidential, and finally we parted as friends. He invited me to visit him again, if I changed my mind and staid over פסח . . . In case I did not remain, I had to promise that I would enter into correspondence with him. . . . I was particularly pleased to find, that Fürst has no intention of accepting baptism, and that he means to promote the cause of Judaism. . . . To work for Judaism, he says, is the prime obligation of every Jew that devotes himself to study, by which he means strictly scientific, possibly also philologic study."

In order not to fritter away all his time while traveling, Graetz began to study Greek, and the Greek conjugations served to beguile dreary hours, banishing remembrance of the mishaps that could not fail to befall one with straitened means on so long a journey, and counteracting the despondency which in consequence often seized upon him. In a miserable village, in which he was forced to spend a whole day on account of the Sabbath, he found a copy of the New Testament, and read it for the first time. He describes the impression made upon him by this first reading in the following words:

"Despite the many absurdities and inconsistencies, the mildness of the character of Jesus attracted me; at the same time I was repelled, so that I was altogether confused."

On May 8, finally, he arrived in Oldenburg, where a new world opened before him.

In Samson Raphael Hirsch he met a man whose spiritual elevation and noble character compelled his profound reverence, and who fully realized all the expectations that he had harbored concerning him. Hirsch was a man of modern culture, and his manner was distinguished, even aristocratic, although he kept aloof from all social intercourse. He was short of stature, yet those who came in contact with him were strongly impressed by his external appearance, on account of his grave, dignified demeanor, forbidding familiarity. With great intellectual gifts and rare qualities of the heart, he combined varied theological attainments and an excellent classical education. Comprehensive or

deep ideas cannot be said to have been at his disposal, but he scintillated with original observations and suggestive sallies, which put his new pupil into a fever of enthusiasm. He was the only teacher from whom Graetz's self-centered being received scientific stimulation; perhaps the only man to exercise, so far as the stubborn peculiarity of Graetz's nature permitted it, permanent influence upon his reserved, independent character.

On his arrival in Oldenburg, the new-comer was most kindly received by Hirsch, and was at once installed in his house, of which thenceforth he was an inmate. Instruction was begun on the very next day. The forenoons were devoted to the Talmud, the late afternoons to the Psalms. The disciple was singularly attracted and stimulated, fairly elevated by the brilliant, penetrating method applied to the exegesis of these works. Plan, order, and coherence were now imposed upon his scientific acquirements. Hirsch took true fatherly interest in his protegé; he exerted himself to discipline his mind and fix his moral and religious standards. At the same time, as though even then a suspicion of the unusual force and talent of this youth panting for knowledge and instruction had dawned upon him, he guarded against assuming the airs of a domineering pedagogue. Despite the difference in age between them he treated him as an equal. He was endowed with truly marvelous power to stir his disciple's soul-life to its depths. Every chord of Graetz's being was set in vibration, and he solemnly vowed to remain a true son and an honest adherent of Judaism under all circumstances. Added years may have contributed to the result; but at all events it is certain that Graetz developed visibly under this master's guidance.

The services required of him in the house of his teacher were mainly those of an assistant. He accompanied the District Rabbi on his tours of

inspection, the tedium of their journeys being relieved with discussions on Talmudic and Biblical subjects. He revised with Hirsch the last part of the latter's "Horeb," helped him read the proof of the last sheets of the book, which delighted and thrilled the young man, and assisted him in various similar ways. How flattering an opinion the punctilious rabbi must have held of his assistant is proved by the fact, that when he had to go to a resort for the restoration of his undermined health, he authorized him to render decisions on questions of religious law (שאלות) during his absence. The assistant fulfilled his duties so conscientiously that the responsibility oppressed him. He confessed that he had imagined the rendering of correct decisions much easier. His enthusiasm burst into flame when he received the following affectionate letter from Hirsch:

"My dear Graetz:—I still owe you cordial thanks for your kind lines. I am delighted to hear that you are industrious, and that you keep to my time-schedule so well. Continue to study, for I, on my part, shall soon have forgotten how to study, and literally shall have to begin to learn all over again. Before my departure, I wanted to call your attention to something, and I do now what I then forgot. I have frequently seen you read the works of Bayle. They are a treasury of learning, and much information can be derived from them, but the man takes peculiar pleasure in laying stress upon דברי ערוה;[1] things of that kind are טמא and מטמא[2]. Pass lightly over such passages; they are unprofitable and harmful; read only what is purely scientific. Follow my advice, etc., etc."

Such friendly and tactful admonitions, permitting the pupil to follow out his own bent, were always employed by Hirsch, and they but served to enkindle Graetz's enthusiasm anew. In spite of the young man's critical propensities combined with a sanguine temperament, his devoted attachment to his master by no means waned under the strain of daily intimate intercourse, not even when he could no longer doubt his ideal's lack of historic depth

[1] Erotic matters. [2] Unclean and contaminating.

and scientific, or rather philosophic insight. Graetz's nature strongly impelled him to form friendships, and his attachments were fervent. He always felt a lively interest in what went on about him, and even at that early time he was fond of taking an active part in shaping the occurrences of the day, whenever he thought, that by assuming the rôle of Providence he might be useful to his friends in the ordering of their affairs—a disposition that redounded later to the benefit of many of his pupils. In January, 1837, for instance, the belated news reached him from his home, with which he kept up a steady correspondence, that the Chief Rabbi Akiba Eger had died in Posen. Without being commissioned to do so, he wrote to the directors of the Posen congregation, and brought Hirsch, whose yearning for a wide sphere of activity he knew, to their notice. When the directors entered into negotiations with Hirsch he broke out into jubilation. In fact, a party favoring the pretensions of the Oldenburg District Rabbi formed in Posen, but nothing more resulted. The procedure was repeated when the Wollstein rabbinate fell vacant in 1840, except that Hirsch, to his disciple's great disappointment, would not share Graetz's enthusiasm for Wollstein. From this it appears that Graetz was not a recluse nor a bookworm. In Oldenburg, as everywhere, he sought to meet people and cultivate friendly intercourse with them, and his joyous nature readily yielded to the innocent gayety of social pleasures.

At the same time he neglected neither his duties nor his studies. While with Hirsch he acquired the English language, and finding some Syriac books in the rabbi's library, he began to devote himself to Syriac. The study of the former language his master seems to have encouraged, but not of the latter. Hirsch met his disciple with uniform kindness, and returned his enthusiastic devotion with fatherly

benevolence. Graetz was treated as a member of his family. In the third year of his Oldenburg sojourn, his relations with the mistress of the house were disturbed by slight discords, such as cannot fail to arise in long-continued, familiar intercourse, and tend now to strengthen, now to abridge intimacy. With Graetz's proud sense of independence they finally sufficed to ruffle the tranquillity of a soul wholly absorbed by the present. Anxiety about his future began to disquiet him. The desire to decide definitely upon a career and the longing to see his parents, who in the meantime had removed from Zerkow to Kosten near Posen, a somewhat larger town, united to make his departure from Oldenburg seem advisable.

III.

THE JOURNEYMAN.

THE adieux were said with touching cordiality, and after an absence of more than three years Graetz set his face homeward, and arrived in Kosten in the middle of August, 1840. The younger people everywhere received Hirsch's disciple with joyous welcome, and induced him to preach at Wollstein, Kosten, and Zerkow. His sermons, to be sure, did not transport his audiences with enthusiasm, but they were ample guarantees of the preacher's fund of knowledge and originality. All his friends, therefore, agreed, that it would be advisable for Graetz to "study," in the technical sense of the German word, that is, go through the university and obtain a degree. They adduced the fact that the smaller congregations at least, such as Wreschen, Wollstein, and Kosten, in part had appointed "graduate rabbis" (*studirte Rabbiner*), in part had resolved to fill their rabbinates with them.

To secure means for a university course, he

agreed to accept a position as tutor in Ostrowo, and entered upon his work at the end of 1840. Ostrowo is a little town in the south-eastern part of the Province, the seat of a large Jewish community, which at the time was still completely under the sway of the graceless habits of Ghetto life. Graetz felt thoroughly uncomfortable. His position in the house at which he was engaged to teach did not please him, and in the town he found no one with whom he cared to cultivate friendly intercourse. He had submitted to tutoring, by no means an arduous occupation, in order to lay by money, but he lacked financial talent and the ability to economize. In fact, his devotion to his family connections, his good nature, and his improvidence involved him in pecuniary embarrassments so serious that the monologues in his diary overflow with pessimistic, melancholy reflections. He sought indemnification in frequent excursions to neighboring towns, in composing a Hebrew biography of Mishna teachers under the title תולדת אבות,[1] and, it appears, in reading the works of the Fathers of the Church. On one of his little trips, the occasion being the betrothal of a friend of his, he met the sister of the *fiancée*, a very young girl, who attracted and pleased him, and who was destined to exert decisive and salutary influence upon his life. The meeting acted like a soothing charm upon his ill-humor, though he was far from anticipating the consequences it bore. He remained in his position at Ostrowo for one year and a half, until July, 1842, when a trivial occurrence ruptured the irksome relation in a manner not altogether pleasant.

Now he went straightway to Breslau to the University. As he had not been graduated from a *Gymnasium*, Graetz had to obtain ministerial per-

[1] This biographical work was not printed, and the manuscript could not be found.

mission to attend the University. His petition was granted, and, in October, 1842, he was matriculated. With reverential awe and expectation the self-taught student entered the mysterious lecture halls consecrated to pure science, only to leave them shrugging his shoulders at the wisdom proclaimed, disappointed, his longings unsatisfied. The knowledge of which he was master when he began his University course was richer and more varied than ordinary students are likely to start with, and though it was not systematically ordered nor well-balanced, it formed a unit, and had already begun to crystallize about a center. His apprenticeship years, in short, were over; the maturity of his views and his judgment is unmistakable.

While at the University, he heard lectures on a wide variety of subjects—on history, philosophy, Oriental languages, even physics—but it does not appear that any left deep traces upon his mind. Even Professor Bernstein, an Orientalist of considerable reputation, who drew him into the circle of his close associates, did not understand how to kindle his pupil's zeal, usually so impetuous, for the thorough study of Syriac and Arabic. Apparently Graetz had relinquished the ambition to gain mastery of them. The only one to have success was Professor Braniss, a philosopher in high esteem in his day, with whom also Graetz cultivated intimate relations. He at all events must have been instrumental in acquainting him with the Hegelian system of philosophy, and in imbuing him with the recognition, that even in the world of liberty, that is, man's world of mental endeavor, phases of development succeed each other in conformity with absolute laws, chiefly of an ideal, non-mechanical nature; that therefore the spiritual powers that produce the history of mankind by the realization of ever higher ideas not only follow their indwelling laws, but at the same time submit uncondition-

ally to the law of cause and effect; and that the paradox of opposites, the principle of thesis, antithesis, and synthesis, is particularly helpful in the consideration of historical phenomena.

Though Graetz was immersed in his studies, he did not fail to give close attention to the occurrences in the Breslau Jewish community. The events happening there in those days were not merely of local interest. They cast their light and their shadow far beyond the Silesian frontier, and were the cause of intense excitement in all Jewish circles of Germany. In Breslau the orthodox and the reform views of Judaism for the first time rushed at each other with full force in the struggle for supremacy. Storm and conflict raged violently between the old and the new. Blind to the conditions of the time, orthodoxy stubbornly opposed a *non possumus* to every offer looking to an adjustment of difficulties. The representatives of the two parties, the orthodox Solomon Tiktin on the one side and the progressive Abraham Geiger on the other, sought to get the better of each other with remorseless acrimony. Geiger won the upper hand, and even the disruption of the Breslau congregation caused by Tiktin's defeat did not derogate from the reform champion's victory.

Dr. Abraham Geiger should be classed among the most prominent rabbis of his time. The modern development of the religious life had been proceeding quietly though steadily, when it was convulsed to its depths by the storm announced by his first appearance upon the rabbinical scene. As a speaker and as a writer he handled a popular style with masterful skill, which manifested itself in felicitous copiousness rather than in the concentration of precise, forcible language. One of the best pulpit orators among Jews, he succeeded in holding attention and stimulating thought by his simple manner and brilliant turns of expression.

His published sermons, very limited in number, give not even an approximate idea of the powerful impression produced by his spoken words, totally unaided though they were by charms of person.[1] His scholarly contributions to Jewish science are of pre-eminent and of permanent value. He has rendered particularly valiant service by his researches into the history of literature, a field in which he was master. On the other hand, one sometimes misses thoroughness of scholarly culture in his early productions, especially those of the first part of his Breslau period. Besides, he was fond of obtruding his reform bias. In spite of his scientific attainments, his historical sense lacked profundity, and in spite of his great achievements in the province of modern liturgy, his appreciation of the needs and emotions of the people's spiritual life was neither sufficiently delicate nor sufficiently intense. At bottom he was a doctrinaire rationalist. His religious program and aims, too, were not clearly and definitely put forth. For example, his attitude towards the radical currents at that time rolling their destructive waves over Judaism amounted to more than benevolent neutrality. The observer cannot ward off the impression, that he was inclined to steer straight for ethical deism, and was restrained only by opportunist reasons. At this above all Graetz took umbrage, and by and by his antipathy to Geiger was complete. A good deal of sham and tinsel had probably slipped into the various tentative organizations which Geiger endeavored to call into existence; perhaps they were unavoidable concomitants of such efforts. It is possible, too, that the unpleasant impression was reinforced by a tendency to officiousness observable in Geiger—at

[1] The writer speaks from personal experience, though it is proper to add, that he heard Geiger's sermons in his youth, when one is inclined to enthusiasm and admiration; yet he thinks that the judgment expressed above can be sustained.

worst a pardonable foible. As Graetz was constituted, he felt so strong a repugnance to humbug and pretense that he exercised neither forbearance nor consideration towards such faults. He visited Geiger only once, possibly twice. Immediately after Graetz had made himself at home in the lecture-rooms of his department, he paid his respects to the two rabbinical party-leaders. The entry in his diary is as follows:

"I have made the acquaintance of Rabbi Tiktin. With what reverence I used to stand and look at the mail-clad names of the Tiktins on the first pages of ריפֿים![1] As Charlemagne in his iron armor kept all intruders at a becoming distance, so the dignity of those theologic knights seemed to me to be enhanced by the long beards and the imposing Spanish canes[2] and the Talmudic dust. There was I sitting next to a descendant of those rabbinical נפילים.[3] Ah! what a falling-off there has been! *Tempora mutantur et nos mutamur in illis.* To be sure, there is still the stately stature, still the Spanish cane. But the *ensemble*, a something not to be defined in words, is missing. Next to the rabbi, *nolentes volentes,* I place Dr. Geiger, a spare little man. Why he was so very kind to me I do not know. Of Hirsch we have not yet spoken, and probably shall not speak. But to what depths we have sunk! In the presence of fifty Jews, headed by a רב, Dr. Freund[4] dares utter words like "rabbinically erratic inferences." Cicero and Plato, then, are to be read as antidotes to rabbinical perversions. Zounds! And to-day Geiger delivered his first lecture on the Mishna. The Mishna is a collection of *religious notions, as they were formed and developed from the Exile to R. Jehuda Hanassi.* What insane logic!"

When, in March, 1843, the stiff-necked, tenacious champion of an effete form of Judaism, the lion-warrior Solomon Tiktin, last representative of a race of Talmudic heroes, wounded to the quick by his defeat, was removed from the scene by death, Geiger stood at the zenith of his fame. Since many a day no rabbi's name had been so well-known as Geiger's in all the extent of German Jewry, none

[1] The Talmudic works of R. Isaac Alfassi.

[2] A great, heavy cane with ornamental knob was carried in Poland as the badge of the rabbinical office.

[3] Heroes.

[4] A philologist of repute, whose contributions to Latin lexicography are of considerable value.

was so frequently mentioned. In Silesia there was no more popular rabbi, and in Breslau his word was potent, influential, and feared by his adversaries. His scientific eminence was generally acknowledged; his eloquence dominated the pulpit no less than the minds of his hearers. Who dared attack him was badly used, and bore ridicule as well as injury from the fray.

In the course of the year 1844, the first signs of a slowly crystallizing reaction became noticeable. Various germinating forces looking to the formation of a new theologic party on a conservative platform consolidated in that year under the leadership of Zacharias Frankel. From this place and that, single barbed arrows, followed by more and sharper ones, winged by irony and hard to parry, came whizzing through the air, striking Geiger and his followers in the most sensitive spots. A well-known weekly Jewish journal, *Der Orient*, under the editorship of Dr. Fürst, published reports of the more important occurrences in the Breslau community. The descriptions of the anonymous correspondent were graphic, pungent, and critical. Th. articles naturally aroused attention. In Breslau, as they continued to appear week after week, they created a veritable sensation. The two parties looked forward to each issue of the "Orient" with equal expectancy, though otherwise with opposite feelings. In the orthodox camp there was exultation. At last an expert writer had appeared, who laid bare all sorts of evils fearlessly and unsparingly, and who seemed to serve the cause of conservatism by his bold opposition to Geiger. But who was the archer that sped his arrow with aim so true and poise so elegant? Guesses were hazarded, a narrow search was instituted, and especially the ranks of the Jewish students of theology at that time gathered in Breslau, mostly about Geiger, were sharply inspected. It was established beyond

a doubt, that it was a *homo novus*, a student from the Province—Graetz, who, proudly independent of every sort of patronage, was earning a scant livelihood by giving lessons. The amazement grew when Graetz, nearly simultaneously with the just mentioned contributions to the "Orient," published a critical review, valuable even at this late day, of Geiger's "Textbook of the Mishnic Language."[1] This critique, auspiciously ushering him into the scientific world,[2] was begun in the literary supplement of the "Orient" at the end of 1844, and continued as a series of articles in the following year. It gave him the opportunity of expounding his own views upon the subject and displaying advantageously a fund of information, mastery of the material, philological tact, scientific instincts, and considerable talent as a stylist. His criticism of the book is often to the point, but rather severe and not entirely free from animosity. It was characteristic of Graetz to express his opinion clearly and directly. Geiger replied to the challenge in "The Israelite of the Nineteenth Century"[3] in still more acrimonious articles, which likewise are not wholly objective. In fact, they contain approaches to personalities, and dwell upon slips and trivial details, thus demonstrating the importance attached to the appearance of his young antagonist in the arena. In any event, Graetz had drawn the attention of a wider circle to himself, and in Breslau he had become at one bound the central topic of interest in *Karlsstrasse*. The orthodox partisans made advances to him, although he did not for a moment leave

[1] *Lehrbuch zur Sprache der Mishnah.*

[2] An anonymous article in the "Orient," 1843, p. 391 ff., may be accounted his introduction into the world of letters. It treats of the question then mooted, "On the Sanctity of Jewish Cemeteries" (*Ueber die Heiligkeit der jüdischen Begräbnissplätze*), and is dated Breslau, November 22. The skirmish with Geiger began in the "Orient," 1844, p. 21.

[3] *Israelit des 19ten Jahrhunderts.*

them in doubt about his disapproval of their program and his dissent from their religious views. He told them that he was pursuing his own original ideas, and that his guiding principle was unalterable loyalty to positive Judaism. However, he restrained them from many a foolish and fanatic step. In the face of orthodox opposition Geiger had energetically organized a religious school, which was prospering. Graetz therefore advised the adherents of orthodoxy not to permit themselves to lose touch with the younger generation, but to build up a similar institution on conservative lines. The advice seems to have fallen on fruitful soil. It was intimated to the counselor, that the intention was to entrust him with the organization and superintendence of a school of that kind, provided he obtained his University degree before its opening. Besides, his name was beginning to be mentioned in connection with vacant rabbinates. It was therefore necessary to hasten his graduation. After a few weeks of severe application, he finished his thesis, *De auctoritate et vi, quam gnosis in Judaismum habuerit*, which secured him the doctorate from the University of Jena in April, 1845. Under the title, "Gnosticism and Judaism,"[1] the dissertation was published in that year as the first original product of his pen. The work in every respect bears the peculiar stamp of his scientific character. It is distinguished by familiarity with patristic literature; by his method of explaining Talmud statements, commonly taken to be general, as particular historical cases; by lucidity of arrangement and presentation; and by his happy gift of divining the occult relation between things, which enabled him to shed the first rays of light upon the כפר יצירה,[2] the most enigmatic book of rabbinical literature. The thesis was received kindly, and it gave him a place in the Jewish world of scholarship.

[1] *Gnostizismus und Judenthum.*

[2] "Book of Creation."

Such surprising successes swelled the breast of the literary novice, who had worked his way to the front by arduous toil, with justifiable and happy hopes. The halcyon days of young fame, at the remembrance of which his face lighted up with pleasure even in old age, he planned to spend with his parents. On his way home he passed through Krotoschin. There, in his friend's house, he met the half-grown girl of other days, now in the flush of young womanhood. Her image, faint though it had become in the background of his memory, had not faded entirely. She was the daughter of Monasch, the proprietor of the well-known Hebrew printing establishment. Each made a deep impression upon the other, and encouraged to believe that his future might be considered assured, Graetz did not conceal his feelings. They were requited, and the young people plighted their troth. Graetz did not suspect that he had won a strong womanly heart that would be his beacon and a prop to which he would cling for support during the dark days soon to break over him.

All sorts of vague, undefined hopes arose before his view, and some of them gradually assumed shape. The prospect of an honorable position, such as he had longed for and aspired to, seemed about to be realized. The rabbinate of Gleiwitz, one of the larger congregations of Upper Silesia, taking rank in wealth and perhaps in size after Breslau, was vacant, and the authorities were looking out for a man equipped with rabbinic lore, standing upon the height of modern culture, and favoring a sober, moderate reform movement. All entitled to a voice in the matter fixed upon Graetz, whose reputation as a writer had spread to them. He seemed the most suitable incumbent. By virtue of his native talent and his attainments, it was thought that he would be able to overrule or to meet the manifold, rather hazy views and demands of the

members of the congregation. The leading spirits among them declared themselves in favor of his election. Nothing more was necessary than to attract all the other circles of the community by proving his homiletic ability in several trial sermons, the success of which seemed a foregone conclusion. Before the great Holy Days of 1845 (5606) Graetz received a Hebrew communication from the directors of the Gleiwitz congregation, couched in the most flattering terms, assuring him of the reversion of the rabbinate, and inviting him to preach the sermons in their synagogue on the Day of Atonement.

At the appointed time, on the eve of the sacred day, he ascended the pulpit, and the result was—a thoroughly unexpected fiasco, the more deplorable as it shattered his own confidence in his oratorical powers. He had forgotten his memorandum completely. Losing his presence of mind, he had to leave the pulpit after saying a few words. His friends and followers stood by him loyally, and did their utmost to secure for him the opportunity of repairing the damage. He succeeded in rehabilitating himself only partly; the ground lost could not be recovered. The surprising mishap, it must be confessed now after the lapse of time, was a stroke of good fortune for the ambitious scholar and his life-work, ungentle though the impetus was that forced him into the path for which he was peculiarly equipped and gifted. In those days of universal fermentation, the religious life of Jewish communities was crossed and agitated by opposite, confused, and stormy currents. A man of uncontrollable impulse to be active and to exert independent, direct influence whenever it might seem necessary, and prone to give utterance to his convictions in truthful, incisive, and caustic language—a quality of dubious value—would hardly have succeeded in steering his rabbinical boat among the

crags of party strife, usually carried on with fanatic violence. He would either have had to become faithless to his nature and genius, or, if that were not possible, eventually be wrecked. At best, in case he had a high degree of tact and prudence at his disposal, he would have consumed his finest powers in putting more or less salutary measures into effect on a restricted field. Graetz, who knew himself thoroughly, had always feared that he would not be in his proper place in a rabbinical position. From the first he had felt a shrinking at the thought of the duties and responsibilities of a rabbi. A few days before he left for Gleiwitz he wrote in his diary:

> "Of all positions I am least adapted for that of rabbi; in every way I lack force of manner, an imposing presence. My knowledge, too, is highly defective, but my will is strong, energetic. If God's service can be performed by an instrument of such caliber, then here am I ready for it, body and soul. But the preaching!"

In very truth the preacher's Pegasus serves the noble enthusiasm of the elect willingly and ardently, and as willingly lends his back to mediocrity to execute more or less doubtful tricks before the eyes and ears of the many-headed crowd. Graetz it threw in the critical moment, and the fall affected him deeply and painfully. He who only a short time before, almost without effort, had won literary triumphs, and who as a rule shrank from no difficult undertaking, now despaired of ever being able to wield the living word with the power with which he directed the pen. In fact, he had been denied the external qualifications of an orator. It cannot be said to have been his appearance that stood in the way of success; he was of average height and well-knit frame. But in loud speech his voice lacked modulation, and his manner was ineffectual. Above all, he was incapable of posing; in his character there was not the slightest trace of the actor, who, as Goethe says, "might give points to a preacher."

IV.

SCHOLAR AND TEACHER.

THE above incident put a hopeless end to all the prospects he had entertained. Again care for his daily bread stalked by his side like a specter. The most deplorable aspect of his case was that his strength did not emerge from this severe contest, as from former ones, steeled and braced by cheering hopes for the future. Besides, he reproached himself for having drawn another and a beloved person into his forlorn life. Then the high-mindedness and unselfish devotion of the woman of his choice sustained him, refreshing his weary soul with consolation and encouragement, and calming the tumult of his wounded feelings. His animal spirits rose again under the stimulus of an honorable invitation, extended by Zacharias Frankel, to join a conference of conservative rabbis called by him to meet at Dresden in September,[1] 1846, for the purpose of discussing the religious problems of the day and uniting for concerted action.

At the very beginning of his career in Dresden, Dr. Zacharias Frankel had developed fruitful activity in connection with the removal of the political and civil disabilities, especially with regard to oaths, under which his coreligionists in Saxony were laboring. None the less he was essentially a scholar. Master of comprehensive knowledge of the Talmud, which he had acquired with critical thoroughness, he laid the foundations for the modern analysis of this work of literature. He made it his life-task to promote the scientific study of the Talmud and trace the evolution of the *Halakha*. The first-fruits of his literary endeavor betrayed the serious, thorough scholar by the accuracy, the scrupulous nicety, and

[1] Originally October 15 had been appointed, but many of the participants considered September a more suitable time.

the trustworthiness of his research, and secured for him a high and undisputed position in the scientific world. When the reform agitation within the Jewish community of Germany developed into a rapid stream whose waters grew more and more turbulent; when, on the one side, rabbinical conferences were planned for the purpose of systematizing and sanctioning projected innovations, and, on the other, distrust of the progressive leaders inspired the fear that the resolutions and professions of such assemblies might throw dangerous, inflammable material into the different congregations; Frankel deemed it prudent to give up his reserve and actively influence the religious movement. In 1844, accordingly, he began to publish the quarterly "Journal for the Religious Interests of Judaism."[1] It was to bear a strictly scientific character, and at the same time discuss the religious topics of the day. A sober, experienced, and tolerant theologian, Frankel held the position, that in matters of faith as in the other concerns of life the exigencies of the times have to be considered, but that concessions to the modern spirit may not remove us from historic ground, and that all modifications must result from a scientific appreciation of the essence and traditions of Judaism.

All this appealed strongly to Graetz, and no sooner had he come into public notice, in the year following the first appearance of the journal, than he sought to establish relations with Frankel. The latter met his advances with cordiality, and invited the young scholar to become a contributor to his quarterly review. Graetz responded with a brilliant and suggestive article, "The Septuagint in the Talmud."[2] It affords a striking example of his peculiar method of comparing Talmud and Midrash passages with each other and with the statements

[1] *Zeitschrift für die religiösen Interessen des Judenthums.*
[2] *Die Septuaginta im Talmud.*

and quotations of the Fathers of the Church, thus determining the historical elements of the Talmudic account and building theories upon it. In the same year (1845), Frankel had gone to Frankfort-on-the-Main, to the second rabbinical conference, with the hope of infusing a spirit of moderation and conciliation into its proceedings and measures. But he abandoned the hope on the passage of the resolution, that the retention of Hebrew as the language of the synagogue service was only "advisable," not "essential" (*objektiv-nothwendig*). He, therefore, withdrew from the conference in a public manner, and justified his action in a formal declaration, equally dignified and firm.

On all sides Frankel's course met with hearty approval. Its effect was to startle the conservatives of every shade of opinion out of their apathy. Numerous prominent communities sent him flattering addresses, conveying their thanks and their unreserved commendation of his resolute policy. Graetz had written an enthusiastic document, which was circulated in Breslau, and was quickly covered with signatures. In collecting them, he had not been able to resist the malicious prompting to secure the names of notorious adherents of Geiger. The latter had taken deep offense at Frankel's secession, and had been betrayed into abuse by his declaration. It is impossible to say now, why Frankel did not at once utilize the disposition in his favor to gather a large conservative party about himself. Only in the following year, 1846, he took steps looking to this end. He issued invitations to the conservative theologians of modern bias, summoning them to a convention at Dresden, with the purpose perhaps of devising an effective opposition to the third reform conference of rabbis to meet at Breslau in July of the same year. But even this effort was not made with the energy characteristic of Frankel and necessary to accomplish the desired

result. When Graetz arrived in Dresden in September, 1846, he was amazed to find that no one else had put in appearance. Samson Raphael Hirsch, at that time District Rabbi of Emden, had from the first refused co-operation with the movement, inasmuch as he denied the authority, natural or conferred, of the modern rabbi to modify the religious cult. Rapoport of Prague had declined the invitation for reasons not specified. It is well-known that his interests were enlisted only in scientific pursuits. Michael Sachs of Berlin had excused himself on the plea of routine duties. For most of the others the time and place of convention were not convenient. To sue for support was out of the question with Frankel's aristocratic temperament. It was repugnant to him, or he did not know how, to create sentiment in his own favor by agitation or self-advertisement. He could not attract a party to his leadership by seductive wiles, nor infuse fanatic factionalism into its ranks. Relying solely on the justice of his cause, and appealing exclusively to the convictions of his followers, he scorned petty tricks and artifices. That Graetz was the only one to render unconditional obedience to his summons must naturally have produced a deep impression upon him. The two men, so different in years, disposition, and endowments, but at one in views and aims, were brought close to each other by the personal meeting. By tacit agreement they became companions in arms from that moment unto the end. Graetz, at all events, recognizing that their religious principles approximated each other, was resolved to take his position in theological affairs by Frankel's side, whenever so doing involved no loss of independence. Frankel in turn evinced a sense of their religious affinity by conferring upon Graetz, at his request, the formal authorization for the exercise of rabbinical functions (התרת הוראה). At the end of 1846, Frankel gave up

the publication of his journal to save his strength for a better future. To this third and last annual series, Graetz had contributed, besides several reviews, one of his important treatises, that discussing "The Construction of Jewish History"[1] in several articles. Bright and vivid in style and replete with fine thoughts which even homiletes drew upon in various ways, the essay defines clearly and sharply the considerations and points of view of essential importance in a complete presentation of Jewish history. But the author was still so prejudiced in favor of the technically philosophic terminology and conceptions of his time that he was betrayed into giving undue prominence to the transcendence of God as compared with the monotheistic idea.

Though Graetz had won high respect by his scholarly productions especially in theologic circles, he vainly looked about for a position, no matter how modest, in which to strike root. At last the sky seemed to grow brighter ; he was cheered by the prospect of soon being able to establish a home of his own, a prospect that proved a *fata morgana*. By the end of 1846 the orthodox party in Breslau resumed energetic operations. They had accepted as their rabbi Gedaliah, the son of the deceased Solomon Tiktin, who had inherited from his father only his tall stature, and they were preparing to open a religious school for the propaganda of their principles. Its organization and superintendence were entrusted to Graetz.[2] The Breslau community was no longer a unit, the orthodox members

[1] *Die Konstruktion der jüdischen Geschichte.*

[2] To accept this trust Graetz needed the permission of the municipal authorities, obtainable only by means of a duly accredited teacher's diploma. He therefore attended the Catholic Normal School at Breslau for some time as "student by courtesy" (*Hospitant*). On November 4, 1847, after having taken an examination, he was given a diploma testifying to his ability to fill the position of teacher and rector at an elementary school. It is the only official certificate of examination Graetz could show.

having separated from the congregation. But the seceders had no legally valid right to form a body corporate. Moreover, on July 23, 1847, the law defining the status of the Prussian Jews appeared, and it could not be determined how conditions would be modified by it. Wealthy individuals in their private capacity therefore assumed responsibility in the business contracts of the orthodox party, particularly in the matter of the new school. Then the political storms of 1848 swept over the Prussian provinces. Economic disturbances occurred, and apprehensive of still more serious ones, the wealthy patrons of the orthodox party recalled their pledges. The complete collapse of the religious school followed as the first sacrifice in orthodox circles claimed by the political flood, whose waves carried destructive change to the most remote relations between men. Graetz was again left stranded, without an occupation, without a livelihood.

At that time all eyes were turned towards Vienna, where the popular uprising had assumed vast dimensions and won surprising victories. Democracy stood in battle array, and had gained possession of the Austrian capital. It was fondly hoped that the fortune of war would decide there in favor of the democratic party. A friend of Graetz, Dr. B. Friedmann,[1] later rabbi in Mannheim, was at that time prominent in Breslau as an effective popular speaker, and was a member of the editorial staff of the democratic organ, the *Oder-zeitung*. By his intervention the curious proposi-

[1] This same Friedmann and Graetz appear as the joint authors of an article in Baur and Zeller's Theologic Year-book for 1848 (Vol. VII, p. 338), "On the Alleged Continuance of the Jewish Sacrificial Cult after the Destruction of the Second Temple" (*Ueber die angebliche Fortdauer des jüdischen Opferkultus nach der Zerstörung des zweiten Tempels*). Friedmann's share in the essay cannot be determined. The introduction plainly bears the marks of Graetz's manner and style, and Graetz was in the habit of considering the work his own. It is the only production published by him between 1846 and 1851.

tion was made to Graetz to go to Vienna as correspondent of the journal just mentioned. In his forlorn state he acquiesced, though not without reluctance. On his journey to Vienna, he felt impelled to leave the direct route and stop off at Nikolsburg to pay a visit to his former teacher, Samson Raphael Hirsch, who had meantime resigned the District Rabbinate of Emden for that of Nikolsburg. Letters had passed between them constantly since the Oldenburg days, and although Graetz was not in sympathy with the rigidly traditional point of view occupied by Hirsch, and no longer viewed the theologic attitude of his old guide with youthful enthusiasm, but rather with critical, sober judgment, their friendly relations of other times had suffered no diminution in cordiality. Graetz's love and reverence for Hirsch had not in the least evaporated, and Hirsch still felt strongly attracted to the younger man. He was not disposed to sanction his project of going to Vienna, the hot-bed of revolution, and Graetz, who had little love and desire for the calling of a political reporter, was easily persuaded to stay in Nikolsburg and content himself with a subordinate place at the religious school of the town. In the background, to be sure, the reversion of a teacher's position at a theologic seminary, projected and seriously considered by Hirsch, loomed up before him.

Hirsch had long cherished the idea of founding a Jewish theologic institute. He shared this dear ambition with the other prominent rabbis of his generation, who hoped thus to further their wish to perpetuate each one his own theologic bias. The establishment of a theologic seminary was, in fact, one of the burning questions of the day. Nikolsburg, where a popular Talmud school had flourished from time immemorial, seemed to lend itself to the execution of Hirsch's plan. It was only necessary to use the existing institution as a foun-

dation, make the proper changes in its management, and infuse the new spirit into it. Graetz was at once induced by his patron to give a course of lectures on Jewish history to the students at Nikolsburg, who were well versed in the Talmud, but whose training had been wholly dialectic. The character of his auditors suggested the subject to the lecturer. He treated the time of the Mishna and the Talmud, a period of which he had previously made a thorough study, and to which he again devoted serious research with a view to his academic purpose. Despite the zeal with which he applied himself to his lectures and studies, his main expectation suffered disappointment. The painfulness of his precarious position became more pronounced as time passed. The fanatics of the Nikolsburg Ghetto found fault even with the scrupulously religious conduct of their District Rabbi; as for his disciple, he went up and down among them a strange, repellant figure. Denunciations led the local authorities to suspect him of democratic leanings, and he was thus branded with the darkest stigma that could be fastened upon any one, but particularly upon a foreigner, in the Austria of that day. All the influence possessed by his friends had to be exerted to ward off ugly complications and immediate expulsion.

It became more and more evident that the rabbinical seminary, upon which Graetz had staked all his hopes, was only a bubble. Whether the circumstances of place and time were unpropitious, or whether Hirsch dropped the plan for other reasons, is doubtful.[1] Moreover, the friendly rela-

[1] In his *curriculum vitæ* (among the archives of the Board of Curators of the Bequests of the royal commercial councilor Fränkel, "relative to Graetz, teacher at the Seminary"), Graetz makes the following statements: "In 1849 I obeyed the summons of the District Rabbi of Moravia to participate in the establishment of, and to act as teacher at, a rabbinical seminary for Moravian and Austrian communities. But the institution did not come into existence; the

tions between the two men began to be somewhat strained. Therefore, the proposal to undertake the organization and superintendence of a school, made him by the directors of the Jewish community of Lundenburg, a little town in the Nikolsburg district in the neighborhood of Vienna, was hailed by Graetz as release from an untenable position. Negotiations were quickly concluded, and on September 12, 1850, he was appointed director and superintendent of the Jewish school at Lundenburg.

Before entering upon the duties of his office he hastened home, and in the beginning of October, 1850, solemnized his marriage with the loyal woman whose patience had never failed, who had never been discouraged by hope deferred, and had never lost confidence in his ability. He could not have found a truer, a braver comrade than the wife who shared the fortunes of the rest of his career. By her harmonious, temperate, and loving nature, she not only glorified his home and cheered cloudy days, but also restrained his impetuous disposition, and moderated his proneness to sharp, caustic, aggressive words. She understood the needs of his inmost soul, in the recesses of which a reverberation was sometimes heard as of vague, unfulfilled longings. His personality was made up of many an incommensurable factor that baffled explanation. With all his communicativeness he was reserved; the most intimate emotions of his heart were never revealed. To outsiders he always appeared wholly unruffled and serene, and no one suspected the thoughts and feelings stormily surging through his being under its placid surface. But in order to preserve his equanimity, he stood in need of frank ex-

unsettled condition of affairs in Austria, especially the permanent temporariness to which the position of the Israelites there had become a prey, prolonged the discussions on the execution of the plans for a seminary of the kind. I was therefore compelled to accept provisionally the superintendence of a Jewish public school at Lundenburg near Vienna."

pression to some one or in some way. It was the outlet and the purification of the easily excited and strongly reacting emotions of a nature responding quickly to external pressure. Probably the leaves of his diary served this purpose; most of them were written under the stimulus of tense passion. From the day of his marriage the record becomes more and more attenuated, until it ceases entirely. In his life-companion he had found the responsive being devoted to him in boundless veneration and sympathy, whose sentiments were a perfect echo, clearer usually than the original sound, of his thought and feeling. And as she took part in his soul-life, so she shared in his intellectual plans. She made her husband's scientific interests her own, and in his scholarly research afforded him the efficient help of a careful assistant.

The new principal began his work in Lundenburg on October 15 with zeal and love for his task—he superintended, classified, taught, and delivered solemn addresses. Apparently success was not lacking, for he met with encouraging applause. In the shelter of his modest but happy home, he resumed his literary plans and work. While preparing his Nikolsburg lectures, he had gathered together an abundance of material on the Talmudic era, which he now meant to put to use.

Before long, however, gray clouds cast a shadow on his idyllic condition. The relation between him and Hirsch almost suffered an open breach. When the newly married couple came to Nikolsburg to pay their respects to him, Hirsch demanded that the young wife, in accordance with a Talmudic custom, cover her beautiful hair with a sort of wig, called *Scheitel*. She resisted the bidding politely but firmly, with the pride of an offended woman. Graetz upheld his wife energetically, and the two parties separated little pleased with each other. The low-hanging mist apt to develop in the atmosphere of

narrow, undisciplined Ghetto life, particularly in a small Austrian community, was more oppressive even and harder to bear. The Lundenburg rabbi, a narrow-minded Talmudist, who feared to have his fame overshadowed by Graetz's, now and again asserted his official superiority unpleasantly. Small town rivalries were fomented to annoy the notabilities of the congregation by means of attacks upon the measures and the men they favored. Such conditions made Graetz feel by their hidden venom that unmixed joy is the portion of no mortal, least of all of the principal of an Austrian communal school. Denunciations of him were again rife. Those before the district court representing him as a democrat incarnate were particularly troublesome. Happily the charges were dismissed without in the least injuring him.

The year 1851 heightened his happiness; it brought him the joys of fatherhood. A daughter was born to him, the only one in a family of five children. His relation to her was always peculiarly close and affectionate. In the same year Zacharias Frankel re-entered the theologic arena with a monthly journal, which, unlike his earlier venture, the *Zeitschrift*, was to be devoted first and foremost to scientific interests. Graetz received a most honorable invitation to become a contributor, and he gladly ranged himself under Frankel's banner. In quick succession he published in the first year of the "Monthly Journal for the History and Science of Judaism"[1] (October, 1851–December, 1852) a series of historical monographs: "Jewish Historical Studies;"[2] a review of Rapoport's Encyclopedia; "Talmudic Chronology and Topography;"[3] and "The Removable Highpriests of the Second Temple Period"[4]—all of which evinced great erudition, clear

[1] *Monatsschrift für Geschichte und Wissenschaft des Judenthums.*
[2] *Jüdisch-geschichtliche Studien.*
[3] *Die talmudische Chronologie und Topographie.*
[4] *Die absetzbaren Hohepriester während des zweiten Tempels.*

grasp of the subject, and mature judgment. They are of the nature of special studies in preparation and as a foundation for a connected account of the events from the downfall of the Jewish state until the completion of the Talmud. He had long cherished the idea of such a work, and he now reduced it to writing with great rapidity.

In the meantime, in the course of the year 1852, the complexion of the district court seems to have changed, or the wind was blowing from another quarter; at all events, Graetz suddenly and with painful surprise became aware that unceasing intrigues and malicious denunciations had at last taken effect upon the district governor. He found himself exposed to serious annoyances and humiliations. No effort to ward them off promising success, he resigned his position at Lundenburg.

He felt impelled to return to his native Prussia, and determined to remove to Berlin with his family. The decision was inspired by the hope of easily finding in the capital a publisher for his history of the Talmudic epoch, which was almost ready for the press. He was furthermore actuated by the consideration, that in the prosecution of the plan of writing a complete history of the Jews, already taking shape in his mind, he could not well do without the libraries to be found only in large cities. In the latter half of September, 1852, he arrived in Berlin, and was kindly received by Dr. Michael Sachs and other friends willing to serve him. Through Dr. Sachs he became acquainted with the excellent Dr. Veit, who undertook the publication of his work. During the winter *semester* 1852–53 the directors of the Berlin congregation invited him to deliver, for a honorarium, a number of historical lectures before students of Jewish theology, in a course in which the other speakers were Zunz and Sachs. His lectures were received with ap-

proval.[1] At the close of one of them, delivered in the middle of February, he was approached by Joseph Lehmann, railway director and editor of a journal in good standing, "Magazine for Foreign Literature,"[2] a man justly enjoying high respect. Acting under the instructions of the Board of Curators of the Fränkel Bequests in Breslau, Lehmann asked Graetz, whether he would be disposed to become a member of the faculty of the rabbinical seminary to be established at Breslau. At the

[1] J. Lehmann, whose zeal in behalf of the founding of the seminary was highly commendable, reports (Archives of the Board of Curators of the Fränkel Bequests. I, Vol. 1, relative to the Seminary) as follows: "Every evening between 7 and 8, in the building of the Boys' School of the Jewish community, a lecture is delivered before Jewish divinity students, Dr. Zunz lecturing on Rabbinic Literature, Dr. Graetz on Jewish History, and Dr. Sachs on the Proverbs of Solomon. The lectures are well attended by about twenty-five or thirty prospective rabbis, who take notes industriously, and by a dozen Jewish scholars who come as visitors (*Hospitanten*) . . . Zunz was obviously making an inspiring impression upon his audience; his dry subject was rendered spicy by piquant observations on Eisenmenger and Karpzow, Wagenseil and Richard Simon, and not a few innuendoes touching the present. On the evening when I heard Sachs, he had just begun the introduction to the exegesis of the Proverbs. It seemed to me that on the whole he was a little too abstruse, although there was no dearth of beautiful thoughts expressed in a manner still more beautiful. Dr. Graetz is a young man, who is very much praised by competent judges. Report says that his lectures bristle with new data and results; I myself have not yet heard him. He is said to have lived in Breslau at one time, and he came here from Lundenburg, his last residence, at the suggestion of Dr. Sachs. The institution of these three lecture courses on six evenings was proposed by the school trustees of the Jewish community. They have appropriated the means for carrying them on (about 1200 *Reichsthaler*) from the legacy fund of the *Talmud-Torah* School. Their right to do this has been contested in certain quarters, but for the present they are supported by the authorization of the communal directors and the approval of the intelligent. I have madè this preface to enable you to estimate to what extent the judgment of those consulted by me with regard to the Breslau project is based upon what has been done here, inadequate though it be. . . . At first, Sachs, who recently received a letter from Frankel in Dresden inquiring into the feasibility of establishing a Rabbinical Institute for Berlin and Dresden in common, also intended to put down his opinion in writing for me, etc."

[2] *Das Magazin für die Litteratur des Auslandes.*

same time he told him, that negotiations with Dr. Frankel, Chief Rabbi of Dresden, were pending with regard to the directorship, and that Frankel, among other conditions of his acceptance, had demanded Graetz's engagement as teacher. The Board of Curators had assented cheerfully, and now desired Graetz's answer. Graetz made his consent dependent upon Frankel's final, favorable decision, which was received soon after. These preliminaries over, the troublesome discussions on the organization of the seminary began. In the first place, no model or scheme whatsoever existed that might serve as a guide in the organization of a rabbinical academy, with regard to such matters as the time-schedule, the curriculum, and the choice of subjects. Its creation was pioneer work, in furtherance of which there was no available experience; yet the arrangements determined upon under such peculiar circumstances were to bear within themselves the guarantee of practical and immediate success. Besides, the will of the founder, Jonas Fränkel, contained certain clauses, the execution of which, in view of the changed times, might become a menace to the new institution.[1] The plan, curriculum, and methods of the future seminary were determined by Zacharias Frankel alone, who recognized the aim to be pursued with clearness and practical insight, and so created the basis for the Jewish theology of the present. His wish to secure a professionally trained man, whose assistance might be freely drawn upon by himself and the Board of Curators, was all the more willingly complied with, as from many considerations an intermediary between the business and the pedagogic heads seemed not superfluous. Frankel had parted from Dresden

[1] Cmp. "The Jewish Theological Seminary founded by Fränkel at Breslau on the 25th Anniversary of its Existence, August 10, 1879," p. 5.

with a heavy heart, and was inclined to seize the first fairly just pretense to recall his word to the Curators. Thus it came about that Graetz entered the service of the projected seminary on July 1, 1853, with the assurance of being employed, under Frankel's directorship, as one of the principal teachers,[1] in case the statutes and the plans for the institution met with governmental approval, which seemed not at all doubtful.

V.

THE MASTER HISTORIAN.

At the same time Graetz's book issued from the press under the title: "History of the Jews from the Downfall of the Jewish State to the Completion of the Talmud."[2] This was really the sub-title. The chief title-page ran as follows: "History of the Jews from the Earliest Times until the Present Day. Volume IV,"[3] indicating that the author had conceived more than the first sketchy plan of a complete history of the Jews, and that the publication of the fourth volume first was merely an accident in the order of production. Beginning with

[1] The Curators as well as Joseph Lehmann entertained the cordial wish and made earnest efforts to obtain a place for Geiger on the teaching staff of the Seminary. But Frankel met every demand looking to this end with abrupt refusal. Even Joseph Lehmann, who had a decided inclination towards Geiger, could not help making the following frank admission in an earlier letter (February 3, 1853) addressed to the Board of Curators: "The communication of the Rabbinical Conference of 1846, which I shall return to you, unfortunately has no value for us, because none of the five signers (Geiger, Holdheim, Philippson, Salomon, and Stein) continues to enjoy the authority in Germany necessary to secure the confidence of the class of Jews chiefly to be considered in the launching of an undertaking like this."

[2] *Geschichte der Juden vom Untergange des jüdischen Staates bis zum Abschluss des Talmud.*

[3] *Geschichte der Juden von den ältesten Zeiten bis auf die Gegenwart. Vierter Band.*

the account of the Talmudic time turned out a happy hit. If the two literary events admit of comparison, Graetz's first important work has its only counterpart in the biography of Rashi, with which Zunz, the creator of the science of Judaism, inaugurated his notable activity. The enthusiasm of Zunz's contemporaries is said to have been kindled when Rashi, the eminent interpreter of Bible and Talmud, familiar to them from their childhood days, and esteemed an indispensable guide and companion in exegesis, appeared to them divested of the vaporous halo of supernatural glory, and translated into the sphere of human reality. Similarly the effect was electrifying when a flood of brilliant light suddenly scattered the mist of the dark epoch in which Mishna and Talmud, the authoritative books of post-Biblical Judaism, were composed, and revealed to sight life-size the rabbi-authors of those works, whose names and maxims were matter of common knowledge. The pen of our historian had charmed them out of the unreality of their existence. They had been habitually looked upon as abstractions, doctrines incarnate. Not much more had been known of them than that they had said, asked, and sometimes wailed. At best, people had been inclined to imagine them a sort of Kabbalists or Polish itinerant rabbis. Now it was seen that hot blood and throbbing life pulsated in their veins. Their clear-cut, mental features with their characteristic excellencies and shortcomings distinguished one from the other. They stood before the reader in checkered array, true knights by the grace of intellect, antique figures, glowing with patriotism, of inflexible will and indestructible faith. With equal vividness the author depicted the spiritual atmosphere of the time with its humors, passions, fermentation, and struggles ; the surging and seething of ideas, factions, opinions, and aims in wild disorder and violent opposition to one another ; and the

final evolution of the impelling forces which determine the course of historical events by the exchange of thrust and counterthrust. Graetz wanted to make the heart-beat of the period perceptible to the senses. Therefore, he was little concerned about the technical correctness of his style and diction. He did not shrink from brusqueness in words, nor from luridness and voluptuousness in coloring. Without regard to sensitive feelings he chose the plainest, the most striking expressions, that he might be understood by all; that no doubt as to his opinion might suggest itself; that personages and events might appear upon the canvas in a clear light and in the proper position, as they were mirrored in his mind.

The book naturally aroused a great sensation upon its appearance. It at once created an audience for itself with which it found a rich measure of favor and applause. On the other hand, most of the author's scholarly colleagues at first reserved their opinions. They were taken aback by the new data, which—as, for instance, the formation of Christian sects—had been boldly pressed into service to complete the picture, and they could not reconcile themselves to the description of ancient conditions by means of modern catchwords and turns of expression peculiar to the lighter forms of literature. For example, Graetz characterizes Nachum of Gimso, in whose life mishap after mishap redounded to his benefit, as the Candide[1] of the Tanaitic world of legend. He seeks to reconstruct the details of the Bar-Cochba revolt, the chapter on which is one of the most beautiful and touching in his "History," from single names and widely scattered debris. He goes so far as to speak of two lines of defense, the Esdraelon line and the Tur-Malka line.[2] He

[1] *Geschichte der Juden*, Vol. IV (Ed. 1), p. 22.
[2] *Ibid.* p. 169 (American Edition, II, p. 414).

charges the eminent teacher Judah ha-Nassi with irritability and sensitiveness.[1] Relying on Talmudic accounts, he refuses to credit the Romans with a civilizing mission in Asia, and describes their influence in Western Asia in particular as destructive of culture and detrimental to morality. Such features of the work confounded the critics and judges. They did not venture to decide whether the boldness of genial originality was asserting itself, or only the uncouthness of fantastic sensationalism, whose tinsel would not stand the test of time. Moreover, the two religious parties looked askance and with dissatisfaction at a book written to serve the truth only and not available for any sort of propaganda. Loud and public quarrel between them had ceased in the face of the world-stirring events of 1848 and their consequences, but they were as sharply divided as ever. The adherents of the reform party reproached the author with having glorified the Talmud and its teachers, and with having omitted to touch in "a single word"[2] upon the sorest spot, "the petrifaction and ossification of Judaism" brought about by the code and its exponents. The rigidly orthodox, on the other hand, were incensed at the criticism, unwarranted in their eyes, to which he subjected the bearers of tradition and at his effort to prove the body of traditional doctrine the product of historical processes.[3]

But no voice dissented from the opinion, that in Graetz Jewish science had gained an eminent promoter with astonishing scholarship at his disposal. His qualifications and achievements were too extraordinary to be belittled on account of the unavoidable errors that had slipped into his history. It could not be denied, that research had received a decided impetus, and that the sum of historical

[1] *Ibid.* p. 236 (American Edition, II, p. 454).
[2] L. Stein, *Der israelitische Volkslehrer*, V, 1855, p. 37.
[3] S. R. Hirsch, *Jeshurun*, II and III.

knowledge had been considerably increased by Graetz's results, which he had obtained by his mastery over the two Talmuds and the Midrash literature; by his close acquaintance with patristic works; by his effective way of bringing these two widely separated literary spheres close to each other, permitting the one to shed light on the other, and thus clearing up critical points; by his happy gift first of discerning, in spite of the rectification they frequently stood in need of, that certain data scattered over various by-paths of literature were complementary, and then of combining them with each other; and by his acuteness in detecting with unerring glance, animating with spirit, and applying to good purpose, long disused geographical names and obsolete terms lying forgotten in some dark corner and buried under debris.[1] In view of the fact that it required rare courage to venture upon the elaboration of one of the obscurest and most difficult portions of Jewish history, thoroughly neglected at that time in the way of special research and monographs, even his opponents could "not help confessing that on the whole he had fulfilled his task satisfactorily."[2] There was evidence, to be sure, of still higher courage in Graetz's announcement, made without fear or diffidence, on the title-page and in the preface of his book, designated as the fourth volume, that he intended to publish a complete history of the Jews, written in the same spirit of critical research and in the same style. The promise gave occasion for ironical insinuations. How could a single individual hope to accomplish so great an undertaking? Was Graetz endowed with the creative, plastic power of the genuine historian? Or, perhaps he expected to obtain the laurels of the historian on credit!

[1] Cmp. *Geschichte der Juden,* Vol. IV, Note 20 (in later editions, Note 16).

[2] *Der israelitische Volkslehrer,* as cited above.

On the whole, circumstances shaped themselves in a way favorable to him, and facilitated the execution of his bold undertaking. It should not be imagined that a community, or—still more extravagant idea—a Mæcenas offered to furnish him with the means indispensable for the accomplishment of a task such as he had set himself. Brilliant as his achievement was, how much greater it might have been, if he, with his genius for work, had been put in a position to examine and use at his leisure the manuscript treasures of the various European libraries! Up to the present day such good fortune has not befallen Jewish science. It seems as though the Jewish race, endowed with an understanding heart and an open hand for humane interests in general, has not yet awakened to a full recognition of the debt of honor it owes its own past. Graetz, however, was well content to be relieved of the irksome care for his daily bread by the ratification, on April 10, 1854, on the part of the Prussian government, of the statutes, the plan, and the teaching staff of the Rabbinical Seminary. He returned to Breslau, where his literary star had first risen, and where he had once tried vainly to establish himself permanently. Thenceforth he remained there in the congenial position of a regularly appointed teacher at the first Jewish theologic institution, which was inaugurated, with Z. Frankel as director, on August 10, 1854, under the name of "The Jewish Theological Seminary founded by Fränkel."[1]

It must be looked upon as providential that the task of first impressing the modern spirit upon the theologic training for the rabbinical office fell to the share of men of such eminent distinction as Frankel, the director of the new institution, and Graetz and Jacob Bernays, its regular teachers. The personality of each of the three was strongly

[1] *Jüdisch-theologisches Seminar, Fränkel'sche Stiftung.*

marked. Each one was a *homo trium litterarum*, in the sense that in subordination to his specialty, he had acquired mastery over the Hebrew-rabbinic, the classical, and the modern literature. By deep and earnest thought each had arrived at a conservative view of Judaism. Of the three, Jacob Bernays,[1] a scholar of far-reaching fame in classical philology, doubtless possessed greatest ability as a teacher, which, however, demanded talented pupils for its effective exercise. Frankel's forte lay in his tact as an organizer and in his practical gifts; he exerted wholesome authority over his disciples in religious as well as scientific matters. Both desired to impress their scientific bias upon those that came under their influence. Graetz, on the other hand, heeded the individuality of his pupils, and in his activity as teacher had in mind especially their stimulation and encouragement. Frankel was desirous of transferring to the Theological Seminary the rigid discipline and detailed supervision of an elementary school,[2] because his dearest object was to turn out thorough Talmudists and professionally well-equipped rabbis. Bernays aspired to the romantic splendor of a theologic faculty, and wanted to educate scholarly theologians. With correct and healthy instinct, Graetz endeavored to reconcile these opposite aims and identify the Seminary with a middle course. Although Frankel grasped the rudder with a firm hand, he was sensible enough to consider prudent counsel and kindly enough to give scope to the wishes and views of his colleagues. In this way harmony prevailed among the Seminary teachers, which reacted beneficially upon the stu-

[1] A son of the Hamburg rabbi, or, as he called himself, Chacham, Isaac Bernays.

[2] This tendency was justified by the circumstance, that under existing conditions admission to the Seminary had to be granted on attainments not more than sufficient for the second class of a Prussian *Gymnasium*, and pupils were to be received at the early age of fourteen.

dents. As long as he lived, Frankel justly maintained what officially and morally was the dominant position in the Seminary. The prosperity of the institution he considered the consummation of his life-work, and being childless, he regarded his pupils as his children, and took a truly paternal interest in their fortunes. Next to him Graetz exercised the most generous hospitality towards the students. He was ever ready to serve any one of them that needed help and advice. Especially such as had aroused his interest, or had impressed him favorably with their ability and character enlisted his sympathy, which he manifested with all the ardor of his temperament. Like Frankel, he identified himself completely with the Breslau Seminary. After many thwarted plans and years of anxious uncertainty, he felt that, at last, through his position as teacher at the Seminary, his vessel had floated into deep, navigable waters, that he could venture to ply the oars with full force, unfurl all the sails, and, favored by wind and weather and propelled by the buoyant courage peculiar to his sanguine nature, steer straight for the destination whither impulse drew him. It was the first time that his official duties coincided with his inner vocation. Faithful, zealous performance of the service he was engaged to do promoted the work he had set himself as the goal of his life. In regular, uninterrupted succession, volume after volume of his "History" now began to appear in complete realization of his plan.

In 1856 the *third* volume was published under the title, "History of the Jews from the Death of Judas Maccabæus to the Downfall of the Jewish State."[1] It formed the complement and justification of his view of the Talmudic epoch, the one with which he had begun as being the period "least understood in its inner relations." At the same time

[1] *Geschichte der Juden von dem Tode Juda Makkabis bis zum Untergang des jüdischen Staates.*

the third volume distinctly bounds the spiritual territory in which the Jewish history of the diaspora is rooted. For he intended to dispose of the Jewish history of the diaspora down to the present time before beginning the account of the Biblical and the early post-Biblical periods. Therefore, when he published his fifth volume, "History of the Jews from the Completion of the Talmud (500) to the Beginnings of Jewish-Spanish Culture (1027),"[1] he had, as he said in the preface, "got back on the right track." Now every doubt was bound to vanish; after many years a genuine historian had arisen unto Judaism.

The historian must not be confounded with the scholar. The chief tasks of the latter are the critical examination of historical records, the determining and grouping of facts, the identifying and differentiating of persons, the demarcation of time and place, and the defining and demonstrating of the causal relation between events, their succession, and their interaction. The minute details to which his research happens to be devoted at any moment are as important in his eyes as great and comprehensive principles. Style, form, and manner, moreover, are minor considerations with the scholar; he aims only at accuracy and lucid presentation adapted to the subject-matter. The demands made upon the historian are more numerous and more exacting. He must constantly carry the whole in mind, he must have the ability to mould the historical material with an artist's creative power and restore the faded features of the past by the life-bestowing word. First of all, he must be equipped with unlimited mastery over the existing material and with easy and sure grasp of all the phases of the historical process, in order to be able to estimate every phenomenon duly, according to its intrinsic value and

[1] *Geschichte der Juden vom Abschluss des Talmud* (500) *bis zum Aufblühen der jüdisch-spanischen Kultur* (1027).

its external effect, emphasize characteristic and significant points, and allot to persons and events their proper place in the historical succession. He cannot, of course, dispense with the acumen that intuitively arrives at the inwardness of every detail. For it is needful, not only to determine with critical penetration the trustworthiness of existing traditions and documents, but also to discern and demonstrate, as one traces the course of a stream with its tributaries and branches, the presence of the primal forces at work under the surface of things, giving them impetus and direction, and of the factors that impede, strengthen, or divert the action of these forces. From investigations of this kind the historian should derive the chief points of view, those which grow naturally and logically out of the course of events. The true historian must be endowed to a high degree with a faculty for presaging, amounting almost to divination, that he may, like a "backward-looking prophet," overcome the inadequacy and incompleteness of the material transmitted to him; restore the defective parts by means of his plastic fancy; and everywhere recognize as well as bring to the recognition of his readers, that historical events in their connection are developments from within outward, the outcome, not of a game of chance, but of the workings of absolute law. For such results of his research and insight the historian must then find adequate expression. His presentation of them must serve as the clear, polished mirror reflecting the play of many-hued, chaotic details in distinct and simply grouped pictures, and permitting the peculiarities and characteristics of single persons and events to be apparent, as the warp and the woof are distinguishable in the finished fabric. Real life as it throbbed in the happenings of the past must stand renewed before our eyes, and its fresh, warm breath as it brushes us must constrain our souls to respond at once to its humors and passions.

These qualities are the distinction of Graetz. By reason of their possession and exercise he is a master historian, and his art manifests itself in each of the twelve comprehensive volumes in which he has thrown light upon the history of the Jewish race from its early beginning to the present, a period of more than three thousand years, with every part of the earth as the scene of its events. But we have not yet come to the end of Graetz's accomplishments as an historian. The lack of special studies in the province of Jewish history made his attempt to write a history of the Jews appear untimely and the prospect of successful execution slight. His undertaking seemed to be opposed not only by well-nigh insuperable inner and outer obstacles, but also by stubborn prejudices. Graetz heeded nothing of all this. Unaided by any committee or corporation, simply by virtue of his exuberant genius, he executed the apparently impossible work. He created the history of their race for his brethren-in-faith, and awakened in the general public sympathetic interest in the past of Judaism. With bold hand he ventured to brush aside the layer of dust and mould encrusting the darkened portraits of the past, and restore freshness and color to the faded, pale contours and forms.

The most important particulars upon which the value and influence of his work depend deserve analysis.

Above all, Graetz, though he did not create it, was the first to define and occupy the point of view from which the historical development of Judaism must be judged. He cleared the whole historical field, so as to be able to examine the various phases of this development with ease and accuracy. As an historian, Graetz had had but a single predecessor[1] who must be taken into account, Isaac Marcus

[1] The Protestant clergyman and diplomat, Jacob Basnage (d. 1723), historiographer of the Netherlands, was the first to write a history of the Jews down to his own time. The means at his command were

Jost. In 1820, the latter began to publish a "History of the Israelites from the Time of the Maccabees."[1] Nine years later nine volumes had appeared, bringing the history down to his own time. Under the title, "Universal History of the Israelitish People,"[2] he published, in 1850, a two-volume epitome with corrections and improvements, covering in addition the period from Abraham to the Maccabees. He did not prove himself a real pioneer in either work. Jost was a scholar, but not an historian; a noble man with admirable qualities, whose varied knowledge gave a considerable impetus to Jewish historical work, but he had not been singled out as the proclaimer of an historical revelation to be spread far and wide in joyful, vigorous utterance. In view of the fact, however, that no monographs on special phases of the subject existed at his time, Jost's achievement cannot be sufficiently admired. He sought out and arranged the more or less obvious, but widely scattered data, appraising their value and assigning to each its due place. He thus produced a manual for the chaos of confusing details and facts. In respect to manner, his presentation of the subject makes the impression of an herbarium. His work consists of a collection of persons and events, heaped up without reference to their inner relations and classified only according to superficial and accidental marks of resemblance. His speculations are prosy, and do not touch the essence of their subject. His style is dry, diffuse, and monotonous, destitute of fire and force, with nothing to indicate that the author had a lively

inadequate and his historical insight hazy, yet he produced a connected account, which Jost took as a guide. The second attempt of the kind was made by an American woman, a Christian, Hannah Adams of Boston (1818), who was able to use only secondary sources. Cmp. for the predecessors of Graetz, his *Geschichte*, XI, p. 452 ff. (American Edition, V, p. 593).

[1] *Geschichte der Israeliten seit der Zeit der Makkabäer.*

[2] *Allgemeine Geschichte des israelitischen Volkes.*

realization of the past. An admirer of the Roman system and impregnated with Christian ideas, he was unconsciously oppressed by the fear that he was not abreast of the times, and dreaded the charge of partiality if he gave due credit to Judaism and Rabbinism. This accounts for his misrepresentation of the Pharisees and their successors, the Rabbis, and for his false, almost caricature-like treatment of the Talmud and the literature depending upon it. He felt that the consideration of Judaism from the point of view of history at once becomes a glorification thereof, and under no circumstances did he care to incur the imputation of being its apologist.[1]

Graetz entertained no such scruples. In the formation of his opinions fear or timidity had no part; they did not curtail the expression of his judgment regardless of the feelings of friend or foe. He was the first to divest himself wholly of Christian prejudices in the consideration of the Jewish past; the first to try to explain the development of Judaism on inherent principles, as all similar phenomena are explained. He was thus able to distribute light and shade justly, without any attempt to gloss or slur facts. Graetz had been in Berlin but a short time when he met Zunz at the house of Michael Sachs. The two visitors had not yet made each other's personal acquaintance. The host presented Graetz, adding in praise of him, that he was about to publish a Jewish history. "Another history of the Jews?" Zunz asked pointedly. "Another history," was Graetz's retort, "but this time a *Jewish* history."[2] And, in truth,

[1] His last historical work, "The History of Judaism and its Sects" (*Geschichte des Judenthums und seiner Sekten*, 3 vols., 1857-59), Jost wrote in a different key. Influenced by Graetz's work, he tended towards the adoption of the younger historian's point of view.

[2] Zunz considered the attempt to write a history of the Jews premature. When he asked the question, he probably had in mind the bungling "History of the Israelites" by Dr. J. H. Dessauer (1846), and in the allusion to it, covert though it was, lay the sting.

Graetz was the first to vindicate the fair claims of Jewish history; he did pioneer work in establishing the validity of the Jewish point of view. Christianity considers the belief in the Messiahship of the Son of God and in the miracles reported in connection with his birth and death the completion and fulfillment of the Law of Moses and of the prophetical promises. Only what springs from this dogma can rise to a proper conception of God, to the heights of true morality, and is capable of promoting the advancement of civilization. Accordingly, having begotten Christianity, Judaism fulfilled its religious mission, and the loss of Jewish national independence occurring almost simultaneously with the rise of Christianity, its spiritual importance was extinguished and its historical progress arrested. Its development since then, it is maintained, bears the marks of decrepitude and degeneration—is nothing more than idolatry of the *Torah* and religious formalism. To this consciously or unconsciously biased view Graetz wished to oppose a faithful presentation of facts, free from partiality, personal predilections, or specious coloring. He held, that an objective, unprejudiced account sufficed to demonstrate the vitality of Judaism, asserting itself again and again in the midst of distress and persecution; continuing to develop its monotheistic doctrines and its ethical system undisturbed by the loss of a national background, and borne onward only by virtue of its spirituality and ideality; producing thinkers, poets, and even statesmen despite untold suffering; and contributing zealously to the solution of the problems of human civilization, uprooted and dispersed though its adherents were. This point of view Graetz assumed energetically and applied consistently in the elaboration of Jewish history, with the result that we owe to him our conscious acquaintance with the various aspects of Judaism in all their abundance and suggestiveness.

Besides making new sources available, Graetz gained fresh points of view and surprising information from the old ones. He was particularly successful in restoring to Jewish accounts that had become hazy or sounded incredible a freshly colored background and life-like reality, or at least in laying bare their kernel of fact, by the discovery of hardly recognizable parallel passages and proofs in non-Jewish authors. He sought everywhere, and was more or less successful in finding and inserting in their place, connecting links and complementary pieces. When he approached his bold undertaking with the courage inspired by enthusiasm, Jewish history was a vast field of debris, over which volcanic events had poured out their lava, and the centuries had scattered their dust. Here and there a gigantic ruin, some literary production, towered in solitude over the wide stretches of the pathless, dismal waste, the only guide-posts to direct the wanderer through the labyrinth of ruins and underbrush. The great creators of Jewish science, to be sure, Zunz and Rapoport, whose extraordinary deserts are not yet duly appreciated by their brethren-in-faith, had already given the world their excellent works of fundamental importance; yet the great tracts explored and made arable by them seemed no more than smaller or larger islands in a vast sea of rubbish. They did not afford vantage-ground from which the whole could be overlooked. Rarely leaving the domain of literary history, these scholars did not lead up to the positions that dominated the field. In this respect particularly Graetz proved himself a pioneer. Whatever epoch he may be considering, and however much he may seem to be absorbed in details, he never takes his eye from the grand whole. His purpose always is to clear a path through the rank underbrush, or to trace on the exposed surfaces of shattered remains the lines and veins that indicate the essential character and the

trend of the historical process. He was endowed with a number of qualities that enabled him to introduce light, order, system, and classification into the chaos of the historical material at his disposal. With rare energy he plunged into the consideration of vast systems of thought, and almost without an effort assimilated and grouped them. In his learned notes he opposes varying accounts, proofs, and hints to one another, and with an adroit hand and a perspicacious mind grasps the main idea firmly and unravels the knotted thread. Finally, fear of error did not deter him from taking a decided stand towards events and persons and giving frank and vigorous expression to his views upon them. Let the reader examine the essays that serve as introductions to certain parts of his work, as, for instance, those in the fourth, fifth, and seventh volumes, and he will appreciate the unerring eye that espies and never loses from sight the motive ideas and the dominating points of view, which not merely are sketched in a general, comprehensive way, but are applied in detail. His "History" affords numerous illustrations of the way in which Graetz promoted and enriched historical research. For example, Saadiah Gaon had been discovered, as it were, by Rapoport, and Geiger had made valuable contributions to our knowledge of him, but the chapter about him in the "History"[1] first fully revealed his epoch-making importance and his rich literary activity. Graetz was the first to recognize and appreciate the notable influence exerted by Chasdaï Crescas[2] upon philosophy and social conditions. The great Disputation of Tortosa, of which we have a trustworthy Jewish account, was nevertheless not understood in its historical bearing and political effect until Graetz ingeniously con-

[1] *Geschichte*, Vol. V (American Edition, Vol. III, pp. 188-207).
[2] *Ibid.*, Vol. VIII (American Edition, Vol. IV, pp. 145-147, 191-193).

fronted the Jewish source with Christian reports.[1] The cloud of legend enveloping the enthusiasts David Reubeni and Solomon Molcho,[2] whom students were inclined to regard as no more than hallucinations or phantasmagoria, he resolved into the reality of their fantastic adventures. In short, coupled with rare sagacity in perceiving the true meaning of a mutilated text and emending it accordingly, he had a remarkable instinct for piercing to the reality of facts, no matter how grotesque they might appear.

Such endowments qualified Graetz to translate the Talmudic method of thought and expression into the terms of modern feelings and views, and give a model illustration of the critical examination of the literature of Talmudic times and its use as a valuable historical source. Non-Jewish scholars and sciolists were quick to brand the apparently unintelligible or the curious passages abounding in rabbinic literature as evidences of Talmudic ignorance or rabbinic folly, and the Jews of the emancipation period, if they did not subscribe to this verdict, at least hesitated whether or not to endorse it. Graetz showed plainly that precisely the text of the historical narratives had become wretchedly corrupted and would have to be restored. Besides, he called attention to various features of the historical tradition as told by the rabbis. Either they were treated pragmatically, with their causes and results, or their presentation was intentionally biased, or layers of legend had deposited themselves about the kernel of fact, which awaited release from its envelopes. Over and above all this, he urged that the concrete, figurative expressions of the rabbis, derived from a sphere of thought foreign to us, must be translated into modern concepts. For instance, in an ancient rabbinic chronicle, the *Seder olam rabba*, it is

[1] *Ibid.*, Vol. VIII (American Edition, Vol. IV, pp. 207-216).
[2] *Ibid.*, Vol. IX (American Edition, Vol. IV, pp. 491-511).

reported that the war of Vespasian is separated from that of Titus by an interval of twenty-two years. Aside from the consideration that it is neither historical nor justifiable to distinguish between a war of Vespasian and a war of Titus, it is impossible to give a satisfactory explanation of the period of twenty-two years. The same incomprehensible distinction between Vespasian's and Titus' war occurs in the Mishna at the end of the tractate *Sota*. Graetz changed a single letter, ט into ק, and instead of טיטוס (Titus), he reads קיטוס (Kitus), *i. e.* Quietus. In this way he discovered a rebellion in Palestine against Lucius Quietus. We know none of its details, but its occurrence is beyond the peradventure of a doubt. The conjecture, as simple as it is ingenious, has been corroborated by a manuscript reading.[1] A narrative in tractate *Sabbath* 17[a] is no less curious: "A sword was thrust into the academy, with the words: Whoever desires may go in, but none may come out," etc. Graetz explains the enigma thus: in the first year of the rebellion against Nero a terrorist synod was dominated by the Shammaites.[2] In general, he considered the opposition between the schools of Hillel and Shammai not merely theoretic but also political, and he identified the rabid Zealots with extreme Shammaites.

"Graetz is deserving of great praise for having established this fact [the existence of the terrorist synod], until then not sufficiently appreciated. In itself it is an extremely important result, and its value is heightened by reason of the data growing out of it. . . . At all events, Herr Graetz has won a second distinction of equally great importance by his use of the *Megilla Taanith* as a historical source and his verification of its statements, even though many remain dubious."

This is the opinion of the historian[3] Jost, surely a competent judge in such matters.

[1] Cmp. *Geschichte*, Vol. IV, 2 Ed., Note 14.
[2] *Geschichte*, Vol. III, 2 Ed., Note 26.
[3] Jost, *Geschichte des Judenthums und seiner Sekten*, Pt. 1, p. 437, Note 2.

Where so much light is radiated, there cannot fail to be some shadows. Graetz's admirable qualities have a reverse side. He often permits subjective views to obtrude themselves too much, and in stating his hypotheses he is apt to clothe them in terms too positive and incisive, not heeding that events dovetail into each other; that men yield to changeful humors and motives, often of a contradictory nature; and that illogical, even irrational turns of language and thought may occasionally occur in the texts. It surely is not astonishing to find inaccuracies, human errors, and misconceptions here and there in a gigantic work of twelve bulky volumes. Faults and shortcomings vanish into forgetfulness by the side of the multiplicity of his results and the grandeur of his achievement. Perspective, life-like characterization, distinct outline, glowing color—these Jewish history owes solely to Graetz's rich fancy. He opened up new problems, created the historical types, constructed the framework of Jewish history. But his greatest achievement, one that cannot be rated sufficiently high, is that of having procured a hearing with all strata of his coreligionists by means of his charming, easy style. He revived the consciousness of an illustrious past, glorious in spite of persecution and degradation, and the belief in a future of spiritual triumph for Israel. Energetic and ardent as his temperament was, he merged his being in the past of his race, as it were, giving devoted study to the most hidden emotions of the national soul. He associated with the rabbis, philosophers, and poets whose features and forms he draws as with companions and intimate friends. When storms are imminent in the course of the history, he is visibly swayed by hope and fear, and when a catastrophe has overwhelmed his people, he is bowed down with anguish and grief. The reader sees his suffering, and cannot withhold passionate

sympathy. For instance, he trembles at the thought of the disgrace and misfortune threatening Israel on account of the aberrations of the pseudo-Messiah Sabbataï Zevi, and consoles himself with the brilliant light of Jewish origin irradiating the world through Spinoza. According to his favorite method of setting men and events over against each other and permitting them to elucidate each other by their very opposition, he sharply contrasts the two figures. He represents both as the product of the Jewish passion for speculation on the infinite, and shows how in the end both sever their connection with Judaism; the one, lured on by the will-o'-the-wisp mysticism, to sink into the abyss of deception and immorality; the other, borne upward by philosophic thought, to soar to the calm but cold heights of an ideal sage.[1] His creative, life-dispensing power wafted the warm, liberating breath of spring over the dull apathy settling like an icy crust on the soul-life of the Jewish brotherhood. He re-awakened general interest in the spirit and the history of Judaism. The most popular writer in the field of Jewish science, he could boast of success phenomenal for a Jewish author; in a comparatively short time, his voluminous work, apparently intended for scholars, attained the distinction of a third, in parts even of a fourth, edition, and in its English, French, Russian, and, last though not least, Hebrew translations,[2] it has become the common possession of all the author's brethren-in-faith.

[1] *Geschichte,* Vol. X, chaps. 6 and 7 (American Edition, Vol. V, Chap. 4).

[2] The French, English, and Hebrew translations of the "History" were superintended by Graetz, and most of the proof-sheets were read by him. The French translation was made by his friend M. Hess, a Socialistic journalist, who by reason of his book, *Rom und Jerusalem,* may be counted among the Zionists. The third volume, the first translated, appeared under the title, *Sinai et Golgatha* (Paris, 1867). The sixth followed, and was called, *Les Juifs d'Espagne* (Paris, 1872). The Franco-Prussian war, which alienated the German and French Jews from each other, interrupted the work, and it

The only help extended to Graetz in the prosecution of his comprehensive plan proceeded from the "Institute for the Promotion of Israelitish Literature,"[1] founded in 1855 by Dr. Ludwig Philippson, the most genial and most productive journalist among rabbis. In return for a modest subscription price several books were issued annually, among which a volume of Graetz's "History" usually formed the chief attraction. Through the "Institute," a large circulation was secured for the "History" from the first. The Society in turn was so dependent upon Graetz's work for its popularity that when, on account of a misunderstanding with Philippson, Graetz refused to have the last (eleventh) volume published by the "Institute," it could not maintain itself long.

On the other hand, there was not lack of hostility, jealousy, and petty annoyances. His work was used everywhere, but not infrequently without an open acknowledgment of its helpfulness. Especially at first the faultfinders and finical critics plied their trade vigorously on his work, as though any Talmudist considered a scholar in his small circle needed but to dip his pen into ink to write a history superior to Graetz's. Even later, when recognition could not be withheld, praise was given grudgingly, in half-hearted accents. The young theologians of both parties, of the right and of the left wing, were indefatigable in picking flaws of all kinds in his details. They did not realize how effectually they

was not resumed until some time in the "eighties." The first volume translated into English was the fourth, by the Rev. James K. Gutheim, under the auspices of the second "American Jewish Publication Society" (New York, 1873). After Graetz's visit to London in 1887, the English translation of the complete work was undertaken there. Both the French and the English translations were revisions of the German original, in which Graetz not only incorporated the results of the latest researches, but also tried to pay particular attention to the history of the Jews of the nations into whose language the work was rendered.

[1] *Institut zur Förderung der israelitischen Litteratur.*

were thus demonstrating his pre-eminence, and failed to understand that so monumental a work cannot by any possible means escape blemishes and malformations.

The "History" completed the breach between Graetz and his sometime teacher, Samson Raphael Hirsch. The latter had left Nikolsburg to act as the rabbi of a wealthy private congregation in Frankfort-on-the-Main. Soon after his removal, he began to issue a monthly journal, *Jeshurun*. In the second and third volumes of the magazine appeared a passionate, violent review of the two parts of the "History" then published, in which Hirsch sat in judgment on Graetz's heresies. The soreness of the critic is unmistakable. It is doubtful whether his thrusts were not meant to strike the Jewish Theological Seminary at Breslau rather than the "History." Personal attacks usually left Graetz unmoved, though he was in the habit of repelling them with caustic brevity. But he never forgave hostility towards the young institution. Thus the last slender ties that had still bound the two men to each other were snapped asunder forever. For the rest, active and joyous as his nature was, he did not trouble himself about his critics, nor did they thwart the success of his work; its triumph was complete. On the other hand, he was frankly proud of the distinction conferred upon him by the Prussian government in making him, in December, 1869, honorary professor of the Breslau University. This governmental recognition went far towards compensating him for the lack of regular professional advancement in his academic career, the sore point in his life, at which spiteful antagonists delighted to aim their shafts.

With the eleventh volume, published in 1870, he brought the history of the Jews since the Maccabean struggle down to the present time (1848); nine volumes had appeared in uninterrupted succession.

To complete and crown the work it was necessary to give an account of ancient Jewish history covering the Biblical and three centuries and a half of post-Biblical times. Graetz devoted scrupulous care to this portion of his work. He considered its importance paramount, and regarded the treatment of the early epochs as a most difficult task, requiring for its adequate performance exegetical studies and original text criticism. Graetz thought himself particularly qualified and endowed for such work; it had always been his favorite pursuit. But before attacking the history of Israel and ancient Judæa, he determined to satisfy his longing to behold the Holy Land with his bodily eye, as he had often sought to picture it to his mental eye. With equal force his artistic impulse drew him to Palestine. He hoped to derive local color and inspiration for the description of hoary events from the sight of consecrated places, which had been their scenes and their witnesses. As early as 1865, he had formed the plan of a journey to Palestine, the execution of which became possible only in March, 1872, when two friends joined him. Limited to his private resources and hampered by consideration for his traveling companions, he was not able to make his trip thoroughly satisfactory from a scientific point of view. After all he obtained what he had journeyed abroad to find; he brought back impressions, enthusiasm, inspiration. In quick succession the two, or more accurately, three[1] parts of his work treating of the Biblical and early post-Biblical time appeared between 1874 and 1876, and his historical work was complete according to the plan he had sketched for himself. It was the brilliant fulfillment of the promise "to furnish a history of the Jews from the most ancient times to the

[1] The second volume assumed such proportions that it had to be divided into two parts, each of which reached the respectable number of 500 pages.

present day elaborated from the original sources," which he had made in 1854, when he began his career as an historian with the publication of the fourth volume of his "History." Grand in conception, clear and perspicuous in execution, riveting attention by its charming style, the work has not failed to find entrance into the hearts of the author's brethren-in-faith. It remains unsurpassed in the present, and the future historian will realize that he cannot deviate from the great lines laid down in it. The little blemishes and errors of various kinds that disfigure all human creations do not affect the impression made by the work as a whole. The discovery of hidden sources, now unsuspected, may necessitate additions and changes in details, but the great points of view, the pragmatic conception, the underlying thoughts, as he deduces them from the intricate complexity of Jewish history, will never be superseded. Graetz's "History of the Jews," voluminous though it is, will forever remain an integral part of Jewish literature.

VI.

THE EXEGETE.

THE first two, or rather three, parts of the "History" form the transition to Graetz's exegetical studies. In their excellencies as well as in their shortcomings they betray all the characteristics of his work in Bible exposition. Obviously Graetz had only awaited the completion of the history of Judaism from the end of the Maccabean struggle to the present time to enter, with all the vigor of his intellect, upon the *second phase of his activity as a writer*, that devoted to Bible exegesis and textual criticism. Exegetical studies, no less than historical research, were a distinct life-aim with him. They were begun in 1871, and continued without inter-

ruption until unexpected death snatched the pen from his hand. To be accurate, the second phase of his literary activity should be dated from 1869. In that year Zacharias Frankel, wishing to devote all his energy to his work on the so-called Jerusalem Talmud, transferred the *Monatsschrift* to Graetz. He marked the beginning of his editorial management with an essay on "The Ebionites in the Old Testament,"[1] the first of a series in Old Testament exposition and Hebrew philology. In part, they may be regarded as monographs in preparation for his history of the Biblical times. The series was continued uninterruptedly, year after year, until 1887, when Graetz discontinued the publication of the *Monatsschrift*.

In view of the narrow compass of Biblical literature, comprising the whole residue of ancient Israelitish writings and therefore the whole treasury of the Hebrew language at our disposal, even those expounders that cling to the word and to tradition with slavish faithfulness are granted wide scope for individual judgments and subjective hypotheses, depending for their acceptance not upon precise proof, but upon the inquirer's will and disposition. It is natural, then, that Graetz with his strongly developed subjectivity, his delicately attuned ear, and his gift of bold conjecture, should have reached conclusions sharply contrasting with all accepted views and incapable of logical, scientific demonstration. His results and explanations, the outcome of a passionate desire for clearness and consistency, are often of startling originality. All sorts of new questions were set on foot by him, many fruitful suggestions may be traced to him, and he bore many a trophy from the battlefields of textual criticism. The boldness of his exegesis is illustrated by his treatment of the two Hagiographic

[1] *Die Ebjoniten des alten Testaments.*

books, Ecclesiastes and the Song of Songs, which, published in quick succession in 1871, introduced him to the world as an exegete. He attributes the composition of *Koheleth* (or the Preacher, translation and critical commentary)[1] to the reign of Herod, and places the author of *Shir ha-Shirim* (or the Song of Songs, translation and critical commentary)[2] in the Macedonian-Syrian time. Though the hypotheses concerning the time of the composition of the two books and many other propositions are curious, and overwhelm the reader by their pronounced deviation from all opinions hitherto advanced; still it must be confessed, that the conjecture with regard to the origin of Ecclesiastes is engaging in the extreme, and it cannot be denied, that the translations are good and in unexceptionable taste, that the remarks and references are instructive, and that the older versions were used with care and attention. In the commentary on Ecclesiastes, decidedly more valuable than that on the Song of Songs, he offers besides interesting data with regard to the Greek translation. Moreover, Graetz frequently adduced analogies from the Mishna and the Talmud, made exhaustive use of whatever was advantageous for textual criticism in the Talmudic literature, and thus brought to light new material in such a way as to make it available for the "higher criticism." This, in fact, constitutes his real and permanent distinction as an exegete.

His expositions were guided by two chief assumptions, both rooted in the depths of his character. He held that in every Biblical work an historical background can be discerned with more or less ease; that even generalizations and reflections cannot conceal their connection with special facts, which

[1] *Kohelet (-oder der salomonische Prediger, übersetzt und kritisch erläutert).*

[2] *Schir-ha-Schirim (-oder das salomonische Hohelied, übersetzt und kritisch erläutert).*

must be deduced and determined. Again, he was of the opinion, that a contradiction or obscurity in a Biblical passage cannot be resolved by a twisting of words and phrases or by far-fetched analogies in remote though related idioms. They were evidence to him that the text had come to grief, and that the original text could be restored only by a conjecture, which might be disengaged from the context, or patterned on a Talmudic parallel, or deduced from older translations. He did not doubt that catastrophes, the centuries, and perhaps also the incompetence of copyists, had mutilated the original Bible text, and wrenched it out of shape, and he thought that even later, when it had been fixed with scrupulous care, all sorts of errors might have crept in.

According to these principles Graetz treated the Psalms. In 1881 he published a German translation of them, and in 1882–83 followed a "Critical Commentary to the Psalms with Text and Translation. 2 vols."[1] The commentary is designed on a generous scale, and gives abundant evidences of ripe scholarship. But by the side of its excellent features it contains many hazardous guesses and vague, even though ingenious hypotheses. Justus Olshausen, an Orientalist highly esteemed on account of his learning and his sobriety, who was occupied with the critical examination of the Old Testament text for philological purposes, says the following about the commentary on the Psalms in a letter to the author:[2]

"On account of its boldness your commentary will certainly arouse serious objections with the larger number of exegetes, themselves overbold in exegesis, but weak in criticism. As for me, you know that I am not affrighted by boldness in criticism when coupled with knowledge of the language and the subject-matter, with acumen, and,

[1] *Kritischer Kommentar zu den Psalmen nebst Text und Uebersetzung.*
[2] Quoted in Rippner, *Zum siebzigsten Geburtstag des Professors Dr. H. Graetz*, p. 31.

above all, with sound common sense. Doubtless, I shall not be able to agree with you in every case in which, overconfident perhaps, you may believe that you have hit upon the correct solution of a difficulty. That, however, does not prevent me from recognizing that your book, by reason of its abundance of excellent emendations, is a valuable addition to exegetical literature."

Graetz undoubtedly hit upon many a happy guess, and applause was not lacking, but in general his results met with opposition so decided that we may surely expect a later generation to review the judgment of our time and separate the chaff from the wheat. Not in the least intimidated by the adverse criticism upon his exegetical methods, he was resolved to remove the difficulties attaching to the Old Testament language by all the means at his command. He thought himself justified in his confidence in himself in matters of textual criticism, upon which chiefly he concentrated his explanations in the course of time. He grew more and more unrestrained in his efforts to restore approximately the original text of the Bible by means of audacious conjectures, which his sympathetic mind was never weary of devising. In other fields he was always careful to keep in connection and in touch with tradition; destructive tendencies were not at all characteristic of him. But in his textual criticism he permitted his zeal to run away with him, until he lost the solid ground of the Bible text and of reality from under his feet. His acumen displayed and dissipated itself chiefly in the blinding pyrotechnics of rocket-like emendations. Of this character are his exegetical studies on the prophet Jeremiah,[1] on the Proverbs of Solomon,[2] and his fine essay on Bible exegesis.[3]

This kind of work was so attractive to him, that in the latter years of his life he set about the execution of a long-cherished and widely compre-

[1] *Monatsschrift*, 1883, vol. 32. [2] *Ibid.*, 1884, vol. 33.
[3] *Ibid.*, 1886, vol. 35.

hensive plan for the critical examination and the emendation of the text of the whole Bible. The realization of this plan was to be the consummation and crown of his life's labors. But he was not destined to celebrate such unquestioned and brilliant successes in this field as in that of history, where he had earned and received the laurels due a pioneer. Yet, we must be careful not to underrate his exegetical and critical achievements as to their intrinsic value and their influence. His exegetical works and essays are replete with new points of view and interesting suggestions. Many a germ that has since proved fruitful can be traced to them, and they have had a lasting effect upon the development of Bible exegesis. His works of this class, original and important enough to fill a life of scholarly research, would suffice to secure to their author an honorable name and a prominent place in the history of Jewish science.

VII.

LAST YEARS.

From year to year Graetz received an increasing number of proofs of the recognition and veneration paid him by a large circle of readers and admirers and a growing band of friends and aspiring disciples. But the enjoyment of his success was not to be unalloyed. In 1879 the feeling against Jews in Germany, always on the point of breaking out, was set free in the shape of an anti-Semitic movement, to serve as an unfailing instrument for political agitation. Heinrich von Treitschke, an historian characterized by patriotic ardor rather than scrupulous adherence to word and truth, a writer with affecting, oratorical pathos and a brilliant style at his command, soon assumed the rôle of challenger in the fray. He was scandalized by the boasting

spirit which, he alleged, was in the ascendant in Jewish circles, and was to be regarded as a menace to the German empire. He illustrated his strictures by references to Graetz, who, he maintained, made use of intemperate language in his polemics against Christianity, and in his "History" had been guilty of applying disrespectful expressions to the German nation.[1] Graetz replied, and Treitschke in turn made him the subject of an article,[2] in which he tried to prove his allegations. He quoted passages from the "History," tearing them from their context, and resorted to all sorts of sophistry. The leaders of the intelligent portion of Berlin Jewry probably did not realize the gravity of the situation. At all events, they were far from having a clear idea of the means necessary for stemming the rapidly swelling tide. They were disinclined, however, to suffer Treitschke's attacks to pass unrepulsed, for they had reason to suppose them to be more than the venomous utterances of a professor. Thereupon H. B. Oppenheim, a well-known politician and writer on political economy, and highly esteemed for his disinterested and noble character, adopted the mistaken course of sacrificing Graetz to Treitschke's aggressive charges without examining them. Confessedly he had not read Graetz's works, yet he disposed of their author summarily as "a man without tact and fanatically one-sided, whose great learning has been rendered nugatory by the absurdity of his practical deductions."[3] This peculiar defense of Judaism, to be sure, did not excite distressful feeling in any one, but later events prove it to have been symptomatic of the opinions and the mental constitution of the intellectual notabilities of the Berlin Jewish community.

A Berlin Jew had been put at the head of the

[1] *Preussische Jahrbücher*, 1879, vol. 44, p. 572 ff. [2] *Ibid.*, p. 660.
[3] *Die Gegenwart*, edited by Lindau, 1880, vol. 17, p. 18 ff.

"Union of German Israelitish Congregations,"[1] when its headquarters had been moved from Leipsic to Berlin. Active and clever in practical affairs, he invested the "Union" with dignity, and stirred it up to work and enterprise. With his help all sorts of useful undertakings were executed; among them, in 1885, a plan to promote the science of Judaism, hitherto wholly neglected, along definite lines. A commission was to be appointed to make means and sources for research into the history of the Jews of Germany available under the protection of the "Union." The project was hailed with satisfaction by Jewish scholars. It was hoped that it would eventually furnish the center from which other scientific endeavors might radiate. All hopes of this kind were early doomed to grievous disappointment. The leaders of the "Union" lacked perception of the needs of the situation; they permitted an ambitious young scholar of the Jewish faith, an "extraordinary" professor at the University of Berlin, to become the governing spirit. He was familiar with the mediæval government offices, and did valiant service in the study of documents. But he was destitute of the most elementary knowledge of Hebrew, and therefore could have no conception of the peculiar difficulties the writer of Jewish history has to grapple with. Besides, he had so completely identified himself with his specialty and with the academic world of professors that a realizing sense of the condition and needs of German Judaism was out of the question. Under these circumstances serious mistakes were inevitable. In the first place Graetz was disregarded, completely ignored, when the commission which was to organize and superintend the historical investigations was made up. The arbitrary exclusion of the only or, at all events, the most eminent historian the Jews can boast of must be considered a gross offense

[1] *Der deutsch-israelitische Gemeindebund.*

against good manners. What is more, the good work was thereby deprived of the best and most valuable guarantee of success. Personal animosity may have contributed to bring about the deplorable action, but that does not alter the fact that Graetz was most familiar with the field of work to be cultivated. None recognized more clearly than he the desiderata[1] that occupied the attention and guided the efforts of the scholars interested in Jewish history at the time. Besides, he was an indefatigable, impulsive worker, and his name was one to conjure with. The slight put upon Graetz called forth decided ill-humor among his numerous friends and disciples, a large portion of whom were the rabbinical heads of respected congregations. Their irritation could not long remain without tangible effect. Moreover, though the commission was composed of highly esteemed scholars, among them Christians who were master historians of the first rank, there was not one member who had attained to more than respectable dilettanteism in his acquaintance with Jewish literature, a thorough knowledge of which was indispensable for the proper realization of the plan, and only one member who had given evidence of his special interest in Jewish history by a work of note. This exception was Professor Stobbe, a humane Christian scholar and eminent jurist, who has described the historico-legal status of the German Jews in "The Jews in Germany during the Middle Ages,"[2] a book that has not yet been superseded. The absence of Jewish scholars, specifically of Jewish historians, awakened distrust in the ability of the

[1] One of these desiderata, but dimly discerned at the time, because its value was not in the least realized, was the publication of the "Memoirs of Glückel von Hameln," since published in an excellent edition, without the help of a commission and without any ostentation by a pupil of Graetz, the learned Professor D. Kaufmann of Buda-Pesth. This remarkable book, which no one should fail to read, was fairly rediscovered by Professor Kaufmann.

[2] *Die Juden in Deutschland während des Mittelalters.*

commission. In fact, its achievements, as displayed in the "Journal for the History of the Jews in Germany"[1] and in separate publications, are far from realizing the expectations awakened by the boastful, arrogant tone of scientific conceit in which the leaders announced the undertaking, and are out of all proportion to the expenditures incurred. The most ambitious production, "Documents on the History of the Jews, etc.,"[2] is a fragment. Quietly, unnoticed, the experiment died one day in the year 1892.[3]

The inconsiderate treatment accorded him by the Berlin coterie or other circles did not cause Graetz much heart-ache, and whatever soreness it may have produced was completely healed by London, whence he received the flattering invitation to open the Anglo-Jewish Historical Exhibition with a lecture. The honorable reception accorded him in the English capital, the persons whose acquaintance he made, and the impressions he carried home with him, all this refreshed him, and put him into a buoyant frame of mind. The visit to England he accounted one of the happiest and most enjoyable events of his life. The experiences gathered there strengthened the hope, to which he had often given expression, that salvation would arise for Judaism out of England and America.

On October 31, 1887, he celebrated the seventieth anniversary of his birth. His disciples and friends made it the occasion for an extraordinary ovation, and from all countries and climes homage was laid at his feet. An overwhelming number of addresses, gifts, congratulatory letters, and poems proved that his achievements were in the mind and his honor in the keeping of the whole body of intelligent Jews.

[1] *Zeitschrift für die Geschichte der Juden in Deutschland.*
[2] *Regesten zur Geschichte der Juden u. s. w.* [3] *See* Note p. 86.

A particularly gratifying surprise came in the shape of a diploma announcing that on October 27, 1888, he, the Jew, who had not dealt leniently with the Spanish nation in his historical writings, had been elected an honorary member of its section in history by the Spanish Academy at Madrid.

Until the very last his body and mind retained remarkable elasticity and vigor; time seemed to pass him by unnoticed. His indestructible working powers and his literary fertility continued to be astonishing.[1] Even after concentrating his efforts on exegetical research, he was a vigilant reader of the monographs in whatever civilized language, bearing, however remotely, on problems of the science of Judaism. He gave the conclusions reached in them a critical examination, and either noted them for the enrichment and correction of a new edition of his "History," or refuted them in special articles, if they seemed sufficiently important. For, besides his historical and exegetical works, in number and bulk an imposing array, he published numberless essays and *Programmschriften* on the most various subjects, many of them real gems, models of clear writing and deep scholarship. In some of them daring theories are advanced, as, for instance, the one which he would never abandon, that the Massora originated with the Karaites, from whose literary works the Rabbanites derived it.

[1] As late as 1888 he published a *Volksthümliche Geschichte der Juden* ("Popular History of the Jews") in three volumes, in response to numerous and frequently repeated requests for a short and popular history. He put all his historical matter into a concise form, constantly bearing in mind the needs of the intelligent laity. At the same time he did not fail to make use of newly determined data. The shorter work has peculiar value, inasmuch as Graetz lays down in it his opinion of men of his own generation whom he had passed over in silence in his eleventh volume published in 1870. He had adopted the rule of not considering living persons in his historical presentation. But from 1870 to 1888 many prominent figures had been removed from the arena by death, and he was left free in the later work to express his judgment upon their character and achievements.

The conjecture was received with a great display of indignation, but its refutation was not equally emphatic, and it cannot be denied that certain evidences may be interpreted in its favor.

Among his *Programmschriften* the following deserve to be singled out: "Visigothic Legislation with Regard to the Jews,"[1] in the annual report of the Jewish Theological Seminary for 1858; "Frank and the Frankists,"[2] in that for 1868; and "The Kingdom of Mesene and its Jewish Population,"[3] in that for 1879. In the *Monatsschrift für Geschichte und Wissenschaft des Judenthums*, of which, as mentioned above, he was the editor from 1869, the greater part of the articles issued from his pen. There is but one way of accounting for his numerous achievements: he understood to perfection the art of utilizing every moment.

Five o'clock in the morning found Graetz at his desk. Until nine he gave uninterrupted attention to his literary work. After that hour he was in the habit of devoting himself to his lectures. He carried on an extensive correspondence, found leisure for all sorts of things, and was fond of the innocent gayeties of social life. He retired late, and in general needed but little sleep. His sound, almost invincible nervous system was supplemented by a constitution calculated to supply his extraordinary capacity for work with a proper physical basis. He was of average height, and habitually bent forward his lean and spare, but sinewy, muscular figure, built upon a strong bony frame. His face was somewhat marred by pock-marks, but his head made a massive, unusual impression. Soft, chestnut-brown, later gray hair, in fair though not clustering abundance, crowned his board-like, square forehead. His sharp, observant eyes, grayish-brown in color, be-

[1] *Die westgothische Gesetzgebung in Betreff der Juden.*
[2] *Frank und die Frankisten.*
[3] *Das Königreich Mesene und seine jüdische Bevölkerung.*

tokened the owner's enjoyment of life, and a somewhat large, prominent nose with its delicate nostrils, quivering like "feelers," gave his long, oval, bony face its characteristic searching expression. Sometimes sadness played about his lips, but usually they were curled by mockery, irony, and defiance, as though sarcastic words might dart out at any moment. In point of fact, sharp satire occasionally spiced his conversation, which, as a rule, however, was far from fulfilling the expectations aroused by his writings. In his younger years happy moments found him full of jokes and pranks for the delectation of his domestic circle, and at all times he displayed unquenchable zest for life and cheerful optimism. Love of family was a dominant trait in him. Towards his wife his bearing was always tender and attentive, as though the honeymoon had not passed; towards his daughter it was marked by the perfection of gallantry; towards his sons he exercised forbearance and self-sacrificing devotion, and his aged father he met with the filial respect of Talmudic times. He enjoyed and cultivated intercourse with friends. For a friend, for any person or cause that had enlisted his sympathy, he was ready to pledge himself. Deeply moved by the sad conditions prevalent in Palestine, he had brought thence a plan for the education of Jewish orphans in Jerusalem. He and his traveling companions founded a society, and he exerted himself to secure a fund, small though it might be, for the promotion of its object. For this purpose he took journey after journey, delivered lectures, at first much against his inclination, in many cities, and even accepted an invitation to go to Galicia, where he was received with joyful demonstrations and overwhelmed with flattering homage. Encouraged by such successes, he persisted, until he had put the society upon a modest but secure basis, which enables it to continue its good work to this day.

Robust and vigorous as he felt himself, he undertook in his old age a work in which he meant to sum up his Bible studies of a critical and exegetical character. He counted, not upon the sympathy of his contemporaries, but upon the appreciation of a late posterity. All subordinate occupations were dropped. In 1888 he even discontinued the publication of the *Monatsschrift*, none of his pupils being able then to assume the editorial management. In order to give a clear, comprehensive review of the results of his Biblical text studies, he proposed to print the Hebrew Bible in its entirety with emendations and short notes justifying them. In 1891 all preparatory work was completed, and the printing was begun. How he cherished this life-work of his is evident from the prospectus. Contrary to his custom, he addresses himself to his friends, and requests them to assist him in his venture.

"At the end of my life," he says in the prospectus, "I have undertaken the laborious task of *summarizing* the emendations of the text of the Holy Scriptures, the admissibility and justification of which no less than the necessity for which the accompanying prospectus sets forth. . . . I beg you to aid my efforts . . . in order that the pecuniary risk incurred may not too far transcend my means."

This prospectus appeared in July, 1891, and it was the last word that issued from the author's untiring pen for publication.

Although he was escaping the infirmities and ailments of the old, and considered himself perfectly well, and certainly felt vigorous, age had crept upon him insidiously. The action of his heart was so much impaired that his physicians became anxious about his condition. According to his annual custom he went to Carlsbad for the cure of minor indispositions. Thence he had planned to go to Munich on a few days' visit to his oldest son, who occupied the position of "extraordinary" professor of physics at the University there, and then spend some time resting at Reichenhall with his

son's family. Shortly before the time set for his departure from Carlsbad, where he had not taken care of himself, he had a fainting spell of so serious a nature that the physician urged Mrs. Graetz to return to Breslau without delay. He considered the precaution exaggerated, and when he finally yielded, he refused to forego the trip to Munich. There, at his son's house, he suffered, in the night between the sixth and the seventh of September, a violent attack of colic. Under the influence of opium administered by a physician the pain passed away, and he dropped to sleep. When his wife arose early in the morning to observe his condition, she found him lying in bed lifeless. His heart had ceased to act, and so a life replete with work and rich in attainment had too soon come to an end. His remains were transported to Breslau, and three days later, in the presence of a numerous gathering of his pupils and friends and amid demonstrations of general sympathy, they were consigned to the grave in the Jewish cemetery.

His wife, whose days are devoted to the memory of her celebrated husband, considered it incumbent upon her to publish his last work, the manuscript of which was all but complete, but of which only a few sheets had issued from the press at the time of Graetz's death. The editor is Professor W. Bacher of Buda-Pesth, one of Graetz's disciples, who has won honorable repute by his editions and his studies in the history of Hebrew grammar and exegesis. Besides the editorial work proper, he has been forced to supply from memoranda a considerable piece in the Prophets, which by some mischance had gone astray. On the whole, this critical Bible edition, by which the departed author set great store, has been pursued by peculiar ill-luck. Unlike his other productions it must miss the author's pruning and correcting hand as it passes through the press. It is doomed to appear as an incomplete

because a posthumous work. The title is: *Emendationes in plerosque Sacræ Scripturæ Veteris Testamente libros secundum veterum versiones nec non auxiliis criticis cæteris adhibitis. Ex relicto defuncti auctoris manuscripto edidit Guil. Bacher. 3 Pts. Breslau, 1892–1894.* The Hebrew text of the Bible is treated boldly and subjectively. But it remains for a later generation to pass final judgment upon the value of Graetz's contributions to the critical determination of the Bible text. There can be no doubt that Graetz was as much a master in the field of exegesis as in that of history.

The time will come when his contemporaries will be envied for the privilege of having stood face to face with one so great and noble. Those days, to be sure, will not know the grief and sorrow that befell us when unexpectedly and without warning the revered teacher was removed from our sight. Still less will there be a suspicion of the self-reproaches that assail us too late for having frequently had a keen eye for the detection of minute shortcomings and inadequacies, the inherent foibles of the human kind, rather than a willing, attentive ear to listen to the suggestions and solutions so lavishly offered. After all, the most beautiful blossoms put forth by him, the best fruits produced by his mind, are in his writings; he that can read may enjoy them.

NOTE.—While this *Memoir* was passing through the press, the commission on the history of the Jews of Germany, spoken of on pp. 78-80, after five years of inactivity again showed signs of life in the form of a valuable publication by a rabbi: *Das Martyrologium des Nürnberger Memorbuches* by Dr. S. Salfeld. At the same time, the promise of the completion of *Die Regesten zur Geschichte der Juden, etc.*, is held out.

TABLES OF JEWISH HISTORY.

TABLES OF JEWISH HISTORY.

CHRONOLOGICAL TABLE OF JEWISH HISTORY.

		PAGE
PERIOD I.	The Patriarchal Age	90
II.	The Exodus	90
III.	The Conquest of Canaan	90
IV.	The Era of the Judges	90
V.	The Kingdom (1067–977 B. C. E.)	91
VI.	Judah and Israel until the Capture of Samaria (977–719 B. C. E.)	92
VII.	Judah until the Destruction of Jerusalem (719–586 B. C. E.)	94
VIII.	The Captivity (586–516 B. C. E.)	95
IX.	The Age of Ezra, Nehemiah, and the Scribes (516–332 B. C. E.)	96
X.	The Age of the Ptolemies and the Seleucidæ to Antiochus IV (332–175 B. C. E.)	97
XI.	The Age of the Maccabees (175–140 B. C. E.)	98
XII.	The Hasmonæan Dynasty (140–37 B. C. E.)	100
XIII.	The Herodian Dynasty (37 B. C. E.–72 C. E.)	102
XIV.	The Epoch of the Mishna and the Tanaites (72–219 C. E.)	104
XV.	The Epoch of the Talmud, the Amoraim, and the Saboraim (219–550 C. E.)	106
XVI.	From the Completion of the Talmud to the End of the Gaonate (550–1038 C. E.)	108
XVII.	The Age of Gebirol, Halevi, Rashi, and Maimonides (1038–1204 C. E.)	111
XVIII.	From the Death of Maimonides to the Expulsion from Spain (1204–1492 C. E.)	114
XIX.	From the Expulsion from Spain to the Persecution in Poland (1492–1648 C. E.)	120
XX.	From the Persecution in Poland to the Present Time (1648–1873 C. E.)	123

I. THE PATRIARCHAL AGE.

B.C.E.

1500(about). **Abraham** leaves Ur of the Chaldees.
Supreme power of *Joseph* in Egypt.
Jacob and his household occupy Goshen in Egypt.

II. THE EXODUS.

Birth of **Moses**.
The **Exodus**.
Revelation at Mount Sinai.
Worship of the Golden Calf.
Rebellion of Korah.
Death of Miriam and AARON.
The Israelites defeat the Emorite king Sihon at Jahaz.
Og, king of Bashan, defeated at Edreï.
The prophecy of Balaam.
Reuben, Gad, and half of Manasseh settle in the land east of the Jordan (Peræa).
DEATH OF MOSES.

III. THE CONQUEST OF CANAAN.

Leadership of JOSHUA.
Passage of the Jordan.
Capture of Jericho.
Submission of the Gibeonites.
Division of the land among the tribes.
The *Jebusites* and others permitted to keep their territory.
The TABERNACLE at Shiloh.
Death of Joshua.

IV. THE ERA OF THE JUDGES.

JUDGES.

1. Othniel,	6. Abimelech,	11. Ibzon,
2. Ehud,	7. Thola,	12. Elon,
3. Shamgar,	8. Jair,	13. Abdon,
4. Deborah and Barak,	9. Jephthah,	14. Eli,
5. Gideon,	10. Samson,	15. Samuel.

Othniel delivers the southern tribes from an Idumæan king.
Ehud routs Eglon, king of Moab.
Shamgar opposes the Philistines.
DEBORAH and Barak defeat Sisera, Jabin's general, at Mount Tabor.
GIDEON routs the Midianites under Zebah and Zalmunna.

B.C.E.

Abimelech leader of the Shechemites.

JEPHTHAH repulses the Ammonites in the trans-Jordanic provinces.

SAMSON keeps the Philistines at bay.

Eli, priest and judge.

The Ark captured by the Philistines at **Aphek.**

Samuel, judge and prophet.

Levitical and prophetical schools formed.

V. THE KINGDOM.

(1067–977 B. C. E.)

KINGS.

Saul, David, Solomon.

1067. **Saul** anointed king.

The Philistines defeated at Michmash.

Jabesh-Gilead saved from the Ammonites.

Agag, king of Amalek, defeated.

David anointed king.

The Gibeonites massacred by order of Saul.

David slays Goliath.

David flees before Saul, and leads the life of an outlaw. He is on friendly terms with the king of Moab, with Nahash, the Ammonite king, and Achish, the Philistine king.

ZADOK high priest.

1055. Saul and Jonathan die in a battle with the Philistines near Mount Gilboa.

1055. David king of Judah; Ishbosheth king of the trans-Jordanic tribes.

1051–1049. Civil war between the houses of Saul and David.

David sole king of the whole people; reigns at Hebron for seven years.

Nathan and Gad prophets.

Jerusalem made the capital after the conquest of the Jebusites.

The Philistines defeated at Mount Baal-Perazim.

Abiathar high priest in Jerusalem; Zadok in Gibeon.

The descendants of Saul, except Mephibosheth, killed by the Gibeonites.

David victorious over Moabites, Ammonites, and others.

Revolt of Absalom.

Sheba's insurrection.

Solomon anointed king by Nathan.

1015. Death of David; succession of Solomon.

1014. Solomon begins the first Temple.

Zadok sole high priest.

B.C.E.

1007. THE FIRST TEMPLE CONSECRATED.

Solomon establishes a fleet. Roads built. Commerce extended. Foreign alliances.

The kingdom at its greatest extent. Literature flourishes. Idolatry introduced.

Rebellion of JEROBOAM.

977. Death of Solomon.

VI. JUDAH AND ISRAEL UNTIL THE CAPTURE OF SAMARIA.

(977–719 B. C. E.)

(*See the Table of the Kings of Judah and Israel, p. 127.*)

977. Rehoboam king of Judah.

Jeroboam king of Israel; rules at Shechem.

Rehoboam allies himself with the king of Damascus.

Shemaiah, prophet, averts a civil war.

972. Shishak, king of Egypt, ally of Jeroboam, enters Jerusalem.

Jeroboam institutes calf-worship at Bethel and Dan; Ahijah prophet.

960. Abijam, son of Rehoboam, king of Judah.

957. Asa, son of Rehoboam, king of Judah.

955. Nadab, son of Jeroboam, king of Israel.

954. Baasha destroys the house of Jeroboam, and rules at Tirzah.

Asa forbids the worship of Astarte in Judah.

Baasha, assisted by Ethiopians and Syrians, makes war upon Asa.

933. Elah, son of Baasha, king of Israel.

932. The house of Baasha exterminated by Zimri.

932–928. Civil war between Omri and Tibni.

928. Omri, the first king in Samaria, introduces the worship of Baal and Astarte.

Alliance between Israel and Phœnicia. Jezebel marries Ahab.

922. AHAB king of Israel.

920(about). Elijah and the prophets persecuted by Jezebel.

918. Jehoshaphat king of Judah.

Micah (I) (Michaiah) prophesies.

904. Ahab victorious over Ben-hadad II, king of Aram (Syria).

Alliance between Jehoshaphat and Ahab.

901. Ahaziah, son of Ahab, king of Israel.

899. Jehoram, son of Ahab, king of Israel.

Jehoram and Jehoshaphat defeat Mesa of Moab.

894. Joram, son of Jehoshaphat, king of Judah.

888. Ahaziah, son of Joram and Athaliah, king of Judah.

Elisha and Jehu.

B.C.E.

887. Jehu kills Jehoram and exterminates the house of Omri; his followers kill Ahaziah.

Jehu king of Israel.

Athaliah queen of Judah; she has male members of the house of David executed.

881. Joash, son of Ahaziah, only surviving male descendant of David in the direct line, king of Judah.

864. The Temple repaired.

Hazael, king of Syria, conquers the trans-Jordanic provinces of Israel.

860. Jehoahaz, son of Jehu, king of Israel.

Joash submits to Hazael.

845. Jehoash, son of Jehoahaz, king of Israel.

Samaria besieged by Ben-hadad III; Jehoash victorious.

843. Amaziah, son of Joash, king of Judah.

Amaziah victorious over the Idumæans.

840. Death of Elisha.

Amaziah of Judah taken prisoner by Jehoash of Israel at Beth-Shemesh; Jerusalem ransacked and its walls destroyed.

830. Jeroboam II, son of Jehoash, king of Israel.

Jeroboam II re-conquers districts taken by the Aramæans.

Jonah prophesies.

815. Amaziah killed at Lachish.

The Idumæans invade Judah, and sell Judæan captives as slaves. *First dispersion of Judæans.*

805. Uzziah, son of Amaziah, king of Judah.

Earthquake and drouth.

Uzziah re-conquers districts lost since Solomon's time.

Jeroboam II takes Damascus and Hamath; peoples become tributary to him.

Luxury in Samaria under Jeroboam II.

800(about). *Amos*, *Joel*, and *Hosea* (*I*) prophesy.

769. Zechariah, son of Jeroboam II, king of Judah.

768. Shallum kills Zechariah and exterminates the house of Jehu.

Shallum king of Israel.

768. Menahem kills Shallum and reigns over Israel.

Uzziah usurps the offices of the high priest in the Temple.

Pul, king of Assyria, invades the kingdom of Israel, acquires booty, and carries off prisoners.

757. Pekahiah, son of Menahem, king of Israel.

756. Pekah kills Pekahiah.

755. Pekah king of Israel.

Isaiah utters his first prophecy.

B.C.E.

754. Jotham, son of Uzziah, king of Judah.
Zechariah (I) prophesies.

739. Ahaz, son of Jotham, king of Judah.
Pekah allies himself with Rezin of Damascus against Tiglath-pileser II.
Ahaz disregards the warning of Isaiah and offers to become a vassal of Tiglath-pileser II.

738. FIRST DEPORTATION OF ISRAELITISH CAPTIVES TO ASSYRIA by Tiglath-pileser II.
Ahaz introduces Assyrian worship into Judah.
Micah (II) prophesies.

736. Pekah killed by Hoshea.

727. *Hoshea* last king of Israel.
Shalmaneser IV, king of Assyria, invades Israel.
Hosea (II) prophesies.
Hoshea refuses the yearly tribute to Shalmaneser IV.

724. HEZEKIAH, son of Ahaz, king of Judah.

719. Shalmaneser IV **captures Samaria**, puts an end to the kingdom of Israel, and DEPORTS MOST OF ITS SUBJECTS—THE SO-CALLED **Ten Lost Tribes**—TO ASSYRIAN PROVINCES.

VII. JUDAH UNTIL THE DESTRUCTION OF JERUSALEM.

(719–586 B. C. E.)

(*See the Table of the Kings of Judah and Israel, p. 127.*)

Hezekiah tries to banish idolatry.
Isaiah advises neutrality between Assyria and Egypt.
Shebna dictates the foreign policy.
Micah and Isaiah predict a glorious future for Israel.

711(about). Sennacherib invades Judah and demands tribute. Destruction of the Assyrian army.
Hezekiah makes a treaty with Merodach-baladan, king of Babylon.
Literature flourishes.

695. Manasseh, son of Hezekiah, king of Judah.
Idolatry flourishes.
Esarhaddon, king of Assyria, takes Manasseh captive.
Manasseh restored.
Esarhaddon COLONIZES SAMARIA WITH CUTHÆANS.

640. Amon, son of Manasseh, king of Judah.

638. JOSIAH, son of Amon, king of Judah.
Zephaniah prophesies.
Scythian invasion of Judah.

627. Josiah repairs the Temple.
Jeremiah (b. 645–640, d. 580–570) prophesies.

B.C.E.

621. Hilkiah, high priest, finds a copy of the **Book of the Law** in the Temple.
Huldah prophesies.

608. Necho, king of Egypt, *defeats Josiah at Megiddo;* Josiah killed.
Jehoahaz (Shallum), second son of Josiah, king of Judah.

607. Jehoiakim (Eliakim), oldest son of Josiah, made king by Necho.
Idolatry flourishes. *Habakkuk* prophesies.

607–604 Uriah, prophet, beheaded.
Jeremiah's life imperiled; Baruch his secretary.

600. Jehoiakim pays tribute to Nebuchadnezzar, king of Babylon.

598. Jehoiakim allies himself with Egypt against Nebuchadnezzar.

596. Jehoiachin, youngest son of Jehoiakim, king of Judah.
Judah overrun by Nebuchadnezzar, Jerusalem besieged by a Babylonian general, Jehoiachin taken prisoner. FIRST DEPORTATION OF JUDÆANS TO BABYLONIA.

596. Nebuchadnezzar makes Zedekiah (Mattaniah), youngest son of Josiah, king of Judah.

593. Jeremiah advises submission to Nebuchadnezzar.

591. Zedekiah renounces allegiance to Babylonia.

587. THE FINAL SIEGE OF JERUSALEM BEGUN.
The siege of Jerusalem interrupted by the battle between the Chaldæan army and Hophra, king of Egypt.

586, Tammuz 9. First breach in the walls of Jerusalem.
Zedekiah taken prisoner and blinded; Seraiah, high priest, and others beheaded by Nebuchadnezzar at Riblah.

586, Ab. 9. The Temple razed, and Jerusalem destroyed by Nebuzaradan, general of Nebuchadnezzar.
SECOND DEPORTATION OF JUDÆANS TO BABYLONIA.

VIII. THE CAPTIVITY.

(586–516 B. C. E.)

BABYLONIAN KINGS.	PERSIAN KINGS.
605. Nebuchadnezzar,	558. Cyrus,
561 Evil-merodach,	529. Cambyses,
559. Neriglissar,	522. Pseudo-Smerdis,
556. Laborosoarchod,	521. Darius I Hystaspis.
555. Nabonad and Belshazzar.	

586. Gedaliah appointed governor of the remnant of Judah by Nebuchadnezzar.

B.C.E.

586. Jeremiah at Mizpah with Gedaliah.
Gedaliah murdered by Ishmael, son of Nethaniah.
Obadiah prophesies against Edom, which possesses itself of southern Judæa.
Jeremiah and Baruch in Egypt with Johanan, son of Kareah.

582. THIRD DEPORTATION OF JUDÆANS TO BABYLONIA by Nebuchadnezzar.
Ezekiel (620–570) prophesies.

561 (about). Jehoiachin honored by Evil-merodach.
Descendants of the Ten Tribes deported by the Assyrian kings mingle with the captives from Judah.

555 (about). The historical books of the Bible compiled in Babylonia; literature flourishes.
Nabonad of Babylonia persecutes the exiles.
The **Babylonian Isaiah** prophesies.

538. CYRUS takes Babylon, and PERMITS THE EXILES IN BABYLONIA TO RETURN TO PALESTINE.

537. ZERUBBABEL AND JOSHUA BEN JEHOZEDEK LEAD THE FIRST RETURN.
Foundation of the second Temple laid.

520. *Haggai* and *Zechariah* (*II*) prophesy.

516. THE SECOND TEMPLE CONSECRATED.

IX. THE AGE OF EZRA, NEHEMIAH, AND THE SCRIBES.

(516–332 B. C. E.)

PERSIAN KINGS.

521. Darius I Hystaspis,
486. Xerxes I,
465. Artaxerxes I Longimanus,
425. Xerxes II,
425. Sogdianus,
425. Darius II Nothus,
405. Artaxerxes II Mnemon,
359. Artaxerxes III Ochus,
338. Arses,
336. Darius III Codomannus.

The Samaritans accuse the Judæans of disloyalty to Persia.
The Judæans contract marriages with their heathen neighbors.

459. EZRA LEADS THE SECOND RETURN with the permission of Artaxerxes I Longimanus.

457 (about). *Ezra prevails upon the people to repudiate their heathen wives.*
The Samaritans under Sanballat engage in hostilities against the Judæans.

444. NEHEMIAH LEADS THE THIRD RETURN.
The Samaritans intrigue against Nehemiah.
Internal reforms by Nehemiah.

B.C.E.

Ezra reads the Law to the people at Jerusalem.
The wall of Jerusalem rebuilt.
Beginnings of the GREAT ASSEMBLY (Keneseth ha-Gedolah).

432. Nehemiah returns to Persia.
MALACHI THE LAST OF THE PROPHETS.

430–424. Nehemiah returns to Jerusalem, and continues his reforms.

420(about). The Samaritan Temple built on Mount Gerizim.
Synagogues established; the Law studied, and the *present form of divine service introduced*, probably by the Council of Seventy (Synhedrion) (*Dibre Sopherim*).

361–360. Artaxerxes II banishes Judæans to Hyrkania.

338(about). Bagoas, general of Artaxerxes III, lays the Judæans under tribute.
The Books of Chronicles written.

332. *Alexander the Great in Judæa.*

X. THE AGE OF THE PTOLEMIES AND THE SELEUCIDÆ TO ANTIOCHUS IV.

(332–175 B. C. E.)

(*See the Table of the High Priests, p. 128.*)

EGYPTIAN KINGS.	SYRIAN KINGS.
323. Ptolemy I Soter,	312. Seleucus I Nicator,
285. Ptolemy II Philadelphus,	280. Antiochus I Soter,
247. Ptolemy III Euergetes,	261. Antiochus II Theos,
222. Ptolemy IV Philopator,	246. Seleucus II Callinicos,
205. Ptolemy V Epiphanes,	226. Seleucus III Ceraunus,
181. Ptolemy VI Philometor.	223. Antiochus III the Great,
	187. Seleucus IV Philopator.

323. Death of Alexander the Great.

320. Jerusalem entered by Ptolemy I Soter. A large number of Judæan prisoners carried to Egypt.

312. THE BEGINNING OF THE SELEUCIDÆAN ERA (Battle of Gaza).

301. Judæa, a subdivision of Cœlesyria, tributary to Egypt (Battle of Ipsus); the high priest the political chief. Judæan colonies in Græco-Macedonian countries; Greek colonies in Judæa.

300(about). SIMON THE JUST high priest and the last of the MEN OF THE GREAT ASSEMBLY.

240. After a struggle between the Ptolemies and the Seleucidæ, Cœlesyria again adjudged to Egypt.
Onias II, high priest, refuses to pay tribute to Egypt.

B.C.E.

230(about). *Joseph, son of Tobiah*, and grandson of Simon the Just, represents the Judæans at the court of Ptolemy III Euergetes and Ptolemy IV Philopator, and is made farmer of taxes.

Joseph introduces *Greek feasts and games at Jerusalem.*

218. Judæa sides with Egypt against Antiochus III the Great.

209(about). Hyrcanus, son of Joseph, Judæan representative at the court of the Ptolemies.

The "Song of Songs" composed.

203. The Tobiades, the elder brothers of Hyrcanus, Syrian partisans. Judæa tributary to Antiochus III the Great.

The HELLENISTS and the CHASSIDIM (Assidæans) begin to oppose each other.

200(about). *Jesus Sirach* writes the apocryphal book *Ecclesiasticus.*

176(about). Heliodorus, treasurer to Seleucus IV Philopator, attempts to confiscate the Temple treasures.

XI. THE AGE OF THE MACCABEES.

(175–140 B. C. E.)

(*See the Table of the High Priests, p. 128.*)

EGYPTIAN KINGS.	SYRIAN KINGS.
181. Ptolemy VI Philometor,	175. Antiochus IV Epiphanes,
146. Ptolemy VII Physcon *and* Ptolemy VIII Lathurus.	164. Antiochus V Eupator,
	162. Demetrius I Soter,
	150. Alexander I Balas,
	146. Demetrius II Nicator *and* Antiochus VI (son of Alexander Balas), Diodotus Tryphon, *and* Antiochus VII Sidetes.

175. Antiochus IV Epiphanes ascends the throne of Syria.

174. The Hellenists induce Antiochus IV to divest Onias III of the high-priestly dignity, and under Jason obtain citizenship for Judæans trained for the Greek combats.

Gymnasiums and the Greek games at Jerusalem.

172. Menelaus (Onias) the Benjamite made high priest by Antiochus IV.

171. Death of Onias III; Menelaus guilty of Temple robbery, but exonerated by Antiochus IV.

168. Antiochus IV attacks Jerusalem, and desecrates the Holy of Holies.

168, Tammuz 17 A STATUE OF JUPITER PLACED IN THE TEMPLE by the Syrians.

B.C.E.

	The Chassidim suffer martyrdom.
	Mattathias the Hasmonæan resists the Syrian overseer.
167.	**Judas Maccabæus** victorious in his first battle with the Syrians under Apollonius.
166.	Judas Maccabæus victorious over Heron at Beth-horon.
	The Book of Daniel written.
	Judas Maccabæus victorious over Gorgias at Emmaus.
165.	Judas Maccabæus victorious over Lysias at Bethzur.
165, Kislev 25.	THE TEMPLE RE-DEDICATED (Chanukah).
	Judas Maccabæus and his brothers victorious over the Idumæans, Ammonites, and Philistines.
164.	Death of Antiochus IV Epiphanes.
163.	Judas Maccabæus retreats before Lysias at Beth-Zachariah; his brother Eleazar Hauran killed.
	Jerusalem besieged by Lysias.
	Judas Maccabæus high priest.
162(about).	The *Onias Temple* built at Leontopolis in Egypt by Onias IV, son of Onias III, the first *Alabarch.*
	The Hellenists calumniate Judas Maccabæus before Demetrius I. Alcimus made high priest. Factions under Judas and Alcimus.
160.	Judas Maccabæus victorious over Nicanor at Caphar-Salama and Adarsa. *He makes overtures to the Romans.*
	The Judæans defeated at Eleasa by the Syrians under Bacchides; JUDAS MACCABÆUS KILLED.
	Parties in Judæa: Chassidim, Hasmonæans, Hellenists.
	Jonathan Haphus, brother of Judas, defends himself unsuccessfully against Bacchides; his brother Johanan Gadi killed in a skirmish with the Bene Amri.
159.	Judæa evacuated by the Syrians.
157.	The Syrian war renewed at the instigation of the Hellenists.
152.	Jonathan Haphus high priest; his friendship sought by Demetrius I and Alexander Balas.
152–143.	The Judæans under Jonathan Haphus participate in the struggles between Alexander Balas, his son Antiochus VI, Diodotus Tryphon, and Demetrius II for the Syrian crown.
150(about).	The Pentateuch translated into Greek: **the Septuagint.**
143.	Jonathan Haphus executed by Diodotus Tryphon.
143.	Simon Tharsi, last of the Hasmonæan brothers, made high priest and leader by the people.
141.	End of the Hellenist party.
140.	JUDÆA AND ROME ALLIES.

XII. THE HASMONÆAN DYNASTY.

(140–37 B. C. E.)

(*See the Genealogical Table of the Hasmonæan Dynasty, p. 130.*)

EGYPTIAN KINGS.	SYRIAN KINGS.
146. Ptolemy VII Physcon *and* Ptolemy VIII,	137. Antiochus VII Sidetes (*alone*),
117. Ptolemy VIII Lathurus *and* Alexander I,	128. Demetrius II (*restored*) *and* Alexander II Zabina,
81. Alexander II,	125. Seleucus V,
80. Ptolemy IX Auletes,	125. Antiochus VIII Grypus *and* Antiochus IX Cyzicenus,
51. Ptolemy X *and* Cleopatra VI,	95. Seleucus VI, Antiochus X Eusebes, Philip, Demetrius III Eucærus, Antiochus XI Epiphanes, Antiochus XII Dionysius,
47. Cleopatra VI [*and* Ptolemy XI *and* Ptolemy XII],	83. Tigranes, king of Armenia,
30. Egypt a Roman Province.	69. Antiochus XII Asiaticus,
	64. Syria a Roman Province.

B.C.E.	
140.	Simon made hereditary high priest and Nassi (Prince).
139.	Simon stamps coins by permission of Antiochus VII Sidetes.
	Cendebæus, general of Antiochus Sidetes, makes war upon Simon.
135.	Simon slain by his son-in-law; accession of JOHN HYRCANUS I.
135–123.	Wars with the rulers of the Seleucidæan house.
133(about).	Embassy to Rome. Rome calls upon Antiochus VII to make restitution to Judæa.
120(about).	Samaria reduced; the Temple on Mount Gerizim destroyed.
	Conquest of the Idumæans and their conversion to Judaism.
	John Hyrcanus again appeals to Rome in his difficulties with Antiochus IX Cyzicenus.
	John Hyrcanus victorious over the allies, Antiochus IX Cyzicenus and Ptolemy VIII Lathurus.
109.	Samaria destroyed; Judæa at the height of prosperity; John Hyrcanus has coins struck.
	Formation of the three sects: **Pharisees, Sadducees, Essenes**; outbreak of hostilities between the Pharisees and the Sadducees.
106.	Accession of Aristobulus I. Discord in the family of the king.
	War with the Ituræans and Trachonites; Judæa enlarged.
105.	Accession of *Alexander* (*I*) *Jannæus.*
98–96.	The seaport towns taken by Ptolemy VIII Lathurus regained with the help of the Egyptian king's mother.

B.C.E.

94–89. Contentions between the Pharisees and the Sadducees; Alexander Jannæus opposed to the Pharisees. 800 Pharisees executed.

Alexander Jannæus adds trans-Jordanic territory to Judæa.

79. *Salome Alexandra*, wife of Alexander Jannæus, ascends the throne.

SIMON BEN SHETACH and JUDAH BEN TABBAI, Pharisee leaders, reorganize the Synhedrion, and exclude the Sadducæans. The queen favors the Pharisees.

70. Accession of *Hyrcanus II*.

69. Aristobulus II co-regent; quarrels between the brothers.

Antipater the Idumæan becomes the counselor of Hyrcanus II.

66. Aretas, king of the Nabathæans, ally of Hyrcanus II against Aristobulus II, takes Jerusalem.

Scaurus, the Roman legate, at the instance of Aristobulus II, forces Aretas to raise the siege of Jerusalem.

63. *Pompey captures Jerusalem;* Hyrcanus II made Ethnarch; Aristobulus II a prisoner.

Alexander (II), son of Aristobulus II, enters Jerusalem; subdued by Aulus Gabinius, Roman governor of Syria.

60. *Shemaya* and *Abtalion* presidents of the Synhedrion.

56. Aristobulus II escapes from Rome, opposes the Romans in Judæa, and is taken captive a second time.

55. Alexander (II) routed by the Romans at Mount Tabor.

53. CRASSUS PLUNDERS THE TEMPLE.

Aristobulus II, set free by Julius Cæsar, is poisoned by the followers of Pompey; Alexander (II) decapitated.

47. At the petition of Antipater, Cæsar proclaims Hyrcanus II high priest and Ethnarch.

The *Judæans of Alexandria* governed by their own Ethnarch, or *Alabarch*.

Phasael, oldest son of Antipater, governor of Jerusalem; HEROD, second son of Antipater, governor of Galilee.

Ezekias of Galilee decapitated by Herod.

Herod before the Synhedrion, protected by Hyrcanus II; made governor of Cœlesyria by Sextus Cæsar, Roman governor of Syria.

43. Antipater poisoned.

42. Herod and Phasael made Tetrarchs by Mark Antony.

B.C.E.

40. Barzaphernes, Parthian general, takes Jerusalem, proclaims Antigonus king, and incapacitates Hyrcanus II for the high-priestly office by mutilating his ears.

HEROD PROCLAIMED KING BY THE ROMAN SENATE.

37. *Herod marries Mariamne*, granddaughter of Hyrcanus II. Jerusalem besieged and taken by Herod and Sosius, Mark Antony's general; Antigonus executed.

XIII. THE HERODIAN DYNASTY.

(37 B. C. E.–72 C. E.)

(*See the Genealogical Table of the Herodian Dynasty, p. 134, and the Table of the High Priests, p. 129.*)

EMPERORS OF ROME.	PROCURATORS OF JUDÆA (Subalterns to the Roman Legates or the Governors of Syria).
B. C. E. 31. Augustus,	C. E. 6. Coponius,
C. E. 14. Tiberius,	9. Marcus Ambivius,
37. Caligula,	13. Annius Rufus,
41. Claudius,	15. Valerius Gratus,
54. Nero,	26. Pontius Pilate,
68. Galba,	36. Marcellus (?)
69. Otho,	37. Marullus (?)
69. Vitellius,	[41. *Agrippa I king*],
69–79. Vespasian.	44. Cuspius Fadus,
	47. Tiberius Julius Alexander,
	48. Cumanus,
	52. Felix,
	60. Festus,
	62. Albinus,
	64–66. Gessius Florus.

37. Herod I king.

35. *Aristobulus* (*III*), brother of Mariamne, high priest, *killed* by order of Herod.

31. Hyrcanus II executed.

30 (about). HILLEL president of the Synhedrion; SHAMMAI deputy. Herod in favor with Augustus, the first Roman emperor.

29. *Mariamne executed.*

20 (about). *Herod rebuilds the Temple.*

Asinai and Anilai found a small Jewish state in Nahardea.

6. Execution of Mariamne's sons, Alexander and Aristobulus.

4. Death of Herod. *Archelaus* possessor of Judæa and Samaria; *Herod Antipas* Tetrarch of Galilee and Peræa; (Herod) Philip II Tetrarch of Gaulanitis, Batanæa, Trachonitis, and Panias.

3. Revolt against Archelaus; the "War Period of Varus," governor of Syria. Leadership of *Judas the Galilean, founder of the Zealots.*

2. Archelaus recognized as Ethnarch by Augustus.

C.E.

6. Archelaus deposed; Judæa a Roman province; Coponius *the first procurator;* Quirinius, governor of Syria, takes a census for purposes of taxation.

18(about). Izates and Helen of Adiabene embrace Judaism. Conversions to Judaism in Rome.

26. *Pontius Pilate* procurator.
John the Baptist.

30(about). JESUS OF NAZARETH. **Rise of Christianity.**

33. Philip's tetrarchy falls to Rome.

37. *Agrippa I*, favorite of Caligula, made king of Philip's tetrarchy.

38. The Jews of Alexandria persecuted by Flaccus.

40. PHILO JUDÆUS, ambassador to Caligula. The emperor's statue set up in the Temple.
Herod Antipas deposed; his tetrarchy added to King Agrippa I's territory.

41. Claudius restores the Alabarchate in Alexandria to *Alexander Lysimachus*, brother of Philo.
AGRIPPA I receives Judæa and Galilee, Archelaus' possessions, from Claudius, and IS KING OF THE WHOLE OF PALESTINE.
GAMALIEL I THE ELDER, president of the Synhedrion.

43. Helen of Adiabene in Jerusalem.

44. Death of Agrippa I. *Herod II, prince of Chalcis, titular king of Judæa.*
Theudas, a false Messiah.

48. SAUL OF TARSUS, THE APOSTLE PAUL, converts the heathen to Christianity. Death of Herod II.

49. AGRIPPA II, prince of Chalcis, TITULAR KING OF JUDÆA.
The Zealots and the Sicarii commit depredations.

52. Hostilities between Jews and the heathen at Cæsarea.

53. Agrippa II king of Philip's tetrarchy.

63. *Joshua ben Gamala*, high priest, establishes **elementary schools** in Judæa.

64. *Gessius Florus*, the last of the procurators.

66. The census taken by Cestus Gallus, governor of Syria, at Jerusalem; the *Passover of the Crushing.*
Renewed hostilities between the Jews and the heathen of Cæsarea.
REBELLION AGAINST GESSIUS FLORUS in Jerusalem; the Zealots under Eleazar ben Ananias.
End of the Roman garrison in Jerusalem.
Race hostilities between the Jews and the heathen in Judæa, Syria, and Alexandria.
Cestius Gallus besieges Jerusalem.
Cestius Gallus retires from Jerusalem; Judæa ruled by the Synhedrion, Simon II ben Gamaliel president.

C.E.

66. The prohibition of "*The Eighteen Things*" enacted by the school of Shammai in consequence of the continued hostilities between the Jews and the heathen.

War in Galilee; FLAVIUS JOSEPHUS governor of Galilee.

66. *John of Gischala* accuses Josephus of duplicity before the Synhedrion.

67. Gabara taken by Vespasian.

Fall of Jotapata. Josephus surrenders to the Romans. Fall of Gamala.

The fall of Gischala completes the *conquest of Galilee* by the Romans.

The Idumæans enter Jerusalem as the allies of the Zealots; civil war in Jerusalem; reign of terror under the Zealots; the Synhedrion ceases to exist.

68. Peræa taken by Vespasian.

Simon bar Giora enters Jerusalem, and renews the civil war.

69. Vespasian proclaimed emperor; he leaves Judæa. TITUS commander of the army in Judæa.

Civil dissension continues in Jerusalem.

70. TITUS BEGINS THE SIEGE OF JERUSALEM.

Fall of the outer wall of Jerusalem; Bezetha in the hands of the Romans.

Fall of the Tower of Antonia.

Famine in Jerusalem. Sacrifices cease to be brought in the Temple.

BURNING OF THE TEMPLE. Titus in the Holy of Holies.

Zion, the upper city, burnt by Titus. **Complete destruction of Jerusalem.**

An academy founded in Jamnia by JOCHANAN BEN ZAKKAI.

71. The fortresses Herodium and Machærus taken by Bassus. Titus' triumph; execution of Simon bar Giora.

72. Masada taken by Silva; the last Zealots fall; JUDÆA COMPLETELY CONQUERED. Death of Agrippa II.

The *Fiscus judaicus* instituted by Vespasian.

XIV. THE EPOCH OF THE MISHNA AND THE TANAITES.

(72–219 C. E.)

72. Rebellion of the fugitive Zealots in Egypt and Cyrene. The Onias Temple closed.

80. GAMALIEL II Patriarch, or president of the Synhedrion at Jamnia; his colleagues ELIEZER BEN HYRCANUS and JOSHUA BEN CHANANYA. Excommunication first used.

C.E.

	The daily prayers ('Eighteen Benedictions") first formulated.
	The Minæan curse introduced into the prayers. Jewish Christians (Nazarenes, Ebionites), heathen Christians, and Gnostics.
93.	JOSEPHUS completes his history of the Jews, THE ANTIQUITIES.
95 (about).	Death of Josephus.
115.	The Jews of Babylonia, Palestine, Egypt, Cyprus, Cyrene, and Lybia rise against Trajan.
118.	The Jews of Palestine rise against Trajan and Hadrian; "War of Lucius Quietus."
	Joshua ben Chananya president of the Synhedrion.
119.	AKYLAS, proselyte, makes a Greek translation of the Scriptures.
130.	AKIBA BEN JOSEPH president of the Synhedrion; collects the Halachoth (*Mishna of R. Akiba*).
133.	**Rebellion of Bar-Cochba against Hadrian; restoration of the Jewish State.**
134.	Magdala taken by Julius Severus.
135.	FALL OF BETHAR; end of Bar-Cochba.
	Persecutions by Turnus Rufus; Jerusalem called Ælia Capitolina.
	Akiba ben Joseph dies a martyr; the ten martyrs; *Elisha ben Abuya* (Acher) informs against observing Jews.
138.	Hadrian's decrees revoked by Antoninus Pius. The fugitive disciples of the Law return from Babylonia, and organize a Synhedrion at Usha.
140.	*Simon III*, son of Gamaliel II, president of the Synhedrion, assisted by MEÏR, Judah ben Ilaï, Nathan of Babylon, José ben Chalafta, and SIMON BEN YOCHAI.
161.	Revolution in Palestine against Antoninus Pius.
	Verus Commodus, co-emperor with Marcus Aurelius, persecutes the Jews of Palestine.
165.	JUDAH I, THE HOLY, RABBI, PRESIDENT OF THE SYNHEDRION.
189.	**Compilation of the Mishna** (*Mishna di Rabbi Judah*); Judah I and Nathan of Babylon the last of the Tanaites.
200.	Severus prohibits heathens from becoming Jews.
210.	Gamaliel III, son of Judah I, president of the Synhedrion.
	The apocryphal Mishnas (Boraïtoth) compiled.

XV. THE EPOCH OF THE TALMUD, THE AMORAIM, AND THE SABORAIM.

C.E. (219–550 C. E.)

219. ABBA AREKA (RAB) OPENS THE ACADEMY AT SORA; MAR-SAMUEL, principal of the academy at Nahardea, declares the law of the land binding on the Jews.

225. *Judah II*, son of Gamaliel III, president of the Synhedrion, influences Alexander Severus to revive the privileges of the Jews, and mitigates the rigor of the Law.

Jochanan bar Napacha, *Simon ben Lakish*, and Joshua ben Levi, Palestinian Amoraim.

247. *Huna*, principal of the Sora academy.

JUDAH BEN EZEKIEL FOUNDS AN ACADEMY AT PUMBEDITHA.

259. Odenathus destroys Nahardea. *Sheshet founds an academy at Silhi.*

279. *Ami and Assi*, heads of the college of Tiberias.

280. Judah III, son of Judah II, Patriarch, collects a tax from foreign communities.

297. Judah ben Ezekiel, general Resh Metibta (principal of both Sora and Pumbeditha).

299. Chasda principal of the Sora academy; Huna ben Chiya, of the Pumbeditha academy.

309. *Rabba bar Nachmani*, principal of Pumbeditha; Rabba bar Huna, principal of Sora.

315. *Emperor Constantine issues the first of his anti-Jewish decrees.*

320. *The Council of Illiberis (Spain) forbids intercourse between Jews and Christians.*

325. The first *Church Council at Nice* completely severs Judaism and Christianity by making *the celebration of Easter independent of the Jewish calendar.*

327. Teachers of the Law banished from Palestine by Constantine.

330. *Joseph ben Chiya*, principal of the Pumbeditha academy, makes a Chaldaic translation of the Prophets.

333. Abayi Nachmani, principal of Pumbeditha.

338. *Raba bar Joseph bar Chama, principal of the academy at Machuza.*

339. *Constantius forbids the marriage of a Jew with a Christian woman, and the circumcision of Christian and heathen slaves, under the penalty of death.*

351. Religious persecutions in Palestine by the emperors Constantius and Gallus and the Roman general Ursicinus.

C.E.

352. Nachman ben Isaac, principal of the Pumbeditha academy.

355. *Papa bar Chanan founds an academy at Nares.*

356. Chama of Nahardea, principal of the Pumbeditha academy.

359. HILLEL II, PATRIARCH, INTRODUCES A FINAL, FIXED CALENDAR.

361. Restoration of the Temple at Jerusalem under Julian the Apostate.

364. Valentinian I and Valens extend toleration to the Jews.

375. ASHI, THE REDACTOR OF THE BABYLONIAN TALMUD, restores the Sora academy. At about this time THE PALESTINIAN, OR JERUSALEM, TALMUD IS COMPLETED.

390. Amemar re-opens an academy at Nahardea.

393. Theodosius I confirms the exceptional position of the Jews in the Roman empire.

400. Moses, the false Messiah of Crete.

415. Gamaliel VI deposed by Theodosius II.

Cyril, bishop of Alexandria, drives the Jews from Alexandria.

Jews excluded from state offices in the Empire of the East under Theodosius II.

425. EXTINCTION OF THE PATRIARCHATE.

427. DEATH OF ASHI, who, in the latter half of his life, collected and arranged the explanations, deductions, and amplifications of the Mishna, included under the name **Talmud (Babylonian Talmud)**.

455. Persecution of the Babylonian Jews under Jezdijird III.

Mar bar Ashi continues the compilation of the Talmud.

465. The Council of Vannes (Gaul) prohibits the clergy from taking part in Jewish banquets.

471. Persecution of the Babylonian Jews under Firuz (Pheroces). The Exilarch Huna Mari and others suffer martyrdom.

490. Babylonian Jews emigrate to India under Joseph Rabban, and found a little *Jewish state in Cranganor.*

499. Death of Rabina, the last of the Amoraim; COMPLETION OF THE TALMUD COLLECTION.

500(about). *Abu-Kariba, Himyarite king, adopts Judaism*, and converts his army and his people.

511. Mar-Zutra II, Prince of the Captivity (Exilarch), establishes an independent Jewish state in Babylonia under the Persian king Kobad.

517. *The Council of Epaone forbids Christians to take part in Jewish banquets.*

518. Persecution of the Jews by Kobad, king of Persia.

530. Death of Zorah Yussuf Dhu-Nowas, *last Jewish Himyarite king.*

C.E.

531. Giza in Sora and Semuna in Pumbeditha, the last Saboraim.

532. Justinian I decrees that *the testimony of Jews shall be valid only in Jewish cases.*

538. *The Council of Orleans forbids Jews to appear on the street at Eastertide.*

550(about). **Final redaction of the Babylonian Talmud.**

XVI. FROM THE COMPLETION OF THE TALMUD TO THE END OF THE GAONATE.

(550–1038 C. E.)

Samuel ben Adiya (500–560), Jewish poet in Arabia.

553. Justinian I decrees that the Scriptural portions in the Synagogue liturgy be read in translation, and orders the omission of alleged anti-Trinitarian sentences from the liturgy.

581. Hormisdas IV, king of Persia, persecutes his Jewish subjects; the teachers of the Law flee from the Babylonian academies.

Chilperic, Merovingian king, forces baptism on the Jews.

589. Reccared, Visigothic king, imposes irksome restraints upon the Jews, and *completely isolates them from Christians.*

Bahram Tshubin, usurper of the Persian throne, friendly to the Jews; Pumbeditha re-opened by Chanan of Iskia.

590. Pope Gregory I discountenances the forced conversion of Jews.

612. Sisebut, Visigothic king, forces the Jews to accept baptism or to emigrate.

614. The Jews of Palestine join the Persians in a war against Emperor Heraclius.

624. The Benu-Kainukaa, a Jewish-Arabic tribe, driven from Arabia by Mahomet.

625. The Benu-Nadhir, a Jewish-Arabic tribe, driven from Arabia by Mahomet.

627. Extermination of the Benu-Kuraiza, a Jewish-Arabic tribe.

Emperor Heraclius *forbids Jews to enter Jerusalem*, and in other ways harasses the Palestinian Jews.

629. Dagobert orders the Jews of the Frankish empire to accept baptism or to emigrate.

633. The Council of Toledo under Sisenand, Visigothic king, and Isidore of Seville, forces backsliding converts back into Christianity.

638. Chintila enacts that only professing Catholics shall remain in Visigothic Spain; Jews emigrate.

C.E.

640. Omar, the second Caliph, *banishes all Jews from holy Arabia.* The "*Covenant of Omar*" imposes restrictions upon Jews in the whole Mahometan world.

642(about). BOSTANAÏ, Exilarch, acknowledged by Omar.

654. Judaizing Christians of Toledo under Receswinth, Visigothic king, swear loyalty to the Catholic Church.

658. BEGINNING OF THE GAONATE; Mar-Isaac, head of the Sora academy, takes the title GAON.

670. Hunaï, Gaon of Sora, and Mar-Raba, principal of Pumbeditha, *reform the divorce laws.*

681. Judaizing Christians re-affirm their adherence to Christianity under Erwig, Visigothic king.

693. Egica, Visigothic king, *forbids Jews to hold real estate.*

700(about). RISE OF THE MASSORA AND OF NEO-HEBRAIC LITURGIC POETRY. José bar José Hayathom the first Poetan.

712. Jews open the gates of Toledo to Tarik, the Mahometan general.

719. Natronaï ben Nehemiah (Mar-Yanka), principal of Pumbeditha.

720. Serene, the Syrian Messiah.

Omar II, Ommiyyade Caliph of Damascus, re-enacts the "*Covenant of Omar.*"

723. Persecution of the Jews of the Byzantine Empire under Leo the Isaurian.

745(about). ELEAZAR BEN KALIR (KALIRI), poetan.

The Chazars under Bulan accept Judaism.

749. Obaiah Abu-Isa ben Ishak, precursor of the Messiah in Ispahan.

759. *Jehuda the Blind,* Gaon of Sora, author of a Talmudic compendium, *Halachoth Ketuoth.*

761. Dudaï principal of Pumbeditha.

The Karaite schism led by Anan ben David.

787. Charlemagne removes the Kalonymos family from Lucca to Mayence to encourage Jewish learning in the Frankish Empire. He introduces a *Jewish oath.*

797. Isaac sent by Charlemagne on an embassy to Haroun Alrashid.

800(about). Judah Judghan, founder of a sect, introduces Mutazilist philosophy into Judaism.

Benjamin ben Moses of Nahavend, founder of the Maghariyites, spreads the Mutazilist philosophy among the Karaites.

807. Haroun Alrashid introduces THE JEW BADGE into the Abbasside Caliphate.

825. Contest for the Exilarchate between David ben Judah and Daniel.

Rise of Karaite sects: Akbarites, Tiflisites, and the followers of Moses of Baalbek.

C.E.

827(about). Eberard, *Magister Judæorum*, under Louis I the Pious, king of the Franks, protects the Jews against Agobard, bishop of Lyons.

842. The title GAON assumed also by the Pumbeditha principals; Paltoi ben Abayi *the first Gaon of Pumbeditha.*

845. The Council of Meaux under Amolo, bishop of Lyons, enacts anti-Jewish decrees, renewing those of Constantine and Theodosius II.

853. The Abbasside Caliph Al-Mutavakkil *introduces Jew badges*, and re-enacts the "*Covenant of Omar.*"

869. Mar-Amram ben Sheshna, Gaon of Sora, at the request of a Spanish community, arranges the **order of prayers** in use among European Jews.

872. Mar-Zemach I ben Paltoi, Gaon of Pumbeditha, author of the *first Talmudic Dictionary.*

880(about). ELDAD HA-DANI.

881. *Nachshon ben Zadok*, Gaon of Sora, *discovers the key to the Jewish calendar.*

900(about). Simon of Cairo writes the *Halachoth Gedoloth*, a polemic against Karaism.

JOSIPPON compiled.

Isaac ben Israeli I Suleiman (845–940), physician and philologist at Kairuan.

913. SAADIAH BEN JOSEPH (892–942) attacks Karaism.

917. Mar-Kohen-Zedek II ben Joseph, Gaon of Pumbeditha, tries to bring about the fall of the Exilarchate and the academy of Sora. Hostilities against Mar-Ukba.

921. *David ben Zaccaï* made Exilarch.

928. *Saadiah installed as Gaon of Sora.* His controversies with the Karaite *Solomon ben Yerucham*, and his *translation of the Scriptures into Arabic.*

930. Hostilities between Saadiah and David ben Zaccaï.

934. Saadiah writes his religious-philosophical work EMUNOTH WE-DEOTH.

940. Death of David ben Zaccaï, the last Exilarch of influence. END OF THE EXILARCHATE a few years later.

940(about). MOSES AND AARON BEN ASHER, Massorets.

942. Death of Saadiah.

945(about). *Four scholars are sent from Sora to gather contributions for the academy:* Shemarya ben Elchanan settles in Cairo; CHUSHIEL, in Kairuan; Nathan ben Isaac Kohen, in Narbonne; and MOSES BEN CHANOCH, IN CORDOVA.

Abusahal Dunash ben Tamim (900–960), physician in Kairuan.

946. *Sabbataï Donnolo* (913–970), physician in Italy.

CHASDAÏ BEN ISAAC IBN-SHAPRUT (915–970), diplomat under Abdul-Rahman III, Nagid of the Jews of the Cordova Caliphate, patron of Jewish learning.

C.E.

950(about). The Karaite controversialists Abulsari Sahal ben Mazliach Kohen and Jephet Ibn-Ali Halevi.

Menachem ben Saruk (910–970) and *Dunash ben Labrat* (Adonim, 920–970), the first Hebrew grammarians. NEO-HEBRAIC POETRY FLOURISHES.

980. SHERIRA (920–1000), Gaon of Pumbeditha; his "LETTER" a chronicle of Jewish events from the conclusion of the Talmud to his time.

985. Chanoch ben Moses (940–1014) and Joseph Ibn-Abitur, Cordova Talmudists.

Jacob Ibn-Jau, prince of the Jews of the Cordova Caliphate.

990. JEHUDA IBN-DAUD (CHAYUJ), Hebrew grammarian.

998. HAÏ (969–1038), Gaon of Pumbeditha.

1000(about). GERSHOM BEN JEHUDA (960–1028), promoter of Talmud study at Mayence, INTERDICTS POLYGAMY.

Simon ben Isaac ben Abun poetan.

1002. NATHAN BEN YECHIEL COMPILES THE ARUCH, A TALMUDIC LEXICON.

1008. The Fatimide Caliph Hakim *decrees a Jew badge*, and persecutes the Jews in various ways.

1012. Jews driven from Mayence by Emperor Henry II.

1020. ABULVALID MERVAN IBN-JANACH (995–1050), Hebrew grammarian.

1027. SAMUEL HALEVI IBN-NAGRELA (993–1055), minister to King Habus of Granada, Nagid of the Jews, patron of Jewish learning, and Talmudic author.

1034. Death of Samuel Chofni, *last of the Sora Geonim*.

1038. The death of HAÏ, Gaon of Pumbeditha, marks the END OF THE GAONATE.

XVII. THE AGE OF GEBIROL, HALEVI, RASHI, AND MAIMONIDES.

(1038–1204 C. E.)

1038(about). Chananel ben Chushiel and Nissim ben Jacob Ibn-Shahin (1015–1055), Talmudists in Kairuan.

1045. **Solomon Ibn-Gebirol (Avicebron,** 1021–1070), poet and philosopher, author of the "Kether Malkuth" and the "Mekor Chayim."

1050(about). *Bachya Ibn-Pakuda*, philosopher, writes the "Guide to the Duties of the Heart."

1055. *Abu Hussain Joseph Ibn-Nagrela* (1031–1066), minister to Badis of Granada, Nagid of the Jews, and patron of Jewish learning.

1056. ISAAC BEN JACOB ALFASSI (1013–1103), Talmudist.

1066. Banishment of the Jews from Granada. *First persecution of the Jews of Spain* since its conquest by the Mahometans.

C.E.

1069. Isaac ben Baruch Ibn-Albalia (1035–1094), astronomer to Al-Mutamed in Cordova, Nassi of the Jews, Talmudist.

1070. **Rashi** (Solomon Yizchaki, 1040–1105), exegete and Talmudist.

1078. Pope Gregory VII (Hildebrand) promulgates the canonical *law against Jews' holding offices in Christendom.*

1095. Emperor Henry IV issues a decree against the forcible baptism of Jews.

1096. THE FIRST CRUSADE: Suffering of the Jews of Rouen, Treves, Speyer, Worms, Cologne, Ratisbon, Prague, etc.

1099. The Jews of Jerusalem burnt in a synagogue by the crusaders under Godfrey of Bouillon.

1100. Abraham ben Chiya Albargeloni (1065–1136), astronomer.

1110. **Moses Ibn-Ezra** (1070–1139), liturgical and erotic poet.

Joseph ben Meïr Ibn-Migash Halevi (1077–1141), Talmudist.

1120. **Jehuda ben Samuel Halevi** (1086–1142), poet and philosopher, author of the Zion songs and of the Chozari.

1141. Jehuda Halevi leaves Spain for Palestine.

THE TOSSAFISTS: the family of Rashi, especially his grandsons JACOB TAM (1100–1171), and Samuel ben Meïr (Rashbam, 1100–1160).

1146. *Beginning of the Almohade persecution* in northern Africa and southern Spain. Jews flee, or pretend to accept Islam.

1147. THE SECOND CRUSADE. Pope Eugenius III absolves crusaders from the payment of interest on debts owing to Jews.

The crusaders attack the Jews of the Rhine country, South Germany, and France.

In consequence of their protection by Emperor Conrad III, the Jews are considered **servi cameræ.**

1149. Jehuda Ibn-Ezra, of Toledo, Nassi, steward of the palace under Alfonso VII Raimundez. He persecutes the Karaites.

1150(about). ABRAHAM BEN MEÏR IBN-EZRA (1088–1167), poet, exegete, philosopher.

1160(about). *Jacob Tam calls the first rabbinical synod.*

Abraham Ibn-Daud Halevi (1110–1180), philosopher and historian.

The Exilarchate revived by Mahomet Almuktafi. Solomon (Chasdaï) Exilarch.

C.E.

1160(about). *David Alrui* pretends to be divinely appointed to lead the Jews of the Bagdad Caliphate to Jerusalem.

1164(about). **Moses ben Maimun** (Rambam, Maimonides, 1135–1204), philosopher, writes his "Letter of Consolation."

1165. *Benjamin of Tudela* begins his travels in the East.
Serachya Halevi Gerundi (1125–1186), Talmudist.

1168. *Maimonides finishes his Arabic commentary on the Mishna.*

1170(about). Meshullam ben Jacob, Provençal patron of Jewish learning.
Judah ben Saul Ibn-Tibbon (1120–1190), physician and translator.
DAVID KIMCHI, grammarian and exegete.
Abraham ben David of Posquières (Rabed II, 1125–1198), Talmudist, Maimonides' opponent.

1170(about). Jonathan Cohen of Lünel, Talmudist.
Jacob ben Meshullam, first promoter of THE KABBALA.

1171. The Jews of Blois burnt ON THE CHARGE OF HAVING USED HUMAN BLOOD IN THE PASSOVER. The **blood accusation,** or charge of ritual murder, preferred for the first time.
Death of Jacob Tam.
Isaac ben Samuel (Ri) of Dampierre, Tossafist.

1172. Persecution of the Jews of Yemen. Messianic excitement.

1175(about). Petachya of Ratisbon, traveler.
Samuel ben Ali Halevi, Gaon of Bagdad, opponent of Maimonides.

1177. *Maimonides rabbi of Cairo.*

1179. The Third Lateran Council passes decrees protecting the religious liberty of the Jews.

1180. Maimonides finishes his MISHNE TORAH, or YAD HA-CHAZAKA.

1181. *Philip II Augustus of France banishes the Jews from his hereditary province.*

1187, Saladin *permits Jews to enter Jerusalem.*

1189. *Attack on the Jews of London* at Richard I's coronation. The excitement spreads to Lynn, Norwich, Stamford, York, and Bury St. Edmund's.

1190(about). Maimonides issues the "**Guide of the Perplexed,**" dedicating it to Joseph Ibn-Aknin.
Abraham Ibn-Alfachar (1160–1223), diplomat under Alfonso VIII of Castile.
Ephraim ben Jacob of Bonn (1132–1200), liturgical poet and author of a martyrology.
Massacre of the Jews of Germany from the Rhine to Vienna under Emperor Henry VI.
Samuel Ibn-Tibbon (1160–1239), translator.

C.E.

1190(about). Süsskind of Trimberg, Jewish minnesinger.

Judah Sir Leon ben Isaac, the Pious (1166–1224), Tossafist, author of the "*Book of the Pious.*"

Samson ben Abraham of Sens, Tossafist.

Isaac the Younger (Rizba), Tossafist; Jacob of Orleans, Tossafist.

1197. *Hillali*, the oldest Hebrew copy of the Bible in Spain, taken by the Almohades.

Sheshet Benveniste (1131–1210), philosopher, physician, Talmudist, diplomat, and poet.

1198. The Jews of France forbidden to move from province to province.

1204. DEATH OF MAIMONIDES.

XVIII. FROM THE DEATH OF MAIMONIDES TO THE EXPULSION FROM SPAIN.

(1204–1492 C. E.)

1209. The Council of Avignon issues restrictive measures against the Jews.

1210(about). Isaac the Blind, founder of **the Kabbala**. Disciples: Azriel and Ezra.

JEHUDA ALCHARISI, poet.

1210. The Jews of England imprisoned by King John.

1211. *French and English rabbis emigrate to Palestine.*

1212. The Jews of Toledo killed by crusaders under the Cistercian monk Arnold. *First persecution of Jews in Castile.*

1215. THE FOURTH LATERAN COUNCIL under the pope INNOCENT III, among many anti-Jewish measures, decrees the **Jew badge**.

1222. The Council of Oxford imposes restrictions on the English Jews.

1223. The rabbinical synod of Mayence regulates the payment of the Jew taxes.

1227. The Council of Narbonne re-enacts the anti-Jewish decrees of the Fourth Lateran Council.

1229. Pope Gregory IX antagonizes the Jews.

1232. The Jews of Hungary excluded from state offices.

Meïr ben Todros Halevi Abulafia (1180–1244) attacks Maimonides' doctrine of the immortality of the soul.

1233. Solomon ben Abraham of Montpellier, Jonah ben Abraham Gerundi, and David ben Saul ally themselves with the Dominicans, who BURN MAIMONIDES' WORKS IN MONTPELLIER AND PARIS.

1235. *Abraham Maimuni* (1185–1254), physician and philosopher.

C.E.

1235. MOSES BEN NACHMAN (Ramban, 1195–1270), Talmudist, exegete, Kabbalist, anti-Maimunist.

Jacob ben Abba Mari ben Simon (Anatoli), Jewish scholar at the court of Frederick II.

BERACHYA BEN NATRONAÏ NAKDAN (Crispia), fabulist and punctuator.

1235. Gregory IX confirms the *Constitutio Judæorum* of Innocent III.

1236. Crusaders attack the Jewish communities of Anjou, Poitou, etc.

1239. On the charges of the apostate Nicholas-Donin, Gregory IX orders the Dominicans and Franciscans to examine the Talmud, and burn it, if necessary.

1240. *Disputation before Louis IX* of France between Nicholas-Donin and the Jews, represented by Yechiel of Paris, MOSES OF COUCY, Talmudist and itinerant preacher, and two others.

1240. A Jewish Parliament assembled by Henry III.

1242. THE TALMUD BURNT AT PARIS.

1244. *Archduke Frederick I the Valiant, of Austria, grants privileges to the Jews.*

1246. The Council of Béziers *forbids Jews to practice medicine.*

1247. *Pope Innocent IV issues a bull disproving the blood accusation against the Jews.*

1254. *The Jews expelled from his dominions by Louis IX of France. End of the Tossafists.*

1257. *Alfonso X, the Wise, of Castile, compiles* a code, containing a section of *anti-Jewish laws.*

1263. MOSES BEN NACHMAN opposes Pablo Christiani AT THE DISPUTATION OF BARCELONA.

1264. The Jews of London attacked under Henry III.

1267. The Council of Vienna re-enacts the anti-Jewish decrees of the Fourth Lateran Council.

1271 (about). Pope Gregory X issues a bull deprecating the forced baptism of Jews.

1278. The Jews of England imprisoned on the charge of counterfeiting coin.

1279. The Council of Buda enacts anti-Jewish measures.

SOLOMON BEN ADRET (Rashba, 1245–1310), Talmudist.

David Maimuni (1233–1300), grandson of Maimonides.

1283. Beginning of the massacres of the Jews of Germany on the blood accusation.

Moses ben Chasdaï Taku (1250–1290), anti-Maimunist.

1286. MEÏR BEN BARUCH OF ROTHENBURG (1220–1293), chief rabbi of Germany, imprisoned when about to emigrate.

1288. *Saad Addaula*, minister of finance of the Persian empire under Argun.

C.E.

1289. *Maimonides' works burnt at Accho.* Solomon Petit, anti-Maimunist and Kabbalist; Hillel ben Samuel of Verona (1220–1295), Talmudist and Maimunist.

1290. THE JEWS BANISHED FROM ENGLAND.

1291. The Jews of Accho imprisoned or executed by the Sultan of Egypt.

1295 (about). Publication of the **Zohar** by Moses de Leon; Kabbalistic studies flourish.

1298. Persecution of the Jews in Germany instigated by *Rindfleish;* Mordecai ben Hillel a martyr.

1305. THE BAN AGAINST THE STUDY OF SCIENCE pronounced by Abba-Mari ben Moses; authorized by SOLOMON BEN ADRET; urged by ASHER BEN YECHIEL (Asheri); opposed by the Tibbonides led by *Jacob ben Machir* (Profatius) and the poet *Yedaya Penini Bedaresi.*

1306. *The first expulsion of the Jews from France* under Philip IV the Fair.

1310. *Asheri compiles his Talmudic code.*

1313. The Council of Zamora renews the canonical laws hostile to the Jews.

1315. Louis X of France recalls the Jews.

1320. The *Pastoureaux* persecutions in France (Gesereth ha-Roïm).

1321. The *Leper* persecution in France (Gesereth Mezoraim). *The second expulsion of the Jews from France.*

1328. Persecution of the Jews of Navarre.

1334. *Casimir III the Great of Poland issues laws friendly to the Jews.*

1336. Disputation at Valladolid between the Jews and the apostate Abner-Alfonso. Alfonso XI of Castile forbids the use of *alleged blasphemous expressions in the Hebrew prayers.*

Persecution of the Jews in Germany by the *Armleder.*

1337. Joseph of Ecija and Samuel Ibn-Wakar favorites of Alfonso XI of Castile. Gonzalo Martinez plans the destruction of the Jews of Castile.

1340. JACOB BEN ASHERI (Baal ha-Turim, 1280–1340) compiles his Talmudic code.

Nissim Gerundi ben Reuben (1340–1380), rabbi of Barcelona.

1342. LEVI BEN GERSON (Gersonides, Maestro Leon de Bagnols, 1288–1345), physician and philosopher.

1348. Persecution of the Jews in Europe on account of the **Black Death.** Pope Clement VI issues two bulls protecting the Jews.

1350. *Moses ben Joshua Narboni* (Maestro Vidal, 1300–1362), philosopher.

C.E.

1350. Aaron II ben Elia Nicomedi (1300–1369), Karaite philosopher.

Santob de Carrion (1300–1350), Jewish-Spanish troubadour.

Samuel Abulafia, minister to Pedro the Cruel of Castile.

1351. The cortes of Valladolid ask the abolition of the judicial autonomy of Spanish-Jewish communities.

1355. The "Golden Bull" by Emperor Charles IV confers the privilege of holding Jews on the Electors.

1357. Completion of the synagogue at Toledo built by Samuel Abulafia.

1360. Samuel Abulafia dies under torture on the charge of peculation.

Participation of the Jews of Castile in the civil war (1360–1369) between Pedro the Cruel and Henry de Trastamare, chiefly on the side of the former.

Manessier de Vesoul obtains from King John a decree permitting Jews to dwell in France.

1370(about). Meïr ben Baruch Halevi of Vienna introduces the conferring of authorization for the exercise of rabbinical functions (*Morenu*). He and his disciples, principally *Isaac of Tyrnau, compile the customs* (*Minhagim*) *of the communities.*

1371. The Jews of Castile under Henry II compelled to wear badges and give up Spanish names.

1375. Disputation at Avila between the apostate John of Valladolid and Moses Cohen de Tordesillas.

1376. Disputation at Pampeluna between John of Valladolid and Shem-Tob ben Shaprut.

Samuel Abrabanel at court under Henry II of Castile.

Chayim ben Gallipapa (1310–1380), innovator; Menachem ben Aaron ben Zerach (1310–1385), rabbinical author; Isaac ben Sheshet Barfat (Ribash, 1310–1409), Talmudist; CHASDAÏ BEN ABRAHAM CRESCAS (1340–1410), philosopher.

1379. Joseph Pichon, receiver-general of taxes in Seville, murdered, probably at the instigation of Jews, against whom the fury of the populace is turned.

1380. Juan I restricts the judicial autonomy of the Castilian Jewish communities.

1381. A synod at Mayence regulates the rabbinical marriage laws (Tekanoth Shum).

1385. Juan I of Castile revives the canonical restrictions against the Jews.

1389. The charge of host desecration leads to the massacre of the Jews of Prague.

C.E.

1391. Ferdinand Martinez incites the mob against the Jews of Seville. THE MASSACRE AND PLUNDER OF THE JEWS SPREADS FROM CASTILE TO ARAGON, MAJORCA, AND OTHER PARTS OF SPAIN. Many Jews converted to Christianity: **Marranos.** Solomon Levi of Burgos (Paul de Santa Maria, 1350–1435), begins his machinations against Judaism.

1392. Joao I of Portugal forbids force in the conversion of Jews.

1394. *Third and last expulsion of the Jews from France*, under Charles VI.

1396(about). Writings in defence of Judaism by Joshua ben Joseph Ibn-Vives Allorqui (Geronimo de Santa Fé), Chasdaï Crescas, and *Profiat Duran.*

1399. Persecution of the Jews of Prague at the instigation of the apostate Pessach; Lipmann of Mühlhausen among the sufferers.

1408. *Alfonso X's anti-Jewish laws revived* under Juan II of Castile.

Don Meïr Alguades, rabbi and physician, executed on the charge of host desecration.

Kabbalistic studies flourish in Spain.

1408. Simon Duran (1361–1444), rabbi of Algiers.

1410. *Chasdaï Crescas publishes his religio-philosophic work.*

1412. Juan II issues an edict of twenty-four articles designed to reduce the social prestige of the Jews. Vincent Ferrer preaches Christianity in the synagogues, and inflames the populace against the Jews. SECOND GENERAL MASSACRE OF JEWS IN ALL THE SPANISH PROVINCES. Numerous Jews submit to baptism.

1413. *Religious disputation at Tortosa* arranged by Pope Benedict XIII between Geronimo de Santa Fé (Joshua Lorqui), and Vidal ben Benveniste Ibn-Labi and *Joseph Albo.* Many Jews submit to baptism.

1415. Benedict XIII forbids the study of the Talmud, and *ordains the Jew badge* and *Christian sermons for Jews.*

1419. Martin V issues a bull deprecating the forced conversion of Jews.

1420. Persecution of the Jews of Austria.

1421. *Jacob ben Moses Mölin Halevi* (*Maharil*, 1365–1427), compiler of the German synagogue liturgy and melodies.

1426. The Jews of Cologne banished.

1428. JOSEPH ALBO (1380–1444) publishes his philosophical work IKKARIM.

1431. The Jews of South Germany persecuted on account of the blood accusation.

C.E.

1431. Menachem of Merseburg (Meïl Zedek) regulates divorce proceedings.

1432. A synod at Avila under Abraham Benveniste Senior provides for an *educational system for Jewish Spain* (the law of Avila).

Moses ben Isaac (Gajo) da Rieti (1388–1451), Italian Jewish poet and physician.

1434. The COUNCIL OF BASLE renews old and devises new canonical restrictions against Jews.

Annihilation of the Jews of Majorca.

1441. The Jews expelled from Augsburg.

1442. Eugenius IV issues a bull enforcing all the old canonical restrictions against the Jews of Leon and Castile.

1445. *The first Hebrew concordance* by Isaac ben Kalonymos Nathan.

1447. Nicholas V makes Eugenius IV's bull applicable to Italian Jews.

Casimir IV of Poland grants unusual privileges to Jews.

1450. The Jews of Bavaria persecuted.

1451. Nicholas de Cusa enforces the wearing of Jew badges in Germany.

Pope Nicholas V authorizes the appointment of inquisitors for Marranos.

1453. The persecution of the Jews of Germany, Silesia, and Poland at the instigation of John of Capistrano.

The Jews favored in Turkey. Moses Kapsali chief rabbi.

1454. The privileges of the Polish Jews revoked.

1460. Alfonso de Spina publishes an attack upon Judaism.

1468. The Jews of Sepulveda charged with the blood accusation.

1470. The Marranos of Valladolid attacked.

1472. The Marranos of Cordova attacked.

1474. The Marranos of Segovia attacked.

1475. Bernardinus of Feltre preaches against the Jews in Italy.

The Jews charged with the murder of *Simon of Trent* for ritual purposes; a persecution of the Jews of Ratisbon follows.

1480(about). *Pico di Mirandola* the first Christian scholar to devote himself to Hebrew literature.

1480. **The Inquisition against the Marranos** established in Seville and at other places in Castile.

1482. Pope Sixtus IV denounces the cruelties of the Spanish Inquisition.

1482. THE INQUISITION AGAINST MARRANOS ESTABLISHED IN ARAGON, THOMAS DE TORQUEMADA CHIEF INQUISITOR.

Elias del Medigo (1463–1498), scholar.

C.E.

1483. TORQUEMADA MADE INQUISITOR-GENERAL OF SPAIN.

1484. ISAAC BEN JEHUDA ABRABANEL (1437–1509), minister of finance to Ferdinand and Isabella.

1492. Expulsion of the Jews from Spain.

XIX. FROM THE EXPULSION FROM SPAIN TO THE PERSECUTION IN POLAND.

(1492–1648 C. E.)

1493 *Most Spanish Jews leave Portugal;* all remaining behind are sold as slaves.

Simon Duran II (1439–1570), rabbi of Algiers.

1494. ISAAC ABRABANEL, minister of finance to two kings of Naples.

1496. Manoel of Portugal orders the Jews to accept baptism or leave the country.

1497. Manoel seizes Jewish children and has them baptized; many Jews accept baptism; **all others banished from Portugal.**

1498. THE EXILES SETTLED IN NAVARRE BANISHED.

1499. The Jews of Nuremberg banished.

1502. *Judah Leon Abrabanel* (Medigo, 1470–1530) writes his "Dialogues of Love."

Asher Lämmlein proclaims himself the forerunner of the Messiah.

1503 (about). Abraham Farissol (1451–1525), scholar at the court of Ferrara.

Gershon Cohen Soncinus establishes a *Hebrew printing office* in Prague.

Jacob Polak (1460–1530), the alleged originator of the PILPUL METHOD OF TALMUD STUDY.

1504. *Abraham Zacuto* finishes his chronicle, "Sefer Yochasin."

1506. Massacre of Marranos in Lisbon.

1507. Beginning of the feud between JOHN REUCHLIN and the Humanists on the one side and, on the other, PFEFFERKORN, the tool of the Dominicans led by Hoogstraten, Victor von Karben, Arnold von Tongern, Ortuinus Gratius, and the theological faculties of various universities. The Talmud and the Jews attacked and defended before Maximilian I, Popes Alexander VI and Leo X. The last publication by Pfefferkorn in 1521, near the beginning of Luther's Reformation.

1507 (about). Obadiah Sforno, Jacob Mantin, Abraham de Balmes, and ELIAS LEVITA (1468–1549), Hebrew grammarians, teachers of Hebrew to Christians. Introduction of Hebrew studies into German and French universities through the efforts of Egidio de Viterbo, Reuchlin, and Augustin Justiniani.

C.E.

1514 (about). *Obadyah di Bertinoro* (1470–1520), Talmudist and preacher, improves Jerusalem.

1516. VENICE SETS APART A SPECIAL QUARTER FOR A GHETTO.

1517 (about). David Ibn-Abi Zimra (1470–1573) *abolishes the Seleucidæan era* for the Egyptian Jews.

1518 (about). *Samuel Abrabanel* (1473–1550) employed as financier by the viceroy of Naples; *Benvenida Abrabanela.*

1519 (about). *Joseph ben Gershon Loans* (Joslin of Rosheim, 1478–1554), representative and protector of the German Jews.

1520 (about). *Elias Mizrachi* (1455–1527), chief rabbi of Turkey.

1523 (about). *Elias Kapsali* (1490–1555), historian.

1524. The Jews of Cairo threatened with destruction by Achmed Shaitan, viceroy of Egypt.

João III of Portugal employs Henrique Nunes (Firme-Fé) as a spy upon the Marranos.

David Reubeni in Rome under the protection of Pope Clement VII.

1529. SOLOMON MOLCHO (Diogo Pires, 1501–1532) begins his Messianic agitation.

1530 (about). Portuguese Marranos burnt by order of the Bishop of Ceuta.

1531 CLEMENT VII ISSUES A BULL ESTABLISHING THE PORTUGUESE INQUISITION FOR MARRANOS.

1532. Marranos forbidden to leave Portugal.

Molcho burnt by Emperor Charles V at Mantua.

Clement VII stops the proceedings of the Portuguese Inquisition at the instance of Marranos.

1535. Eighteen hundred Marranos liberated from the Portuguese Inquisition in obedience to a bull of Paul III.

1535 (about). Moses Hamon (1490–1565), physician to Sultan Selim I.

1536. Paul III sanctions the Portuguese Inquisition.

1538. *The ordination of rabbis* (*Semicha*) re-introduced by *Jacob Berab.*

1541. Most of the Jews leave Naples, where they are threatened with social degradation.

1542. The Jews of Prague banished.

Luther attacks the Jews.

1548. Portuguese Marranos again liberated on the interference of Paul III.

1550. The Jews banished from Genoa.

1552. *Samuel Usque* finishes his "Consolations for the Sorrows of Israel."

1553. The Talmud confiscated under Julius III in Italy.

1554. **Joseph Karo** (1488–1575), Kabbalist and Talmudist, finishes his code, the **Shulchan Aruch.**

1555. Paul IV issues a severe bull against the Jews.

The Marranos of Ancona imprisoned and tried by the **Inquisition.**

C.E.

1555. *Amatus Lusitanus* (1511–1568), physician.

1556. Sultan Solyman demands from Paul IV the release of Turkish Marranos; *Donna Gracia Mendesia* (1510–1568).

1559. The Talmud burnt at Cremona; prayer books burnt in Vienna.

1560(about). JOSEPH BEN JOSHUA COHEN (1496–1575), historian, writes his "Annals."

JOSEPH IBN-VERGA completes the martyrology "Shebet Jehuda," begun by his grandfather and father.

1561. The Jews of Prague banished.

1564. *Pius IV permits the publication of the Talmud without its name, and after having been submitted to censorship.*

1566. Pius V enforces all the canonical restrictions against the Jews.

Joseph Nassi (d. 1579) made Duke of Naxos by Sultan Selim II.

1568. ISAAC LURYA LEVI (1534–1572), Kabbalist, pretends to be the Messiah of Joseph.

CHAYIM VITAL CALABRESE (1543–1620), Kabbalist, associate of Lurya.

1569. All the Jews in the Papal States except those of Rome and Ancona expelled.

1570. AZARYA BEN MOSES DEÏ ROSSI (1514–1578), scholar.

1570(about). *Solomon Lurya* (1510–1573) and MOSES BEN ISRAEL ISSERLES (1520–1572), author of the "MAPPA," the continuation of the Shulchan Aruch, Polish Talmudists.

1574. Solomon ben Nathan Ashkenazi negotiates peace between Venice and Turkey.

1576. Stephen Bathori allows the Jews of Poland to carry on trade without restrictions.

1579. Gracia Nassi establishes a Hebrew printing press in Turkey. Esther Kiera, Turkish court-Jewess, publishes Hebrew books.

1581. Gregory XIII forbids the employment of Jewish physicians, re-ordains the confiscation of Hebrew books, and re-introduces the *compulsory Christian sermon for Jews.*

1586. Sixtus V permits Jews in the Papal States and the printing of the Talmud.

David de Pomis (1525–1588), physician.

1586(about). The Jews of Poland establish the SYNOD OF THE FOUR COUNTRIES; Mordecai Jafa probably its first president.

1587. *Gedalya Ibn-Yachya* (1515–1587), historian, has his work printed.

C.E.

1592. DAVID GANS (1541–1613) publishes his history.

1593. Isaac ben Abraham Troki (1533–1594), Karaite, publishes his "CHISUK EMUNAH."

Clement VIII expels the Jews from all the Papal States except Rome and Ancona.

THE FIRST MARRANO SETTLEMENT MADE IN HOLLAND AT AMSTERDAM under Jacob Tirado.

1597. The Jews expelled from various Italian principalities; Ferrara ceases to harbor Marranos.

1604. Clement VIII issues a bull of absolution for imprisoned Portuguese Marranos.

1612. *Portuguese Jews granted right of residence in Hamburg.*

1614. Vincent Fettmilch's attack upon the Jews of Frankfort.

1615. The Jews of Worms banished.

1616. Jews re-admitted into Frankfort and Worms.

1617. *Lipmann Heller* (1579–1654) completes his "*Tossafoth Yomtob.*"

1619. Permission accorded the Jews of Amsterdam to profess their religion.

1621 (about). *Sara Copia Sullam* (1600–1641), poetess.

1623. *Excommunication of Uriel da Costa* (1590–1640).

1630. Suffering of the Jews during the Thirty Years' War (1618–1648).

1639 (about). A *Talmud Torah* opened in Amsterdam. Saul Levi Morteira, Isaac Aboab de Fonseca, and MANASSEH BEN ISRAEL, rabbis of Amsterdam.

1641 (about). LEO BEN ISAAC MODENA (1571–1649); Joseph Solomon Delmedigo (1591–1655); and Simone Luzzatto (1590–1663), scholars not wholly in accord with the Judaism of their time.

1646. The Jews in Brazil side with the Dutch in their war with the Portuguese.

1648. Beginning of the COSSACK PERSECUTIONS OF THE JEWS IN POLAND UNDER CHMIELNICKI.

XX. FROM THE PERSECUTION IN POLAND TO THE PRESENT TIME.

(1648–1873 C. E.)

1649 (about). Christian scholars in Holland devote themselves to Hebrew literature.

1655. MANASSEH BEN ISRAEL goes to London to obtain from Cromwell THE RE-ADMISSION OF THE JEWS INTO ENGLAND.

1657. Cromwell permits Sephardic Jews settled in London to open a burial ground.

1665. Sabbataï Zevi (1626–1676) publicly accepted as the Messiah; his followers and opponents.

C.E.

1670. BARUCH SPINOZA (1632–1677) publishes his "Theologico-Political Treatise"; contemporary Marrano poets and authors in Amsterdam.

The Jews banished from Vienna by Emperor Leopold I.

The Jews permitted to settle in the Mark Brandenburg by Elector John George.

1678 (about). Richard Simon, Father of the Oratory, makes Rabbinical literature known to Christians.

1679. Mordecai of Eisenstadt renews the Sabbatian craze.

1686 (about). *Jacob Querido* represents himself as the successor of Sabbataï Zevi.

1690 (about). Swedish scholars study the history of the Karaites.

1695 (about). Berachya represents himself as the successor of Sabbataï Zevi; his sect, *the Donmäh.*

1698. *William Surenhuysius translates the Mishna into Latin.*

1700. John Andrew Eisenmenger attempts the publication of his "*Judaism Unmasked.*"

1707. Jacob Basnage publishes his "History of the Jewish Religion."

1713. Nehemiah Chiya Chayon (1650–1726), Sabbatian, causes a quarrel in the Amsterdam community; Solomon Ayllon and *Chacham Zevi* (Zevi ben Jacob Ashkenazi, 1656–1678).

1743. MOSES CHAYIM LUZZATTO (1707–1747), poet and Kabbalist, publishes his drama La-Yesharim Tehilla.

1745. The Jews of Prague placed under severe restrictions by Maria Theresa.

1750 (about). **Chassidism** founded by ISRAEL BAALSHEM (1698–1759) and BEER OF MIZRICZ (1700–1772); ELIJAH WILNA GAON (1720–1797), its antagonist.

1751. Contest between JONATHAN EIBESCHÜTZ (1690–1764) and JACOB EMDEN ASHKENAZI (1698–1776).

1755. **Moses Mendelssohn** (1728–1786) publishes his first work.

1759 (about). *Jacob Frank*, Sabbatian leader, founder of the Frankist sect.

1762. Isaac Pinto publishes his "Reflections" in answer to Voltaire's defamation of Judaism.

1778. Mendelssohn publishes the first part of his **Pentateuch translation.**

1779. *Lessing* publishes his "*Nathan the Wise.*"

1781. *Christian William Dohm* (1751–1820) publishes his work "Upon the Civil Amelioration of the Condition of the Jews."

JOSEPH II of Austria abolishes the Jewish poll-tax, and grants civil liberties to the Jews.

1783. Mendelssohn publishes "*Jerusalem, or upon Ecclesiastical Power and Judaism.*"

C.E.

1783. *Ha-Meassef* founded by Mendelssohn's followers (*Measfim*).

1787. Mirabeau publishes his work "Upon Mendelssohn and the Political Reform of the Jews."

1788. The poll-tax removed from the Jews of Prussia.

1789. Abbé Grégoire publishes his "Proposals in Favor of the Jews."

1790. The French National Assembly grants citizenship to the Sephardic Jews.

1791. The French National Assembly grants full civil rights to the Jews.

1796. The Batavian National Assembly decrees citizenship for the Jews.

1803. Israel Jacobson and Wolff Breidenbach agitate the abolition of the poll-tax for Jews.

1804. Alexander I of Russia exempts certain classes of Jews from the exceptional laws.

1806. NAPOLEON I SUMMONS THE ASSEMBLY OF JEWISH NOTABLES; Abraham Furtado, president. Twelve Questions propounded to the Assembly.

1807. THE GREAT SYNHEDRION CONVENED BY NAPOLEON; Joseph David Sinzheim president.

1808. The Jews of Westphalia and of Baden emancipated.

1811. The Jews of Hamburg emancipated.

1812. The Jews of Mecklenburg and Prussia emancipated.

1818 (about). Consecration of the Temple of the HAMBURG REFORM UNION, Gotthold Salomon, preacher.

1819. The beginning of the "Hep, hep!" persecutions.

Formation of the Society for the Culture and Science of the Jews; Zunz, Gans, and Moser.

1821. Chacham Bernays opposes the Reform Temple Union in Hamburg.

1822. *Isaac Marcus Jost* (1793–1860) begins to publish his history of the Jews.

1825. *Isaac Noah Mannheimer* (1793–1864), rabbi in Vienna, champion of the moderate party.

1831. Louis Philippe ratifies the law for the complete emancipation of the French Jews.

Gabriel Riesser (1806–1860), champion of the emancipation of the German Jews.

Solomon Ludwig Steinheim (1790–1866), Jewish religious philosopher.

Nachman Cohen Krochmal (1785–1840), *Solomon Jehuda Rapoport* (1790–1867), *Samuel David Luzzatto* (1800–1865), Isaac Erter (1792–1851), scholars, regenerators of Jewish science and Hebrew style.

1832. LEOPOLD ZUNZ (1794–1886) publishes his first epoch-making work.

C.E.

1833. The *Kerem Chemed*, a Hebrew journal for Jewish science. established.

1835. *Abraham Geiger* (1810–1876), scholar and preacher.

1836. Franz Delitzsch publishes his "*History of Neo-Hebraic Poetry.*"

1839. Sultan Abdul Meg'id grants citizenship to Turkish Jews.

1840. THE DAMASCUS BLOOD ACCUSATION; *Moses Montefiore* (1784–1885); *Adolf Crémieux* (1796–1880); *Solomon Munk* (1802–1867).

1842. The "Society of the Friends of Reform" founded in Frankfort.

1844. The first Rabbinical Conference at Brunswick; Samuel Holdheim (1806–1860).

1845. The REFORM ASSOCIATION formed in Berlin.

The second Rabbinical Conference at Frankfort; Zachariah Frankel (1801–1875).

Michael Sachs (1808–1864) publishes his "Religious Poetry of the Jews of Spain."

1848. The emancipation of the Jews in the German states.

1854. The Breslau Jewish Theological Seminary founded.

1858. The oath "on the true faith of a Christian" abolished in England; Jewish disabilities removed.

The Mortara abduction case.

1860. The ALLIANCE ISRAÉLITE UNIVERSELLE founded.

1871. The Anglo-Jewish Association founded.

1873. The Union of American Hebrew Congregations established.

THE KINGS OF JUDAH AND ISRAEL.

(1067–586 B. C. E.)

SAUL 1067
DAVID 1055
SOLOMON 1015

Judah.		*Israel.*
REHOBOAM	—977—	JEROBOAM I
ABIJAM	—960	
ASA	—957	
	955—	NADAB
	954—	BAASHA
	933—	ELAH
	932—	OMRI-TIBNI
	928—	OMRI
	922—	AHAB
JEHOSHAPHAT	—918	
	901—	AHAZIAH
	899—	JEHORAM
JORAM	—894	
AHAZIAH	—888	
ATHALIAH	—887—	JEHU
JOASH	—881	
	860—	JEHOAHAZ
	845—	JEHOASH
AMAZIAH	—843	
	830—	JEROBOAM II
PERIOD OF ANARCHY	—815	
UZZIAH	—805	
	769—	ZECHARIAH
	768—	SHALLUM
	768—	MENAHEM
	757—	PEKAHIAH
	755—	PEKAH
JOTHAM	—754	
AHAZ	—739	
	736—	PERIOD OF ANARCHY
	727—	HOSHEA
HEZEKIAH	—724	
	719—	SAMARIA DESTROYED
MANASSEH	—695	
AMON	—640	
JOSIAH	—638	
JEHOAHAZ	—608	
JEHOIAKIM	—607	
JEHOIACHIN	—596	
ZEDEKIAH	—596	

586 DESTRUCTION OF THE FIRST TEMPLE.

THE HIGH PRIESTS.

(FROM THE CAPTIVITY TO THE DISPERSION.)

Period.	*High Priest.*		*Civil Ruler.*
VIII			
586–516 B. C. E.	Jehozedek		Babylonian Kings and Cyrus
	Joshua b. Jehozedek		Zerubbabel (Cyrus and Darius I)
IX			
516–332 B. C. E.	Jehoiakim		Xerxes I
	Eliashib		Nehemiah (Artaxerxes I)
	Joiada		Nehemiah (Darius II)
	Johanan b. Joiada		Artaxerxes III
	Jaddua		Alexander the Great
X			
332–175 B. C. E.	Onias I		Ptolemy I Soter
	Simon I the Just (300–270)		Ptolemy I Soter
	Eleazar (br. of Simon I)	during the minority of Onias II.	Ptolemy II Philadelphus
	Manasseh (br. of Onias I)		Ptolemy II Philadelphus
	Onias II (240)		Ptolemy III Euergetes
	Simon II		Ptolemy IV Philopator
	Onias III (Jason his deputy)		Ptolemy V Epiphanes and Antiochus III
XI			
175–140 B. C. E.	Jason (174)		Antiochus IV Epiphanes
	Menelaus (Onias IV, 172. Lysimachus his deputy)		Antiochus IV Epiphanes
	Judas Maccabæus (163)		Antiochus V Eupator
	Alcimus (162–159)	*appointed by*	Demetrius I Soter
	Jonathan Haphus (152–143)		Alexander Balas
	Simon (III) Tharsi (143–135)		Simon Tharsi
XII			
140–37 B. C. E.	Hyrcanus I (135–106)		Hyrcanus I
	Aristobulus I (106–105)		Aristobulus I
	Alexander Jannæus (105–79)		Alexander (I) Jannæus
	Hyrcanus II (79–40)		Alexandra, Hyrcanus II, Aristobulus II, and Roman governors
	Antigonus (40–37)		Antigonus

THE HIGH PRIESTS.

(FROM THE CAPTIVITY TO THE DISPERSION.)

[*Continued.*]

Period.	*High Priest.*	*Appointee.*
XIII		
37 B. C. E.–	ANANEL (37–35)	Herod I
72 C. E.	ARISTOBULUS (III) (35)	Herod I
	ANANEL (34, second term)	Herod I
	JOSHUA, of the family Phabi	Herod I
	SIMON (IV) B. BOËTHUS	Herod I
	MATTHIAS B. THEOPHILUS (Joseph b. Ellem his deputy)	Herod I
	JOASER B. SIMON (b. Boëthus)	Herod I
	ELEAZAR (brother of Joaser)	Archelaus
	JOSHUA, of the family Sié	Archelaus
	JOASER (second term)	Archelaus
	ANAN, of the family Seth	Quirinius, governor of Syria
	ISHMAEL I PHABI	Valerius Gratus, procurator
	ELEAZAR B. ANAN	Valerius Gratus, procurator
	SIMON (V) B. CAMYTH	Valerius Gratus, procurator
	JOSEPH CAIAPHAS (26–36)	Valerius Gratus, procurator
	JONATHAN B. ANAN	Vitellius, governor of Syria
	THEOPHILUS B. ANAN (brother of preceding)	Vitellius, governor of Syria
	SIMON (VI) B. BOËTHUS, of the family Cantheras (41)	Agrippa I
	MATTHIAS B. ANAN (brother of Jonathan)	Agrippa I
	ELIONAI B. HAKOPH (44)	Agrippa I
	JOSEPH B. CAMYTH (45)	Herod II
	ANANIAS B. NEBEDEUS (48)	Herod II
	ISHMAEL II PHABI (59–61)	Agrippa II
	JOSEPH CABI (61)	Agrippa II
	ANAN, of the family Anan	Agrippa II
	JOSHUA B. DAMNAI	Agrippa II
	JOSHUA B. GAMALA	Agrippa II
	MATTHIAS B. THEOPHILUS	Agrippa II
	PHINEAS B. SAMUEL (67, 68)	The People

THE HASMO

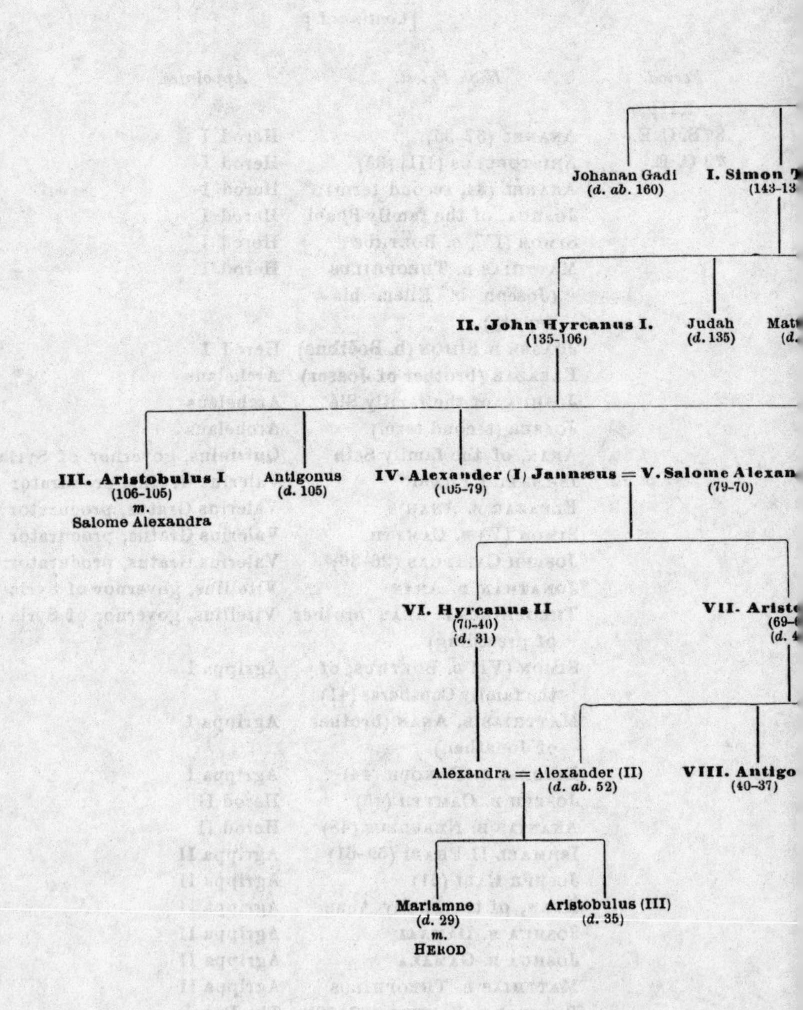
Johanan Gadi
(d. ab. 160)
I. Simon T
(143-13
II. John Hyrcanus I.
(135-106)
Judah
(d. 135)
Matt
(d.
III. Aristobulus I
(106-105)
m.
Salome Alexandra
Antigonus
(d. 105)
IV. Alexander (I) Jannæus = V. Salome Alexan
(105-79)
(79-70)
VI. Hyrcanus II
(70-40)
(d. 31)
VII. Aristo
(69-
(d. 4
Alexandra = Alexander (II)
(d. ab. 52)
VIII. Antigo
(40-37)
Mariamne
(d. 29)
m.
Herod
Aristobulus (III)
(d. 35)

STY (143– B. C. E.)

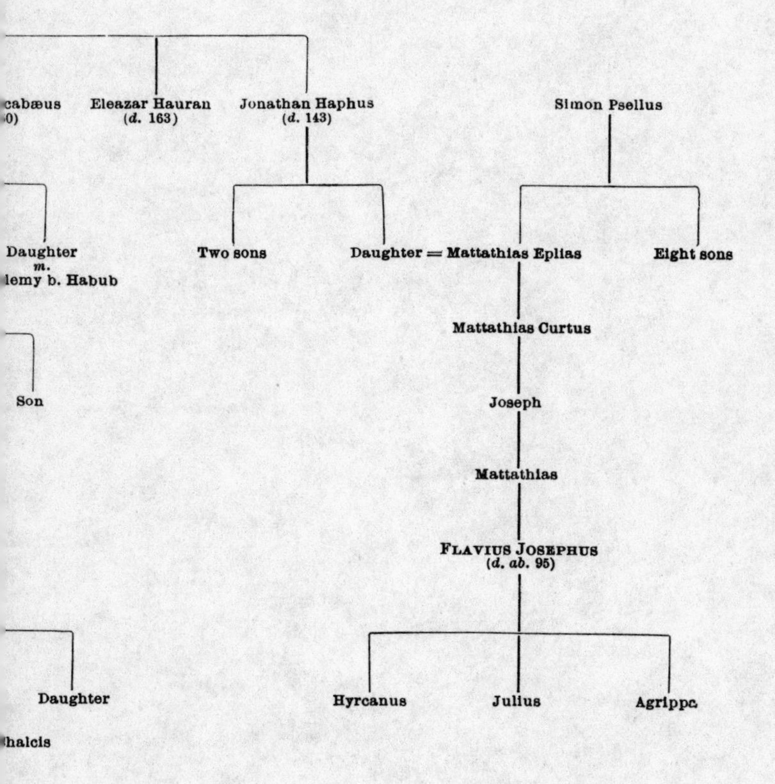
smonai
ıan
thias
67)
cabæus
0)
Eleazar Hauran
(d. 163)
Jonathan Haphus
(d. 143)
Simon Psellus
Daughter
m.
lemy b. Habub
Two sons
Daughter = Mattathias Eplias
Eight sons
Mattathias Curtus
Son
Joseph
Mattathias
FLAVIUS JOSEPHUS
(d. ab. 95)
Daughter
Hyrcanus
Julius
Agrippa
halcis

THE HERODIAN D

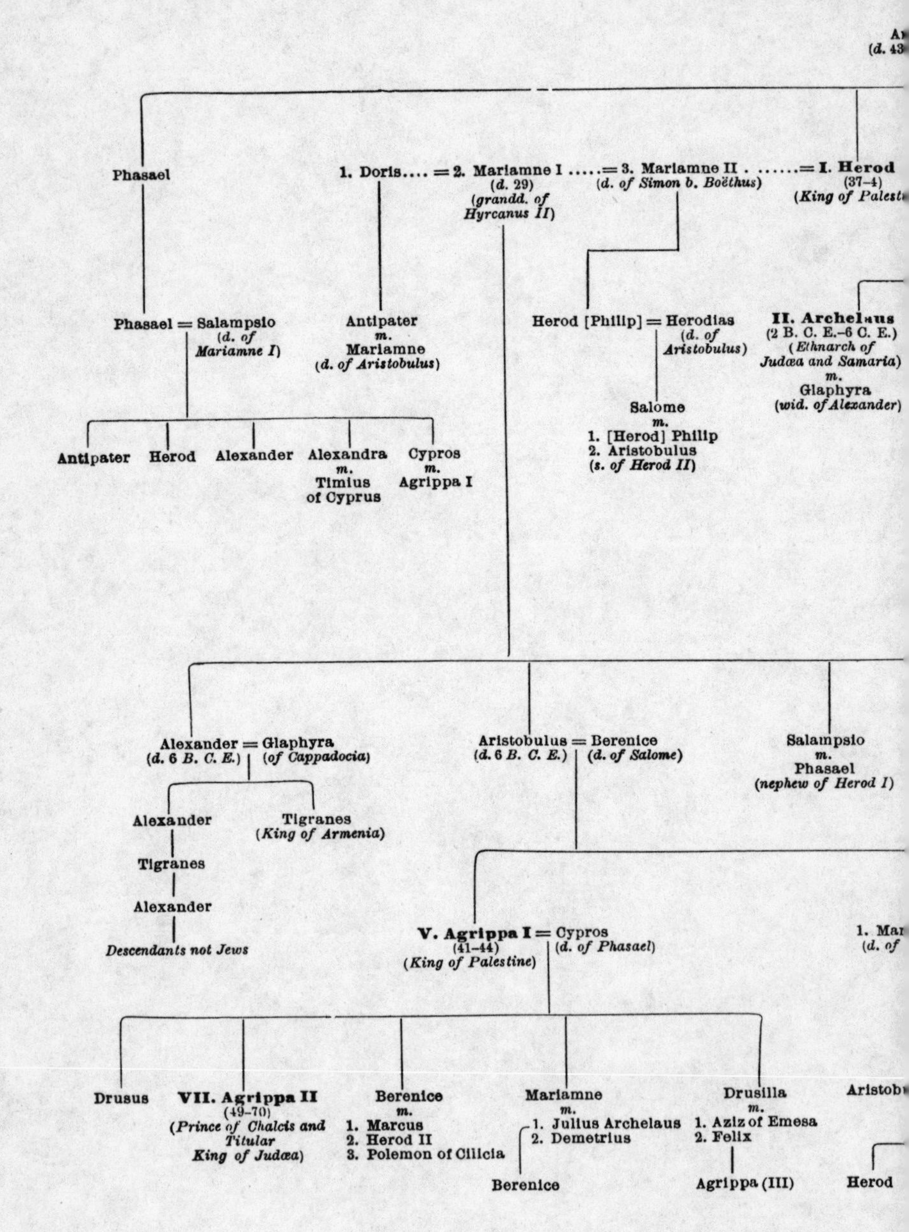

. C. E.-70 C. E.)

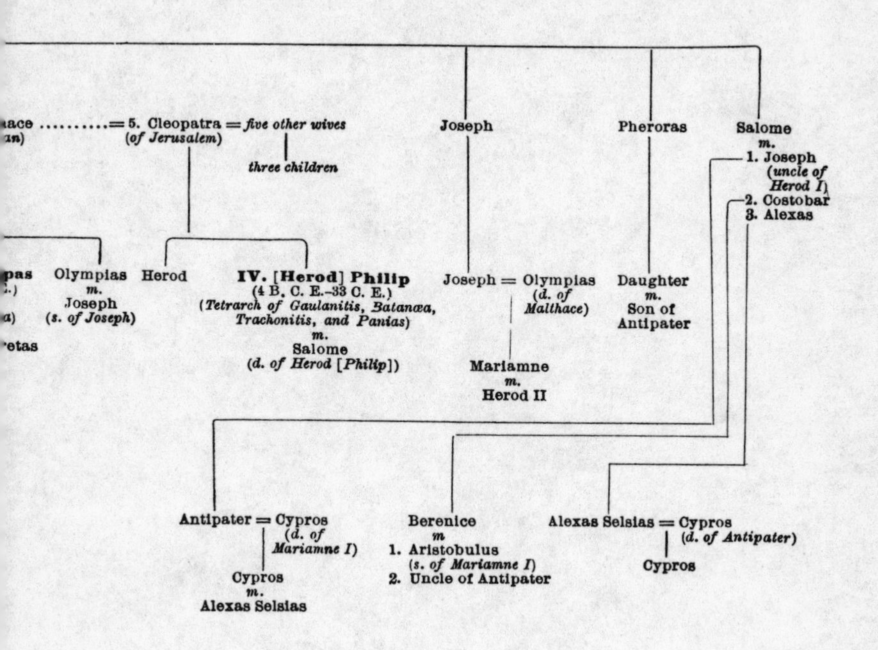

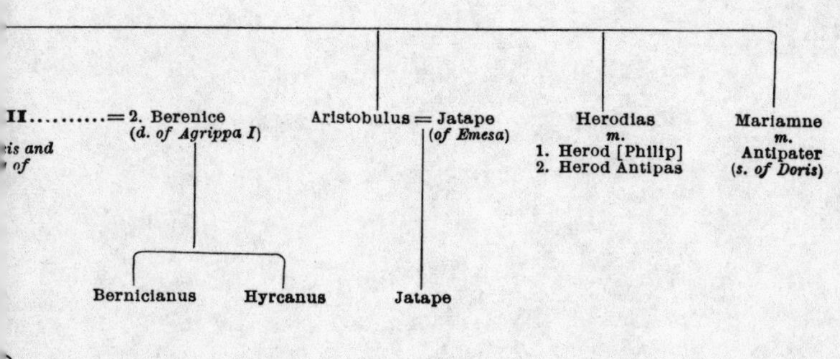

obulus

INDEX.

INDEX.

Explanatory Notes.

For the complete index of references to *Jews*, see under *Israelites* until 586 B. C. E. (the Babylonian Captivity) and under *Judæans* until 70 C. E. (the Dispersion), as well as under *Jews* and *the Jews of* and *the Judæans of* the various cities and countries.

Persons living before 1600 will be found under their forenames. The rule has been violated by indexing certain Spanish Rabbis and Marranos living before this date under their surnames, and certain Germans and Poles living after it under their forenames. In these cases cross-references have been made.

Persons with the same descriptive cognomen, as *Gerundi*, *Ibn-Ezra*, *Abrabanel*, *Abulafia*, are enumerated under it, but the references are indexed as above.

Persons bearing the same forename, as *Abraham*, *Jacob*, etc., are arranged in the order adopted by Joseph Zedner in his "Catalogue of the Hebrew Books in the Library of the British Musuem" (1867):

"1. Those distinguished by an epithet *only*, derived from their birthplace, rank, or occupation, arranged after the alphabetical order of the epithets.

"2. Those followed by the word *ben* (son of) [in our Index preceded by those with the Aramaic form *bar*, and followed by those with the Arabic form *ibn* and the English *son of*], arranged according to the name of the father.

"3. Compound names of first and family names, as *Jacob Berab*, or two first names, as *Jacob Zeeb*, [or of first name and birthplace when the latter follows without a preposition, or is modified to include *of*, as *Jacob Tus*, *Abraham Bedaresi*].

"4. Family names, as *Jacob (Henry)*."

This arrangement of Zedner's is, however, subordinate to the class-divisions adopted by indexers and cataloguers in general, namely: 1. Popes, according to numbers; 2. Emperors; 3. Kings and Sovereign Princes, by countries and by number in each country; 4. Others by appellatives, neglecting prepositions and articles.

The subjoined Table will enable the student approximately to refer from the index of the American Edition of the "History" to the German, when it is desirable to consult the notes and other additional matter contained in the original.

American Edition.			German.
Volume I,	p. 1–178	=	Volume I.
Volume I,	p. 179–487	=	Volume II.
Volume I, Volume II,	p. 487–531 p. 1–320	=	Volume III.
Volume II,	p. 321–635	=	Volume IV.
Volume III,	p. 1–250	=	Volume V.
Volume III,	p. 250–493	=	Volume VI.
Volume III, Volume IV,	p. 494–650 p. 1–126	=	Volume VII.
Volume IV,	p. 127–381	=	Volume VIII.
Volume IV,	p. 382–675	=	Volume IX.
Volume IV, Volume V,	p. 676–708 p. 1–290	=	Volume X.
Volume V,	p. 291–703	=	Volume XI.

Lists of Names, etc., in the Index.

Academies, the Babylonian.
Alliances, Jewish.
Amoraim, the.
Anti-Maimunists, the.
Apostates.
Astronomers and Mathematicians, Jewish.
Church Councils.
Codes, general, defining the status of the Jews.
Codes, Jewish religious.
Council, the Great, couples at the head of.
Exilarchs, the.
Fabulists, the.
Frankists, the.
Grammarians and Lexicographers, Jewish.
Hasmonæan Dynasty, the, the members of.
Herodian Dynasty, the, the members of.
High Priests, the.
Historians, Jewish.
Historians of the Jews.
Israel, the kings of.
Israelites, the, the kings of.
Journals, Jewish.
Judah, the kings of.
Judæa, the Roman governors of.
Judaism, the sects of.
Judges, the.
Kabbalistic terms, the.
Kabbalists, the.
Karaite sects, the.
Karaite writers, the.
Maimunists, the.
Massorets.
Measfim, the.
Messiahs, the.
Nahardea, the academy of, principals of.
Patriarchs, the.
Philosophers, Jewish.
Physicians, Jewish.
Poets, Jewish.
Procurators of Judæa.
Prophets, the.
Pumbeditha, the academy of, principals of.
Rabbis.
Rabbis, itinerant.
Sabbataï Zevi, the followers of.
Sabureans, the.
Sora, the academy of, Geonim of.
Sora, the academy of, principals of.
Synhedrion, the, presidents of.
Syria, the Roman governors of.
Talmudists.
Tanaites, the.
Travelers, Jewish.
Writers (Historians, Pamphleteers, Scholars, etc.), non-Jewish, on Jewish subjects.

An almost complete biographical history of the Jews can be collated by following up through the Index the biographies of the persons grouped below. The column on the left consists of the class-names of the secular chiefs of the Jewish community; the column on the right, of those of the spiritual chiefs; the middle column, whether connecting the other two or replacing them, of those whose position, powers, and influence were, or were supposed to be, both spiritual and secular.

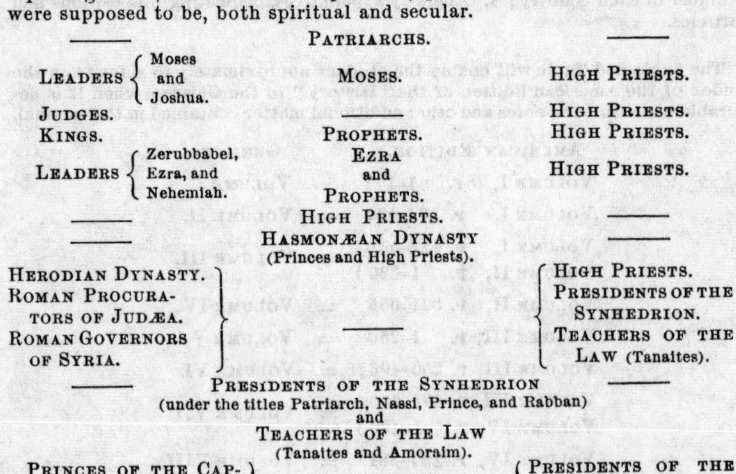

A

Aaron, high priest, member of the tribe of Levi, **1,** 12.
countenances idolatry, **1,** 14.
meets Moses on Horeb, **1,** 15.
descendants of. *See* Aaronides.

Aaron de la Papa. *See* Papa, Aaron de la.

Aaron of York, chief rabbi of England, **3,** 588.
sums paid to Henry III by, **3,** 591.

Aaron ben Asher, Massoret, criticised by Saadiah, **3,** 196, 207.
corrects Bible manuscripts, **3,** 207.
as a poet, **3,** 223.

Aaron (II) ben Elia Nicomedi (1300–1369), Karaite philosopher, **4,** 95.

Aaron (I) ben Joseph, the Elder (1270–1300), Karaite physician, disciple of Nachmani, **3,** 607; **4,** 71.
fixes the Karaite prayer book, **4,** 71.

Aaron ben Meshullam (1170–1210), scholar, **3,** 396.
Maimunist, attacks Meïr Abulafia, **3,** 524.

Aaron ben Zerach, martyr, **4,** 144.

Aaron ben Zion Ibn-Alamâni, physician at Alexandria, **3,** 340.

Aaron Ibn-Sarjadu (943–960), opponent of Saadiah, **3,** 194, 195, 196, 200.
reconciled with Saadiah, **3,** 200–1.
Gaon of Pumbeditha, **3,** 202.
death of, **3,** 207–8.
in Sherira's "Letter," **3,** 233.

Aaron Cohen, of Narbonne, elegy by, **4,** 49.

Aaron Halevi (1235–1300), Talmudist, **3,** 621.

Aaronides, the, oppose idolatry under Manasseh, **1,** 283.
dismissed for not participating in idolatrous worship, **1,** 284.
massacred at the first fall of Jerusalem, **1,** 314.
return with Zerubbabel, **1,** 352.
rejected by Nehemiah, **1,** 378.
provided for, under Ezra, **1,** 382.
exiled by Nehemiah, **1,** 386.
officiate on Gerizim, **1,** 390.
honor Judah I's remains, **2,** 467.
in charge of Judah II's remains, **2,** 487.
in Arabia, **3,** 55.
make Abraham ben David's grave, **3,** 490.
See also High priests, the; Priests, the.

Ab, the Ninth of, celebration of, by Sabbataï Zevi, **5,** 152, 159.

Abaka (Abagha), Tartar king in Persia, **3,** 638.

Abayi Nachmani (280–338), Babylonian Amora, **2,** 560.
disciple of Rabba bar Nachmani, **2,** 575, 580, 583.
principal of the Pumbeditha Academy, **2,** 583.
youth of, **2,** 583–4.
integrity of, **2,** 584.
decrease of students under, **2,** 584–5.
dialectics of, **2,** 585.
death of, **2,** 585.
rebukes Raba bar Joseph, **2,** 586.

Abba of Accho, ordination of, **2**, 540.
modesty of, **2**, 541.
Abba bar Abba, Amora, father of Mar-Samuel, **2**, 511.
Abba-Areka (Rab), Amora, authorized to teach in Babylon, **2**, 454, 479, 511.
adds supplements to the Mishna, **2**, 470.
opposed to the purchase of oil from heathens, **2**, 484.
reception of, in Babylonia, **2**, 512.
made Agora-nomos, **2**, 512.
introduces excommunication into Babylonia, **2**, 517.
compared with Hillel, **2**, 517.
wife of, **2**, 517.
modesty of, **2**, 517–18.
descendants of, **2**, 518, 544.
opposes Persian innovations, **2**, 521.
yields to Magian demands, **2**, 526.
influence of, on Jewish Babylonia, **2**, 544.
Abba-Mari ben Isaac, sheriff of St. Gilles, **3**, 399.
Abba-Mari ben Moses (Don Astruc En-Duran), follower of Nachmanides, **4**, 27–8.
appeals to Ben Adret, **4**, 28, 29.
fails to win Jacob ben Machir's aid, **4**, 31.
aggressive anti-Maimunist, **4**, 32.
adherents of, **4**, 33–4.
secures the support of Asheri, **4**, 38.
draws up the ban against the study of science, **4**, 38, 39.
opposed by the Tibbonides, **4**, 41–2.
in Perpignan, **4**, 50.
Abba Saul, a Tanaite, **2**, 330.
Abbadides, the, in Seville, **3**, 315.
Abbahu, a Palestinian Amora, **2**, 531.
and the observance of the Law in Samaria, **2**, 534.
secular culture of, **2**, 537–8.
education of the daughter of, **2**, 537.
and Diocletian, **2**, 538.
Hebrew style of, **2**, 538.
attacks Christian dogmas, **2**, 539–40.
modesty and generosity of, **2**, 540–1.
on the Greek theatre, **2**, 542.
makes Cæsarea an academic city, **2**, 543.
sons of, **2**, 543.
Abbasside Caliphate (Caliphate of the East, Bagdad Caliphate), the, weakness of, in the twelfth century, **3**, 431.
conquered by Hulagu, **3**, 606.
Abbasside Caliphate, the, the Jews of, in the ninth century, **3**, 145–6, 176–80.
under Al-Mutadhid, **3**, 183.
in the twelfth century, **3**, 428–33.
Abbassides, the, opponents of the Ommiyyades, **3**, 125.
Ab-beth-din, president of the Council of Seventy, **1**, 395.
deputy of the president of the Synhedrion, **2**, 360, 404.
office of, ceases, **2**, 453.
Abdallah Ibn-Allah, vizir, prevents the forced conversion of Jews to Islam, **3**, 312.
Abdallah Ibn-Hakam, murders the king of Saragossa, **3**, 266.
Abdallah Ibn-Sabâ, partisan of Ali, **3**, 90.

Abdallah Ibn-Salâm, Jewish disciple of Mahomet, **3,** 73.
Abdallah Ibn-Tumart, incites the Moors against the Almoravides, **3,** 357–8.
founds the Almohades, **3,** 358.
Abdallah Ibn-Ubey, opponent of Mahomet, **3,** 75.
protects the Benu-Kainukaa, **3,** 77.
promises aid to the Benu-Nadhir, **3,** 78.
Abdallah, son of Saura, Jewish opponent of Mahomet, **3,** 74.
Abdallah Almamun (813-833), son of Haroun Alrashid, at war with his brother, **3,** 145.
prosperity of the Abbasside Caliphate under, **3,** 146.
adopts the Mutazilist theology, **3,** 147.
appealed to by rival parties in the Pumbeditha academy, **3,** 155.
the last of the tolerant caliphs of the East, **3,** 176.
reduces the power of the Exilarchs, **3,** 177.
Abdel-latif, Mahometan physician, on Maimonides, **3,** 473, 488.
Abdon, judge, **1,** 66.
Abdul-Malik, Ommiyyade caliph, tolerance of, **3,** 110.
Abdul Meg'id, sultan of Turkey, **5,** 634.
emancipates the Jews, **5,** 641, 664.
orders a revision of the Rhodes trial, **5,** 647.
secures the Turkish Jews against the blood accusation, **5,** 662.
Abdulmumen, Almohade ruler of northern Africa, tries to force Islam upon his subjects, **3,** 358–60, 451.
Abdul-Rahman III, Ommiyyade caliph, appealed to in behalf of Moses ben Chanoch, **3,** 209–10.
Moslem culture under, **3,** 214.
appoints Chasdaï Ibn-Shaprut interpreter, **3,** 216.
death of, **3,** 222.
Abel, Psychic type of the Gnostics, **2,** 377.
Abel. *See* Abel-Bethmaachah.
Abel-Bethmaachah, refuge of Sheba, **1,** 149–50.
the region of, subjugated by Ben-hadad I, **1,** 191.
Abelè-Zion, ascetic Karaites in Jerusalem, **3,** 182. *See also* "Mourners of Zion," the.
Abenacar, Isaac (Manuel Pimentel), first Jew buried at Ouderkerk, **4,** 672.
Abendana, Jacob, rabbi of London, **5,** 214.
Abenhuacar. *See* Samuel Ibn-Wakar.
Abensur, Daniel, millionaire in Hamburg, **5,** 205.
Abia, king of Arabia, at war with Izates of Adiabene, **2,** 217–18.
Abiathar, the family of, under David's protection, **1,** 100.
partisan of David, **1,** 107, 112.
made high priest, **1,** 120.
on the persecution of the Gibeonites, **1,** 123.
against Absalom, **1,** 141.
urges the recall of David, **1,** 146.
supports Adonijah, **1,** 152.
of the priestly house of Ithamar, **1,** 155.
deposed, **1,** 160.
Abi-Ezri. *See* Eleazar ben Joel Halevi.
Abigail, wife of David, **1,** 134.

Abijah, son of Samuel, judge, **1,** 79.

Abijam, son of Rehoboam, king of Judah, **1,** 189.

Abilene, given to Agrippa II, **2,** 245.

Abimaï, son of Abbahu, **2,** 543.

Abimelech, judge, **1,** 63.

Abin, Amora, emigrates from Judæa, **2,** 567.

Abinadab, guards the Ark of the Covenant, **1,** 119.

Abinadab, son of Saul, death of, **1,** 103.

Abinerglus (Abennerig), father-in-law of Izates, **2,** 216.

Abishag, wife of David, and Adonijah, **1,** 160.

Abishai, brother of Joab, kills Abner, **1,** 111.
saves David, **1,** 117.
commander in the Ammonite war, **1,** 127.
conducts the Idumæan war, **1,** 128–9.
against Absalom, **1,** 141, 144.
conducts the war against Sheba, **1,** 149.

Ablaat, astronomer, friend of Mar-Samuel, **2,** 521.

Abner, cousin of Saul, qualities of, **1,** 84–5.
frees Israel from the Philistines, **1,** 108.
makes Ishbosheth Saul's successor, **1,** 108.
actual founder of the kingdom of the Ten Tribes, **1,** 108.
jealous of Joab, **1,** 109.
power of, **1,** 109.
kills Asahel, **1,** 110.
accused of coveting Rizpah, **1,** 110.
joins David, **1,** 110–11.
murdered, **1,** 111–12.

Abner of Burgos. *See* Alfonso Burgensis.

Aboab, Immanuel, defends Rabbinical Judaism, **5,** 55.

Aboab, Isaac, rabbi of Toledo, friend of Isaac Abrabanel, **4,** 341.
negotiates for the settlement of Spanish exiles in Portugal, **4,** 352, 365.
death of, **4,** 366.

Aboab, Isaac, de Fonseca (1606–1693), rabbi at Amsterdam, instructs at the Talmud Torah, **4,** 681.
member of the first Rabbinical college, **4,** 682.
as a preacher, **4,** 682–3.
vacillating character of, **4,** 683.
goes to Brazil, **4,** 693.
on the war in Brazil, **4,** 694.
devotee of the Kabbala, **5,** 52.
translates Kabbalistic works, **5,** 54, 88.
and Spinoza, **5,** 92.
Sabbatian, **5,** 139, 160.

Aboab, Samuel, rabbi at Venice, and Luzzatto, **5,** 240.

Aboda Zara, Mishnic treatise on idolaters, **2,** 477.

Abodah, the, Day of Atonement Temple service, poem on, **3,** 114–15.

Aboget, alleged poisoner of wells, **4,** 102.

Abrabanel. *See* Dormido; Isaac ben Judah; Isaac II, son of Isaac; Isaac III, son of Judah Leon; Judah Leon; Samuel I; Samuel II.

Abrabanel family, the, descended from David, **3,** 43.

Abrabanela. *See* Benvenida.

Abradhi, caliph of the East, vizir of, favors Saadiah, **3,** 200.

Abraham, disciple of Meïr of Rothenburg, **4,** 74.
Abraham, monk, convert to Judaism, **3,** 21.
Abraham, patriarch, acquires Machpelah, **1,** 4.
monotheist, **1,** 5.
virtues of, **1,** 6.
revered by the Israelites, **1,** 6–7.
impresses Mahomet, **3,** 71.
in the Zohar, **4,** 23.
Abraham of Aragon, oculist, **3,** 583.
Abraham de Balmes, physician and grammarian, **4,** 411.
instructs Christians in Hebrew, **4,** 473.
Abraham de Beya, traveler in Portuguese employ, **4,** 368.
Abraham of Granada, Kabbalist, **4,** 196–7.
Abraham de Herrera. *See* Herrera, Abraham de.
Abraham ben Chasdaï, Maimunist, as poet, **3,** 388, 560.
denounces Solomon of Montpellier, **3,** 544.
epigram by, **3,** 544.
Abraham ben Chiya Albargeloni (1065–1136), astronomer, **3,** 313; **4,** 120.
Abraham ben David of Posquières (Rabed II, 1125–1198), Talmudist, as a controversialist, **3,** 389, 399.
disciple of Abraham ben Isaac, **3,** 392.
friend of Judah Ibn-Tibbon, **3,** 397.
writes a Mishna commentary, **3,** 399.
criticises Maimonides' Mishne-Torah, **3,** 490.
death of, **3,** 490.
alleged founder of the Kabbala, **3,** 547.
Abraham ben Isaac, head of the college of Narbonne, **3,** 392.
son-in-law of, **3,** 399.
Abraham ben Meïr Ibn-Ezra (1088–1167), personality of, **3,** 366–7, 381.
attitude of, towards the Karaites, **3,** 366.
and Jehuda Halevi and Moses Ibn-Ezra, **3,** 367.
poetry of, **3,** 367–8.
as an exegete, **3,** 368, 370–1, 371–3.
poverty of, **3,** 368–9.
in the East, **3,** 369.
in Rome, **3,** 369–71.
as a grammarian, **3,** 371, 374.
adheres to the Massora, **3,** 371.
at Mantua and Lucca, **3,** 371.
in southern France, **3,** 373.
poem on, by Jacob Tam, **3,** 373, 376.
in London, **3,** 373–4.
as philosopher, **3,** 373.
defends the Sabbath eve, **3,** 374.
last years of, **3,** 374–5.
son of, **3,** 375.
influence of, on Italian Jews, **3,** 423.
attacked by Nachmani, **3,** 534, 608.
the works of, used by Raymund Martin, **3,** 622.
denounced as a heretic, **3,** 624.
admired by Yedaya Bedaresi, **4,** 43.
the works of, studied in the fourteenth century, **4,** 143–4.
the Pentateuch commentary by, commented upon, **4,** 144.
commentary on the works of, **4,** 191.
exegesis of, praised by Reuchlin, **4,** 442.
commentary by, in the Bomberg Bible, **4,** 476.
studied by Spinoza, **5,** 88.

Abraham ben Samuel Abulafia (1240-1291), Kabbalist, **4**, 3, 11, 622.
youth and ideals of, **4**, 4–5, 19.
system of, **5**, 5–6, 14.
disciples of, **4**, 6, 8, 10.
in Italy, **4**, 6.
imprisoned, **4**, 7.
Messianic claims of, **4**, 7–8.
works of, **4**, 8.
declared a heretic, **4**, 625.
Abraham ben Sherira. *See* Mar-Abraham.
Abraham Ibn-Alfachar (1160–1223), favorite of Alfonso III of Castile, **3**, 384–5.
ambassador to Morocco, **3**, 385.
encourages Talmud study, **3**, 386.
Abraham Ibn-Daud Halevi (1110-1180), physician, philosopher, and historian, **3**, 363–6.
parentage of, **3**, 364.
attainments of, **3**, 364.
as an historian, **3**, 364, 365–6.
as a scientist, **3**, 364.
as a philosopher, **3**, 364–5.
style of, **3**, 366.
death of, **3**, 386.
the work of, consulted by Basnage, **5**, 196.
Abraham Ibn-Shoshan, scholar, Spanish exile in Egypt, **4**, 393.
Abraham Ibn-Zarzal, physician and astrologer, **4**, 116.
Abraham, son of Manessier de Vesoul, **4**, 150.
Abraham Bedaresi, poet, elegy by, **3**, 579.
compared with his son, **4**, 42.
Abraham Benveniste Senior, dignitary at the court of Juan II of Castile, **4**, 228.
frames the law of Avila, **4**, 229.
Abraham Benveniste Senior (*continued*), promotes the marriage of Isabella of Castile, **4**, 280.
friend of Isaac Abrabanel, **4**, 341.
accepts baptism, **4**, 351.
See also Coronel.
Abraham Bibago, favorite of John II of Aragon, **4**, 275.
Abraham Farissol (1451–1525), Bible commentator and geographer, **4**, 411–12.
protegé of Hercules d'Este I, **4**, 412–13.
polemic writings of, **4**, 413.
Abraham Israel, excommunicates Eibeschütz's opponents, **5**, 264.
Abraham Klausner, compiles the customs of various communities, **4**, 134.
Abraham Levi, Spanish exile, Kabbalist, **4**, 481.
Abraham (Abulmeni) Maimuni (1185–1254), son of Maimonides, his successor, **3**, 493.
Talmudist and philosopher, **3**, 495.
visited by rabbis emigrating to Palestine, **3**, 505.
and the attacks upon his father, **3**, 525–6, 545.
Abraham Maimuni II, great-grandson of Maimonides, converts Karaites to Rabbanism, **4**, 71–2.
Abraham Menz, director of the Padua college, **4**, 410.
Abraham Saba, Kabbalist, leaves Portugal, **4**, 381.
Abraham Yizchaki, anti-Sabbatian, **5**, 220–1.
Abraham Zacuto, disciple of Isaac Aboab, pronounces his funeral oration, **4**, 366.
author of an astronomical calendar, **4**, 367, 372.

Abraham Zacuto (*continued*), escapes from Portugal, **4**, 378.
at Tunis, **4**, 391.
writes the Sefer Yochasin, **4**, 391.
flees to Turkey, **4**, 392.
compared with Elias Kapsali, **4**, 407.
chronicle of, published, **4**, 608, 629.
great-grandson of, **4**, 678.

Abraham Zacuto Lusitano (1576–1642), physician, honor paid to, **4**, 678.

Abrianim, transgressors of the Law, addressed by Jesus, **2**, 152.

Absalom, son of David, instigates the murder of Amnon, **1**, 134.
seeks refuge with Talmai of Geshur, **1**, 134–5.
pardoned, **1**, 136.
plots with Ahithophel, **1**, 136, 138–44.
description of, **1**, 137.
hailed as king in Hebron, **1**, 139.
in Jerusalem, **1**, 142–3.
accepts Hushai's advice, **1**, 143.
killed, **1**, 144–5.
mourned by David, **1**, 145.
monument of, **1**, 145.
children of, **1**, 145.

Absalom, son of John Hyrcanus, **2**, 34.
in Pompey's triumph, **2**, 67.

Abt, friend of Mendelssohn, **5**, 303.

Abtalion (Pollion), head of the Synhedrion, **2**, 71–2.
maxims of, **2**, 72; **3**, 573.
disciples of, **2**, 72, 96.
opposed to Antigonus, **2**, 85–6.
counsels submission to Herod, **2**, 88.
spared by Herod, **2**, 89.
death of, **2**, 90.

Abu-Abdullah Mahomet Alnasir, Almohade caliph, invades Andalusia, **3**, 506–7.
decrees Jew badges, **3**, 512.

Abu-Afak, poet, opponent of Mahomet, **3**, 74.

Abu Amr Joseph ben Chasdaï. *See* Joseph ben Chasdaï.

Abu-Amr Joseph ben Zadik Ibn-Zadik (1080–1148), philosopher, **3**, 314–15.
as a poet, **3**, 315.
death of, **3**, 361.

Abu-Amran Moses, founder of a Karaite sect, **3**, 157–8.

Abu-Amranites, Karaite sectaries, **3**, 158.

Abu-Amrun Musa ben Maimun Obaid Allah, Arabic name of Maimonides, **3**, 447.

Abu Ayub (Solomon Ibn-Almuallem), poet and physician, **3**, 312.

Abu Ayub Sulaiman Ibn-Yachya. *See* Solomon Ibn-Gebirol.

Abu-Bekr, Mahomet's general, repulsed at Kamus, **3**, 82.

Abudiente, Abraham Gideon, Sabbatian, **5**, 155.

Abu Fadhl Chasdaï (1040), Arabic Jewish poet, vizir to the king of Saragossa, **3**, 280.

Abuhajaj Joseph Ibn-Ezra, brother of Moses Ibn-Ezra, **3**, 319.
son of, **3**, 361.

Abu Hussain Joseph Ibn-Nagrela. *See* Joseph Ibn-Nagrela.

Abu-Ibrahim Isaac Ibn-Ezra, brother of Moses Ibn-Ezra, **3**, 318.

Abu Ibrahim Isaac Ibn-Kastar ben Yasus (Yizchaki, 982–1057), physician and philosopher, **3**, 273.

Abu-Isa. *See* Obaiah Abu-Isa ben Ishak.
Abu Ishak al-Elviri, Mahometan poet, enemy of the Jews of Granada, **3,** 278.
Abu Ishak Ibn-Mohajar, vizir to the Almoravide Ali, **3,** 312.
Abu Jacob Yussuff Almostansir, Almohade ruler of Morocco, **3,** 385.
Abu-Jafar Ibn-Aljezzar, Mahometan disciple of Isaac Israeli, **3,** 181.
Abu Jafar Almansur, caliph, imprisons Anan ben David, **3,** 129–30.
Abu-Kariba Assad Toban, king of Yemen, besieges Yathrib, **3,** 62.
convert to Judaism, **3,** 63.
end of, **3,** 63.
sons of, **3,** 64.
Abulafia. *See* Abraham ben Samuel; Abulafia, Moses; Joseph ben Todros; Levi ben Todros; Meïr ben Todros Halevi; Samuel ben Meïr Allavi; Todros ben Joseph.
Abulafia, Marrano, agent of Ferdinand and Isabella, opposes the Inquisition, **4,** 313.
burnt at the stake, **4,** 317.
Abulafia, Moses, accused of ritual murder, **5,** 636.
tortured, **5,** 636–7.
turns Mahometan, **5,** 638.
Abulafia family, the, of the nobility of Jewish Spain, **3,** 236; **4,** 116.
members of, perish during the Black Death, **4,** 113.
Abul-Ala, Arabic poet, **3,** 199.
Abul Arab Ibn-Moïsha, Mahometan theologian and poet, friend of Maimonides, **3,** 456.
Abul Arab Ibn-Moïsha (*continued*), accuses Maimonides of apostasy from Islam, **3,** 474.
Abul-Barkat Hibat-Allah ben Malka. *See* Nathaniel.
Abulhassan, king of Morocco, at war with Castile, **4,** 84.
Abulhassan Abraham ben Meïr Ibn-Kamnial, physician, vizir to the Almoravide Ali, **3,** 312.
patron of Moses Ibn-Ezra, **3,** 320.
Abulhassan Jehuda ben Samuel Halevi (Ibn-Allevi). *See* Jehuda Halevi.
Abulhassan Jehuda Ibn-Ezra, brother of Moses Ibn-Ezra, **3,** 318.
Abulkasim Ibn-Alarif, vizir of Habus, patron of Samuel Ibn-Nagrela, **3,** 256.
Abulkassim Mahomet. *See* Al-Mutamed.
Abulmeni Abraham Maimuni. *See* Abraham Maimuni.
Abulsari Sahal ben Mazliach Kohen, propagandist for Karaism, **3,** 203–5.
as controversialist, **3,** 204–5.
Hebrew style of, **3,** 204, 206.
Abulvalid Mervan Ibn-Janach. *See* Jonah Marinus.
Abu Mansur Samuel ben Chananya, Nagid, invites Jehuda Halevi to Cairo, **3,** 340–1.
successor of, **3,** 443.
Abumelik, leads a Moorish army against Castile, **4,** 84.
killed, **4,** 85.
Abunassar Azaria, son of Joseph Ibn-Nagrela, flees to Lucena, **3,** 279.
death of, **3,** 284.
Abu-Sahal Ali (835–853), medical writer, **3,** 146.

Abusahal Dunash ben Tamim. *See* Dunash ben Tamim.

Abu Said ben Chalfon Halevi, friend of Jehuda Halevi, **3,** 340.

Abu-Yussuf Chasdaï ben Isaac Ibn-Shaprut. *See* Chasdaï Ibn-Shaprut.

Abu-Yussuff Almansur, Almohade prince, introduces a garb for apostate Jews, **3,** 511–12.

Abuzurj-Mihir, inventor of chess, **3,** 7.

Abydos, Sabbataï Zevi imprisoned at, **5,** 148, 151.
enriched by the Sabbatians, **5,** 149.

Academies, the Babylonian, authority of the principals of, **2,** 547.
closed under Kobad, **3,** 4.
re-opened, **3,** 5.
work of, **3,** 6.
give religious instruction to the Arabian Jews, **3,** 59.
principals of, deposed by the Exilarchs, **3,** 91.
independent of each other in internal affairs, **3,** 96.
organization of, under the caliphs, **3,** 96–7.
office of the president of, not hereditary, **3,** 96.
meetings of, in Adar and Elul, **3,** 97.
income of, **3,** 97–8.
prayers for the departed at, **3,** 101.
the heads of, excommunicate Anan ben David, **3,** 134.
the Karaites on, **3,** 134–5.
and the election of the Exilarch, **3,** 137.
hold aloof from Islam theology, **3,** 148.

Academies, the Babylonian (*continued*), respect paid to, in the ninth century, **3,** 160.
See also under Pumbeditha *and* Sora.

Academies, the Babylonian, list of:

Firuz-Shabur, Machuza, Nahardea, Nares, Nisibis, Pumbeditha, Shekan-Zib, Silhi, Sora.

Academies, the Palestinian, origin of, **2,** 324.
established by the disciples of Jochanan ben Zakkai, **2,** 335.
frequented by Babylonian students, **2,** 511, 531.
decline of, **2,** 543, 548, 560.
method of, **2,** 557–8.
See under Acbara; Bekiin; Cæsarea; Emmaus; Jamnia; Lydda; Sepphoris; Tiberias; Schools.

Academy at Jerusalem, founded by the Vegas, **5,** 126.

Academy of Sciences at Berlin, prize of, won by Mendelssohn, **5,** 303–4.
Mendelssohn proposed as member of, **5,** 308.

Acbara, seat of Jannaï's academy, **2,** 470.

Accho (Acco; Acre; Ptolemais; St. Jean d'Acre), built by the Canaanites, **1,** 3.
surrenders to Shalmaneser, **1,** 264.
fortifications of, destroyed by Ptolemy I, **1,** 417.
the inhabitants of, threaten the Galilean Judæans, **1,** 475.
Jonathan Haphus meets Demetrius at, **1,** 496.

Accho (*continued*), Jonathan Haphus taken prisoner at, **1**, 499.
surrenders to Ptolemy VIII, **2**, 40.
Vespasian prepares for his Judæan campaign at, **2**, 285.
Talmudists in, in the twelfth century, **3**, 427.
Maimonides at, **3**, 456.
Nachmani at, **3**, 605.
Kabbalist center, **3**, 626.
Kabbalists of, burn the "Guide of the Perplexed," **3**, 631.
Maimonides' tomb at, desecrated, **3**, 631.
Maimunists in, **3**, 631.
David Maimuni at, **3**, 632-3.
the Jews of, blotted out, **3**, 650.
Acha of Diphta, proposed as principal of the Sora academy, **2**, 627.
Acha ben Jacob, on Chama of Nahardea, **2**, 595.
Achaï bar Huna, Amora, compiler of the Babylonian Talmud, **2**, 631.
Achaia, Paul establishes Christian communities in, **2**, 227.
Achbâr, teacher of the Law among the Arabic Jews, **3**, 59.
Acher. *See* Elisha ben Abuya.
Achiab, prevents Herod from committing suicide, **2**, 116.
Achish, Philistine king, in friendly relations with David, **1**, 101-2.
acknowledges David king, **1**, 108.
Achitub, grandson of Eli, high priest at Nob, **1**, 79.
Achiya, first Exilarch known, **2**, 509.
Achiya. *See also* Chiya.
Achmed I, sultan, Jewish women under, **4**, 629, 630.
Achmed Shaitan, viceroy of Egypt, treachery of, **4**, 395.
avenges himself on the Jews of Cairo, **4**, 395-6.
Achunaï. *See* Chananya.
Acosta, Uriel (Gabriel). *See* Costa, Uriel da.
Acra, the, a part of Jerusalem, burnt by Titus, **2**, 308.
Acra (Acrapolis; Baris; Birah), the, the Temple citadel, built by Nehemiah, **1**, 382, 585.
garrisoned by Scopas, **1**, 433.
Greek games taught in, **1**, 445.
refuge of the Hellenists, **1**, 454.
occupied by Menelaus, **1**, 470, 478.
besieged by Judas Maccabæus, **1**, 478.
Hellenists leave, **1**, 480.
reinforced by Bacchides, **1**, 491.
besieged by Jonathan Haphus, **1**, 496.
surrenders to Simon Tharsi, **1**, 523.
the towers of, taken down, **1**, 524.
called Birah, **1**, 524-5.
wife and children of Aristobulus II imprisoned in, **2**, 58.
called Antonia, **2**, 106.
See Antonia.
Acrabatene, the Samaritans of, slaughtered by the Zealots, **2**, 243.
Acrabattine, the Idumæans driven out of, by Judas Maccabæus, **1**, 474.
invested by Simon bar Giora, **2**, 293.
Acrapolis, the. *See* Acra, the.
Acre. *See* Accho.

Actian games, the, introduced into Jerusalem, **2,** 105.
Actium, the battle of, won by Octavius, **2,** 96.
Ada, a Babylonian Amora, **2,** 579.
Adalbert, bishop of Prague, and the slave-trade of Jews, **3,** 305.
Adam, the book of, Sibylline chronicle, quoted, **2,** 462.
Adam Kadmon, Kabbalistic term, the original man, **5,** 121, 143.
Adamantius, apostate Jew in Alexandria, **2,** 619.
Adams, Hannah, history of the Jews by, **5,** 593.
Adarsa, the battle of, won by Judas Maccabæus, **1,** 485.
Adath Jeshurun, the body of advanced Jews in Amsterdam, innovations of, **5,** 457.
Aden, the Jews of, in the twelfth century, **3,** 436.
Adher-Baijan (Aserbeidsan), Samuel Ibn-Abbas in, **3,** 442.
Adher-Baijan, the Jews of, in the twelfth century, **3,** 430–33.
urged to join David Alrui, **3,** 431.
followers of David Alrui, **3,** 433.
Adiabene, description of, **2,** 216.
the nobles of, conspire against Izates, **2,** 217–18.
the people of, friendly to the Judæans, **2,** 219.
in alliance with the Zealots, **2,** 256.
the royal house of, aids Judæa against Rome, **2,** 264.
the princes of, the only Judæan insurgents spared by Rome, **2,** 311.
conquered by Trajan, **2,** 393–4.
laid waste by Severus, **2,** 464.
Adido, Simon Tharsi assembles his forces at, **1,** 500.
Adiya, father of the poet Samuel, **3,** 68.
Adnan, ancestor of the Arabs, **3,** 61.
Adolph of Nassau, emperor, refuses to surrender Meïr of Rothenburg's body, **4,** 35.
war of, with Albrecht, **4,** 35.
death of, **4,** 36.
Adonijah, son of David, opposes Absalom, **1,** 135.
rebels, **1,** 151–4.
supporters of, **1,** 152.
royal display of, **1,** 152.
Nathan opposed to, **1,** 153.
acknowledged king, **1,** 153.
pays homage to Solomon, **1,** 154.
killed, **1,** 160.
Adonim. *See* Dunash ben Labrat.
Adoniram, superintendent of the building of the first Temple, **1,** 163, 172.
accompanies Rehoboam to Shechem, **1,** 181.
killed, **1,** 182.
Adonis, Baal of the Phœnicians, **1,** 54.
statue of, worshiped at Bethlehem, **2,** 422.
Adora, Idumæan fortress, demolished by John Hyrcanus, **2,** 8.
Adoyot, the oldest Mishna compilation, **2,** 343, 460.
Adraat, chief town of Batanæa, **3,** 77.
Benu-Nadhir settle in, **3,** 79.
Adrammelech, son of Sennacherib, murders him, **1,** 280.
Adramyttium, treasure-house in, for the half-Shekel contributions, **2,** 53.

Adrianople, Karaites move to, **4**, 269.
the Spanish exiles in, **4**, 405.
Joseph Karo at, **4**, 557.
Sabbataï Zevi at, **5**, 154–66.
Nathan Ghazati at, **5**, 158–9, 161.
Sabbatians of, devoted to Sabbataï, **5**, 163.
Cardoso at, **5**, 207.
Sabbatians in, **5**, 210.
Adrianople, the Jews of, divided into national groups, **4**, 478.
consider trading with Pesaro, **4**, 579.
Adullam, David at, **1**, 116.
Adultery, ritual for suspected cases of, abolished, **2**, 238.
laws against, inviolate, **2**, 424.
"**Advice** to the Representatives of the People," by Van Swieden, against the emancipation of the Dutch Jews, **5**, 453–4.
Ælia Capitolina, name of Jerusalem under Hadrian, **2**, 421–2.
Ælius Hadrian. *See* Hadrian.
Afia, Aaron, scientist in Salonica, **4**, 405.
Africa (northern), Karaites influential in, in the tenth century, **3**, 207.
Jewish captives transported to, **3**, 213.
students from, at the Cordova Talmud school, **3**, 228.
part of the Fatimide Caliphate, **3**, 248.
Talmud authorities of, in the eleventh century, **3**, 248–9.
Abraham Ibn-Ezra in, **3**, 369.
asylum for persecuted Jews in the fifteenth century, **4**, 197–8.
Africa, northern (*continued*), the Sephardic liturgy adopted in, **4**, 198.
Portuguese conquests on the coast of, **4**, 218.
Marranos flee to, **4**, 318.
Spanish exiles in, **4**, 352, 358, 361–2, 389–96.
descendants of Portuguese Marranos in, **4**, 381.
Spanish spoken in, by the exiles, **4**, 389.
emigration of Portuguese Marranos to, forbidden, **4**, 508.
Africa (northern), the Jews of, conspire against the Visigothic empire, **3**, 108.
aid Tarik, **3**, 109.
persecuted, **3**, 357–60, 451.
Africa, Visigothic, the Jews of, enjoy civil and political equality, **3**, 45.
Agada, the, popular exposition of the Prophets and historical writings, **2**, 328–9.
of Jochanan ben Zakkai, **2**, 329.
used by R. Meïr, **2**, 440.
the study of, preferred in Judæa, **2**, 540.
cultivated by the brothers of Rabba bar Nachmani, **2**, 575–6.
cultivated under Theodosius II, **2**, 623.
in the synagogue forbidden by Justinian I, **3**, 14.
manifests the spirit of Judaism, **3**, 15.
frequent use of, in the synagogues of the East, **3**, 16.
cultivated among the Arabic Jews, **3**, 59.
replaced by neo-Hebraic poetry, **3**, 116.

Agada, the (*continued*), cultivated by Eleazar ben Kalir, **3**, 117.
studied by French and Italian Jews in the ninth century, **3**, 160.
used by Rashi, **3**, 288.
used by the Tossafists, **3**, 345.
effect of, on Asiatic Jews, **3**, 440.
contains philosophical doctrines according to Maimonides, **3**, 479.
reconciled with philosophy by Abraham Maimuni, **3**, 495.
rejected by Maimonides, **3**, 523, 533.
accepted literally by Solomon ben Abraham, **3**, 527–8.
view of, held by Nachmani, **3**, 533, 535, 599–600.
in the Kabbala, **3**, 549, 552.
used by Pablo Christiani, **3**, 599.
rationalized by Solomon ben Adret, **3**, 619.
used by Raymund Martin, **3**, 622.
authority of, **4**, 214.
declared without authority by Chayim Ibn-Musa, **4**, 237.
quoted, **4**, 242.
reviled by Aaron Margalita, **5**, 194.
used by Mannheimer, **5**, 581.
Agag, Amalekite king, defeated by Saul, **1**, 91–2.
killed, **1**, 93.
Agape, the meal of the Nazarenes, **2**, 223.
Agen, meeting-place of the Pastoureaux, **4**, 56.
Agobard, bishop of Lyons, incites rebellion again Louis the Pious, **3**, 164.
refuses to restore a runaway slave to a Lyons Jew, **3**, 164.
Agobard (*continued*), tries to set Louis the Pious against the Jews, **3**, 165–8.
joins the conspiracy against the empress, **3**, 168.
successor to, **3**, 170.
Agora-nomos, inspector of markets, Abba-Areka appointed as, **2**, 512.
choice of, left to the Jews, **2**, 616.
Agriculture, among the Jews of the Frankish and Burgundian kingdoms, **3**, 35.
occupation of the Jews of Crissa, **3**, 424.
Jews restricted to, by Frederick II, **3**, 569.
occupation of the immigrants in Palestine, **4**, 74.
See also Real estate.
Agrigentum, Jews in, in the sixth century, **3**, 28.
Agrippa I (10 B. C. E.–44 C. E.), grandson of Mariamne, distinguished by Caligula, **2**, 175.
educated with the son of Tiberius, **2**, 175.
appointed to an office in Tiberias, **2**, 175.
courtier of the governor of Syria, **2**, 175.
supplanted by his brother, **2**, 175.
assisted by Alexander Lysimachus, **2**, 175–6.
kindly treated by Tiberius, **2**, 176.
imprisoned, **2**, 176.
released, **2**, 177.
king of Philip's tetrarchy, **2**, 177.
accuses Herod Antipas of treachery to Caligula, **2**, 177.

Agrippa I (*continued*), ruler of Galilee and Peræa, **2,** 177.
rouses the resentment of the Alexandrian Greeks, **2,** 181–182.
and Caligula's edict concerning images, **2,** 188–9.
king of all Palestine, **2,** 190.
coins in honor of, **2,** 190, 194.
change in the character of, **2,** 191.
popularity of, **2,** 191–2.
piety of, **2,** 192.
sends gifts to Athens, **2,** 193.
favors Cæsarea and Sebaste, **2,** 194.
plans of, for Judæa, **2,** 194–5.
hampered by Vibius Marsus, **2,** 195.
allied with Eastern princes, **2,** 195–6.
death of, **2,** 196.
memory of, insulted, **2,** 196–7.

Agrippa II (27–92), son of Agrippa I, proposed as king of Judæa, **2,** 196.
introduces Judæan envoys to Claudius, **2,** 198.
prince of Chalcis, **2**, 235.
and his sister, **2,** 235.
titular king of Judæa, **2,** 236.
king of Philip's tetrarchy, **2,** 245.
given four towns and Tiberias, **2,** 245–6.
accused of encroaching upon the privileges of the Temple authorities, **2,** 247–8.
bribed to make Joshua ben Gamala high priest, **2,** 249.
summons all Judæans to Jerusalem for the Passover of 66, **2,** 251.
opposed to revolutionary measures, **2,** 257–8.
flees from Jerusalem, **2,** 258.

Agrippa II (*continued*), sends troops to Jerusalem, **2,** 259.
palace of, burnt, **2,** 260.
sends a contingent to the Roman army, **2,** 264–5.
Tiberias under, **2,** 273.
Varus representative of, **2,** 274–5.
the inhabitants of Gamala revolt against, **2,** 275.
relation of, to Josephus, **2,** 278.
meets Vespasian, **2,** 285.
lacks patriotism, **2,** 288–9.
pays homage to Galba, **2,** 299.
helps Titus in the siege of Jerusalem, **2,** 302.
spectator at the death of Judæans in the arena of Cæsarea Philippi, **2,** 312.
fall of, **2,** 317.
and Justus of Tiberias, **2,** 319–20.
alleviates the burdens of the conquered Jews, **2,** 332, 333.
Galilee given to, **2,** 333.
treatment of, by Titus, **2,** 388.
death of, **2,** 388.

Agrippina, wife of Claudius, favorable to the Herodians, **2,** 245.

Aguilar, Baron de, saves the Jews of Moravia from exorbitant taxes, **5,** 252.
intercedes for the Moravian and Bohemian Jews, **5,** 253.

Aguilar, de, governor of Palma, asks for Gibraltar as a refuge for Marranos, **4,** 282.

Aguilar, Raphael Moses d', Sabbatian, **5,** 139, 160.

Aguilar, the Jews of, destroyed, **4,** 125.

Ahab, son of Omri, wife of, **1,** 194, 196–7.

Ahab (*continued*), ascends the throne of Israel, **1**, 196.
character of, **1**, 196.
builds an ivory palace, **1**, 201–2.
reproved by Elijah, **1**, 202–3.
a famine announced to, **1**, 203.
summons the priests of Baal to Carmel, **1**, 203–4.
stops the persecution of the prophets, **1**, 204.
imprisons Michaiah, **1**, 205.
ally of Ben-hadad II, **1**, 205.
ally of Jehoshaphat, **1**, 206.
death of, **1**, 206.
destruction of the house of, **1**, 211–12.

Ahasuerus. *See* Xerxes.

Ahaz, king of Judah, character of, **1**, 257.
ally of Tiglath-Pileser, **1**, 258.
warned by Isaiah, **1**, 258–9.
introduces Assyrian idolatry into Judah, **1**, 260–1.
not buried in the royal mausoleum, **1**, 267.

Ahaziah, son of Ahab, reign of, over Israel, **1**, 206–7.

Ahaziah, son of Joram, king of Judah, killed by Jehu's followers, **1**, 211.

Ahijah, of Shiloh, prophet, at the consecration of the Temple, **1**, 167.
rebukes Solomon, **1**, 175.
prophesies success to Jeroboam, **1**, 175.
prophesies the end of Jeroboam's line, **1**, 188.

Ahikam, father of Gedaliah, **1**, 319.

Ahikam, son of Shaphan, saves Jeremiah, **1**, 303.

Ahimaaz, messenger from Hushai to David, **1**, 143.

Ahinoam, wife of Saul, **1**, 95.

Ahishar, Solomon's major-domo, **1**, 172.

Ahithophel, councilor of David, **1**, 122–3.
grandfather of Bathsheba, **1**, 133.
opposed to Solomon's succession, **1**, 135.
plots with Absalom, **1**, 136, 138–43.
with Absalom in Jerusalem, **1**, 142.
advice of, rejected by Absalom, **1**, 143.
suicide of, **1**, 143.

Ahmed, khan of the Mongol kingdom in Persia, **3**, 638.

Ahmed Coprili, Turkish grand vizir, orders the arrest of Sabbataï Zevi, **5**, 146.
imprisons Sabbataï at Abydos, **5**, 148.

Ahriman. *See* Angro-Mainyus.

Ahunai, teacher of the Law, during Kobad's persecutions, **3**, 4.

Ahura-Mazda, Persian god of light, influence of the conception of, on Judaism, **1**, 402.

Ai, attacked by the Israelites, **1**, 33.

Aibu, father of Abba-Areka, **2**, 511.

Aibu, son of Abba-Areka, **2**, 518.

Aidug, Arab king, defeats Zorah Yussuf, **3**, 64.

Ain-tab, the new-moon announced at, **2**, 458.

Airvi (Eravi), king of Cranganor, and the Jews of India, **3**, 630.

Aix-la-Chapelle, the Jews of, oppose the study of science, **4**, 33.

Aix-la-Chapelle (*continued*), the Congress of, the emancipation of the Jews discussed by, **5**, 525–7.

Ajubides, the, make Egypt the Islam center, **3**, 457.

Akbara, Karaite center, **3**, 157.
- the Jews of, in the twelfth century, **3**, 429.

Akbarites, the, a Karaite sect, **3**, 157.

Akiba ben Joseph, teacher of the Law, suggested as successor to Gamaliel II, **2**, 342.
- effects the re-instatement of Gamaliel II, **2**, 345.
- informs Eliezer ben Hyrcanus of his excommunication, **2**, 347.
- legends concerning the youth of, **2**, 350–1.
- intellectual development of, **2**, 351–2.
- system of, **2**, 352–3.
- arranges the Halachas in groups, **2**, 353.
- disciples and wife of, **2**, 354–5.
- in the Jamnia Synhedrion, **2**, 355.
- and Ishmael ben Elisha, **2**, 355–6.
- theosophist, **2**, 381.
- saying of, **2**, 381.
- opposes Gnostic influences, **2**, 382.
- disciples of, proselytes, **2**, 384.
- and Akylas, **2**, 385.
- and Flavius Clemens, **2**, 387, 389, 391.
- influences Nerva, **2**, 392.
- opposes reckless charity, **2**, 405.
- prepares for the revolt against Hadrian, **2**, 408; **5**, 724–5.
- attracted to Bar-Cochba, **2**, 409.
- at Lydda, **2**, 423.

Akiba ben Joseph (*continued*), evades Roman spies, **2**, 424.
- martyrdom of, **2**, 428–9.
- disciples of, ordained, **2**, 429.
- disciples of, return to Judæa, **2**, 433.
- favorite disciple of, **2**, 436.
- dialectics of, adopted by Meïr, **2**, 438–40.
- first compiler of the Mishna, **2**, 460.
- position of, compared with Rabba bar Nachmani's, **2**, 579.

Akko. *See* Accho.

Akra di Coche, a Babylonian fortification, **2**, 507.

Akrabattine. *See* Acrabattine.

Akrish. *See* Isaac ben Abraham Akrish.

Akylas (Aquila), convert to Judaism, translates the Scriptures into Greek, **2**, 385.
- superintends the rebuilding of Jerusalem, **2**, 401.
- mourns for Gamaliel II, **2**, 404.

Akylas, translation of the Scriptures by, literal, **2**, 386.
- used by Jews and Ebionites, **2**, 387.
- used by Origen, **2**, 489.
- Targum Onkelos based on, **2**, 581.
- recommended to Jewish congregations by Justinian I, **3**, 14.

Alabarch (Arabarch, Ethnarch), the, prince of the Judæans in Egypt, **1**, 507, 510.
- office of, confirmed by Cæsar, **2**, 76.
- controls the Nile harbor, **2**, 102.
- dignity of, restored by Claudius, **2**, 191.

Alabarch, the (*continued*). *See also* Alexander Lysimachus; Ethnarch.
Al-ablak, castle of Samuel Ibn-Adiya, **3**, 68, 69.
Aladhid, last Fatimide caliph of Egypt, **3**, 443.
Aladil, sultan, receives emigrant rabbis kindly, **3**, 506.
Alagon, Blasco de, conspires against Pedro Arbues, **4**, 329.
Alami. *See* Solomon Alami.
Alani, the, of the Crimea, friendly to the Jews, **3**, 123.
Alarcos, Alfonso VIII defeated at the battle of, **3**, 387.
Alashkar. *See* Moses ben Isaac Alashkar.
Albalag. *See* Isaac Albalag.
Albalia. *See* Ibn-Albalia.
Albanian Gates, the, Jews settle in, **3**, 124.
Albargeloni. *See* Abraham ben Chiya Albargeloni.
Albergeloni. *See* Isaac ben Reuben Albergeloni.
Albert I, emperor, war of, with Adolph of Nassau, **4**, 35.
punishes the Rindfleisch followers, **4**, 36.
demands a ransom for Meïr of Rothenburg, **4**, 37.
claims authority over the French Jews, **4**, 47.
Albert II, emperor, imprisons the Jews of Austria, **4**, 223.
banishes the Jews from Austria, **4**, 224.
hostile to the Jews, **4**, 249.
son of, cruel to the Jews, **4**, 262–3.
Albert, duke of Bavaria, under the influence of John of Capistrano, **4**, 258.
Albert von Brandenburg, archbishop of Mayence, convenes a diet to consider the Jewish question, **4**, 463.
ordered to drop the Jewish question, **4**, 464.
Albert of Munich, son-in-law of Maximilian I, **4**, 428.
Albertina, the. *See* Königsberg, the university of.
Albertus Magnus, the works of, translated, **4**, 69.
Albi. *See* Alby.
Albigenses, the, origin of, **3**, 390.
in Béziers, **3**, 394, 395.
relation of, to the Jews, **3**, 501.
crusade against, **3**, 501–2.
and the council of Montpellier, **3**, 508.
and the Fourth Lateran Council, **3**, 509.
the war against, ended, **3**, 519.
extirpation of, by the Inquisition, **3**, 542.
Albinus, procurator of Judæa, appointed by Nero, **2**, 248.
appealed to against Anan, **2**, 248–9.
taxes Judæa heavily, **2**, 249.
punishes the Sicarii, **2**, 249.
Albo. *See* Joseph Albo.
Albrecht I. *See* Albert I.
Alby, the council of, forbids Jews to practice medicine among Christians, **3**, 582, 583.
the Jews of, perish, **4**, 57.
Alcala, the academy at, **4**, 145.
the Jews of, ridiculed, **4**, 181.
Alcana, street in Toledo occupied by Jews, **4**, 118.
Alcañiz, the Jews of, converted, **4**, 214.
Alcantara, the Order of, and Gonzalo Martinez, **4**, 85–6.
Alcharam. *See* Mecca.

Alcharisi. *See* Jehuda Alcharisi.
Alcimus (Jakim), leader of the Hellenists, appointed high priest, **1,** 482.
slays sixty Chassidim, **1,** 483.
attracts the Hellenists, **1,** 483.
fears Judas Maccabæus, **1,** 483.
appeals to Demetrius I, **1,** 484.
informs against Nicanor, **1,** 484.
withdraws from Jerusalem, **1,** 485.
takes possession of Jerusalem, **1,** 487.
has the "Soreg" destroyed, **1,** 492.
death of, **1,** 492, 508.
Alcolea, the Jews of, converted, **4,** 214.
Aldea de los Judios, village given to Jewish soldiers, **3,** 592.
Aldobrandini, prevents the expulsion of the Ferrara Jews, **4,** 660.
Aleman, Jochanan, Kabbalist, teacher of Pico di Mirandola, **4,** 291.
Alembert, d', approves of Pereira's sign language, **5,** 343.
Alenu prayer, the, misrepresented by Pessach-Peter, **4,** 178.
attacked by Wülfer, **5,** 185.
denounced by apostates, **5,** 191.
exonerated by Michaelis, **5,** 191.
regulations concerning, **5,** 192.
Aleppo (Haleb), the Jews of, in the twelfth century, **3,** 426.
Jehuda Ibn-Abbas settles at, **3,** 442.
the Jewish liturgy of, changed, **3,** 466.
Aleppo (*continued*), taken by Hulagu, **3,** 606.
the battle of, gives Egypt to the Turks, **4,** 393.
Sabbataï Zevi in, **5,** 133.
Alessandria, the Jews of, in the sixteenth century, **4,** 653.
Alexander III, pope, convenes a Church Council, **3,** 376.
orders the enforcement of anti-Jewish decrees, **3,** 400.
finances of, managed by a Jew, **3,** 421.
Alexander VI (Borgia), pope, and the Aragon Inquisition, **4,** 319.
banishes the Jews from Rome, **4,** 363.
the favor of, bought by the Portuguese Marranos, **4,** 379.
friendly to the Jews, **4,** 407.
employs a Jewish physician, **4,** 407–8.
Reuchlin at the court of, **4,** 434.
Alexander I, of Judæa. *See* Alexander Jannæus.
Alexander II, of Judæa, son of Aristobulus II, marries Hyrcanus II's daughter, **2,** 58.
seizes Jerusalem, **2,** 70.
has coins struck, **2,** 70.
subdued by Aulus Gabinius, **2,** 70–1.
rebels against Rome, **2,** 73.
beheaded, **2,** 75.
Alexander the Great, of Macedon, destroys the Persian empire, **1,** 412.
legends about, **1,** 412–13.
tolerance of, **1,** 413, 415.
favors the Judæans, **1,** 414–15, 418.
conquests of, **1,** 415.
confusion after the death of, **1,** 416.

Alexander, of Poland, hostile to the Jews, **4**, 419.
Alexander I, of Russia, inquires into the condition of the Jews, **5**, 472-3.
enforces attendance at schools, **5**, 473.
and the emancipation of the Jews, **5**, 525, 527.
Alexander, apostate, accuses Jews of blasphemy, **4**, 591.
Alexander, son of Mariamne, designated successor to Herod, **2**, 112.
marriage of, **2**, 112.
executed, **2**, 113.
Alexander, Zealot leader, **2**, 238.
attacks the Samaritans of Acrabatene, **2**, 243.
Alexander Balas, pretender to the Syrian throne, ally of Jonathan Haphus, **1**, 494, 496.
marriage of, **1**, 496.
death of, **1**, 496.
son of, on the throne, **1**, 497-8.
Alexander (I) Jannæus (105-79), third son of Hyrcanus I, **2**, 34.
banished to Galilee, **2**, 38-9.
favors the Pharisees, **2**, 39.
military character of, **2**, 39.
defeated by Ptolemy VIII, **2**, 40.
ally of Ptolemy VIII's mother, **2**, 41.
takes Gaza, **2**, 41.
mediates between the Pharisees and Sadducees, **2**, 42.
sides with the Sadducees, **2**, 42-3.
refuses to offer the water libation, **2**, 43.
defeated by the Nabathæan king, **2**, 44.
Pharisees revolt against, **2**, 44.
defeated by Eucærus, **2**, 44.
Alexander (I) Jannæus (*continued*), forces Eucærus to retreat, **2**, 45.
crucifies eight hundred Pharisees, **2**, 45.
conquests of, **2**, 45-6.
coins of, **2**, 46.
builds fortresses, **2**, 46, 315.
end of, **2**, 47.
appoints his wife his successor, **2**, 47.
sons of, **2**, 47.
towns conquered by, declared free, **2**, 67.
Alexander Lysimachus, Alabarch of Alexandria, aids Agrippa I, **2**, 175-6, 181.
brother of Philo, **2**, 185.
released from prison, **2**, 190.
sons of, **2**, 198, 235.
descendant of, **2**, 395.
Alexander Polyhistor, writer friendly to the Judæans, **2**, 179.
Alexander Severus (222-235), emperor, friendly to Jews and Judaism, **2**, 481-3.
and Judah II, **2**, 482.
presents a gold candlestick to a synagogue, **2**, 482.
taught Jewish customs by Romanus, **2**, 482.
anarchy after the death of, **2**, 486, 526.
Alexander, Tiberius Julius. *See* Tiberius Julius Alexander.
Alexander Zabina, rival of Demetrius Nicator for the Syrian throne, **2**, 6.
disputes the Syrian throne with Antiochus VIII, **2**, 6.
acknowledged king by Hyrcanus I, **2**, 6.
fall of, **2**, 7.
Alexandra. *See* Salome Alexandra.

Alexandra, daughter of Aristobulus II, marries two princes of Chalcis, **2,** 75.
Alexandra, daughter of Hyrcanus II, marries the son of Aristobulus II, **2,** 58.
betroths her daughter Mariamne to Herod, **2,** 81.
obtains Mark Antony's favor for her son, **2,** 91.
accuses Herod of her son's murder, **2,** 92.
threatened with death, **2,** 93.
imprisoned, **2,** 94, 96.
death of, **2,** 105.
Alexandria, Judæans settle in, **1,** 418.
center of the Egyptian Judæans, **1,** 504–5.
busts of Caligula placed in the synagogues of, **2,** 182.
wheat imported from, for Jerusalem, **2,** 218.
study of the Law in, **2,** 359.
synagogue of, destroyed, **2,** 398.
Karaite community in, **3,** 182.
Jehuda Halevi at, **3,** 339–40.
Spanish spoken at, by the exiles, **4,** 388.
rabbis of, favor the establishment of schools, **5,** 663.
See also under Egypt.
Alexandria, the Jews of, rebel against Trajan, **2,** 396.
punished by Martius Turbo, **2,** 398.
ill-treated by Cyril, **2,** 618–19.
receive fugitives from Palestine, **3,** 23.
in the twelfth century, **3,** 444.
object to Maimonides' Mishne-Torah, **3,** 472.
appeal to Mehemet Ali in the Damascus affair, **5,** 647.
rejoice over the release of the Damascus prisoners, **5,** 660.
Alexandria, the Judæans of, influence those of Jerusalem, **1,** 427.
occupy the Delta district, **1,** 504.
under Ptolemy VII, **1,** 519.
under Ptolemy VIII, **2,** 12.
well treated by Cæsar, **2,** 76.
unkindly treated by Cleopatra, **2,** 94.
antagonized by the Greeks, **2,** 178, 181.
conspiracies against, **2,** 181–2.
forced into the harbor, **2,** 182–3.
forced to worship Caligula's statues, **2,** 183–4.
send envoys to Caligula, **2,** 186–7; **5,** 654.
well treated by Claudius, **2,** 190–1.
have a synagogue in Jerusalem, **2,** 201.
impregnated with Greek views, **2,** 208–9.
apostasy among, **2,** 209.
massacred, **2,** 263–4.
undisturbed by the Roman war, **2,** 313.
fugitive Zealots betrayed by, **2,** 317–18.
and the closing of the Temple of Onias, **2,** 322.
Alexandrian school of philosophy. *See* Judæo-Alexandrian school.
Alexandrion, fortress, built by Alexander Jannæus, **2,** 46.
surrenders to Pompey, **2,** 64.
garrisoned by Aristobulus II, **2,** 73.
Mariamne confined in, **2,** 96.
fire signals on, **2,** 363.
Alfachar. *See* Ibn-Alfachar.
Alfadhel, vizir of Saladin, employs Maimonides, **3,** 472–3, 489.

Alfadhel (*continued*), acquits Maimonides of apostasy, **3**, 474.
Alfarda, Strangers' Tax, in Spain, **4**, 344.
Alfassi. *See* Isaac ben Jacob Alfassi.
Alfonsine Tables, the, used by scientists, **4**, 367.
Alfonso I, of Aragon, conquers Saragossa, **3**, 316.
Alfonso II, of Aragon (1162–1196), the Jews under, **3**, 387–8.
Alfonso VI, of Castile, employs Jews on diplomatic missions, **3**, 291–2.
the Jews under, **3**, 292–3.
admonished to dismiss Jews from state offices, **3**, 294.
conquers Toledo, **3**, 294.
opposed by a Mahometan league, **3**, 295–6.
Alfonso VII Raimundez, of Castile (1126–1157), rebels against his parents, **3**, 316.
Jewish favorite of, **3**, 361.
death of, **3**, 363, 366.
Alfonso VIII (III), of Castile (the Noble, 1166–1214), minority of, **3**, 363.
the Jews under, **3**, 384–7.
employs a Jew as ambassador, **3**, 385.
Jewish mistress of, **3**, 386.
assisted by the Toledo Jews against the Almohades, **3**, 386–7.
defeated at Alarcos, **3**, 387.
reproached for his humane treatment of the Jews, **3**, 499.
appeals to Innocent III against the Mahometans, **3**, 507.
protects the Jews of Toledo, **3**, 507.
Alfonso X, of Castile (the Wise, 1252–1284), the Jews under, **3**, 592–6.
patron of learning, **3**, 592.
gives a village to his Jewish soldiers, **3**, 592.
and the Jews of Seville, **3**, 592–3.
employs Jews, **3**, 593–4, 615.
reproached by Nicholas III, **3**, 594, 615.
degrades the Jews, **3**, 594–5.
Jews in the code of, **3**, 595–6.
code of, in Spanish America, **3**, 596.
executes his Jewish Almoxarif, **3**, 616.
imprisons the Jews, **3**, 616.
son of, rebels, **3**, 616.
death of, **3**, 616.
anti-Jewish statutes of, revived, **4**, 194–5.
Alfonso XI, of Castile (1325–1380), the Jews prosperous under, **4**, 52, 75–6.
Jewish favorites of, **4**, 79–80.
petitioned against usury, **4**, 80.
makes a Jew farmer of revenues, **4**, 80.
Jews accused before, **4**, 83.
accuses Gonzalo Martinez of treason, **4**, 85.
besieges Valencia, **4**, 86.
death of, **4**, 113.
bastard sons of, oppose Pedro the Cruel, **4**, 113.
wife of, **4**, 114.
law of, renewed, **4**, 193.
Alfonso II, of Ferrara, death of, **4**, 660.
Alfonso IX, of Leon, does not compel the Jews to wear a badge, **3**, 513.
Alfonso II, of Naples, patron of Isaac Abrabanel, **4**, 360, 383–4.

Alfonso III, of Portugal (1248-1279), the Jews under, **3**, 618.
Alfonso V, of Portugal, takes Jews captive at Arzilla, **4**, 286-7, 339.
employs Isaac Abrabanel, **4**, 337-8.
prosperity of the Jews under, **4**, 338-9.
code of, **4**, 339.
Jewish favorites of, **4**, 339.
death of, **4**, 340.
Alfonso, brother of Henry IV, of Castile, crowned, **4**, 278.
death of, **4**, 279.
Alfonso, duke of Poitou, employs a Jewish oculist, **3**, 583.
Alfonso, Infante of Portugal, releases Marranos, **4**, 517.
Alfonso of Aragon, archbishop, protects Marranos, **4**, 330.
Alfonso de Cartagena, influences Eugenius IV against the Jews, **4**, 249-50.
Alfonso de Spina, Franciscan, attacks the Spanish Jews, **4**, 276.
confessor of Alvaro de Luna, **4**, 271.
writes a work against the Jews, **4**, 277.
anti-Jewish work by, reprinted, **4**, 415.
Alfonso of Valladolid. *See* Alfonso Burgensis.
Alfonso Burgensis (Abner of Burgos, Alfonso of Valladolid, 1270-1346), apostate, hostile to the Jews, **4**, 81, 342.
infidel, **4**, 81-2.
sacristan, **4**, 82.
attacks the Jews in Hebrew, **4**, 82.
reply to, by Isaac Pulgar, **4**, 82.
Alfonso Burgensis (*continued*), accuses the Jews before Alfonso XI, **4**, 83.
disciple of, **4**, 141-2.
work of, refuted, **4**, 143.
charges of, repeated, **4**, 213.
Algazi, Moses Joseph, rabbi of Cairo, seconds Munk's efforts to establish schools, **5**, 664.
Algazi, Solomon, opposes the Sabbatian movement, **5**, 144.
Alghazali, mystic philosopher, Mahometan, **3**, 273, 357.
Algiers, refuge for the Jews of Spain, **4**, 197.
tax imposed on Marrano fugitives in, **4**, 199.
the Spanish exiles in, **4**, 361, 390-1.
Alguades, Meïr. *See* Meïr Alguades.
Alhakem, Ommiyyade caliph, employs Chasdaï Ibn-Shaprut, **3**, 222, 227.
obtains an Arabic translation of the Mishna, **3**, 237.
appealed to in behalf of Chanoch ben Moses, **3**, 238.
appealed to by Joseph Ibn-Abitur, **3**, 238.
death of, **3**, 239.
founds a medical school at Cordova, **3**, 261.
Ali, Mahomet's general, defeats Marhab, **3**, 82.
the Judæo-Babylonian community under, **3**, 90.
the candidate of a party, **3**. 90.
aided by Jews and Christians, **3**, 90.
house of, and the Ommiyyades, **3**, 92.
Ali (1106-1143), the second Almoravide ruler, the Jews under, **3**, 312.

Ali Ibn-Isa, vizir of Abradhi, favors Saadiah, **3**, 200.
Ali Ibn-Rahmadan, mathematician, and Joseph Delmedigo, **5**, 76.
Ali Halevi, Gaon of Bagdad, **3**, 429.
son of, **3**, 438.
Ali Ikbal Addaula, prince of Denia, patron of Yizchaki, **3**, 273.
Alice of Montmorency, persecutes the Toulouse Jews, **3**, 514.
Alkabez. *See* Solomon Alkabez.
Alkadir, caliph of the East, Sherira arraigned before, **3**, 233–4.
Alkalaï. *See* Isaac ben Jacob Alfassi.
Alkamel, sultan, employs a Jewish physician, **3**, 495.
Alkuti (Chepez), Jewish philosopher, sayings of, used by Ibn-Gebirol, **3**, 267.
Allatif. *See* Isaac ben Abraham Ibn-Latif.
Allebrandus, bishop of Worms, protects the Jews, **3**, 301–2.
offers the Jews baptism, **3**, 302.
Allegorical poems in Hebrew literature, **1**, 158–9.
Allegorists, the, Alexandrian Jewish school of Scripture interpreters, **2**, 208–9, 329.
Philo among, **2**, 210.
misrepresentations of, accentuate the legal side of Judaism, **2**, 471.
compared with the Mutazilists, **3**, 147.
Allegorization, the, of the Scriptures by the mystics and the philosophers, **4**, 23–4.
"Alliance Israélite Universelle," the outgrowth of Crémieux's activity in the East, **5**, 664.
founders of, **5**, 701.
Alliances, Jewish, value of, **5**, 704. *See:*

Alliance Israélite Universelle,
Anglo-Jewish Association,
Israelitische Allianz,
Union of American Hebrew Congregations.

Allorqui. *See* Joshua ben Joseph Ibn-Vives.
"Al-Luma', Rikmah," grammar and exegesis by Ibn-Janach, **3**, 263.
Almagest, the, translated into Arabic, **3**, 146.
Almaida, Manuela Nuñez da, poetess, **5**, 203.
Almalek Alashraf, Egyptian sultan, besieges Accho, **3**, 650.
Almamun. *See* Abdallah Almamun.
"Almansor," dramatic poem by Heine, **5**, 548–9.
Almanzi, Italian Jewish scholar, **5**, 622.
Almeida, Lopes de, Portuguese ambassador to Sixtus IV, **4**, 340.
Almeirin, residence of the Portuguese king, **4**, 493.
Almeria, captured by the Almohades, **3**, 448.
Almohades (Almovachides, Unitarians), the, a Mahometan sect, **3**, 358.
under Abdulmumen, **3**, 358–9.
take Andalusia, **3**, 360–1.
persecute the Spanish Jews, **3**, 360–2.
irruptions of, into Christian territory, **3**, 363.
drive the Jews from Andalusia, **3**, 384.

Almohades, the (*continued*), attack Castile, **3**, 386–7.
drive the Jews from Ceuta, **3**, 424.
drive the Ibn-Abbas to Asia, **3**, 442.
capture Cordova, **3**, 447–8.
capture Almeria, **3**, 448.
Jewish fugitives from, received in Sicily, **3**, 569.
Almoravides, the, the Jews well treated by, **3**, 296, 311–13.
attack the Arabs of Andalusia, **3**, 316.
rebellion against, **3**, 357.
dynasty of, destroyed by Abdulmumen, **3**, 358.
Almosnino. *See* Moses Almosnino.
Almotassem, of Almeria, invades Granada, **3**, 278.
Almovachides, the. *See* Almohades, the.
Almoxarif, treasurer in Castile, **3**, 593; **4**, 75, 79, 138, 160, 169.
Jews excluded from the position of, **4**, 158.
Alms-giving, in Judæa after Ezra and Nehemiah, **1**, 393–4.
Al-Muktadir (908–932), caliph of the East, banishes Mar-Ukba, **3**, 184.
restores the Exilarch to office, **3**, 185.
appealed to by the partisans of Saadiah and of David ben Zaccaï, **3**, 195–6.
death of, **3**, 196.
Al-muktadir Billah, king of Saragossa, patron of Abu Fadhl Chasdaï, **3**, 280.
Almustadhi, Abbasside caliph, and the Exilarch Daniel, **3**, 438.
Almustanjid, Abbasside caliph, and the Exilarch Daniel, **3**, 438.
Al-Mutadhid (892–902), caliph of the East, the Jews under, **3**, 183.
Al-Mutamed Ibn-Abbad (Abulkassim Mahomet), king of Seville, patron of Isaac Ibn-Albalia, **3**, 283, 284.
ally of Alfonso VI of Castile, **3**, 294.
kills Alfonso's ambassador, **3**, 295.
joins the Mahometan league against Alfonso, **3**, 295–6.
Al-Mutavakkil (849–856), caliph of the East, re-enacts Omar's laws against the Jews, **3**, 176–7.
Almuthadid, king of Seville, receives Jewish fugitives kindly, **3**, 279–80.
Alnakvah family, the, of the nobility of Jewish Spain, **3**, 235.
Alnasir Ledin Allah, Abbasside caliph, patron of David of Mosul, **3**, 506.
Alphabet, the Phœnician, adopted by other nations, **1**, 3.
the Assyrian, adopted by the Judæans, **1**, 395–6.
Alroy, or Alrui. *See* David Alrui.
Alsace, the Jews of, suffer during the Armleder persecutions, **4**, 97.
declared outlaws, **4**, 107.
abasement of, **5**, 347–8.
taxes paid by, **5**, 348, 446.
forced into usury, **5**, 349.
blackmail levied on, **5**, 349.
receipts from, forged, **5**, 350.
protected by Louis XVI, **5**, 350–1.
memorialize the crown, **5**, 351, 352.
Mendelssohn's Pentateuch translation among, **5**, 430.

Alsace, the Jews of (*continued*), petition for alleviation of burdens, **5**, 431.
complaints of and charges against, **5**, 434.
number of, **5**, 435.
complain to the National Assembly, **5**, 436.
attacked, **5**, 437, 524, 542.
appeal to Grégoire, **5**, 437.
exposed to attack, **5**, 440.
emancipation of, opposed, **5**, 441, 447.
under special protection, **5**, 446.
relieved of taxes, **5**, 446.
occupations of, **5**, 475–6.
in danger of massacre, **5**, 477.
equality of, restored, **5**, 525.
Alsaid Ibn-Sina Almulk, poet, on Maimonides, **3**, 473.
Al Tanchik, by Ibn-Janach, **3**, 263.
Altiflisi. *See* Abu-Amran Moses.
Altona, the Jewish cemetery at, **4**, 688.
Judah Chassid in, **5**, 213.
printing press in, **5**, 255.
Altona, the council of, espouses Eibeschütz's cause, **5**, 264–5.
punished for its treatment of Jacob Emden, **5**, 265.
urges Eibeschütz to submit to a rabbinical court, **5**, 268.
Altona-Hamburg, the rabbis of, and Moses Meïr Kamenker, **5**, 230.
Alva, the duke of, barbarity of, **4**, 601.
and the Jews, **4**, 662.
Alvalensi. *See* Samuel Alvalensi.
Alvarez, Alfonso, de Villasandino, Spanish satirist, **4**, 181.
Alvernes de Gras. *See* Suasso, Isaac.
Alypius, of Antioch, oversees the rebuilding of the Temple, **2**, 599, 600.
Amadeus, duke of Savoy, imprisons Jews on account of the Black Death, **4**, 103–4.
Amadia, birthplace of David Alrui, **3**, 430, 431, 432.
Amalarich of Bena, philosopher, disciples of, burnt, **3**, 503.
Amalasuntha, daughter of Theodoric, **3**, 31.
Amalekites, the, dwell with the tribe of Judah, **1**, 39.
war of, with Saul, **1**, 91–2.
burn Ziklag, **1**, 106–7.
Amali, the, a Gothic family, **3**, 27.
Amalrich of Jerusalem, campaign of, **3**, 444.
Amantius, governor of the East, punishes rioters, **3**, 17.
Amasa, cousin of David, joins Absalom, **1**, 139.
lacks military genius, **1**, 143.
influences the men of Judah, **1**, 146.
commander against Sheba, **1**, 148.
killed by Joab, **1**, 149.
Amasia (Amazia), the Spanish exiles in, **4**, 405.
the Jews of, accused of murder, **4**, 553.
Amasis, reigns over Egypt, **1**, 327.
opponent of Cyrus, **1**, 343.
Amatus (Chabib) Lusitanus (João Rodrigo de Castel-Branco), physician, **4**, 569–70.
medical works by, **4**, 570.
in Salonica, **4**, 580.
death of, **4**, 610.
Amaziah, of Judah, re-conquers Edom, **1**, 222–3.

Amaziah (*continued*), respects the Law, **1**, 223.
at war with Jehoash of Israel, **1**, 224–5.
taken prisoner, **1**, 225.
conspiracy against, **1**, 226.
murder of, **1**, 226.
interred in Jerusalem, **1**, 228.
Amaziah, high priest of the bull-worship under Jeroboam II, **1**, 233.
opposes Amos, **1**, 236–7.
Ambivius, Marcus, second procurator of Judæa, **2**, 135.
Ambrosius of Milan, bishop, incites persecutions of Arians and Jews, **2**, 612–13.
rebukes mild treatment of Jews, **2**, 614.
accuses the Jews, **2**, 614.
Amemar (390–420), Amora, opens an academy at Nahardea, **2**, 606.
subordinates himself to Ashi, **2**, 606.
at the court of Jezdijird, **2**, 610.
Amemar bar Mar-Janka (469–70?), Amora, executed, **2**, 629.
Am-ha-Arez, the ignorant, addressed by Jesus, **2**, 152.
Ami, Amora, defends a political offender, **2**, 529–30.
subordinates himself to the Babylonian authorities, **2**, 531, 537.
investigates the educational institutions of Judæa, **2**, 532.
investigates the observance of the Law in Samaria, **2**, 534.
appeals to Abbahu, **2**, 538.
meets the corpse of Huna, **2**, 548.
disciples of, **2**, 560.
Amigo, Abraham, Talmudist and Kabbalist, **5**, 126.
Ammon, an Egyptian god, **1**, 9.
Ammonite district, the, governed by Aretas, **1**, 447.
Ammonites, the, idolatry of, **1**, 55.
attack Ephraim and Judah, **1**, 64.
defeated by Jephthah, **1**, 64–5.
invade the territory of Gad and Manasseh, **1**, 80.
besiege Jabesh-Gilead, **1**, 89–90.
at war with David, **1**, 126–7.
subdued by David, **1**, 128–9.
declared bondmen by Solomon, **1**, 163.
attracted to Palestine, **1**, 173.
regain independence, **1**, 185.
urge Zedekiah to revolt, **1**, 310.
in friendly relations with the Judæans, **1**, 362.
hostile to the Judæans during the Syrian invasion, **1**, 474.
defeated by Judas Maccabæus, **1**, 474.
as proselytes, **2**, 343, 383–4.
Amnon, eldest son of David, killed, **1**, 134.
Amolo, bishop of Lyons, adversary of the Jews, **3**, 171, 172–3.
Amon, of Judah, idolatry under, **1**, 285–6.
murdered, **1**, 286.
Amoraim, the, connection of, with the Tanaites, **2**, 479.
expounders of the Mishna, **2**, 489.
compared with the Tanaites, **2**, 490, 590.
decisions of, **2**, 515.
of Galilee, methods of, **2**, 557.
last, in Judæa, compile the Jerusalem Talmud, **2**, 612.
Babylonian, create Talmudic dialectics, **2**, 635.

Amoraim, the (*continued*), loss of creative power in the disciples of (*See* Sabureans, the), **3,** 5.
See also Law, the, the teachers of.

Amoraim, the, list of:
Abayi Nachmani,
Abba of Accho,
Abba bar Abba,
Abba Areka (Rab),
Abbahu,
Abin,
Acha of Diphta,
Acha ben Jacob,
Achaï bar Huna,
Ada,
Amemar,
Amemar bar Mar-Janka,
Ami,
Ashi, son of Simaï,
Assi,
Chaggaï,
Chama of Nahardea,
Chananya,
Chanina bar Chama,
Chasda of Cafri,
Chiskiya ben Chiya,
Chiya bar Abba,
Chiya bar Abba-Areka,
Dimé,
Huna,
Huna ben Chiya,
Huna ben Joshua,
Isaac bar Joseph,
Jannaï,
Jeremiah,
Jochanan bar Moryah,
Jochanan bar Napacha,
Jonah II,
Jonathan ben Amram,
José (Babylonian),
José (Palestinian),
Joseph ben Chiya,
Joshua ben Levi,
Judah II,
Judah III,
Judah ben Chiya,
Judah ben Ezekiel,
Kama,
Levi bar Sissi,
Mar bar Ashi,
Mar-Sheshet,
Mar-Ukban,
Mar-Zutra,
Meshershaya bar Pacod,
Nachman ben Isaac,
Nachman ben Jacob,
Papa bar Chanan,
Raba bar Joseph bar Chama,
Rabba bar Abbahu,
Rabba bar Chana,
Rabba bar Huna (Rab Abba),
Rabba bar Matana,
Rabba bar Nachmani,
Rabina,
Samuel,
Samuel (Arioch),
Samuel bar Bun,
Samuel bar Judah,
Shila,
Simaï bar Ashi,
Simlaï,
Simon bar Abba,
Simon bar Kappara,
Simon ben Lakish,
Tanchuma bar Abba,
Ulla,
Ushaya the Elder,
Ushaya the Younger,
Zeïra.

Amorites, the, a subdivision of the Canaanites, **1,** 3.
defeat the tribe of Dan, **1,** 39.

Amos, prophet, depicts the debauchery in Israel, **1,** 234.
beauty of the prophecies of, **1,** 235–6.
intrepidity of, **1,** 237.
prophesies concerning Judah, **1,** 237.
prophesies concerning Israel, **1,** 247.

Amram. *See* Mar-Amram ben Sheshna.

Amram ben Isaac Ibn-Shalbib, physician and secretary to Alfonso VI of Castile, **3,** 292.
ambassador to Seville, **3,** 295.

Amram Efrati, rabbi of Valencia, **4,** 162.

Amru, king of Yemen, **3,** 64.

Amschel, promotes the emancipation of the Frankfort Jews, **5,** 505.

Amschel, Talmudist, opponent of Israel Bruna, **4,** 302.

Amsterdam, the first Portuguese Marranos in, **4,** 665–75.
the first synagogue in, **4,** 667.
the second synagogue in, **4,** 671.
Hebrew printing press in, **4,** 675.
called new Jerusalem, **4,** 676.
the first synagogue of, honored, **4,** 678.
third synagogue of, **4,** 680.
German Jews settle in, **4,** 680–1.
union of the Portuguese congregations of, **4,** 681.
Jewish school in, **4,** 681–2.
Polish-Jewish fugitives in, **5,** 16.
the synagogue of, visited by an English ambassador, **5,** 33–4.

Amsterdam (*continued*), Joseph Delmedigo at, **5**, 79.
the secular authorities of, and Spinoza, **5**, 95.
the Sabbatian movement in, **5**, 139, 150.
stagnation of the trade of, **5**, 149.
new synagogue at, **5**, 166-7.
Chayon at, **5**, 220.
repudiates Chayon, **5**, 231.
Luzzatto at, **5**, 242.
split in the Jewish community of, **5**, 457-8.
the German rabbi of, opposes the Reform movement, **5**, 571.
rabbinical college at, **5**, 700.
Amsterdam, the Jews of, religious government of, **4**, 684-5.
influence of, **4**, 685.
branches of, **4**, 685, 693; **5**, 50.
desirous of settling in England, **5**, 18.
mourn for Isaac de Castro-Tartas, **5**, 32.
alarmed at Spinoza's scepticism, **5**, 90-1, 92.
try Spinoza, **5**, 92.
lay him under the lesser ban, **5**, 93.
lay him under the greater ban, **5**, 94.
culture of, **5**, 109.
and Sabbataï Zevi, **5**, 155.
warned against Sabbatian emissaries, **5**, 220.
marriages of, **5**, 453.
oppose their own emancipation, **5**, 454, 457.
number of, **5**, 455.
send messengers to the French Synhedrion, **5**, 496.
Amsterdam, the Portuguese Jews (Marranos) of, disturbed in their religious exercises, **4**, 666.
pay a tax on corpses, **4**, 673.
intolerant treatment of, **4**, 673.
culture of, **4**, 674, 677-8.
invited to settle in Denmark, **4**, 675.
early in the seventeenth century, **4**, 677.
wealth of, **4**, 677; **5**, 205.
devotion of, to Judaism, **4**, 678-9.
found benevolent institutions, **4**, 679.
morality of, **4**, 679-80.
espouse Chayon's cause, **5**, 223, 225.
abuse Chacham Zevi, **5**, 224.
urged to oppose Chayon, **5**, 225.
Chacham Zevi summoned before the council of, **5**, 226.
send Chayon to the East, **5**, 227.
hold aloof from the Eibeschütz controversy, **5**, 264.
Amsterdam, the rabbis of, mediocrity of, **4**, 682.
Poles, **5**, 17, 206.
try Spinoza, **5**, 92-4.
sentence Moses Meïr Kamenker, **5**, 230.
Anabaptists, the, enthusiasm of, **4**, 470.
Anahita (Anaitis), Persian goddess of love, **1**, 408.
Anakim, the aboriginal inhabitants of Canaan, **1**, 2.
Anan (Seth), a family of high priests, **2**, 237.
Anan, governor of the Temple, envoy to Rome, **2**, 244.
Anan (Ananias, son of Eleazar?) of the family of Anan, high priest under Agrippa II, **2**, 236

Anan (*continued*), favors Sadducæism, **2**, 248, 271.
dismissed, **2**, 248–9.
house of, burnt, **2**, 260.
important post of, **2**, 271.
supports the charges against Josephus, **2**, 281.
incites a civil war, **2**, 295.
party of, overpowered, **2**, 295–6.
executed, **2**, 296.
Anan, of the family of Seth, high priest, **2**, 135.
Anan ben David, aspirant to the Exilarchate, **3**, 128.
opponents and adherents of, **3**, 129.
imprisoned, **3**, 129.
permitted to emigrate, **3**, 130.
opposes the Talmud, **3**, 130; **5**, 727.
works of, **3**, 131.
uses Mishnic rules of interpretation, **3**, 131.
abolishes the fixed calendar, **3**, 131.
rigor of, **3**, 132–3.
exegesis by, **3**, 133.
accepts Jesus and Mahomet, **3**, 133–4.
excommunicated, **3**, 134.
the Exilarch of the Karaites, **3**, 135.
memorial service for, **3**, 135.
mediocrity of, **3**, 135.
son of, his successor, **3**, 136.
characterized by Saadiah, **3**, 189.
descendants of, **3**, 444.
Anan ben Jonathan, advises the surrender of Jerusalem, **2**, 265.
Ananel, high priest, appointed by Herod, **2**, 90.
deposed, **2**, 91.
re-appointed, **2**, 92.
Ananel (*continued*), successor to, **2**, 107.
Ananel di Foligno, apostate, denounces the Talmud, **4**, 564.
Anania, merchant, converts Izates of Adiabene, **2**, 216.
Anania, physician to Izates of Adiabene, **2**, 217.
Ananias, high priest. *See* Anan of the family of Anan.
Ananias, son of Onias IV, Egyptian general, sides with Cleopatra, **2**, 10, 12.
prevents an invasion of Judæa, **2**, 41.
Ananites, the, appeal to the caliph, **3**, 129.
exiles, **3**, 134.
differ with their founder on various points, **3**, 136.
See Karaites, the.
Anastasius, the Sinaite, Patriarch at Antioch, killed by the Jews, **3**, 18.
Anathoth, birthplace of Jeremiah, **1**, 289, 290.
Anatoli, Jacob. *See* Jacob ben Abba Mari ben Simon Anatoli.
Anavim, the (the Gentle), disciples of Isaiah, **1**, 254.
and Hezekiah, **1**, 267.
sufferings of, under Manasseh, **1**, 283–4.
spread the doctrines of God, **1**, 286.
nucleus of a nationalistic party in Babylonia, **1**, 337–8.
Anbar. *See* Firuz-Shabur.
Ancona, Marranos permitted to settle in, **4**, 408, 500.
Solomon Molcho at, **4**, 501.
Marranos well treated in, **4**, 525, 526.
refuge of the Neapolitan Jews, **4**, 544.

Ancona (*continued*), trade of, diverted to Pesaro, **4**, 579, 580.
Jews of, try to regain their trade, **4**, 579.
Jews permitted to remain in, on their expulsion from the Papal States, **4**, 591, 659.
Ancona, the Marranos of, protected by three popes, **4**, 568.
persecuted by Paul IV, **4**, 568–9.
tried by the Inquisition, **4**, 570–1.
Andalusia, broken up into small kingdoms, **3**, 255.
Berbers and Arabs at war in, **3**, 316.
conquered by the Almohades, **3**, 360.
Jews driven from, **3**, 384.
invaded by the Almohades, **3**, 506–7.
taxation of the Jews of, **3**, 617.
the Marranos of, taught by Jews, **4**, 334–5.
expulsion of the Jews from, proposed, **4**, 336.
See also under Spain; Spain, Visigothic.
Andalusian school, the, of Jewish poetry, **3**, 223–4.
Andrade, Abraham, rabbi, deputy to the Assembly of Jewish Notables, **5**, 484, 490.
Andreas, of Hungary, excommunicated for employing Jews, **3**, 521.
Andreas Beltran, Marrano, denounces the Talmud, **4**, 213.
Andreias (Lucuas), leader of the Jews of Cyrene, **2**, 395.
Andrew, disciple of Jesus, **3**, 153.
Andro, Joseph Nassi duke of, **4**, 596.
Andromachos, governor of Cœlesyria, killed by the Samaritans, **1**, 414.
Andronicus, lieutenant of Antiochus Epiphanes, murders Onias III, **1**, 448.
Andronicus, son of Messalam, Judæan champion, **1**, 516.
Angels, imported into Judaism, **1**, 403.
Angiel, one of the Sefiroth, **4**, 17.
"Anglo-Jewish Association," the, founders and work of, **5**, 703.
Angoulême, the Jews of, maltreated, **3**, 570.
Angro-Mainyus, Persian god of darkness, and Judaism, **1**, 402.
transformed into Satan, **1**, 403.
Anilaï (Chanilai), robber chieftain, **2**, 202.
Anjou, rabbis from, at the first rabbinical synod, **3**, 377.
Anjou, the Jews of, observe a fast, **3**, 380.
under Henry II, **3**, 409.
maltreated, **3**, 570.
Anna, wife of Joceus of York, death of, **3**, 415.
"Annals of Persecution, The," by Joseph Cohen, **4**, 590.
"Annals of the Kings of France and of the house of Othman, The," by Joseph Cohen, **4**, 556.
Ano, wife of Jeroboam I, **1**, 184.
Ansar, allies of Mahomet, **3**, 73.
Anteri, Jacob, rabbi of Damascus, charged with ritual murder, **5**, 638.
translates Talmud passages, **5**, 640.
Anthropomorphists, literalist expounders of the Koran, **3**, 148.

Anthropomorphists (*continued*), among the Jews, **3**, 152.
Antigonus, Macedonian general, and Ptolemy I, **1**, 417.
Antigonus of Soho, disciple of Simon the Just, saying of, **1**, 422.
Antigonus, son of Aristobulus II, graces Pompey's triumph, **2**, 67.
escapes from Rome, **2**, 72.
second captivity of, **2**, 73.
protected by Ptolemy of Chalcis, **2**, 75.
seeks the aid of Cæsar, **2**, 75–6.
plots against Herod, **2**, 80–1.
king of Judæa, **2**, 82–3.
has coins struck, **2**, 83.
character of, **2**, 85.
dissension between, and the Synhedrists, **2**, 85–6.
declared an enemy of Rome, **2**, 86.
beheaded, **2**, 89.
sister of, **2**, 94.
Antigonus, son of John Hyrcanus, besieges Samaria, **2**, 10.
alleged murder of, **2**, 36–7.
campaign of, against the Ituræans and Trachonites, **2**, 37.
death of, **2**, 38.
Anti-Maimunists, the, opponents of Moses ben Maimun, **3**, 523–4.
led by Solomon ben Abraham, **3**, 527.
excommunicated by the Jews of Aragon, **3**, 537.
invite the Dominicans into the controversy, **3**, 542–3.
subdued by the burning of the Talmud, **3**, 579–80.
of Palestine, excommunicated, **3**, 632–3.
See also under Maimunist controversy, the; Maimunists, the.
Anti-Maimunists, list of:
Daniel ben Saadiah,
David ben Saul,
Jehuda bar Joseph Ibn-Alfachar,
Jonah ben Abraham Gerundi (the Elder),
Meïr ben Todros Halevi Abulafia,
Moses ben Chasdaï Taku,
Moses ben Nachman,
Samson ben Abraham,
Solomon ben Abraham,
Solomon Petit,
Tossafists, the, of northern France, **3**, 529.
Antioch, Judæans settle in, **1**, 419.
gladiatorial combats introduced in, **1**, 444.
partly destroyed by Judæans, **1**, 497.
Verus Commodus at, **2**, 47.
number of Judæans in, **2**, 201–2.
Nazarenes in, **2**, 222–3.
Judæan Christians of, **2**, 231.
the Judæans of, protected by Titus, **2**, 313.
residence of Niger, **2**, 463.
Antioch, the Jews of, interest Christians in Judaism, **2**, 613–14.
dispossessed of their synagogues, **2**, 621–2.
murdered by the green faction, **3**, 10–11.
massacre the Christians, **3**, 18.
subdued, **3**, 18.
in the twelfth century, **3**, 426.
Antiochus, of Commagene, favorite of Caligula, **2**, 189.
allied with Agrippa I, **2**, 195.
son of, **2**, 195, 235.
Antiochus III, the Great, of Syria, defeated at Raphia, **1**, 425–6.
takes Egypt, **1**, 432.
enters Jerusalem, **1**, 432.
besieges the Acra, **1**, 433.
repairs the Temple, **1**, 433.

Antiochus III (*continued*), defeated by the Romans, **1**, 434.
death of, **1**, 434.
Antiochus IV Epiphanes, of Syria, hostage at Rome, **1**, 434, 442–3.
characterization of, **1**, 442–3.
accession of, described in Daniel, **1**, 443–4.
introduces gladiatorial combats into Syria, **1**, 444.
petitioned to admit Judæan athletes to citizenship, **1**, 444–5.
makes Menelaus high priest, **1**, 447.
summons Menelaus to justify himself, **1**, 448.
punishes Onias III's murder, **1**, 448.
exonerates Menelaus, **1**, 449.
war of, with Egypt, **1**, 450–1.
desecrates the Temple, **1**, 451, 455.
calumniates Judaism, **1**, 452–3.
treats the Judæans cruelly, **1**, 453–4.
orders the worship of the Greek gods in Jerusalem, **1**, 454–5.
sacrifices ordered on the birthday of, **1**, 456.
dependencies of, revolt, **1**, 463.
determines to exterminate the Judæans, **1**, 463–4.
son of, entrusted to Lysias, **1**, 463.
in the East, **1**, 466.
death of, **1**, 477.
appoints a regent, **1**, 477.
persecutes the Samaritans, **1**, 516.
Antiochus V Eupator, of Syria, accession of, **1**, 477.
appealed to by the Hellenists, **1**, 478.
Antiochus V Eupator (*continued*), treaty of, with the Judæans, **1**, 480, 488.
makes Judas Maccabæus high priest, **1**, 481.
Rome displeased with, **1**, 482.
Antiochus VI, of Syria, on the throne, **1**, 497–8.
cause of, espoused by the Hasmonæans, **1**, 498, 499.
Antiochus VII Sidetes, of Syria, assisted by Simon Tharsi, **1**, 525.
permits Simon to strike coins, **1**, 525, 528.
hostile to Simon, **1**, 528–9.
investigates Simon's assassination, **1**, 530.
abandons the assassin, **1**, 531.
besieges John Hyrcanus, **2**, 3–4.
grants a truce, **2**, 4.
counselors of, advise the suppression of Judaism, **2**, 4.
yields up Judæan fortresses, **2**, 4–5.
seeks the alliance of John Hyrcanus, **2**, 5.
death of, **2**, 5.
Antiochus VIII Grypus, of Syria, succession of, opposed, **2**, 6.
poisons his mother, **2**, 6.
harasses the Idumæans of Samaria, **2**, 9.
Antiochus IX Cyzicenus, of Syria, hostile to John Hyrcanus, **2**, 9.
forbidden by Rome to molest the Judæans, **2**, 9.
aids Samaria, **2**, 10.
defeated by the sons of John Hyrcanus, **2**, 10.
allied with Ptolemy VIII, **2**, 10.
Antiparo, Joseph Nassi duke of, **4**, 596.

Antipas I. *See* Herod Antipas, son of Malthace and Herod I.
Antipas, of the Herodian family, wickedness of, **2**, 236.
Antipas, treasurer of the Synhedrion, suspected of Roman proclivities, **2**, 294.
Antipater, the Idumæan, counselor of Hyrcanus II, **2**, 59.
intrigues against Aristobulus II, **2**, 59.
bribes Scaurus, **2**, 62.
envoy to Pompey, **2**, 63.
governor of Judæa, **2**, 66–7.
supports Rome, **2**, 70.
causes the death sentence of Pitholaus, **2**, 75.
offers his services to Cæsar, **2**, 75.
tries to coerce the Judæans into loyalty to Cæsar, **2**, 77.
wife and sons of, **2**, 77.
warns Herod, **2**, 78.
urges mild measures upon Herod, **2**, 79.
poisoned, **2**, 80.
Antipater, son of Herod I, conspires against the sons of Mariamne, **2**, 112–13.
conspires against Herod, **2**, 113.
convicted of attempted parricide, **2**, 114.
executed, **2**, 116.
Antipater, son of Jason, envoy to Rome, **1**, 526.
"**Anti-Phædon**," by John Balthasar Kölbele, **5**, 316.
Anti-Semitism, prevalence of, **5**, 704.
Antitaktes, an extreme sect of Jewish Christians, **2**, 370.
Anti-Talmudists. *See* Frankists.
Anti-Trinitarians, a Christian sect of the Reformation period, **4**, 541.
in Poland, **4**, 647.
Anton, Charles (Moses Gerson Cohen), apostate, descent and history of, **5**, 267.
writes a panegyric on Eibeschütz, **5**, 267.
denies the existence of Sabbatians, **5**, 271.
Antonia, daughter of the triumvir, ward of Alexander Lysimachus, **2**, 176.
Antonia, sister-in-law of Tiberius, advocate of the Judæans, **2**, 172.
patroness of Agrippa I, **2**, 176.
Antonia, fortress of the Temple, named for Mark Antony, **2**, 106.
communicates with the Temple, **2**, 109, 111.
vestments of the high priests kept in, **2**, 129.
pontifical robes removed from, **2**, 172.
strengthened by Agrippa I, **2**, 195.
invested by Cumanus, **2**, 242.
first wall of, taken by Titus, **2**, 305.
See also Acra, the.
Antoninus, a Jew recommended by Pope Gelasius, **3**, 29.
Antoninus, name of Alexander Severus in Jewish sources, **2**, 482.
Antoninus Pius, emperor, clemency of, **2**, 432.
revokes Hadrian's decrees, **2**, 433.
revolution in Judæa under, **2**, 447.
death of, **2**, 447.
Antony, Mark, member of the second triumvirate, favors Herod, **2**, 81, 87.
beheads Antigonus, **2**, 89.
interested in Aristobulus (III), **2**, 91, 93.

Antony, Mark (*continued*), fall of, **2**, 96.
Antwerp, Amatus Lusitanus at, **4**, 569.
the Jews of, expelled, **4**, 662.
Anusim, forced converts, **4**, 179.
See Marranos, the.
Anzarbi, Arabic medical authority, taught by Jews, **3**, 146.
Apamea, treasure house in, for the Temple contributions, **2**, 53.
Apelles, of Ascalon, favorite of Caligula, **2**, 187.
Apelles, Syrian overseer, resisted by the Maccabees, **1**, 459.
Aphek, battle of, between Israelites and Philistines, **1**, 70.
Apherema, taken by the Samaritans, **1**, 410.
Aphrodite, worshiped by the Persians, **1**, 108.
Apion, Greek writer, misrepresents Judaism, **2**, 180–1.
envoy to Caligula, **2**, 186.
contrasted with Philo, **2**, 187.
charges of, refuted by Josephus, **2**, 390.
Josephus' work against, translated, **4**, 608.
Apis, black bull, worshiped by the Egyptians, **1**, 9.
Apocalypse, the Christian, by John, **2**, 369.
Apocrypha, the, rejected from the Canon, **2**, 344.
translated into Greek, **2**, 359.
considered part of the Canon by Christians, **2**, 359, 488.
canonized by the Council of Nice, **2**, 624.
Apollo, Onias III takes refuge in the temple of, at Daphne, **1**, 448.
Apollonius, ambassador to Rome, **2**, 4–5.
Apollonius, commander of Cœlesyria, confiscates the Temple treasures, **1**, 438.
Apollonius, Syrian general, in the war with Jonathan Haphus, **1**, 496.
Apollonius, Syrian general, takes Jerusalem, **1**, 453–4.
defeated by Judas Maccabæus, **1**, 462.
Apollonius Malo, Greek writer, maligns Judaism, **2**, 178–9.
Apollonius Molo, Greek writer, hostile to the Judæans, **2**, 68.
Apollos, of Alexandria, Christian teacher, **2**, 231.
"**Apology** for the Honorable Nation of the Jews," by Edward Nicholas, **5**, 28–9.
Apostasy to Christianity among Jews after the destruction of Jerusalem, **2**, 322.
in the early Christian centuries, **2**, 377.
under Constantine, **2**, 562–3.
in Hamburg, **4**, 687, 690.
in Vienna, **4**, 706.
among the Chassidim, **5**, 213.
among the Frankists, **5**, 287.
among the Jews of Germany, **5**, 420.
in Berlin, **5**, 587.
See also under Conversions to Christianity; Marranos, the.
Apostasy to Islam among Jews in the East in the twelfth century, **3**, 441–2.
among Sabbatians, **5**, 153–4, 211.
among Chassidim, **5**, 213.
See also under Conversions to Islam.
Apostasy to paganism among Jews in Alexandria, **2**, 184.

Apostate, an, the disappearance of, causes annoyance to the Jews of Paris, **4,** 175.
in Breslau, charges the Jews with host desecration, **4,** 261.
Apostates, account of, by Philo, **2,** 184.
in Alexandria, **2,** 209.
act as spies upon the Jews under Hadrian, **2,** 425.
Constantine protects the Jews against, **2,** 564.
excommunicated by the later Patriarchs, **2,** 612–13.
decisions concerning, by Natronaï ben Nehemiah, **3,** 122.
repentant, kindly received by Gershom ben Jehuda, **3,** 264.
permitted by Emperor Henry IV to return to Judaism, **3,** 306.
returning, unkindly treated by the Jews, **3,** 308–9.
forbidden to retain Jewish customs, **3,** 510.
house for, in England, **3,** 644.
validity of the evidence of, **4,** 36–7.
force the Jews to attend church, **4,** 132.
inform against Marranos, **4,** 180.
in Spanish satiric literature, **4,** 181.
favored by the Council of Basle, **4,** 246.
employed as censors, **4,** 566, 659.
annoy the Jews of the Papal States, **4,** 581, 584.
refrain from defending the German Jews, **5,** 533.
Heine on, **5,** 548–9, 551–2.
assert the falsity of the blood accusation, **5,** 650.
See also under Apostasy; Conversions; Marranos, the.

Apostates, list of:

Abraham Senior, the family of
Abulafia, Moses
Adamantius,
Alexander,
Alfonso Burgensis,
Ananel di Foligno,
Anton, Charles
Asher of Udine,
Astruc Raimuch,
Astruc Sibili,
Baptista, John
Bonafoux, Daniel Israel
Börne, Ludwig
Chananya, nephew of Joshua,
Chayon, Nehemiah, son of
Cohen, Nehemiah
Diego de Valencia,
Donin (Nicholas),
Drusilla,
Du Vallié, Paul
Eliano, Victor
Ferrus, Pero
Frank, Jacob
Friedländer, David, the family of
Gans, Edward
Gershom ben Jehuda, son of
Gerson, Christian
Guidon,
Heine, Heinrich
Herz, Henrietta
Isaac of Mayence,
Isaac Ibn-Ezra,
John of Valladolid,
Joseph.
Joseph de Vesoul,
Joshua ben Joseph Ibn-Vives,
Juan de España,
Kahtz, Christian
Karben, Victor von
Levi ben Shem Tob,
Levi, Wolf
Levin, Rachel
Machault, Denys
Margalita, Aaron
Margaritha, Anton
Mendelssohn, Dorothea
Mendelssohn, Henrietta
Moro, Joseph
Nathaniel (Hibat-Allah),
Neander, Augustus
Nunes, Henrique
Pablo Christiani,
Paul, apostle,
Pedro de la Caballeria,
Pessach-Peter,
Pfefferkorn, Joseph
Riccio, Paul
Sabbataï Zevi,
Samuel Ibn-Abbas,
Samuel Abrabanel (Juan de Seville),
Schwarz, Peter
Sixtus Senensis,
Solomon Levi of Burgos (Paul de Santa Maria),
Tiberius Julius Alexander,
Uriah of Mayence,
Vayol, Hans
Wenzel, Francis
Wolfkan of Ratisbon.

Apostles, the twelve, trusted disciples of Jesus, **2,** 158.
sent out by the early Christians, **2,** 220.
Apostole, mission tax, collected by the Patriarchs, **2,** 487.

Apostoli, messengers of the Synhedrion, **2,** 535.
Appian, historian, persecuted by Jewish rebels, **2,** 396.
Apries (Hophra), of Egypt, at war with Nebuchadnezzar, **1,** 312.
defeated, **1,** 313.
ally of Judah, **1,** 318.
receives Judæans kindly, **1,** 324.
dethroned, **1,** 327.
Apulia, the Jews of, liable to curial duties, **2,** 616.
invaded by the Mahometans, **3,** 212.
Jews from, form a congregation in Constantinople, **4,** 402.
Aquet, suspected of well poisoning, **4,** 104.
Aquila. *See* Akylas.
Aquinas, Thomas, works of, translated, **4,** 69.
studied by Solomon Levi, **4,** 183.
Aquitania, rabbis from, at the first rabbinical synod, **3,** 377.
gathering place of crusaders, **3,** 570.
Arabarch. *See* Alabarch, the.
Arabia, trade with, under Uzziah, **1,** 230.
(Auranitis) Paul flees to, **2,** 226.
Jewish fugitives flee to, **2,** 317, 319, 419.
Jews settle in, **2,** 629; **3,** 54–5.
Babylonian Jews emigrate to, **3,** 4.
position of Jews in, in the sixth century, **3,** 53.
See also Auranitis.
Arabia, the Jews of, similarity of, to the Arabs, **3,** 56.
alienate Mahomet's followers, **3,** 74–5.
Arabia, the Jews of (*continued*), rejoice at Mahomet's death, **3,** 84.
possess good taste, **3,** 111.
find the authority of the Talmud irksome, **3,** 119–20.
in the twelfth century, **3,** 436–7.
Arabia, northern (Hejas), inhabitants of, descended from Ishmael, **3,** 60, 61.
Arabia, northern (Hejas), the Jews of, 3, 54–6.
lead a Bedouin life, **3,** 57.
distinguish themselves in poetry, **3,** 57–8.
intelligence of, **3,** 58.
religious affairs among, **3,** 58–9.
relation of, to the Arabs, **3,** 60–1.
history of, **3,** 67–71.
dispossessed by Mahomet, **3,** 76–83.
in the twelfth century, **3,** 436–7.
Arabia, southern, inhabitants of, descended from Yoktan, **3,** 60.
called Kachtanites, **3,** 61.
See also Himyarites, the; Yemen.
Arabia, southern, the Jews of, 3, 56.
the Jews of, trade with India, **3,** 57.
a Jewish kingdom in, **3,** 62–7. *See under* Yemen.
Arabia Felix, southern Arabia, **3,** 56.
Arabic, spoken by Jews of Mahometan countries, **3,** 110–11.
used by the Gaon of Sora officially, **3,** 178.
translation of the Bible into, **3,** 189–90.

Arabic (*continued*), used in Sherira's responses, **3**, 232.
spoken by the Jews of Andalusia, **3**, 235.
the Mishna translated into, **3**, 237.
spoken by Italian Jews in the twelfth century, **3**, 423.
translations from, made by Jews, **3**, 593.
taught as a means of conversion, **3**, 597; **4**, 245.
forgotten by the Spanish Jews, **4**, 60.

Arabic poetry influences neo-Hebraic poetry, **3**, 116, 224.

Arabs, the, love the Scriptures, **3**, 59.
adopt the Jewish calendar, **3**, 59–60.
relation of, to the Jews, **3**, 60.
supremacy of, **3**, 86–7.
helped by the Jews and Samaritans, **3**, 87.
enthusiasm of, for their language, **3**, 110–111.
obtain access to scientific literature through Jews, **3**, 111.
influence the revival of Hebrew, **3**, 111.
at war with the Chazars, **3**, 138.
defeated by the Chazars, **3**, 139.
unkindly treated by the Spanish Berbers, **3**, 261.
See also under Mahometans, the; Nabathæans, the.

Arach, the family of, intermarries with the Ammonites, **1**, 362.

Aradus, built by the Canaanites, **1**, 3.
refuses obedience to Antiochus IV, **1**, 463.

Aragon, Jews in, in the twelfth century, **3**, 384.
ally of Castile against the Almohades, **3**, 387.
forced converts in, relapse into Judaism, **4**, 180.
Ferdinand of Castile becomes king of, **4**, 205, 206.
the Inquisition established in, **4**, 319.
opposed to the Inquisition, **4**, 319, 328.
privileges of, canceled, **4**, 326.
inquisitors appointed for, **4**, 326.
exiles from, form a congregation in Constantinople, **4**, 402.

Aragon, the Jews of, under Alfonso II, **3**, 387–8.
under Pedro II, **3**, 497–8.
prevent anti-Jewish legislation, **3**, 508.
exempt from wearing the Jew badge, **3**, 514–15.
in the Maimunist controversy, **3**, 530, 536, 537.
letter to, denouncing Solomon of Montpellier, **3**, 544.
under Jayme I, **3**, 596–7.
regarded as "servi cameræ," **3**, 597.
debate with Pablo Christiani, **3**, 602.
persecuted in the fourteenth century, **4**, 77.
massacred on account of the Black Death, **4**, 102–3.
helped by the higher classes, **4**, 103.
under Pedro IV and Juan I, **4**, 145.
possess penal jurisdiction, **4**, 155.
persecuted in 1391, **4**, 170–1, 172.
converted, **4**, 206, 214.

Aragon, the Jews of (*continued*), at the disputation of Tortosa, **4**, 214.
under John II, **4**, 274, 275.
warned of approaching danger, **4**, 336.
proclamation expelling, **4**, 347–8.
possessions of, sequestrated, **4**, 350.
Aragon, the Marranos of, 4, 309.
try to suppress the Inquisition, **4**, 329.
Aram, home of Abraham, **1**, 4. *See* Syria.
Arama, Isaac. *See* Isaac Arama.
Aramæans, the, help the Ammonites against David, **1**, 126–7.
See under Damascus, the kingdom of; Syria.
Aramaic, learnt by the Judæans in Babylon, **1**, 330–1.
spoken by the Judæans in Hasmonæan times, **2**, 14, 15.
spoken in Galilee, **2**, 149.
words in the Mishna, **2**, 461.
Aranda, Counts de, try to suppress the Aragon Inquisition, **4**, 329.
Aranda, de, Marrano bishop, burnt by Torquemada, **4**, 333.
Arari, David, accused of ritual murder, **5**, 636, 638.
persecuted, **5**, 636–7.
Araunah. *See* Ornah.
Arbachshter. *See* Ardashir.
Arbues, Pedro, de Epila, inquisitor in Aragon, **4**, 326.
plot against, by the Marranos, **4**, 329.
killed in church, **4**, 330.
honor paid to the memory of, **4**, 330–1.
Marranos concerned in the murder of, sheltered in Navarre, **4**, 357.
Arcadius (395–408), emperor of the East, insignificance of, **2**, 615.
the Jews under, **2**, 616.
Archelaus, of Cappadocia, daughter of, **2**, 112, 128.
Archelaus (Herod II), son of Herod I, sovereign of Judæa and Samaria, **2**, 119.
promises to abolish unjust laws, **2**, 120–1.
attacks those offering the Passover sacrifices, **2**, 121.
forbids the celebration of Passover, **2**, 122.
puts Jerusalem under Quintilius Varus, **2**, 122–3.
ethnarch of Judæa, **2**, 127.
deposes the high priest Joasar, **2**, 127.
war of, against Athronges, **2**, 128.
marries Glaphyra, **2**, 128.
exiled by Augustus, **2**, 128.
property of, confiscated by Augustus, **2**, 129.
Archelaus, Julius, brother-in-law of Agrippa II, **2**, 235.
Archipelago, the, Cardoso in, **5**, 207.
Archisynagogus, title of the rabbi of Speyer, **3**, 297.
Architecture, under Herod, **2**, 106–7, 118.
Ardashir (Arbachshter), establishes the dynasty of the Sassanides, **2**, 513, 523.
restores the Zoroastrian doctrine, **2**, 524.
Ardashir, populated with Jews, **2**, 507. *See also* Ctesiphon.
Ardebil, Armenian fortress, taken by the Chazars, **3**, 139.
"Are philosophical truths susceptible of mathematical demonstration?" prize essay by Mendelssohn, **5**, 303–4.

" **Are there means** to make the Jews happier and more useful in France?" prize question of a Metz society, **5**, 434–5.
Areobindus, minister of Justinian I, **3**, 15.
Aretas, Nabathæan king, and the high priest Jason, **1**, 447, 481.
Aretas, Nabathæan king, overthrown, **2**, 45.
Aretas, Nabathæan king, helps Hyrcanus II, **2**, 59.
besieges Aristobulus II, **2**, 60.
raises the siege of Jerusalem, **2**, 62.
defeated by Aristobulus II, **2**, 62.
attacked by Scaurus, **2**, 70.
Aretas, Nabathæan king, aids Quintilius Varus, **2**, 126.
Aretas, Nabathæan king, at war with Herod Antipas, **2**, 173.
Aretas Philodemus, Nabathæan king, creates the office of Judæan ethnarch, **2**, 202.
Argent, d', marquis, friend of Mendelssohn, **5**, 304.
Argentière, the Jews of, oppose the study of science, **4**, 33.
Argob, fortress, besieged by Alexander Jannæus, **2**, 47.
Argun (1284–1291), khan of the Perso-Mongolian realm, employs Saad-Addaula as physician and financier, **3**, 638, 646.
distinguishes Saad-Addaula, **3**, 647.
enters into diplomatic connections with Europe, **3**, 647.
sickness and death of, **3**, 649.
Arianism, toleration of, under Valentinian I, **2**, 603; **3**, 44.
hostility to, by Ambrosius of Milan, **2**, 612.
Arianism (*continued*), less hostile to Jews than Catholicism, **3**, 26.
persecuted in Spain, **3**, 46.
Arias Montana, publishes a polyglot Bible, **4**, 651.
Arias, Jean, instigates a persecution, **4**, 279.
Arias, Joseph Szemach, translator of Josephus, **5**, 113.
uninfluenced by Spinoza, **5**, 117.
Arioch. *See* Samuel.
Aristides, Church teacher, demonstrates the independence of Christianity, **2**, 431.
Aristobulus (Judah) I, son of John Hyrcanus, defeats Antiochus IX, **2**, 10.
removes his mother from the regency, **2**, 35.
first Hasmonæan to assume a royal title, **2**, 35.
coins of, **2**, 35.
dissensions under, **2**, 36.
imprisons his mother and brothers, **2**, 36.
hostile to the Pharisees, **2**, 36.
accused of matricide and fratricide, **2**, 36–7, 38.
campaign of, against the Ituræans and Trachonites, **2**, 37.
death of, **2**, 37–8.
Aristobulus II, son of Alexander Jannæus, **2**, 47.
protects the Sadducees, **2**, 55.
conspires against Hyrcanus, **2**, 56.
character of, **2**, 58.
made king, **2**, 58.
besieged, **2**, 60.
bribes Scaurus, **2**, 62.
defeats Aretas, **2**, 62.
has coins struck, **2**, 62.
bribes Pompey, **2**, 62–3.

Aristobulus II (*continued*), summoned to Damascus by Pompey, 2, 63.
at war with Pompey, 2, 64–7.
in Pompey's triumph, 2, 67.
escapes from Rome, 2, 72.
garrisons Alexandrion, 2, 73.
surrenders Machærus, 2, 73.
second captivity of, at Rome, 2, 73.
freed by Cæsar, 2, 75.
poisoned, 2, 75.
wife and daughters of, in Chalcis, 2, 75.
Aristobulus (III), brother of Mariamne, high priest, 2, 91.
popularity of, 2, 92.
murdered, 2, 92.
Aristobulus, brother of Agrippa I, supplants him, 2, 175.
opposes Caligula, 2, 188.
wife of, 2, 195.
begs for a truce, 2, 197.
Aristobulus, son of Mariamne, designated successor to Herod, 2, 112.
marriage of, 2, 112.
executed, 2, 113.
Aristotle, the Ten Categories of, compared with the Ten Commandments, 3, 197.
sayings of, used by Ibn-Gebirol, 3, 267.
system of, as presented by Jehuda Halevi, 3, 328.
dominance of, in the twelfth century, 3, 331.
works of, translated into Hebrew, 3, 398.
popular among Jews, 3, 448–9.
philosophy of, interpreted by Ibn-Sina, 3, 478.
theories of, in Jewish writings, 3, 479.
denounced by Nachmani, 3, 534.
Aristotle (*continued*), works of, translated into Latin, 3, 566–7.
in Immanuel Romi's work, 4, 66.
opposed by Gersonides, 4, 93.
authority of, questioned by Chasdaï Crescas, 4, 146.
Ethics of, translated, 4, 193.
quoted by Jewish preachers, 4, 232.
writings of, expounded by Judah ben Yechiel, 4, 289.
system of, expounded by Elias del Medigo, 4, 290.
studied by Polish Jews, 4, 633.
Ark of the Covenant, the, 1, 23, 41.
taken by the Philistines, 1, 70–2.
made by Achitub, 1, 79.
removed to Jerusalem, 1, 119–120.
transferred to the Temple, 1, 166.
Arles (city), Jews participate in battles before, 3, 36.
Jews remain in, after their banishment from France by Charles VI, 4, 177.
Arles (district), first Jewish settlement of Gaul in, 3, 35.
Arles, kingdom of, demanded by Albrecht I, 4, 47.
Armada, the, collapse of, 4, 663.
Armenia, the Jews of, taken by Shabur II, 2, 591.
invaded by the Chazars, 3, 138.
visited by Petachya, 3, 421.
Armenians (Tartars?), converted to Judaism, 3, 439–40.
Armentarius, name borne by Gallic Jews, 3, 36.
Armleder (Leather-arms) persecutions, the, of the German Jews, 4, 97–8.
Arnheim, adviser of the duke of Alva, 4, 662.

Arnim, representative of the romantic school, **5**, 515.
Arnold, cardinal bishop of Cologne, protects the Jews, **3**, 352.
Arnold of Brescia, denounces the popes, **3**, 370.
Arnold of Citeaux, organizes the crusade against the Albigenses, **3**, 502.
organizes a crusade against the Spanish Mahometans, **3**, 507.
instigates an attack upon the Toledo Jews, **3**, 507.
Arnoldists, the, party opposed to Reuchlin, **4**, 456.
Arnstadt, the Jews of, persecuted, **3**, 611.
Arnstein, Nathan Adam von, wife of, **5**, 414.
Ar-Rabbi Mor (Arraby Moor), title of the chief rabbi of Portugal, **3**, 618; **4**, 158–9, 380.
duties, assistants, and jurisdiction of, **4**, 159.
Arsaces, the dynasty of, fall of, **2**, 513, 523.
Arsaces, satrap of Parthia, revolts from Antiochus IV, **1**, 463.
Arsenios, Samaritan favorite of Empress Theodora, **3**, 17.
Arta (Larta), the Jews of, in the twelfth century, **3**, 424.
Spanish exiles in, **4**, 406.
the Jews of, split up into national groups, **4**, 478.
Artaban, fined for using Mezuzzoth, **2**, 424.
Artabanus, of Parthia, invites Izates to act as arbitrator, **2**, 217.
Artabanus IV (211–226), of Parthia, and Abba-Areka, **2**, 513.
overthrown, **2**, 523.
Artaxerxes I Longimanus, of Persia, assists Ezra, **1**, 366.
influenced by Judæan favorites, **1**, 371.
makes Nehemiah governor of Judæa, **1**, 373.
Artaxerxes II Memnon, of Persia, Egypt rebels against, **1**, 407.
banishes Judæans, **1**, 408.
killed, **1**, 409.
Artaxerxes III Ochus, of Persia, **1**, 407.
Artaxias, of Armenia, independent of Antiochus IV, **1**, 463.
Artemion, leader of a Jewish rebellion on Cyprus. **2**, 397.
Artemion, the school of, deface the Septuagint, **2**, 386.
Artisans, among the Alexandrian Judæans, **1**, 505.
among the teachers of the Law, **2**, 344, 348, 441, 442, 575.
See Handicrafts; Trades.
Aruch, Talmudic dictionary, by Mar-Zemach I ben Paltoi, **3**, 179.
by Nathan ben Yechiel, **3**, 290, 421.
See also Lexicon, Talmudical.
Arverna. *See* Auvergne.
Arzilla, Jews taken captive at, **4**, 286, 339.
Portuguese Marranos in, **4**, 381.
Asa, king of Judah, accession of, **1**, 189.
forbids the worship of Astarte, **1**, 190.
at war with Baasha, **1**, 190–1.
ally of Ben-hadad I, **1**, 191.
Asahel, Joab's brother, killed by Abner, **1**, 110.
Asaph, psalmist, **1**, 79, 120–1.
Asaphites, descendants of Asaph, **1**, 120.

Asara be-Tebeth. *See* Fast of Tebeth.
Ascalon (Askelon), Philistine port, **1**, 54.
left in the possession of the Philistines by David, **1**, 117.
Ascalona, the Jews of, exterminated, **4**, 170.
Ascarelli, Deborah, poetess, **5**, 68.
Ascarelli, Joseph, husband of the preceding, **5**, 68.
Ascension, the dogma of, attacked by Abbahu, **2**, 539–540.
Ascetics, among the Arabian Jews, **3**, 437.
Asclepiadotus, lawyer, opposes Belisarius, **3**, 32.
murdered, **3**, 32.
Ashdod (Azotus), Philistine port, **1**, 54.
the Ark of the Covenant at, **1**, 71.
left in the possession of the Philistines by David, **1**, 117.
conquered by Uzziah, **1**, 231.
destroyed, **1**, 496.
revenue from, left to Salome, **2**, 120.
Asher, the tribe of, acquires land in the north, **1**, 37.
relation of, to the Phœnicians, **1**, 53.
twenty towns of, given to Hiram, **1**, 164.
descendants of, around Nishabur, **3**, 433.
Asher, tribesmen of, join Gideon, **1**, 62.
join Solomon's fleet, **1**, 170.
Asher of Udine, apostate, charges Jews with blasphemy, **4**, 584.
Asher ben Jehuda, hero of Solomon Ibn-Sakbel's romance, **3**, 318.
Asher ben Meshullam, ascetic, **3**, 396–7.
Asher ben Yechiel (Asheri, 1250–1327), Tossafist, **4**, 34–5.
accepts the evidence of baptized Jews, **4**, 37.
settles in Toledo, **4**, 37.
opposed to the study of science, **4**, 37–8, 39, 50, 86–7.
opinion of, sought by Abba-Mari, **4**, 38.
influence of, on the Spanish Jews, **4**, 51.
as Talmudist, **4**, 51.
severity of, **4**, 53.
sons of, **4**, 87.
prefers Germany, **4**, 90, 96.
See also Asheri family, the.
Asher Lämmlein, poses as the forerunner of the Messiah, **4**, 482.
adherents of, **4**, 483.
Asher, Saul, deplores the decay of morality among the Jews, **5**, 419.
writes against Fichte, **5**, 463.
Asheri. *See* Asher ben Yechiel; Jacob ben Asheri; Jehuda ben Asher I; Jehuda ben Asher II.
Asheri family, the, loses members by the Black Death, **4**, 113.
members of, martyrs in 1391, **4**, 169–70.
See Asher ben Yechiel.
Ashi (352–457), principal of the Sora academy, wealth of, **2**, 605.
re-builds the academy of Sora, **2**, 606.
receives the title of Rabbana, **2**, 606.
authority of, **2**, 606.
makes Sora the center of Jewish life, **2**, 607.
collects the Talmud, **2**, 607–9.

Ashi (*continued*), completes the work of Judah I, **2**, 609.
decisions of, **2**, 609.
at the court of Jezdijird, **2**, 610.
suppresses the Messianic hope, **2**, 610–11.
death of, **2**, 611.
successors of, **2**, 626.
son of, **2**, 626.
Ashkabá, prayer for the departed at the Babylonian academies, **3**, 101.
Ashkenasi. *See* Saul Cohen Ashkenasi.
Ashkenazi. *See* Solomon ben Nathan.
Ashkenazi, Jacob, Talmudist and Sabbatian, **5**, 150.
Ashkenazi, Jacob Emden. *See* Emden, Jacob.
Ashkenazi, Zevi. *See* Zevi Ashkenazi.
Ashmodai, a demon introduced from Magianism, **1**, 403.
Ashmun, a Canaanite god, **1**, 54.
Ashura, name for the Atonement Day among the Arabian Jews, **3**, 58.
fast day instituted by Mahomet, **3**, 73.
Asia, the Jews of, esteem Mahometans, **3**, 88–9.
loses the leadership of Judaism, **3**, 207.
Karaites obtain influence in, **3**, 207.
low estate of Judaism in, **3**, 440.
Messianic hopes in, **4**, 497.
See also East, the; Abbasside Caliphate, the.
Asia Minor, conquered by Alexander the Great, **1**, 412.
votive offerings from, seized by Flaccus, **2**, 68–9.
Asia Minor (*continued*), women in, converted to Judaism, **2**, 215.
Greek-Christian communities in, **2**, 227.
study of the Law in, **2**, 358–9.
chief seat of the Pagan Christians, **2**, 367.
districts of, rebel against Hadrian, **2**, 399.
the Spanish exiles in, **4**, 405–6.
Asia Minor, the Jews of, celebrate two days of the new-moon, **2**, 363.
in the twelfth century, **3**, 426.
molested by Greek Catholics, **4**, 552–3.
Sabbatians, **5**, 137.
Asia Minor, the Judæans of, send contributions to the Temple, **2**, 52.
protected by Cæsar, **2**, 76.
have a synagogue at Jerusalem, **2**, 201.
make annual pilgrimages to Jerusalem, **2**, 220.
Asinaï (Chasinaï), robber chief near Nahardea, **2**, 202.
"**Asiré ha-Tikwah**," drama by Joseph Penso, **5**, 113.
Askaloni, Joseph, manager of Reyna Nassi's printing press, **4**, 628.
Askelon. *See* Ascalon.
Asma, poetess, satirizes Mahomet, **3**, 76.
Asochis. *See* Sichin.
Assad, teacher of the Law, converts the Yemenites to Judaism, **3**, 62–3.
Assassins, the, plot against Saad-Addaula, **3**, 648–9.
Assembly, the Great. *See* Great Assembly, the.
Asser, deputy to the Synhedrion, **5**, 497.

Asser, Carolus and Moses, members of the Felix Libertate, **5,** 452.
zealous in the emancipation struggle, **5,** 454.
Assi, Palestinian Amora, subordinates himself to the Babylonian authorities, **2,** 531, 537.
investigates the educational institutions of Judæa, **2,** 532.
investigates the observance of the Law in Samaria, **2,** 534.
appeals to Abbahu, **2,** 538.
meets Huna's corpse, **2,** 548.
disciples of, **2,** 560.
Assidæans, the. *See* Chassidim, the; Hasmonæans, the; Maccabees, the.
Assyria, doom of, predicted by Isaiah, **1,** 272–3.
invaded by the Scythians, **1,** 287.
power of, declines, **1,** 287, 296.
fall of, **1,** 303.
Assyrian customs introduced into Judah, **1,** 260–1.
characters used for the Scriptures, **1,** 395–6.
Assyrians, the, extend their territory, **1,** 246.
host of, destroyed at Lachish, **1,** 277.
defeat the Medes, **1,** 287.
Astarte, worship of, by the Canaanites, **1,** 54.
in Samuel's time, **1,** 75.
under Solomon, **1,** 175.
under Rehoboam, **1,** 189.
under Omri, **1,** 195.
under Jeroboam II, **1,** 233.
under Hezekiah, **1,** 269.
See also Idolatry.
Asti, French exiles settle in, **4,** 177.
Astorga, the Jews of, converted by Vincent Ferrer, **4,** 205.
Astronomers and mathematicians, Jewish, list of:
Abraham ben Chiya Albargeloni,
Abraham ben Meïr Ibn-Ezra,
Abraham Zacuto,
Bonet de Lates,
David Gans,
Isaac ben Baruch Albalia,
Isaac ben Joseph Israeli II,
Jacob ben Machir Tibbon,
Judah ben Moses Cohen,
Judah Ibn-Verga,
Levi ben Gerson,
Meïr Alguades,
Moses ben Israel Isserles,
Profiat Duran,
Sahal Rabban,
Samuel Ibn-Abbas,
Simon ben Zemach Duran,
Vecinho, Joseph
Zag Ibn-Said.
Astronomical knowledge, the, of the teachers of the Law, **2,** 336, 344–5, 349, 521.
Astronomy, studied in Portugal, **4,** 367–8.
studied by Polish Jews, **4,** 633.
Astruc En-Duran. *See* Abba-Mari ben Moses.
Astruc Levi, at the Tortosa disputation, **4,** 208.
ascribes no authority to the Agada, **4,** 214.
refuses to accept baptism, **4,** 215.
Astruc Raimuch (Francisco God-flesh, Dios-Carne), apostate, expounds Christian dogmas, **4,** 182.
Astruc Sibili, informs against the Palma Jews, **4,** 246.
imprisoned and baptized, **4,** 247.
Astruc, Aristides, founder of the "Alliance Israélite Universelle," **5,** 701.
Astyages, of Media, dethroned by Cyrus, **1,** 342.
Asverus, name of Alexander Severus in the Jewish sources, **2,** 482.
Atel. *See* Volga.

Athaliah, Ahab's daughter, marriage of, **1**, 206.
introduces idolatry into Judah, **1**, 209.
upholds Baal worship in Jerusalem, **1**, 212, 214.
executes members of the house of David, **1**, 213.
six years' rule of, **1**, 215.
murder of, **1**, 216.
Athenion, favorite of Ptolemy II, envoy to Jerusalem, **1**, 423.
and Joseph, son of Tobiah, **1**, 424, 425.
Athenion, general of Cleopatra, sent against Herod, **2**, 95.
Athens, gifts sent to, by Judæan kings, **2**, 193.
Judæans in, **2**, 203.
the Jews of, oppose Sabbataï Zevi, **5**, 124.
Athias, editor of the Ferrara Spanish Bible, **4**, 576.
Athias, Isaac, Chacham of Hamburg, **4**, 689.
Athronges, a shepherd, assumes the royal title, **2**, 125.
war of, with Archelaus, **2**, 128.
Atonement, Day of, forbidden to be observed, **2**, 572.
among the Arabs, **3**, 58.
liturgy of, **3**, 113–14.
a second, **4**, 626.
Atra, besieged by Trajan, **2**, 399.
Attalus, of Pergamus, proclaims Antiochus IV king of Syria, **1**, 443.
Attaman. *See* Hetman.
Atzbaha. *See* Elesbaa.
Aubriot, Hugues, prevôt of Paris, protects the Jews, **4**, 151.
Auerbach, Jacob, fair-preacher in Leipsic, **5**, 573.
Heine on, **5**, 577.
Auerstädt, defeat of, **5**, 495.
"**Augenspiegel**," the, Reuchlin's pamphlet against Pfefferkorn, **4**, 446–8.
excitement created by, **4**, 448.
adverse opinions of, **4**, 450.
charges against, **4**, 451.
burning of, ordered, **4**, 451–2.
cleared of the charge of heresy, **4**, 455.
declared heretical by the University of Paris, **4**, 460.
translation of, **4**, 460.
Augsburg, the Jews of, saved from the Rindfleisch persecution, **4**, 36.
perish during the Black Death persecutions, **4**, 110.
imprisoned, **4**, 163.
re-admission of, petitioned for, **4**, 127–8.
expelled, **4**, 249, 413.
August, of Brunswick, has Templo's work translated, **5**, 114–15.
Augustine, Church Father, hates the Jews, **2**, 625.
Augustus (Octavius), member of the second triumvirate, **2**, 81.
favors Herod, **2**, 86.
wins the battle of Actium, **2**, 96.
confirms Herod's royal dignity, **2**, 101–2.
favors the Egyptian Judæans, **2**, 102–3.
favors the Roman Judæans, **2**, 103.
increases Herod's territory, **2**, 103.
power of, over Herod, **2**, 105.
statue of, erected in Cæsarea, **2**, 106.
asked to ratify Antipater's death-sentence, **2**, 114.
condemns the execution of Herod's sons, **2**, 116.

Augustus (*continued*), excutor of Herod's will, **2,** 120.
appealed to by the Herodians, **2,** 122.
seizes Herod's treasures, **2,** 123.
makes Judæa an ethnarchy, **2,** 126–7.
exiles Archelaus, **2,** 128.
instructions of, to the governor of Syria, **2,** 129.
death of, **2,** 135.
Augustus III, of Poland, and the Frankists, **5,** 283.
Auranitis (Hauran, Havvoth Jair), the Gileadites take possession of, **1,** 64.
Paul flees to, **2,** 226.
given to Agrippa II, **2,** 245.
cavalry from, sent to Jerusalem, **2,** 259, 260.
See also Arabia.
Aurelian, emperor, conquers Zenobia, **2,** 530.
Aurum coronarium (crown money), tax imposed on Judæa, **2,** 463.
collected by the Patriarchs, **2,** 487, 535.
Austrasia, the Jews of, in the sixth century, **3,** 40.
Austria, Frederick the Valiant's Jewish statute confirmed for, **3,** 635.
Jews emigrate to, from Hungary, **4,** 111.
John of Capistrano in, **4,** 258.
Jewish exiles from, take refuge in Poland, **4,** 263, 420.
Polish Jewish fugitives in, **5,** 16
at war with Prussia, **5,** 251.
willing to grant citizenship to the Jews, **5,** 518.
protects the Frankfort Jews, **5,** 520.
Austria (*continued*), in the Quadruple Alliance, **5,** 658.
Jews concerned in the reorganization of, **5,** 697.
Jewish association in, **5,** 703.
Austria, the Jews of, fill offices, **3,** 516, 567.
protected by Frederick the Valiant's Jewish statute, **3,** 567–9.
suffer during the Rindfleisch persecution, **4,** 36.
suffer from the Deggenburg persecution, **4,** 98.
accused of well poisoning, **4,** 110.
suffer during the Hussite agitation, **4,** 222–4.
charged with host desecration, **4,** 223–4.
banished, **4,** 224, 427.
restrictions placed on, **4,** 585.
threatened with expulsion, **4,** 652.
condition of, improved by Joseph II, **5,** 357–8.
letter addressed to, by Wessely, **5,** 368.
continued abasement of, **5,** 461.
freed from the poll-tax, **5,** 464.
new taxes imposed on, **5,** 508.
under Francis I, **5,** 523.
influence of Mannheimer on, **5,** 579.
growing self-respect of, **5,** 582.
Austria, Lower, the Jews of, banished, **4,** 585.
Austrian Succession, the, War of, and the Jews of Prague, **5,** 251–2.
Autobiography of Josephus, **2,** 390.
of Uriel da Costa, **5,** 64–5.
of Solomon Maimon, **5,** 409.
Auto-da-fé, the first, of Marranos, **4,** 317.

Auto-da-fé (*continued*). *See also* Marranos, the; Inquisition, the.
Auvergne (Arverna), Jews in, in the sixth century, **3**, 35.
Auxerre, rabbi of, at the first rabbinical synod, **3**, 377.
Averroës (Ibn-Roshd), commentaries by, on Aristotle, translated, **3**, 566–7.
views of, opposed by Gersonides, **4**, 93.
admired by Narboni, **4**, 94.
quoted by Jewish preachers, **4**, 232.
system of, expounded by Elias del Medigo, **4**, 290.
Avesta, the, laws of clean and unclean in, **1**, 402.
Avicebrol (Avicebron), name of Solomon Ibn-Gebirol among the schoolmen, **3**, 271.
Avicenna. *See* Ibn-Sina.
Avigedor Kara, rabbi of Prague, on friendly terms with Emperor Wenceslaus, **4**, 166.
Avignon, the council of, forbids the employment of Jews in state offices, **3**, 503–4.
the papacy at, **4**, 162.
Jews remain in, after their banishment from France, **4**, 177, 659.
David Reubeni in, **4**, 499.
the Sabbatian movement in, **5**, 141.
Jews in, during the French Revolution, **5**, 436.
Avignon, the Jews of, oppose the study of science, **4**, 33.
tolerated by the popes, **4**, 177.
expelled, **4**, 592.
honor Crémieux and Montefiore, **5**, 658.
Avila, de, Marrano bishop, burnt by Torquemada, **4**, 333.
Avila, the Messiah of, **4**, 8–9, 9–10.
religious disputation at, **4**, 140–2.
Henry IV deposed at, **4**, 278.
law of, **4**, 229.
Avila, the Jews of, under Sancho, **3**, 617.
converted by Vincent Ferrer, **4**, 205.
Avitus, bishop, presides over the council of Epaone, **3**, 37.
forcibly converts the Jews of Clermont, **3**, 38–9.
celebrated in a poem, **3**, 39.
Avran, commander under Lysimachus the Benjamite, **1**, 449.
Ayllon, Solomon (1667–1728), Sabbatian, profligacy of, **5**, 210.
youth of, **5**, 214.
rabbi of London, **5**, 214.
rabbi of Amsterdam, **5**, 215.
on Chacham Zevi, **5**, 221.
mistrusted by the Portuguese community, **5**, 222.
supports Chayon's cause, **5**, 222–3.
refuses reconciliation with Chacham Zevi, **5**, 224.
acquits Chayon of heresy, **5**, 224–5.
Brieli writes to, **5**, 225.
summons Chacham Zevi before the Council, **5**, 226.
abandons Chayon, **5**, 231.
Azael, name of a Sefirah, **4**, 17.
Azariah. *See* Uzziah.
Azariah, general of Judas Maccabæus, **1**, 476.
Azariah, high priest, contest of, with Uzziah, **1**, 245.
Azariah ben Zadok, high priest under Solomon, **1**, 167.
Azarya ben Moses deï Rossi (1514–1578), attainments of, **4**, 614.

Azarya ben Moses deï Rossi (*continued*), connects the Talmud with other ancient writings, **4**, 614.
works by, **4**, 615.
as a critic, **4**, 615.
declared a heretic, **4**, 616.
Azeka, offers opposition to Nebuchadnezzar, **1**, 311.
"**Azharoth**," composed by Isaac ben Reuben Albergeloni, **3**, 284.
Aziz, of Emesa, husband of Drusilla, **2**, 235.
Azotus. *See* Ashdod.
Azriel, Kabbalist, reduces the Kabbala to a system, **3**, 548; **4**, 14.
history of, unknown, **3**, 548.
clothes the Kabbala in philosophical language, **3**, 549, 556.
Azzel Ibn-Samuel, one of the Benu-Kuraiza, **3**, 81.

B

Baal, altar to, in Samaria, **1**, 197.
priests of, assemble by order of Elijah, **1**, 203–4.
Baal, the worship of, among the Canaanites, **1**, 54.
by Ammonites and Moabites, **1**, 55.
at Ophrah, **1**, 62.
in Samuel's time, **1**, 75.
under Omri, **1**, 195.
under Athaliah, **1**, 212, 214.
removed from Jerusalem, **1**, 216–17.
under Jeroboam II, **1**, 233.
abolished by Menahem, **1**, 244.
See also Astarte; Idolatry.
Baal ha-Turim. *See* Jacob ben Asheri.
Baal-Peor. *See* Peor.
Baal-Perazim, mount, scene of a Philistine defeat, **1**, 116.
Baal-Shem. *See* Israel of Miedziboz.
Baal-Zebub, idol, consulted by Ahaziah, **1**, 207.
Baalbek, a Karaite center, **3**, 158.
captured by Hulagu, **3**, 606.
Baalis, king of Ammon, protects Judæan fugitives, **1**, 318.
instigates Gedaliah's murder, **1**, 322.
Baaltis. *See* Astarte.
Baasha, of Israel, kills Nadab, **1**, 189.
ascends the throne, **1**, 190.
allied with the king of Egypt, **1**, 190.
at war with Asa, **1**, 190–1.
allied with Ben-hadad I, **1**, 191.
takes Ramah, **1**, 191.
death of, **1**, 191.
Bab al Abwab, Persian wall against the Chazars, **3**, 138.
Baba ben Buta, follower of Shammai, **2**, 133.
Babenberg, the princes of, permit Jews to fill state offices, **3**, 567.
Babylon, inhabitants of, colonized in Samaria, **1**, 285.
description of, **1**, 330.
fall of, **1**, 349–50.
the goddess of love worshiped in, **1**, 408.
the Judæans of, aid Judæa against Rome, **2**, 264.
study of the Law in, **2**, 358.
Babylonia, the scene of Jewish activity, **2**, 503–4, 531, 537; **3**, 160; **5**, 726.
three meanings of, in Jewish history, **2**, 504–5.

Babylonia (*continued*), resembles the Holy Land, **2**, 544.
Jewish public life in, **2**, 547.
independent of Judæa, **2**, 548.
rise of, **2**, 557.
the study of the Law flourishes in, **2**, 574–5.
called Irak by the Arabs, **3**, 89.
loses intellectual supremacy, **3**, 193, 210, 228.
Jewish communal life in, in the tenth century, **3**, 194.
visited by Petachya, **3**, 421.

Babylonia, Jewish, described, **2**, 504.
compared with Judæa, **2**, 505.
districts of, **2**, 505.
towns of, **2**, 505–8.
fertility of, **2**, 507–8.
scene of the war between Julian and Shabur II, **2**, 601.
Sora the center of, **2**, 607.
constitution of, **3**, 93–101.
communal constitution of, **3**, 98–100.
power of, **3**, 100–1.
mystic doctrines flourish in, **3**, 154.

Babylonia, the Jews of, resist Trajan, **2**, 393, 397.
favorable position of, **2**, 508.
political chief of, **2**, 508–11.
needs of, produce a new development of the Law, **2**, 511.
resort to the academies of Galilee, **2**, 511, 531.
religious ignorance of, **2**, 513.
immorality of, **2**, 516–17, 579.
establish the sanctity of the law of the land, **2**, 520.
suffer under Magian supremacy, **2**, 524–5.
on friendly terms with the Magi, **2**, 525–6.
injured by Odenathus, **2**, 527.
luxurious habits of, **2**, 588.

Babylonia, the Jews of (*continued*), oppressed by Shabur II, **2**, 591–2.
favor Julian the Apostate, **2**, 597.
well treated by Jezdijird, **2**, 609–10.
persecuted, **2**, 626, 627–8; **3**, 8.
suffer under Zendik communism, **3**, 2–3.
rebel under Mar-Zutra II, **3**, 3–4.
independence of, **3**, 3–4.
kindly treated by Bahram Tshubin, **3**, 8–9.
prosperous under Chosru II, **3**, 9–10.
help the Arabs, **3**, 89.
form a separate community under the Exilarch, **3**, 89.
oppose Moawiyah, **3**, 90, 92.
ill-treated by the caliphs of the East, **3**, 176–7.

Babylonia, the Judæans of, kindly treated, **1**, 329–30, 331.
government and possessions of, **1**, 330.
easily learn Aramaic, **1**, 330–1.
practice idolatry, **1**, 332.
cherish Hebrew literature, **1**, 334–6.
joined by the descendants of the Ten Tribes, **1**, 335–6.
mourning of, **1**, 337–8.
make proselytes, **1**, 338–9.
adopt Chaldæan superstitions, **1**, 339–40.
occupations and wealth of, **1**, 339–40.
literature produced by, **1**, 340–2.
not desirous of returning to Palestine, **1**, 340, 341.
beg for permission to return to Palestine, **1**, 342–3.
hate Babylon, **1**, 343.
persecuted, **1**, 343–4.

Babylonia, the Judæans of (*continued*), divided into the worldly and the pious, **1**, 349.
interested in the war with Cyrus, **1**, 349.
cured of idolatry by the fall of Babylon, **1**, 350.
permitted to return to Palestine, **1**, 351.
number of, returning under Cyrus, **1**, 352.
sympathy of, with the returning exiles, **1**, 354–5.
national enthusiasm of, **1**, 363–5.
accompany Ezra to Palestine, **1**, 366.
send contributions to the Temple, **2**, 52.
welcome Hyrcanus II, **2**, 90.
own large tracts of land, **2**, 202.
in Batanæa, **2**, 274.
massacred by Varus, **2**, 275.
retreat to Gamala, **2**, 275.
Bacchides, Syrian general, sent to Jerusalem, **1**, 482.
slays Judæans at Beth-Zachariah, **1**, 483.
encamps before Jerusalem, **1**, 486.
defeats the Judæans at Eleasa, **1**, 487.
reduces the whole country, **1**, 491.
leaves Judæa, **1**, 492.
makes a truce with Jonathan Haphus, **1**, 493–4.
Bacchus, worshiped in Alexandria, **1**, 428.
Bacharach, the Jews of, massacred, **3**, 636.
Bachiel Ibn-Alkonstantini, physician, Maimunist, **2**, 536, 537.
Bachurim, Talmud students, **4**, 640; **5**, 567.
Bachya Ibn-Pakuda, moral philosopher, system of, **3**, 271–2.
ascetic, **3**, 272.
work of, translated, **3**, 392, 397.
Badajoz, Henrique Nunes murdered at, **4**, 490.
attacked by Spanish Marranos, **4**, 498.
Baden, the Jews of, the blood-accusation against, **3**, 564.
obtain political freedom, **5**, 502–3.
persecuted, **5**, 530–1.
honor Riesser, **5**, 601.
Badis, Berber king, supported by Samuel Ibn-Nagrela, **3**, 258.
makes him vizir, **3**, 258.
makes him chief of the Granada congregations, **3**, 259.
avenges Balkin's death, **3**, 275.
orders the massacre of the Granada Arabs, **3**, 276.
mistrusts Joseph Ibn-Nagrela, **3**, 277.
Baffa, sultana, favorite of, **4**, 629.
Bagdad, a scientific center, **3**, 146.
the Mutazilist theology taught at, **3**, 147.
in the Pumbeditha district, **3**, 156.
Saadiah at, **3**, 196.
Sabbataï Donnolo at, **3**, 213.
birthplace of Dunash ben Labrat, **3**, 226.
Abraham Ibn-Ezra in, **3**, 369.
Bagdad, the Jews of, prosperous under Al-Mutadhid, **3**, 183.
in the twelfth century, **3**, 428.
Talmudical college of, **3**, 429, 438.
invited to join David Alrui, **3**, 431.

Bagdad, the Jews of (*continued*), enthusiastic for David Alrui, **3**, 432.
Maimunists, **3**, 633.
attacked by the Mongols, **3**, 649–50.
Bagdad Caliphate, the. *See* Abbasside Caliphate, the.
Bagoas (Bagoses), Syrian commander, murders Artaxerxes III, **1**, 409.
levies a tax on the daily sacrifice, **1**, 409–10.
Bahir, a Kabbalistic manuscript, **3**, 556, 557.
Bahram Tshubin, Persian general, ascends the throne, **3**, 8.
friendly to the Jews, **3**, 8–9.
dispossessed by Chosru II, **3**, 9.
Bahurim, David passes through, **1**, 142.
Bail, defends the Jews, **5**, 522.
Bailly, mayor of Paris, favors the emancipation of the Jews, **5**, 445.
Bairut. *See* Beyrout.
Bajazet (Bajasid) II, sultan, censures the expulsion of the Spanish Jews, **4**, 356.
receives Spanish exiles kindly, **4**, 364, 400.
Jews under, **4**, 402.
Baki, Simon, rabbi, superstition of, **5**, 201–2.
Balaam, magician, employed against the Israelites, **1**, 28.
Balak, king of Moab, hostile to the Israelites, **1**, 28.
"Balance, The," grammatical work by Abraham Ibn-Ezra, **3**, 371.
Balanyiar, Jews settle in, **3**, 124, 139.
Balch, birthplace of Chivi Albalchi, **3**, 198.
Baldwin IV, of Jerusalem, banishes the Jews, **3**, 427.
Baldwin, archbishop of Canterbury, induces Richard I to dismiss the Jews from his palace, **3**, 410.
and Benedict of York's baptism, **3**, 411.
Balkin (Bologgin), of Granada, abdicates in favor of Badis, **3**, 258.
death of, **3**, 258, 275.
partisans of, leave Granada, **3**, 258.
Joseph Ibn-Nagrela secretary to, **3**, 274.
Bamberg, the council of, enforces Jew badges, **4**, 255.
the Jews of, persecuted, **5**, 529.
Band of Virtue, the, founded by Berlin Jewesses, **5**, 423, 425.
Bandito, suspected of well poisoning, **4**, 104.
Baptism, the moral meaning of, taught by John the Baptist, **2**, 146.
value of, examined by Chasdaï Crescas, **4**, 188.
Baptista, John (Solomon Romano), grandson of Elias Levita, apostate, denounces the Talmud, **4**, 564.
Bar, the Jews of, slaughtered by Cossacks, **5**, 11.
Barak, judge, leads the Israelites against Jabin, **1**, 61.
Barbaro, Mark Antonio, Venetian consul, and Solomon Ashkenazi, **4**, 605.
Barbary states, the, Marranos emigrate to, **4**, 485.
Polish-Jewish fugitives in, **5**, 16.
Barbastro, the Jews of, converted, **4**, 214.

Barbastro (*continued*), the Marranos of, conspire against Arbues, **4**, 330.
Barcelona, the disputation at, **3**, 598–601.
bishop of, appointed censor of the Talmud, **3**, 603.
report of the disputation at, **3**, 603–4.
Kabbala taught in, **4**, 6.
Marranos from, in Algiers, **4**, 199.
the Inquisition established in, **4**, 332.
Jews disappear from, **4**, 354.
exiles from, form a congregation in Constantinople, **4**, 402.
Barcelona, the Jews of, the leaders of northern Spain, **3**, 387–8.
entreat Nachmani to break off the disputation, **3**, 600–1.
opposed to the study of science, **4**, 29, 33, 40.
charged with causing the Black Death, **4**, 102–3.
persecuted, **4**, 171–2.
Bar-Chanina, teacher of Jerome, **2**, 623–4.
Bar-Cochba, attacks Akiba, **2**, 409.
described as the Messiah, **2**, 410.
confidence of, **2**, 411.
victories of, **2**, 411.
coins of, **2**, 411.
hostile to Christians, **2**, 412.
restores the Jewish state, **2**, 412, 413.
strongholds of, **2**, 414–15.
particulars of the revolt of, **2**, 415–16.
loses the strongholds of the north, **2**, 416.
causes the death of Eleazar of Modin, **2**, 418.
Bar-Cochba (*continued*), end of, unknown, **2**, 419.
Barebones Parliament. *See* Parliament, the Short.
Bar-Eleaza, son-in-law of Judah I, **2**, 455–6.
Barfat Crescas, imprisoned, **4**, 150.
Barfat. *See* Isaac ben Sheshet Barfat; Zarak.
Bari, the four Sora emissaries captured at, **3**, 203.
Baris. *See* Acra, the; Antonia.
Bar-Kappara. *See* Simon bar Kappara.
Bar-Kasha, and Rab, **2**, 518.
Bar-Kosiba, real name of Bar-Cochba.
Barlæus, Caspar, Socinian, and Manasseh ben Israel, **5**, 22.
Barnabas. *See* Jose Barnabas.
Barnave, favors the emancipation of the Jews, **5**, 441.
Barrios, Miguel (Daniel) de, historian, **5**, 202.
versifier, **5**, 204.
Bartholomaion, demon exorcised by Simon ben Yochaï, **2**, 449.
Baruch, ancestor of the Ibn-Albalias, early settlement of, in Spain, **3**, 43.
Baruch of Benevento, Kabbalist, **4**, 481.
Baruch ben Samuel, Talmudist, member of the Mayence synod, **3**, 517.
Baruch Ibn-Albalia, birth of the son of, **3**, 322.
Baruch, son of Neriah, reads Jeremiah's prophecies in the Temple, **1**, 304.
taken prisoner by the Chaldæans, **1**, 315.
attends Jeremiah in Mizpah, **1**, 320.
taken captive by Ishmael, **1**, 322.

Baruch, son of Neriah (*continued*), rescued, **1**, 323.
in Egypt, **1**, 324.
in Babylon, **1**, 328.
brings Jeremiah's writings to Babylon, **1**, 336.
writes a history of Israel, **1**, 336–7.
Letter of, translated, **2**, 359.
Baruch Gad, Palestinian emissary, on the Sons of Moses, **5**, 126.
Baruch Yavan, carries the Eibeschütz controversy to Poland, **5**, 262–3.
Baruch, Jacob, Börne's father, deputy to the Congress of Vienna, **5**, 513.
Baruch, Löb (Louis). *See* Börne, Ludwig.
Barzaphernes, Parthian commander, **2**, 82.
Barzillai, aids David, **1**, 144.
Bashan, the inhabitants of, appeal to Judas Maccabæus, **1**, 474–5.
Basilius (850–866), emperor, tries to convert the Jews, **3**, 175–6.
Basilius, Jewish slave-dealer, and Pope Gelasius, **3**, 29.
Basle, the Talmud printed at, **4**, 589.
Alsatian Jews escape to, **5**, 437.
Basle, the Council of, renews the anti-Jewish measures of previous councils, **4**, 245, 248, 251, 264.
excludes Jews from university degrees, **4**, 245.
favors baptized Jews, **4**, 246.
degrades Eugenius IV, **4**, 249, 250.
decree of, concerning Jewish physicians disregarded, **4**, 407.
Basle, the Jews of, protected from the Black Death persecutions, **4**, 106, 108.
banishment of, demanded, **4**, 106–7.
burnt, **4**, 107.
Basmath, daughter of Solomon, **1**, 177.
Basnage, Jacob (1653–1723), historian of the Jewish dispersion, **5**, 195, 593.
on the persecutions of the Jews, **5**, 195–6.
consults Jewish historians, **5**, 196.
faults of the history by, **5**, 196–7.
prejudiced, **5**, 197.
importance of the history by, **5**, 197.
disciples of, **5**, 197.
history of, suggested by Manasseh ben Israel, **5**, 202.
Bassan, Isaiah, teacher of Moses Chayim Luzzatto, **5**, 235.
espouses Luzzatto's cause, **5**, 238, 241.
makes Luzzatto promise not to teach Kabbala, **5**, 239.
has Luzzatto's writings in safekeeping, **5**, 239.
permits Luzzatto to publish Kabbalistic works, **5**, 239.
Bassora, under the jurisdiction of the Sora academy, **3**, 98.
the Mutazilist theology taught in, **3**, 147.
the Gaon of Sora at, **3**, 202.
the Jews of, in the twelfth century, **3**, 437.
Bassus, Vespasian's governor of Judæa, **2**, 315.
Basula, Moses. *See* Moses Basula.
Batanæa, given to Philip by Herod's will, **2**, 119.

Batanæa (*continued*), under Philip, 2, 137.
given to Agrippa II, 2, 245.
cavalry from, sent to Jerusalem, 2, 259, 260.
Babylonian Judæans in, 2, 274.
Porphyry a native of, 2, 502.
the Benu-Kainukaa settle in, 3, 77-8.
Batavian Republic, the, the Jews of, emancipation of, 5, 452.
number of, 5, 453, 455.
disabilities of, 5, 453.
writings hostile to, 5, 453.
hold aloof from the National Assembly, 5, 454.
emancipated, 5, 456-7.
appointed to public offices, 5, 458.
protection of, in Germany, 5, 458, 463.
See also Emancipation of the Dutch Jews; Holland.
Bath-Kol, heavenly voice, 2, 337, 338.
Bathori, Stephen, election of, as king of Poland, 4, 642.
the Jews prosperous under, 4, 642-3.
Bathsheba, wife of Uriah the Hittite, becomes David's wife, 1, 132.
sons of, 1, 133.
made first queen, 1, 134.
pleads for Solomon's succession, 1, 153.
Bathyra, Judæan fortress in Batanæa, 2, 274.
Baudin, suppresses evidence in favor of the Damascus Jews, 5, 637.
Bavaria, John of Capistrano in, 4, 258.
the poll-tax abolished in, 5, 468.
Bavaria, the Jews of, suffer from the Rindfleisch persecution, 4, 35-6.
suffer from the Hartmann von Deggenburg persecution, 4, 98.
during the Black Death persecutions, 4, 110.
accused of aiding the Hussites, 4, 222.
assaulted by the imperial army, 4, 225.
expelled, 4, 253-4.
during John of Capistrano's visit, 4, 258.
taxed for the defense of the Ratisbon Jews, 4, 305.
take refuge in Poland, 4, 420.
accused of child-murder, 4, 545-6.
partial emancipation of, 5, 508.
Bayonne, the kings of Castile and of France meet at, 4, 2.
Bayonne, the Jews of, addressed in behalf of the Moravian and Bohemian Jews, 5, 253.
in Malesherbes' commission, 5, 432.
prosperity of, 5, 436.
emancipated, 5, 442-3.
Bayreuth, the Jews of, persecuted, 5, 530.
Beatrice, wife of Juan I of Castile, heir to Portugal, 4, 158.
proposes David Negro as chief rabbi, 4, 161.
Beaucaire (Belcaire), the Jews of, in the twelfth century, 3, 400.
Be-Chatim, home of Achaï bar Huna, 2, 631.
Bechinath ha-Dath, work of Elias del Medigo, 4, 293.
Bechinath Olam, by Yedaya Bedaresi, 4, 49.
Bedaresi. *See* Abraham; Yedaya En-Bonet.

Bedr, battle of, between Mahomet and the Koraishites, **3,** 76.
Beer of Mizricz (Berish, 1700–1772), founder of new Chassidism, **5,** 375, 379.
learning of, **5,** 379.
habits of, **5,** 379–80.
pilgrimages to, **5,** 380, 407.
simulates inspiration, **5,** 380–1.
emphasizes the importance of the Sabbath, **5,** 381–2.
apostles of, **5,** 383.
adopts the Portuguese ritual, **5,** 386–7.
death of, **5,** 392.
a relative of, supreme Zaddik, **5,** 393.
sayings by, **5,** 393.
disciples of, **5,** 393.
Beer, Jacob, private synagogue of, in Berlin, **5,** 563.
Beersheba, frontier town of ancient Israel, **1,** 129.
pilgrimages to, **1,** 232.
Behaim, Martin, at João II's astronomical congress, **4,** 367.
Bekashoth ha-Memin, prayer by Yedaya Penini, **4,** 43.
Bekiin, center for the teaching of the Law under Gamaliel II, **2,** 335, 348.
Bel, temple of, rebuilt by Alexander the Great, **1,** 415.
Bela IV, of Hungary, invites Jewish agents into his country, **3,** 613.
introduces Frederick the Valiant's Jewish statute, **3,** 613–14.
Belgium, Jews in, in the sixth century, **3,** 35.
the Jews of, during the Black Death persecutions, **4,** 112.
Catholic agitators in, hostile to the Jews, **5,** 655.
"**Belief of the Universe, The,**" by Chayon, **5,** 219–20.
Belillos, Jacob, rabbi of Venice, and Luzzatto, **5,** 239.
Belisarius, Jewish soldiers fight against, **3,** 4.
removes the Temple vessels to Constantinople, **3,** 26.
in Italy, **3,** 31.
opposed by the Jews of Naples, **3,** 32.
Belkis, supposed name of the Queen of Sheba, **1,** 173.
"**Bellerophon,**" satire by Lefrank, **5,** 471–2.
Bellieta, suspected of well poisoning, **4,** 104.
Belmonte, Bienvenida Coen, Jewish poetess, **5,** 203.
Belmonte, Jacob Israel, poet, interested in the Amsterdam Marranos, **4,** 665.
Belmonte, Manuel, poet, founder of an academy of poetry, **5,** 113.
Belmontes, the, millionaires at Amsterdam, **5,** 205.
Belvedere, the Nassi palace at Constantinople, **4,** 597.
Hebrew printing press at, **4,** 628.
Ben-Adret. *See* Solomon ben Abraham ben Adret.
Benaiah, commander of David's mercenaries, **1,** 122.
in the Ammonite war, **1,** 126.
opposes Absalom, **1,** 141.
acknowledges Solomon king, **1,** 153.
kills Adonijah and Joab, **1,** 160.
Ben Asai (Azai). *See* Simon ben Asai.
Ben Asher. *See* Moses and Aaron ben Asher.
Benavente, the Jews of, converted by Vincent Ferrer, **4,** 205.

Ben-Batiach, Zealot leader, aids Jochanan ben Zakkai, **2,** 323.
Bendama, and the Jewish Christians, **2,** 370.
Ben David, Messiah, **2,** 144.
Ben-David, Lazarus (1762–1832), philosopher, **5,** 405.
admires Kant's philosophy, **5,** 409.
lectures on Kant, **5,** 410.
deplores the decay of morality among Jews, **5,** 419.
leaves attacks on Judaism unanswered, **5,** 469.
influences Heine, **5,** 546.
member of the Society for Culture, **5,** 583.
Bene Amri, the, attack the Hasmonæans, **1,** 491.
Bene Bathyra, presidents of the Synhedrion, **2,** 90, 358.
resign in favor of Hillel, **2,** 99.
Bene-Berak, home of Akiba, **2,** 355.
Benedict XII, pope, unable to protect the Jews, **4,** 99.
Benedict XIII (Pedro de Luna), pope, debates with Shem-Tob ben Isaac Shaprut, **4,** 142.
confers ecclesiastic offices upon Solomon Levi, **4,** 184, 190.
employs a Jewish physician, **4,** 200.
plans the conversion of the Spanish Jews, **4,** 206–7.
arranges the disputation at Tortosa, **4,** 207.
plans the annihilation of the Talmud, **4,** 209.
and Jewish delegates to Tortosa, **4,** 210.
pomp displayed by, **4,** 210–11.
refuses to release the Jews from the disputation, **4,** 211.
Benedict XIII (*continued*), presides over the disputation, **4,** 212.
threatens the Jewish delegates with death, **4,** 213, 239.
issues a bull against the Talmud and the Jews, **4,** 215–16.
deposed by the council of Constance, **4,** 216, 228.
sets up a papal court at Peñiscola, **4,** 217.
originates the sermon for Jews, **4,** 655.
Benedict XIV, pope, acquits the Jews of the blood accusation, **5,** 282.
Benedict of York, accepts baptism, **3,** 411.
returns to Judaism, **3,** 411.
death of, **3,** 413.
house of, burnt, **3,** 413.
Bene Korach. *See* Korah, the sons of.
Bene Mikra. *See* Karaites, the.
Benet, Mordecai, leader of the orthodox party, **5,** 567, 572.
Benevento, the Jews of, in the twelfth century, **3,** 424.
the Inquisition for Marranos at, **4,** 385.
Benfelden, the council at, banishes the Jews of the upper Rhine, **4,** 107.
Ben-hadad I, of Damascus, ally of Israel and Judah, **1,** 191.
defeats Omri, **1,** 195.
Ben-hadad II, of Damascus, besieges Samaria, **1,** 205.
defeated by Ahab, **1,** 205.
treachery of, **1,** 205.
defeats Ahab and Jehoshaphat, **1,** 206.
murdered, **1,** 210.
Ben-hadad III, of Damascus, defeated, **1,** 221–2.

Benisch, Abraham, founder of the "Anglo-Jewish Association," **5,** 703.
Benjamin, the tribe of, acquires Gibeon, **1,** 38.
holds assemblies at Shiloh, **1,** 41.
opposed to intermarriages with the heathen, **1,** 56.
aids Ehud against the Moabites, **1,** 60.
attacked by the Philistines, **1,** 64.
aids Saul, **1,** 85.
accuses David of destroying the house of Saul, **1,** 124.
sides with Absalom, **1,** 139–40.
hesitates to recall David, **1,** 146.
meets David at the Jordan, **1,** 147.
closely united with Judah, **1,** 174.
loyal to Rehoboam, **1,** 182.
members of, return from the Captivity, **1,** 352.
Benjamin of Canterbury, Tossafist, **3,** 409.
Benjamin of Fermo, patron of Immanuel Romi, **4,** 68.
Benjamin of Tiberias, and Emperor Heraclius, **3,** 19, 22.
Benjamin ben Jonah of Tudela, traveler, **3,** 388–9; **4,** 127.
Benjamin ben Moses of Nahavend (800–820), spreads the Mutazilist philosophy, **3,** 150–1.
founder of the Makariyite sect, **3,** 151.
Benjamin Assia, physician, scorns the teachers of the Law, **2,** 589–90.
Ben-Kafren (Ephraim), defends Menachem ben Saruk, **3,** 227.
Ben Kohelet, work by Samuel Ibn-Nagrela, **3,** 260.
Ben Mishle, work by Samuel Ibn-Nagrela, **3,** 260.
Ben-Naphtali, criticises the Ben Ashers, **3,** 207.
Ben-Nazar. *See* Odenathus.
Ben Shaltiel-Chen. *See* Serachya ben Isaac.
Ben Soma. *See* Simon ben Zoma.
Ben Tehillim, work by Samuel Ibn-Nagrela, **3,** 260.
Benu-Aus, the, Arabic family, relations of, to the Jews, **3,** 55.
conversions among, to Judaism, **3,** 61.
hostile to Jewish rule, **3,** 67.
the Jews of Yathrib dependent on, **3,** 68.
feuds of, **3,** 70–1.
Benu-Bachdal, the, Jewish-Arabic tribe, **3,** 54–5.
Benu-Kainukaa, the, Jewish tribe in northern Arabia, **3,** 55.
invited to accept Islam, **3,** 74, 76–7.
forced to surrender to Mahomet, **3,** 77.
settle in Batanæa, **3,** 77–8.
preserve love for Arabic, **3,** 111.
object to Talmudic restraints, **3,** 119.
Benu-Kinanah, the, Arab tribe converted to Judaism, **3,** 61.
Benu-Kuraiza, the, a Jewish-Arabic tribe, **3,** 54–5.
threatened by Mahomet, **3,** 77.
make war upon Mahomet, **3,** 80.
slaughtered, **3,** 81.
Benu-Nadhir, the, a Jewish-Arabic tribe, **3,** 54–5.
threatened by Mahomet, **3,** 77.
meditate treachery against Mahomet, **3,** 78.

Benu-Nadhir, the (*continued*),
forced to emigrate, **3,** 78-9.
war with, justified in the Koran, **3,** 79.
organize an alliance against Mahomet, **3,** 79-80.
rouse the Jews of Chaibar to resist Mahomet, **3,** 82.
preserve love of Arabic, **3,** 111.
object to Talmudic restraints, **3,** 119.

Ben Usiel, champion of the orthodox party, **5,** 627.

Benvenida Abrabanela, wife of Samuel II Abrabanel, character of, **4,** 409.
friend of the duchess of Tuscany, **4,** 410, 544.
supports David Reubeni, **4,** 493.
prevents the banishment of the Naples Jews, **4,** 543.

Benveniste. *See* Abraham Benveniste Senior; Benveniste Ibn-Labi; Benveniste, Chayim; Isaac; Joseph ben Ephraim Ibn-Benveniste Halevi; Judah; Sheshet; Vidal ben Benveniste Ibn-Labi.

Benveniste Ibn-Labi, part translator of Aristotle's Ethics, **4,** 193.

Benveniste, Chayim (1603-1673), rabbi of Smyrna, Sabbatian, **5,** 136.
disappointed in Sabbataï Zevi, **5,** 155.

Benveniste family, the, of the nobility of Jewish Spain, **3,** 236.
Gracia Mendesia of, **4,** 571.

Ben Yasus. *See* Abu Ibraham Isaac Ibn-Kastar ben Yasus.

Ben-Zeeb, one of the Measfim, **5,** 400.

Be-Rab, Abba-Areka's school, **2,** 514.

Berab. *See* Jacob Berab.

Berachoth, the eighteen, introduced by Gamaliel II, **2,** 363.

Berachya ben Natronaï Nakdan (Crispia, 1230-1270), fabulist, **3,** 560.

Berachya, son of Jacob Querido, Messiah, followers of, **5,** 211.
soul of, in Jacob Frank, **5,** 274.
prayers addressed to, **5,** 274.

Berber princes, the, receive Jewish refugees kindly, **4,** 198

Berbers, the, establish themselves in southern Spain, **3,** 256.
hostile to the Spanish Arabs, **3,** 261, 276, 316.
incensed against the Jews, **3,** 275.
slay Joseph Ibn-Nagrela, **3,** 278.

Berdaa. *See* Derbend.

Berenice, daughter of Agrippa I, marriage of, **2,** 235.
Drusilla envious of, **2,** 236.
appeals to Gessius Florus, **2,** 254.
popularity of, **2,** 257.
palace of, burnt, **2,** 260.
captivates Titus, **2,** 289, 299.
wins Tiberius Alexander to Vespasian's side, **2,** 300.
influence of, over Titus, **2,** 302, 307.
in the arena of Cæsarea Philippi, **2,** 312.
honored at the court, **2,** 317.
fall of, **2,** 317.
obtains pardon for Justus of Tiberias, **2,** 319-20.
consoles her conquered coreligionists, **2,** 333.
abandoned by Titus, **2,** 388.

Berenice, Herod's niece, marriage of, **2,** 112.
friend of Antonia, **2,** 176.

Bergamo, Bernardinus of Feltre in, **4,** 296.
Berish. *See* Beer of Mizricz.
Berlin, settlement of Jews in, **5,** 174.
Chayon at, **5,** 218–20.
subscribers to Mendelssohn's Pentateuch translation in, **5,** 329.
the Free School of, **5,** 416.
the progressive party in, **5,** 418.
Jewish physicians of, a class, **5,** 461.
the University of, arbiter between the Jews and the Senate of Frankfort, **5,** 520.
Jacobson transplants the Reform movement to, **5,** 562–3.
private synagogues in, closed, **5,** 563.
appoints no rabbi, **5,** 566.
a German Jewish church in, **5,** 683.
rabbinical colleges at, **5,** 700.
Berlin, the Jews of, threatened with expulsion, **4,** 652.
under Frederick I, **5,** 190.
split into two parties, **5,** 219.
culture of, **5,** 294–5.
enterprises of, **5,** 396–7.
devoted to literary pursuits, **5,** 397.
encourage the Meassef, **5,** 399.
influenced by Herz, **5,** 407.
disseminators of culture, **5,** 410–11.
the salons of, **5,** 412–13, 422–23.
millionaires, **5,** 414.
begin the emancipation struggle, **5,** 414–16.
influence of, **5,** 416–17.
apostasy among, **5,** 420, 587.
procure an order against anti-Jewish pamphlets, **5,** 469.
object to Napoleon's Synhedrion, **5,** 494–5.
Berlin, the Jews of (*continued*), antipathy to, weakened, **5,** 691.
See also Reform of Judaism, the.
"Berlin religion," the, opposition to, **5,** 333.
Bernal, Abraham Nuñes and Marcus da Almeyda, Marranos, martyrs, **5,** 92.
Bernaldez, Andreas, pastor, on the Spanish Jewish exiles, **4,** 349.
Bernard of Clairvaux, abbot, preaches the second crusade, **3,** 349.
preaches the repudiation of Jewish debts, **3,** 349.
prevents a persecution of the French Jews, **3,** 351, 356.
appealed to, by the archbishop of Mayence, **3,** 352.
denounces Rudolph, **3,** 353.
influences Rudolph, **3,** 353.
Bernard of Sienna, master of John of Capistrano, **4,** 257.
Bernard, Isaac, Mendelssohn's employer, **5,** 296, 303.
Bernardinus of Feltre, Franciscan, preaches against the Jews in Italy, **4,** 296.
failure of, **4,** 296–7.
in Trent, **4,** 297.
raises the blood accusation, **4,** 298.
Bernardo, Dominican, incites the mob against Marranos, **4,** 487.
Bernays, Isaac (1792–1849), opposes the Hamburg reforms, **5,** 574.
characteristics of, **5,** 574–5, 577.
chief work by, **5,** 575.
criticises Mendelssohn and his school, **5,** 575.
appointed to the Hamburg rabbinate, **5,** 576.

Bernays, Isaac (*continued*), character of the sermons by, **5,** 577.
Heine on, **5,** 577.
respected by the orthodox, **5,** 577–8.
influence of, in Germany, **5,** 582.
influence of, on Steinheim, **5,** 602.
Ben Usiel disciple of, **5,** 627.
forbids the use of the Reform Temple prayer book, **5,** 673.
attacked by the Reform Temple Union, **5,** 673.
supported by the rabbi of Altona, **5,** 674.
Bernays, Jacob, founder of the Breslau seminary, **5,** 700.
Berne, the Jews of, accused of well poisoning, **4,** 104–5.
consuls of, spread the charge against the Jews, **4,** 105.
Bernhard, treasurer of the Frankish empire, friendly to the Jews, **3,** 162.
rebellion against, **3,** 166.
Bernstorff, Danish minister, decides against Eibeschütz, **5,** 265.
Bernstorff, deputy to the Congress of Vienna, favors the emancipation of the Jews, **5,** 519.
on the emancipation of the Jews at Aix, **5,** 527.
Berr, Berr Isaac (1744–1828), member of Malesherbes' commission, **5,** 431.
a representative French Jew, **5,** 436.
delegate to the National Assembly, **5,** 438, 440.
on the emancipation of the French Jews, **5,** 448–9.
projects a French Bible translation, **5,** 449.
Berr, Berr Isaac (*continued*), son of, **5,** 460.
deputy to the Assembly of Jewish Notables, **5,** 482.
opposes Sabbath sessions, **5,** 486.
candidate for the presidency, **5,** 487.
answers the imperial commissioners, **5,** 490.
Berr, Cerf (Herz Medelsheim, 1730–1793), representative of the Alsatian Jews, **5,** 351.
character of, **5,** 430.
services of, to the Alsatian Jews, **5,** 430, 431.
services of, to the government, **5,** 430.
draws Jews to Strasburg, **5,** 431.
member of Malesherbes' commission, **5,** 431.
a representative French Jew, **5,** 436.
accused of bribing, **5,** 447.
culture of the family of, **5,** 476.
brother-in-law of, **5,** 484.
Berr, Lipmann Cerf, speaks in the Assembly of Jewish Notables, **5,** 487.
Berr, Michael (1780–1843), first Jewish attorney in France, addresses the princes of Europe, **5,** 460.
deputy to the Assembly of Jewish Notables, **5,** 482.
a state officer in Westphalia, **5,** 500.
member of the Westphalian Consistory, **5,** 501.
addresses the Congress of Aix on the emancipation of the Jews, **5,** 527.
Berthold, bishop of Strasburg, at the council of Benfelden, **4,** 107.

Bertinoro. *See* Obadiah di Bertinoro.
Bertolio, abbé, favors the emancipation of the Jews, **5,** 445.
Bertrand, cardinal-legate, forbids baptized children to return to Judaism, **3,** 514.
Berytus. *See* Beyrout.
Besht. *See* Israel of Miedziboz.
Bessarabia, Frankists in, **5,** 283.
Bethany, Jesus in, **2,** 160.
the Synhedrion removed to, **2,** 240.
suburb of Jerusalem, **2,** 292.
Bethar, fortress, **2,** 414.
Bar-Cochba retreats to, **2,** 416–17.
legends about, **2,** 417.
siege of, **2,** 417–19.
fall of, **2,** 418–19.
Betharamata. *See* Beth-Ramatha.
Beth-Din, name of the Synhedrion, **2,** 325.
Bethel, taken by the Ephraimites, **1,** 34.
description of, **1,** 45.
Samuel holds assemblies at, **1,** 78.
a center of idolatry, **1,** 186.
an association of prophets at, **1,** 205, 234.
visited by Elijah, **1,** 208.
bull-worship at, **1,** 233.
capital of Jeroboam II, **1,** 233.
Amos at, **1,** 235, 236.
Cuthæans worship at, **1,** 285.
purged of idolatry, **1,** 294.
priests of, killed, **1,** 295.
military station under Hadrian, **2,** 419.
Bethhagla, fortress, besieged by Bacchides, **1,** 493.
Beth-Haran, balm of Gilead found near, **1,** 43.
Beth-horon, battle of, won by Judas Maccabæus, **1,** 462.
Beth-horon (*continued*), camp of Nicanor at, **1,** 485.
Cestius Gallus retreats from, **2,** 266–7.
Beth Israel, third Amsterdam synagogue, **4,** 680.
Beth Jacob, first Amsterdam synagogue, **4,** 667, 671.
poem in honor of, **4,** 678–9.
Bethlehem, birthplace of David, **1,** 95–6.
camp of the Philistines, **1,** 116.
children of, murdered by Herod, **2,** 116.
the expected birthplace of the Messiah, **2,** 161.
statue of Adonis worshiped at, **2,** 422.
nunnery at, **2,** 623.
the Jews of, in the twelfth century, **3,** 427.
Bethmaon, Josephus and the men of Tiberias meet at, **2,** 279.
Bethome, Pharisee fortress, **2,** 45.
Bethoron. *See* Beth-horon.
Bethpage, suburb of Jerusalem, **2,** 292.
Beth-Ramatha (Betharamata), palace of, destroyed, **2,** 125.
re-named Livia, **2,** 138.
Bethsaida, Jesus in, **2,** 157.
Bethsan (Bethshan). *See* Bethshean.
Bethshean (Bethsan, Scythopolis), bodies of Saul and Jonathan dishonored at, **1,** 104.
Greek citizens of, resist Joseph, **1,** 425.
refuge of Antiochus IX, **2,** 10.
recovered by the sons of John Hyrcanus, **2,** 11.
Judæans of, massacred, **2,** 262–3.
sparsely inhabited by Jews in the sixth century, **3,** 12.

Bethshearim, temporary seat of the Synhedrion, **2**, 452.
Beth-Shemesh, battle of, between the kings of Israel and Judah, **1**, 224–5.
Bethsur. *See* Beth-Zur.
Beth-Waad, religious school in the Sopheric age, **1**, 396.
Beth-Zachariah, the battle of, Judas Maccabæus defeated at, **1**, 479.
Judæans slain at, by Bacchides, **1**, 483.
Beth-Zur (Bethsur), Judas Maccabæus victorious at, **1**, 469–70.
stronghold against the Idumæans, **1**, 473.
garrison of, surrenders to Lysias, **1**, 479.
reinforced by Bacchides, **1**. 491.
Hellenists take refuge in, **1**, 494.
garrisoned by the Hasmonæans, **1**, 498.
under Simon Tharsi, **1**, 523, 524.
Alexander Jannæus and Cleopatra make a league at, **2**, 41.
Beugnot, Napoleon's state councilor, favors Jewish emancipation, **5**, 480.
helps to frame the Westphalian constitution, **5**, 500.
Beyrout, the Judæans of, perish in the arena, **2**, 312.
Beyrout (Bairut, Berytus), the **Jews of**, in the twelfth century, **3**, 426.
protected by European consuls, **5**, 641.
appeal to European Jews, **5**, 651.
Bezalel Masserano, requests permission for Jews to own Talmud copies, **4**, 658.
Bezetha, suburb of Jerusalem, fortified by Agrippa, **2**, 195.
destroyed by Cestius Gallus, **2**, 265.
seized by the Romans, **2**, 303.
Béziers (Biterræ), Jews in, in the sixth century, **3**, 35.
synagogue of, sold, **4**, 48.
Béziers, the council of, inflicts hardships upon the Albigenses, **3**, 581.
renews ancient restrictions against the Jews, **3**, 581–2.
prohibits Jews from practicing medicine among Christians, **3**, 582, 583.
Béziers, the Jews of, attacked at Eastertide, **3**, 173–4, 394.
in the twelfth century, **3**, 394–5.
under Count Roger, **3**, 395.
suffering of, during the Albigensian crusades, **3**, 502–3.
excommunicate Solomon of Montpellier, **3**, 530.
Bible, the. *See* Law, the; Old Testament, the; Pentateuch, the; Scriptures, the; Septuagint, the; Translation; Vulgate, the; *and under its various books.*
Bible exegesis. *See* Exegesis.
“**Bible for Israelites**,” by Sachs, **5**, 693.
“**Biblical Orient, The**,” ascribed to Isaac Bernays, **5**, 575.
on the symbolism of Judaism, **5**, 575–6.
emphasizes the historical mission of the Jews, **5**, 576.
Bidkar, follower of Jehu, **1**, 211.
Biester, admirer of Mendelssohn, **5**, 372.
Bilbeïs, the Jews of, in the twelfth century, **3**, 444.

Bing, Isaiah Berr (1759-1805), writes a defense of the Jews, **5,** 434.
Birah, the. *See* Acra, the; Antonia.
Birath, camp of Bacchides, **1,** 486.
Birchath ha-Minim, curse of the Jewish Christians, **2,** 379-80.
Biri, religiousness of the inhabitants of, **2,** 480.
Birtha. *See* Bitra.
Biterræ. *See* Béziers.
Bither. *See* Bethar.
Bitra, the Jews of, hostile to Julian the Apostate, **2,** 601-2.
Black Death, the, ravages of, **4,** 100, 133, 135.
Jews charged with having caused, **4,** 101-2, 188; **5,** 728.
in southern France, **4,** 102.
in Spain, **4,** 102-3, 112-13.
in Switzerland, **4,** 103-5, 106-7.
in Germany, **4,** 105, 111, 133.
in Austria, **4,** 110.
in Hungary, **4,** 111.
in Poland, **4,** 111-12.
in Belgium, **4,** 112.
in Catalonia, **4,** 112-13.
in Castile, **4,** 113.
Black Forest, the, the Jews of, molested by Lutheran peasants, **4,** 542-3.
Black Prince, the. *See* Edward, prince of Wales.
Black Sea, the, Jews settle on the shores of, **3,** 123.
serfs on, **5,** 2.
Blanche, mother of Louis IX, at the disputation on the Talmud, **3,** 576.
refuses to banish the Jews, **3,** 585.
Blanche de Bourbon, wife of Pedro the Cruel, **4,** 116-17.
Blanche de Bourbon (*continued*), party of, **4,** 117.
meditates the banishment of the Spanish Jews, **4,** 117.
murder of, resolved on, **4,** 121-2.
death of, attributed to the Jews, **4,** 122.
illegality of the marriage of, **4,** 122.
Blandrata, disciple of Servetus, **4,** 647.
Bloch, Mattathias, emissary of Sabbataï Zevi, **5,** 133, 137.
Blois, the Jews of, charged with the blood accusation, **3,** 378-81.
fast prescribed for, **3,** 380-1.
Blood accusation, the, first preferred in Blois in 1171, **3,** 378-81.
under Philip Augustus, **3,** 402.
in Germany in the twelfth century, **3,** 418.
preferred by Innocent III, **3,** 499.
against the Baden Jews, **3,** 564.
in Germany and France in the thirteenth century, **3,** 583-5.
disproved by Innocent IV, **3,** 584-5, 635.
in England under Henry III, **3,** 591.
believed by Alfonso X, **3,** 596.
under Rudolph of Habsburg, **3,** 635-7.
at Mayence, **3,** 636.
at Munich, **3,** 636-7.
in England, **3,** 643.
against the Jews of Austria, **4,** 223-4.
in South Germany, **4,** 227.
against the Jews of Palma, **4,** 246-7.
against the Jews of Silesia, **4,** 261-2.

Blood accusation, the (*continued*), forbidden by Casimir IV of Poland, **4**, 264.
against the Jews of Trent, **4**, 298–9, 304, 307.
in Ratisbon, **4**, 301–2, 304–5.
not believed by Emperor Frederick III, **4**, 305.
the Jews of Castile charged with, **4**, 343–4.
the Jews of Neuburg charged with, **4**, 545.
injustice of, shown by a Lutheran pastor, **4**, 545–6.
preferred by Dr. John Eck, **4**, 546–7.
preferred by Luther, **4**, 550.
denounced by Stephen Bathori, **4**, 642.
preferred by William Prynne, **5**, 45.
Manasseh ben Israel defends the Jews from, **5**, 47–9.
the Jews of Metz charged with, **5**, 174–5.
Richard Simon disproves, **5**, 175–6.
Moses Germanus disproves, **5**, 177.
denounced by John Wülfer, **5**, 185.
denounced by Wagenseil, **5**, 187.
endorsed by Eisenmenger, **5**, 187, 188.
preferred by the Frankists, **5**, 279.
Jews acquitted of, by Benedict XIV, **5**, 282.
Jews acquitted of, by Clement XIII, **5**, 285.
believed by the papal nuncio Serra, **5**, 286.
not refuted at Lemberg, **5**, 287.
threatened to be brought in Damascus, **5**, 633.

Blood accusation, the (*continued*), the Damascus Jews charged with, **5**, 636.
alleged to be proved from the Talmud, **5**, 639.
brought against the Jews of Rhodes, **5**, 640–1.
a Jülich Jew charged with, **5**, 642.
groundlessness of, asserted by apostates, **5**, 650.
groundlessness of, asserted by the London rabbis, **5**, 654–5.
refuted by Mehemet Ali, **5**, 661.
firman securing the Turkish Jews against, **5**, 662.
refuted by Zunz, **5**, 669.
See also Child-murder; Host-desecration.

Boabdil. *See* Muley Abu-Abdallah.

Bodenlaube, castle, Süsskind of Trimberg at, **3**, 420.

Bodo, bishop, accepts Judaism, **3**, 168–9.
hatred of, towards Christians, **3**, 169.

Boëthius, a notability of the sixth century, **3**, 31.

Boëthus, a family of high priests, **2**, 108, 237.

Boëthusans, a Sadducee sect, **2**, 108.

Bohemia, Jews in, in the ninth century, **3**, 144.
a Talmud center, **3**, 420–1.
adopts Frederick the Valiant's Jewish statute, **3**, 569.
Jews emigrate to, from Hungary, **4**, 111.
Austrian exiles settle in, **4**, 224.
Polish Jewish fugitives in, **5**, 16.
Jewish exiles from Vienna settle in, **5**, 173.

Bohemia (*continued*), the Sabbatian movement in, **5**, 208, 228.
Jews excluded from parts of, **5**, 523.
rabbis of, oppose the Brunswick conference, **5**, 682.
Bohemia, the Jews of, carry on the slave trade, **3**, 305.
suffer during the first crusade, **3**, 305.
determine to emigrate, **3**, 307.
plundered, **3**, 308.
suffer during the second crusade, **3**, 356.
address Solomon ben Adret on religious questions, **3**, 620.
suffer during the Hartmann von Deggenburg persecution, **4**, 98.
charged with host-desecration, **4**, 164–6.
threatened with expulsion, **4**, 417.
take refuge in Poland, **4**, 420, 631–2.
charged with incendiarism, **4**, 544.
exiled, **4**, 544.
recalled, **4**, 545.
submit religious questions to the Polish Talmudists, **4**, 639.
heavily taxed, **4**, 652, 702; **5**, 508.
rights of, extended, **4**, 707.
suspected of treason, **5**, 252.
banished, **5**, 252.
modify their synagogue service, **5**, 582.
Böhme, Jacob, mystic, disciple of, **5**, 24.
Boleslav Pius, confirms Frederick the Valiant's Jewish statute, **4**, 111, 263.
Bologgin. *See* Balkin.
Bologna, synod at, **4**, 218.
Jewish printing house in, **4**, 289.
Marranos well treated at, **4**, 525.
Bologna, the Jews of, expelled, **3**, 421.
persecuted by Pius V, **4**, 590–1.
flee to Ferrara, **4**, 591.
Bomberg, Daniel, publishes the Babylonian Talmud, **4**, 468.
a rabbinical Bible, **4**, 476.
Bonafides, character in "Nathan the Wise," **5**, 325.
Bonafoux Vidal, opposes the study of science, **4**, 28.
Bonafoux, Daniel Israel, Sabbatian, **5**, 207.
convert to Islam, **5**, 208.
Bonald, Louis Gabriel Ambroise, French reactionary leader, and the emancipation of the Jews, **5**, 477–9.
maligns the Jews, **5**, 478, 485.
in league with Molé, **5**, 479.
Bonastruc de Porta. *See* Moses ben Nachman.
Bonastruc Desmaëstre, at the Tortosa disputation, **4**, 208.
Bonastruc, Isaac. *See* Isaac Bonastruc.
Bonet. *See* David Bonet Buen-Giorno.
Bonet, a Jew of Montpellier, **3**, 395.
Bonet de Lates, physician, to Pope Alexander VI, **4**, 407–8.
to Leo X, **4**, 408.
letter to, from Reuchlin, **4**, 453, 454.
espouses Reuchlin's cause, **4**, 454.
Bonfed. *See* Solomon ben Reuben Bonfed.
Bonifaccio, Balthasar, accuser of Sarah Sullam, **5**, 70.

Boniface VIII, pope, at odds with Philip IV of France, 4, 44.
Boniface IX, pope, forbids the forcible baptism of Jews, 4, 173.
Bonnet, Caspar, work of, translated by Lavater, 5, 309.
works of, criticised by Mendelssohn, 5, 312–13, 314–15.
disclaims connection with Lavater, 5, 313–14.
Bonosus, governor of the East, subdues the Jews of Antioch, 3, 18.
"**Book of Creation**, The," commentary on, 3, 197.
"**Book of Riches**, The," work by Samuel Ibn-Nagrela, 3, 261.
"**Book of the Pious**, The," by Judah Sir Leon ben Isaac, 3, 408.
Book of the Wars of God, early Hebrew poetry, 1, 29.
"**Book of Wisdom**, The," against paganism, 2, 205–8.
Boppard, the blood accusation in, 3, 418, 637, 639.
Boraïta, an apocryphal Mishna, 2, 470.
Boraïtas, explained by Abba-Areka, 2, 515.
by Rabba bar Nachmani, 2, 578.
Bordeaux, the Marranos in, 5, 341.
German Jews in, 5, 342.
struggle in, between German and Portuguese Jews, 5, 342–3.
foreign Jews ejected from, 5, 343–4.
Bordeaux, the Jews of, maltreated by crusaders, 3, 570.
perish during the Pastoureaux massacres, 4, 56.
Bordeaux, the Jews of (*continued*), addressed in behalf of the Moravian and Bohemian Jews, 5, 253.
in Malesherbes' commission, 5, 432.
number of, 5, 435.
prosperity of, 5, 436.
join the National Guard, 5, 438.
on the Jewish question, 5, 442.
emancipated, 5, 442–3.
not affected by Napoleon's restrictive laws, 5, 499.
Borgia, cardinal. *See* Alexander VI, pope.
Börne, Ludwig (1786–1837), employed in the Frankfort ducal police, 5, 505, 541.
defends the German Jews, 5, 533.
as a Jew, 5, 536.
as a German, 5, 536–7.
apostle of liberty, 5, 537, 538–9.
resemblance of, to Mendelssohn, 5, 538.
despises the Jews of his time, 5, 538, 540.
sobriety of, 5, 538.
life of, in Frankfort, 5, 539.
style of, 5, 539.
feeling of, for Jews, 5, 539–40.
insults offered to, as a Jew, 5, 540–1.
defends the Jews, 5, 541–2.
publishes a journal, 5, 542.
becomes a Christian, 5, 542.
wit of, 5, 542.
on the "hep, hep!" persecutions, 5, 542–3.
answers Dr. Holst, 5, 543–4.
compared with Heine, 5, 544.
early home-life of, 5, 545.
debt of the Jews to, 5, 556.
debt of Germany to, 5, 556.

Börne, Ludwig (*continued*), compared with Erter, **5,** 615.
Boso, king of Burgundy, and the Jews, **3,** 175.
Bosporus, the, Jews settle on, **3,** 123.
a Karaite community on, **3,** 182.
Bosporus (Kertch), capital of the Crimea, **3,** 222.
Bossuet, bishop, applauds Richard Simon's exegesis, **5,** 179.
Bostanaï, Exilarch, restores the office to power, **3,** 10.
recognized as chief of the Jews, **3,** 89.
marries a daughter of Chosru, **3,** 89.
vassal of the Mahometans, **3,** 89.
permitted to wear a signet ring, **3,** 89–90.
dissensions among the sons of, **3,** 91.
descendants of, and the college presidents, **3,** 91.
descendants of, inherit the Exilarchate, **3,** 94.
Sherira a descendant of, **3,** 232.
line of, described in Sherira's "Letter," **3,** 233.
Bostra, birthplace of Simon ben Lakish, **2,** 495.
Botarel, Moses. *See* Moses Botarel.
Bourbon dynasty, the, restored to the French throne, **5,** 512, 596.
Bourges, the archbishop of, anti-Jewish sentiments of, **3,** 171.
"**Bow and Buckler,**" polemic by Simon ben Zemach Duran, **4,** 238.
Brabant, soldiers of, enlisted against the Hussites, **4,** 225.
Brahe, Tycho, astronomer, and David Gans, **4,** 638.
Brancas, duke of, given the Jews of Metz, **5,** 348, 446.
Brandenburg, the Mark of, Jews settle in, **5,** 173–4.
Brandenburg, the Mark of, the Jews of, accused of host-desecration, **4,** 439–40.
charged with child murder, **4,** 440.
burnt, **4,** 440.
threatened with expulsion, **4,** 652.
Bray, the Jews of, suffer martyrdom, **3,** 404.
Brazil, Paul de Pina in, **4,** 670.
the Jewish community in, **4,** 693–4.
Breidenbach, Wolff (1751–1829), interested in the abolition of the poll-tax, **5,** 467, 468, 472.
Bremen, Jews admitted into, **5,** 507.
Bremen, the Jews of, threatened with banishment, **5,** 512.
banished, **5,** 520.
Brendel, professor, attacked for defending the Jews, **5,** 528.
Brentano, representative of the romantic school, **5,** 515.
Breslau, the clergy of, upbraided by John of Capistrano, **4,** 260–1.
Chayon at, **5,** 218.
anti-Jewish pamphlets published in, **5,** 470.
rabbi of, opposes the Reform movement, **5,** 571.
the Hamburg reforms adopted in, **5,** 573.
a German-Jewish church in, **5,** 682.
a Jewish seminary at, **5,** 699. 700.

Breslau, the Jews of, during the Black Death persecutions, **4**, 109–10.
engaged in money-lending, **4**, 260.
charged with host-desecration, **4**, 261.
tortured, **4**, 261.
burnt or banished, **4**, 262–3.
join the "Society of Friends," **5**, 418.
apostasy among, **5**, 420.
Bresselau, Mendel J., Hebrew style of, **5**, 398.
establishes a society and a journal, **5**, 398, 399.
compiles a liturgy, **5**, 564.
scourges the orthodox party, **5**, 572.
secretary of the Reform Temple Union, **5**, 672.
Bretagne, the Jews of, under Henry II, **3**, 409.
"**Bridle** for the Jews, The," by Raymund Martin, **3**, 622.
Brieli, Jehuda Leon (1643–1722), rabbi of Mantua, innovations of, **5**, 200.
opponent of the Kabbala, **5**, 200.
opposes Chayon, **5**, 225.
Bristol, a Jew of, tortured by King John, **3**, 505.
Britain, rebels against Hadrian, **2**, 399.
Brody, the Chassidim in, **5**, 388.
ban against the Chassidim published in, **5**, 392.
Chassidistic writings burned in, **5**, 393.
beginnings of culture among the Jews of, **5**, 612.
Broglie, Duc de, opposes the emancipation of the Jews, **5**, 447.
Bromet, Herz, member of the Felix Libertate, **5**, 453.
Bromet, Herz (*continued*), zealous for the emancipation of the Dutch Jews, **5**, 454.
deputy to the National Assembly, **5**, 458.
Broussa, the Spanish exiles in, **4**, 405.
the Jews of, and the Pesaro trade, **4**, 579.
Brühl, Saxon minister, Jewish agent of, **5**, 263.
and Eibeschütz's supporters, **5**, 263.
indifferent about Polish affairs, **5**, 282.
Bruna, Israel. *See* Israel Bruna.
Brunetta, a Jewess of Trent, on friendly terms with Christians, **4**, 297.
charged with the blood accusation, **4**, 298.
Brunhilde, of Austrasia, permits Jews to own slaves, **3**, 34.
Brünn, the Jews of, banished, **4**, 263.
Israel Bruna exiled from, **4**, 302.
Jews under restrictions in, **5**, 523.
Brunswick, rabbinical conference at, **5**, 677–8, 681–2.
Brunswick, the duke of, honors Mendelssohn, **5**, 308.
commends Mendelssohn's reply to Lavater, **5**, 313.
conversation of, with Mendelssohn, on Christian dogmas, **5**, 315.
Brunswick, the Jews of, expelled, **4**, 652.
deprived of civil rights, **5**, 512.
Brunswick-Lüneburg abolishes the poll-tax, **5**, 467.
Bruria (Valeria), wife of Rabbi Meïr, **2**, 436.

Brussels, the Jews of, during the Black Death persecutions, **4**, 112.
expelled, **4**, 662.
Brutus, Roman leader, suicide of, **2**, 81.
Buchholz, opposes Jewish emancipation, **5**, 468, 472.
Buda, the council of, anti-Jewish decrees of, **3**, 614–15.
Buda-Pesth, rabbinical college at, **5**, 700. *See also* Pesth.
Budnians, anti-Trinitarian sect, **4**, 647.
Budny, Simon, translates the Bible into Polish, **4**, 647.
Buen-Giorno. *See* David Bonet Buen-Giorno.
Buffon, praises Pereira's sign language, **5**, 343.
Bugia (Buja), refuge for Spanish Jews, **4**, 197.
suffering of Spanish exiles in, **4**, 361.
Bulan, king of the Chazars, convert to Judaism, **3**, 139–40, 327.
Bulgarians, the, friendly to the Jews, **3**, 123.
vassals to the Chazars, **3**, 138.
Bulls, papal, by Benedict XIII, **4**, 215–16.
Boniface IX, **4**, 173.
Clement IV, **3**, 602.
Clement VI, **4**, 103, 105, 173.
Clement VII, **4**, 507, 515, 516.
Clement VIII, **4**, 671.
Eugenius III, **3**, 349–51.
Eugenius IV, **4**, 229, 250, 251.
Gregory IX, **3**, 564.
Gregory X, **3**, 635.
Innocent III, **3**, 497.
Innocent IV, **3**, 584–5; **4**, 165.
Julius III, **4**, 565.
Martin V, **4**, 219–20, 226.
Nicholas V, **4**, 253, 254, 256, 287.
Bulls, papal (*continued*), Paul III, **4**, 516, 522, 526.
Paul IV, **4**, 566.
Pius IV, **4**, 588, 589.
Pius V, **4**, 591.
Sixtus IV, **4**, 311, 319, 321, 322.
Sixtus V, **4**, 655–6, 658.
against the immigration of Jews in Palestine, **4**, 274.
Buol Schauenstein, Count von, protects the Frankfort Jews, **5**, 530.
Burgos, Kabbala taught in, **4**, 6.
disputation at, **4**, 140.
coronation of Juan I at, **4**, 156.
Burgos, the cortes of, make the Jews responsible for the civil war, **4**, 124–5.
oppose the employment of Jews, **4**, 229.
Burgos, the Jews of, under Sancho, **3**, 617.
taxed heavily, **4**, 123, 124.
persecuted, **4**, 170.
converted, **4**, 205.
Burgundians, the, the empire of, the Jews of, not considered a distinct race, **3**, 35.
occupations of, **3**, 35–6.
discriminated against, **3**, 37.
Burgundy, the Jews of, presented to the Church, **3**, 175.
Burnt-offerings, Samuel on the importance of, **1**, 74.
Jochanan ben Zakkai on, **2**, 324, 325.
Burrus, Nero's secretary, bribed to oppose the Judæans, **2**, 247.
Bury St. Edmunds, the Jews of, butchered, **3**, 415.
Busche, Hermann von, partisan of Reuchlin, **4**, 456.

Buxtorf, John, senior (1564-1639), renders rabbinical studies accessible to Christians, **5,** 21.
Buxtorfs, the, introduce rabbinical literature to Christians, **5,** 179.
Byk, Jacob Solomon, Hebrew style of, **5,** 617.
Byron, quoted, **4,** 127.
Byzantine emperors, the, Jews under, **5,** 725-6.
Byzantine empire, the, attacked by the Agadists, **3,** 16.
in fear of the Chazars, **3,** 138.
fall of, **4,** 267.
Byzantine empire, the (*continued*), toleration of, **4,** 285.
Byzantine empire, the, the Jews of, under Arcadius, **2,** 615-16.
forbidden to build synagogues, **2,** 617.
treated with hostility, **3,** 10.
forced into Christianity, **3,** 122-3.
emigrate, **3,** 123-4.
in the ninth century, **3,** 175-6.
in the twelfth century, **3,** 424-8.
not admitted to military offices, **3,** 425.
brutal treatment of, **3,** 425.
poets among, **3,** 426.

C

Cabades. *See* Kobad.
Caballeria, Alfonso de, Marrano, tries to suppress the Aragon Inquisition, **4,** 329.
Caballo, Jules, founder of the "Alliance Israélite Universelle," **5,** 701.
Cabiri, the seven planets worshiped by the Canaanites, **1,** 54.
Cabrera, governor of the castle of Segovia, **4,** 283.
Cabul, fortress, **2,** 414.
fall of, **2,** 416.
religiousness of the inhabitants of, **2,** 480.
Caceres, Simon de, opens a Jewish burial-ground in London, **5,** 49.
Cacina, Roman consul, and Titus, **2,** 317.
Cadiz, Marranos flee to, **4,** 313.
victims of the Inquisition in the archbishopric of, **4,** 317.
taken by the English, **4,** 665.
Cæsar, Julius, in the first triumvirate, **2,** 73.
Cæsar, Julius (*continued*), frees Aristobulus II, **2,** 75.
favors Antipater, **2,** 75-6.
kindly disposed to the Judæans, **2,** 76, 179.
hated by the Judæans of Palestine, **2,** 77.
murder of, **2,** 79.
remits the tax during the Sabbatic year, **2,** 469.
Cæsar, Sextus, governor of Syria, honors Herod, **2,** 78.
makes Hyrcanus II responsible for the life of Herod, **2,** 78.
Cæsarea (Mazaca). *See* Mazaca.
Cæsarea (Straton), beautified by Herod, **2,** 106.
trade and shipping of, **2,** 118.
seat of the procurator, **2,** 129.
residence of Herod (Philip), **2,** 173.
favored by Agrippa I, **2,** 194.
destroyed by an earthquake, **2,** 408-9.
made an academic city, **2,** 543.
anti-Christian riot in, **3,** 17.

Cæsarea (*continued*), played into the hands of the Arabs, **3,** 87.
Cæsarea (Straton), the Greek inhabitants of, rejoice over Agrippa I's death, **2,** 196.
hate the Judæans, **2,** 246–7.
quarrel with the Judæans, **2,** 252–3.
Cæsarea (Straton), the Jews of, Greek culture of, **2,** 538.
devoted to circus sports, **2,** 626.
Cæsarea (Straton), the Judæans of, deprived of civil rights, **2,** 247.
exterminated, **2,** 262.
perish in the arena, **2,** 312.
Cæsarea Philippi, built by the tetrarch Philip, **2,** 138.
capital of Philip's tetrarchy, **2,** 158.
Judæans of, perish in the arena, **2,** 312.
Cæsars, the, sacrifices offered for, **2,** 103.
Cafri, native town of Rabba bar Chana, **2,** 454.
Cain, the Choic type of the Gnostics, **2,** 377.
Cainites, a Gnostic sect, **2,** 375.
Cairo (Fostat), a Karaite community in, **3,** 182.
Talmud study encouraged in, **3,** 208, 210.
Jehuda Halevi at, **3,** 340–1.
two synagogues of, **3,** 444.
Karaites of, **3,** 444; **4,** 71.
Maimonides at, **3,** 457–92.
hospital at, **3,** 495.
Spanish spoken at, **4,** 388.
Spanish exiles in, **4,** 392–96.
Purim of, **4,** 396.
Joseph Delmedigo at, **5,** 76.
Cairo, the Jews of, in the twelfth century, **3,** 444.
maltreated, **4,** 396.
Cairo, the Jews of (*continued*), establish schools, **5,** 664.
reconciled with the Karaites, **5,** 664.
Calabrese. *See* Chayim Vital Calabrese.
Calabria, the Jews of, subject to curial duties, **2,** 616.
invaded by the Mahometans, **3,** 212.
Calahorra, Abraham Ibn-Ezra dies at, **3,** 374.
Calatayud, the Marranos of, conspire against Pedro Arbues, **4,** 330.
Calatayud, the Jews of, excommunicate anti-Maimunists, **3,** 537.
converted, **4,** 214.
Calatrava, fortress, taken by Jehuda Ibn-Ezra, **3,** 361.
Calderon, dramatist, **5,** 112.
Calderon, the Jewish, 5, 110–11.
Calendar, the, arranged by the Jamnia Synhedrion, **2,** 326.
fixed by astronomical calculations, **2,** 336.
fixed by the Patriarchs, **2,** 362–3.
corrected by Akiba's disciples, **2,** 433.
arranged by Chananya, **2,** 443.
drawn up by Mar-Samuel, **2,** 521–2, 574.
the computation of, forbidden, **2,** 571.
fixed adopted by Hillel II, **2,** 572–4.
method of calculating, **2,** 573.
Jewish, adopted by the Arabs, **3,** 59–60.
fixed, abolished by Anan ben David, **3,** 131.
fixed, rejected by the Tiflisites, **3,** 158.
key to, by Nachshon ben Zadok, **3,** 179.

Calendar, the (*continued*), Karaite, attacked by Saadiah, **3**, 190–1.
rules of, collected by Saadiah, **3**, 196.
work on, by Dunash ben Tamim, **3**, 211, 217.
Isaac Ibn-Albalia on, **3**, 283.
accuracy of, demonstrated, **3**, 313.
work on, by Maimonides, **3**, 451.
used by the Karaites, **4**, 270.
See also Ibbur.
Caligula, emperor, distinguishes Agrippa I, **2**, 174–5, 176.
divine honor to the images of, **2**, 183–4.
hates the Judæans, **2**, 187.
statues of, in the Temple, **2**, 188–9.
assassinated, **2**, 189.
Judaism defended before, **5**, 654.
Caliphate of the East, the. *See* Abbasside Caliphate, the.
Calixtus, pope, convenes a Church Council in France, **3**, 376; **4**, 275.
Callimandrus, Egyptian general against the Judæans, **2**, 11.
Calliopas, charioteer, causes a riot, **3**, 11.
"**Calumniator, The**," sobriquet of Joshua Lorqui, **4**, 217.
Calvin, and Michael Scotus, **4**, 541.
Cambridge, the Jews of, expelled, **3**, 641.
Cambyses, of Persia, death of, **1**, 358.
Camith, family of high priests, **2**, 237.
Campanton. *See* Isaac ben Jacob Campanton.
Campeggio, cardinal, on the commission on the Portuguese Inquisition, **4**, 514.
Campo Formio, peace of, and the poll tax of French Jews in Germany, **5**, 464.
Campo-Mayor, refuge for Spanish Marranos, **4**, 498.
"**Can the Jews remain in their present condition without harm to the state?**" anti-Jewish pamphlet, **5**, 469–70.
Canaan, entry of Israelites into, **1**, 1, 32.
description of the coast of, **1**, 2–3.
claimed by the Israelites, **1**, 4–5.
rapid conquest of, **1**, 39–40.
becomes the Holy Land, **1**, 41.
not entirely conquered, **1**, 50–1.
See Palestine.
Canaanites, the, description of, **1**, 2–4.
subdivisions of, **1**, 3.
trade of, **1**, 3.
cities of, **1**, 3.
at war with Asher and Naphtali, **1**, 37.
dwell with the tribe of Judah, **1**, 39.
in dread of the Israelites, **1**, 40.
heathenism of, **1**, 51.
idol worship of, **1**, 54.
relations of, to the Israelites, **1**, 56–8.
suffer under David, **1**, 131.
help to build the Temple, **1**, 163.
See Gibeonites; Jebusites; Philistines, etc.
Candia. *See* Crete.
Canea, the Jews of, importance of, **4**, 406.
Canon, the, of the Holy Writings, completed, **2**, 344. *See* Scriptures, the.

Cansino family, the, dragomans in Oran, **5**, 169.
Cantheras, family of high priests, **2**, 237.
Caorsini (Ultramontanes), usury practiced by, **3**, 510.
Capernaum (Kephar Nahum), Jesus successful in, **2**, 153–7.
the first church at, **2**, 565.
Capets, the first, the Jews oppressed under, **3**, 241–2.
Caphar-Salama, the battle of, Judas Maccabæus victorious at, **1**, 484.
Caphtor, the original home of the Philistines, **1**, 54.
Capistrano. *See* John of Capistrano.
Capnion. *See* Reuchlin, John.
Capo d'Istrias, Russian plenipotentiary, and the emancipation of the Jews, **5**, 527.
Cappadocia, study of the Law in, **2**, 358.
the Jews of, under Shabur I, **2**, 520, 526.
"Captives of Hope, The," drama by Joseph Penso, **5**, 113.
Captivity, the, the return from, **1**, 351–6.
See Babylonia, the Judæans of.
Captivity, the, Princes of. *See* Exilarchate, the; Exilarchs, the.
Capua, the Jews of in the twelfth century, **3**, 424.
Hillel of Verona in, **3**, 629.
Carabas, impersonates Agrippa I, **2**, 182.
Caracalla, emperor, vices of, **2**, 468.
relation of, to the Jews, **2**, 468–9.
exacts the tax during the Sabbatic year, **2**, 469.
Caraffa, Pietro. *See* Paul IV, pope.
Çarca, Samuel. *See* Samuel Çarça.
Carcassonne, Jews in, in the sixth century, **3**, 35.
Cardoso, Abraham Michael (1630–1706), Marrano, resumes Judaism, **5**, 163.
occupations and morality of, **5**, 164.
figures as a Sabbatian prophet, **5**, 164–5.
proclaims himself Sabbataï's successor, **5**, 207.
writings of, **5**, 208, 248.
writings of, burned, **5**, 220.
Cardoso, (Isaac) Fernando (1615–1680), Marrano physician, resumes Judaism, **5**, 163.
occupations and life of, **5**, 164.
anti-Sabbatian, **5**, 164, 165.
Sachs compared with, **5**, 688.
Cardozo, Elihu Aboab, erects a synagogue at Hamburg, **4**, 689.
Carenton, the Jews of, attacked by crusaders, **3**, 355.
Carians, the, mercenary troops employed by Athaliah, **1**, 214.
in sympathy with Joash, **1**, 215–6.
Carinthia, the Jews of, expelled, **4**, 427.
Carlovingians, the last, the Jews oppressed under, **3**, 241–2.
Carlsruhe, the Jews of, persecuted, **5**, 530.
the Hamburg reforms adopted in, **5**, 573.
Carmel, Mount, description of, **1**, 44.
considered holy by the Canaanites, **1**, 51.

Carmel, Mount (*continued*), Elijah lives on, **1,** 203.
Elisha lives on, **1,** 208.
north-western limit of Judæa under Alexander Jannæus, **2,** 46.
Carmelite district, the, of Paris, commends the Jews, **5,** 444.
Carmona, the Marranos of, resist the Inquisition, **4,** 313.
conspirators of, burnt, **4,** 317.
Carpentras, rabbi of, at the first rabbinical synod, **3,** 377.
Carpentras, the Jews of, not banished by Charles VI, **4,** 177.
wealth of, **4,** 592.
number of, **5,** 436.
honor Crémieux and Montefiore, **5,** 658.
Carrion, the Jews of, under Sancho, **3,** 617.
persecuted, **4,** 170.
Carthage, captured by Genseric, **2,** 611.
the Temple vessels removed from, **3,** 26.
Carvajal, Fernandez (Isaac), a Jew secretly living in London, **5,** 38.
opens a Jewish burial ground, **5,** 49.
Casalmaggiore, the Jews of, number of, **4,** 653.
Casimir III, the Great, of Poland, extends the privileges of the Jews, **4,** 111, 263.
protects the Jews, **4,** 111.
Jewish mistress of, **4,** 112.
Casimir IV, of Poland, extends the privileges of the Jews, **4,** 263–5, 419.
under Capistrano's influence, **4,** 265–6.
revokes the privileges of the Jews, **4,** 266.
sons of, **4,** 419, 631.
Casimir IV (*continued*), statute of, confirmed by Sigismund III, **4,** 643.
Caspe, the Jews of, converted, **4,** 214.
Caspian Sea, the, Jews settle on the coast of, **3,** 123.
island in, refuge of the Chazars, **3,** 222.
Cassander, ally of Ptolemy I, at the battle of Ipsus, **1,** 417.
Cassel, meeting place of the Westphalian consistory, **5,** 501.
Cassiodorus, minister of Theodoric, **3,** 30.
homiletic exposition of the Psalms by, **3,** 31.
on the Jews, **3,** 31.
Cassius, Avidius, rebel, death of, **2,** 463.
Cassius Longinus, Caius, legate of Crassus, retreats before the Parthians, **2,** 74.
defeats the Judæan army, **2,** 74.
governor of Syria, forces contributions from Judæa, **2,** 80.
suicide of, **2,** 81.
Cassius Longinus, Caius, governor of Syria, occupies Jerusalem, **2,** 197.
Castel-Branco, João Rodrigo de. *See* Amatus Lusitanus.
Castellane, de, deputy to the National Assembly, **5,** 439.
Castel-Narbonnais, refuge of the Jews from the Pastoureaux, **4,** 56.
Castile, lacks Talmud schools in the twelfth century, **3,** 322.
Jews in, in the twelfth century, **3,** 384.
war of, with Morocco, **4,** 84.

Castile (*continued*), civil war in, **4**, 118–19, 120–2, 123–6.
union of, with Portugal, **4**, 161.
quarrel about the rabbinate of, **4**, 161–2.
forced converts in, relapse into Judaism, **4**, 180.
Marranos of, **4**, 309. *See under* Marranos.
exiles from, form a congregation in Constantinople, **4**, 402.
See also under Spain.
Castile, the Jews of, under Alfonso VI, **3**, 292–3.
under Alfonso Raimundez, **3**, 361, 363.
oppose the Almohades, **3**, 387.
under Alfonso VIII, **3**, 499.
first persecution of, **3**, 507.
in the Maimunist controversy, **3**, 530, 536, 544.
under Alfonso X, **3**, 592–6.
under Ferdinand III, **3**, 592.
employed at court, **3**, 593–4.
degraded by Alfonso X, **3**, 594–6.
fined, **3**, 616.
under Sancho, **3**, 616–17.
taxed, **3**, 617; **4**, 125–6.
send deputies to Huete, **3**, 617.
number of, **3**, 617.
opponents of science, **4**, 38.
in the fourteenth century, **4**, 51–3.
leaders of the Spanish-Jewish community, **4**, 75.
under Alfonso X, **4**, 75–6.
guilty of usury, **4**, 80.
Gonzalo Martinez conspires against, **4**, 84–5.
neglect Jewish science, **4**, 86–7, 91.
not held responsible for the Black Death, **4**, 113.
Castile, the Jews of (*continued*), under Pedro the Cruel, **4**, 113–26.
aid Maria de Padilla, **4**, 117.
in the civil war, **4**, 118–19, 120–2, 123–6.
Pedro's opponents hostile to, **4**, 120–1.
held responsible for the civil war, **4**, 124–5, 167.
reduced to beggary by the civil war, **4**, 137.
under Henry II, **4**, 137–8.
hostility to, **4**, 138.
degraded by outward signs, **4**, 139.
forced into religious debates, **4**, 140–2.
possess penal jurisdiction, **4**, 155.
deprived of criminal jurisdiction, **4**, 157.
accusations against, **4**, 157.
under Henry III, **4**, 193.
under Juan II, **4**, 194, 203–4, 205–6, 228–9.
assaulted, **4**, 204–5.
bull against, **4**, 250–1.
appeal to Juan II, **4**, 251.
insecurity of, under Juan II, **4**, 252–3.
under Henry IV, **4**, 274–6.
low position of, in Henry IV's statute book, **4**, 278.
indispensable as financiers, **4**, 279–80.
warned of approaching danger, **4**, 336.
protected by Isaac Abrabanel, **4**, 343–4.
help the Marranos, **4**, 344.
proclamation expelling, **4**, 347–8.
See also under Spain.
Castile, New, the Jews of, taxed, **3**, 617.

Castro, an English Jew, and the Damascus affair, **5**, 653.
Castro, de, a noble Castilian family, **3**, 363.
Castro, Abraham de, Selim I's master of the mint, benevolence of, **4**, 393.
informs against the Egyptian viceroy, **4**, 395.
Castro, Balthasar (Isaac) Orobio de (1620–1687), Marrano, professor of metaphysics at Salamanca, tortured, **5**, 116.
professor of medicine at Toulouse, **5**, 117.
associates with Spinoza, **5**, 117.
refutes Spinoza's views, **5**, 167.
prominence of, **5**, 199–200.
Castro, Bendito (Baruch Nehemiah) de, physician, Sabbatian, **5**, 140, 150.
Castro, Moses de, antagonist of Jacob Berab, **4**, 534–5.
Castro, Rodrigo de (1560–1627), Marrano physician, ability of, **4**, 686–7.
owns landed property, **4**, 688.
Castro-Tartas, Isaac de, Marrano, martyrdom of, **5**, 31–2.
Casuistry, in the Mishna, **2**, 475–6.
Catalina of Lancaster, regent for Juan II of Castile, **4**, 193.
issues edicts concerning the Jews, **4**, 203–4, 205–6, 275.
death of, **4**, 217, 228.
Catalonia, part of Aragon, **3**, 387.
Catalonia, the Jews of, in the Maimunist controversy, **3**, 530.
massacred, **4**, 102–3.
provide against the Black Death persecutions, **4**, 112–13.
Catalonia, the Jews of (*continued*), possess penal jurisdiction, **4**, 155.
persecuted in 1391, **4**, 172.
converted, **4**, 214.
loyal to their faith, **4**, 215.
possessions of, sequestrated, **4**, 349.
Catechumens, the house of, supported by the Jews, **4**, 566.
Catherine, empress of Russia, member of the Berlin Academy, **5**, 308.
at war with Poland, **5**, 388.
Catherine, of Portugal, hostile to the Marranos, **4**, 489.
Catherine de Medici, queen mother in France, and Joseph Nassi, **4**, 598.
proposes her son for the Polish throne, **4**, 604.
Catholic Church, the, rise of, **2**, 500.
Catholic Church, the German, established, **5**, 682.
Catholic reaction, the, **4**, 650–1.
the Jews suffer under, **4**, 652–3.
Catholicism, more hostile to the Jews than Arianism, **3**, 26.
overthrown in England, **4**, 541.
and the romantic movement, **5**, 516.
See Christianity.
Catholics, the, toleration of, under Valentinian I, **2**, 603.
hate Theodoric, **3**, 29, 30.
antagonized by the Arian Visigoths, **3**, 44–5.
in the Damascus affair, **5**, 650–1, 662.
See Christians, the.
Catholics, the Greek, molest the Turkish Jews, **4**, 552–3.

Cathunho, Isaac, Marrano in Pernambuco, **4,** 693.
Catullus, Roman governor of Cyrene, executes Zealots, **2,** 318.
Caucasus, the, Jews settle in, **3,** 123.
under the Exilarch's jurisdiction, **3,** 429.
Cavilhão, Jewish center in Portugal, **4,** 159.
Ceba, Ansaldo, priest and poet, tries to convert Sarah Sullam, **5,** 69–70.
Cendebæus, Syrian general, invades Judæa, **1,** 529.
Ceneda, wagers a pound of his own flesh, **4,** 657.
Cenedæus, of Adiabene, relatives of, aid Judæa against Rome, **2,** 264.
Censorship of the press introduced by Caraffa, **4,** 563.
in Germany, **5,** 532.
Censorship of the Talmud under Jayme I of Aragon, **3,** 603.
advised by two popes, **4,** 658.
abuses of, **4,** 659, 660.
See under Talmud, the.
Census, a, taken by David, **1,** 137–8.
of Judæans ordered by Augustus, **2,** 129.
arouses terror and dissension, **2,** 130.
resisted by the Zealots, **2,** 133–4.
in 66, **2,** 251.
"Centuries," by Amatus Lusitanus, **4,** 570.
Cervera, the Jews of, persecuted, **4,** 94, 103.
Cesis, de, cardinal, on the commission on the Portuguese Inquisition, **4,** 514.
Ceuta, the Jews of, emigrate, **3,** 424.
battle of, **4,** 390.
Ceylon, the Jews of, in the twelfth century, **3,** 436.
Chabar, teacher of the Law among the Arabian Jews, **3,** 59.
Chaberim, fellows, **2,** 364.
Chabib. *See* Amatus Lusitanus.
Chabulon. *See* Cabul.
Chaburah, order, **2,** 364.
Chacham, officer of the Synhedrion, **2,** 360.
office of, ceases, **2,** 453.
title of the Amsterdam rabbis, **4,** 681.
title of the Hamburg rabbis, **4,** 689; **5,** 577.
Chacham Zevi. *See* Zevi Ashkenazi.
Chacon, Castilian farmer of taxes, **4,** 275.
Chadija, wife of Mahomet, **3,** 71.
Chages, Jacob (1620–1674), recluse at Jerusalem, **5,** 126.
teacher of Nathan Ghazati, **5,** 131.
threatens Sabbataï Zevi with excommunication, **5,** 132.
Chages, Moses, denounces Chayon's work as heretical, **5,** 222.
excommunicates Chayon, **5,** 224.
abused by the Amsterdam Portuguese Jews, **5,** 224.
excommunicated and driven from Amsterdam, **5,** 226.
in Altona, **5,** 231.
opposes Luzzatto's Kabbala, **5,** 238.
threatens Kabbalistic writers with the ban, **5,** 239.
forbids the study of Kabbala to young men, **5,** 241.

Chages, Moses (*continued*), deprecates leniency towards Eibeschütz, **5,** 249–50.
opposes the Eibeschütz Talmud edition, **5,** 251.
returns to Palestine, **5,** 256.
Chaggai (Haggai), teacher of the Law, attacks Judah II, **2,** 485.
a Palestinian Amora, **2,** 560.
member of the last Synhedrion, **2,** 567.
Chaibar, Israelites settle in, **3,** 54.
the Benu-Nadhir settle in, **3,** 79.
Chaibar, the Jews of, descendants of the Rechabites, fortifications held by, **3,** 55.
threatened by Mahomet, **3,** 81–2.
roused against Mahomet, **3,** 82–3.
driven away by Omar, **3,** 85.
preserve love for Arabic, **3,** 111.
object to Talmudic restraints, **3,** 119.
in the twelfth century, **3,** 437.
Chaifa, burial place of Nachmani and Yechiel of Paris, **3,** 608.
"**Chain of Tradition, The,**" by Gedalya Ibn-Yachya, **4,** 616.
Chaireas, commander of the fortress Joazer, **1,** 474.
Chakan (Chagan), title of the Chazar kings, **3,** 138.
Chalafta, member of the Jamnia Synhedrion, **2,** 357.
Chalcis, prince of. *See* Herod II.
Chaldæan garrison in Judah, **1,** 321.
Chaldæans, the. *See* Nebuchadnezzar.
Chaldaic translations of Scriptures, **2,** 581–2.
Chaldee, taught as a means of conversion, **4,** 245.
Chalil, vizir, tries to save Esther Kiera, **4,** 630.
Chama of Nahardea (356–377), Amora, **2,** 593.
principal of the Pumbeditha academy, **2,** 594.
insignificance of, **2,** 594–5.
Chama ben Anilaï, a Jew of Sora, **2,** 545–6.
Chamath, military station under Hadrian, **2,** 419.
Chambéry, supposed center of the well poisoners, **4,** 102.
Chamiz, Joseph, physician, and Leo Modena, **5,** 67.
Kabbalist, **5,** 74.
Champagne, the home of Talmud studies after Rashi, **3,** 289.
Talmud college of, **3,** 403.
Chanan, prince of the Jews of Taima, **3,** 437.
Chanan of Iskia, restores the Pumbeditha academy, **3,** 9.
Chananel ben Chushiel, recognized as a Talmud authority, **3,** 211, 248.
busies himself with the Jerusalem Talmud, **3,** 249.
consults Haï Gaon, **3,** 252.
eulogizes Haï Gaon, **3,** 253.
Alfassi disciple of, **3,** 285.
writings of, the basis of Nathan ben Yechiel's lexicon, **3,** 290.
Chananel Ibn-Askara, Kabbalist, **4,** 74.
Chananya, Agadist, **2,** 575–6.
Chananya (Achunaï), brother of Anan ben David, candidate for the Exilarchate, **3,** 129.
death of, **3,** 137.
Chananya, nephew of Joshua ben Chananya, joins Christianity, **2,** 370.

Chananya (*continued*), withdrawn from Jewish Christian influences, **2**, 443.
establishes a Synhedrion at Nahor-Pakod, **2**, 443.
arranges the calendar, **2**, 443.
and Simon II, **2**, 443–4.
dissolves his Synhedrion, **2**, 444.
Chananya, principal of the Sora academy, **3**, 10.
Chananya. *See also* Chanina.
Chanceller, Jewish Portuguese official, **4**, 159.
Chanilaï. *See* Anilaï.
Chanina, teacher of the Law, **2**, 330.
Chanina. *See* Mar-Chanina.
Chanina bar Chama, refused permission to teach, **2**, 456.
to be appointed teacher by Gamaliel III, **2**, 466.
the oldest of the Amoraim, **2**, 490.
work of, **2**, 490–1.
compared with Eliezer ben Hyrcanus, **2**, 491.
deserted by his disciples, **2**, 491.
veneration for, **2**, 491.
characterizes the people of Sepphoris, **2**, 491–2.
old age of, **2**, 492.
protects Mar-Samuel's daughter, **2**, 528.
disciples of, **2**, 531.
Chanina ben Abbahu, at Tiberias, **2**, 543.
Chanina (Chananya) ben Teradion, member of the Jamnia Synhedrion, **2**, 357.
refuses obedience to Hadrian's decrees, **2**, 427.
suffers martyrdom, **2**, 429.
wife and daughter of, **2**, 429, 436.
Chaninaï, Babylonian Jewish judge, declares Bostanaï's son legitimate, **3**, 91.
Chaninaï, Exilarch, **3**, 10.
Chaninaï, principal of the Pumbeditha academy, **3**, 10.
Chaninaï Kahana ben Huna (765–775), Gaon of Sora, **3**, 137.
Chanoch ben Moses (940–1014), attainments of, **3**, 229.
rabbi of Cordova, **3**, 230.
chief of the Andalusian Jews, **3**, 236.
dispute about the position of, **3**, 237–8.
deposed and re-instated, **3**, 240.
on the death of Jacob Ibn-Jau, **3**, 241.
death of, **3**, 241.
Chanukah (Hanukkah), Feast of Lights, instituted, **1**, 472–3.
introduced into Egypt, **2**, 6–7.
observed by pagans, **2**, 384.
abolished by Anan ben David, **3**, 132.
Charag, poll-tax of the Babylonian Jews, **2**, 508.
Chares, leader of the Zealots in Gamala, **2**, 289.
Charisi. *See* Jehuda Alcharisi.
Charlemagne, predecessors of, and the Jews, **3**, 40.
contributes to the advancement of the Jews, **3**, 141, 143.
protects the Jews, **3**, 142.
embassy of, to Haroun Alrashid, **3**, 143.
oath imposed by, on Jews testifying against Christians, **3**, 144.
Charles IV, emperor, protects the Jews, **4**, 106.

Charles IV (*continued*), gives the Jews of Worms to the town, **4**, 108.
at war with Gunther of Schwarzburg, **4**, 109.
punishes the murderers of Jews, **4**, 109–10.
and the Jews of Nuremberg, **4**, 110.
asked to permit Jews to return to Augsburg, **4**, 127–8.
grants "servi cameræ" to the electors, **4**, 128.
deed of, concerning the Jews, **4**, 695.
Charles V, emperor, ambassador of, employs a Jewish physician, **4**, 411.
opposed to Reuchlin, **4**, 464.
adherents of, **4**, 468.
declares Luther an exile, **4**, 469.
refuses freedom of belief to Marranos, **4**, 484.
empowers the Inquisition to proceed against Lutherans, **4**, 485.
Nunes sent to, to learn about the Inquisition, **4**, 490.
threatens the liberty of Italy, **4**, 492.
treats Rome as a hostile city, **4**, 497.
liberates Reubeni from the Spanish Inquisition, **4**, 499.
crowned king of Italy, **4**, 503.
instrumental in the establishment of the Portuguese Inquisition, **4**, 507, 509, 517, 518.
delivers Molcho and Reubeni to the Mantua Inquisition, **4**, 510.
imprisons Reubeni, **4**, 511.
hated by Clement VII, **4**, 514.
victorious at Tunis, **4**, 517.
hostile to Paul III, **4**, 526.
Charles V (*continued*), banishes the Jews from Naples, **4**, 544.
renews the privileges of the Jews, **4**, 547.
in debt to the Mendes bank, **4**, 572.
orders the Mendes property to be seized, **4**, 573.
expels the Jews from the Netherlands, **4**, 661–2.
Charles VII, anti-emperor, occupies Prague, **5**, 251.
Charles of Anjou, king of Sicily, employs a Jewish physician, **3**, 628.
Charles, of Baden, grants the Jews political freedom, **5**, 502–3.
Charles I, of England, promotes the cause of liberty, **5**, 25.
Charles II, of England, the Jews under, **5**, 141.
Charles II, the Bald (843), king of the western Franks, friendly to the Jews, **3**, 170, 172.
condition of the Jews under, **3**, 170–4.
Charles III, the Simple (899–914), of France, grants the possessions of the Narbonne Jews to the Church, **3**, 175.
Charles IV, of France, death of, **4**, 77.
Charles V, of France, permits Jews to return, **4**, 129.
increases the privileges of the Jews, **4**, 131, 133.
prohibits forced attendance of Jews at churches, **4**, 132.
death of, **4**, 150.
Charles VI, of France, protects the Jews, **4**, 152.
and the rights of Jewish creditors, **4**, 174.
banishes the Jews, **4**, 175–6.
protects the exiles, **4**, 176.

Charles VIII, of France, conquers Naples, **4**, 360.
alliance against, **4**, 373.
Charles IX, of France, and the election of a Polish king, **4**, 604.
Charles X, of France, the emancipation of the Jews under, **5**, 596.
Charles III, of Navarre, employs a Jewish physician, **4**, 184.
Charles X, of Sweden, at war with Poland, **5**, 15.
Charles XI, of Sweden, inquires into Karaism, **4**, 182.
Charles XII, of Sweden, inquires into Karaism, **4**, 184.
Chasda of Cafri (217–309), a Babylonian Amora, **2**, 545.
disciple of Rab, **2**, 552–3.
good fortune of, **2**, 553, 576, 585.
estrangement between, and Huna, **2**, 553.
principal of the Sora academy, **2**, 553.
death of, **2**, 553, 583.
Chasdaï (670–730), Exilarch, **3**, 92.
Chasdaï ben Abraham Crescas (1340–1410), philosopher, **4**, 145–7.
as Talmudist, **4**, 146.
exposes the weakness of Aristotelianism, **4**, 146.
disciple of Nissim Gerundi, **4**, 146.
character of, **4**, 147.
orthodoxy of, **4**, 149.
authority of, **4**, 149–50, 230.
imprisoned, **4**, 150, 155.
appealed to about the French rabbinate, **4**, 150, 153.
son of, martyr, **4**, 172.
describes the persecution of 1391, **4**, 172.
Chasdaï ben Abraham Crescas (*continued*), intrigue against, **4**, 185.
attacks the Christian dogmas, **4**, 187–8.
influences Profiat Duran, **4**, 190.
religious philosophy of, **4**, 191–3, 240.
creed of, **4**, 193.
disciple of, **4**, 208, 239.
anti-Christian polemic by, translated, **4**, 235.
views of, endorsed by Isaac Abrabanel, **4**, 342.
studied by Spinoza, **5**, 88.
Chasdaï ben Solomon of Tudela, rabbi, denounces Chayim ben Gallipapa, **4**, 149.
ambition of, **4**, 162.
Chasdaï Ibn-Shaprut (915–970), makes science a principle of Judaism, **3**, 187.
first representative of Judæo-European culture, **3**, 188.
protects Moses ben Chanoch, **3**, 209–10, 228.
corresponds with Dunash ben Tamim, **3**, 211, 217.
the founder of Judæo-Spanish culture, **3**, 215, 223.
modern character of, **3**, 215–16.
attainments of, **3**, 216.
as diplomat, **3**, 216, 218–19.
homage paid to, **3**, 217.
corresponds with Dossa, son of Saadiah, **3**, 217.
translates the work of Dioscorides, **3**, 218.
grieves over the Jewish dispersion, **3**, 219.
communicates with the king of the Chazars, **3**, 219–22.
honored by Alhakem, **3**, 222.
inspires poets, **3**, 223–4.
and Menachem ben Saruk, **3**, 224–5, 226–7.

Chasdaï Ibn-Shaprut (*continued*), invites Dunash Ibn-Labrat to Cordova, **3,** 226.
encourages the study of the Talmud in Spain, **3,** 227–8.
favors Chanoch ben Moses, **3,** 230.
death of, **3,** 230.
unique in Spanish-Jewish history, **3,** 313.

Chassidim (Chasidim, Assidæans), the, Nazarites under Simon the Just, **1,** 422.
opposed to the Hellenists, **1,** 435–6.
piety of, **1,** 436, 490.
exponents of the teachings of, **1,** 436.
incite the Judæans to steadfastness, **1,** 457.
hiding-places of, betrayed, **1,** 457–8.
killed in the caves, **1,** 458.
follow Mattathias the Hasmonæan, **1,** 460.
betrayed by Alcimus, **1,** 483.
a distinct party, **1,** 489.
compared with the Hasmonæan party, **1,** 489–90.
incensed at the destruction of the "Soreg," **1,** 492.
withdraw from public life, **2,** 16.
called Essenes, **2,** 16. *See* Essenes, the.
give rise to the Pharisees, **2,** 16. *See* Pharisees, the.
See also under Hasmonæans, the; Maccabees, the.

Chasinaï. *See* Asinaï.

Chassidim, the, Polish Sabbatian sect, emigrate, **5,** 212.
exhort to penance, **5,** 212.
supported by Samuel Oppenheim, **5,** 213.
accept Islam and Christianity, **5,** 213.

Chassidim, the (new), mock at the Talmudists, **5,** 379.
form a brotherhood, **5,** 383–5.
introduce innovations, **5,** 386.
divide into two branches, **5,** 388.
slander Elijah Wilna, **5,** 391.
excommunicated, **5,** 391–2.
conduct of, under persecution, **5,** 392–3.
put themselves under "Rebbes," **5,** 392.
read only Chassidistic works, **5,** 393.
second interdict against, **5,** 393–4.
writings of, burned, **5,** 393.
resist the opening of secular schools, **5,** 394.
writings of, forbidden in Galicia, **5,** 394.
efforts to suppress, **5,** 394.
persecute readers of non-Hebrew books, **5,** 608, 611.
attacked by Joseph Perl, **5,** 612.
joined by Erter, **5,** 613.

Chassidism, the (new), opposed to Rabbinical Judaism, **5,** 375, 379.
founders of, **5,** 375.
character of, **5,** 380–1.
the leaders of, **5,** 381–3.
circumstances favoring the spread of, **5,** 383–6, 387.
opposed by the Mendelssohnians, **5,** 394.
prevents the spread of culture among Russian Jews, **5,** 473.
revolt from, and culture in Galicia, **5,** 611.

Chastelard, the Jews of, suspected of well poisoning, **4,** 104.

Chateaubriand, on Judaism, **5,** 427, 428.

Chateaubriand (*continued*), reactionary influence of, **5,** 477, 478.
Chatel, the Jews of, suspected of well poisoning, **4,** 103–4.
Châtelet, refuge of the Jews of Paris, **4,** 151.
Chaumette, instrumental in setting up the religion of Reason, **5,** 450.
Chaves, Jacob de, pupil of Luzzatto, **5,** 242.
Chaves, Moses de, patron of Luzzatto, **5,** 242.
Chaya, daughter of Elias Schor, Frankist, **5,** 275.
Chayim of Landshut, appoints three rabbis for Germany, **4,** 227.
Chayim of Lublin, excommunicates Eibeschütz's opponents, **5,** 261, 262.
deprived of his rabbinate, **5,** 263.
Chayim ben Gallipapa (1310–1380), rabbi of Pampeluna, proposes innovations, **4,** 148–9.
Chayim Ibn-Musa (1390–1460), polemic writer against Christianity, **4,** 235–7.
controversy of, with a Christian, **4,** 236.
refutes Nicholas de Lyra's charges, **4,** 237.
rules by, for religious controversies, **4,** 237.
Chayim Benveniste. *See* Benveniste, Chayim.
Chayim Cohen, disciple of Jacob Tam, **3,** 381.
Chayim Malach, leader of a Sabbatian sect, **5,** 212.
doctrines of, **5,** 213.
joins the Donmäh, **5,** 214.
travels of, **5,** 214.
Chayim Vital Calabrese (1543–1620), Kabbalist, youth of, **4,** 623.
meets Isaac Lurya, **4,** 623–4.
spreads reports about Lurya's gifts, **4,** 624.
usurps authority over Lurya's disciples, **4,** 625.
alleged forerunner of the Messiah, **4,** 625; **5,** 53.
in Palestine and Syria, **5,** 52–3.
invites Kabbala enthusiasts to Damascus, **5,** 53.
alleges possession of Lurya's manuscripts, **5,** 53.
brother and son of, **5,** 53.
writings of, sought, **5,** 54.
Messianic speculation in the Kabbala of, **5,** 120–1.
adherents of, in Jerusalem, **5,** 125.
descendant of, **5,** 267.
disfigures Judaism, **5,** 559.
Chayon, Nehemiah Chiya (1650–1726), Sabbatian, education of, **5,** 215.
character of, **5,** 215–16.
doctrines of, **5,** 216–17.
excommunicated, **5,** 216.
publishes a pamphlet, **5,** 217.
preaches Sabbatian doctrines at Prague, **5,** 217–18.
submits his work to Naphtali Cohen, **5,** 218.
enters into relations with Löbele Prosnitz, **5,** 219.
prints his work in Berlin, **5,** 219–20.
at Amsterdam, **5,** 220.
denounced, **5,** 221–2.
work of, denounced, **5,** 222.
supported by Ayllon and Pinto, **5,** 223.
work of, examined by a Portuguese committee, **5,** 223.
excommunicated, **5,** 224, 231.
acquitted of heresy, **5,** 224–5.

Chayon, Nehemiah Chiya (*continued*), homage paid to, **5,** 225.
opposed by Brieli, **5,** 225.
calumniates his opponents, **5,** 226.
exposed, **5,** 227.
disgrace of, **5,** 227.
ban removed from, **5,** 228.
returns to Europe, **5,** 230–1.
death of, **5,** 231.
son of, **5,** 231.
influences Eibeschütz, **5,** 248.
Chayuj. *See* Jehuda Ibn-Daud.
Chayyat. *See* Judah ben Jacob Chayyat.
Chazanuth, synagogue chanting, **3,** 118.
Chazaria, the Crimean peninsula, **3,** 138.
the Ten Tribes in, **3,** 141.
Chazars, the, friendly to the Jews, **3,** 123.
Jews settle in the capital of, **3,** 124.
found a kingdom, **3,** 138.
warlike, **3,** 138.
conquer the Crimea, **3,** 138.
converted to Judaism, **3,** 139–40, 327–30.
victorious over the Arabs, **3,** 139.
taught the Bible and Talmud, **3,** 140.
influences of Judaism on, **2,** 141.
judicial system of, **3,** 141.
information about, brought to Spain, **3,** 219–20.
power of, in the tenth century, **3,** 221.
flee before Sviatislav, **3,** 222.
Jewish princes of, take refuge in Spain, **3,** 254.
the land of, visited by Petachya, **3,** 421.
Chazraj, the, Arabic family, relations of, to the Jews, **3,** 55.
Chazraj, the (*continued*), conversions among, to Judaism, **3,** 61.
hostile to Jewish rule, **3,** 67.
Jews of Yathrib, dependent on, **3,** 68.
feuds of, **3,** 70–1.
Chebrath Dorshe Leshon Eber, society for the promotion of the Hebrew language, **5,** 398–9.
Chelebi, Raphael Joseph, mintmaster at Cairo, benevolence of, **5,** 124–5.
devotee of the Kabbala, **5,** 125.
interested in Sabbataï Zevi, **5,** 125, 127.
the Jerusalem Jews appeal to, **5,** 127–8.
Sabbataï Zevi married in the house of, **5,** 129.
letter to, from Nathan Ghazati, **5,** 131.
rewarded by Sabbataï Zevi, **5,** 145.
encourages the Italian Sabbatians, **5,** 160.
Chemnitz, leader hostile to the Jews of Worms, **4,** 698.
Chemosh, Ammonite and Moabite god, **1,** 55.
worshiped on the Mount of Olives, **1,** 175.
Chepez Alkuti. *See* Alkuti.
Cherem. *See* Excommunication.
Cherethites, the, mercenary troops under David, **1,** 122.
in the Ammonite war, **1,** 126.
employed against Sheba, **1,** 149.
attend Solomon, **1,** 153.
Chesheb-Efod, mathematical work by Proflat Duran, **4,** 191.
Chess, inventor of, **3,** 7.
Chiddush, a novelty in Talmud explanations, **4,** 641.

Chiddushim, Talmudic explanations by Nachmani, **3,** 532.
Chiddushim, theoretic discussion of the Talmud, **3,** 345.
Child-murder, charged against Israel Bruna, **4,** 302–5.
Manasseh ben Israel exonerates the Jews from, **5,** 42.
Child-murder, the charge of against the Jews, of Zurich, **4,** 105.
of Spain, **4,** 276.
of Sepulveda, **4,** 278–9.
of Trent, **4,** 298–9.
discredited by the Doge of Venice, **4,** 299.
of Frankfort, **4,** 299–300.
forbidden in Portugal, **4,** 372.
believed by Maximilian I, **4,** 414.
of the Mark of Brandenburg, **4,** 440.
See also Blood accusation, the.
Childebert I, forbids the Jews to appear on the street at Eastertide, **3,** 37.
anti-Jewish decrees of, revived, **3,** 171.
Chillon, the Jews of, suspected of well poisoning, **4,** 103–4.
the castellan of, spreads evidence against the Jews, **4,** 108.
Chillukim, hair-splitting Talmudic discussions, **4,** 641.
Chilperic, Merovingian king, forces Christianity upon the Jews, **3,** 39.
Chindaswinth (642–652), Visigothic king, kindly disposed towards the Jews, **3,** 101–2.
Chinon, college of, sold, **4,** 48.
the Jews of, martyrs, **4,** 57–8.
Chintila (638–642), Visigothic king, forces Jews into Catholicism, **3,** 51–2, 101.
Chinuch Nearim, Berlin Free School, curriculum of, **5,** 416.
Chios, the Jews of, in the twelfth century, **3,** 424.
prophets on, silenced by Sabbataï's apostasy, **5,** 157.
Nathan Ghazati on, **5,** 160.
Chiskiya, Gaon of Pumbeditha and Exilarch, executed, **3,** 254.
sons of (Ibn-Daudi), in Spain, **3,** 254, 275.
Chiskiya, prince of the Cairo Karaites, **3,** 444.
Chiskiya ben Chiya, offends Judah ha-Nassi, **2,** 457.
adds supplements to the Mishna, **2,** 470.
disciple of Judah I, **2,** 511.
Chiskiya ben Reuben, member of the Mayence synod, **3,** 517.
Chivi Albalchi, the first rationalistic Bible critic, **3,** 199.
Chiya, a Babylonian buried in Palestine, **2,** 548.
Chiya (Achiya) bar Abba, Amora, characterization of, **2,** 454, 531.
punished by Judah I, **2,** 455.
sons of, **2,** 457, 470, 511.
announces the new-moon at Ain-tab, **2,** 458.
adds supplements to the Mishna, **2,** 470.
Mishnic compilation of, authoritative, **2,** 471.
intercedes for Abba-Areka, **2,** 512.
investigates the Judæan educational institutions, **2,** 532.
collects the Patriarch's tax, **2,** 536.
supported by Beth-Silvani, **2,** 536.

Chiya (Achiya) bar Abba (*continued*), leaves Judæa, **2**, 536.
ignorant of the Bible, **2**, 536.
rigor of, **2**, 536–7.
appeals to Abbahu, **2**, 538.
Agadist, **2**, 540.
Chiya, son of Abba-Areka, learned in the Law, **2**, 518.
Chmielniecki, Bogdan (1595–1657), grievances of, against Jews, **5**, 7.
organizes the Haidamak troops, **5**, 8.
conditions of peace, proposed by, **5**, 12, 14.
Chochmoth, the sciences, studied under Measfim influence, **5**, 402–3.
Chocim, Jacob Frank at, **5**, 27.
Chodar-Warda, son of Jezdijird III, at war with his brother, **2**, 628.
Choics. *See* Gnosticism.
Chorazin, Jesus in, **2**, 157.
Choreas, Caligula's murderer, **2**, 189.
Chorin, Aaron, aids the Reform movement, **5**, 571.
recalls his approval of the movement, **5**, 571.
Chosru (Chosroes) I Nushirvan, of Persia, imposes a poll-tax upon the Jews, **3**, 5.
son of, **3**, 7.
protects his dominions against the Chazars, **3**, 138.
Chosru II (590–628), of Persia, supplanted, **3**, 8–9.
protected by Mauritius, **3**, 9.
prosperity of the Jews under, **3**, 9–10.
at war with the Byzantine empire, **3**, 19.
incapacity of, **3**, 22.
death of, **3**, 22.
Chozari (Chosari), philosophical work by Jehuda Halevi, **3**, 327–36, 338.
translated into Hebrew, **3**, 397.
Chrestus, apostle at Rome, **2**, 202, 231.
Christ, the. *See* Messiah, the.
Christian IV, of Denmark, invites Jews to settle there, **4**, 675.
employs a Jewish physician, **4**, 692; **5**, 115.
Christian VII, of Denmark, subscribes to Mendelssohn's Pentateuch translation, **5**, 334.
"Christian Denunciation, The," by Wagenseil, **5**, 186.
Christian dogmas, in the Zohar, **4**, 23.
debated at Avila, **4**, 141.
expounded by Astruc Raimuch, **4**, 182.
in the Kabbala, **4**, 292.
belief in, threatened, **5**, 682.
Christian dogmas, the, criticised, by Abbahu, **2**, 539–40.
Solomon Bonfed, **4**, 182.
Joshua Ibn-Vives, **4**, 186–7.
Chasdaï Crescas, **3**, 187–8.
Profiat Duran, **4**, 189.
Joseph Ibn-Shem Tob, **4**, 235.
See also under Disputation; Polemical works against Christianity.
Christian names forbidden to Jews, in Spain, **4**, 52, 139.
in Prussia, **5**, 630.
Christian nurses, Jews forbidden to employ, **3**, 294, 400, 508, 582; **4**, 566.
Christian servants, Jews forbidden to keep, by the third Lateran Council, **3**, 400, 418, 422.

Christian servants, Jews forbidden to keep (*continued*), by the Council of Avignon, **3,** 504.
by French Church Councils, **3,** 508.
by the Council of Oxford, **3,** 516.
by the Council of Béziers, **3,** 581, 582.
by the code of Alfonso X, **3,** 595.
by the Council of Vienna, **3,** 611.
under Juan II, of Castile, **4,** 203, 205.
by Eugenius IV, **4,** 250, 253.
by Paul IV, **4,** 566.
by Pius IV, **4,** 588.
Christian servants, Jews keep, under Charles the Bold, **3,** 172.
in Speyer, **3,** 298.
Christian slaves, not permitted to become Jews, **2,** 564, 567, 615; **3,** 46, 171–2.
become Jews in Visigothic Spain, **3,** 45.
Christian slaves, Jews forbidden to keep, by the Theodosian code, **2,** 617; **3,** 28–9.
by Gregory I, **3,** 33–4.
by Reccared, **3,** 46.
by Sisebut, **3,** 48.
by the Council of Rouen, **3,** 294.
in Hungary, **3,** 521.
See also Slave-trade, the; Slaves.
Christian state, the, founded by Constantius, **2,** 568.
Christianity, Essenism with foreign elements, **2,** 142.
origin of, in Messianic longings, **2,** 142–3.
helped by the exegesis of the Pharisees, **2,** 166.
averse to Phariseeism, **2,** 171.
power of, over Rome, **2,** 174.
Christianity (*continued*), indebted to the apostle Paul, **2,** 225, 365.
does not appeal to cultivated Greeks, **2,** 229.
relation of, to Judaism, according to Paul, **2,** 229–30.
schism in, **2,** 230, 232, 365.
influences the Jewish peasants, **2,** 364.
development of, belongs to Jewish history, **2,** 365.
equivalent to the teaching of Paul, **2,** 373.
elements of, **2,** 373–4.
as viewed by the Gnostics, **2,** 377.
influences Judaism, **2,** 380–1.
mocked at by Hadrian, **2,** 407–8.
independent of Judaism, **2,** 431.
laws hostile to, promulgated by Severus, **2,** 464.
admired by Alexander Severus, **2,** 481.
becomes the Catholic Church, **2,** 500.
new dogmas of, **2,** 500–1.
oppresses Judaism and Samaritanism, **2,** 535.
proselytizing efforts of, **2,** 539.
persecuted by Diocletian, **2,** 539.
triumphant, **2,** 559, 560.
influence of, on Constantine, **2,** 561–2.
completely separated from Judaism, **2,** 563–4.
shaped by Constantius, **2,** 566.
confined by Julian the Apostate, **2,** 596.
and Magianism, **2,** 627.
forced upon the Samaritans, **3,** 16–17.

Christianity (*continued*), tolerant in western Europe, **3,** 34.
among the Chazars, **3,** 139–40.
barbarous during the Middle Ages, **3,** 187.
objections of, to Judaism answered by Saadiah, **3,** 198.
contest of, with Islam, **3,** 297.
characterized by Jehuda Halevi, **3,** 328–9, 330.
belief of, in the supernatural, **5,** 305.
dethronement of, by the French thinkers, **5,** 305–6.
Mendelssohn on, **5,** 313–14.
characterized by Heine, **5,** 552.
See also Christian dogmas; Christians; Polemical works against Christianity.

Christianity, conversions to. *See* Apostasy; *and under* Conversion.

Christianity, Pauline, hostility of, accentuates the legal character of Judaism, **2,** 471.
produces the Talmud, **3,** 127.

Christians, the, regarded as conjurors, **2,** 170.
consider the Apocrypha part of the Bible, **2,** 359, 489.
accuse Jews of cursing Jesus, **2,** 380.
propaganda of, in the pagan world, **2,** 383.
tamper with the Septuagint, **2,** 385–6.
of Judæa, receive Hadrian with servility, **2,** 406.
accounts by, of Bar-Cochba, **2,** 412.
persecuted by Hadrian, **2,** 430–1.
separate themselves from the Jews, **2,** 431.
appeal to Marcus Aurelius, **2,** 449.

Christians, the (*continued*), intercourse of, with the heathen interdicted, **2,** 476–7.
complain of the indifference of the Jews, **2,** 483.
primitive sects of, merged into the Catholic Church, **2,** 500.
persecuted by the Magi, **2,** 524.
persecuted by Diocletian, **2,** 533, 539.
called Galilæans by Julian, **2,** 596.
reproached for having forsaken Judaism, **2,** 597.
malign Julian, **2,** 599.
object to the rebuilding of the Temple, **2,** 600–1.
well treated by Jezdijird, **2,** 609–10.
oppress Judæa, **2,** 611.
refuse to recognize the authority of the Patriarchs, **2,** 612–13.
forbidden to trade with Jews, **2,** 620.
controversies with, interest the Jews in Scripture studies, **2,** 623.
persecuted by Jezdijird III, **2,** 627–8.
of Babylonia suffer from Zendik communism, **3,** 2–3.
persecuted by Hormisdas IV, **3,** 8.
in possession of Palestine, **3,** 11.
Jewish witnesses cannot testify against, **3,** 12, 102, 520; **4,** 250.
of Jerusalem perish at the hands of Persians and Jews, **3,** 19.
forbidden to eat at Jewish banquets in Gaul, **3,** 36, 37.

Christians, the (*continued*), forbidden to hold intercourse with Jews, **3**, 36, 37, 407, 499, 595, 611; **4**, 216, 245, 250, 560, 590.
forbidden to marry Jews in Spain, **3**, 44, 46.
ill-treated in Yemen, **3**, 64, 65.
Mahomet's revelation against, **3**, 78.
driven out of Najaran, **3**, 85.
restrictions against, in the covenant of Omar, **3**, 87–8.
Jewish testimony against, accepted, **3**, 144.
persecuted under the sons of Haroun Alrashid, **3**, 145.
Frankish, respect Judaism, **3**, 163.
antagonized by Bishop Bodo, **3**, 169.
called Mozarabs among the Mahometans, **3**, 215.
persecuted by Hakim, **3**, 247.
invade Mahometan Spain, **3**, 291.
persecuted by Abdulmumen, **3**, 359.
permitted to testify against Jews, **3**, 422.
deny equal rights to the Marranos, **4**, 256–7.
study Hebrew, **4**, 471–4.
interested in the Kabbala, **4**, 481.
devote themselves to Hebrew literature, **5**, 21–2.
interested in the Sabbatian movement, **5**, 137, 151.
interested in Judaism and the Jews, **5**, 176.
attracted by Jewish literature, **5**, 178–9.
Hebraists, attack the Jews, **5**, 184.
and the Eibeschütz-Emden controversy, **5**, 262.

Christians (*continued*), subscribers to Mendelssohn's Pentateuch translation, **5**, 329.
See also Christianity; Ebionites; Greek Christians; Jewish Christians; Judæan Christians; Nazarenes; Pagan Christians.

Christians, the early. *See* Jewish Christians, the; Judæan Christians, the; Nazarenes, the, etc.

Christians, the Judaizing, under Receswinth, **3**, 104.
under Erwig, **3**, 106–7.
forbidden to own real estate, **3**, 107–8.
See also Marranos, the.

Christians, the Nestorian, help the Arabs in Babylonia, **3**, 89.
side with Ali, **3**, 90.

Christians, the Syrian, and the science of grammar, **3**, 7.
make scientific literature accessible to the Arabs, **3**, 111.

Christina, of Sweden, student of Hebrew, **5**, 21.
Manasseh ben Israel recommended to, **5**, 22, 23.
Manoel Texeira's guest, **5**, 140.
intercedes for the Jews of Vienna, **5**, 171.

Chronicles, the Books of, written by a Levite, **1**, 411.

Chrysostom. *See* John Chrysostom.

Church appurtenances, Jews forbidden to buy, **3**, 377.

Church councils, occupied with the Jewish question, **3**, 25.
discuss the slave-trade of the Jews, **3**, 40.
convened in France by the fugitive popes, **3**, 376–7.

Church councils, list of:

Alby,
Avignon (1209),
Bamberg (1451),
Basle (1431-1443),
Béziers (1246),
Buda (1279),
Clermont (1095),
Constance (1414),
Epaone (517),
Exeter (1287),
Illiberis (320),
Lateran, the third (1179)
Lateran, the fourth (1215)
Lateran, the fifth (1512-1517)
Lyons (829),
Mâcon (581),
Meaux (845),
Montpellier,
Narbonne (1227),
Nice (325),
Orleans (538, 545),
Oxford (1222),
Paris (615, 846, 1212),
Rome (1078),
Rouen (1231),
Toledo (589, 633, 652?),
Tours (1231),
Trent (1545),
under Chintila (638),
under Erwig,
under Wamba,
Vannes (465),
Vienna (1267),
Zamora (1313).

Church Fathers, the, works of, connected with the Talmud, **4,** 614.

"**Church of the Mother of God,**" synagogue in Constantinople, **3,** 26.

Chushiel (950–980), emissary from Sora, settles in Kairuan, **3,** 208, 210.
title of, **3,** 211.
disciples of, **3,** 211.

Chuzpit, interpreter of the Jamnia Synhedrion, **2,** 357, 429.

Cicero, animosity of, to Judæans, **2,** 68–70.
indebted to Greek writers, **2,** 179.

Cidellus, Jewish adviser of Alfonso VI of Castile, **3,** 292.

Cilicia, mercenaries of, hired by Alexander Jannæus, **2,** 39.
Greek-Christian communities in, **2,** 227.
the Jews of, punish an apostate, **2,** 565.

Cincinnati, rabbinical college at, **5,** 700.

Circumcision, observed by Babylonian proselytes, **1,** 339.
observed by Babylonian Judæans, **1,** 364.
whether optional or imperative with proselytes, **2,** 384–5.
forbidden by Hadrian, **2,** 422, 424.
permitted by Antoninus Pius, **2,** 433.
of slaves, forbidden, **2,** 567, 615; **3,** 46.
practiced by the heathen Arabs, **3,** 61.
discussed in Frankfort, **5,** 676–7.
See also under Proselytes.

"**Citizen's Cry** against the Jews, The," published in Metz, **5,** 434.

Citizenship granted to Judæans in Egypt, **1,** 418, 503.
granted to Judæans in Antioch, **1,** 419.
granted to Judæan athletes, **1,** 445.
withdrawn from the Alexandrian Judæans, **2,** 182.
restored to the Alexandrian Judæans, **2,** 191.
Judæans of Cæsarea deprived of, **2,** 247.
Roman, under Caracalla, **2,** 468.
Roman, of the Jews, guarded by Gregory I, **3,** 33.
accorded to the Jews of Gaul, **3,** 35.
enjoyed by the Jews of Castile, **3,** 292–3.
obtained by the Jews of Tudela, **3,** 388.
enjoyed by the Jews of Messina, **3,** 423.
enjoyed by Jews in the Holy Roman Empire, **4,** 443.

Citizenship (*continued*). *See also* Emancipation of the Jews, the.
Civil offices, Honorius III objects to Jews in, **3**, 515.
Henry II of Castile refuses to exclude Jews from, **4**, 125.
exclusion from, requested in Lisbon, **4**, 160.
Civil offices, Jews excluded from, by Theodosius II, **3**, 28, 171.
by the Council of Toledo, **3**, 46.
by the Council of Mâcon, **3**, 39, 171.
in the Empire of the East, **3**, 175, 425.
by the Arabs, **3**, 216.
by Gregory VII, **3**, 293.
by Innocent III, **3**, 400.
by the Council of Avignon, **3**, 504.
by the Fourth Lateran Council, **3**, 510.
in Hungary, **3**, 521.
by Frederick II, **3**, 567, 569.
by the Council of Béziers, **3**, 582.
by Alfonso X, **3**, 595.
by the Council of Vienna, **3**, 611.
by the Council of Buda, **3**, 614.
by Rudolph of Habsburg, **3**, 635.
by Juan II, **4**, 194–5, 203, 228, 229.
by Benedict XIII, **4**, 216.
by the Council of Basle, **4**, 245.
by Eugenius IV, **4**, 250.
by Henry IV, **4**, 278.
See Magisterial offices.
Civil offices, Jews fill, under Al-Mutadhid, **3**, 183.
in Moslem Spain, after Abdul-Rahman III, **3**, 234–5.
Civil offices, Jews fill (*continued*), under Alfonso VIII of Castile, **3**, 384.
in Messina, **3**, 423.
in Toulouse, **3**, 501, 514.
in Austria, **3**, 516–17, 567.
under Alfonso X, **3**, 593, 596, 615.
See Magisterial offices.
Civil war, between the houses of Saul and David, **1**, 109–10.
David and Absalom, **1**, 138–44.
the Zealots and the Peace Party in Jerusalem, **2**, 259–70.
the Zealots and the Moderates in Jerusalem, **2**, 295.
the Zealots and the Sicarii, **2**, 297–9.
Pedro the Cruel and Henry de Trastamare, **4**, 118–26.
"Claims of the Jews to German Citizenship," by Rühs, **5**, 517.
Claudius, emperor, makes Agrippa I king over Palestine, **2**, 190.
makes Herod II prætor and prince of Chalcis, **2**, 190.
treats the Judæans well, **2**, 190–1, 193.
and the fortification of Jerusalem, **2**, 195.
and Agrippa II, **2**, 196.
makes the governor of Judæa independent of the governor of Syria, **2**, 197.
makes Herod II titular king of Judæa, **2**, 198.
names Tiberius Julius Alexander governor of Judæa, **2**, 198.
expels Judæans from Rome, **2**, 202.
makes Agrippa II king of Chalcis, **2**, 235.

Claudius (*continued*), makes Felix governor of Galilee, **2**, 242.
banishes Cumanus, **2**, 245.
gives Agrippa II a kingdom, **2**, 245.
death of, **2**, 245.
Clemens of Alexandria, Father of the Church, critical spirit of, **2**, 488.
Clemens, Flavius, proselyte, sons of, proclaimed Cæsars, **2**, 387.
and four teachers of the Law, **2**, 387, 389, 391.
condemned to death, **2**, 389.
and Josephus, **2**, 389, 391.
Clement III, pope, resists the return of forced converts to Judaism, **3**, 306, 308.
orders the confiscation of the Talmud, **3**, 602.
Clement IV, pope, appealed to against Nachmani, **3**, 605.
Clement VI, pope, has Gersonides' astronomical treatise translated, **4**, 93.
arrests the Black Death persecutions, **4**, 103.
declares the Jews innocent of well poisoning, **4**, 105.
forbids the forced baptism of Jews, **4**, 173.
Clement VII, pope, friendly to the Jews, **4**, 407.
grants David Reubeni an audience, **4**, 492.
efforts of, for the liberty of Italy, **4**, 492.
treats Reubeni with distinction, **4**, 492–3.
addressed on the Portuguese Inquisition, **4**, 500.
permits Marranos to profess Judaism, **4**, 500.
intercourse of, with Molcho, **4**, 503.
Clement VII (*continued*), honors Molcho publicly, **4**, 505.
opposes the Portuguese Inquisition, **4**, 505.
saves Molcho from the stake, **4**, 507.
establishes the Portuguese Inquisition, **4**, 507.
sympathizes with the Marranos, **4**, 509.
innocent of Molcho's death, **4**, 512.
stays the Portuguese Inquisition, **4**, 513.
absolves Marranos for leaving the Church, **4**, 513–14.
motive of, in protecting the Marranos, **4**, 514.
appoints a commission on the Portuguese Inquisition, **4**, 514.
death of, **4**, 515.
briefs of, enforced by Paul IV, **4**, 516.
absolves the Marranos of Ancona, **4**, 568.
Clement VIII, pope, grants an amnesty to the Marranos, **4**, 528.
expels the Jews from the Papal States, **4**, 659.
forbids the reading of the Talmud, **4**, 659.
incorporates Ferrara with the Papal States, **4**, 660.
absolves Portuguese Marranos, **4**, 671.
Clement IX, pope, death of, **5**, 171.
Clement XIII, pope, acquits the Jews of the blood accusation, **5**, 285–6.
Clemente, Philip, Marrano, tries to suppress the Aragon Inquisition, **4**, 329.

Cleopatra I, sister of Antiochus IV, wife of Ptolemy V, **1,** 450.
Cleopatra II, sister and wife of Ptolemy VI, claimant of the Egyptian throne, **1,** 506.
marries Ptolemy VII Physcon, **1,** 518.
Cleopatra III, second wife of Ptolemy VII, mother of Ptolemy VIII, espouses the cause of Judæa, **2,** 10.
defended by Judæan soldiers, **2,** 12.
sends an army against her son, **2,** 40–1.
in league with Alexander Jannæus, **2,** 41.
Cleopatra VI, friendly to Herod, **2,** 86.
favors Aristobulus (III), **2,** 92.
summons Herod to answer for Aristobulus' death, **2,** 92–3.
receives the district of Jericho, **2,** 93.
unkind to the Alexandrian Judæans, **2,** 94.
schemes against Herod, **2,** 94–5.
death of, **2,** 102.
body-guard of, given to Herod, **2,** 103.
Cleopatra, wife of Demetrius Nicator, kills her son, **2,** 6.
Cleopatra of Jerusalem, wife of Herod, **2,** 119.
Clermont, the Jews of, and Bishop Avitus, **3,** 38–9.
the council of, resolves upon a crusade, **3,** 297.
Clermont-Tonnerre, Count, defends the Jews, **5,** 440.
favors the emancipation of the Jews, **5,** 441.
Closener of Strasburg, historian, on the persecution of the Jews, **4,** 106.
Clotaire II, Merovingian king, hostile to the Jews, **3,** 40.
Clovis, founder of the Frankish kingdom, **3,** 35.
Jews in the army of, **3,** 36.
converted, **3,** 36.
Coblenz, the Jews of, persecuted, **3,** 611.
Cochelet, French consul-general, interferes in the Damascus affair, **5,** 647.
ordered to stop the Damascus trial, **5,** 649.
hinders Montefiore and Crémieux in Egypt, **5,** 659, 660.
Codes, general, defining the status of the Jews. *See under*
Alfonso X of Castile,
Alfonso V of Portugal,
Henry IV of Castile,
Napoleon,
Theodosius,
Visigothic.
Codes, Jewish religious. *See*
Asher ben Yechiel,
Mishna, the
Mishne Torah,
Mordecai Jafa,
Moses ben Israel Isserles,
Shulchan Aruch,
Turim.
Cœlesyria, Macedonian province, Judæa belongs to, **1,** 414.
conquered by Ptolemy I, **1,** 416.
revolts from Ptolemy II, **1,** 423.
Joseph, tax-gatherer of, **1,** 425.
Herod governor of, **2,** 79.
Cohen, Aaron. *See* Aaron Cohen.
Cohen, Chayim. *See* Chayim Cohen.
Cohen, Daniel, scientist, **4,** 405.

Cohen (Soncino), Gershon, establishes a printing house in Prague, **4,** 418.
Cohen, Isaac. *See* Isaac Cohen Shalal.
Cohen, Jehuda. *See* Jehuda ben Solomon Cohen Ibn-Matka.
Cohen, Jonathan. *See* Jonathan Cohen.
Cohen, Joseph ben Joshua. *See* Joseph ben Joshua Cohen.
Cohen, Joshua Falk, president of the Synod of the Four Countries, **4,** 645.
Talmudist, **4,** 703.
Cohen, Judah. *See* Judah ben Moses Cohen.
Cohen, Malachi, rabbi of Leghorn, espouses the cause of Eibeschütz, **5,** 264.
Cohen, Moses. *See* Moses Cohen de Tordesillas; Moses ben Judah.
Cohen, Moses Gerson. *See* Anton, Charles.
Cohen, Naphtali, Kabbalist, patron of Chayon, **5,** 217.
approves of Chayon's work, **5,** 218.
refrains from exposing Chayon, **5,** 219.
exposes Chayon, **5,** 227.
Cohen, Nehemiah, announces the approach of the Messiah, **5,** 152.
summoned by Sabbataï Zevi, **5,** 152.
disagrees with Sabbataï, **5,** 153.
turns Mahometan, **5,** 153.
betrays Sabbataï, **5,** 153.
returns to Poland, **5,** 154.
Cohen, Nehemiah Vital, rabbi of Venice, and Luzzatto, **5,** 239.
Cohen, Perachyah, physician and scientist, **4,** 405.
Cohen, Raphael (1722–1803), rabbi of the "three communities," opposes Mendelssohn's Pentateuch translation, **5,** 330, 331, 333.
objects to the study of the sciences, **5,** 402.
retirement of, **5,** 566.
son-in-law of, **5,** 570.
grandson of, **5,** 598.
Cohen, Sabbataï, commemorates the Cossack massacres, **5,** 13.
Cohen, Samuel. *See* Samuel Cohen ben Daniel.
Cohen, Saul. *See* Saul Cohen Ashkenazi; Saul Astruc Cohen.
Cohen, Shalom, employed by the Hamburg Dayanim, **5,** 573.
Cohen, Simcha. *See* Simcha Cohen.
Cohn, Isidore, founder of the "Alliance Israélite Universelle," **5,** 701.
Coimbra, the Inquisition at, **4,** 508.
Coin, counterfeiting of, denounced by the Mayence synod, **3,** 517.
clipping of, charged against the English Jews, **3,** 642.
Coinage, the right of, enjoyed by the Jews of Hungary, **3,** 521.
Coins struck by Simon Tharsi, **1,** 525, 528.
by John Hyrcanus, **2,** 12.
by Aristobulus I, **2,** 35.
by Alexander Jannæus, **2,** 46.
by Salome Alexandra, **2,** 48.
by Aristobulus II, **2,** 62.
by Alexander, son of Aristobulus II, **2,** 70.
by Antigonus, **2,** 83.
for Agrippa I, **2,** 190, 194.
by the Zealots, **2,** 268.

Coins (*continued*), in honor of Simon ben Gamaliel, **2**, 269.
Judæan, under Vespasian, **2**, 292.
commemorating Titus' victory, **2**, 314.
by Nerva, **2**, 392.
by Hadrian, **2**, 407, 419.
by Bar-Cochba, **2**, 411.
Collectants, a Dutch sect, **5**, 94.
Colleges, established in Spain by the law of Avila, **4**, 229.
Colleges, Rabbinical, at Metz, **5**, 597–8, 700.
at Padua, **5**, 624, 700.
at Breslau, **5**, 699–700.
at various places, **5**, 700.
Colleges, Talmudical, at Narbonne, **3**, 143, 242, 392.
in western countries founded by emissaries from Sora, **3**, 208.
at Cordova, **3**, 209, 228.
in Egypt and the Fatimide Caliphate, **3**, 210.
at Kairuan, **3**, 210–11, 248.
in Spain, **3**, 236.
at Mayence, **3**, 243, 247.
at Lucena, **3**, 322.
at Toledo, **3**, 338, 362.
in Spain, closed, **3**, 361, 384.
at Dampierre, **3**, 403.
at London, **3**, 409.
at Bagdad, **3**, 429, 633.
in France, closed, **4**, 48.
at Paris, **4**, 133.
at Alcala, **4**, 145.
at Padua, **4**, 410.
in Poland, **4**, 420, 634, 639.
at Cremona, **4**, 582.
at Prague, **5**, 249.
the decay of, **5**, 566–7, 569.
See also under Academies; Schools.
Collegium Germanicum, propagandist seminary, **4**, 654.
Collier, Thomas, refutes anti-Jewish charges, **5**, 46.
"Colloquium Middelburgense," controversial work, **4**, 691.
Colmar, the Jews of, banished, **4**, 416.
Cologna, Abraham Vita di (1755–1832), deputy to the Assembly of Jewish Notables, **5**, 488, 490.
second vice-president of the Synhedrion, **5**, 495.
member of the French consistory, **5**, 502.
conservative, **5**, 559.
Cologne, fair of, visited by Jews, **3**, 243.
university of, and the confiscation of Hebrew books, **4**, 437, 441.
theologians of, sanction the burning of the "Augenspiegel," **4**, 452.
Cologne, the Dominicans of. *See* Dominicans, the, of Cologne.
Cologne, the Jews of, privileges of, abolished by Constantine, **2**, 563.
settlement of, **3**, 41.
protected during the first crusade, **3**, 304.
massacred at Neus, **3**, 304–5.
persecuted during the second crusade, **3**, 352.
represented at the first rabbinical synod, **3**, 377.
protected during the Black Death persecutions, **4**, 106, 108.
banished, **4**, 227, 413.
Columbus, aided by Joseph Vecinho, **4**, 368.
Comet, a, orbit of, calculated by Joshua ben Chananya, **2**, 349.
Comino, the isle of, Abraham Abulafia on **4**, 8.

"**Commentary**," Talmudical work by Rashi, **3**, 288.

Commerce, under Uzziah, **1**, 230.
pursued by Alexandrian Judæans, **1**, 504.
under the Herodians, **2**, 118.
between Jews and Christians forbidden, **2**, 620; **4**, 203, 216.
among the Jews of the Frankish and Burgundian kingdoms, **3**, 35.
in the hands of Jews in the eighth century, **3**, 142-3.
international, in the hands of Jews, **3**, 162.
in the hands of the Jews under the Saxon emperors, **3**, 242-3.
the, of southern France, carried on by Jews, **3**, 391.
the, of Venice, in the fifteenth century, **4**, 285.
of the Turkish Jews, **4**, 401.
of the Jews in Poland, **4**, 419.
capacity for, an argument for the admission of Jews into England, **5**, 40-1.
the, of the Jews, described by Simone Luzzatto, **5**, 82-3.
stagnation of, during the Sabbatian movement, **5**, 149.
forbidden partly to the Jews of Alsace, **5**, 348.
the, of Jews under the Napoleonic law, **5**, 524-5.

Commercial Hall, meeting place of the Synhedrion in Bethany, **2**, 239.

Commodus, emperor, profligacy of, **2**, 447.
death of, **2**, 448, 463.

"**Communities of the Friends of Light**," Protestant societies, **5**, 682, 683.

"**Compositions**," grammatical work by Yizchaki, **3**, 273.

"**Concerning the Jews and their Lies**," by Luther, **4**, 548-9.

"**Concerning the superstitions of the Jews**," letter addressed to Louis the Pious, **3**, 167-8.

Conciliador, the, by Manasseh ben Israel, translated, **5**, 22.

Concordance of the Bible, by Isaac Nathan ben Kalonymos, **4**, 234-5,

Condottieri, Italian mercenaries, **4**, 286.

Confederation War, the, Jews suffer during, **5**, 387-8.

Confession of Faith, the, recital of, forbidden, **3**, 15.

Confessional, the, discussed by the Jews of France, **3**, 343.

"**Confessions**," by Heine, **5**, 553-5.

Confirmation, the rite of, introduced into German Jewish communities, **5**, 562, 573.

Confiscation and burning, the, of Hebrew books, by the Dominicans, **3**, 542-3.
by Gregory IX, **3**, 574-6, 578-9.
by Pfefferkorn, **4**, 429-31, 437-8, 441, 444.
under Julius III, **4**, 565.
under Paul IV, **4**, 567, 583, 584-5.
under Pius V, **4**, 590.
under Gregory XIII, **4**, 654.
at Kamieniec, **5**, 282.
See also under Talmud, the.

"**Conflict of Duties, the, Letter on**," by Solomon Duran I, **4**, 238.

Conforte, David, itinerant rabbi and historian, **5**, 202.

Congress. *See* Aix-la-Chapelle; Rastadt; Vienna.

Coniah. *See* Jehoiachin.

Conrad III, emperor, protects the Jews during the second crusade, **3**, 351, 416.
joins the second crusade, **3**, 353, 354.
Conrad of Wintertur, exculpates the Jews from the charge of well poisoning, **4**, 106, 108.
Consistorial organization, in France, approved by Napoleon, **5**, 498.
established in Westphalia, **5**, 501–2.
“ **Consolation for the Sorrows of Israel**,” by Samuel Usque, **4**, 558–61.
Constance, the Council of, and Benedict XIII, **4**, 212, 216.
condemns Ferrer, **4**, 217.
anarchy during, **4**, 218.
elects Martin V pope, **4**, 219.
condemns John Huss to death, **4**, 221.
expenses of, borne by the Jews, **4**, 248.
Constance (Costnitz), the Jews of, charged with well poisoning, **4**, 105.
wait on Martin V, **4**, 219.
Constance (lake), the cities on, the Jews of, charged with well poisoning, **4**, 105.
Constantia, queen-mother, contends for the regency in Castile, **4**, 52.
Constantine I, emperor, puts Judaism on an equality with Christianity, **2**, 561.
under the influence of Christianity, **2**, 561–2.
abolishes the privileges of the Jews, **2**, 563; **5**, 725.
closes Jerusalem to the Jews, **2**, 564; **3**, 11–12.
protects the Jews against apostates, **2**, 564.
Constantine I (*continued*), anti-Jewish restrictions of, revived, **3**, 23, 171.
Constantine VIII (944–949), Byzantine emperor, and Abdul-Rahman III, **3**, 218.
Constantine, African town, refuge for Spanish Jews, **4**, 197.
Constantine Dragosses, last Byzantine emperor, **4**, 267.
Constantinople, the Temple vessels in, **3**, 26–7.
Karaite center, **4**, 69, 71, 269.
fall of, **4**, 267.
Spanish spoken at, by the exiles, **4**, 388.
the Spanish exiles in, **4**, 402–4.
the Mendes-Nassi family in, **4**, 577.
rabbis of, advise the diversion of Jewish trade from Ancona, **4**, 580.
rabbis of, excommunicate Daud, **4**, 599.
description of, by Moses Almosnino, **4**, 608.
Joseph Delmedigo at, **5**, 76.
Sabbataï Zevi at, **5**, 145–8.
effect of Sabbataï's apostasy in, **5**, 157.
Sabbatians excommunicated in, **5**, 157, 159.
Sabbataï Zevi banished to, **5**, 166.
Cardoso at, **5**, 207.
Chayim Malach banished from, **5**, 214.
Chayon at, **5**, 227–8.
rabbis of, espouse the cause of Eibeschütz, **5**, 264.
a rabbi of, accused of using human blood, **5**, 640.
revision of the Rhodes trial at, **5**, 647.
Constantinople, the Jews of, inhabit a separate quarter, **3**, 26.

Constantinople, the Jews of (*continued*), expelled, **3,** 26.
in the twelfth century, **3,** 425.
divided into national groups, **4,** 402, 478.
taxed, **4,** 402.
have a political representative, **4,** 404.
collect a ransom for Polish-Jewish captives, **5,** 8.
appeal to the European Jews, **5,** 651.

Constantius, emperor, influence of, on the Church, **2,** 566.
teachers of the Law banished from Judæa under, **2,** 566–7.
hostile to the Jews, **2,** 567–8.
founder of the Christian state, **2,** 568.
re-enacts Hadrian's edicts against the Jews, **2,** 571.
makes Julian co-emperor, **2,** 595.
law of, with regard to the slaves of Jews revived, **2,** 615.
law of, concerning the Patriarchs re-enacted, **2,** 616.

Constitutio Judæorum, issued by Innocent III, **3,** 497.

Constitution of the Directory, the, recognizes the emancipation of the Jews, **5,** 452.

Constitution, the French, ratified by Louis XVI, **5,** 447.

"**Constitutions,** The," code of the Inquisition compiled by Torquemada, **4,** 326–8.
introduced into Portugal, **4,** 508.

Conti, Vincent, prints the Zohar, **4,** 583.

Contra-Remonstrants, the, a Dutch sect, **4,** 673.

"**Contrasts** and Greatness of Constantinople," by Moses Almosnino, **4,** 608.

Controversial literature, in Spain in the fifteenth century, **4,** 232–8.
See also Polemical works against Christianity.

"**Conversations** and Recollections," by Moses Ibn-Ezra, **3,** 320.

Conversion, the, of the Himyarites, **3,** 56.

Conversion, the, of the Jews to Christianity, promoted by Constantine, **2,** 562, 564.
desired by Theodoric, **3,** 29–30.
hoped by Bernard of Clairvaux, **3,** 353.
means used for, by Raymond de Penyaforte, **3,** 520.
encouraged by Louis IX, **3,** 570.
projected by Benedict XIII, **4,** 206–7.
designed by the Council of Basle, **4,** 245–6.
attempted in Ratisbon, **4,** 301.
measures for, devised by Pfefferkorn, **4,** 425–6.
unpopular, **4,** 426–7.
measures for, devised by Gregory XIII, **4,** 654–5, 706.
hoped for by Cromwell, **4,** 43.
agitated by Charles XI of Sweden, **5,** 182.
agitated by Wagenseil, **5,** 186.
urged by Rühs, **5,** 517.
See also Apostasy; Apostates.

Conversion, the forced, of Jews to Christianity, objected to by Gregory I, **3,** 33.
objected to by Henry IV, **3,** 298.
forbidden by the third Lateran Council, **3,** 421.
deprecated by Gregory IX, **3,** 570.
deprecated by Gregory X, **3,** 635.

Conversion, the forced, of Jews to Christianity (*continued*), advised by Duns Scotus, **3**, 644; **4**, 277.
forbidden by Clement VI, **4**, 103, 173.
deprecated by Innocent IV, **4**, 165.
forbidden by Boniface IX, **4**, 173.
deprecated by Martin V, **4**, 220.
advocated by John of Capistrano, **4**, 277.
condemned by Ferdinand Coutinho, **4**, 375.
attempted by Manoel of Portugal, **4**, 377.
objected to by Paul III, **4**, 517–18.
See also Marranos, the.
Conversions, forced, of Jews to Christianity, in Magona, **2**, 619–20.
in Clermont, **3**, 38–9.
under Chilperic, **3**, 39.
under Sisebut, **3**, 48, 49–50.
under Chintila, **3**, 51–2, 101.
under Receswinth, **3**, 102–4.
under Erwig, **3**, 106–7.
under Leo the Isaurian, **3**, 122–3.
under Basilius, **3**, 176.
in Mayence, **3**, 246, 303.
in Treves, **3**, 300.
in Worms, **3**, 301–2.
in Bohemia, **3**, 305, 356.
in Blois, **3**, 380.
in France, **3**, 403, 570; **4**, 48, 56.
in Toulouse, **3**, 514.
during the Rindfleisch persecution, **4**, 36.
in Speyer, **4**, 107.
in Strasburg, **4**, 108.
in Hungary, **4**, 111.
in Castile, **4**, 126, 137, 205.
Conversions, forced, of Jews to Christianity (*continued*), in Seville, **4**, 169.
in Cordova, **4**, 169.
in Toledo, **4**, 170.
in Valencia, **4**, 171.
in Gerona, Barcelona, and Lerida, **4**, 172.
in Aragon, **4**, 206, 214.
in Austria, **4**, 224.
in Palma, **4**, 247.
in Bavaria, **4**, 254.
of children in Breslau, **4**, 262.
in Trent, **4**, 298.
in Spain at the expulsion, **4**, 351.
in Navarre, **4**, 358.
in Genoa, **4**, 363.
in Malaga, **4**, 370.
of children at San Thomas, **4**, 371.
in Portugal, **4**, 374, 375–6, 378.
in the Mark of Brandenburg, **4**, 440.
in Poland, **5**, 7–8.
See also Apostasy; Apostates; Marranos, the.
Conversions, forced, of Jews to Islam, by Omar, **3**, 120.
decreed by Hakim, **3**, 247–8.
in Morocco, **3**, 358–9.
in northern Africa, **3**, 359–60.
in Lucena, **3**, 311–12, 361.
under Abdulmumen, **3**, 451–6.
in Yemen, **3**, 461.
Maimonides on, **3**, 462–4.
See also Apostasy; Apostates.
Conversions, forced, of Jews to Magianism, **2**, 629.
Conversions to Judaism, in Babylon, **1**, 338–9.
under Zerubbabel, **1**, 356.
made by Alexander Jannæus, **2**, 46.
among the Romans under Tiberius, **2**, 136–7.

Conversions to Judaism (*continued*), among the heathen, **2,** 215–19, 383–5.
among the Roman soldiers of Titus, **2,** 306.
Tacitus and Josephus on, **2,** 384.
forbidden by Antoninus Pius, **2,** 433.
forbidden by Constantine, **2,** 562.
among slaves forbidden, **2,** 564, 567–8, 615; **3,** 46.
during the Persian occupation of Palestine, **3,** 21.
forbidden by the councils of Orleans, **3,** 37.
among the Arabs, **3,** 61–3.
punishable with death by the code of Alfonso X, **3,** 595.
See also Circumcision; Proselytes.

Conversions to Paganism in Alexandria, **2,** 184.

Converts, forced, to Christianity, a menace to the Spanish Jews, **4,** 179.
emigrate from Spain, **4,** 179.
relapse into Jewish ceremonies, **4,** 180.
See Marranos, the.

Converts, forced, to Judaism, the Idumæans under John Hyrcanus, **2,** 8–9.
the Ituræans and Trachonites under Aristobulus I, **2,** 37.

Converts to Christianity, cannot return to Judaism, **3,** 49–50, 306, 308.
See also Apostates; Christians, Judaizing; Marranos, the.

Converts to Judaism. *See* Circumcision; Conversions to Judaism; Proselytes.

Copenhagen, the Jews of, persecuted, **5,** 531.

Copia, Sarah. *See* Sullam, Sarah Copia.

Copia, Simon, father of Sarah Sullam, **5,** 69.

Coponius, first procurator of Judæa, **2,** 129.
administration of, **2,** 135.

Cordova, ancient gateway in, **3,** 42.
Jews masters of, **3,** 109.
seat of a Talmud school, **3,** 210, 228, 236.
birthplace of Samuel Ibn-Nagrela, **3,** 255.
taken by Suleiman, **3,** 255, 262.
medical school at, **3,** 261.
home of the Albalias, **3,** 283.
synagogues of, destroyed, **3,** 360.
Talmud school of, destroyed, **3,** 384.
taken by the Almohades, **3,** 447–8.
the Inquisition in, **4,** 325.
Jews disappear from, **4,** 354.
exiles from, form a congregation in Constantinople, **4,** 402.
disturbance in, caused by the Inquisition, **4,** 484.
autos-da-fé in, **5,** 91, 92.

Cordova, the Jews of, ransom Moses ben Chanoch, **3,** 209.
choose him as their rabbi, **3,** 209.
appeal to Abdul-Rahman III, **3,** 209–10.
Chasdaï Ibn-Shaprut political chief of, **3,** 217.
prosperity of, **3,** 229.
side against Joseph Ibn-Abitur, **3,** 238.
Jacob Ibn-Jau chief of, **3,** 239.
emigrate, **3,** 255.
murdered in 1391, **4,** 169.

Cordova, the Marranos of, attacked, **4,** 281–2.

Cordova, the Marranos of (*continued*), flee to Granada, **4**, 351.
Corfu, the Spanish exiles in, **4**, 363–4.
Isaac Abrabanel at, **4**, 384.
rites of the Jews of, followed in Greece, **4**, 406.
Nathan Ghazati at, **5**, 160.
honors shown to Crémieux in, **5**, 668.
Corinth, Judæans in, **2**, 203.
Paul establishes a Christian community in, **2**, 228.
the Jews of, in the twelfth century, **3**, 424.
Cornelianus, Atidius, governor of Syria, defeated by the Parthians, **2**, 447.
Cornelius, Judæan envoy to Claudius, **2**, 197–8.
Coronel, baptismal name of Abraham Senior's family, **4**, 351.
Coronel, David Senior, Marrano in Pernambuco, **4**, 693.
Coronello, Joseph Nassi's deputy, **4**, 597.
Correa, Isabel, Marrano poetess, **5**, 114.
"**Correction** of the False Teacher," by Isaac Nathan ben Kalonymos, **4**, 234.
Cosmas, bishop of Prague, protects the Jews during the first crusade, **3**, 305, 307.
Cossacks, the, origin and independence of, **5**, 2.
efforts to convert, **5**, 2–3.
highly taxed, **5**, 3.
Jews further the enslavement of, **5**, 6.
insurrections of, **5**, 6, 7.
organized into Haidamak troops, **5**, 8.
massacres of the Jews by, **5**, 9–12.
Cossacks, the (*continued*), make peace with the Poles, **5**, 12.
attack the Jews, **5**, 14, 15.
second treaty with, **5**, 14.
losses inflicted upon the Jews by, **5**, 15.
persecutions by, influence Judaism, **5**, 16–17.
ravages of, in Poland, **5**, 388.
Costa, Duarte Nuñes da, Portuguese agent in Hamburg, **4**, 692.
Costa, Emanuel da, Marrano, martyrdom of, **4**, 520–1.
Costa, Isaac Atias da, civic honors of, **5**, 458.
Costa, Joseph da, and Manasseh ben Israel, **5**, 34.
Costa, Uriel (Gabriel) da (1590-1640), as a Marrano, **5**, 56.
studies the Scriptures, **5**, 57.
returns to Judaism, **5**, 57.
at odds with Amsterdam Judaism, **5**, 58–9.
excommunicated, **5**, 59.
attacked by Samuel da Silva, **5**, 59.
publishes a work hostile to Judaism, **5**, 59–60.
retracts, **5**, 60–1.
formulates a natural religion, **5**, 61.
fails to conform to Jewish usages, **5**, 62.
restrains Christians from becoming Jews, **5**, 62.
refuses to do penance, **5**, 62.
penance imposed upon, **5**, 63–4.
autobiography of, **5**, 64–5.
suicide of, **5**, 64.
violence of, **5**, 84.
case of, compared with Spinoza's, **5**, 92, 93, 97.
Costnitz. *See* Constance.
Costobar, prevents the escape of fugitives from Jerusalem, **2**, 89.

Costobar, of the Herodian family, wickedness of, **2,** 236.
accuses Gessius Florus before Nero, **2,** 268.

Cotys, king of Armenia Minor, ally of Agrippa I, **2,** 195.

Cotys, Byzantine commander, subdues the Jews of Antioch, **3,** 18.

Council of Elders, the, instituted by Moses, **1,** 25–6.

Council of Seventy, the. *See* Council, the Great.

Council, the Great, of Seventy, work of, **1,** 394–5.
institutes Chanukah, **1,** 472–3.
informs the Egyptian Judæans of the independence of Judæa, **1,** 522.
composed of Sadducees, **2,** 42.
chief post in, given up to the Pharisees, **2,** 48–9.
reorganized, **2,** 50.
called the Great Synhedrion, **2,** 71.
See Synhedrion, the.

Council, the Great, couples at the head of:

José, son of Joëzer.	José, son of Johanan.
Joshua, son of Perachia.	Matthai of Arbela.
Judah ben Tabbai.	Simon ben Shetach.
Shemaya.	Abtalion.
Hillel I.	Shammai.

Councils, Church. *See* Church Councils.

"**Counsels and Lessons,**" by Santob de Carrion, **4,** 115.

Couples. *See* Council, the Great.

Courts of justice, held on Mondays and Thursdays in Judæa, **1,** 394.
restored to the Jews by Alexander Severus, **2,** 482.
purified by Abba-Areka, **2,** 517.

Courts of Justice (*continued*). *See also* Jurisdiction, Jewish, autonomous.

Coutinho, Ferdinand, bishop of Algarve, opposes the forcible baptism of Jews, **4,** 375.
describes the baptism of Jewish children, **4,** 376.
opposes the Portuguese Inquisition, **4,** 500.

Cracow, Jews massacred in, on the charge of well poisoning, **4,** 111.
the Jews of, number of, **4,** 632.
the German population of, **5,** 3.
Chassidistic writings burned in, **5,** 393.

Cranganor, destroyed, **2,** 630.

Crassus, member of the first Triumvirate, receives Syria. **2,** 73.
robs the Temple, **2,** 74.
slain, **2,** 74.

Creation, Kabbalistic theory of, **3,** 552–3.
theory of, held by Isaac Lurya, **4,** 619.

Creed, the, by Albo, **4,** 240.
by Chasdaï Crescas, **4,** 193.

Creed, the, by Maimonides, 3. 459–60.
effect of, **3,** 469, 470.
objected to, by Chasdaï. Crescas, **4,** 193.

Creizenach, Michael (1789–1842), advocate of the Reform movement, **5,** 674–5.

Crémieux, Adolf (1796–1880), espouses the cause of the Damascus Jews, **5,** 643–4.
acts in conjunction with the English Jews, **5,** 645, 651.
appeals to Louis Philippe, **5,** 645.
announces the faithlessness of Louis Philippe, **5,** 651.

Crémieux, Adolf (*continued*), appeal to, from Damascus, **5**, 651.
sent to Egypt, **5**, 652.
at the London meeting, **5**, 653.
hampered by the French ministry, **5**, 658.
sets out for Egypt, **5**, 658.
honors shown to, **5**, 658–9, 667–8.
introduces himself to Mehmet Ali, **5**, 659.
influences the European consuls and Mehmet Ali, **5**, 660.
tries to establish schools in Egypt, **5**, 663, 671.
services of, acknowledged, **5**, 669–72.
declines a medal, **5**, 671.
president of the "Alliance Israélite Universelle," **5**, 702.
Cremona, the Talmud burnt at, **4**, 582–3.
Cremona, the Jews of, number of, **4**, 653.
expelled, **4**, 660.
Crescas, Barfat, imprisonment of, **4**, 150.
Crescas, Chasdaï. *See* Chasdaï ben Abraham Crescas.
Crescas Vidal, opposes the study of science, **4**, 28–9.
reproaches Samuel Sulami for harboring a heretic, **4**, 29.
Crete (Candia), the Judæans of, make annual pilgrimages to Jerusalem, **2**, 220.
a false Messiah in, **2**, 610–11.
restored to Turkey, **5**, 661.
the Spanish exiles in, **4**, 363–4, 406.
the Talmud burnt in, **4**, 565.
Cardoso on, **5**, 207.
Crimea, the, Jews of the Byzantine empire settle in, **3**, 123–4.
the Karaites spread to, **3**, 182.
Crimea (*continued*), the land of the Chazars, **3**, 222.
the Karaites in, in the twelfth century, **3**, 435.
Karaites emigrate from, **4**, 269.
Jews of Poland transported to, **5**, 8.
Crispia. *See* Berachya ben Natronaï Nakdan.
Crissa, the Jews of, in the twelfth century, **3**, 424.
"Critical History of the Old Testament, The," by Richard Simon, **5**, 179.
Croatia, the Jews of, proscribed, **3**, 614.
Crœsus, at war with Cyrus, **1**, 343.
Cromwell, Oliver, obtains religious liberty for England, **5**, 25–6.
inspired by the Old Testament, **5**, 26, 27.
regards the Jews favorably, **5**, 27.
dissolves the Long Parliament, **5**, 34.
Protector, **5**, 35.
favors the re-settlement of Jews in England, **5**, 35, 42–3.
invites Manasseh ben Israel to England, **5**, 38.
receives Manasseh, **5**, 38–9.
hopes to convert the Jews, **5**, 43.
assembles a commission on the Jewish question, **5**, 43–5.
followers of, favor the admission of Jews, **5**, 44.
reported the Messiah of the Jews, **5**, 45.
dismisses Manasseh honorably, **5**, 49.
acquits the Marrano Robles, **5**, 49.

Cromwell, Oliver (*continued*), permits a Jewish burial ground in London, **5**, 49.

Crossen, the duchy of, Jews settle in, **5**, 173.

Crown money. *See* Aurum coronarium.

Crusade, a, against the Albigenses, **3**, 501–3.
against the Mahometans in Spain, **3**, 507.
preached by order of Gregory IX, **3**, 570.
organized by Louis IX with Jewish money, **3**, 585.

Crusade, the first, Jews during, **3**, 298–305, 308, 309.
disgraceful end of, **3**, 306.

Crusade, the second, Jews during, **3**, 349–56.

Crusade, the third, participators in, **3**, 404, 411, 418.
preached by Fulko de Neuilly, **3**, 405.

Crusade, the fourth, and the Jews, **3**, 496–7.

Crusaders, fall upon Jews in the English towns, **3**, 412–13.

Crusades, the, begin with massacres of the Jews, **4**, 222.

Crzemieniec, Jewish children slaughtered in, **5**, 12.

Ctesiphon (Ardashir), capital of the Parthians, **2**, 506.
populated with Jews, **2**, 507.
escapes seizure by Julian the Apostate, **2**, 602.

Cuenca, the Jews of, under Sancho, **3**, 617.
autos-da-fé in, **5**, 91, 92.

Cuenqui, Abraham, Sabbataï Zevi's biographer, **5**, 212.

Cumanus (48–52), procurator of Judæa, **2**, 241.
places a cohort in the Temple, **2**, 242.

Cumanus (*continued*), punishes the profanation of the Scriptures, **2**, 242–3.
sides with the Samaritans, **2**, 243.
hated in Jerusalem, **2**, 244.
called to Rome to justify himself, **2**, 244.
banished, **2**, 245.

Curiel, Jacob, unites the Portuguese congregations of Amsterdam, **4**, 681.
Portuguese agent in Hamburg, **4**, 692.

Cuthæans, the, a mixed population colonized in Samaria, **1**, 285.
See Samaritans, the.

Cyaxares, of Media, defeats the Assyrians, **1**, 287.
puts an end to Assyria, **1**, 303.

Cyclades, the, Joseph Nassi duke of, **4**, 596.

Cycle of Rabbi Nachshon, the, key to the Jewish calendar, **3**, 179.

Cydonia, original home of the Philistines, **1**, 54.

Cypros, wife of Agrippa I, appeals to Herodias, **2**, 175.
hostage for her husband, **2**, 176.

Cypros, wife of Antipater, **2**, 77.

Cyprus, refuge of Ptolemy VIII, **2**, 12.
seized by Ptolemy VIII, **2**, 40.
wheat imported from, for Jerusalem, **2**, 218.
the Judæans of, make annual pilgrimages to Jerusalem, **2**, 220.
promised to Joseph Nassi, **4**, 600.
taken by the Turks, **4**, 601.
as a Jewish state, **4**, 611.

Cyprus, the Jews of, rebel against Trajan, **2**, 394.

Cyprus, the Jews of (*continued*), Martius Hurbo sent against, **2,** 398.
join an expedition against the Christians of Tyre, **3,** 20.
in the twelfth century, **3,** 424-5.
Cyrenaica, the Judæans of, have a synagogue in Jerusalem, **2,** 201.
the Jews of, rebel against Trajan, **2,** 394, 395, 396.
Cyrene, Judæans settle in, **1,** 419.
position of the Judæans in, **1,** 503.
given to Ptolemy VII, **1,** 507.
the Judæans of, make annual pilgrimages to Jerusalem, **2,** 220.
Zealots take refuge in, **2,** 317, 318.
Jewish revolt in, **2,** 331.
the Jews of, revolt from Trajan, **2,** 395, 397.
Cyril, bishop of Alexandria, ill-treats the Jews, **2,** 618-19; **3,** 23.
Cyrus, of Persia, dethrones the Median king, **1,** 342.
at war with Crœsus, **1,** 343.
called the instrument of God by Isaiah, **1,** 348.
conquers Babylon, **1,** 349-50.
proclaims himself king of Babylon, **1,** 350.
permits the Judæans to return to Palestine, **1,** 351-2.
sends an escort with the returning exiles, **1,** 355.
Czarnicki, Polish general, ill-uses the Jews, **5,** 15.
Czechowic, Martin, Polish Unitarian, writes against Judaism, **4,** 648.
Czenstochow, Frank imprisoned at, **5,** 288, 289.
Czernigov, the Jews of, massacred, **5,** 10.

D

Dabaritta, the Judæans of, plunder Agrippa II's agent, **2,** 279.
Dævas, Persian evil spirits, **1,** 403.
Dafiera. *See* Solomon Dafiera.
"**Dagger of Faith, The,**" anti-Jewish work by Raymund Martin, **3,** 622-3.
Dagobert (629), Merovingian king, hostile to the Jews, **3,** 40.
Dagon, Philistine god, **1,** 55.
temple of, burnt, **1,** 496.
Dâi, forerunner of the Messiah, **3,** 124.
Dalalat al Haïrin. *See* "Guide of the Perplexed, The."
Dalberg, Karl von, imperial chancellor, aids Breidenbach, **5,** 468.
favors the emancipation of Jews, **5,** 504.
grants civil rights to the Jews of Frankfort, **5,** 505.
Dalburg, bishop of Worms, refuses to judge the Reuchlin case, **4,** 454.
Dallim (Ebionim), disciples of Isaiah, **1,** 254.
Dalmatia, the Jews of, proscribed, **3,** 614.
Damascus (Aram, Syria), belongs to the king of Israel, **1,** 127.
king of, defeated by David, **1,** 127.

Damascus (*continued*), taken by Rezon, **1,** 177, 183.
king of, makes a treaty with Rehoboam, **1,** 183.
extended by Tabrimon, **1,** 183.
conquered by Jeroboam II, **1,** 232.
besieged by Tiglath-Pileser, **1,** 259.
subdued by Sennacherib, **1,** 270.
the goddess of love, worshiped in, **1,** 408.
taken by the Hasmonæans, **1,** 498.
number of Judæans in, **2,** 202.
women of, adopt Judaism, **2,** 215.
the Nazarene community in, **2,** 222-3.
the apostle Paul in, **2,** 226, 227.
Jehuda Halevi at, **3,** 342.
captured by Hulagu, **3,** 606.
the Spanish exiles in, **4,** 399-400.
Chayim Vital Calabrese in, **5,** 52-3.

Damascus affair, the, reported in the French journals, **5,** 642.
taken up by Crémieux, **5,** 644.
considered in England, **5,** 645.
the Austrian report on, **5,** 646.
in the hands of Mehmet Ali, **5,** 647.
tried by a court of European consuls, **5,** 648.
trial of, stopped by Thiers, **5,** 649.
in the French Chamber of Deputies, **5,** 649-50.
view of, among Catholics, **5,** 650-1.
in Parliament, **5,** 652-3.
discussed by London Jews, **5,** 653-4.

Damascus affair, the (*continued*), a Mansion House meeting protests against, **5,** 656-7.
rejoicing at the termination of, **5,** 667, 669.
plans for commemorating, **5,** 669, 670, 671.
account of, by Erter, **5,** 671.
Munk on, **5,** 671-2.

Damascus, the Jews of, in an expedition against the Christians of Tyre, **3,** 20.
in the twelfth century, **3,** 426-7.
liturgy of, changed, **3,** 466.
cause of, espoused by various governments, **5,** 633.
number of, **5,** 634.
suspected of ritual murder, **5,** 635, 636.
arrested and tortured, **5,** 636-7.
houses of, destroyed, **5,** 637.
evidence favoring, suppressed, **5,** 637.
confess under torture, **5,** 638.
pronounced guilty by Ratti Menton, **5,** 640.
appeal to the European Jews, **5,** 642, 651.
torture of, stopped, **5,** 648.
release of, **5,** 660-1.
new crusade against, incited by Catholics, **5,** 662.

Dan, the tribe of, late settlement of, **1,** 39.
isolation of, **1,** 51.
attacked by the Philistines, **1,** 64.
oppressed by the Philistines, **1,** 66.
around Nishabur, **3,** 433.

Dan, northern frontier town of Israel, **1,** 129.
occupied by Sheba's followers, **1,** 149-50.

Dan (*continued*), center of idolatry, **1**, 186, 233.
subjugated by Ben-hadad I, **1**, 191.
"**Danger** to the Welfare and Character of the Germans through the Jews," by J. F. Fries, **5**, 521.
"**Dangerous** Courses, The," by Joseph Penso, **5**, 113.
Daniel, the supposed grave of, causes a quarrel, **3**, 434–5.
Daniel, the **Book** of, written during the Maccabæan struggle, **1**, 465–6.
language of, **1**, 465.
consolations offered by, **1**, 465.
prophesies the end of the Syrian power, **1**, 465–6.
additions to, **2**, 359.
prophecy of, thought to be verified, **2**, 482–3.
explained by Jochanan bar Napacha, **2**, 494–5.
as explained by Christians, **2**, 502.
commentary on, by Porphyry, **2**, 502.
a verse of, applied to Odenathus, **2**, 527.
a prophecy of, applied to Julian the Apostate, **2**, 598.
commentary on, by Abraham Ibn-Ezra, **3**, 373.
Nissim Gerundi on, **4**, 120.
Gallipapa on, **4**, 149.
commentary on, by Isaac Abrabanel, **4**, 482.
Simone Luzzatto on, **5**, 81.
Daniel, friend of Immanuel Romi, **4**, 66.
Daniel, Karaite, candidate for the Exilarchate, **3**, 155.
Daniel ben Saadiah, anti-Maimunist, **3**, 525–6.
excommunicated, **3**, 526.
Daniel, son of Solomon (Chasdaï?, 1165–1175), Exilarch, **3**, 438.
death of, **3**, 439.
Dante, friend of Immanuel Romi, **4**, 65.
imitated by Immanuel Romi, **4**, 66, 67.
quoted, **4**, 325.
Danz, Frankfort deputy to the Congress of Vienna, objects to the emancipation of the Jews, **5**, 519.
Daphne, Verus Commodus at, **2**, 447.
Darius, king of Persia, permits the rebuilding of the Temple, **1**, 359.
Darius, commander of Agrippa II's troops, **2**, 259.
"**Dark Age**," the Jewish, **4**, 617.
Darke ha-Talmud, work by Isaac Campanton, **4**, 230.
Darmstadt, the Jews of, persecuted, **5**, 530.
Daroca, the Jews of, converted, **4**, 206, 214.
Darshanim, Jewish preachers, deliver sermons in the vernacular, under Louis the Pious **3**, 163.
Daub, professor, protects the Jews of Heidelberg, **5**, 531.
Daud, physician, traduces Joseph Nassi, **4**, 598–9.
banished and excommunicated, **4**, 599.
Dauphiné, Jews remain in, after the expulsion by Charles VI, **4**, 177.
David, king, anointed, **1**, 95–6.
poetic talent of, **1**, 96.
under Samuel's influence, **1**, 96–7.
and Goliath, **1**, 97.
soothes Saul's melancholy, **1**, 98.

David (*continued*), victorious over the Philistines, **1**, 98–9.
attacked by Saul, **1**, 99.
marries Michal, **1**, 100.
outlawed, **1**, 100.
in friendly relations with Ammonites and Philistines, **1**, 100–2.
at Ziklag, **1**, 101–2.
to help the Philistines against Saul, **1**, 102.
routs the Amalekites, **1**, 106–7.
chosen king by Judah, **1**, 107.
ally of Achish, **1**, 107–8.
resides at Hebron, **1**, 109.
and Abner, **1**, 110–12.
rules over the whole kingdom, **1**, 112.
subdues the Jebusites, **1**, 113–14.
resides at Jerusalem, **1**, 114.
at war with the Philistines, **1**, 115–18.
at Adullam, **1**, 116.
saved by Abishai, **1**, 117.
ally of Hiram, **1**, 118.
builds a cedar palace, **1**, 119.
makes Jerusalem the center of religious life, **1**, 119–20.
introduces choral song into the religious service, **1**, 120.
as Psalmist, **1**, 120–1.
as king, **1**, 121.
loyalty to, **1**, 121–2.
army of, **1**, 122.
favorite and councilor of, **1**, 122–3.
surrenders Saul's descendants to the Gibeonites, **1**, 123.
buries the remains of Saul and Jonathan, **1**, 124.
at war with the Moabites, **1**, 125–6.
at war with the Ammonites, **1**, 126–7.
at war with the Aramæans, **1**, 127.

David (*continued*), at war with the Ammonites and Idumæans, **1**, 128–9.
enlarges his territory, **1**, 129–30.
faith of, **1**, 130.
lenient towards conquered races, **1**, 131.
betrays Uriah, **1**, 131–2.
rebuked by Nathan, **1**, 133.
and Absalom, **1**, 134–7.
orders a census, **1**, 137–8.
conspiracy against, **1**, 138–44.
leaves Jerusalem, **1**, 140–1.
faithful followers of, **1**, 141–2, 144.
enemies of, **1**, 142.
victorious over Absalom, **1**, 144.
mourns Absalom, **1**, 145.
invited to Jerusalem by the northern tribes, **1**, 146.
pardons Amasa, **1**, 146.
met by embassies of Benjamites and Judæans, **1**, 146–8.
suppresses Sheba's revolt, **1**, 148–50.
returns to Jerusalem, **1**, 150.
restrained from building a Temple, **1**, 150–1.
debility of, **1**, 151.
has Solomon acknowledged king, **1**, 153.
death of, **1**, 154.
summary of the reign of, **1**, 154–5.
number of wives of, **1**, 161.
descendants of, the only ones entitled to the crown, **1**, 527–8.
a descendant of, the Messiah, **2**, 143, 144.
descent from, traced by Spanish families, **3**, 43.
Israelites under, settle in northern Arabia, **3**, 54.

David (*continued*), in Immanuel Romi's work, **4**, 67.
favorite character of the Puritans, **5**, 26.
David, candidate for the Exilarchate, **3**, 439.
David, German immigrant in Turkey, **4**, 271.
David, principino of the Neapolitan Jews, **3**, 424.
David of Mosul, Exilarch in Jerusalem, **3**, 506.
excommunicates Daniel ben Saadiah, **3**, 526.
David de Pomis (1525–1588), physician, employed by Christians, **4**, 653.
attainments of, **4**, 656.
defense of Jewish physicians by, **4**, 656–7.
Talmudic dictionary by, **4**, 657.
David ben Daniel, Exilarch of Mosul, excommunicates Solomon Petit, **3**, 632.
David ben Judah (825–840), Exilarch, **3**, 155–6.
David ben Kalonymos, Tossafist, member of the Mayence synod, **3**, 517.
David ben Maimun, brother of Maimonides, **3**, 451, 457.
David ben Saul, excommunicates the Maimunists, **3**, 529.
excommunicated, **3**, 530, 536–7.
David ben Zaccaï (940), Exilarch, deposes Kohen-Zedek, **3**, 186.
appoints two Geonim of Sora, **3**, 192–3.
excommunicates the congregation of Fars, **3**, 194.
injustice of, **3**, 194–5.
contest of, with Saadiah, **3**, 195–6, 200–1.
cause of, espoused by Aaron Ibn-Sarjadu, **3**, 200.
David ben Zaccaï (*continued*), death of, **3**, 201.
great-grandson of, **3**, 254.
David Ibn-Abi Zimra (1470–1573), scholar, Spanish exile in Cairo, **4**, 393.
rabbi of Cairo, **4**, 394.
abolishes the Seleucidæan era, **4**, 394–5.
reverses the liturgical changes made by Maimonides, **4**, 395.
Kabbalist, **4**, 481.
David Ibn-Albilla, philosopher, **4**, 91.
David Ibn-Yachya, rabbi at Naples, **4**, 410.
David Ibn-Yachya Negro, foresees the expulsion of the Jews from Portugal, **4**, 339.
David Abudarham, a Jew of Castile, **3**, 617.
David Alrui (Alroy, Ibn-Alruchi, Menahem ben Solomon), attainments of, **3**, 430.
summons the Jews of the East to return to Jerusalem, **3**, 431.
imprisoned, **3**, 431–2.
death of, **3**, 433.
David Bonet Buen-Giorna, Marrano, persuaded to remain a Christian, **4**, 188.
epistle to, **4**, 188–90.
David Gans (1541–1613), historian and astronomer, works of, **4**, 638–9.
consulted by Basnage, **5**, 196.
refutes Eibeschütz's defense, **5**, 270.
David Kimchi (1160–1235), grammarian and lexicographer, **3**, 393–4, 561.
grammatical and exegetical work of, **3**, 394.
Maimunist, **3**, 530–1, 540–1.

16

David Kimchi (*continued*), denounces Solomon of Montpellier, **3**, 544.
works of, used by Raymund Martin, **3**, 622.
commentary of, in the Bomberg Bible, **4**, 476.

David Maimuni (1223–1300), grandson of Maimonides, aided by Solomon ben Adret, **3**, 620.
Nagid of Egypt, friend of the Exilarch Yishaï, **3**, 627.
appealed to by Hillel of Verona, **3**, 631.
in the Maimunist controversy, **3**, 632–3.

David Negro Ibn-Yachya, counselor of Ferdinand I of Portugal, **4**, 159–60.
leaves Lisbon, **4**, 160.
chief rabbi of Castile, **4**, 161, 162.

David Rafan, discovers the Zohar to be a forgery, **4**, 20–1.

David Reubeni, travels of, in the East, **4**, 491.
description of, **4**, 491–2.
at Rome, **4**, 492, 493.
honored by the Jews, **4**, 493.
received by João III of Portugal, **4**, 493, 498.
considered the forerunner of the Messiah, **4**, 494, 497–8.
repulses the Marranos and Solomon Molcho, **4**, 495–6.
opposed by Miguel de Silva, **4**, 498–9.
leaves Portugal, **4**, 499.
prisoner in Spain, **4**, 499.
in Avignon, **4**, 499.
and Molcho, **4**, 504.
and the Venetian senate, **4**, 504.
petitions Charles V, **4**, 509–10.
confined by the Spanish Inquisition, **4**, 511.

David's chapel, Franciscan church on Mount Zion, **4**, 274.

Daya, character in "Nathan the Wise," **5**, 324.

Dayan, title of the judges in Jewish Babylonia, **3**, 98.
title of Moses ben Chanoch, **3**, 229.

Dayane-di-Baba, judges of the gate, in Babylonia, **2**, 547.

Dayanim, assistants of the rabbis, **5**, 566, 569.

Dead Sea, the, description of, **1**, 43.

Debir, the, the Holy of Holies, **1**, 165.

Debir (Kirjath-Sepher), taken by the tribe of Judah, **1**, 38.

Deborah, judge, inspires resistance to Jabin, **1**, 61.

Debts owing to Jews, the interest on, repudiated by Eugenius III, **3**, 349, 351.
the repudiation of, not permitted by Maria de Molina, **4**, 52.
the repudiation of, urged by Louis the Rich, **4**, 254.

Decapolis, league of towns, freed from Judæan rule, **2**, 67.

Deckendorf (Deggendorf), the Jews of, massacred, **4**, 98.

"Declaration," by Manasseh ben Israel, concerning the admission of Jews into England, **5**, 39–42.

"Defense of the Rational Worshipers of God," by Reimarus, **5**, 320.

"Definitions and Descriptions," by Isaac Israeli, **3**, 181.

Deï Rossi. *See* Azarya ben Moses deï Rossi.

Deity, the, Israelitish conception of, **1**, 24, 402.

Delaborde, Count, on the Turkish Jews, **5,** 649–50.
"**Delight of all Mankind,**" epithet of Titus, **2,** 304.
Delitzsch, Franz, admires neo-Hebraic poetry, **5,** 628–9.
Della Ruvere, Marco, nuncio in Portugal, **4,** 514.
Della Volta, Samuel Vita, physician and scholar, **5,** 622.
Del Medigo. *See* Elias del Medigo.
Delmedigo, Joseph Solomon (1591–1655), sceptic, **5,** 56, 75–6.
ancestry and education of, **5,** 75.
wanderings of, **5,** 76–80.
mathematical attainments of, **5,** 76.
among Karaites, **5,** 76–7.
as physician, **5,** 76, 80.
defends the Kabbala, **5,** 78.
at Amsterdam, **5,** 79.
preacher, **5,** 79–80.
end of, **5,** 80.
hypocrisy of, **5,** 84.
Delmedigo, Judah, son of Elias, rabbi of Canea, **4,** 406.
Dembowski, Nicolas, bishop of Kamieniec, persecutes the Frankists, **5,** 278.
Frankists make a partial confession of Christianity before, **5,** 279.
favors the Frankists, **5,** 279–80.
consents to disputations between Frankists and Talmudists, **5,** 280, 281–2.
confiscates and burns the Talmud, **5,** 282.
death of, **5,** 282.
Dembowski, Frankist family, **5,** 289.
Demetrius I, of Syria, sent to Rome as hostage, **1,** 443.
Demetrius I (*continued*), throne of, usurped by Antiochus IV, **1,** 443.
plots to depose Antiochus V, **1,** 481.
escapes from Rome, **1,** 482.
kills Antiochus V, **1,** 482.
appoints Alcimus high priest, **1,** 482.
sends Bacchides to Jerusalem, **1,** 482, 486.
sends Nicanor to Judæa, **1,** 484.
leaves the religious freedom of the Judæans undisturbed, **1,** 488, 491–2.
seeks the friendship of Jonathan Haphus, **1,** 494, 495–6.
Demetrius II Nicator, of Syria, contests the throne with Alexander Balas, **1,** 496.
appealed to by the Hellenists, **1,** 497.
exempts the Judæans from taxation, **1,** 497.
besieged in his palace, **1,** 497.
seeks help with Jonathan Haphus, **1,** 497.
flees from Antioch, **1,** 498.
negotiates with Simon Tharsi, **1,** 521.
acknowledges the independence of Judæa, **1,** 521.
expedition of, against Persia, **1,** 525.
defeated by the Parthians, **2,** 5.
deposed by Alexander Zabina, **2,** 6.
death of, **2,** 6.
Demetrius, librarian of Ptolemy II, advises the translation of the Law, **1,** 514.
Demetrius, son of Antigonus, defeated, **1,** 417.
Demetrius, son-in-law of Agrippa I, **2,** 235.

Demiurge, creator of the world, in the Gnostic system, **2**, 375.
Demons, exorcism of, in Galilee, **2**, 148.
by the Essenes, **2**, 151.
by Jesus, **2**, 156–7.
by the disciples of Jesus, **2**, 170.
Denia, home of Isaac Albergeloni, **3**, 284.
Denmark, the Protestant Reformation in, **4**, 469.
Jews invited to settle in, **4**, 675.
rabbis of, willing to excommunicate Luzzatto, **5**, 241.
favors the emancipation of the Jews, **5**, 519, 531.
Derasha. *See* Agada.
Derbend (Berdaa), Jews settle in, **3**, 124.
refuge of the Chazars, **3**, 222.
Derketades, royal Assyrian house, last member of, **1**, 258.
Derush. *See* Agada.
Descartes, philosophy of, studied by Spinoza, **5**, 89.
characteristics of, **5**, 90.
Desfar, Juan, governor of Palma, protects the Jews, **4**, 246, 247.
Dessau, subscribers to Mendelssohn's Pentateuch translation in, **5**, 329.
Deuteronomy, the Book of, found in the Temple, **1**, 289, 292–3. *See under* Law, the.
Deuterosis, code of Rabbi Akiba, **2**, 354.
Deuterotes, the Tanaites, **2**, 371.
Deutz, Menahem, member of the French consistory, **5**, 502.
Deutz, the Jews of Cologne take refuge in, **4**, 227.
De Wette, exegete, **5**, 623, 695.
De Witt, John, friend of Spinoza, **5**, 107, 108.
Deza, archbishop of Seville, second inquisitor general, **4**, 356, 484.
Dhor el-Khedib, highest peak of Lebanon, **1**, 44.
Dialoghi d'amore ("Dialogues of Love"), by Leon Abrabanel, **4**, 480–1.
Dias, André, Marrano, assassin of Henrique Nunes, **4**, 490.
Dibre Sopherim, the work of the Council of Seventy, **1**, 395.
traditional Jewish lore, **2**, 19, 472.
See Law, the oral.
Dictionaries, Chaldean and Rabbinical, by Elias Levita, **4**, 474.
Dictionary. *See* Aruch; Iggaron; Lexicon; Machbereth.
Diderot, praises Pereira's sign language, **5**, 343.
Diebitsch, von, defender of the Jews, **5**, 470.
Diego de Valencia, apostate, Spanish satirist, **4**, 181.
Dietary laws, the, observed by the Babylonian Judæans, **1**, 364.
observed by the Judæan Christians of Antioch, **2**, 231.
obeyed by the Jews of Gaul, **3**, 36.
observed by the Jews of Arabia, **3**, 58.
made severer by Anan ben David, **3**, 132.
not observed by the "Friends of Reform," **5**, 675.
declaration against, withdrawn, **5**, 676.
Dieterich. *See* Theodoric of Burgundy.

Diez, friend of Dohm, on the emancipation of the Jews, 5, 358–9.
Dimé, Palestinian Amora, banished from Judæa, 2, 567.
Dimuh, so-called synagogue of Moses at, 3, 445.
Dina d'malchuta dina, sanctity of the law of the land, 2, 519.
Diniz (1279–1325), of Portugal, Jews under, 3, 618.
Dio Cassius, historian, on the revolt under Bar Cochba, 2, 411.
on the fall of Bethar, 2, 418–19.
Dio Kart, birthplace of Huna, 2, 545.
Diocæsarea. *See* Sepphoris.
Diocletian, emperor, tolerant, 2, 533.
accuses Judah III of disloyalty, 2, 533–4.
and Abbahu, 2, 538.
persecutes Christianity, 2, 539.
Diodorus, ambassador to Rome, 2, 4–5.
Diodotus Tryphon, general of Alexander Balas, puts the latter's son on the throne, 1, 497–8.
friendly to Jonathan Haphus, 1, 498.
seeks to make himself king, 1, 498–9.
takes Jonathan Haphus prisoner, 1, 499.
negotiates with Simon Tharsi for tribute, 1, 500–1.
has Jonathan Haphus executed, 1, 501.
Simon Tharsi hostile to, 1, 521.
at odds with Antiochus Sidetes, 1, 525, 528, 529.
Diogenes, Sadducee, favorite of Alexander Jannæus, 2, 42.
Diogenes (*continued*), advises the crucifixion of Pharisees, 2, 45.
put to death by the Pharisees, 2, 55.
Diokna Kadisha, Kabbalistic term, 4, 538.
Dionysus, worshiped in Alexandria, 1, 428.
festival of, in Judæa, 1, 428, 456–7.
Dios-Carne. *See* Astruc Raimuch.
Dioscorides, work of, translated, 3, 218.
Diospolis. *See* Lydda.
Dioterich. *See* Theodoric.
Disciples, meaning of, 2, 357.
See Law, the, the teachers of.
Dispersion, the, of Judæans under Uzziah, 1, 227.
after the capture of Jerusalem by Nebuchadnezzar, 1, 317–18.
in the lands of the Seleucidæ and the Ptolemies, 1, 420–1.
value of, 2, 200–1.
Disputation, between Judæans and Samaritans in Alexandria, 1, 516–17.
between Donin and four rabbis, 3, 576–8.
between Pablo Christiani and Nachmani, 3, 598–604.
at Burgos, 4, 140.
at Avila, 4, 140–2.
at Pampeluna, 4, 142.
at Tortosa, 4, 207–15.
at Kamieniec, 5, 280–1.
at Lemberg, 5, 285–7.
Disputations, between Jews and Christians, under Basilius, 3, 175–6.
in France in the twelfth century, 3, 343.
See under Polemical works against Christianity.

"**Distinction**," anti-Karaite work by Saadiah, **3**, 192.

"**Diversions**," satire by Joseph ben Sabara, **3**, 559.

Divine Service, the. *See* Liturgy, the.

Divorce, abolished by Obaiah Abu-Isa ben Ishak, **3**, 124.
bills of, criticised after delivery to the wife, **3**, 378.
discussed by the Assembly of Jewish Notables, **5**, 489, 491.
discussed by the French Synhedrion, **5**, 497.

Divorce law, the, as formulated by the Pharisees, **2**, 50.
according to the school of Shammai, **2**, 132.
as interpreted by Meïr, **2**, 439.
alleviations of, proposed by Judah II, **2**, 484.
regulated by Abba Areka, **2**, 516–17.
reformed by Hunaï and Mar-Raba, **3**, 92.
changed by Gershom, **3**, 244.
modified by the Troyes synod, **3**, 378.
changed by Menachem of Merseburg, **4**, 228.

Divorces, frequent among Kabbalists, **4**, 627; **5**, 210.

Djabar, the Jews of, pillaged, **5**, 641.

Dnieper, the, colonies of serfs on, **5**, 2.

Doag, captain of the guard under Saul, **1**, 91.

Dob Beer. *See* Beer of Mizricz.

Dohm, Christian William (1751–1820), friend of Mendelssohn, **5**, 351–2.
plea by, for the amelioration of the condition of the Jews, **5**, 352–62.
inspired by Mendelssohn, **5**, 356, 361, 366.

Dohm, Christian William (*continued*), admits the depravity of the Jews, **5**, 361.
criticised by Mendelssohn, **5**, 361–2.
enlists Mirabeau's sympathies for the Jews, **5**, 366.
fails to impress Frederick the Great, **5**, 414.
helps to frame the Westphalian constitution, **5**, 500.
entertains a distorted view of Jewish history, **5**, 593.

Dok, fortress, Simon Tharsi assassinated in, **1**, 530.
Ptolemy ben Habub shut up in, **1**, 531.

Dolmäh. *See* Donmäh.

Domingo, founder of the Dominican order, **3**, 519.

Dominicans, the, originate in the Fourth Lateran Council, **3**, 509.
persecutions by, in southern France, **3**, 519.
entrusted with the extirpation of the Albigenses, **3**, 542.
interfere in the Maimunist controversy, **3**, 542–3.
preach Jew hatred, **3**, 565.
judges of the Talmud, **3**, 575, 602–3.
at Donin's disputation, **3**, 576.
charge the Jews of England with the blood accusation, **3**, 591.
taught Hebrew and Arabic for conversion purposes, **3**, 597, 621.
in the Barcelona synagogue, **3**, 601.
appeal to Clement IV against Nachmani, **3**, 605.
enforce Jew badges, **3**, 613.
in Hungary, **3**, 614.
and Robert de Redingge's conversion, **3**, 641.

Dominicans, the (*continued*), deliver sermons to the Jews of England, **3**, 643-4.
denounce the Jews of England, **3**, 645.
arouse hatred against the Hussites and the Jews, **4**, 222, 226.
hate the Jews, **4**, 308.
try to convert the Jews of Spain, **4**, 350.
work for the expulsion of the Portuguese Marranos, **4**, 486-7.
incite the mob against the Marranos, **4**, 487.
have the Jews of Genoa banished, **4**, 554.
arouse Cremona against the Jews, **4**, 582.

Dominicans, the, of Cologne, and their crusade against Judaism, **4**, 424-6.
wish to confiscate the Talmud, **4**, 425, 426, 428.
devise measures for the conversion of the Jews, **4**, 426.
urge Maximilian I to deliver the Jews to them, **4**, 428-9.
eager to associate Reuchlin with themselves, **4**, 432.
suspect Reuchlin of heresy, **4**, 435-6.
obtain Maximilian's fourth mandate, **4**, 440-1.
decide upon the burning of the Talmud, **4**, 444.
declare the Hebrew Bible heretical, **4**, 445.
publish a refutation of Reuchlin's defense, **4**, 445-6.
sanction the burning of the "Augenspiegel," **4**, 452.
try to overthrow the Speyer decision against Hoogstraten, **4**, 455-6, 458.

Dominicans, the, of Cologne (*continued*), hatred of, for the Jews, increases, **4**, 457.
threaten to withdraw allegiance from the papacy, **4**, 459.
abuse Maximilian I, **4**, 459.
rejoice over the University of Paris decision, **4**, 460.
have the "Augenspiegel" translated, **4**, 460.
plan the extermination of the Jews of Germany, **4**, 462-3.
complain of the treatment accorded them, **4**, 465-6.

Dominicus Haman Epiphanes, pseudonym of a Jewish champion, **5**, 471.

Domitia, empress, Josephus a favorite of, **2**, 389.

Domitian, emperor, celebration of the birthday of, **2**, 312.
celebrates his triumph over Judæa, **2**, 314-15.
Jews troubled under, **2**, 345, 384, 388-9.
cousin of, convert to Judaism, **2**, 387.
Josephus a favorite of, **2**, 389.
prosecutes Josephus, **2**, 391.

Domitilla, Flavia, convert to Judaism, **2**, 387, 389.

Domna, Julia, wife of Severus, **2**, 468.

Donin (Nicholas), Talmudist, excommunicated by the French rabbis, **3**, 572-3.
apostatizes, **3**, 573.
causes the persecution of the Jews of Poitou, **3**, 573.
brings charges against the Talmud, **3**, 573-4.
disputation of, with four rabbis, **3**, 576-8.
and Pablo Christiani, **3**, 598, 599, 602.
charges of, repeated, **4**, 213.

Donin (*continued*), instigates the burning of the Talmud, **4**, 460.

Donmäh (Dolmäh), the, followers of Berachya, **5**, 211.
descendants of, in Salonica, **5**, 211.
joined by Chayim Malach, **5**, 214.
address prayers to their leaders, **5**, 274.

Donnolo. *See* Sabbataï Donnolo.

Dora, besieged by Antiochus Sidetes, **1**, 528, 529.
Greek youths of, introduce statues into the synagogues, **2**, 193.

Doria, Andrea, doge of Genoa, opposed to the expulsion of the Jews, **4**, 554.
employs a Jewish physician, **4**, 555.

Doria, Gianettino, and Joseph Cohen, **4**, 555.

Doris, first wife of Herod, **2**, 112.

Dormido, David Abrabanel, petitions Parliament to permit Jews to settle in England, **5**, 35.

Dorotheus, Judæan envoy to Rome, **2**, 197–8.

Dortmund, Jews tolerated in, **4**, 686.

Dortus of Jerusalem, tries to incite a rebellion against Cumanus, **2**, 244.

Dositheus, companion of Onias IV, espouses Ptolemy VI's cause, **1**, 506, 507.

Dossa ben Nachman (Archinas), teacher of the Law, **2**, 330.

Dossa ben Saadiah, author, **3**, 202.
in correspondence with Chasdaï Ibn-Shaprut, **3**, 217.

"**Doubts** of the Religion of Jesus," by Joseph Ibn-Shem Tob, **4**, 235.

Dowry, the law of, according to Meïr, **2**, 439.

Draï, the Jews of, persecuted, **3**, 360.

Drama, the, in Jewish literature, **5**, 112.

Dresden, Jews permitted to live in, **5**, 509.

Dresden, the Jews of, assisted by Mendelssohn, **5**, 344.
present an address to the Synhedrion, **5**, 496.

Drome, rabbi of, at the first rabbinical synod, **3**, 377.

Drouth, under Uzziah, **1**, 229–30.

Drusilla, youngest daughter of Agrippa I, affianced to Epiphanes of Commagene, **2**, 195, 235.
married to Aziz, **2**, 235.
married to Felix, **2**, 235, 245.
envious of Berenice, **2**, 236.

Drusus, son of Tiberius, educated with Agrippa I, **2**, 175.

Drusus, a tower on the wall of Cæsarea, **2**, 106.

Dsimma, Mahometan tax, **3**, 110.

Duarte de Pinel. *See* Usque, Abraham.

Dubno, Solomon, writes the commentary to Mendelssohn's Pentateuch translation, **5**, 329, 332.
alienated from Mendelssohn, **5**, 334.

Duchan, Jacob Israel, Sabbatian, **5**, 156.

Dudaï ben Nachman (761–764), principal of Pumbeditha, opponent of Anan ben David, **3**, 129.

Duelling, permitted to Jews under Alfonso VI, **3**, 293.

Du Guesclin, Bertrand, aids Henry de Trastamare, **4,** 123, 124.
cruelty of, to the Jews of Castile, **4,** 126.
kills Pedro the Cruel, **4,** 126.
Dulcigno, Sabbataï Zevi banished to, **5,** 166.
Dunash ben Labrat (Adonim, 920–970), poet, founder of Judæo-Spanish culture, **3,** 215.
introduces meter into the Hebrew language, **3,** 223.
supplements Menachem ben Saruk, **3,** 225.
circumstances of, **3,** 226.
criticises Saadiah's works, **3,** 226.
controversy of, with the disciples of Menachem ben Saruk, **3,** 226–7.
disciples of, grammarians and poets, **3,** 237.
grammar by, known to Rashi, **3,** 289.
Dunash ben Tamim (Abusahal, 900–960), disciple of Isaac Israeli, **3,** 181, 211–12.
admiration of, for Saadiah, **3,** 192.
Dunash ben Tamim (*continued*), physician to a caliph, **3,** 211.
works of, **3,** 211.
and Chasdaï Ibn Shaprut, **3,** 217.
Dunin. *See* Donin.
Duns Scotus, scholastic philosopher, counsels compulsory baptism of Jews, **3,** 644; **4,** 277.
Duport, favors the emancipation of the Jews, **5,** 441, 447–8.
Duran. *See* Profiat; Simon ben Zemach; Simon (II); Solomon (I).
Dury, John, writes against the admission of Jews into England, **5,** 46.
Düsseldorf, the Jews of, persecuted, **5,** 530.
"Duties of the Heart, The," by Bachya Ibn-Pakuda, translated, **3,** 397.
Du Vallié, Antoinette, mother of the next, **5,** 175.
Du Vallié, Paul, apostate, testifies falsely in a blood accusation case, **5,** 175.
Dyeing, trade of the Jews of Jerusalem, **3,** 427, 606.
Dzalski, Frankist family, **5,** 289.

E

Earthquake, under Uzziah, **1,** 229, 236.
under Hyrcanus II, **2,** 61.
under Herod, **2,** 95.
under Hadrian, **2,** 408.
at Lisbon, **4,** 505.
at Ferrara, **4,** 615.
East, the, conversions to Judaism in, **2,** 383.
East, the, the empire of. *See* Byzantine Empire, the.
East, the, the Jews of, affected by Islam theology, **3,** 148.
East, the, the Jews of (*continued*), persecuted, **3,** 245–8.
poor, **5,** 205.
admire the European Jews, **5,** 662–3.
See also under Abbasside Caliphate, the; Byzantine Empire, the.
East, the, the Roman governors of. *See* Amantius; Bonosus.
East India Company, the, Jews interested in, **4,** 677.

Easter, the date of, fixed, **2**, 563–4.
to be celebrated before the Passover, **3**, 13.
tax to be paid at, by Jews, **3**, 510.

Eastertide attacks upon Jews, in France, **3**, 173–4.
in Béziers, **3**, 394.
in Prague, **4**, 164.
in Majorca, **4**, 246.
in Trent, **4**, 298.

Eastertide, Jews forbidden to appear in public during, by the Councils of Orleans, **3**, 37.
by the Council of Mâcon, **3**, 39, 171.
by the Fourth Lateran Council, **3**, 510.
by the Council of Narbonne, **3**, 518.
by the Council of Béziers, **3**, 582.
by the code of Alfonso X, **3**, 595.
in Ratisbon, **3**, 635.
by Eugenius IV, **4**, 250.
by Henry IV of Castile, **4**, 278.

Ebal, mountain, described, **1**, 45.

"Eben Bochan," polemic by Shem-Tob ben Isaac Shaprut, **4**, 142.

Eben ha-Ezer, scene of battles between Israelites and Philistines, **1**, 70, 78.

Eberard, Magister Judæorum, under Louis the Pious, **3**, 161.
and the bishop of Lyons, **3**, 164, 166.

Eberhard von Cleve, Dominican provincial, complains of the treatment of his order, **4**, 465–6.

Ebionim (Dallim), disciples of Isaiah, **1**, 254.

Ebionites (Ebionim), the, followers of Jesus, **2**, 168, 366.
communists, **2**, 220.
disappearance of, **2**, 373.
use Akylas' Scripture translation, **2**, 387.
merged into the Catholic Church, **2**, 500.
See under Jewish Christians, the; Judæan Christians, the.

Ecbatana, taken by Cyrus, **1**, 342.
the goddess of love worshiped in, **1**, 408.

Ecclesiastes, the Book of, holiness of, discussed in the Synhedrion, **2**, 343–4.
exposition of, by Samuel Ibn-Tibbon, **3**, 398.
commentary on, by Nathaniel of Bagdad, **3**, 442.

Ecclesiasticus, the Book of, by Jesus Sirach, **1**, 439–41.
considered apocryphal, **2**, 344.
translated into Greek, **2**, 359.

Ecija, the Jews of, persecuted, **4**, 170.

Eck, Dr. John, writes against the Jews, **4**, 546–7.
accusations of, repeated by Luther, **4**, 548, 549, 550.

Eden, garden of, name applied to Paradise, **1**, 404.

Edessa, destroyed, **2**, 398.
the Christians of, persecuted, **2**, 524.
the Jews of, massacred, **2**, 599.
taken by Nureddin, **3**, 349.

Edict, banishing the Jews from Spain, **4**, 347–8.

Edict of Grace, the, for Marranos, **4**, 315.

Edles, Samuel, Talmudist, **4**, 703.

Edom. *See* Idumæans, the.

Education among the Jews. *See under* Academies; Colleges; Law, the; Schools; Talmud, the; Talmud Torah.
Edward I, of England, Jews under, **3**, 640–6.
stops the denunciations of coin counterfeiters, **3**, 643.
and the charge of blasphemy against the Jews, **3**, 643.
permits the Dominicans to preach to the Jews, **3**, 643–4.
erects a house for Jewish converts, **3**, 644.
banishes the Jews, **3**, 645.
Edward, Prince of Wales (the Black Prince), aids Pedro the Cruel, **4**, 124, 125.
Edzardus, Esdras, Hamburg preacher, and David de Lara, **5**, 115.
and the Sabbatian movement, **5**, 151.
Efodi. *See* Profiat Duran.
Eger, Akiba, reverence paid to, **5**, 567.
Eger, Samuel, protests against reforms, **5**, 562.
Egica, Visigothic king, forbids Jews to hold real estate, **3**, 107–8.
Egidio de Viterbo, cardinal, sides with Reuchlin, **4**, 457.
patron of Elias Levita, **4**, 472, 564.
interested in the Kabbala, **4**, 481, 583.
opposes the Portuguese Inquisition, **4**, 507.
Egilbert, bishop of Treves, forcibly baptizes Jews, **3**, 300, 306.
Eglon, king of Moab, killed by Ehud, **1**, 60.
Eglon, king of, defeated by Joshua, **1**, 34–5.
Egypt, priests of, **1**, 10.
allied with Solomon, **1**, 170.
hostile to Ben-hadad III, **1**, 221.
helps the Idumæans against Uzziah, **1**, 226.
allied with Hoshea, **1**, 263.
allied with Hezekiah, **1**, 270.
counsels resistance to Nebuchadnezzar, **1**, 304, 306, 309.
Judæans take refuge in, **1**, 317, 318, 324.
rebels against Persia, **1**, 407–8.
given to Ptolemy I, **1**, 418.
Judæans settle in, **1**, 419.
taken by Antiochus III and Philip V of Macedon, **1**, 432.
wars of, with Antiochus IV, **1**, 450–1, 452–3.
number of Judæans in, **2**, 201.
Zealots flee to, **2**, 317–18.
study of the Law in, **2**, 359.
succumbs to the Arabs, **3**, 86.
Rabbanites in, in the ninth century, **3**, 180.
Karaites spread to, **3**, 182.
schools founded in, by the emissaries from Sora, **3**, 208, 210.
part of the Fatimide Caliphate, **3**, 248.
Jehuda Halevi in, **3**, 339–41.
Abraham Ibn-Ezra in, **3**, 369.
Maimonides in, **3**, 445, 457.
Louis IX taken prisoner in, **3**, 585.
in the Zohar, **4**, 23.
Karaites of, inclined to Rabbanism, **4**, 72.
the Spanish exiles in, **4**, 392–6.
taken by the Turkish sultan, **4**, 393.
Isaac Lurya in, **4**, 618, 622.
conquered by Napoleon, **5**, 459.
Crémieux's schools in, **5**, 671.

Egypt, the Jews of, celebrate two days of the new-moon, **2,** 363.
rebel against Trajan, **2,** 394, 395–8.
hail the Mahometans as liberators, **3,** 88–9.
in the twelfth century, **3,** 443–5.
governed by a Nagid, **3,** 443.
lack of culture of, **3,** 444–5.
pilgrimages of, **3,** 445.
under Saladin, **3,** 461.
liturgy of, changed by Maimonides, **3,** 465–6.
exhorted to establish schools, **5,** 663.
Egypt, the Judæans of, practice idolatry, **1,** 326–7.
neglected under Amasis, **1,** 327.
settlement of, encouraged, **1,** 503.
equality of, with the Greeks, **1,** 503.
alliance of, sought by Syrians and Egyptians, **1,** 503–4.
faithful to the Ptolemies, **1,** 504.
occupations of, **1,** 504–5.
Greek learning of, **1,** 505.
espouse the cause of Ptolemy VI, **1,** 507.
recognize Onias IV as ethnarch, **1,** 507.
sacrifice in the Temple of Onias, **1,** 509.
maintain connection with the Temple at Jerusalem, **1,** 509; **2,** 52.
pleased with the Septuagint, **1,** 511–12.
originate the sermon, **1,** 515.
dispute with the Samaritans, **1,** 517.
informed of the independence of Judæa, **1,** 522–3.
Egypt, the Judæans of (*continued*), urged to celebrate Chanukah, **2,** 6–7.
prosperous under Cleopatra and Ptolemy VIII, **2,** 12.
devoted to the cause of Octavius, **2,** 102.
control the Nile harbors, **2,** 102.
make annual pilgrimages to Jerusalem, **2,** 220.
go to Jerusalem for the Passover of 66, **2,** 251.
Egyptians, the, culture of, **1,** 8.
pantheon of, **1,** 9.
enslave the Israelites, **1,** 11.
refuse to liberate the Israelites, **1,** 16–17.
at the Red Sea, **1,** 18–19.
Ehud, judge, routs the Moabites, **1,** 60–1.
Eibeschütz, Jonathan (1690–1764), disciple of Nehemiah Chayon, **5,** 218.
supposed Sabbatian, **5,** 229, 248.
early education of, **5,** 246–7.
as a Talmudist, **5,** 247.
mysticism of, **5,** 248.
weakness of the character of, **5,** 248–9.
as teacher in Prague, **5,** 249, 250.
excommunicates the Sabbatians, **5,** 249.
clemency shown towards, **5,** 249–50.
in intercourse with Jesuits, **5,** 250.
obtains the right of printing the Talmud, **5,** 250.
and the rabbinate of Metz, **5,** 251.
accused of treason, **5,** 252.
intercedes for the Jews of Moravia and Bohemia, **5,** 253.

Eibeschütz, Jonathan (*continued*), declared a traitor, **5,** 253.
popular in Metz, **5,** 253.
rabbi of the "three communities," **5,** 254, 256.
distributes amulets, **5,** 257, 260.
called on by Emden to clear himself of the charge of Sabbatianism, **5,** 258.
supported by his disciples, **5,** 258, 259.
cause of, espoused by the "three communities," **5,** 260–1.
opponents of, excommunicated, **5,** 261.
publishes an encyclical, **5,** 261–2.
invited to exculpate himself, **5,** 262, 263.
excommunicated, **5,** 263–4.
cause of, espoused by some rabbis, **5,** 264.
case of, submitted to the king of Denmark, **5,** 265, 268, 269.
letter to, from Ezekiel Landau, **5,** 265–6.
associates himself with an apostate, **5,** 267.
protected by the princes of Brunswick, **5,** 267–8.
before a rabbinical court, **5,** 268–9.
publishes a defense, **5,** 270.
supposed to be a secret Christian, **5,** 270.
again acknowledged rabbi of the "three communities," **5,** 271.
and the Frankists, **5,** 289.
distrust of, **5,** 289.
Eichhorn, exegete, **5,** 623, 695.
Eighteen Benedictions. *See* Berachoth.
"**Eighteen Things,** The," decreed by the school of Shammai, **2,** 270.
permitted by Judah II, **2,** 483–4.
Eisenach, the Jews of, during the Black Death persecutions, **4,** 109.
Eisenmenger, John Andrew, Hebraist, revives the blood accusation, **5,** 187.
title of the book by, against the Jews, **5,** 188.
charges raised against the Jews by, **5,** 188–9.
work of, suppressed, **5,** 190.
death of, **5,** 190.
See "Judaism Unmasked."
"**Eisenmenger the Second,** an open letter to Fichte," by Saul Asher, **5,** 463.
Ekron, Philistine city, **1,** 54.
left in the possession of the Philistines, **1,** 117.
center of Baal-zebub worship, **1,** 207.
given to Jonathan Haphus, **1,** 496.
fortified by the Syrians, **1,** 529.
Elah, king of Israel, dissipation and death of, **1,** 192.
El-Arish, taken by Napoleon, **5,** 459.
El-Arish, the river of Egypt, boundary under David, **1,** 129.
Elath, port on the Red Sea, **1,** 170, 171, 177, 230.
Elchanan ben Isaac, descendant of Rashi, Tossafist, martyr, **3,** 404.
Eldad, Karaite, adventurer, **3,** 182.
spreads the news of the Jewish Chazar kingdom, **3,** 220.
Elder, title of the ordained, **2,** 361.

Elders, Council of the, formed by Moses, **1**, 25-6.
Eleanor, mother of Edward I, hostile to the Jews, **3**, 641, 645.
Eleanor, wife of Edward I, favorably inclined to the Jews, **3**, 644.
Eleanora, wife of Louis VII of France, accompanies him on the second crusade, **3**, 349.
Eleasa, camp of Judas Maccabæus at, **1**, 486.
the battle of, Judas Maccabæus falls in, **1**, 487.
Eleazar, Galilæan Judæan, persuades Izates of Adiabene to be circumcised, **2**, 217.
Eleazar, high priest, and the Septuagint, **1**, 514.
Eleazar, Jewish name of Bishop Bodo, **3**, 169.
Eleazar, one of David's warriors, **1**, 116.
Eleazar of Antioch, refuses to sacrifice to the Greek gods, **1**, 456.
Eleazar of Modin, member of the Jamnia Synhedrion, **2**, 357.
prays for Bethar, **2**, 417.
accused as a spy, **2**, 417-18.
Eleazar ben Ananias, leader of the Zealots, **2**, 256.
brings about the rupture with Rome, **2**, 258-9.
relations of, to the leader of the Sicarii, **2**, 260-1.
destroys the Roman garrison of Jerusalem, **2**, 261.
disinterestedness of, **2**, 261.
governor of Idumæa, **2**, 270.
Eleazar ben Arach, disciple of Jochanan ben Zakkai, **2**, 324, 326.
tries to establish a school at Emmaus, **2**, 334.
Eleazar ben Azariah, president of the Synhedrion, **2**, 342.
vice-president of the Synhedrion, **2**, 345.
and Flavius Clemens, **2**, 387, 389, 392.
influence of, on Nerva, **2**, 392.
Eleazar ben Dinai, Zealot leader, **2**, 238.
exterminates the Samaritans of Acrabatene, **2**, 243.
Eleazar ben Jacob, disciple of Akiba, **2**, 433.
Eleazar ben Jair, grandson of Judas of Galilee, leader of the Sicarii, **2**, 239.
flees from Jerusalem, **2**, 261.
commander of Masada, **2**, 292, 316.
Eleazar ben Jehuda (Rokeach), Kabbalist, at the Mayence synod, **3**, 517.
Eleazar ben Joel Halevi (Abi-Ezri), Talmudist, at the Mayence synod, **3**, 517.
Eleazar ben Joseph of Chinon, martyr, **4**, 49.
Eleazar ben Joseph (ben Chalafta), accompanies Simon ben Jochaï to Rome, **2**, 449.
Eleazar ben Kalir, the greatest of the poetans, **3**, 116-17, 245.
poetry of, rugged, **3**, 223.
Eleazar ben Poira, Pharisee, reproves John Hyrcanus, **2**, 32.
Eleazar ben Shamua, teacher of Judah I, **2**, 451.
Eleazar ben Simon, Zealot leader, treasurer of the Temple, **2**, 270-1, 301.
opposed to the Synhedrion, **2**, 293-4.
Eleazar ben Simon (ben Jochaï), reproaches the Samaritans with having altered the Law, **2**, 457.

Eleazar ben Simon (*continued*), denounces Jewish freebooters to the Romans, **2**, 464–5.
Eleazar Chasma, in the Jamnia Synhedrion, **2**, 357.
Eleazar Hawran, son of Mattathias the Hasmonæan, **1**, 459.
death of, **1**, 479.
Eleazar. *See also under* Eleazer and Eliezer.
Eleazer, commander of Machærus, **2**, 315.
Eleazer ben Nathan of Mayence, at the first rabbinical synod, **3**, 377.
Eleazer ben Simon of Cologne, at the first rabbinical synod, **3**, 377.
Eleazer. *See also under* Eleazar and Eliezer.
Elegabalus, emperor, vices of, **2**, 468.
relations of, to the Jews, **2**, 469–70.
Elesbaa (Atzbaha), king of Ethiopia, at war with the Jewish king of Yemen, **3**, 66.
Elhanan, of Bethlehem, Israelite champion under David, **1**, 117.
Eli, judge, characterization of, **1**, 69.
inveighs against idolatry, **1**, 70.
sons of, **1**, 70.
death of, **1**, 71.
grandson of, **1**, 79.
descendants of, murdered by Saul, **1**, 100.
descendants of, inhabit Mamal, **2**, 575.
Elia. *See* Mar-Elia.
Eliakim, in Speyer, Rashi's Talmud teacher, **3**, 286.
Eliakim, son of Hilkiah, made Sochen, **1**, 272.
Eliakim. *See* Jehoiakim.
Eliam, father of Bathsheba, **1**, 133.
Eliano, Victor, grandson of Elias Levita, apostate, **4**, 564.
defames the Talmud, **4**, 583.
editor of the Cremona Zohar, **4**, 584.
Elias of London, chief rabbi of England, **3**, 588.
asks permission for the Jews to leave England, **3**, 590–1.
deposed, **3**, 591.
Elias del Medigo (Cretensis, 1463–1498), philosopher, **4**, 289, 290–3.
classical culture of, **4**, 290.
teacher of Pico di Mirandola, **4**, 290–1.
umpire chosen by the University of Padua, **4**, 291.
public lecturer on philosophy, **4**, 291.
denounces the Kabbala, **4**, 292; **5**, 78.
views of, on the Talmud and religion, **4**, 292–3.
character of the influence of, **4**, 293.
hostility to, **4**, 293.
and Judah Menz, **4**, 295.
disciple of, **4**, 386.
sons and relatives of, leaders in Canea, **4**, 406.
descendant of, **5**, 75.
Elias ben Elkanah Kapsali (1490–1555), rabbi at Canea, and Judah Delmedigo, **4**, 406.
as an historian, **4**, 406–7.
style of, **4**, 557.
Elias Chendali, husband of Esther Kiera, **4**, 629.
Elias Cretensis. *See* Elias Del Medigo.
Elias Halevi, Rabbanite teacher of Karaites, **4**, 270.

Elias Levita (1468–1549), grammarian, teacher of Christians, **4,** 471, 507.
pupils of, **4,** 472.
publishes a Hebrew grammar, **4,** 472.
mediocrity of, **4,** 472.
on the accents and vowel signs, **4,** 472–3.
declines to go to France, **4,** 473–4.
establishes a Hebrew press at Isny, **4,** 474.
grandchildren of, apostates, **4,** 564.
Elias Mizrachi (1455–1526), rabbi of Constantinople, character and attainments of, **4,** 402–3.
feud of, with the Karaites, **4,** 403.
protects the Karaites, **4,** 403–4.
Elias Montalto, physician, employed by Christians, **4,** 653.
dissuades Paul de Pina from becoming a monk, **4,** 670.
buried at Ouderkerk, **4,** 672–3.
physician to Maria de Medici, **4,** 673.
Eliashib, high priest, countenances marriages between Judæans and Samaritans, **1,** 362.
in friendly communication with the Samaritans, **1,** 383.
dismissed by Nehemiah, **1,** 385.
Eliezer ben Hyrcanus, disciple of Jochanan ben Zakkai, **2,** 326.
teacher of the Law at Lydda, **2,** 335.
opposes decisions by the Bath-Kol, **2,** 338.
brother-in-law of Gamaliel II, **2,** 339.
Eliezer ben Hyrcanus (*continued*), excommunicated, **2,** 339–40, 347–8.
devotion of, to tradition, **2,** 346–7, 356.
called Sinai, **2,** 347.
opposed to Gamaliel II, **2,** 347.
end of, **2,** 348.
ban removed from, **2,** 350.
supposed teacher of Akiba, **2,** 351.
and the Jewish Christians, **2,** 370.
on the admission of proselytes, **2,** 384.
and Akylas, **2,** 385.
mourns for Gamaliel II, **2,** 404.
condemns the instruction of women in the Law, **2,** 474.
compared with Chanina bar Chama, **2,** 491.
Eliezer Kapsali, Rabbanite teacher of Karaites, **4,** 270.
Eliezer. *See also under* Eleazar and Eleazer.
Elijah, the Tishbite, prophet, character of, **1,** 199.
a Nazarite, **1,** 200.
disciples of, **1,** 200.
rebukes Ahab, **1,** 202–3.
announces a famine, **1,** 203.
assembles the priests of Baal, **1,** 203–4.
flees from Jezebel, **1,** 204.
instructed to anoint Jehu, **1,** 204.
chooses Elisha as his successor, **1,** 207.
prophesies the death of Ahaziah, **1,** 207.
disappears, **1,** 207.
result of the activity of, **1,** 208.
precursor of the Messiah, **2,** 143.
in the Zohar, **4,** 12, 16.

Elijah, disciples of, Nazarites, **1,** 200.
persecuted by Jezebel, **1,** 201.
saved by Obadiah, **1,** 201.
on Mount Carmel, **1,** 203.
Elijah Wilna (1720–1797), draws attention to the Scriptures, **5,** 329, 390.
disinterestedness of, **5,** 389.
critical powers of, **5,** 389–90.
simple exegetical method of, **5,** 390.
fondness of, for the Kabbala, **5,** 390–1.
slandered by the Chassidim, **5,** 391.
excommunicates the Chassidim, **5,** 392, 393.
persecutes the Chassidim, **5,** 394.
Elijah Zevi, brother of Sabbataï, **5,** 145.
Elionai, high priest, under Agrippa I, **2,** 198.
Elisha, Essene, punished for the use of Tephillin, **2,** 424.
Elisha, father of Ishmael, **2,** 427.
Elisha, prophet, successor to Elijah, **1,** 207.
accompanies Elijah, **1,** 208.
lives on Mount Carmel, **1,** 208.
hates Jehoram, **1,** 208–9.
disciple of, appoints Jehu king of Israel, **1,** 210.
position of, compared with Elijah's, **1,** 217–18.
in Samaria, **1,** 218.
respected by Jehoash of Israel, **1,** 223–4.
influence of, on Jehoash, **1,** 225.
Elisha ben Abuya (Acher), teacher of the Law, apostate, **2,** 358, 377.
theosophist, **2,** 381.
Elisha ben Abuya (*continued*), assists Hadrian in persecuting the Law, **2,** 426.
and Meïr, **2,** 437.
daughters of, **2,** 452.
Elisha Gallaico, member of Karo's rabbinical college, **4,** 616.
Elishama, keeper of the lists, favors submission to Nebuchadnezzar, **1,** 305.
Elizabeth, of Brunswick, has Templo's work translated, **5,** 114–15.
Elizabeth, of England, and Maria Nuñes, **4,** 664.
Elkanah Kapsali, of Candia, ransoms Spanish exiles, **4,** 364.
Elon, judge, **1,** 66.
Elulai, king of Tyre, subdued by Shalmaneser, **1,** 263.
El-Uz. *See* Usha.
Elvira. *See* Illiberis.
Elymæans, the, have a synagogue in Jerusalem, **2,** 201.
Elymais, falls to Nabopolassar, **1,** 303.
Emancipation of Jews, the, advocated by John Toland, **5,** 197–8.
favored by Mirabeau, **5,** 433–4.
accomplished by the French, **5,** 459.
urged by Michael Berr, **5,** 460–1, 527.
opposed by Fichte, **5,** 462.
dependent on that of French Jews, **5,** 480.
favored by Dalberg, **5,** 504.
favored by Hardenberg, **5,** 507.
favored by Denmark, **5,** 519, 531.
advocated before the Congress of Aix-la-Chapelle, **5,** 525–7.

Emancipation of Jews, the (*continued*), favored by Alexander I, **5,** 527.
urged by Italian Jews, **5,** 527.
advocated by Zunz, **5,** 621.
hindrances to, in Judaism, **5,** 675.
completed by the February revolutions, **5,** 696-7.
See also Citizenship.
Emancipation of the Austrian Jews, the, by Joseph II, **5,** 357-8.
Emancipation of the Baden Jews, the, **5,** 502-3.
Emancipation of the Bavarian Jews, the partial, **5,** 508.
Emancipation of the Dutch Jews, the, celebrated by Friedrichsfeld, **5,** 400.
promoted by French victories, **5,** 452.
opposed by Van Swieden, **5,** 453-4.
opposed by representative Amsterdam Jews, **5,** 454.
Jewish advocates of, **5,** 454-5.
Christian objections to, **5,** 455-6.
favored by Noel, **5,** 456.
passed by the National Assembly, **5,** 456.
does not delight the Jews, **5,** 456-7.
Emancipation of the English Jews, the, **5,** 336-8, 430, 698.
discussed in Parliament, **5,** 601.
advocated by O'Connell, **5,** 653.
Emancipation of the Frankfort Jews, the, **5,** 505.
discussed in the Senate, **5,** 598.
Emancipation of the French Jews, the, promoted by Cerf Berr, **5,** 430, 431.
Emancipation of the French Jews, the (*continued*), discussed by the National Assembly, **5,** 439-41.
favored by the heroes of the Revolution, **5,** 441.
opposition to, **5,** 441-2.
equivocal decision on, **5,** 442.
granted to the Portuguese section, **5,** 442-3, 444-5.
subject of a petition to the National Assembly, **5,** 443.
before the Paris Commune, **5,** 443-5.
Abbé Mulot on, **5,** 443-4.
opposed by the Duc de Broglie, **5,** 447.
advocated by Duport, **5,** 447-8.
passed by the National Assembly, **5,** 448.
celebrated by Berr Isaac Berr, **5,** 448-9.
recognized by the Constitution of the Directory, **5,** 452.
endangered, **5,** 476.
objected to by Bonald, **5,** 478-9.
laid before Napoleon's council, **5,** 479.
determines that of Jews in other countries, **5,** 480.
advocated by Beugnot, **5,** 480.
opposed by Napoleon, **5,** 480.
urged by Regnault and Ségur, **5,** 480-1.
guaranteed by Napoleon, **5,** 492.
curtailed by Napoleon, **5,** 498-9.
under Louis XVIII, **5,** 524-5.
curtailed under the Bourbons, **5,** 596.
considered by Louis Philippe, **5,** 597.
advocated by Mérilhou, **5,** 597.
completed in the Chamber of Peers, **5,** 597.

Emancipation of the German Jews, the, promoted by Dohm's plea, **5,** 356–7.
promoted by the French, **5,** 459.
urged by the Peace Congress of Rastadt, **5,** 463.
writers against, **5,** 468–70, 472.
retarded by the reaction after Napoleon's fall, **5,** 512.
urged before the Congress of Vienna, **5,** 513–14.
favored by Hardenberg and Metternich, **5,** 514.
promised in the constitution drawn up by Humboldt, **5,** 514.
retarded by Teutomania, **5,** 516.
opposed by Rühs, **5,** 517.
promised by the Act of Federation, **5,** 518.
opposed by the Hanse Towns, **5,** 519.
favored by Holstein, **5,** 519.
defeated at the Congress of Vienna, **5,** 519–20.
pamphlet literature against, **5,** 521.
favored by Krämer, **5,** 521–2.
leads to estrangement from Judaism, **5,** 560.
Riesser interested in, **5,** 599–600.
on the programme of the liberal party, **5,** 602.
Emancipation of the Hessian Jews, the, legalized, **5,** 601.
Emancipation of the Italian Jews, the, undone by Pius VII, **5,** 518.
Emancipation of the Jews in the Hanse Towns, the, **5,** 506–7.
Emancipation of the Mecklenburg Jews, the, **5,** 507.
Emancipation of the Prussian Jews, the, struggle for, begun, **5,** 414–16.
partial, **5,** 507.
granted by Frederick William III, **5,** 508, 630.
a dead letter, **5,** 524.
Emancipation of the Turkish Jews, the, by Abdul Meg'id, **5,** 641.
Emancipation of the Westphalian Jews, the, **5,** 500–1.
medal commemorative of, **5,** 501.
Emanuel, Byzantine emperor, and his Jewish physician, **3,** 425.
Embicho, bishop of Würzburg, protects the Jews, **3,** 354.
Emden, Jacob (Ashkenazi, Jabez, 1698–1776), grandson of Jacob Ashkenazi, anti-Sabbatian, **5,** 221.
son of Chacham Zevi, studies of, **5,** 254–5.
character of, **5,** 255.
as rabbi, **5,** 255.
candidate for the rabbinate of the "three communities," **5,** 255–6.
antipathy of, to heretics, **5,** 256.
induced not to expose Eibeschütz, **5,** 257–8.
calls on Eibeschütz to clear himself, **5,** 258.
punished by the Council, **5,** 258–9.
persecuted in Altona, **5,** 260.
excommunicated and flees to Amsterdam, **5,** 261.
returns to Altona, **5,** 265, 266.
historian of the Sabbatian movement, **5,** 266.
maligned by Charles Anton, **5,** 267.

Emden, Jacob (*continued*), refutes Eibeschütz's defense, **5**, 270.
appealed to by the Polish rabbis, **5**, 277-8.
exposes the Zohar as a forgery, **5**, 278.
sanctions Frankist persecutions, **5**, 278.
triumphant, **5**, 289.
refers the Schwerin Jews to Mendelssohn, **5**, 318.
opposes Mendelssohn on the subject of hasty burial, **5**, 318-19.
Emden, Portuguese Marranos arrive at, **4**, 665.
Jews tolerated in, **4**, 686.
Emek ha-Bacha, by Joseph ben Joshua Cohen, **4**, 590, 608.
Emesa, native town of Julia Domna, **2**, 468.
Emicho. *See* Emmerich.
Emim, descendants of the Anakim and Rephaim, **1**, 2.
Emmaus (Gimso), Synhedrion established at, **2**, 71.
burnt, **2**, 126.
effort to establish an academy at, **2**, 334.
destroyed by an earthquake, **2**, 408-9.
Emmerich (Emicho), of Leiningen, leader of the first crusade, massacres the Jews, **3**, 303.
disgraceful end of the crusaders under, **3**, 306.
accused before Henry IV, **3**, 307.
"**Emunoth**," Kabbalistic work by Shem Tob ben Joseph, **4**, 197.
Emunoth we-Deoth, philosophical work by Saadiah, **3**, 197-8.
Endor, camp of Gideon, **1**, 62.
Saul's camp, **1**, 103.
the witch of, **1**, 103.
"**Enemy** of the Jews, The," Pfefferkorn's second pamphlet, **4**, 427-8.
Engadi, Essene center, **2**, 25.
Engel, friend of Mendelssohn, **5**, 372.
England, rabbis of, emigrate to Jerusalem, **3**, 505-6.
Marranos unkindly received in, **4**, 509.
struggles for religious freedom in, **5**, 25-8.
Jews gradually establish themselves in, **5**, 49-50.
anomalous position of Jews in, **5**, 50.
ambassador of, intercedes for the Moravian and Bohemian Jews, **5**, 253.
the first country to emancipate the Jews, **5**, 430.
in the Quadruple Alliance, **5**, 658.
England, the Jews of, protected during the second crusade, **3**, 356.
prosperous under Henry II, **3**, 409.
under Richard I, **3**, 409-16.
abused at Richard's coronation, **3**, 410-11.
massacre of, **3**, 412-16.
under John, **3**, 416, 504-5.
imprisoned, **3**, 505.
wear the Jew badge, **3**, 515, 516.
hated on account of their usurious rates, **3**, 571.
under Henry III, **3**, 587-92.
Christians not permitted to sell food to, **3**, 588.
tax imposed on, **3**, 589.
charges against, **3**, 589.

England, the Jews of (*continued*), pledged to the king's brother, **3**, 590.
restrictions put on, by the Church, **3**, 590.
not permitted to leave England, **3**, 591.
the blood accusation preferred against, **3**, 591.
under Edward I, **3**, 640–6.
the statute of Judaism passed against, **3**, 642.
charged with counterfeiting and clipping coin, **3**, 642.
imprisoned, **3**, 642–3, 645.
forced to listen to Dominican sermons, **3**, 643.
denounced to Honorius IV, **3**, 645.
banished and ill-treated, **3**, 645–6.
take refuge in France, Germany, Spain, **3**, 646.
emancipation of, advocated, **5**, 197–8.
pay the alien duty, **5**, 337.
urge their emancipation, **5**, 337.
naturalization of, **5**, 337–8.
under Polish influence, **5**, 558.
emancipation of, **5**, 601, 653, 698.
act in the Damascus affair, **5**, 644–5, 651–2.
public-spiritedness of, **5**, 703.
number of, **5**, 703.

England, the re-settlement of Jews in, prospects of, **5**, 18–19.
suggested by Messianic hopes, **5**, 28.
negotiations for, interrupted, **5**, 34.
before the Short Parliament, **5**, 34.
the subject of three petitions, **5**, 35.

England, the re-settlement of the Jews in (*continued*), reasons for, stated by Manasseh ben Israel, **5**, 39–42.
favored by Cromwell, **5**, 42–3.
in the hands of a commission, **5**, 43–5.
objections to, **5**, 44–5.
literature on, **5**, 45–6.

Enns, the Jews of, charged with host desecration, **4**, 223.

Enoch, the Book of, Kabbalistic source, **4**, 17.

Enoch Saporta, Rabbanite teacher of Karaites, **4**, 270.

Enriquez, Antonio de Gomez. *See* Paz, Enrique Enriquez de.

En-Rogel, spring south of Jerusalem, **1**, 114.

Ensheim, Moses, one of the Measfim, mathematician, and the emancipation of the French Jews, **5**, 401, 450.

Ensisheim, tower of, Meïr of Rothenburg imprisoned in, **3**, 639.

En-Sof, title of God in the Kabbala, **3**, 550.
emanations of, **3**, 550–1.
in the Zohar, **4**, 14.
the son of heaven, **5**, 124.

En-Vidal Ephraim Gerundi, rabbi of Majorca, **4**, 162.
martyr, **4**, 171.

En-Zag Vidal de Tolosa, rabbi, calumniated, **4**, 155.

Epaone, the council of, forbids Christians to take part in Jewish banquets, **3**, 37.

Épée, de l', Abbé, anticipated by Pereira, **5**, 343.

Ephes-Damim, scene of David's victory over Goliath, **1**, 97.

Ephesus, a Greek-Christian community in, **2**, 227.

Ephesus (*continued*), chief seat of the Pagan Christians, **2,** 367.

Ephoros, Jewish overseer in Greece, Macedonia, Illyria, **3,** 27.

Ephraim, the tribe of, in contact with the Egyptians, **1,** 7.
- takes Bethel, **1,** 34.
- claims the central lands of Canaan, **1,** 35–6.
- and the Danites, **1,** 39.
- holds assemblies at Shiloh, **1,** 41.
- opposes intermarriages with the heathen, **1,** 56.
- keeps worshipers from Shiloh, **1,** 57.
- assists Ehud against the Moabites **1,** 60.
- in conflict with Manasseh, **1,** 63.
- attacked by the Ammonites, **1,** 64.
- quarrels with Jephthah, **1,** 65.
- oppressed by the Philistines, **1,** 71.
- not well disposed towards David, **1,** 114.
- sides with Absalom, **1,** 140.
- persuaded to separate from Solomon, **1,** 176.
- chooses Jeroboam as king, **1,** 182–3.
- end of, **1,** 265–6.

Ephraim of Tyre, head of the Jews of Tyre, **3,** 426.

Ephraim ben Jacob of Bonn (1132–1200), Talmudist and liturgical poet, **3,** 419.

Ephraim, mountain, description of, **1,** 45,

Epicrates, general of Ptolemy VIII, fights against the Judæans. **2,** 11.

Epicurus, teachings of, accepted in Judæa, **1,** 429.

Epiphanes, son of Antiochus of Commagene, affianced to Drusilla, **2,** 195, 235.

Epistles to the Hebrews, the, urge the separation of Jewish Christians from Jews, **2,** 371.

Epistolæ Obscurorum Virorum, by Crotus Rubianus, a Reuchlinist work, **4,** 461–2.
- *See* "Letters of Obscurantists."

Eras used by the Jews, **1,** 417; **2,** 134; **3,** 433; **4,** 394–5.

Erasmus, as humanist, **4,** 432, 433.
- supposed author of the "Letters of Obscurantists," **4,** 462.
- on hatred of the Jews, **4,** 462–3.
- in the pantomime on the Reformation, **4,** 468.

Eravi. *See* Airvi.

Erfurt, refuge of Archbishop Ruthard of Mayence, **3,** 307.

Erfurt, the Jews of, persecuted, **3,** 611.
- during the Black Death persecutions, **4,** 109.

Erfurt, the university of, consulted regarding the confiscation of Hebrew books, **4,** 437, 441.
- theologians of, sanction the burning of the "Augenspiegel," **4,** 452.

Ergas, Joseph, Kabbalist, denounces Chayon, **5,** 227.

Ermengarde, princess of Narbonne, Jews under, **3,** 392.

"**Errors of the Doctrine of the Trinity,**" by Michael Servetus, **4,** 541.

Erter, Isaac (1792–1851), Galician scholar, re-animates the Hebrew language, **5,** 612–13, 617.
education and marriages of, **5,** 613.
self-culture of, **5,** 613–14.
influence of Rapoport and Krochmal on, **5,** 614.
excommunicated, **5,** 614–15.
satirizes Orenstein, **5,** 615.
style of, **5,** 615–16.
poverty of, **5,** 616.
poetry of, compared with S. D. Luzzatto's, **5,** 623.
writes an account of the Damascus affair, **5,** 671.
Erwig, Visigothic king, usurper, enacts anti-Jewish laws, **3,** 106–7.
Esarhaddon, king of Assyria, reduces Babylonia, **1,** 284.
takes Manasseh prisoner, **1,** 285.
Esau, honored by a Gnostic sect, **2,** 375.
Eschenloer, town clerk of Breslau, protests against cruelty towards Jews, **4,** 262.
Escrivao, Jewish-Portuguese official, **4,** 159.
"Eshkol ha-Kofer," Karaite work by Jehuda ben Elia Hadassi, **3,** 362.
Eskapha, Joseph, Talmudist, teacher of Sabbataï Zevi, **5,** 118.
excommunicates him, **5,** 122.
Eskeles, Issachar Berush, intercedes for the Moravian Jews, **5,** 252, 253.
Eski-Crimea. *See* Sulchat.
Esperaindo, Juan de, assassin of Arbues, **4,** 330.
Essenes, the, offshoot from the Assidæan party, **2,** 16–17, 24.
Essenes, the (*continued*), give rise to the Pharisees, **2,** 17.
wherein opposed to the Pharisees, **2,** 18.
allied with the Pharisees, **2,** 24.
rigid celebration of the Sabbath by, **2,** 24.
Nazarite practices of, **2,** 24–5.
celibates, **2,** 25.
settle in Engadi, **2,** 25.
communism of, **2,** 26.
habits of, **2,** 26–7.
mysticism of, **2,** 27–8.
popular, **2,** 29.
fatalists, **2,** 30.
avoid the Temple, **2,** 30.
initiation into the brotherhood of, **2,** 30–1.
prophetic power ascribed to, **2,** 100.
exempt from swearing allegiance to Herod, **2,** 108.
conception of the Messianic age by, **2,** 145.
the first to proclaim the advent of the Messiah, **2,** 145.
Jesus attracted to, **2,** 150–1.
displeased with Jesus, **2,** 162.
followers of Jesus, **2,** 219–20.
Essenism, the kernel of Christianity, **2,** 142.
Essex, Earl of, takes Cadiz, **4,** 665.
Essinger, Samuel, testifies in favor of Eibeschütz, **5,** 262.
Estella, the Jews of, massacred, **4,** 77–8, 144.
Esther (Esterka), mistress of Casimir III, **4,** 112.
"Esther," epic by Ansaldo Ceba, **5,** 69, 70.
Esther, the Book of, additions to, **2,** 359.
read in Spanish translation, **4,** 148.

Estori Parchi, on the suffering of the French Jews, **4**, 48–9.
emigrates to Palestine, **4**, 49.
on the Karaites, **4**, 72.
Etam, springs of, supply the second Temple, **1**, 421.
Etampes, d', Count, protects the French Jews, **4**, 130, 132.
Eternal Punishment, dogma of, in the Kabbala, **4**, 292.
Ethbaal I, of Tyre, allied with Omri of Israel, **1**, 194.
Ethbaal II, of Tyre, vassal of Nebuchadnezzar, **1**, 304.
rebels against Nebuchadnezzar, **1**, 306.
urges war against Nebuchadnezzar, **1**, 309.
Ethics, The, by Aristotle, translated, **4**, 193.
by Spinoza, **4**, 167.
Ethnarch, the prince of the Judæans in Egypt. *See* Alabarch, the.
Ethnarch, office of, created for the Judæans of the Nabathæan kingdom, **2**, 202.
Ethnarch, title of, conferred on Hyrcanus II, **2**, 66, 76.
on Archelaus, **2**, 127.
on the President of the Synhedrion, **2**, 360.
Eucærus, king of Syria, invades Judæa, **2**, 44.
forced to retreat, **2**, 45.
Euchel, Isaac Abraham, Hebrew style of, **5**, 398.
establishes the Chebrath Dorshe Leshon Eber, **5**, 398.
founds a journal, **5**, 399.
mediocrity of, **5**, 417.
founder of the "Society of Friends," **5**, 418.
Eugenius III, pope, absolves the debtors of Jews from payment, **3**, 349–51.
Eugenius IV, pope, exhorts Juan II of Castile to humiliate the Jews, **4**, 229.
hostile to the Jews, **4**, 249, 275.
confirms the privileges of Jews, **4**, 249.
influenced by Alfonso de Cartagena, **4**, 249–50.
revives anti-Jewish restrictions, **4**, 250–1.
issues a bull against the Italian Jews, **4**, 251.
and John of Capistrano, **4**, 257.
Eulæus, guardian of Ptolemy V's sons, rules Egypt, **1**, 450.
Eumenes, king of Pergamus, proclaims Antiochus IV king of Syria, **1**, 443.
Euonymus of Gadara, philosopher, and Meïr, **2**, 437–8.
Euphrates, the, depredations in the district of, **2**, 527.
fortresses on, captured by Hulagu, **3**, 606.
Euphrates, the, district of, the Jews of, rebel against Trajan, **2**, 397.
opposed by Lucius Quietus, **2**, 398–9.
in the twelfth century, **3**, 428–33.
See also under Babylonia.
Eupolemos, Judæan envoy to Rome, **1**, 485.
Eupraxios, Byzantine viceroy, Sabbataï Donnolo, physician to, **3**, 213.
Europe, the seat of Judaism in the twelfth century, **3**, 383.
Europe, the Jews of, in the sixth and seventh centuries, **3**, 24–5.
in the latter half of the eighth century, **3**, 141.
in the tenth century, **3**, 212.

Europe, the Jews of (*continued*), admired by the Jews of the East, **5**, 662–3.
Europe, western, early Jewish settlements in, **3**, 35.
position of the Jews of, **5**, 704.
Eusebius, bishop of Cæsarea, historian, asperses Judaism, **2**, 562.
patron of Joseph the apostate, **2**, 565.
Eusebius, chamberlain of Constantius, burdens the Jews with taxes, **2**, 572.
Eutropius, chamberlain of Arcadius, favorably inclined to the Jews, **2**, 615–16.
fall of, **2**, 616.
Evangelists, the, and the revolt of Bar-Cochba, **2**, 412–13.
describe Hadrian's persecutions, **2**, 431.
Evangels, the, colored by Jewish and Pagan Christian views, **2**, 368–9.
influence of, on Judaism, deprecated by the Tanaites, **2**, 378.
Evil-Merodach, king of Babylon, releases Jehoiachin, **1**, 331.
murdered, **1**, 331.
Evora, Jewish center in Portugal, **4**, 159.
the Marranos of, spied upon, **4**, 490.
tribunal of the Inquisition at, **4**, 508.
Ewald, Heinrich, historian of Israel, **5**, 696.
Ewald, Johann Ludwig, defends the Jews, **5**, 522.
"**Examination** of the Pharisaic Traditions, An," by Uriel da Costa, **5**, 60.
"**Example** of Human Life, An," autobiography of Uriel da Costa, **5**, 64–5.
Exchequer of the Jews, in England, **3**, 588.
Excommunication, as used by Gamaliel II, **2**, 339, 347.
regulated by the Usha Synhedrion, **2**, 405.
practiced by Simon II, **2**, 446.
introduced into Babylonia, **2**, 517.
used by Judah ben Ezekiel, **2**, 551–2.
the right of, granted to the Patriarchs, **2**, 612–13.
as dispensed in Jewish Babylonia, **2**, 99–100.
introduced among the Karaites, **3**, 151.
freely used by Paltoi ben Abayi, **3**, 177.
threatened for violating the secrecy of a letter, **3**, 245.
threatened for reproaching a repentant apostate, **3**, 246.
threatened for accepting an office from Christian authorities, **3**, 518.
pronounced in Poland only with the concurrence of the whole community, **4**, 265.
employed by the rabbis of Turkey, **4**, 599.
objected to by Mendelssohn, **5**, 362–3.
forbidden by the Austrian government, **5**, 614.
Excommunication of, the community of Fars, **3**, 194.
Joseph ben Isaac Ibn-Abitur, **3**, 238.
informers and traitors revived, **3**, 378.
fault-finders with a bill of divorce after its delivery, **3**, 378.
the Maimunists, **3**, 528–9, 535.
the Anti-Maimunists, **3**, 530, 536.

Excommunication of (*continued*), Donin, **3,** 572–3.
students of science, **4,** 39–40.
Uriel da Costa, **4,** 58–63.
Spinoza, **5,** 93, 94.
Sabbataï Zevi, **5,** 122.
Chayim Malach, **5,** 214.
Nehemiah Chayon, **5,** 216, 224.
Chacham Zevi, **5,** 226.
Podolian Sabbatians, **5,** 228.
Sabbatians at Frankfort, **5,** 230.
Moses Chayim Luzzatto, **5,** 240, 242.
Eibeschütz's opponents, **5,** 259, 261.
Eibeschütz, **5,** 263–4.
the Frankists, **5,** 276–7.
Wessely, **5,** 370.
the Chassidim, **5,** 392, 393.
young Galician scholars, **5,** 614.

Exegesis of the Bible, taught Origen by the Jews, **2,** 488.
Simlaï's sober method of, **2,** 499, 501–2.
incorrect, favored by the Talmud, **2,** 633.
by Anan ben David, **3,** 133.
freedom in, the principal dogma of Karaism, **3,** 157.
special study of the Karaites, **3,** 180.
cultivated by the Spanish Jews in the tenth and eleventh centuries, **3,** 235.
by Ibn-Janach, **3,** 262, 263.
by Yizchaki, **3,** 273.
by Rashi, **3,** 288.
by Moses ben Samuel Ibn-G'ikatilia, **3,** 290.
supplanted by the study of the Talmud in Spain, **3,** 317.
by the Tossafists, **3,** 345–6.
by Abraham Ibn-Ezra, **3,** 368, 370–1, 371–3.
by David Kimchi, **3,** 394.

Exegesis of the Bible (*continued*), decay of, in the post-Maimunic time, **3,** 561.
neglected in Spain in the fourteenth century, **4,** 91.
Jewish, praised by Reuchlin, **4,** 441–2.
scientific, founded by Richard Simon, **5,** 178.
by S. D. Luzzatto, **5,** 623–4.
by Sachs, **5,** 692–3.
by the rationalistic school, **5,** 695–6.
See also Scriptures, the, commentary on.

Exeter, the Council of, anti-Jewish decrees of, **3,** 645.

"Exilarch, the, Feast of," court at the Exilarch's, **3,** 95.

Exilarchate, the, on an equality with the Patriarchate, **2,** 454.
extinction of, a condition of the advent of the Messiah, **2,** 457.
in abeyance after Kobad's persecutions, **3,** 4.
from 589 to 640, **3,** 10.
restored to power by Bostanaï, **3,** 10.
hereditary in the house of Bostanaï, **3,** 94, 137.
as viewed by the Jews of distant lands, **3,** 100.
co-extensive with the Ommiyade Caliphate, **3,** 100.
dependent on the Gaonate, **3,** 137.
contests for, **3,** 155, 439.
decay of, **3,** 183, 188.
attachment to, **3,** 185–6.
during Saadiah's Gaonate, **3,** 193–4.
end of, **3,** 201–2.
revived in the twelfth century, **3,** 369, 428.
extent of, **3,** 428–9.

Exilarchate, the (*continued*), revived in the thirteenth century, 3, 627.

Exilarchs, the (Princes of the Captivity, Resh-Galutha), leaders of the Jews in the East, 2, 393.
political chiefs of the Babylonian Jews, 2, 508.
vassals of Persia, 2, 508.
royal position of, 2, 508-9.
descendants of David, 2, 509.
supreme judges of the Jewish community, 2, 509; 3, 93.
revenues of, 2, 509-10; 3, 96.
homage paid to, 2, 510, 515, 606-7.
religious ignorance of, 2, 510.
political and spiritual authority of, 2, 511.
devoted to the study of the Law, 2, 544.
appoint judges, 2, 547; 3, 98, 428.
barbarity of, in the time of the Amoraim, 2, 554.
exercise civil and judicial functions, 3, 89.
depose the principals of the Babylonian academies, 3, 91.
history of, dark, 3, 92.
office of, political, 3, 93.
installation of, 3, 94-5.
annual court at the house of, 3, 95.
authority of, lessened by the Karaite schism, 3, 137.
power of, reduced, 3, 177, 183.
hold public assemblies at Pumbeditha, 3, 177.

Exilarchs, the, list of:
Achiya,
Bostanaï,
Chananya (Achunaï),
Chaninaï,
Chasdaï,
Chiskiya,
Daniel, son of Solomon (Chasdaï ?),
David of Mosul,
David ben Daniel,
David ben Judah,
David ben Zaccaï,

Exilarchs, the, list of (*continued*):
Huna,
Huna-Mari,
Josiah Hassan,
Judah ben David,
Judah ben David, son of
Kafnaï,
Mar-Kahana,
Mar-Ukban,
Mar-Zutra I,
Mar-Zutra II,
Nathan,
Nehemia,
Solomon,
Solomon (Chasdaï ?),
Yishaï ben Chiskiya,
Zaccaï ben Achunaï.

Exile, the Babylonian, described, 5, 720-1. *See* Babylonia, the Judæans of.

Exorcism. *See* Demons, exorcism of.

Ezekias, leads the revolt in Galilee against Rome, 2, 77.
executed, 2, 77-8.
son of, 2, 125.

Ezekiel, prophet, encourages and rebukes the Babylonian exiles, 1, 332-4.
prophecy of, leads to theosophic speculations, 2, 380-1.
pilgrimages to the grave of, 3, 440-1.
in Immanuel Romi's work, 4, 67.

Ezer ha-Emuna, work by Moses Cohen de Tordesillas, 4, 141.

Eziongeber, port on the Red Sea, 1, 170.

Ezobi (Esobi). *See* Joseph Ezobi ben Chanan.

Ezra, descent of, 1, 365.
studies the Law, 1, 365.
leads a company of Judæans to Palestine, 1, 366.
opinion of, on intermarriages, 2, 367-8.
induces the Judæans to repudiate their heathen wives, 1, 368-9
opposition to the severity of, 1, 370.
reads the Law in Jerusalem, 1, 378-80.

Ezra (*continued*), subordinates the priesthood to the Scriptures, **1**, 379.
exacts an oath from the Judæans to observe the Law, **1**, 380–1, 387–8.
at the consecration of the walls of Jerusalem, **1**, 381.
guardian of the Temple, **1**, 382.
regulations ascribed to, **1**, 395.
Ezra (*continued*), the chief of the Scribes, **2**, 19.
Mahomet on, **3**, 76.
pilgrimages to the supposed grave of, **3**, 441.
Ezra, Kabbalist, reduces the Kabbala to a system, **3**, 548.
Ezra Gatiño commentator on Ibn-Ezra's Pentateuch commentary, **4**, 144.

F

Fables, written by Meïr, **2**, 436.
"**Fables** of Ancient Times," by Ibn-Sahula, **3**, 560.
Fabulists, list of:
Berachya ben Natronaï Nakdan,
Ibn-Sahula,
Meïr.
Fadak, submits to Mahomet, **3**, 83.
Fadus, Cuspius, procurator, strengthens Rome in Judæa, **2**, 197.
rising of Theudas under, **2**, 198.
deposed, **2**, 198.
Fagius, Paulus, disciple of Reuchlin, and Elias Levita, **4**, 474.
"**Faith** and Creed," by Saadiah, **3**, 197–8.
Falaquera. *See* Shem-Tob Falaquera.
Falcos, the Jews of, attacked, **4**, 78.
Falero, Abraham Aboab, builds the second synagogue at Hamburg, **4**, 691.
Faliachi, Jacob, Sabbatian, **5**, 156.
Falk, Jacob Joshua, rabbi of Metz and Frankfort, **5**, 251.
against Eibeschütz, **5**, 262, 263, 268, 269.
Falk, Jacob Joshua (*continued*), disciple of, **5**, 263.
Fall, the. *See* Original Sin.
Fall, the, of the **Angels**, dogma of, in the Kabbala, **4**, 292.
Famagusta, besieged by the Turks, **4**, 600.
taken, **4**, 601.
"**Familianten**," privileged Jews, **5**, 253.
Famine, in Israel under Ahab, **1**, 203.
in Judah under Uzziah, **1**, 229–30.
in Jerusalem during the siege of Titus, **2**, 304, 305–6.
under Marcus Aurelius, **2**, 451.
Farchi, Chayim Maalem, Jewish minister at Accho, **5**, 460.
Farchi, Raphael Murad, accused of ritual murder, **5**, 639.
restored to his position, **5**, 661.
Farchi family, the, accused of ritual murder, **5**, 638.
Farissol, Abraham. *See* Abraham Farissol.
Farnese, Alexander. *See* Paul III, pope.
Farnese, Alexander, cardinal, intercedes for the Jews, **4**, 567.

Faro, Count of, friend of Isaac Abrabanel, **4,** 338.
Faro, Jewish center in Portugal, **4,** 159.
Farraj Ibn-Solomon (Farragut), physician to Charles of Anjou, **3,** 628.
Fars. *See* Hamadan.
Farsistan, the Exilarch's income from, **3,** 96.
Fast, proclaimed under Jehoiakim, **1,** 304.
in memory of Gedaliah, **1,** 325.
in memory of the Blois martyrs, **3,** 380–1.
during the disputation with Donin, **3,** 577.
on the anniversary of the burning of the Talmud, **3,** 579.
against Gonzalo Martinez, **4,** 85.
to avert the Black Death persecutions, **4,** 100.
during the Hussite war, **4,** 225–6.
commemorating the Nemirov massacre, **5,** 13.
Fast days, observed by the Babylonian exiles, **1,** 337.
Fast of Tammuz abolished, by Sabbataï Zevi, **5,** 151–2.
by the Sabbatians, **5,** 159.
Fast of Tebeth, abolished by Sabbataï Zevi, **5,** 143.
"**Father of the Judæans.**" *See* Ragesh.
Fatimide Caliphate, the, Talmud schools established in, **3,** 210.
Jewish science in, **3,** 211.
fanaticism of, **3,** 212.
Joseph ben Isaac Ibn-Abitur in, **3,** 238.
the Jews of, persecuted, **3,** 247–8.
Fatimide Caliphate, the (*continued*), extent of, **3,** 248.
consequences of the fall of, **3,** 461.
Fauma Kadin, Sarah Zevi's Mahometan name, **5,** 154.
Fayum, Saadiah's birthplace, **3,** 188.
the Jews of, in the twelfth century, **3,** 444.
Feast of Ingathering, celebrated in the eighth month, **1,** 186. *See* Tabernacles, the feast of.
Feast of Lights. *See* Chanukah.
February revolution, the, completes the emancipation of the Jews, **5,** 696–7.
Federation of the German states, Act of, assures citizenship to the Jews, **5,** 518.
Felgenhauer, Paul, mystic, Messianic speculations of, **5,** 35–6.
Felix, governor of Galilee, husband of Drusilla, **2,** 235, 242, 245.
rouses the Zealots against the Samaritans, **2,** 243.
sides with the Galilæans, **2,** 244.
procurator of Judæa, rapacity of, **2,** 245.
allied with the Sicarii, **2,** 246.
sides with the Greeks against the Judæans, **2,** 247.
Felix Libertate, Dutch club, joined by Jews, **5,** 453.
"**Fence,**" the, about the Law, **1,** 397.
Ferber, von, and the Jews of Dresden, **5,** 344.
Ferdinand I, emperor, permits the expulsion of the Bohemian Jews, **4,** 544.
expels the Jews from Lower Austria, **4,** 585.

Ferdinand I (*continued*), expels the Jews of Prague, **4**, 585–6.
embassy of, negotiates with Joseph Nassi, **4**, 597.
appeals to Joseph Nassi, **4**, 601.
Ferdinand II, emperor, reproves Hamburg for permitting a synagogue, **4**, 689–90.
protects the Jews, **4**, 701–2.
imprisons Lipmann Heller, **4**, 705.
fines him, **4**, 706.
introduces conversion sermons in Vienna, **4**, 706.
Ferdinand III, emperor, extends the rights of the Bohemian Jews, **4**, 707.
Ferdinand I, of Aragon, regent of Castile, **4**, 194.
issues an anti-Jewish edict, **4**, 203–4.
becomes king of Aragon, **4**, 205.
defers to Vincent Ferrer, **4**, 206.
arranges for the disputation at Tortosa, **4**, 207.
advises Benedict XIII to abdicate, **4**, 216.
threatens to besiege Benedict XIII, **4**, 217.
death of, **4**, 217.
Ferdinand II, of Aragon. *See* Ferdinand V, of Castile, the Catholic.
Ferdinand III, of Castile, the Holy, hostile to the Jews, **3**, 519.
employs a Jewish physician, **3**, 537.
Jews under, **3**, 592.
Ferdinand IV, of Castile, employs a Jewish treasurer, **4**, 51–2.
death of, **4**, 52.
Ferdinand V, of Castile (II, of Aragon), the Catholic, marriage of, **4**, 280.
ascends the throne of Castile, **4**, 284.
avarice of, **4**, 310, 318.
sanctions the Inquisition for Marranos, **4**, 310–11.
obtains sanction for the Inquisition in Aragon, **4**, 319.
introduces the Inquisition into his hereditary lands, **4**, 325–6.
inclined to revoke the Jewish edict of banishment, **4**, 348.
confiscates the possessions of the Jews of his hereditary lands, **4**, 350.
threatens Navarre for protecting Marranos, **4**, 357.
urges the expulsion of the Jews from Navarre, **4**, 358.
and Judah Leon Abrabanel, **4**, 384, 385.
establishes the Inquisition at Benevento, **4**, 385.
See also Ferdinand and Isabella.
Ferdinand (V) and Isabella (I), of Castile, establish the Inquisition in Spain, **4**, 309.
appoint the commission to frame the statute for the Inquisition, **4**, 312.
papal letter to, concerning the Inquisition, **4**, 318.
refuse to modify the rigors of the Inquisition, **4**, 322.
ask for an inquisitor-general, **4**, 324.
establish the Inquisition at Seville, **4**, 335.
urged to expel the Jews from Seville, **4**, 336.
protect the Jews from chicanery, **4**, 336.

Ferdinand (V) and Isabella (I) (*continued*), appoint Isaac Abrabanel minister of finance, **4,** 343.
secret treaty of, with Boabdil, **4,** 345.
enter Granada, **4,** 345.
decide on the expulsion of the Jews, **4,** 346–7.
proclamation of, expelling the Jews, **4,** 347–8.
confiscate the treasures of the exiles, **4,** 354–5.
censured for the expulsion of the Jews, **4,** 356.
marry their daughter to Manoel of Portugal, **4,** 372–3.
oppose the Portuguese Marranos at Rome, **4,** 379.

Ferdinand I, of Naples, employs a Jewish physician, **4,** 287.
receives Spanish exiles kindly, **4,** 358–9.
patron of Isaac Abrabanel, **4,** 359, 383.
refuses to expel the Jews, **4,** 359–60.
death of, **4,** 360.

Ferdinand I, of Portugal, prosperity of the Jews under, **4,** 158–9.
Jewish favorites of, **4,** 159–60.
death of, **4,** 160.

Ferdinand, duke of Braganza, friend of Isaac Abrabanel, **4,** 338, 340–1.

Ferdinand de Medici, duke of Tuscany, receives Jewish exiles from the Papal States, **4,** 659.
permits the use of the expurgated Talmud, **4,** 659.

Fermo, residence of Immanuel Romi, **4,** 68.

Fernando, Manuel, de Villa-Real, Marrano, martyr, **5,** 91.

Ferrajo, Lucio, tries to prove the blood accusation out of the Talmud, **5,** 639.

Ferrara, Hillel of Verona in, **3,** 629.
Jewish printing house in, **4,** 289.
Jewish exiles in, **4,** 412–13.
Marranos well treated at, **4,** 526.
refuge of the Neapolitan Jews, **4,** 544.
Samuel Usque at, **4,** 558.
the Talmud burnt in, **4,** 565.
a refuge for Marranos, **4,** 568, 569.
refuge of Gracia Mendesia, **4,** 575.
Marranos of, in distress, **4,** 581.
refuge of the Jewish exiles from the Papal States, **4,** 592.
becomes part of the Papal States, **4,** 660.
no longer a refuge for Marranos, **4,** 661.
earthquake in, **4,** 615.

Ferrara, the Jews of, liberties of, **3,** 628.
appeal for permission to own the Talmud, **4,** 658.
attached to the house of Este, **4,** 660.

Ferrer. *See* Vidal ben Benveniste Ibn-Labi.

Ferrer, Vincent, humility of, **4,** 200–1.
revives flagellation, **4,** 201.
as an orator, **4,** 201.
fanaticism of, **4,** 201–2.
crusade of, against the Jews, **4,** 202.
extorts Christian confession from the Marranos, **4,** 202–3.
influences Jews to accept Christianity, **4,** 204–5, 206, 214.

Ferrer, Vincent (*continued*), procures the crown of Aragon for Ferdinand of Castile, **4,** 205, 206.
denounces Benedict XIII, **4,** 216.
death of, **4,** 217.
refused aid by João I of Portugal, **4,** 218.
in Savoy, **4,** 218.
terror of, spreads to Germany and Italy, **4,** 218.
policy of, adopted by the Council of Basle, **4,** 246.
compared with John of Capistrano, **4,** 257.
compared with Bernardinus of Feltre, **4,** 296.
Ferrus, Pero, apostate, satirist, **4,** 181.
Festus, procurator of Judæa, administration of, **2,** 247–8.
Fettmilch, Vincent, leader of the Frankfort guilds against the Jews, **4,** 696–7.
attacks the Jew quarter, **4,** 697.
hanged, **4,** 699–700.
Fez, Dunash ben Labrat in, **3,** 226.
Maimun's family in, **3,** 451–6.
forced converts emigrate to, **4,** 179.
suffering of Spanish exiles in, **4,** 361–2.
the Spanish exiles in, **4,** 390.
Fez, the Jews of, consult Haï Gaon, **3,** 252.
persecuted, **3,** 360.
fortunes of, **5,** 168.
Fezara, the, Arab tribe, promise assistance to the Jews of Chaibar, **3,** 82.
Fichte, classes Jews with the nobility and clergy, **5,** 461.
opposes the emancipation of the Jews, **5,** 462, 468.
Saul Asher refutes, **5,** 463.
Fields, the blessing of, by Jews, forbidden, **2,** 620; **3,** 44.
Fifth Monarchy, the, believers in, regard the Jews favorably, **5,** 23, 27.
view of, held by Christians, **5,** 37.
as interpreted by Manasseh ben Israel, **5,** 38.
believers in, fix the Messianic year, **5,** 120.
Firme-Fé. *See* Nuñes, Henrique.
First-born, the, Mosaic law of, as interpreted under Ahaz, **1,** 261.
Firuz (Pheroces, 457–484), Sassanian king, persecutes the Jews, **2,** 628–30; **3,** 1.
persecutes the Jews of Ispahan, **2,** 629.
closes the Jewish schools, **2,** 629.
forces Magianism upon Jews, **2,** 629.
death of, **2,** 630.
Firuz-Shabur (Anbar), important Babylonian town, **2,** 505.
the Jews of, in the war between Julian the Apostate and Shabur II, **2,** 601.
academy opened at, **3,** 8, 9.
taken by Ali, **3,** 90.
Fiscus Judaicus, tax instituted by Vespasian, **2,** 316.
extorted from the Jews, **2,** 332.
See Tax.
"Five Evidences of the Faith," Sabbatian work, **5,** 162.
Flaccus, prætor in Asia Minor, seizes upon the votive offerings in the Temple, **2,** 68.
defended by Cicero, **2,** 68–70.
Flaccus, Pomponius, governor of Syria, Agrippa I courtier of, **2,** 175.

Flaccus, Pomponius (*continued*), tool of the Alexandrians, 2, 181.
deprives Judæans of Alexandrian citizenship, 1, 182.
deposed, 2, 183.

Flagellants, the, in Hanover, 4, 111.
under Vincent Ferrer, 4, 201.
condemned by the Council of Constance, 4, 217.

Flanders, Spanish spoken in, by the exiles, 4, 387.
Portuguese Marranos imprisoned in, 4, 509.

Flavian house, the, and the Jews, 2, 388.

Flavio Jacopo de Evora, on Amatus Lusitanus, 4, 610.

Flavius Josephus. *See* Joseph ben Matthias.

Florence, commerce of, in the fifteenth century, 4, 285.
Elias del Medigo lectures on philosophy at, 4, 291.
the Jews of, protected against Bernardinus of Feltre, 4, 297.
the Marranos of, not molested, 4, 500.
the Portuguese Jews of, wealthy, 5, 205.

Florentin, Solomon, Talmudist, supporter of Jacob Querido, 5, 210.

Florus, Gessius (64–66), last procurator of Judæa, rapacity and profligacy of, 2, 249–50.
favors the Sicarii, 2, 250.
bribed by the Judæans of Cæsarea, 2, 252–3.
imprisons Judæan deputies, 2, 253.
demands a part of the Temple treasures, 2, 253.
in Jerusalem, 2, 253–4.

Florus, Gessius (*continued*), plunders the upper town, 2, 254.
appealed to by Berenice, 2, 254.
demands a friendly reception for his troops, 2, 254.
troops of, attack the Temple, 2, 255.
leaves Jerusalem, 2, 255.
Jerusalem rebellious towards, 2, 258.
refuses to aid the Peace party, 2, 259.
refrains from interference between the Zealots and the Roman garrison in Jerusalem, 2, 261–2.
enslaves the Judæans in Cæsarea, 2, 262.
accused before Nero, 2, 268.

Fons Vitæ, philosophical work by Solomon Ibn-Gebirol, 3, 270–1. *See* "Fountain of Life, The."

Fonseca Pinto y Pimentel, Sarah de, Jewish poetess, 5, 203.

Fontaine, de, Countess, owns the Jews of Metz, 5, 348, 446.

Fontanes, reactionary influence of, 5, 477, 479.

"**Fool's Voice, The**," by Leo Modena, 5, 73.

Forli, Hillel of Verona in, 3, 629.
synod at, 4, 218.

"**Fortalitium Fidei**," anti-Jewish work by Alfonso de Spina, 4, 277, 415.

"**Fortress, The**," polemic, 4, 234.

Fortunatus, Venantius, poet, celebrates the achievements of Avitus, 3, 39.

Forum Judicum, Visigothic code, translated into Castilian, 3, 594–5.

Fossano, French exiles settle in, **4**, 177.
Fostat. *See* Cairo.
Fould, Achille, questions Thiers on the Damascus affair, **5**, 649.
" **Fountain of Life, The**," (Mekor Chayim, Fons Vitæ), philosophical work by Solomon Ibn-Gebirol, **3**, 270.
translated into Latin, **3**, 270.
used by the schoolmen, **3**, 271.
Four Countries, the, Synod of (Vaad Arba Arazoth), functions of, **4**, 643–4; **5**, 3–4.
authority of, **4**, 644.
supposed originator of, **4**, 645.
president of, **4**, 645.
and the Kamieniec disputation, **5**, 281.
forbidden to assemble, **5**, 387.
dissolution of, favorable to Chassidism, **5**, 387.
Fourth of August, the, glory of, **5**, 437.
Fox Fables, the, by Berachya ben Natronaï, **3**, 560.
Fraga, the Jews of, converted, **4**, 214.
" **Fragments** of an Unknown," published by Lessing, **5**, 320–1.
effect of, **5**, 321–2.
attributed to Mendelssohn, **5**, 322.
France, Talmud schools established in, **3**, 208.
Talmudists of, imported into Egypt, **3**, 444.
rabbis of, emigrate to Jerusalem, **3**, 505–6.
rabbis of, in sympathy with Solomon Petit, **3**, 627.
refuge of the Jews banished from England, **3**, 646.
quarrel about the chief rabbinate of, **4**, 152–3, 162.
France (*continued*), the Protestant Reformation in, **4**, 469.
professorships for Hebrew instituted in, **4**, 471, 473, 474.
Portuguese Marranos arrested in, **4**, 509.
ambassador of, and Joseph Nassi, **4**, 595, 598–9.
Joseph Nassi seizes the merchant vessels of, **4**, 597.
the Measfim in, **5**, 401.
the first country to emancipate the Jews, **5**, 430.
congregations of, present addresses to the Synhedrion, **5**, 496.
Central Consistory of, keeps aloof from the Reform movement, **5**, 572.
France, the Jews of, participate in the memorial services at the Babylonian academies, **3**, 101.
advanced under Charlemagne, **3**, 141.
devote themselves to the Agada, **3**, 160.
under Charles the Bald, **3**, 170–4.
decrees against, revived, **3**, 171.
tax levied on, **3**, 172.
antagonized by Bishop Amolo, **3**, 172–3.
exposed to Easter attacks, **3**, 173–4.
under Charles the Simple, **3**, 175.
treated as the wards of the king, **3**, 175.
yield precedence to the Jews of Spain, **3**, 236.
oppressed under the last Carlovingians and the first Capets, **3**, 241–2.
the clergy arouse hatred against, **3**, 241.

France, the Jews of (*continued*),
accused of using spells against Christians, **3**, 242.
not creative in the eleventh century, **3**, 281.
occupations of, **3**, 281.
compared with the Christians, **3**, 281.
devoted to the study of the Talmud, **3**, 281, 343–5.
protected during the first crusade, **3**, 299.
beginnings of culture among, **3**, 343.
debts owing to, repudiated, **3**, 349–51.
Louis VII roused against, **3**, 349–50.
a persecution of, prevented, **3**, 351.
martyrdom of, during the second crusade, **3**, 354–6.
Jewish culture of, **3**, 357.
and the secular courts, **3**, 377.
observe a fast for the Jews of Blois, **3**, 380.
banished by Philip Augustus, **3**, 402–3.
charges against, by Innocent III, **3**, 499.
forbidden to employ Christian nurses, **3**, 508.
suffer during Gregory IX's crusade, **3**, 570.
forced into Christianity, **3**, 570.
appeal to Gregory IX, **3**, 570.
under Louis IX, **3**, 570–1.
charged with usury, **3**, 571.
fast during the disputation with Donin, **3**, 577.
charged with the blood accusation, **3**, 583–5.
banished by Louis IX, **3**, 585–6.
return of, **3**, 586.
forced to wear a badge, **3**, 612.

France, the Jews of (*continued*),
address Solomon ben Adret for religious decisions, **3**, 620.
banished by Philip IV, **3**, 646; **4**, 46.
reasons for the exile of, **4**, 47.
suffering of, **4**, 47–9.
emigrate, **4**, 49.
recalled by Louis X, **4**, 53.
conditions for the re-admission of, **4**, 53–4.
privileges of, extended by Philip V, **4**, 54.
massacred by the Pastoureaux, **4**, 55–7.
accused of poisoning wells, **4**, 57.
permitted to return by John the Good, **4**, 129.
privileges granted to, **4**, 129–31, 150.
hostility to, **4**, 131, 132.
attacked by mobs, **4**, 151–2.
refuse to submit to the German chief rabbi, **4**, 152–3.
conditions of the residence of. in France, **4**, 174.
forced into usury, **4**, 174.
banished by Charles VI, **4**, 175–6.
remain in certain towns and provinces, **4**, 176–7.
settle in Germany and Italy, **4**, 177.
number of, **5**, 435.
not united for concerted action, **5**, 436.
petition for admission into the fraternity of the French people, **5**, 438.
Saint Etienne speaks in behalf of, **5**, 439.
improvement of, planned by Berr Isaac Berr, **5**, 449.
interested in the government, **5**, 449–50.

France, the Jews of (*continued*), and the religion of Reason, **5**, 451–2.
recognized as equals by the Constitution of the Directory, **5**, 452.
object to the poll-tax in Germany, **5**, 464–5.
in danger of losing their privileges, **5**, 474.
opposed by the reactionary party, **5**, 477–8.
deprived temporarily of civil equality, **5**, 482.
restrictive laws for, **5**, 498–9
rights of, not curtailed after Napoleon's fall, **5**, 512–13.
restrictions against not renewed, **5**, 524–5.
rapid advance of, **5**, 557.
under Polish influence, **5**, 558.
influenced by the Reform movement, **5**, 582–3.
and the Damascus affair, **5**, 644, 651.
asked to support Crémieux's Eastern schools, **5**, 671.
France, the Jews of, emancipation of. *See* Emancipation of the French Jews, the.
France, northern, home of Talmudic studies after Rashi, **3**, 289.
rabbis of, at Donin's disputation, **3**, 576.
France, northern, the Jews of, devoted to Talmud study, **3**, 289, 290, 345, 407–8.
expect the Messiah, **3**, 298.
prosperous in the twelfth century, **3**, 343.
banished during the third crusade, **3**, 405.
received by Philip Augustus, **3**, 405–6.
not permitted to move from province to province, **3**, 406.
France, northern, the Jews of (*continued*), forbidden to buy property confiscated from Jews, **3**, 406–7.
treated as bondmen, **3**, 407.
naïve faith of, **3**, 549.
wear Jew badges, **3**, 612.
France, southern, Judæans in, **2**, 203.
culture and rulers of, **3**, 390.
tolerance in, **3**, 390.
Spanish culture introduced into, **3**, 392.
Jews from, in Palestine, **3**, 427–8.
rabbis of, renounce Solomon of Montpellier, **3**, 539, 541.
See also Languedoc; Narbonne; Provence.
France, southern, the Jews of, dependent on vassal princes, **3**, 242.
in the twelfth century, **3**, 389–91.
idolize Maimonides, **3**, 488–9.
Maimonides on, **3**, 492.
relation of, to the Albigenses, **3**, 501, 513–14.
suffer during the Albigensian crusade, **3**, 501–3.
not employed as state officials, **3**, 503–4.
send delegates to the Fourth Lateran Council, **3**, 509.
struggle against badges, **3**, 513.
Innocent III's decrees enforced against, **3**, 518.
Maimunists, **3**, 526–7.
excommunicate Solomon of Montpellier, **3**, 530.
philosophical leanings of, **3**, 549
ordered to enter into disputations with Pablo Christiani, **3**, 602.

France, southern, the Jews of (*continued*), obtain the abrogation of the law on badges, **3**, 612.
persecuted in the fourteenth century, **4**, 53.
during the Pastoureaux rising, **4**, 56–7.
massacred on the charge of having caused the Black Death, **4**, 102.
hostility towards, **4**, 132.

Francesco Maria I, duke of Urbino, brings Molcho to Pesaro, **4**, 501.

Francesco Maria II, duke of Urbino, David de Pomis dedicates a book to, **4**, 657.

Francis I, of Austria, emperor, imposes restrictions on the Jews, **5**, 508.
the Jews under, **5**, 523.
intolerance of, **5**, 579.

Francis I, of France, patron of Hebrew learning, **4**, 473.

Franciscans (Minorites), the, order of, originates in the Fourth Lateran Council, **3**, 509.
persecutions by, in southern France, **3**, 519.
in the Maimunist controversy, **3**, 542–3.
judges of the Talmud, **3**, 575.
free English Jews imprisoned on the blood accusation, **3**, 591.
censors of the Talmud, **3**, 603.
in Hungary, **3**, 614.
mock at the Dominicans, **3**, 641.
object to a synagogue on Mount Zion, **4**, 274.
espouse Reuchlin's cause, **4**, 457.

Franciscus of Sardinia, persecutes the Damascus Jews, **5**, 639–40.

Franco, (Christoval) Mordecai Mendes, Marrano in Holland, **4**, 667.

Franco, Nicolo, papal nuncio, urges the Inquisition for Marranos, **4**, 310.

Franco, Samuel, Kabbalist, **4**, 405.

Franconia, the Jews of, suffer during the Rindfleisch persecution, **4**, 35.
privileges granted to, **4**, 259.
banished, **4**, 259–60.
attacked by Lutheran peasants, **4**, 542.
persecuted, **5**, 529.

Frank, Eva, daughter of Jacob Frank, **5**, 289.

Frank, Jacob, roguery of, **5**, 272.
joins the Sabbatians, **5**, 272.
accepts Islam, **5**, 272.
Kabbalistic views of, **5**, 273.
considered an incarnation of the Messiah, **5**, 273, 274.
leader of the Polish Sabbatians, **5**, 273–4.
prayers addressed to, **5**, 274.
emigrates to Turkey, **5**, 276.
advises his followers to accept Christianity, **5**, 278–9, 284.
invited to return to Podolia, **5**, 283.
baptized, **5**, 287–8.
betrayed, **5**, 288.
end of the career of, **5**, 289.

Fränkel, David, rabbi of Berlin, Mendelssohn's teacher, **5**, 293–4.

Fränkel, Jonas, founder of the Breslau Seminary, **5**, 700.

Frankel, Sæckel, compiles Hebrew prayers, **5**, 564.

Frankel, Zachariah (1801–1875). orthodox leader, compared with Holdheim, **5**, 684.

Frankel, Zachariah (*continued*), character and scientific activity of, **5,** 684, 694–5.
attitude of, towards reforms, **5,** 684–5.
at the Frankfort rabbinical conference, **5,** 685.
founder of the Breslau seminary, **5,** 700.
Frankenberg, Abraham von, mystic, on the restoration of Israel, **5,** 24.
Frankfort, duchy of, created, **5,** 505.
Frankfort-on-the-Main, diet at, to consider the Jewish question, **4,** 463, 464.
Jews tolerated in, **4,** 686.
refuses to receive Portuguese Jews, **4,** 695.
Polish-Jewish fugitives in, **5,** 16.
rabbis of, Poles, **5,** 17, 206.
Joseph Delmedigo at, **5,** 80.
"Judaism Unmasked" printed at, **5,** 189.
Judah Chassid at, **5,** 213.
Moses Meïr Kamenker at, **5,** 229–30.
Börne's life in, **5,** 539.
without a rabbi, **5,** 566.
Talmud school of, closed, **5,** 567.
honor shown to Crémieux at, **5,** 668.
the Reform movement in, **5,** 674.
rabbinical conference at, **5,** 683–4, 685–6.
Frankfort-on-the-Main, the Jews of, burn themselves to escape persecution, **4,** 109.
charged with child murder, **4** 299–300.
threatened with expulsion, **4,** 417, 696.
Frankfort-on-the-Main, the Jews of (*continued*), confiscation of the books of, by Pfefferkorn, **4,** 429–30, 438.
appeal to Uriel von Gemmingen, **4,** 430.
send a representative to Maximilian I, **4,** 430–1, 436–7.
extermination of, suggested by Pfefferkorn, **4,** 463.
submit disputes to the Polish Talmudists, **4,** 639.
number of, **4,** 694.
antipathy to, **4,** 694–5.
restrictions imposed on, **4,** 695–6, 700.
houses of labeled, **4,** 696.
attacked by Fettmilch, **4,** 697.
flee, **4,** 697–8.
re-admitted, **4,** 699.
celebrate Purim-Vincent, **4,** 700.
protected by Ferdinand II, **4,** 701.
oppose Eibeschütz's Talmud edition, **5,** 251.
petition for emancipation, **5,** 465–6.
miserable condition of, **5,** 466.
relieved of the poll-tax, **5,** 468.
oppressed, **5,** 503.
freed from the Ghetto, **5,** 504.
new laws for, **5,** 504–5.
emancipation of, **5,** 505.
under restrictions after Napoleon's fall, **5,** 512, 520.
send deputies to the Congress of Vienna, **5,** 513.
rely on Prussia and Austria, **5,** 520–1.
persecuted, **5,** 529.
purchase political rights, **5,** 541.
Frankfort-on-the-Main, the senate of, orders the surrender of Hebrew books, **4,** 429.

Frankfort-on-the-Main, the senate of (*continued*), withdraws aid from Pfefferkorn, **4**, 430.
forbids the sale of Hebrew books, **4**, 431.
protects Hebrew books on sale at the Fair, **4**, 438.
directed to return the Hebrew books, **4**, 439.
discusses the emancipation of the Jews, **5**, 598.
and circumcision, **5**, 676–7.
Frankfort-on-the-Oder, the theological faculty of, permits Jews to live in Hamburg, **4**, 687.
Jews settle in, **5**, 174.
regulations for the Fair at, **5**, 415.
Frankfurter, Naphtali, devotee of the Kabbala, **5**, 55.
complains of the scorn for the Talmud, **5**, 56.
Frankists, the, Sabbatian sect, origin of, **5**, 274.
opposed to Rabbinical Judaism, **5**, 274.
charged with dissoluteness, **5**, 275–6.
excommunicated, **5**, 276–7.
the persecution of, sanctioned by Emden, **5**, 278.
handed over to the Inquisition, **5**, 278.
inclined towards Christianity, **5**, 278–9.
attacked by the Talmud Jews, **5**, 279.
charge the Talmud Jews with the blood accusation, **5**, 279.
favored by Bishop Dembowski, **5**, 279–80.
disputations of, with the Talmudists, **5**, 280, 281, 286–7.
confession of faith by, **5**, 280, 285.
persecuted, **5**, 283.
Frankists, the (*continued*), apply for baptism, **5**, 284.
baptized, **5**, 287.
customs of, **5**, 289.
families descended from, **5**, 289.
regard Eibeschütz as the great Gaon, **5**, 289.
Frankists, list of:
Chaya, daughter of Elisha Schor,
Krysa, Jehuda Leb
Nachman ben Samuel Levi,
Schor, Elisha
Solomon of Rohatyn.
Franks, the, the empire of, independent of the Church, **3**, 37.
Jew hatred introduced into, **3**, 38–9.
extent of, under Charlemagne, **3**, 142.
Jews spread in, **3**, 144.
Franks, the, the empire of, the Jews of, permitted to carry on the slave trade, **3**, 34.
not considered a separate race, **3**, 35.
occupations of, **3**, 35–6.
protected by Charlemagne, **3**, 142.
education of, cared for by Charlemagne, **3**, 143.
oath imposed on, **3**, 144.
under Louis the Pious, **3**, 161–70.
have free access to court, **3**, 162.
synagogues of, visited by Christians, **3**, 163.
and Agobard of Lyons, **3**, 164–8.
Frederick I Barbarossa, emperor, considers the Jews "servi cameræ," **3**, 416–17.
includes Jews in his general peace, **3**, 418.

Frederick II, emperor, Jews under, **3**, 516.
introduces the Jew badge into Naples and Sicily, **3**, 518.
Gregory IX the enemy of, **3**, 519.
patron of learning, **3**, 565.
corresponds with a Jewish scholar, **3**, 565–6.
brings Jacob Anatoli to Naples, **3**, 566–7.
reproached with heterodoxy, **3**, 567, 580.
excludes Jews from public offices, **3**, 567.
censures Frederick the Valiant, **3**, 569.
executes the decrees of the Fourth Lateran Council, **3**, 569.
lays imposts upon Jewish immigrants, **3**, 569.
forces Innocent IV to retire to Lyons, **3**, 584.
the Jews persecuted after the death of, **3**, 611.
Frederick III, emperor, has a Jewish favorite, **4**, 224.
accession of, **4**, 249.
Jews under, **4**, 293–4.
claims the Jews of Ratisbon, **4**, 300, 416.
orders Israel Bruna's release, **4**, 303.
defers Israel Bruna's execution, **4**, 304.
protects the Jews of Ratisbon, **4**, 305–6.
recommends the Jews to his son, **4**, 413.
daughter of, **4**, 428.
Reuchlin at the court of, **4**, 433.
ennobles Reuchlin, **4**, 435.
Frederick V, of Denmark, and the Eibeschütz controversy, **5**, 265, 269, 271
Frederick V (*continued*), wife of, **5**, 267.
reinstates Eibeschütz, **5**, 268.
Frederick I, of Prussia, Jews under, **5**, 190–1.
and the Alenu prayer, **5**, 191–2.
exerts himself in behalf of "Judaism Unmasked, **5**, 192–3.
lays the Midrash Rabba under the ban, **5**, 194–5.
court-Jewess of, **5**, 219.
Frederick II, the Great, of Prussia, at war with Austria, **5**, 251.
reputed patron of the Jews, **5**, 251.
the Jews of Berlin under, **5**, 294.
illiberality of, **5**, 296.
poetry of, criticised by Mendelssohn, **5**, 302.
summons Mendelssohn to Sans-Souci, **5**, 302–3.
makes Mendelssohn a "Schutzjude," **5**, 304.
antipathy of, to Jews, **5**, 304.
objects to Mendelssohn as a member of the Berlin Academy, **5**, 308.
enraged against Voltaire, **5**, 339.
appoints Dohm superintendent of the archives, **5**, 351.
in need of money, **5**, 396.
culture under, **5**, 410–11.
popularizes French literature, **5**, 411.
treatment of the Jews by, **5**, 414, 415.
Frederick the Valiant, archduke of Austria, Jewish statute of, 3, 567–9.
introduced into a number of countries, **3**, 569, 613–14.

Frederick the Valiant, Jewish statute of (*continued*), confirmed by Rudolph of Habsburg, **3,** 635.
confirmed in Poland, **4,** 111.
Frederick, elector palatine, corresponds with Abraham Zacuto Lusitano, **4,** 678.
re-admits the Jews into Worms, **4,** 699.
Frederick the Wise, elector of Saxony, patron of Luther, **4,** 469.
Frederick, commissioner sent by Louis the Pious to Agobard, **3,** 166.
Frederick Franz, duke of Mecklenburg, emancipates the Jews, **5,** 507.
Frederick William, elector of Brandenburg, invites Jewish exiles to his state, **5,** 173–4.
Frederick William I, of Prussia, court Jew of, **5,** 219.
Frederick William II, of Prussia, and the emancipation of the Jews, **5,** 414, 416.
Mirabeau on Prussia under, **5,** 419.
abrogates the poll-tax, **5,** 464.
Frederick William III, of Prussia, tutor of, **5,** 372.
attends Herz's lectures, **5,** 406.
grants some political rights to Jews, **5,** 507, 508.
nullifies the emancipation of the Jews, **5,** 524.
interrupts the Reform movement in Berlin, **5,** 563.
forbids Jews to bear Christian names, **5,** 630.
Free Towns, the. *See* Hanse Towns, the.
Freedom of Conscience, in the French National Assembly, **5,** 439.
Freemasons' Lodge, the first Jewish, hearth of the Reform movement, **5,** 674.
Freiburg, the **Jews** of, protected during the Black Death persecutions, **4,** 106.
burnt, **4,** 107.
French, the, in Naples, **4,** 384.
French literature, attracts the German Jews, **5,** 411.
French Revolution, the, characterized, **5,** 429.
outbreak of, **5,** 435.
excesses of, **5,** 436–7.
progress of, **5,** 441.
Jews take no part in the atrocities of, **5,** 450.
reaction from, **5,** 477–8.
French translation, a, of the Bible projected, **5,** 449.
Frenks, the. *See* Frankists, the.
Fresco, Moses, rabbi of Constantinople, urges the Jews to study Turkish, **5,** 664.
Friedländer, Bärmann, prominent Königsberg Jew, **5,** 397.
Friedländer, David (1750–1834), promotes the revival among Jews, **5,** 397.
successor to Mendelssohn, **5,** 412.
urges the abolition of the Jewish poll-tax, **5,** 414.
representative of the Berlin Jewish community, **5,** 415.
director of the Berlin Free School, **5,** 416.
mediocrity of, **5,** 417.
deplores the decay of morality among Jews, **5,** 419.
makes overtures to the Church, **5,** 421–2, 426.
children of, baptized, **5,** 422.
leaves attacks on Judaism unanswered, **5,** 469.
consulted by Jacobson, **5,** 502.

Friedländer, David (*continued*), efforts of for the emancipation of the Jews, **5**, 508.
on the "hep, hep!" persecutions, **5**, 534.
influence of, on Heine, **5**, 546.
Heine's criticism of, **5**, 547.
followers of, criticised by Bernays, **5**, 574–5.
and Mannheimer, **5**, 580.
member of the Society for Culture, **5**, 583.
Jost a disciple of, **5**, 595.
Friedländer, Meyer, prominent Königsberg Jew, **5**, 397.
Friedländer, Wolf, prominent Königsberg Jew, **5**, 397.
Friedrichsfeld, David, one of the Measfim, **5**, 400.
refutes Van Swieden, **5**, 454.
"Friends of Reform," Society of the, **5**, 675–6.
Fries, J. F., attacks the Jews, **5**, 521.
Friesland, East, Jews live in, **4**, 665.
Frohbach, astronomical work by, **4**, 638.
Fronto, guardian of Jerusalem, **2**, 311.
Fuero juzgo, Visigothic code, translated, **3**, 594–5.
Fueros, Spanish law of custom, grants citizenship to Jews, **3**, 292.
"Fulfillment of Prophecy, The," by Pierre Jurieu, **5**, 176.
Fulko de Neuilly, preaches the third crusade, **3**, 405
Fulvia, Roman patrician, proselyte, **2**, 136, 215.
Funes, the Jews of, attacked, **4**, 78.
Furin al-Mizrayim, Purim of Cairo, **4**, 396.
Furtado, Abraham, member of Malesherbes' commission, **5**, 432.
a representative French Jew, **5**, 436.
deputy of the French Jews, **5**, 438.
ancestry and youth of, **5**, 483.
rôle played by, during the Revolution, **5**, 483.
president of the Assembly of Jewish Notables, **5**, 487.
speech of, in answer to the imperial commissioners, **5**, 489–90.
speeches of, before the Synhedrion, **5**, 495, 497.
view held by, of Judaism, **5**, 496.
informs Napoleon of anti-Jewish agitation, **5**, 498.
Fürth, the Jews of, indifferent to the confiscation of Hebrew books, **4**, 438.
rabbis of, Poles, **5**, 17.
Jewish exiles from Vienna settle in, **5**, 173.
interdicts Mendelssohn's Pentateuch translation, **5**, 331–2.
Talmud school of, closed, **5**, 567.
rabbi of, opposes the Reform movement, **5**, 571.
honor shown to Crémieux at, **5**, 668.
Future life, the, doctrine of, **1**, 404–6.
in the Mishna, **2**, 473.

G

Gabaot, Roman camp under Cestius Gallus, **2**, 265–6.
Gabara, ordered not to protect Josephus, **2**, 281.
taken by Vespasian, **2**, 286.
Gabata, Galilæan fortress, **2**, 56.
Gabinius, Aulus, governor of Syria, subdues Alexander, **2**, 70.
divides Judæa into provinces, **2**, 71.
defeats Alexander, **2**, 73.
Gabriel, the name of an angel, **1**, 403.
makes revelations to Mahomet, **3**, 71.
Gad, Chaldæan god of fortune, **1**, 340.
Gad, prophet, joins David, **1**, 100, 113.
orders David to sacrifice on Mt. Moriah, **1**, 138.
Gad, the tribe of, asks for land east of the Jordan, **1**, 29–30.
appeals to Samuel for help, **1**, 80.
territory of, taken by Hazael, **1**, 220.
descendants of, in Chaibar, **3**, 437.
Gadara, incorporated with Judæa, **2**, 103.
Gaffarelli, Jacob, Christian Kabbalist, taught by Leo Modena, **5**, 71.
Gailan, emir, persecutes Sabbatians, **5**, 151.
oppresses the Jews, **5**, 168.
Galaïgo, Joseph Chayim, addresses Mendelssohn, **5**, 369.
Galaistes, governor of Gabata, assists Aristobulus, **2**, 56.
Galante, Moses, adherent of Sabbataï Zevi, **5**, 132.
Galatia, a Greek-Christian community in, **2**, 227.
Galatino, interested in the Kabbala, **4**, 481, 583.
Galba, emperor, short reign of, **3**, 299.
Galen, writings of, elaborated by Maimonides, **3**, 473.
Galerius, emperor, persecutes Christianity, **2**, 539.
Galicia, the Jews of, proscribed by the Council of Buda, **3**, 614.
resist the opening of secular schools, **5**, 394.
described by Rohrer, **5**, 472.
taxed, **5**, 508.
oppressed, **5**, 523.
affected by the Reform movement, **5**, 582.
beginnings of culture among, **5**, 611–12.
improvement of, undertaken by the "Israelitische Allianz," **5**, 703.
Galician school, the, founders of, **5**, 607.
Hebrew style of, **5**, 617.
contribute to the Kerem Chemed, **5**, 621.
inspire the contributors to the Scientific Journal, **5**, 625.
Galilæan Synod, the, second assembly of the teachers of the Law at Usha, **2**, 434.
Galilæans, name given to Christians, **2**, 596.
Galilee, lake, description of, **1**, 42.
Galilee, province, description of, **1**, 45.
Gelil Haggoyim, **1**, 164.
appeals to Judas Maccabæus, **1**, 475.
rescued by Simon Tharsi, **1**, 475.
Judæans of, emigrate, **1**, 475.
Judæans of, killed, **1**, 486.

Galilee (*continued*), restored to Judæa, **2**, 76.
declares in favor of Antigonus, **2**, 85.
subdued by Herod, **2**, 87.
given to Herod Antipas, **2**, 119.
Roman troops in, to fight Judas the Galilæan, **2**, 126.
under Herod Antipas, **2**, 137.
lack of culture in, **2**, 148.
morality in, **2**, 148.
language of, **2**, 148–9.
Jesus in the towns of, **2**, 157.
a Messiah from, not acceptable, **2**, 161.
given to Agrippa I, **2**, 177.
pilgrims from, murdered, **2**, 243.
under the command of Josephus, **2**, 272, 278–9.
divided into Upper and Lower, **2**, 272.
civil war in, **2**, 282–3.
strength of, broken by Josephus, **2**, 285, 286.
subject to Rome, **2**, 288.
Zealots of, possess three fortified places, **2**, 289.
end of the Roman conquest of, **2**, 290.
fugitives from, in Jerusalem, **2**, 291.
recovers under Jewish governors, **2**, 333.
the seat of the Synhedrion, **2**, 458.
Babylonian students in the academies of, **2**, 511.
first churches in, **2**, 565.
Jews inhabit the cities of, in the sixth century, **3**, 12.
prevalence of mysticism in, **4**, 617.

Galilee, the Jews of, join the Persian general, **3**, 19.
Galilee, the Jews of (*continued*), join an expedition against the Christians of Tyre, **3**, 20.

Galileo, teacher of Joseph Delmedigo, **5**, 75.

Gallaico, Elisha. *See* Elisha Gallaico.

Gallienus, emperor with Odenathus, **2**, 528.

Gallipoli, the Jews of, in the twelfth century, **3**, 424.

Gallus, emperor, campaign of, against the Persians, **2**, 568.
death of, **2**, 572.

Gallus, Cestius, governor of Syria, on the turbulent state of Judæa, **2**, 250–1.
arranges a demonstration in Jerusalem in 66, **2**, 251–2.
in communication with the Peace party, **2**, 257.
sends a deputy to Jerusalem, **2**, 257.
campaign of, near Jerusalem, **2**, 264–6.
retreats, **2**, 266–7.
losses of, **2**, 267.
death of, **2**, 284.

Gama, Vasco da, aided by Joseph Vecinho's instruments, **4**, 367.

Gamala, capital of Gaulanitis, taken by Alexander Jannæus, **2**, 45.
birthplace of Judas the Galilæan, **2**, 125.
focus of insurrection in Galilee, **2**, 273.
impregnable position of, **2**, 274.
refuge of the Babylonian Judæans, **2**, 275.
revolts from Agrippa II, **2**, 275.
taken by Vespasian, **2**, 289–90.

Gamaliel I, the Elder, grandson of Hillel, president of the Synhedrion, **2**, 192–3.

Gamaliel I (*continued*), gentle reforms of, **2**, 193.
grants heathens the right of gleaning, **2**, 478.
Gamaliel II, Patriarch, president of the Jamnia Synhedrion, **2**, 334.
tries to reconcile the schools of Hillel and Shammai, **2**, 335, 336–8.
humanity of, **2**, 336.
regulates the calendar, **2**, 336, 356.
journeys of, **2**, 336.
character of, misunderstood, **2**, 336.
inquires into the character of students of the Law, **2**, 338–9.
uses excommunication, **2**, 339–40, 347.
contest of, with Joshua ben Chananya, **2**, 340–2.
deposed, **2**, 341.
rejects Moabites and Ammonites as proselytes, **2**, 343.
reconciled with Joshua, **2**, 344–5.
reinstated, **2**, 345.
opposes Eliezer ben Hyrcanus, **2**, 347.
death of, **2**, 350, 404, 479.
introduces set prayers, **2**, 363.
supposed relation of, to the Jewish Christians, **2**, 379.
and Akylas, **2**, 385.
journey of, to Rome, **2**, 387.
and Flavius Clemens, **2**, 387, 389, 391.
influences Nerva, **2**, 392.
funeral of, **2**, 404.
sons of, **2**, 404, 479.
Gamaliel III, Patriarch, instructions of his father to, **2**, 466.
recommends trades, **2**, 467.
Gamaliel III (*continued*), advises caution in intercourse with the Romans, **2**, 467–8.
and Abba-Areka, **2**, 512.
Gamaliel IV, Patriarch, scant knowledge of the Law of, **2**, 532.
Gamaliel V, Patriarch, successor to Hillel II, **2**, 612.
Gamaliel VI (Batraah, 370–425), last of the Patriarchs, **2**, 612.
dignities bestowed on, **2**, 617–18.
physician, **2**, 618.
last of the house of Hillel, **2**, 618.
Gans, David. *See* David Gans.
Gans, Edward, apostate, **5**, 551, 587.
founder of the Society for Culture, **5**, 583.
selfishness of, **5**, 585.
reproaches the Jews, **5**, 586.
desires a professorship, **5**, 587.
compared with Riesser, **5**, 600.
compared with Steinheim, **5**, 607.
Gaon, title of the principal of the Sora Academy, **3**, 90–1, 93.
of the principal of the Pumbeditha academy, **3**, 93, 177.
of Isaac Ibn-Sakni, **3**, 285.
of the head of the Bagdad college, **3**, 429.
of Samuel ben Ali Halevi, **3**, 438.
of Eibeschütz, **5**, 289.
of Elijah Wilna, **5**, 389.
See also Gaonate, the; Geonim, the; Pumbeditha, the academy of, principals of; Sora, the academy of, principals of.
Gaon of Castile, Isaac Campanton, **4**, 230.

Gaonate, the, Anan ben David hostile to, **3**, 130.
European and African Jews independent of, **3**, 208, 210.
decline of, **3**, 231, 253.
See also Gaon; Geonim, the.
Garcilaso, Spanish ambassador to Rome, opposes the Portuguese Marranos, **4**, 379.
Gascony, the Jews of, under Henry II, **3**, 409.
banished, **3**, 646.
during the Pastoureaux massacres, **4**, 56.
"**Gate of Heaven, The**," Kabbalistic work by Abraham de Herrera, **5**, 54.
Gates, the, of the second Temple, **2**, 111.
Gath, Philistine city, **1**, 54, 80.
surrendered to the Israelites, **1**, 117.
returned to the Philistines, **1**, 117–18.
conquered by Hazael, **1**, 221.
conquered by Uzziah, **1**, 231.
"**Gatherer**, The," (Ha-Meassef), a Hebrew journal, **5**, 399.
editors of, **5**, 400.
interest in, **5**, 403, 404.
contributors to, in Berlin, **5**, 411.
Gatiño, Ezra. *See* Ezra Gatiño.
Gaucelin, de, lords of Lünel, Jews under, **3**, 396.
Gaul, early Jewish settlements in, **3**, 35.
Gaul, the Jews of, **3**, 35–40.
names borne by, **3**, 36.
intermarry with Christians, **3**, 36.
obey the dietary laws, **3**, 36.
treated with hostility, **3**, 37–40.
Gaulanitis (Gaulonitis), invaded by Alexander Jannæus, **2**, 44, 45.
Gaulanitis (*continued*), **given to** Philip, **2**, 119.
given to Agrippa II, **2**, 245.
a field in, given to Judah II, **2**, 482.
Gauls, body-guard of Cleopatra, given to Herod, **2**, 103.
Gayo da Rieti. *See* Moses ben Isaac da Rieti.
Gayo, Maëstro. *See* Isaac ben Mordecai.
Gaza, Philistine port, **1**, 54.
left in possession of the Philistines, **1**, 117.
frontier town of Israel, **1**, 129.
taken by Necho, **1**, 297.
taken by Alexander the Great, **1**, 412.
battle of, **1**, 417.
Greek citizens of, resist Joseph, **1**, 425.
Jewish prisoners sold at the slave markets of, **2**, 419.
proclaimed the Holy City of the Sabbatians, **5**, 132.
Jews of, flee before Napoleon, **5**, 459.
Gaza, the district of, overrun by Alexander Jannæus, **2**, 40.
surrenders to Ptolemy VIII, **2**, 40.
taken by Alexander Jannæus, **2**, 41.
Gazara, fortified by Bacchides, **1**, 491.
surrenders to Simon Tharsi, **1**, 523.
fortified by Simon Tharsi, **1**, 524.
the son of Simon Tharsi at, **1**, 525.
claimed by Antiochus Sidetes, **2**, 4–5.
a Synhedrion established at, **2**, 71.
Geba. *See* Gibeah.

Gedaliah, son of Ahikam, overseer of the Judæan fugitives, **1**, 315.
governor of Judah, disciple of Jeremiah, **1**, 319.
guardian of Zedekiah's daughters, **1**, 319.
joined by Jeremiah, **1**, 320.
erects a sanctuary at Mizpah, **1**, 321.
informed of Ishmael's treachery, **1**, 322.
murder of, **1**, 322.
a fast on the anniversary of the murder of, **1**, 325.
Gedaliah Levi, quarrels with Vital Calabrese, **5**, 52.
Gedalya Ibn-Yachya (of the Italian branch, 1515–1587), historian, expelled from Ravenna, **4**, 592.
works of, **4**, 616.
consulted by Basnage, **5**, 196.
Gedalya Ibn-Yachya I (of the Turkish branch), patron of Jewish literature, **4**, 609.
Gedalya Ibn-Yachya II, patron of Jewish literature, **4**, 609.
Gehazi, disciple of Elisha, **1**, 218.
recounts Elisha's deeds, **1**, 223.
Ge-henna. *See* Hinnom.
Geiger, Abraham (1810–1874), scholar, characteristics of, **5**, 626.
attitude of, towards the Talmud, **5**, 626, 669.
devoted to the reform of Judaism, **5**, 626.
journal of, **5**, 626, 632.
at the Frankfort rabbinical conference, **5**, 685.
Gelasius, pope, kind to Jews, **3**, 29.
Geldern, Betty von, Heine's mother, **5**, 545.
Gelil Haggoyim, **1**, 164. *See* Galilee.
Gelimer, grandson of Genseric, in the triumph of Belisarius, **3**, 26.
Gemara. *See* Talmud, the Babylonian.
Gemara di Bene Ma'araba. *See* Talmud, the Jerusalem.
Gematria, Kabbalistic term, **4**, 5.
Gemmingen, Uriel von, archbishop of Mayence, the Frankfort Jews appeal to, **4**, 430.
not friendly to Pfefferkorn, **4**, 430, 431.
appointed commissary, **4**, 437.
and the confiscation of Hebrew books, **4**, 437, 441.
favors the Jews, **4**, 438.
delays the execution of the judgment against Reuchlin, **4**, 452.
"General Privilege" for the Jews, issued by Frederick the Great, **5**, 304.
Genesareth. *See* Tiberias, lake.
Genesis, treatise on, by Samuel Ibn-Tibbon, **3**, 398.
Geneva, the lake of, scene of Black Death persecutions, **4**, 103–4.
Genoa, commerce of, in the fifteenth century, **4**, 285.
suffering of the Spanish exiles in, **4**, 362–3.
Judah Leon Abrabanel in, **4**, 384.
Genoa, the Jews of, under the Ostrogoths, **3**, 28.
seek permission to repair the synagogue, **3**, 30.
in the twelfth century, **3**, 424.
banished, **4**, 553–4.
Genseric, the Vandal, carries the Temple vessels to Africa, **2**, 611.

Gentz, Frederick von, on Jewish women, **5,** 413.
immorality of, **5,** 423.
reactionary leader, **5,** 477, 512.
Geonim, the, beginning of the epoch of, **3,** 90–1.
history of, dark, **3,** 92.
duties of, **3,** 93.
power of, as viewed by the Jews of distant lands, **3,** 100.
decisions of, binding, **3,** 118–19.
opposed to the Exilarchs, **3,** 137.
literary works of, in the ninth century, **3,** 178–9.
favor scientific pursuits, **3,** 187.
responses of, criticised, **3,** 198.
chronicle of, by Sherira, **3,** 233.
Talmudic work of, surpassed by Spanish Talmudists, **3,** 282.
See also Gaon; Gaonate, the; Pumbeditha, the academy of, principals of; Sora, the academy of, principals of.
George II, of England, ratifies the naturalization of the Jews, **5,** 337–8.
George, of Hesse, forbids the use of a sentence in the Alenu prayer, **5,** 185.
George, bishop of Speyer, tries the Reuchlin - Hoogstraten case, **4,** 454–5.
Gepidæ, the, overrun Rome, **3,** 27.
Gerasa, besieged by Alexander Jannæus, **2,** 45.
Gere ha-Zedek, true proselytes, in the daily prayers, **2,** 384.
Gerizim, Mount, description of, **1,** 45.
the Samaritan Temple on, **1,** 390.
Gerizim, Mount (*continued*), Temple of, destroyed, **2,** 8.
temple to Jupiter on, **2,** 422.
Gerlach, archbishop of Mayence, obtains Jews as "servi cameræ," **4,** 128.
German-Frankish empire, the. *See* Franks, the, the empire of.
German language, the, carried to Poland by German Jews, **4,** 421.
German merchants antagonize Jews in Poland, **4,** 632.
German translation of the Bible by Luther, **4,** 469, 475.
by Sachs, **5,** 693.
German translation of the Pentateuch by Mendelssohn. *See under* Pentateuch, the.
Germans, the simplicity of, **4,** 422.
purity of, **4,** 423.
Germanus, Moses, proselyte, **5,** 177–8.
Germany, Jewish emigrants from, held up in Lombardy, **3,** 638–9.
refuge of the Jews banished from England, **3,** 646.
preferred to Spain by the Asherides, **4,** 90, 96.
re-admits Jews soon after the Black Death, **4,** 127–8.
French exiles settle in, **4,** 177.
exiles from, take refuge in Poland, **4,** 263.
exiles from, form a congregation in Constantinople, **4,** 402.
professorships for Hebrew instituted in, **4,** 471.
Messianic hopes connected with Solomon Molcho in, **4,** 497.
Portuguese Marranos perish in, **4,** 509.

Germany (*continued*), religious parties in, **5**, 25.
the Sabbatian movement in, **5**, 160, 228.
Chayim Malach in, **5**, 214.
feeling of solidarity developed in, **5**, 515.
the romantic movement in, **5**, 515–16.
debt of, to Börne and Heine, **5**, 556.
See also Franks, the, the empire of.

Germany, the Jews of, in the sixth century, **3**, 40–1.
advanced under Charlemagne, **3**, 141.
yield precedence to the Jews of Spain, **3**, 236.
under the Saxon emperors, **3**, 241, 242–3.
compelled to be tradesmen, **3**, 242–3.
lack of culture among, **3**, 243.
not creative in the eleventh century, **3**, 281.
occupations of, **3**, 281.
compared with the Christians, **3**, 281.
devoted to the study of the Talmud, **3**, 281, 419.
suffer during the crusades, **3**, 297, 351–4.
under Henry IV, **3**, 298.
expect the Messiah, **3**, 298.
dependent on the emperor, **3**, 308.
gloom and bigotry of, **3**, 309.
debts owing to, repudiated by the pope, **3**, 349.
become "servi cameræ," **3**, 356–7, 416–17, 516, 569.
degradation of, **3**, 357.
in the twelfth century, **3**, 416–21.
protected by the emperors during the crusades, **3**, 416.

Germany, the Jews of (*continued*), privileges of, **3**, 417–18.
massacred under Henry VI, **3**, 418–19.
high morality of, **3**, 419.
little affected by the Fourth Lateran Council, **3**, 516–17.
heavily taxed, **3**, 517.
naïve faith of, **3**, 549.
accused of aiding Jenghis-Khan, **3**, 580–1.
charged with the blood accusation, **3**, 583–5, 635.
persecuted after Frederick II's death, **3**, 611–12.
address Solomon ben Adret for religious decisions, **3**, 620.
in the Maimunist controversy, **3**, 624.
piety of, **3**, 625.
determine to emigrate, **3**, 634, 637.
offer to ransom Meïr of Rothenburg, **3**, 639–40.
persecuted by Rindfleisch, **4**, 35–7.
neglect the Talmud in the fourteenth century, **4**, 96.
under Louis IV, **4**, 96–7.
during the Armleder persecutions, **4**, 97–8.
during the Black Death persecutions, **4**, 105–111.
intellectual decay among, **4**, 133–4.
effect of persecution on, **4**, 166.
under Sigismund, **4**, 218.
privileges of, confirmed, **4**, 219.
liturgy of, compiled by Maharil, **4**, 225.
fast during the Hussite wars, **4**, 225–6.
neglect the Talmud in the fifteenth century, **4**, 227.
hatred of, increases, **4**, 248; **5**, 528, 532–3.

Germany, the Jews of (*continued*),
bear the expenses of the Council of Constance, **4**, 248.
under Albert II, **4**, 249.
terrified by John of Capistrano, **4**, 258.
urged to emigrate to Turkey, **4**, 271–3.
under Frederick III, **4**, 293–4, 413.
influence the Jews of Italy, **4**, 294.
speak a corrupt jargon, **4**, 388–9.
representative of, **4**, 414.
uncertain lot of, under Maximilian I, **4**, 414–15.
find a refuge in Poland, **4**, 418, 420.
carry the German language to Poland, **4**, 421.
expulsion of, proposed, **4**, 427.
ordered to submit their books to Pfefferkorn, **4**, 429.
citizens of the Holy Roman Empire, **4**, 443.
the extermination of, planned, **4**, 462–3.
narrow-mindedness of, **4**, 479.
adherents of Asher Lämmlein, **4**, 483.
suffer through the Protestant Reformation, **4**, 542–3.
submit questions to the Polish Talmudists, **4**, 639.
submit disputes to the Synod of the Four Countries, **4**, 644.
during the Catholic reaction, **4**, 652, 653.
seek refuge in Amsterdam, **4**, 680.
in the seventeenth century, **4**, 694–5.
under Matthias, **4**, 700–1.
and the Thirty Years' War, **4**, 701.

Germany, the Jews of (*continued*),
help the Jews of Poland, **4**, 707–8; **5**, 16.
intercede for the Jews of Vienna, **5**, 171.
poverty of, **5**, 205.
Dohm's apology begins the emancipation of, **5**, 356–7.
after Mendelssohn's death, **5**, 395–6.
attracted to French literature, **5**, 411.
apostasy among, **5**, 420.
decay of morality among, **5**, 422.
emancipated by the French, **5**, 459.
not well thought of, **5**, 461–3.
subject to the poll-tax, **5**, 464.
in the constitution drawn up by Humboldt, **5**, 514.
attacked by J. F. Fries, **5**, 521.
defenders of, **5**, 521–3, 533–4.
the "hep, hep!" persecutions of, **5**, 528–32.
writers among, **5**, 534–5.
rapid advance of, **5**, 557.
under Polish influence, **5**, 558.
estranged from Judaism, **5**, 560.
influenced by Bernays and Mannheimer, **5**, 582.
effect of the July Revolution on, **5**, 598, 600.
forced into reforms, **5**, 628.
and the Damascus affair, **5**, 669.
rupture among, **5**, 672, 674.

Germany, the Jews of, emancipation of. *See* Emancipation of the German Jews, the.

Germany, rabbis of, in sympathy with Solomon Petit, **3**, 627.
insignificance of, **4**, 133.
willing to excommunicate Luzzatto, **5**, 241.

Germany, rabbis of (*continued*), oppose the Reform movement, 5, 571.
protest against the Brunswick rabbinical conference, 5, 682.
Germany, North, the Jews of, few in number, 4, 111.
the Protestant Reformation in, 4, 469.
Jews tolerated in the towns of, 4, 686.
Germany, South, the Jews of, charged with the blood accusation, 4, 227.
attacked by Lutheran peasants, 4, 542.
Germany, Young, the creation of Börne and Heine, 5, 556.
compelled to advocate Jewish emancipation, 5, 602.
Gerona, Serachya Halevi Gerundi persecuted by the Jews of, 3, 389.
home of the Kabbala, 3, 556; 4, 1.
the Jews of, persecuted, 4, 172.
Geronimo de Santa Fé. *See* Joshua ben Joseph Ibn-Vives Allorqui.
Gerrick, commissioner of Louis the Pious to Agobard, 3, 166.
Gershom ben Jehuda (960–1028), disciple of Leontin, founds a Talmud school at Mayence, 3, 242, 243.
writes commentaries on the Talmud, 3, 243–4.
authority of, 3, 244, 245.
studies the Massora, 3, 244.
forbids polygamy, 3, 244.
regulates the carrying of letters, 3, 244–5.
penitential hymns by, 3, 246.
son of, an apostate, 3, 246.
Gershom ben Jehuda (*continued*), protects repentant apostates, 3, 246.
memory of, perpetuated by the Mayence community, 3, 247.
consults Haï Gaon, 3, 252.
introduces Talmud study in France and Germany, 3, 281.
Talmudical work of, supplanted by Rashi's, 3, 288.
abrogation of the polygamy ordinance of, 3, 378.
Gerson, Christian, vilifies the Talmud, 5, 181.
Gersonides. *See* Levi ben Gerson.
Gerundi. *See* En-Vidal Ephraim; Jacob ben Sheshet; Jonah ben Abraham; Nissim; Serachya Halevi.
Gerville, Cahier de, favors the emancipation of the Jews, 5, 444–5.
Gesenius, exegete, 5, 623, 695.
Gesereth ha-Roïm. *See* Pastoureaux.
Gesereth Mezoraim, the persecution caused by lepers in France, 4, 57–8.
Ghassanids, the, Arab tribe, 3, 67, 68.
Ghatafan, the, Arab tribe, induced to make war upon Mahomet, 3, 79.
distrustful of their allies, 3, 80.
promise help to the Jews of Chaibar, 3, 82.
Ghazati. *See* Nathan Benjamin Levi.
Ghent, the Jews of, expelled, 4, 662.
Ghetto, Venetian Jew quarter, the first in Italy, 4, 408.
See Jew's quarter.

Ghinucci, Geronimo de, cardinal, and the Portuguese Inquisition, **4**, 507, 516, 520.
Ghirondi, rabbi of Padua, scholar, **5**, 622.
Ghuzz, Turkish tribe, allied with the Jews of Khorasan, **3**, 434.
Gibbethon, Danite city, occupied by the Philistines, **1**, 189.
attacked by Elah's army, **1**, 192.
Omri chosen king at, **1**, 192.
Gibeah (Geba), Philistine garrison of, killed by Jonathan, **1**, 85.
Saul's capital, **1**, 89, 91.
inhabitants of, flee before the Philistines, **1**, 104.
Gibeon, Joshua's victory at, **1**, 34–5.
seat of a high priest, **1**, 120.
Gibeonites, the, submit to Joshua, **1**, 34.
massacre of, under Saul, **1**, 94.
murder the descendants of Saul, **1**, 123.
under Ezra, **1**, 367.
Gibraltar, the fortress of, asked as a refuge for Marranos, **4**, 282.
Gideon, judge, delivers the Israelites from the Midianites, **1**, 62–3.
the ideal of Oliver Cromwell, **5**, 26.
Gihon, river west of Jerusalem, **1**, 114.
Gilboa, mount, description of, **1**, 44.
battle of, between Saul and the Philistines, **1**, 103.
Gilead, balm of, where found, **1**, 43.
description of, **1**, 50.
first scene of Elijah's activity, **1**, 200.
Gilead, the inhabitants of, prosperity of, **1**, 64.
appeal to Judas Maccabæus, **1**, 474–5.
emigrate to Judæa, **1**, 476.
Gilgal, camp of the Israelites, **1**, 32, 40.
Samuel holds popular assemblies at, **1**, 78.
Saul at, **1**, 85–6.
the tribes pay homage to Saul at, **1**, 90.
Samuel reproves Saul at, **1**, 92–3.
David met at, by the men of Judah, **1**, 146, 147.
an association of prophets at, **1**, 205.
visited by Elijah, **1**, 208.
development of the prophetical school at, **1**, 234.
Gilion, Evangels, **2**, 378.
Gil-Nunjoz, bishop of Palma, charges the Jews with the blood accusation, **4**, 246.
Gilo, birthplace of Ahithophel, **1**, 123.
Gimso, explanation of, **2**, 330.
See Emmaus.
Ginæa, murder of Galilæans at, **2**, 243.
Girgashites, the, subdivision of the Canaanites, **1**, 3.
Gischala, the Judæans of, forced into insurrection, **2**, 272–3.
in possession of the Zealots, **2**, 289.
taken by Titus, **2**, 290.
the Jews of, in the twelfth century, **3**, 427.
Giulio, cardinal, and Reubeni, **4**, 492.
Giza, teacher of the Law, flees during Kobad's persecutions, **3**, 4.
principal of the Sora academy, **3**, 5.

Giza (*continued*), Saburean, **3**, 6.
commits the Talmud to writing, **3**, 6–7.
successors to, not known, **3**, 7.
Gladiatorial combats introduced into Antioch, **1**, 444.
Glaphyra, daughter of Archelaus of Cappadocia, wife of Alexander, **2**, 112.
second and third husband and son of, **2**, 128.
Glass-working, occupation of the Antioch Jews, **3**, 426.
Gleaning, the right of, granted to heathens, **2**, 478.
Gleim, admires "Phædon," **5**, 307.
Gley, priest, interested in Napoleon's Synhedrion, **5**, 494.
Glogau, the Jews of, massacred, **4**, 111.
Chayon at, **5**, 218.
Jews from, settle in Brandenburg, **5**, 174.
"**Glorious Stone**, or the Image of Nebuchadnezzar, The," by Manasseh ben Israel, **5**, 37–8.
"**Glory** to the Virtuous," drama by Luzzatto, **5**, 242–4.
Glynn, Lord Chief Justice, on Cromwell's commission for the Jewish question, **5**, 43.
Gnosis, the higher knowledge of God, **2**, 374.
Gnosticism, spread of, **2**, 374.
sects of, **2**, 375.
system of, **2**, 375–7.
influence of, on Judaism, **2**, 377, 380–1.
Akiba deprecates the influence of, **2**, 382.
Gnostics, the, theosophists, **2**, 374–7.
mystic-allegoric language of, **2**, 374.
Gnostics, the (*continued*), the God of, **1**, 375–6.
influence Elisha ben Abuya, **2**, 377.
tamper with the Septuagint, **2**, 386.
hostility of, accentuates the legal character of Judaism, **2**, 471.
God, the name of, not pronounced, **2**, 413.
Godard, and the emancipation of the French Jews, **5**, 443.
God-flesh, Francisco. *See* Astruc Raimuch.
Godfrey, bishop of Würzburg, grants privileges to the Jews, **4**, 259.
banishes the Jews, **4**, 259–60.
Godfrey of Bouillon, takes Jerusalem, **3**, 308.
Goethe, admires "Phædon," **5**, 307.
expresses regard for Solomon Maimon, **5**, 409.
romanticism of, **5**, 423.
prejudices of, against the Jews, **5**, 461, 462.
Goldberg, Samuel Löb, founder of the "Kerem Chemed," **5**, 621.
Goldbergs, the, Hebrew style of, **5**, 617.
"**Golden Bull**," the, issued at the Diet of Nuremberg, **4**, 128.
"**Golden Penny**," the, tax imposed on the Jews, **4**, 96–7, 166.
Goldschmidt, Moritz, founder of the "Israelitische Allianz," **5**, 703.
Goldsmid brothers, the, in the Damascus affair, **5**, 645.
Golgotha, the place of skulls, **2**, 165.
temple to Venus on, **2**, 422.

Goliath, Philistine champion, **1**, 95.
killed by David, **1**, 97.
Gomez, archbishop of Toledo, at the Burgos disputation, **4**, 140.
Gomez, Antonio Enriquez de. *See* Paz, Enrique Enriquez de.
Gomez, Duarte. *See* Usque, Solomon.
Gomez, Isaac, de Sosa, Marrano poet, **5**, 113.
Gonsalvo de Cordova, viceroy of Naples, employs a Jewish physician, **4**, 384–5.
descendant of, a Jewish author, **4**, 385, 666; **5**, 54.
opposes the banishment of the Jews, **4**, 385.
dismissal of, **4**, 385.
Gonzago, Ludovico, duke, employs a Jewish physician, **4**, 287.
Gonzago, Vicenzo, duke of Mantua, permits the use of the expurgated Talmud, **4**, 659.
Gonzalez, Luis, Marrano, tries to suppress the Inquisition, **4**, 329.
Gonzalo de Santa Maria, son of Solomon Levi, Benedict XIII's agent, **4**, 216, 217.
Good Friday. *See* Eastertide.
"Good News of the Messiah for Israel," by Paul Felgenhauer, **5**, 36.
Gorgias, Syrian general, invades Judæa, **1**, 467.
at Emmaus, **1**, 468.
defeated by Judas Maccabæus, **1**, 468–9, 476.
Görres, romanticist, **5**, 516.
Goshen, home of the Israelites in Egypt, **1**, 7.
in the Zohar, **4**, 23.
Gospels, the four, translated into Hebrew, **4**, 143.
Gotha, the Jews of, during the Black Death persecutions, **4**, 109.
Goths, the, invade the Roman empire, **2**, 527.
in Rome, **3**, 27.
Göttingen, Jews tolerated in, **4**, 686.
Gottschalk, crusader, and the Jews, **3**, 298.
Göze, opponent of Lessing, **5**, 326.
Gozolas, name borne by Gallic Jews, **3**, 36.
Gracian. *See* Solomon Gracian.
Gradis, David, member of Malesherbes' commission, **5**, 432.
representative French Jew, **5**, 436, 438.
Graes, Ortuin de (Ortuinus Gratius), inspires anti-Jewish pamphlets, **4**, 424.
writes the "Mirror for Admonition," **4**, 425.
helps Pfefferkorn with "The Enemy of the Jews," **4**, 428.
tool of Hoogstraten, **4**, 450.
"Letters of Obscurantists" directed against, **4**, 461.
Grammar, a Hebrew, by Saadiah in Arabic, **3**, 190.
by Abulsari Sahal ben Mazliach Kohen, **3**, 204.
by Samuel Ibn-Nagrela, **3**, 261.
by Ibn-Janach, **3**, 262–3.
by Yizchaki, **3**, 273.
by Abraham Ibn-Ezra, **3**, 371.
by David Kimchi, **3**, 394.
by Profiat Duran, **4**, 191.
by Judah ben Yechiel, **4**, 289–90.
by Ibn-Gebirol, **3**, 267.
by Reuchlin, **4**, 434.
by Elias Levita, **4**, 472.
Grammar, Hebrew, the study of, stimulated by Karaism, **3**, 136.

Grammar, Hebrew, the study of, (*continued*), among the Spanish Jews, **3,** 235, 317; **4,** 91.
decays in the post-Maimunic period, **3,** 561.

Grammarians and Lexicographers, Jewish, list of:

Aaron ben Asher,
Abraham de Balmes,
Abraham ben Meïr Ibn-Ezra,
Abu Ibrahim Isaac Ibn-Kastar ben Yasus,
Abulsari Sahal ben Mazliach Kohen,
David de Pomis,
David Kimchi,
Dunash ben Labrat,
Elias Levita,
Jacob Tam,
Jehuda Ibn-Balam,
Jehuda Ibn-Daud,
Jephet Ibn-Ali Halevi,
Jonah Marinus,
Joseph ben Isaac Kimchi,
Judah ben Yechiel,
Lara, David Coen de
Mar-Zemach I ben Paltoi,
Menachem ben Saruk,
Moses ben Asher,
Moses ben Samuel Ibn-G'ikatilia,
Moses Kimchi,
Musaphia, Benjamin
Nachshon ben Zadok,
Nathan ben Yechiel,
Profiat Duran,
Saadiah,
Samuel Halevi Ibn-Nagrela,
Solomon Ibn-Gebirol,
Solomon Lurya.

Granada, called the city of the Jews, **3,** 42.
the Jews masters of, **3,** 109.
Talmud school of, **3,** 236.
Cordova Jews emigrate to, **3,** 255.
capital of the Berber kingdom, **3,** 256.
home of the descendants of the Exilarchs, **3,** 275.
massacre of the Arabs of, **3,** 276–7.
invaded by Almotassem, **3,** 278.
Mahometan court of, cultured, **3,** 291.
conspiracy against the Mahometans of, **3,** 316.

Granada (*continued*), home of the Ibn-Ezra brothers, **3,** 318.
Talmud school of, destroyed, **3,** 384.
Samuel Ibn-Wakar farms the import duties of, **4,** 80–1.
at war with Castile, **4,** 84–5.
ally of Pedro the Cruel, **4,** 125, 126.
forced converts emigrate to, **4,** 179, 318, 351.
war of Ferdinand and Isabella with, **4,** 344.
Jewish physicians of, **4,** 344.
fall of, **4,** 345–6.
entered by Ferdinand and Isabella, **4,** 345.
Jews disappear from, **4,** 354.
autos-da-fé in, **5,** 91–2.

Granada, the Jews of, Samuel Ibn-Nagrela chief of, **3,** 259.
enjoy complete equality, **3,** 261.
Joseph Ibn-Nagrela chief of, **3,** 274.
arouse the hatred of the Berbers, **3,** 275, 278.
persecuted by the Berbers, **3,** 278–80, 281.
Arabic scholars, **4,** 60.
protected by Boabdil's treaty, **4,** 345.

Granville, Lord, English ambassador at Paris, presents Montefiore at court, **5,** 668.

Granville, Ranulph de, courtier of Richard I, protects the Jews, **3,** 410.

Grapte, granddaughter of Helen of Adiabene, erects a palace in Jerusalem, **2,** 219.

Grattenauer, opposes the emancipation of the Jews, **5,** 468, 472.
refuted, **5,** 470, 471.

Gratus, Valerius, fourth procurator of Judæa, **2,** 135, 137.

Great Assembly (Keneseth ha-Gedolah), the, under Ezra and Nehemiah, **1,** 381.
a permanent religious council, **1,** 394.
traditional laws ascribed to, **2,** 19.

"**Great Assembly,** the," the court of the Exilarch, **3,** 95.

Greece, Jews from, form a congregation in Constantinople, **4,** 402.

Greece, the Jews of, celebrate two days of the new-moon, **2,** 363.
autonomy of, **3,** 27.
occupations of, **3,** 175.
not permitted to hold office, **3,** 175.
in the twelfth century, **3,** 424-5.
in the sixteenth century, **4,** 406.
molested by the Greek Catholics, **4,** 552-3.

Greek art, under John Hyrcanus, **2,** 14.
under Herod, **2,** 118.

Greek Christian communities, established by Paul, **2,** 227-8.

Greek Christians, the, despise the Judæan Christians, **2,** 231.
differences between, and Judæan Christians, **2,** 232.
See Pagan Christians.

Greek colonies, in Judæa, **1,** 419.

Greek culture, in Judæa in the third century, **1,** 426, 427-9.
acquired by Jews in the Amoraim period, **2,** 537-8.

Greek customs, among the Judæans, **1,** 427, 527.

Greek games, introduced into Judæa, **1,** 445.

Greek islands, the, the Spanish exiles on, **4,** 363-4.

Greek Judæans, the, become Nazarenes, **2,** 219-20, 221.
attack the Law, **2,** 221-2.

Greek language, the, spoken by Judæans in Hasmonæan times, **2,** 15.
study of, forbidden by the teachers of the Law under Hadrian, **2,** 400.
acquirement of, permitted by Jochanan bar Napacha, **2,** 494.
spoken by the Jews of Italy in the twelfth century, **3,** 423.

Greek learning, the, of the Alexandrian Judæans, **1,** 505.

Greek philosophy, an aid to Christianity, **2,** 373.

Greek poems, by a Samaritan and a Judæan, **1,** 517.

Greek translation of the Scriptures, by Akylas, **2,** 385, 386-7.
ordered to be read in the synagogues by Justinian I, **3,** 14-15.
See also Septuagint, the.

Greek translations of Hebrew works, **2,** 359.

Greek words in the Mishna, **2,** 461.

Greeks, the, characteristics of, **1,** 411.
influence of, on the Judæans, **1,** 427-9.
in Judæa, hate the Judæans, **1,** 434; **2,** 246-7.
learn Judaism through the Septuagint, **1,** 512-14.
beyond the Jordan, hostile to Judæa, **2,** 7.

Greeks, the (*continued*), cultured, opposed to Christianity, **2,** 229.
and Jews, contrasted, **5,** 706–8.
Grégoire, Abbé, influenced by Ensheim, **5,** 401.
champion of the Jews, **5,** 432.
competes for the Metz prize on the Jewish question, **5,** 434–5.
in the National Assembly, **5,** 435, 440.
exhorts the Jews to obtain naturalization, **5,** 436.
intercedes for the Alsatian Jews, **5,** 437.
entertains a distorted view of Jewish history, **5,** 593.
Gregory I, pope, protects the Jews against forced conversions, **3,** 25, 33.
forbids Jews to own slaves, **3,** 33, 34.
remits the land-tax of converts, **3,** 33.
praises Reccared for his attitude towards the Jews, **3,** 34, 46.
Gregory VII (Hildebrand), pope, on the venality of the clergy, **3,** 287.
and the Jews, **3,** 293, 298.
forbids Jews to hold offices in Christian countries, **3,** 293–4.
tries to arrest the influence of the Jews at the Castilian court, **3,** 294.
Gregory IX, pope, permits the burning of the Talmud, **4,** 460.
hostile to the Jews, **3,** 519, 520.
enforces the decrees of the Fourth Lateran Council, **3,** 521.
banishes philosophical writings from the University of Paris, **3,** 528.
Gregory IX, pope (*continued*), establishes the Inquisition in France, **3,** 542.
legate of, in the Maimunist controversy, **3,** 542.
re-issues the Jewish constitution of Innocent III, **3,** 564.
reproaches Frederick II with heterodoxy, **3,** 567.
orders a crusade, **3,** 570.
deprecates the compulsory baptism of Jews, **3,** 570.
the Talmud accused before, **3,** 573–4.
orders the confiscation of the Talmud, **3,** 574–5.
Gregory X, pope, protects Jews against forcible baptism, **3,** 635.
Gregory XIII, pope, forbids the employment of Jewish physicians, **4,** 653–4.
puts the Jews under the Inquisition, **4,** 654.
orders the confiscation of the Talmud, **4,** 654.
institutes sermons for Jews, **4,** 654–5, 706.
Gregory, bishop of Tours, charges a poet to celebrate the achievements of Avitus, **3,** 39.
Grimani, Dominico, cardinal, employs a Jewish physician, **4,** 411.
in the Reuchlin-Hoogstraten case, **4,** 458.
Grodno, Mordecai Jafa rabbi at, **4,** 645.
Groede, burial ground of the Dutch Jews at, **4,** 672.
Gröningen, Martin von, translates the "Augenspiegel," **4,** 460.
Grotius, Hugo, studies Hebrew, **5,** 21.

Grotius, Hugo (*continued*), introduced to Manasseh ben Israel, **5,** 22.
Grund, Christian, advocate of Jewish emancipation, **5,** 463, 465–6.
Guarini, work of, translated, **5,** 114.
Gudeo, papal legate, presides over the Council of Vienna, **3,** 611.
Guebres, neo-Persians. *See* Sassanides.
Guglielmo di Portaleone, Italian physician, **4,** 287.
" Guide of the Perplexed, The " (Moréh Nebuchim, Dalalat al Haïrin), religious philosophical work by Maimonides, **3,** 477–85.
addressed to Joseph Ibn-Aknin, **3,** 478.
connects Judaism and philosophy, **3,** 478–9, 485–6.
explains the Jewish doctrine of the universe, **3,** 479.
on the influence of God on the universe of entities, **3,** 480–1.
on the nature of sin, **3,** 481–2.
on the intellectual and moral powers of man, **3,** 482–3.
on the prophetic faculty and the prophets, **3,** 482–4.
on miracles, **3,** 483.
on Moses, **3,** 483–4.
on revelation, **3,** 484–5.
supplants all other Jewish religious-philosophical systems, **3,** 486; **4,** 479.
effect of, on the Mahometan and Christian world, **3,** 486.
Latin translation of, **3,** 486, 542–3; **4,** 60, 474.
weakness of, **3,** 486–7.
condemned by Mahometans, **3,** 488.
" Guide of the Perplexed, The " (*continued*), condemned by Abraham ben David, **3,** 490.
Hebrew translation of, **3,** 490–2.
assailed by anti-Maimunists, **3,** 523.
satirized, **3,** 538.
denounced by Solomon Petit, **3,** 626.
studied by the Italian Jews, **3,** 629.
ordered to be burnt at Accho, **3,** 631.
defended by Shem-Tob Falaquera, **3,** 634
attacked by Aaron ben Elia Nicomedi, **4,** 95.
neglected in Spain in the fourteenth century, **4,** 143.
studied by Moses Isserles, **4,** 638.
studied by Mendelssohn, **5,** 295.
studied by Solomon Maimon, **5,** 407.
Guido Ubaldo, duke of Urbino, permits Marranos to live in Pesaro, **4,** 569, 578.
banishes the Marranos, **4,** 580–1.
Guidon, physician, convert to Islam, employed to convert Sabbataï Zevi, **5,** 153–4.
Guienne, the Jews of, under Henry II, **3,** 409.
wells of, poisoned, **4,** 57.
Guilds, the, antagonize the Jews in Frankfort, **4,** 695, 696.
antagonize the Jews in Worms, **4,** 698–9.
persecute the Jews in Poland, **5,** 1.
arouse passion against the Jews of Prussia, **5,** 191.
Guldberg, von, Danish minister, and Mendelssohn's Pentateuch translation, **5,** 333.

Gumpertz, Aaron Solomon, friend of Mendelssohn, **5,** 295.
Gumprecht, obtains the emancipation of the Jews of Frankfort, **5,** 505.
Gunther of Schwarzberg, at war with Emperor Charles IV, **4,** 109, 110.
Gustavus Adolphus, the daughter of. *See* Christina of Sweden.
Guttenstein, de, count, imprisons Pfefferkorn, **4,** 424.
Gymnasia, introduced into Jerusalem, **1,** 445.

H

Haaja. *See* Haï.
Haarlem, Jews not permitted to settle in, **4,** 685.
Haatakah, tradition, among the Karaites, **3,** 159.
Habakkuk, apocryphal additions to, **2,** 624.
Habor, the Ten Tribes colonized in, **1,** 265.
Habus, king of Granada, vizir of, patron of Samuel Ibn-Nagrela, **3,** 256.
makes Samuel Ibn-Nagrela minister, **3,** 256–7.
poems addressed to, **3,** 257.
parties formed at the death of, **3,** 258.
makes Samuel Ibn-Nagrela chief of the Granada Jews, **3,** 259.
employs Jewish officials, **3,** 319.
Hadad, prince of Idumæa, allied with Shishak, **1,** 176.
regains possession of Idumæa, **1,** 176–7.
Hadadezer, king of Zobah, ally of the Ammonites, defeated by David, **1,** 126–7.
Hadrian, pope, hostile to the Jews, **3,** 142.
Hadrian, emperor, hostile to the Jews, **2,** 350; **5,** 724–5.
rebellions against, **2,** 399.
clemency of, to the rebels, **2,** 400.
Hadrian, emperor (*continued*), deposes and executes Lucius Quietus, **2,** 400–1.
permits the restoration of the Temple, **2,** 401–2.
withdraws the permission, **2,** 402–3.
visits Judæa, **2,** 406.
and Joshua ben Chananya, **2,** 406–7.
coins of, **2,** 407, 419.
projects the rebuilding of Jerusalem as a pagan city, **2,** 407.
mocks at Judaism, **2,** 407–8.
first action of, against Bar-Cochba, **2,** 411.
concerned about the Bar-Cochba rebellion, **2,** 413–14.
sends Julius Severus to Judæa, **2,** 414.
persecutes Jewish prisoners and fugitives, **2,** 419–20.
taxes the Jews heavily, **2,** 420.
decrees laws against Judaism, **2,** 421, 423–6.
sends Turnus Rufus to Judæa, **2,** 421.
rebuilds Jerusalem, **2,** 421–2.
column in honor of, **2,** 422.
erects heathen temples in Judæa, **2,** 422.
tries to graft paganism on Judaism, **2,** 422.
cruelty of, to the dead, **2,** 430.

Hadrian, emperor (*continued*), persecutes the Christians, **2**, 430-1.
death of, **2**, 432.
decrees of, revoked, **2**, 433.
edict of, revived, **3**, 23.
Hagadah, the. *See* Agada, the.
Hagenau, the duke of, Jews of Alsace tributary to, **5**, 348.
Haggaï, Jewish name of Robert de Redingge, **3**, 641.
Haggaï, prophet, urges the completion of the second Temple, **1**, 359.
extols Zerubbabel, **1**, 360.
Haggaï. *See also* Chaggaï.
Haggeth, wife of David, **1**, 135.
Hagin (**Chayim**) **Denlacres**, chief rabbi of England, **3**, 644.
Hagiographa, the, commentaries on, by Solomon ben Yerucham, **3**, 206.
by Joseph Kara, **3**, 346.
Haï ben David (890-897), Gaon of Pumbeditha, **3**, 183.
Haï (**Haaja, Haya**) **ben Sherira** (969-1038), chief judge, **3**, 233, 250.
Gaon of Pumbeditha, **3**, 234, 250.
popularity of, **3**, 234, 250.
authority of, rivaled by Gershom ben Jehuda's, **3**, 244.
character and attainments of, **3**, 250.
compared with Saadiah, **3**, 250.
consults the Patriarch of the Eastern Christians, **3**, 250.
consults the Koran, **3**, 251.
commentary on the Talmud by, **3**, 251.
denounces mysticism, **3**, 251-2.
consulted by African and European Talmudists, **3**, 252, 260.
Haï (**Haaja, Haya**) **ben Sherira** (*continued*), the head of Judaism, **3**, 252.
revives the academy of Sora, **3**, 253.
eulogies on, **3**, 253.
Haï Gaon. *See* Haï ben Sherira.
Haidamaks, the, ravages of, among Polish Jews, **5**, 8-10. 11-12, 388.
See Cossacks, the.
Hakim, Fatimide caliph, decrees the conversion of Jews to Islam, **3**, 247.
ordains Jew badges, **3**, 247-8.
expels the Jews, **3**, 248.
assassination of, **3**, 248.
Halacha, the, oral teaching, **2**, 328, 329.
knowledge of, acquired by pagans, **2**, 384.
cultivated by Rabba bar Nachmani, **2**, 576, 578.
neglected under Theodosius II, **2**, 623.
See also Law, the oral; Mishna, the.
Halacha, the, the study of, scorned by the Nazarenes, **2**, 371.
declines in Judæa, **2**, 540.
new method of, introduced by Judah ben Ezekiel, **2**, 545.
strengthens the judgment, **2**, 625.
Halachas, the, Gamaliel II maintains the authority of, **2**, 338, 339.
arrangement of, by Akiba, **2**, 353, 354.
collected by the half-Tanaites, **2**, 470-1.
See also Law, the oral; Mishna, the.
Halachic development, the, of the Law, **5**, 723-4.
"**Halachoth,**" by Alfassi, **3**, 286.

Halachoth Gedoloth, by Simon of Cairo, **3,** 179.
Halachoth Ketuoth, work by Judah the Blind, **3,** 136.
supplemented by Halachoth Gedoloth, **3,** 179.
Halah, the Ten Tribes colonized in, **1,** 265.
Halberstadt, the Talmud school of, closed, **5,** 567.
Haleb. *See* Aleppo.
Halevi, Aaron. *See* Aaron Halevi.
Halevi, Abraham. *See* Abraham Ibn-Daud Halevi.
Halevi, Abu Said ben Chalfon. *See* Abu Said.
Halevi, Ali. *See* Ali Halevi.
Halevi, Eleazar ben Joel. *See* Eleazar ben Joel Halevi.
Halevi, Elia, French Jewish poet, **5,** 460.
Halevi, Elias. *See* Elias Halevi.
Halevi, Isaac. *See* Isaac ben Asher Halevi; Isaac Halevi.
Halevi, Jacob ben Moses Mölin. *See* Jacob ben Moses.
Halevi, Jehuda. *See* Jehuda Halevi.
Halevi, Jephet Ibn-Ali. *See* Jephet Ibn-Ali Halevi.
Halevi, Joseph ben Ephraim Ibn-Benveniste. *See* Joseph ben Ephraim Ibn-Benveniste Halevi.
Halevi, Joseph ben Meïr Ibn-Migash. *See* Joseph ben Meïr Ibn-Migash.
Halevi, Joseph Amarkala. *See* Joseph Amarkala Halevi.
Halevi, Meïr ben Baruch. *See* Meïr ben Baruch Halevi.
Halevi, Meïr ben Todros. *See* Meïr ben Todros Halevi.
Halevi, Moses Uri. *See* Moses Uri Halevi.
Halevi, Samuel. *See* Samuel ben Abraham Ibn-Chasdaï; Samuel ben Ali Halevi; Samuel Halevi; Samuel Halevi Ibn-Nagrela.
Halevi, Serachya. *See* Serachya Halevi Gerundi; Serachya Halevi Saladin.
Halfen, Azaria and Solomon, rabbis at Damascus, charged with ritual murder, **5,** 638.
ordered to translate suspicious Talmud passages, **5,** 640.
Halicz, Karaites in, **5,** 182.
Halle, Aaron. *See* Wolfsohn, Aaron.
Halles district, the, of Paris, opposes the emancipation of the Jews, **5,** 445.
Hamadan (Fars), center of the Judghanites, **3,** 149-50.
the community of, excommunicated, **3,** 194.
the Jews of, in the twelfth century, **3,** 434.
Hamath, the inhabitants of, colonized in Samaria, **1,** 285.
Hamburg, settlement of Jews in, **4,** 685-8.
the Lutherans of, object to Jews, **4,** 685, 687, 691-3.
refuses permission to German Jews to settle there, **4,** 685-6.
harbors Portuguese Jews as "traders," **4,** 686-7.
admits Jews under restrictions, **4,** 688.
bank of, supported by Jews, **4,** 689.
synagogues at, **4,** 689-90, 691.
German Jews in, **4,** 691.
posts of honor occupied by Jews in, **4,** 692.
called "little Jerusalem," **4,** 693.

Hamburg (*continued*), Joseph Delmedigo at, **5,** 78.
the Sabbatian movement in, **5,** 139, 140–1, 150, 151, 155.
stagnation of trade in, **5,** 149.
Jews from, settle in Brandenburg, **5,** 174.
Portuguese Jews of, wealthy, **5,** 205.
rabbis of, Poles, **5,** 206.
Lessing at, **5,** 319–20.
the Reform movement in, **5,** 563–4.
Talmud school of, closed, **5,** 567.
the Dayanim of, oppose the Reform Temple, **5,** 570, 573.
the "hep, hep!" persecution in, **5,** 573.
Bernays appointed to the rabbinate of, **5,** 576–7.
conflagration in, **5,** 674.
See also Reform Temple Union, the.
Hamburg, the Jews of, described by John Miller, **4,** 690.
wish to settle in England, **5,** 18.
emancipated, **5,** 506.
Ha-Meassef, a Hebrew journal, **5,** 339. *See* "Gatherer, The."
Hamma, Jews tolerated in, **4,** 686.
Hammuna, friend of Chanina bar Chama, **2,** 456.
Hamon, Isaac, physician in Granada, power of, **4,** 344.
Hamon, Joseph, physician to Selim I, **4,** 401.
Hamon, Moses, physician to Solyman I, patron of Jewish literature, **4,** 401.
family of, exempt from taxes, **4,** 402.
protector of the Turkish Jews, **4,** 553.
Hamon, Moses (*continued*), disposes the sultan in favor of the Mendes family, **4,** 575.
Hanameel, cousin of Jeremiah, **1,** 290.
Hananel, gate, tower at, in Jerusalem, **1,** 231.
Hanania. *See* Chananya.
Hananiah, informs Nehemiah of the distress of the Judæans, **1,** 372.
commander of the Birah, **1,** 382.
Hanau, Solomon, teacher of Wessely, **5,** 367.
Hanau, Jews permitted to settle in, **4,** 695.
rabbi of, opposes the Reform movement, **5,** 571.
Handicrafts, Jews engage in, **3,** 401, 425, 426, 427, 606.
Jews forbidden to engage in, **4,** 203, 205, 216.
discussed by the French Synhedrion, **5,** 497.
See Artisans; Trades.
"**Handspiegel,**" by Pfefferkorn, Reuchlin's reply to, **4,** 446–8.
Hanna Bachari Bey, opponent of the Damascus Jews, **5,** 633, 635.
Hannah, mother of Samuel, **1,** 73.
Hanover, the flagellants in, **4,** 111.
Jews tolerated in, **4,** 686.
Chayon at, **5,** 231.
the Jews of, deprived of civil rights, **5,** 512.
Hanse Towns, the, object to the emancipation of the Jews, **5,** 519.
Hanse Towns, the, the Jews of, emancipated under French influence, **5,** 506.

Hanse towns, the, the Jews of (*continued*), send a deputy to the Congress of Vienna, **5**, 513.
oppression of, disapproved of, **5**, 514.
deprived of the rights secured by French influence, **5**, 519.

Hanukkah. *See* Chanuka.

Hanun, king of the Ammonites, at war with David, **1**, 126–7, 129.

Haphtarah, the lesson from the Prophets, **1**, 400.

Haquinet, son of Manessier de Vesoul, **4**, 150.

Hardenberg, Prussian minister, and the emancipation of the Jews, **5**, 507, 527.
disapproves of the oppression of the Jews, **5**, 514.
carelessness of, **5**, 519–20.

Hariri of Basra, Arabic poet, imitated by Solomon Ibn-Sakbel, **3**, 318.

Harith Ibn-Abu Shammir, kills the Jewish chiefs of Yathrib, **3**, 67.
feud of, with Samuel Ibn-Adiya, **3**, 68, 69.

Harith Ibn-Amru, Kendite prince, proselyte, **3**, 63.

"**Harmony of Heaven**, The," by Judah Leon Abrabanel, **4**, 480.

Haroun Alrashid, Abbassid caliph, and Charlemagne, **3**, 143.
re-enacts the "covenant of Omar," **3**, 145.
death of, **3**, 145.

Harp, Lake of the. *See* Tiberias.

Harrach, count, patron of Ben-David, **5**, 410.

Harrison, General, Jewish spirit of, **5**, 34.

Hartmann von Deggenburg, leads a massacre of Jews, **4**, 98.

Hartmann, Frederick Traugott, opponent of the Jews, **5**, 359, 361.

Hasmonæan dynasty, the, the members of:

Alexander I Jannæus,
Alexander (II),
Antigonus,
Aristobulus I,
Aristobulus II,
Hyrcanus I, John
Hyrcanus II,
Salome Alexandra,
Simon Tharsi.

Hasmonæan party, the, leaders of, **1**, 489.
comparison of, with the Assidæans, **1**, 489.
aims of, **1**, 489–90.
attacked by the Bene-Amri, **1**, 491.
defeated by Bacchides, **1**, 491.
fight for Antiochus VI, **1**, 498.

Hasmonæans, the, and Greek art, **2**, 14.
palace of, in Jerusalem, **2**, 14.
mausoleum of, **2**, 14.
hated by the Pharisees, **2**, 33.
assume the royal title, **2**, 35.
contrast between the first and the last, **2**, 84.
temporary character of the rule of, **2**, 143.
See also Maccabees, the.

Hasselbauer, bishop of Prague, friend of Eibeschütz, **5**, 250.

Hathor, an Egyptian goddess, **1**, 9.

Hatti Sherif, firman emancipating the Turkish Jews, **5**, 641, 664.

Hauran (Havvoth Jair). *See* Auranitis.

"**Havayot d'Abayi ve Raba**," **1**, 585.

Haya. *See* Haï ben Sherira.

Hazael, of Damascus, at war with Jehoram of Israel, **1**, 210.
gains territory from Jehu, **1**, 220–1.
at war with Jehoahaz and Joash, **1**, 221.
Hazor, rallying place of the Canaanites, **1**, 37.
Heathen, the, view held by, of Judæans and Judaism, **2**, 203.
adopt Judaism, **2**, 215–19.
disgusted with the deification of human beings, **2**, 228.
Judæans forbidden to deal with, **2**, 270.
join the Bar-Cochba rebellion, **2**, 410.
intercourse with, regulated by the Mishna, **2**, 476–8.
intercourse with, interdicted by Tertullian, **2**, 476–7.
permitted to glean, **2**, 478.
purchases from, permitted by Judah II, **2**, 483–4.
become acquainted with Jewish literature, **2**, 502.
relaxing of the laws against, **2**, 525.
Heber, the Kenite, in Charisi's Tachkemoni, **3**, 559.
Hebert, sets up the religion of Reason, **5**, 450.
Hebrew alphabet, the, Assyrian characters of, **1**, 395.
"**Hebrew Chrestomathy**," by Adam Martinet, **5**, 628, 629.
Hebrew grammar. *See* Grammar.
Hebrew language, the, cherished by the Babylonian exiles, **1**, 340, 364.
Judæans ignorant of, **1**, 386.
cultivated under the Hasmonæans, **2**, 14–15.
called New-Hebrew (Neo-Hebrew), **2**, 15.
Hebrew language, the (*continued*), used in the historical writings, **2**, 16.
mispronounced in Galilee, **2**, 149.
of the Mishna, **2**, 461.
spoken in Judæa, **2**, 461–2.
learnt by Origen, **2**, 488.
in the Amoraim period, **2**, 538–9.
interest in, under Theodosius II, **2**, 623, 625.
Jews forbidden to teach Christians, **2**, 624.
revived under Arab influence, **3**, 111–12.
furnished with vowel points, **3**, 112.
neglected in the ninth century, **3**, 157.
studied by Menachem ben Saruk, **3**, 224–5.
promoted by the controversy under Chasdaï Ibn-Shaprut, **3**, 226–7.
improvement in, in the twelfth century, **3**, 317.
taught as a means for conversion, **3**, 597, 640–1; **4**, 245.
words of, used by Spanish satirists, **4**, 181.
study of, introduced into Germany by Reuchlin, **4**, 432, 433, 434.
panegyric on, by Reuchlin, **4**, 433–4, 436.
study of, at the German universities advised by Reuchlin, **4**, 443.
studied by Egidio de Viterbo, **4**, 457.
professorships for, instituted, **4**, 471, 473, 474.
studied by Christians, **4**, 471–4, 651.
widely studied in Holland, **5**, 21.

Hebrew language, the (*continued*), society for the promotion of, **5,** 398–9.
a bond for the Jews of western Europe, **5,** 402.
love of, prevents apostasy, **5,** 420.
importance of, in the Jewish liturgy, **5,** 562.
omission of, from the divine service objected to, **5,** 564.
Portuguese pronunciation of, adopted in Hamburg, **5,** 571.
retained in the Vienna Temple, **5,** 580.
renaissance of, through Erter, **5,** 613, 616.
banishment of, from the liturgy proposed by Holdheim, **5,** 680.
abolition of, in the liturgy discussed, **5,** 685.
See also Grammar, Hebrew; Literature, Jewish.
Hebrew literature, allegories in, **1,** 158–9.
under Hezekiah, **1,** 279.
during the Babylonian Captivity, **1,** 334–6, 340–2.
in the Persian period, **1,** 410–11.
translated into Greek, **2,** 359.
See also Literature, Jewish; Judæo-Greek literature; Poetry.
"Hebrew Physician, The," by David de Pomis, **4,** 656–7.
"Hebrew Rites, The," by Leo Modena, **5,** 71–2, 180.
Hebrew writings. *See* Confiscation and burning of Hebrew books.
Hebron, king of, defeated by Joshua, **1,** 34–5.
chief city of Judah, **1,** 38, 77.
residence of David, **1,** 109.
David leaves, **1,** 114.
Hebron (*continued*), Absalom declared king in, **1,** 139.
owned by Idumæans, **1,** 435, 474.
Jewish prisoners sold at the slave markets of, **2,** 419.
Maimonides in, **3,** 457.
occupations of the Jews of, **4,** 75.
Sabbataï Zevi at, **5,** 128.
Hechal, the Holy Place, **1,** 165.
Hegel, influence of, on Edward Gans, **5,** 583.
on Young Israel, **5,** 585.
Heidelberg, the Jews of, persecuted, **5,** 530–1.
Heidelberg, the University of, on the confiscation of Hebrew books, **4,** 437, 441.
Spinoza offered a professorship at, **5,** 108.
Heidenheim, Wolf, one of the Measfim, Massoretic studies of, **5,** 400.
Heilmann, rabbi, opponent of Eibeschütz, **5,** 262, 263, 268, 269.
Heilperin, Jechiel, historian, **5,** 202.
Heine, Heinrich (1799–1854), as a Jew, **5,** 536, 544.
as a German, **5,** 537.
as poet, **5,** 537.
as a thinker, **5,** 544–5.
character of, **5,** 545, 555–6.
love of, for his mother, **5,** 545.
Jewish education of, **5,** 545–6.
pride of, in his race, **5,** 546.
attitude of, towards Judaism, **5,** 546.
influence of Berlin Jewish society on, **5,** 546.
joins the Society for the Culture of Jews, **5,** 547.
criticises the Jews, **5,** 547–8.

Heine, Heinrich (*continued*), contempt of, for apostates, **5,** 548–9, 551–2.
glorifies Jewish history in the "Rabbi of Bacharach," **5,** 549–50.
baptism of, **5,** 550–1.
characterizes Judaism and Christianity, **5,** 552.
on Shylock, **5,** 552–3.
on Moses, **5,** 553–5.
inspired by Jewish poetry, **5,** 555, 694.
on the "hep, hep!" persecutions, **5,** 556.
debt of the Jews to, **5,** 556.
debt of Germany to, **5,** 556.
on Isaac Bernays, **5,** 577.
on Moses Moser, **5,** 583.
on the journal of the Society for Culture, **5,** 586.
on Edward Gans's apostasy, **5,** 587.
compared with Steinheim, **5,** 607.
compared with Erter, **5,** 615–16.
on Hellenism and Judaism, **5,** 688.
Hejas, the Jews settle in, **3,** 54. *See* Arabia, northern.
Hejira, the, Mahomet's flight from Mecca, **3,** 73.
Helam, the battle of, the Aramæans defeated at, **1,** 127.
Helen, queen of Adiabene, proselyte, **2,** 216–17.
visits Jerusalem, **2,** 218, 224.
gift of, to the Temple, **2,** 218.
mausoleum of, **2,** 219.
Helicon, favorite of Caligula, **2,** 187.
Heliodorus, treasurer of Seleucus II, tries to force his way into the Temple, **1,** 438.
murders Seleucus, **1,** 443.
Heliopolis (Onion), district containing the Temple of Onias, **1,** 508.
revenues of, devoted to the Temple, **1,** 508.
called the Arabian province, **1,** 510.
Helisachar, incites the sons of Louis the Pious against their step-mother, **3,** 166.
Helkias, son of Onias IV, general, sides with Cleopatra, mother of Ptolemy VIII, **2,** 10, 12.
death of, **2,** 41.
Hell, attorney, levies blackmail on the Jews of Alsace, **5,** 349.
prevents debtors from paying Jews, **5,** 350.
banished, **5,** 350.
Hell, belief in, derived from Magianism, **1,** 403.
Hellenism, the attacks of, accentuate the legal character of Judaism, **2,** 471.
Hellenists, the, aims of, **1,** 435–6.
Onias III opposed to, **1,** 437.
persecute Onias III, **1,** 438–9, 444.
condemned by Jesus Sirach, **1,** 440–1.
invite the interference of Antiochus IV, **1,** 444.
introduce games and gymnasia into Judæa, **1,** 444–6.
refuse to sacrifice to Hercules, **1,** 446.
procure Jason's dismissal, **1,** 446–7.
disapprove of Menelaus as high priest, **1,** 447.
take refuge in the Acra, **1,** 454.
betray the hiding places of the Chassidim, **1,** 457–8.

Hellenists, the (*continued*), appeal to Antiochus V, **1**, 478.
lose favor at the Syrian court, **1**, 480.
oppose Judas Maccabæus, **1**, 480, 482.
fear Judas Maccabæus, **1**, 483.
masters of Palestine, **1**, 488.
called "Traitors of the Covenant," **1**, 489.
plan to deliver Jonathan and Simon to the Syrians, **1**, 493.
deserted by Bacchides, **1**, 494.
take refuge in Bethzur, **1**, 494.
appeal to Demetrius II, **1**, 497.
driven out of Bethzur, **1**, 498.
secret understanding of, with Diodotus Tryphon, **1**, 500.
driven from their strongholds, **1**, 523.
seek refuge in Egypt, **1**, 523.
end of, **1**, 523–4.

Heller, Lipmann (1579–1654), Talmudist, character and attainments of, **4**, 703.
commentary on the Mishna by, **4**, 704.
rabbi of Vienna and Prague, **4**, 704–6.
apportions the war tax, **4**, 704.
accused and imprisoned, **4**, 705.
fined and deprived of his office, **4**, 706.
relaxes the Jewish marriage law, **5**, 13.
draws up penitential prayers, **5**, 13.

Heman, grandson of Samuel, psalmist, **1**, 79, 120–1.

Hengstenberg, exegete, **5**, 695.

Henna. *See* Hinnom.

Hennigs, Augustus von, Danish state councilor, interested in Mendelssohn's Pentateuch translation, **5**, 333, 334.

Henrique, bishop of **Ceuta**, and the prosecution of Marranos, **4**, 499.

Henrique, Infante of Portugal, grand inquisitor, deposition of, demanded by Paul III, **4**, 521.
sends a list of Marrano delinquencies to Rome, **4**, 523.

Henry II, emperor, banishes the Jews from Mayence, **3**, 245–6.

Henry IV, emperor, and the Jews of Worms, **3**, 293.
issues a decree in favor of the Jews, **3**, 298.
permits Jews forcibly baptized to return to Judaism, **3**, 306.
grants protection to the Jews, **3**, 308, 416.

Henry VI, emperor, Jews massacred under, **3**, 418–19.

Henry of Anjou (III of France), candidate for the Polish throne, **4**, 604, 605.

Henry II (de Trastamare), of Castile, rival of Pedro the Cruel, **4**, 114.
gains allies against Pedro, **4**, 122.
maligns his brother, **4**, 122–3.
begins war with his brother, **4**, 123.
taxes the Jews of Burgos, **4**, 123, 124.
gains Toledo and Seville, **4**, 124.
leaves Spain, **4**, 124.
takes northern Spain, **4**, 124.
refuses to exclude Jews from state offices, **4**, 125.
taxes the Jews, **4**, 125–6.
victorious at Montiel, **4**, 126.
accession of, **4**, 136.
attitude of, towards Jews, **4**, 137, 138.

Henry II, of Castile (*continued*),
decrees Jew badges, **4**, 139.
discriminates against Jewish creditors, **4**, 139.
forces Jews into religious debates, **4**, 140.
Jewish courtiers of, **4**, 156.
death of, **4**, 156.
Jews hated under, **4**, 167.

Henry III, of Castile, discord early in the reign of, **4**, 167.
regents for, quell the riot against the Jews of Seville, **4**, 168.
confers dignities upon Solomon Levi, **4**, 184.
employs Jewish physicians, **4**, 185, 190.
advised not to employ Jewish officials, **4**, 185.
Jews under, **4**, 193.
death of, **4**, 193, 196.
appoints Solomon Levi executor of his will, **4**, 194.

Henry IV, of Castile, the Jews under, **4**, 274–6.
plunders the houses of Jews and Marranos, **4**, 274.
employs Jewish officials, **4**, 275.
forbids the Jews to dress luxuriously, **4**, 275–6.
disproves the charge of child murder against the Jews of Spain, **4**, 276.
punishes the murderers of the Jews of Medina del Campos, **4**, 278.
statute book of, assigns a low position to the Jews, **4**, 278.
deposed, **4**, 278.
reproached with partiality towards the Jews, **4**, 279–80.
protects the Marranos of Valladolid, **4**, 281.
death of, **4**, 283.

Henry IV, of Castile (*continued*),
opposes the establishment of the Inquisition, **4**, 310.

Henry I, of England, grants privileges to the Jews, **3**, 504.

Henry II, of England, the Jews prosperous under, **3**, 409.

Henry III, of England, the Jews under, **3**, 570–1, 587–92.
the minority of, **3**, 587–8.
appoints a chief rabbi, **3**, 588.
restrains the intolerance of the Church, **3**, 588.
summons a Jewish Parliament, **3**, 589–90.
refuses the Jews permission to leave England, **3**, 591.
deposes Elias of London, **3**, 591.
protects the Jews of London, **3**, 592.

Henry VIII, of England, overthrows Catholicism, **4**, 541.

Henry II, of France, Obadiah de Sforno dedicates his works to, **4**, 411.
treats Neapolitan Jews kindly, **4**, 544.
confiscates the Mendes property, **4**, 574.
refuses to pay the Mendes-Nassi family his debt, **4**, 596, 597.

Henry III, of France. *See* Henry of Anjou.

Henry IV, of France, and Manuel Pimentel, **4**, 672.

Henry of Orange, well disposed towards Jews, **4**, 678.

Henry de Trastamare. *See* Henry II, of Castile.

Henry I, archbishop of Mayence, protects the Jews during the second crusade, **3**, 352–3.

Henry, bishop of Ratisbon, enforces anti-Jewish restrictions, **4**, 301.
attempts to convert the Jews, **4**, 301.
charges Israel Bruna with child-murder, **4**, 303.
urges an inquiry against the Jews, **4**, 304.
Henry Julius, duke of Brunswick, expels the Jews, **4**, 652.
"Hep, hep!" cry, the, against the Jews, **5**, 528–32.
Rachel Levin on, **5**, 534.
"Hep, hep!" persecutions, the, Börne on, **5**, 542–3.
Heine on, **5**, 556.
in Hamburg, **5**, 573.
Hephzi-bah, wife of Hezekiah, **1**, 280.
Heraclius, emperor of the East, sues for peace with Chosru II, **3**, 19.
allies himself with the Jews, **3**, 21–2.
makes peace with the Persians, **3**, 22.
persecutes the Jews of Palestine, **3**, 22–3, 47.
forbids Jews to enter Jerusalem, **3**, 23.
Hercules d'Este I, duke of Ferrara, patron of Abraham Farissol, **4**, 412–13.
Hercules d'Este II, duke of Ferrara, friend of the Jews, **4**, 544.
protects the Marranos, **4**, 569.
protects Gracia Mendesia, **4**, 575.
Hercules, chief of the Jewish community of Arta, **3**, 424.
Hercules, demi-god, Jason sacrifices to, **1**, 446.
Herder, admires "Phædon," **5**, 307.
Herder (*continued*), aversion of, to Jews, **5**, 462.
Heresy, signs of, enumerated by the Inquisition, **4**, 315–16.
Hermandad, the, union of Spanish towns, enforces anti-Jewish measures, **4**, 251.
Hermann III, bishop of Cologne, protects the Jews during the first crusade, **3**, 304.
Hermann the Carpenter, leader of the first crusade in Cologne, **3**, 303, 306.
"Hermitage" (Stübel), the Zaddik's room, **5**, 382.
Hermon (Anti-Lebanon), mountain, description of, **1**, 44.
Jesus at, **2**, 158.
Herod I (37–3), son of Antipater, governor of Galilee, **2**, 77.
subdues Ezekias, **2**, 77–8.
honored by Sextus Cæsar, **2**, 78.
before the Synhedrion, **2**, 78–9.
governor of Cœlesyria, **2**, 79.
assassinates Malich, **2**, 80.
betrothed to Mariamne, **2**, 81.
tetrarch of Judæa, **2**, 81.
opposed by the Parthians, **2**, 82.
escapes to Rome, **2**, 83, 86.
favored by Antony, **2**, 86.
proclaimed king of Judæa by the Roman Senate, **2**, 86.
struggle of, with Antigonus, **2**, 87.
marries Mariamne, **2**, 87.
besieges Jerusalem, **2**, 87–8.
has Antigonus beheaded, **2**, 89.
policy of, **2**, 89.
kills the Synhedrists, **2**, 89.
appoints Ananel high priest, **2**, 90.

Herod I (*continued*), tries to obliterate his Idumæan descent, **2**, 90.
fears Hyrcanus and Aristobulus (III), **2**, 90–1.
brings Hyrcanus to Jerusalem, **2**, 91.
proclaims Aristobulus (III) high priest, **2**, 91.
has him murdered, **2**, 92.
accused before Cleopatra, **2**, 92–3.
orders the murder of Mariamne, **2**, 93.
threatened by a sister of Antigonus, **2**, 94.
at war with Malich, **2**, 94–5.
orders the execution of Hyrcanus II, **2**, 96.
confines Mariamne in Alexandrion, **2**, 96.
appoints Hillel president of the Synhedrion, **2**, 96, 99.
appoints Menahem deputy, **2**, 100.
received with favor by Octavius, **2**, 101–2.
territory of, increased, **2**, 103.
executes Mariamne, **2**, 104.
quells Alexandra's sedition, **2**, 105.
submits to Augustus, **2**, 105.
ornaments Sebaste and Cæsarea, **2**, 106.
exhausts the people by taxation, **2**, 107.
degrades the high priesthood, **2**, 107.
marries Mariamne II, **2**, 107.
requires an oath of allegiance from his subjects, **2**, 108.
remodels the Temple, **2**, 109–11.
distrustful of his family, **2**, 112.
appoints Antipater his successor, **2**, 112, 113.

Herod I (*continued*), executes Mariamne I's sons, **2**, 113.
conspiracy against, **2**, 113.
appoints Herod Antipas his successor, **2**, 114.
contest of, with the Pharisees, **2**, 114–15.
attempts suicide, **2**, 115–16.
executes Antipater, **2**, 116.
orders executions for the day of his death, **2**, 116.
death of, **2**, 117.
territory added to Judæa by, **2**, 118.
will of, **2**, 119–20.
sends gifts to Athens, **2**, 193.
palace of, stormed by the Zealots, **2**, 260.
palace of, in Galilee destroyed by Josephus, **2**, 279.
Herod II, brother of Agrippa I, prætor and prince of Chalcis, **2**, 190.
allied with Agrippa I, **2**, 196.
opposes Cuspius Fadus, **2**, 197.
asks for a truce, **2**, 197.
titular king of Judæa, **2**, 198.
death of, **2**, 199, 235.
widow of, **2**, 235.
Herod ben Gamala, partisan of Rome, **2**, 274.
Herod ben Miar, partisan of Rome, **2**, 274.
Herod (Antipas), son of Cleopatra of Jerusalem and Herod I, disinherited, **2**, 119.
Herod (Philip), son of Mariamne II and Herod I, disinherited, **2**, 119.
wife of, **2**, 173.
Herod Antipas (Antipas I), son of Malthace and Herod I, successor to Herod I, **2**, 114.
ruler of Galilee and Peræa, **2**, 119.
envious of Archelaus, **2**, 120.

Herod Antipas (*continued*), builds Tiberias, **2**, 137–8.
character of, **2**, 138.
beheads John the Baptist, **2**, 147.
pursues Jesus, **2**, 160.
abandons his wife to marry Herodias, **2**, 173.
defeated by the Nabathæans, **2**, 173.
assisted by Vitellius, **2**, 173.
procures an office for Agrippa I, **2**, 175.
banished to Lyons, **2**, 177.

Herod Philip, son of Cleopatra of Jerusalem. *See* Philip, tetrarch.

Herodian dynasty, the, the members of:

Agrippa I,	Herod I,
Agrippa II,	Herod II,
Archelaus,	Herod Antipas,
Philip.	

Herodian time, the, characterized, **5**, 723.

Herodians, the, appeal to Augustus, **2**, 122.
petition for the removal of obnoxious emblems from the Roman standard, **2**, 139.
oppose John the Baptist, **2**, 147.
morality of the opponents of, **2**, 151.
immorality of, **2**, 236.

Herodias, wife of Herod (Philip), daughter of, **2**, 147.
illegal marriage of, with Herod Antipas, **2**, 173.
appealed to by Cypros, **2**, 175.
envious of Agrippa I, **2**, 177.
banished to Lyons, **2**, 177.

Herodium, fortress, burial place of Herod I, **2**, 117.
surrenders to Bassus, **2**, 315.

Heron, Syrian commander, defeated by Judas Maccabæus, **1**, 462.

Herrera, Abraham (Alonzo) de, descendant of Gonsalvo de Cordova, in Amsterdam, **4**, 666.
identifies the Kabbala with Neo-platonism, **5**, 54, 88.

Herrera, Pedro de. *See* Pedro de Herrera.

Herrera, prophetess of, burnt, **4**, 494.

Herschel, Solomon, rabbi of London, repeats Manasseh ben Israel's oath concerning ritual murder, **5**, 654–5.

Heruli, the, overrun Rome, **3**, 27.

Herz Medelsheim. *See* Berr, Cerf.

Herz, Henrietta, influence of, in Berlin, **5**, 412–13.
salon of, **5**, 413, 422–3, 540.
influence of romanticism on, **5**, 423.
relation of, to Schleiermacher, **5**, 423.
and Dorothea Mendelssohn, **5**, 424.
apostasy of, **5**, 425–6.

Herz, Leb, Sabbatian, **5**, 152.

Herz, Marcus (1747–1803), physician, translates the "Vindiciæ Judæorum," **5**, 362.
youth and education of, **5**, 405.
distinguished by Kant, **5**, 405–6.
as a physician, **5**, 406.
marriage of, **5**, 406.
lectures on Kant's philosophy, **5**, 406.
influences Berlin Jews, **5**, 407.
house of, a center of culture, **5**, 412.
mediocrity of, **5**, 417.
disapproves of Dorothea Mendelssohn, **5**, 424.

Heschels, Leb, rabbi, opposes Eibeschütz, **5**, 262, 263, 268, 269.
Hesychius, consular agent, accused by Gamaliel V, **2**, 613.
Hess, Hermann, chancellor of the University of Mayence, and the confiscation of Hebrew books, **4**, 437.
Hess, Isaac, introduces Mendelssohn to Lessing, **5**, 297.
Hesse, the Jews of, deprived of civil rights, **5**, 512.
emancipated, **5**, 601.
Hetman (Attaman), Cossack chieftain, **5**, 2.
Hewn-stone Hall, meeting place of the Synhedrion in Jerusalem, **2**, 239.
Hexapla, parallel texts of Bible versions by Origen, **2**, 488–9.
Hezekiah, king of Judah, virtues of, **1**, 266–7.
limited power of, **1**, 267–8.
banishes idolatry, **1**, 267.
celebrates the Passover, **1**, 268.
allied with Egypt, **1**, 270.
assures Sennacherib of his submission, **1**, 274.
refuses to surrender to Sennacherib, **1**, 274–5.
illness of, **1**, 276.
recovers, **1**, 277.
honors Merodach-baladan's embassy, **1**, 278–9.
marriage of, celebrated, **1**, 279.
Hebrew literature under, **1**, 279.
burial of, **1**, 280.
Hibat-allah. *See* Nathaniel.
Hiel of Bethel fortifies Jericho, **1**, 201.
Hieronymus. *See* Jerome.
High priests, the, seat of, in Shiloh, **1**, 41.
dignity of, raised under Joash, **1**, 219.
High priests, the (*continued*), heads of the Council of Seventy, **1**, 394.
considered political chiefs, **1**, 418.
installed by the Roman procurator, **2**, 129, 137.
vestments of, kept in the Antonia, **2**, 129.
chosen by the Roman governor, **2**, 172, 197.
chosen by Herod II, **2**, 198.
chosen from certain families, **2**, 237.
feuds among, **2**, 237.
power of, under Agrippa II, **2**, 246.
short terms of, **2**, 249.
deputy to, **2**, 330.
See also Aaronides; Priests.
High priests, the, list of:
Aaron,
Abiathar,
Achitub,
Alcimus,
Alexander Jannæus,
Amaziah (Bethel),
Anan, of the family Seth,
Anan, of the family Anan,
Ananel,
Ananias,
Antigonus,
Aristobulus I,
Aristobulus II,
Aristobulus III,
Azariah,
Azariah ben Zadok,
Eleazar,
Eli,
Eliashib,
Elionai,
Hilkiah,
Hyrcanus I, John
Hyrcanus II,
Ishmael II,
Jaddua,
Jason,
Jehoiada,
Jehoiakim,
Joaser,
Johanan, son of Joiada,
Joiada,
Jonathan ben Anan,
Jonathan Haphus,
Joseph, of the house of Camyth,
Joseph Caiaphas,
Joshua, of the family of Phabi,
Joshua, of the family of Sié,
Joshua ben Damnai,
Joshua ben Gamala,
Joshua, son of Jehozedek,
Judas Maccabæus,
Manasseh,
Matthias ben Theophilus,
Menelaus the Benjamite,
Onias I,
Onias II,
Onias III,

High priests, the, list of (*continued*):

Phineas,	Simon, son of Boëthus,
Phineas ben Samuel,	Simon Tharsi,
Seraiah,	Uriah,
Simon I,	Zachariah ben Jehoiada,
Simon II,	Zadok.

High-roads, the king's, built by Solomon, **1**, 171–2.

"**High Tower, The,**" drama by Luzzatto, **5**, 235.

Hilchetha Gabriatha, Talmud commentary by Samuel Ibn-Nagrela, **3**, 259.

Hildebrand. *See* Gregory VII.

Hilderic of Nismes, governor of Septimania, revolts against Wamba, **3**, 104–5.
promises the Jews religious liberty, **3**, 105.

Hildesheim, Jews tolerated in, **4**, 686.
the Jews of, deprived of civil rights, **5**, 512.

Hildesheimer, the Frankfort deputy to the Synhedrion, **5**, 497.

Hilduin, incites the sons of Louis the Pious against their step-mother, **3**, 166.

Hilkia, treasurer of the Temple, envoy to Nero, **2**, 248.

Hilkiah, high priest, charged with the repairs of the Temple, **1**, 289.
finds the Book of the Law, **1**, 292.
counsels Josiah, **1**, 293.
ancestor of Ezra, **1**, 365.

Hillali, oldest copy of the Bible in Spain, destroyed, **3**, 387.

Hillel I, appointed president of the Synhedrion, **2**, 96, 99.
disciple of Shemaya and Abtalion, **2**, 96.
character of, **2**, 96–7.
maxims of, **2**, 97–8.

Hillel I (*continued*), justifies the oral law, **2**, 98.
justifies new laws, **2**, 99.
enacts the Prosbol, **2**, 100.
followers of, swear allegiance to Herod, **2**, 108.
death of, lamented, **2**, 130.
descendants of, presidents of the Synhedrion, **2**, 130, 192.
spreads the knowledge of the Law in Judæa, **2**, 149.
the model of Jesus, **2**, 149–50.
quoted by Philo, **2**, 213.
compared with Philo, **2**, 214.
followers of, support the Peace party, **2**, 256.
the founder of Talmudic Judaism, **2**, 327.
laws of interpretation by, **2**, 327, 338.
laws of interpretation by, supplemented, **2**, 331, 356.
reverence paid to the house of, **2**, 360.
compared with Abba Areka, **2**, 517.
end of the house of, **2**, 618.

Hillel, disciples of, distinguished, **2**, 131.
conception of the Messiah held by, **2**, 144.
morality of, **2**, 151.

Hillel, the school of, 2, 101.
conciliatory, **2**, 131.
disputes with the school of Shammai under Gamaliel II, **2**, 333, 336–8.
deductions of, condemned by Joshua ben Chananya, **2**, 350.
estimation of, by the Nazarenes, **2**, 372.
extends the application of tradition, **2**, 462.

Hillel II, brother of Judah II, censured for irreligiousness, **2**, 480.
Agadist, **2**, 487.

Hillel II (*continued*), maxim of, **2,** 487.
consulted by Origen, **2,** 487.
versed in the Scriptures, **2,** 487, 488.
Patriarch, unselfishness of, **2,** 560.
defamed by Joseph the apostate, **2,** 566.
adopts a fixed calendar, **2,** 572–4.
honored by Julian the Apostate, **2,** 597, 598.

Hillel ben Samuel of Verona (1220–1295), Talmudist, founder of Italian Jewish culture, **3,** 629; **4,** 59.
Maimunist, **3,** 629, 630.
accomplishments of, **3,** 629.
tries to prevent a renewal of the Maimunist controversy, **3,** 631–2.

Himyar, ancestor of the Arabs, **3,** 61, 62.

Himyara, part of southern Arabia, **3,** 54.

Himyarite kingdom, the Jewish, **3,** 62–7.

Himyarites, the, conversion of, to Christianity projected, **4,** 298.

Hinderbach, bishop of Trent, charges the Jews with child murder, **4,** 298.

Hinkmar, bishop of Rheims, anti-Jewish feelings of, **3,** 171.
favorite of Charles the Bald, **3,** 172.

Hinnom (Ge-henna), the vale of, south of Jerusalem, **1,** 115.
tower at the gate of, **1,** 231.
Ahaz sacrifices to Moloch in, **1,** 260–1.
sacrifices in, under Manasseh, **1,** 283.

Hinnom, the vale of (*continued*), Moloch worship in, under Jehoiakim, **1,** 300.
gives its name to hell, **1,** 404.

Hippicus, tower in the wall of Jerusalem, refuge of the Roman garrison, **2,** 260.
left undemolished by Titus, **2,** 309.

Hippodrome, the, in Jerusalem, occupied during the disturbance by Sabinus, **2,** 123.

Hippos, incorporated with Judæa, **2,** 103.

Hiram, of Tyre, allied with David, **1,** 118.
allied with Solomon, **1,** 162.
supplies material for the Temple, **1,** 164.
supplies Solomon with sailors, **1,** 170.

Hiram, artist in bronze, employed in the building of the Temple, **1,** 165.

Hiram, brother of Merbal, king of Phœnicia, **1,** 342.

Hirsch (Hirschel), Berlin jeweler, excites Voltaire's animosity, **5,** 339.

Hisham, Ommiyyade caliph, **3,** 239.
releases Jacob Ibn-Jau, **3,** 241.

Historians, Jewish, consulted by Basnage, **5,** 196.

Historians, Jewish, list of:

Abraham Ibn-Daud Halevi,
Abraham Zacuto,
Almosnino, Moses
Barrios, Miguel de
Baruch,
Conforte, David
David Gans,
Elias ben Elkanah Kapsali,
Ephraim ben Jacob,
Gedalya Ibn-Yachya,
Heilperin, Jechiel
José ben Chalafta,
Joseph ben Joshua Cohen,
Joseph ben Matthias (Josephus),
Josephus, pseudo-
Joseph Ibn-Verga,
Jost, Isaac Marcus
Justus, son of Pistus,

Historians, Jewish, list of (*continued*):

Lōwisohn, Solomon
Luzzatto, Samuel David
Profiat Duran,
Rapoport, Solomon Jehuda
Samuel Shulam,
Sherira,
Usque, Samuel
Usque, Solomon.

Historians of the Jews, list of:

Adams, Hannah
Basnage, Jacob
Ewald, Heinrich.

Historical writings of the Jews, the, carried into the Babylonian Exile, **1,** 335.
compiled by Baruch, **1,** 336–7.
collected by the Sopherim, **1,** 400.
translated into Greek, **1,** 514.

History, Jewish, cultivated in Hasmonæan times, **2,** 15–16.
beginnings of, **4,** 554.
in the "Moniteur," **5,** 485.
distorted, **5,** 592–3.
by Christians, **5,** 593.
by Jews, **5,** 593–6.
as viewed by Krochmal, **5,** 609–10.
the "Kerem Chemed" devoted to, **5,** 621.
a review of, **5,** 705–31.

"**History** of neo-Hebraic Poetry," by Franz Delitzsch, **5,** 628–9.

"**History** of the Jews," by Gedalya Ibn-Yachya, **4,** 616.

"**History** of the People of Israel, The," by Ewald, **5,** 696.

"**History** of the Religion of the Jews," by Jacob Basnage, **5,** 197.

"**History** of the World," by Gedalya Ibn-Yachya, **4,** 616.

Hittites, the, subdivision of the Canaanites, **1,** 3.
suffer under David, **1,** 131.
mercenary troops under David, **1,** 137.

Hittites, the (*continued*), declared bondmen by Solomon, **1,** 163.
king of, hostile to Ben-hadad III, **1,** 221.

Hivites, the, subdivision of the Canaanites, **1,** 3.
submit to Joshua, **1,** 34.
declared bondmen by Solomon, **1,** 163.

Hochmeister, title of rabbis in Franconia, **4,** 259.

Hochstraten. *See* Hoogstraten, Jacob.

Hodges, English consul-general, services of, in the Damascus affair, **5,** 653, 659.

Hodki, Haidamak leader, **5,** 10.

Holdheim, Samuel (1806–1860), Talmudist, at the Brunswick rabbinical conference, **5,** 678, 681.
opposes Talmudic Judaism, **5,** 678, 680–1.
secular studies of, **5,** 678.
temperament of, **5,** 679.
chief rabbi of Mecklenburg-Schwerin, **5,** 679.
view held by, of Judaism, **5,** 680–1.
compared with Frankel, **5,** 684.
at the Frankfort rabbinical conference, **5,** 685.
preacher of the Berlin Reform Association, **5,** 686.
innovations of, **5,** 686–7.
compared with Sachs, **5,** 687–8, 692.
Sachs's opinion of, **5,** 691.

Holland, soldiers of, in the imperial army against the Hussites, **4,** 225.
a refuge for Jews, **4,** 661, 676–7, 678.
second Jewish colony of, **4,** 685.

Holland (*continued*), learning in, **5**, 20–1.
war of, with England, and the re-settlement of Jews in England, **5**, 34.
displeased with the efforts to settle Jews in England, **5**, 46.
rabbis of, prepared to excommunicate Luzzatto, **5**, 241.
ambassador of, intercedes for the Moravian and Bohemian Jews, **5**, 253.
funds advanced to, by Isaac Pinto, **5**, 340.
the Measfim in, **5**, 400–1.
See also Amsterdam; Batavian Republic, the.
Holmes, Nathaniel, Puritan, attitude of, towards the Jews, **5**, 27.
on the place of the Jews in the Messianic time, **5**, 29–30.
Holst, Ludwig, attacks the Jews, **5**, 543.
Holstein, favors the emancipation of the Jews, **5**, 519.
Holwan, the Exilarch's income from, **3**, 96.
Holy City, the, beginnings of, **1**, 114. *See* Jerusalem.
Holy Days, the, kept by the Babylonian Judæans, **1**, 364.
Holy Ghost, the, dogma of, introduced into Christianity, **2**, 500–1.
Holy Land, the. *See* Palestine.
Holy of Holies, the, Debir, **1**, 165.
entered by Antiochus Epiphanes, **1**, 451–2.
entered by Pompey, **2**, 66.
the Romans desecrate, **2**, 124.
entered by Titus, **2**, 308.
Holy Place, the, Hechal, **1**, 165.
Holy Roman Empire, the, dismembered, **5**, 465. *See* Rome; Germany.
Holy Sepulcher, the, Church of, fear that Jews will gain possession of, **4**, 272, 274.
Holy Week. *See* Eastertide.
Homberg, Herz, assists Mendelssohn in his Pentateuch translation, **5**, 334.
teacher in an Austrian school, **5**, 369.
one of the Measfim, **5**, 401–2.
Homel, the Jews of, massacred, **5**, 10.
Homem, Gaspar Lopez, Portuguese Marrano, **4**, 664.
Homem, Mayor Rodrigues, Marrano, sends her daughter to Holland, **4**, 664–5.
emigrates to Holland, **4**, 667.
Homer, read by the Alexandrian Judæans, **1**, 505.
Greek views of the world in, **2**, 208.
"**Homilies of the Jews in Divine Worship**," by Zunz, **5**, 620–1.
Honorius III, pope, enforces anti-Jewish decrees, **3**, 513.
exempts the Toulouse Jews from wearing badges, **3**, 514.
prevents the employment of Jews as diplomats, **3**, 514.
Honorius IV, pope, bids the English clergy proceed against the Jews, **3**, 645.
Honorius, emperor of the West, and the Jews, **2**, 616–17, 622.
forbids the collection of the Patriarch's tax, **2**, 617.
forbids Jews to enter military service, **2**, 617.
Hooghe, Romein de, poet, on the Amsterdam synagogue, **5**, 167.
Hoogstraten, Jacob, Dominican general in Cologne, **4**, 424.
and the confiscation of Hebrew books, **4**, 437, 441

Hoogstraten, Jacob (*continued*), decides that the Talmud ought to be burnt, **4,** 444.
proposes the indictment of the Jews, **4,** 444.
accuses Reuchlin of heresy, **4,** 450.
tries Reuchlin and the "Augenspiegel," **4,** 451.
orders the burning of the "Augenspiegel," **4,** 451–2.
the examination of, ordered by Leo X, **4,** 454.
fails to appear for trial, **4,** 454.
convicted of slander, **4,** 455.
appeals to Leo X, **4,** 455.
tries to have the Speyer judgment overturned, **4,** 458.
summoned to Rome, **4,** 458.
satirized in the "Letters of Obscurantists," **4,** 461.
asks for a decision by council, **4,** 464.
influences Leo X to suspend his case, **4,** 465.
leaves Rome in disgrace, **4,** 465.
life of, endangered, **4,** 465.
Hoornbeek, John, anti-Jewish author, **5,** 46.
Hophni, son of Eli, character and death of, **1,** 70.
Hophra. *See* Apries.
Horeb, mount, scene of the first revelation to Moses, **1,** 15.
Hormisdas IV, of Persia, character of, **3,** 7–8.
persecutes the Jews, **3,** 8.
murdered, **3,** 8.
Hosannas, Day of, a second Day of Atonement, **4,** 626.
Hosea (I), prophet, under Jeroboam II, prophecies of, **1,** 240–2.
Hosea (II), prophet, under Hoshea, **1,** 251.
Hoshea, son of Elah, murders Pekah, **1,** 260.
king of Israel, **1,** 263.
ally of Egypt and vassal to Shalmaneser, **1,** 263.
withdraws his tribute from Shalmaneser, **1,** 264.
fortifies Samaria, **1,** 264.
imprisoned for life, **1,** 264.
Hosiander, probable author of the "Little Book about the Jews," **4,** 545.
Host desecration, the charge of, believed by Maximilian I, **4,** 414.
Host desecration, charged against the Jews of Röttingen, **4,** 35.
of Deckendorf, **4,** 98.
of Prague, **4,** 164–6.
of Segovia, **4,** 195–6.
of Austria, **4,** 223.
of Silesia, **4,** 261.
of Passau, **4,** 306.
of the Mark of Brandenburg, **4,** 437, 440.
See also Blood accusation, the; Child murder.
Hosts, God of, meaning of, **1,** 130–1.
House of Commons, the, passes the Statute of Judaism, **3,** 642.
"**House of God, The,**" Kabbalistic work by Abraham de Herrera, **5,** 54.
"**House of Jacob,**" first Amsterdam synagogue, **4,** 667.
House of the Forest of Lebanon, Solomon's armory, **1,** 108.
Howan, the Temple of, Jewish children brought up as Magians in, **2,** 629.
Howdon, Lord, on the Damascus affair, **5,** 656.
Hubmaier, Balthasar, Anabaptist, agitates against the Jews, **4,** 542–3.

Huesca, the Jews of, excommunicate the anti-Maimunists, **3,** 537.
the Marranos of, conspire against Pedro Arbues, **4,** 330.
Huet, Peter Daniel, and Manasseh ben Israel, **5,** 22.
Huete, meeting of the deputies of Castile congregations at, **3,** 617.
the Jews of, persecuted, **4,** 170.
Hufnagel, translates Wessely's "Songs of Glory," **5,** 404.
Hugh, chaplain of Toulouse, and the Jews, **3,** 174.
Hugh Capet, of France, death of, said to have been caused by the Jews, **3,** 242.
Hujej Ibn-Achtab, chief of the Benu-Nadhir, **3,** 78.
induces Arabian tribes to make war against Mahomet, **3,** 79, 80.
killed, **3,** 81.
daughter of, **3,** 83.
Hulagu, Tartar sultan, ravages of, **3,** 606.
founder of the Mongol kingdom in Persia, **3,** 638.
Huldah, prophetess under Josiah, **1,** 286, 293.
Humanists, the, espouse Reuchlin's cause, **4,** 456.
courted by Leo X, **4,** 465.
favor Charles V's election, **4,** 468.
Humboldt, Wilhelm von, relation of, to Henrietta Herz, **5,** 423.
draws up a constitution for Germany, **5,** 514.
Huna, on the refugees from Sepphoris, **2,** 571.
Huna (212–297), Babylonian Amora, chief teacher at Sora, **2,** 545.
Huna (*continued*), agriculturist, **2,** 545.
and Chama ben Anilaï, **2,** 546.
charitableness of, **2,** 546.
presides over the Metibta, **2,** 547–8.
death of, **2,** 548.
and Judah ben Ezekiel, **2,** 552.
and Chasda, **2,** 553.
and Mar-Sheshet, **2,** 553–4.
Huna, Exilarch, buried in Judæa, **2,** 455, 509.
Huna bar Nathan, at the court of Jezdijird, **2,** 610.
Huna ben Chiya, principal of the Pumbeditha academy, wealth of, **2,** 576.
opposition to, **2,** 577.
death of, **2,** 577.
Huna ben Joshua, teacher at the academy of Nares, **2,** 593–4.
Huna-Mar (488–508), Exilarch, Amora, **2,** 631; **3,** 3.
Huna-Mari, Exilarch, executed by Firuz, **2,** 629.
learned in the Law, **2,** 631.
Hunaï, Gaon of Sora, reforms the divorce law, **3,** 92.
Hundt, Hartwig, pamphlet by, against the Jews, **5,** 532.
Hungary, adopts Frederick the Valiant's Jewish statute, **3,** 569.
Jews invited into, **3,** 613.
Jewish exiles from, take refuge in Poland, **4,** 263.
Messianic hopes connected with Solomon Molcho in, **4,** 497.
Polish-Jewish fugitives in, **5,** 16.
the Sabbatian movement in, **5,** 208.
rabbis of, protest against the Brunswick rabbinical conference, **5,** 682.

Hungary, the Jews of, condition of, in early days, **3,** 520.
possess the right of coinage, **3,** 521.
farmers of salt mines and taxes, **3,** 521.
kindly treated by Andreas, **3,** 521.
the decrees of the Fourth Lateran Council enforced against, **3,** 521.
indispensable to the prosperity of the country, **3,** 613.
proscribed by the Council of Buda, **3,** 614–15.
banished by Louis I, **4,** 111.
liturgy of, arranged by Maharil, **4,** 225.
urged to emigrate to Turkey, **4,** 271–2.
Sabbatians, **5,** 149.
modify their divine service, **5,** 582.
Huns, the, incursions of, **2,** 604.
aid Kobad, **3,** 2.
Huozmann. *See* Rüdiger.
Hurwitz, Isaiah (Sheloh), devotee of the Kabbala, **5,** 52, 55.
Hurwitz, Phineas Levi (1740–1802), rabbi of Frankfort, opposes Mendelssohn's Pentateuch translation, **5,** 331.
death of, **5,** 566.
Hurwitz, Sabbataï, draws up penitential prayers, **5,** 13.
Hurwitz, Salkind, competes for the Metz prize on the Jewish question, **5,** 434..
in the National Guards, **5,** 443.
Hushai, David's favorite, **1,** 122.
faithful to David in Absalom's rebellion, **1,** 141–2.
pretends to submit to Absalom, **1,** 142–3.
Huss, John, attacks the papacy, **4,** 221.
condemned to death, **4,** 221–2.
Hussite war, the, and the Jews, **4,** 222.
cruelties of, **4,** 224–6.
German Jews in sympathy with, **4,** 226.
Hussites, the, hated by Emperor Albert II, **4,** 249.
excite Catholic bigotry, **4,** 258.
protect the Jews of Ratisbon, **4,** 301.
the Dominicans threaten to ally themselves with, **4,** 459.
Hutten, Ulrich von, agent at the imperial court, instructed to aid the Jews, **4,** 431.
espouses Reuchlin's cause, **4,** 456–7.
supposed author of the "Letters of Obscurantists," **4,** 462.
enemy of ecclesiastical domination, **4,** 465.
favors Charles V, **4,** 468.
in the pantomime on the Reformation, **4,** 468.
Hypatia, killed by monks, **2,** 619.
Hyrcanion, fortress, built by John Hyrcanus, **2,** 46.
held by a sister of Antigonus, **2,** 94.
Hyrcanists, the, Hyrcanus II's party, defend the Temple, **2,** 65.
Hyrcanus I, John, son of Simon Tharsi, **1,** 520.
lives at Gazara, **1,** 525.
defeats Cendebæus, **1,** 529.
escapes from Ptolemy ben Habub, **1,** 530–1.
mother of, imprisoned, **1,** 531; **2,** 2.
reign of, **2,** 1.
contest of, with Ptolemy ben Habub, **2,** 2–3.

Hyrcanus I, John (*continued*), besieged by Antiochus Sidetes, **2**, 3–4.
sends an embassy to Rome, **2**, 4–5.
furnishes Syria troops against Parthia, **2**, 5.
acknowledges Alexander Zabina king of Syria, **2**, 6.
Samaritan campaign of, **2**, 7–8.
destroys the Temple on Gerizim, **2**, 8.
converts the Idumæans forcibly to Judaism, **2**, 8–9.
appeals to Rome, **2**, 9.
besieges Samaria, **2**, 9.
destroys Samaria, **2**, 10.
conquests of, **2**, 11–12.
has coins struck, **2**, 12.
worldly ambition of, **2**, 13.
erects a mausoleum at Modin, **2**, 14.
employs Pharisees and Sadducees, **2**, 31.
offended by the Pharisees, **2**, 32–3.
fills the high offices with Sadducees, **2**, 33.
death of, **2**, 33.
sons of, **2**, 34.

Hyrcanus I, John, the wife of, queen, supplanted by Aristobulus I, **2**, 35.
imprisonment and death of, **2**, 36.

Hyrcanus II, son of Alexander Jannæus, **2**, 47.
proclaimed high priest, **2**, 48, 76.
conspiracy against, **2**, 56.
accession and character of, **2**, 57.
defeated at Jericho by Aristobulus, **2**, 58.
deprived of the royal dignity, **2**, 58.

Hyrcanus II (*continued*), aided by the Nabathæan king, **2**, 59.
refuses to supply the sacrificial lamb during the siege of Jerusalem, **2**, 60.
summoned to Damascus, **2**, 63.
favored by Pompey, **2**, 64.
made ethnarch, **2**, 66, 76.
leaves Jerusalem, **2**, 70.
petitioned to punish Herod, **2**, 78.
permits the Synhedrion to summon Herod, **2**, 78.
reproved by Shemaya, **2**, 79.
adjourns the Synhedrion, **2**, 79.
takes counsel with Malich, **2**, 80.
mutilated, **2**, 82.
dethroned, **2**, 82–3.
taken captive to Babylon, **2**, 83.
welcomed by the Babylonian Judæans, **2**, 90.
returns to Palestine, **2**, 91.
executed, **2**, 96.
descendants of, in Nahardea, **2**, 551.

Hyrcanus, son of Joseph, his father's representative in Egypt, **1**, 429–30.
favored by Ptolemy IV, **1**, 430.
rebuked for extravagance, **1**, 430.
successor of his father, **1**, 431–2.
flees to Alexandria, **1**, 432.
in favor with Ptolemy V, **1**, 437.
wealth of, **1**, 437.
betrayed by the Hellenists, **1**, 444.
tax-collector for the king of Egypt, **1**, 444.

Hyrkania, Judæans banished to, **1**, 408.

I

Ibbur, impregnation of the soul, Kabbalistic term, **4**, 621.
Ibbur, work on the calendar by Isaac Ibn-Albalia, **3**, 283.
See also Calendar.
Iberia, early Jewish settlements in, **3**, 35. *See* Spain.
Ibleam, Zechariah, king of Israel, murdered at, **1**, 243.
Ibn-Abbas. *See* Jehuda and Samuel Ibn-Abbas.
Ibn-Abbas, plots to depose Samuel Ibn-Nagrela, **3**, 258.
Ibn-Abi Musa, plots to depose Samuel Ibn-Nagrela, **3**, 258.
Ibn-Abi Obsaibiya, physician, colleague of Abraham Maimuni, **3**, 495.
Ibn-Abitur. *See* Joseph ben Isaac Ibn-Abitur.
Ibn-Abitur family, the, opposes Chanoch ben Moses, **3**, 238.
Ibn-Albalia. *See* Baruch Ibn-Albalia; Isaac ben Baruch Albalia.
Ibn-Albalia family, the, early settlement of, in Spain, **3**, 43.
Ibn-Alfachar. *See* Abraham Ibn-Alfachar; Jehuda bar Joseph Ibn-Alfachar.
Ibn-Alfachar family, the, of the nobility of Jewish Spain, **3**, 235, 537.
Ibn-Alfara, Arabic poet, elegy by, **3**, 279.
Ibn-Aljami. *See* Nathaniel.
Ibn-Alruchi (Arruchi). *See* David Alrui.
Ibn-Benveniste Halevi. *See* Joseph ben Ephraim Ibn-Benveniste Halevi.
Ibn-Chabib. *See* Jacob Ibn-Chabib.
Ibn-Chasdaï. *See* Abraham ben Chasdaï; Samuel ben Abraham Ibn-Chasdaï.
Ibn-Daud. *See* Abraham Ibn-Daud Halevi; Jehuda Ibn-Daud (Chayuj).
Ibn-Daud family, the, traces descent from David, **3**, 43.
Ibn-Daudi, the, descendants of the last Exilarch, settle in Spain, **3**, 254.
Ibn-Ezra. *See* Abraham ben Meïr; Abuhajaj Joseph; Abu-Ibrahim Isaac; Abulhassan Jehuda; Isaac ben Abraham; Jacob; Jehuda; Moses.
Ibn-Ezra family, the, Chasdaï Ibn-Shaprut a member of, **3**, 215.
of the nobility of Jewish Spain, **3**, 235.
Ibn-Falyaj family, the, of the nobility of Jewish Spain, **3**, 236.
Ibn-Farussal. *See* Solomon Ibn-Farussal.
Ibn-Gebirol. *See* Solomon Ibn-Gebirol.
Ibn-Giat. *See* Isaac ben Jehuda; Judah.
Ibn-Giat family, the, of the nobility of Jewish Spain, **3**, 236.
Ibn-G'ikatilia. *See* Isaac Ibn-G'ikatilia; Moses ben Samuel Ibn-G'ikatilia.
Ibn-Janach. *See* Jonah Marinus.
Ibn-Jau. *See* Jacob Ibn-Jau.
Ibn-Kamnial. *See* Abulhassan Abraham ben Meïr Ibn-Kamnial.
Ibn-Labi. *See* Vidal ben Benveniste Ibn-Labi.
Ibn-Migash. *See* Joseph ben Meïr; Meïr ben Joseph.
Ibn-Migash family, the, of the nobility of Jewish Spain, **3**, 236.

Ibn-Misha'l, Jewish diplomat, **3**, 284.
Ibn-Nagrela. *See* Joseph Ibn-Nagrela; Samuel Halevi Ibn-Nagrela.
Ibn-Raz, assailant of Rabbinical Judaism in Leo Modena's work, **5**, 73–4.
Ibn-Roshd. *See* Averroës.
Ibn-Rumahis, Moorish admiral, captures and sells the four emissaries from Sora, **3**, 203, 208, 209.
Ibn-Sahal. *See* Joseph ben Jacob Ibn-Sahal.
Ibn-Sahula (1245), fabulist, **3**, 560.
Ibn-Said (Sid). *See* Zag Ibn-Said.
Ibn-Sakbel. *See* Solomon Ibn-Sakbel.
Ibn-Sakviyah, Karaite writer, opposed by Saadiah, **3**, 192.
Ibn-Satanas. *See* Joseph ben Isaac Ibn-Abitur.
Ibn-Shalbib. *See* Amram ben Isaac Ibn-Shalbib.
Ibn-Shem Tob. *See* Joseph ben Shem Tob; Shem Tob ben Joseph Ibn-Shem-Tob.
Ibn-Shoshan. *See* Abraham; Joseph ben Solomon Ibn-Shoshan; Solomon ben Joseph Ibn-Shoshan.
Ibn-Shoshan family, the, members of, die from the Black Death, **4**, 113.
Ibn-Sina (Avicenna), Mahometan interpreter of Aristotle, **3**, 478.
Ibn-Tibbon. *See* Jacob ben Machir; Judah ben Moses; Judah ben Saul; Moses; Samuel.
Ibn-Verga. *See* Joseph; Judah; Solomon.
Ibn-Vives. *See* Joshua ben Joseph Ibn-Vives.
Ibn-Wakar. *See* Jehuda; Samuel.
Ibn-Yachya. *See* David; David Negro; Gedalya; Gedalya I; Gedalya II; Joseph; Moses; Solomon Ibn-Gebirol.
Ibn-Yachya family, the, Turkish branch of, **4**, 609.
Italian branch of, **4**, 616.
Ibn-Yachya-Negro. *See* David; Judah.
Ibn-Yachya-Negro, two brothers, favorites of Alfonso V, of Portugal, **4**, 339.
Ibn-Yaish, prominent at the court of Alfonso XI, of Castile, **4**, 84.
Ibn-Zachariah Yachya Chayuj. *See* Jehuda Ibn-Daud.
Ibn-Zadik. *See* Abu-Amr Joseph ben Zadik Ibn-Zadik.
Ibrahim, sultan, war of, with Venice, **5**, 119.
Ibzan, judge, **1**, 66.
Icabo, character in Samuel Usque's work, **4**, 558, 559, 560.
Idolatry, among the Egyptians, **1**, 9–10.
practiced by the Israelites in Egypt, **1**, 11.
among the Israelites in the desert, **1**, 23–4.
of the Israelites at Baal-Peor. **1**, 28.
the Israelites reclaimed from, by Samuel, **1**, 75–6.
under Solomon, **1**, 175.
under Jeroboam, **1**, 186–7.
under Omri, **1**, 195–6.
under Jezebel, **1**, 197–8.
under Joram, **1**, 209.
under Jeroboam II, **1**, 233.
under Menahem, **1**, 244, 247.
under Ahaz, **1**, 260–1.
removed by Hezekiah, **1**, 268.
under Manasseh, **1**, 282–3.

Idolatry (*continued*), uprooted by Josiah, **1**, 294–5.
relapse into, under Jehoiakim, **1**, 299–300.
under Jehoiachin, **1**, 306.
practiced by Judæans in Egypt, **1**, 326–7.
among the Babylonian exiles, **1**, 332, 339, 340.
stamped out among the Judæans by the fall of Babylon, **1**, 350.
laws against, inviolate under all circumstances, **2**, 424.
regulations against, in the Mishna, **2**, 476–8.
practiced by the Arabs, **3**, 72.
See also Astarte; Baal, the worship of.

Idumæa, urges Zedekiah to revolt from Nebuchadnezzar, **1**, 310.
ruled by procurators, **2**, 137.
Eleazar ben Ananias governor of, **2**, 270.

Idumæan, applied to Herod and Rome, **2**, 114–15.

Idumæans, the, antagonize the Israelites in the desert, **1**, 27.
characteristics of, **1**, 55.
relations of, to the Israelites, **1**, 56–9.
routed by Othniel, **1**, 60.
attracted to Palestine under Solomon, **1**, 173.
gain independence, **1**, 185.
revolt of, from Judah, **1**, 209.
conquered by Amaziah, **1**, 222–3.
attack Jerusalem under Uzziah, **1**, 226–7.
defeated by Uzziah, **1**, 230.
allies of Nebuchadnezzar, **1**, 314.
molest fugitive Judæans, **1**, 318.

Idumæans, the (*continued*), appropriate Judæan territory, **1**, 325–6.
settled to the south of Judæa, **1**, 355.
in possession of Judæan territory, **1**, 435.
hostile to the Judæans during the Syrian invasions, **1**, 473, 474.
defeated by Judas Maccabæus, **1**, 474.
hostile to Judæa under John Hyrcanus, **2**, 7.
forcibly converted to Judaism, **2**, 8–9.
colony of, in Samaria, **2**, 9, 10.
expeditions of, against Simon bar Giora, **2**, 293.
help the Zealots against Anan, **2**, 295–6.
disliked by the Zealots and the Moderates, **2**, 296.
allied with the aristocratic party, **2**, 298.
one of the factions in Jerusalem, **2**, 301.
try to make terms with Titus, **2**, 309.

Ifra-Ormuzd, mother of Shabur II, leans towards Judaism, **2**, 580, 592–3.
generous towards the Pumbeditha academy, **2**, 581.
protects the Jews, **2**, 592.
assists Raba bar Joseph, **2**, 592.

Iggaron, Hebrew lexicon by Saadiah, **3**, 190.

Iggeret Teman, by Maimonides, **3**, 462–4.

Ignatius, Christian martyr, **2**, 621.

Ijon, subjugated by Ben-hadad I, **1**, 191.

Ikkarim, work by Joseph Albo, **4**, 239.

Ilai, member of the Jamnia Synhedrion, **2,** 357.
Ilhas Perdidas. *See* San Thomas.
Illiberis (Elvira), the Council of, forbids Christians to trade with Jews, **2,** 620.
anti-Jewish decrees of, **3,** 43, 44.
Illyria, synagogues of, protected by Arcadius, **2,** 616.
the Jews of, autonomous, **3,** 27.
Ilpha, companion of Jochanan bar Napacha, **2,** 493.
Imam, founder of the Fatimide dynasty, **3,** 212.
Imamate, the, the high priesthood among the Mahometans, **3,** 110.
Immaculate Conception, the, dogma of, attacked by Chasdaï Crescas, **4,** 187.
Immanuel ben Solomon Romi (1265–1330), poet, under Maimunist influence, **3,** 630; **4,** 60.
characterization of, **4,** 63–4.
position of, in the Roman Jewish community, **4,** 64–5.
friend of Dante, **4,** 65.
works of, **4,** 65–7.
place of, in neo-Hebraic poetry, **4,** 67; **5,** 112.
in Fermo, **4,** 68.
on the poets of his time, **4,** 68.
Immorality, under Jeroboam II, **1,** 233–4.
under Jotham, **1,** 249–50.
under Ahaz, **1,** 261.
under Jehoiakim, **1,** 300.
under Zerubbabel, **1,** 358.
of the Judæan aristocracy, **2,** 234.
of Judæans under the Roman dominion, **2,** 237–8.
among the Jews of Babylonia, **2,** 516–17, 579.
Immorality (*continued*), among the Marranos at Amsterdam, **4,** 680.
among the Jews of Prussia, **5,** 419–20, 422.
Immortality of the soul, the dogma of, in the "Guide of the Perplexed," **3,** 482, 488.
Maimonides' treatment of, attacked, **3,** 524.
in the Kabbala, **3,** 554.
doubt cast upon, by the French thinkers, **5,** 305–6.
Mendelssohn tries to restore the belief in, **5,** 306–7.
Imnestar, the Jews of, punished for Purim pleasantry, **2,** 621.
Imrulkais Ibn-Hojr, Arabic poet, protected by Samuel Ibn-Adiya, **3,** 68–9.
"In Praise and Honor of Emperor Maximilian," anti-Jewish pamphlet by Pfefferkorn, **4,** 439.
"In Refutation of Anan," by Saadiah, **3,** 189.
Incarnation, the dogma of, refuted by Moses Cohen de Tordesillas, **4,** 141.
expounded by Astruc Raimuch, **4,** 182.
refuted by Solomon Bonfed, **4,** 182.
attacked by Chasdaï Crescas, **4,** 187.
criticised by Joseph Ibn-Shem Tob, **4,** 235.
in the Kabbala, **4,** 292.
Jews averse to, **5,** 420.
belief in, threatened, **5,** 682.
Index expurgatorius, the, Kabbalistic writings on, **4,** 584.
India, trade with, under Solomon, **1,** 170.
Uzziah revives the trade with, **1,** 230.
Jews settle in, **2,** 629–30.

India (*continued*), south Arabian Jews trade with, **3**, 54, 57.
under the Exilarch's jurisdiction, **3**, 429.
the Jews of, in the twelfth century, **3**, 435-6.
desire of the Portuguese to reach, **4**, 367.
Infessura, chancellor of Rome, on Sixtus IV, **4**, 321.
Informers, among the Jewish Christians, **2**, 378-9.
during Hadrian's persecutions, **2**, 425-6.
under Severus, **2**, 464-5.
against the Jews of Sepphoris, **2**, 570.
the excommunication of, revived, **3**, 378.
decree against, by the Mayence synod, **3**, 517.
against Jews in Spain, **4**, 155-6.
Innocent II, pope, convenes a Church Council in France, **3**, 376.
Innocent III, pope, persecutes Raymond VI of Toulouse, **3**, 400, 501-2.
preaches the third crusade, **3**, 405.
refuses to sanction Philip Augustus' marriage, **3**, 406.
baneful influence of, **3**, 496.
protects the Jews against the crusaders, **3**, 496-7.
and Pedro II of Aragon, **3**, 497-8.
reproaches Philip Augustus with disregard of anti-Jewish decrees, **3**, 498-9.
reprimands Alfonso III of Castile for kindly treatment of Jews, **3**, 499.
threatens excommunication for intercourse with Jews, **3**, 499.
Innocent III (*continued*), threatens Count Nevers for favoring the Jews, **3**, 500.
organizes the Albigensian crusade, **3**, 502.
asked to decree a crusade against the Mahometans, **3**, 507.
convokes the Fourth Lateran Council, **3**, 508-9.
introduces Jew badges, **3**, 511-12.
death of, **3**, 513.
anti-Jewish decrees of, enforced in southern France, **3**, 518.
anti-Jewish decrees of, in Hungary, **3**, 520-1.
degrades the Jews, **3**, 563.
Jewish constitution of, re-issued, **3**, 564.
anti-Jewish decrees of, confirmed, **3**, 611.
Innocent IV, pope, appealed to, in behalf of the Talmud, **3**, 579.
condemns the blood accusation, **3**, 583-5, 635.
opposes the forcible baptism of Jews, **4**, 165.
Innocent VII, pope, opposes the expulsion of the Jews, **4**, 346.
Innocent VIII, pope, urges the establishment of the Portuguese Inquisition, **4**, 368.
Innocents, the, legend concerning the slaughter of, **2**, 116.
"**Inquiry** into Light and Truth," directed against Mendelssohn, **5**, 363.
"**Inquiry** into Probability," essay by Mendelssohn, **5**, 299.
Inquisition, the, established in France, **3**, 542.
meets opposition in Navarre, **4**, 357.

Inquisition, the (*continued*), established at Benevento, **4**, 385.
condemns Molcho to the stake, **4**, 506-7.
at Rome authorized, **4**, 525.
burns the Talmud and other Hebrew writings in Italy, **4**, 565.
tries the Marranos of Ancona, **4**, 568, 570.
permits the printing of the Zohar, **4**, 583.
persecutes the Bologna Jews, **4**, 590-1.
in the Netherlands, **4**, 601, 662.
the Jews of Italy put under, **4**, 654.
cruelties of, to Jews, recounted by Manasseh ben Israel, **5**, 31-2.
Inquisition, the Portuguese, commission for the establishment of, **4**, 365.
planned by João III, **4**, 490
idea of, abandoned, **4**, 490-1.
plans for, mooted, **4**, 499-500.
establishment of, opposed, **4**, 500, 505.
established by Clement VII, **4**, 507.
inhumanity of, complained of by the Marranos, **4**, 509.
proceedings of, stopped by Clement VII, **4**, 513.
power of, abrogated by Clement VII, **4**, 514.
commission on, **4**, 514-15.
reconsideration of, ordered by Paul III, **4**, 516.
arrested by Paul III, **4**, 517.
sanctioned by Paul III, **4**, 518, 527.
cruelty of, **4**, 519-20.
practically abrogated by Paul III, **4**, 520.
rules of, enforced, **4**, 521.
Inquisition, the Portuguese (*continued*), crippled, **4**, 522.
described by Samuel Usque, **4**, 522.
described by an assembly of cardinals, **4**, 523.
imprisons Marranos, **4**, 670.
Inquisition, the Spanish, first germs of, **4**, 167.
deals with Judaizing Marranos, **4**, 256.
and the Jews, **4**, 308.
established by Ferdinand and Isabella, **4**, 309.
views on the establishment of, **4**, 310.
authorized by Sixtus IV, **4**, 311.
commission to frame the statute for, **4**, 312.
statute of, ratified, **4**, 312.
judges of, **4**, 312.
established in Seville, **4**, 312-13.
distrust of, **4**, 313.
orders the surrender of fugitive Marranos, **4**, 313-14.
first victims of, **4**, 314.
publishes the Edict of Grace, **4**, 315.
heresy defined by, **4**, 315-16.
first auto-da-fé ordered by, **4**, 317.
cruelty of, censured by Sixtus IV, **4**, 318-19.
established in Aragon, **4**, 319, 330.
opposition to, in Aragon, **4**, 319, 328-9.
opposition to, in Sicily, **4**, 319-20.
judges of, cannot be Marranos, **4**, 321.
rigors of, modified by Sixtus IV, **4**, 322.
confined at first to the southern part of the country, **4**, 323.

Inquisition, the Spanish (*continued*), description of, by Samuel Usque, **4,** 324–5.
tribunals of, established by Torquemada, **4,** 325.
in Ferdinand's hereditary lands, **4,** 325–6.
code of, by Torquemada, **4,** 326–8.
the introduction of, resisted by the northern provinces, **4,** 332.
increase of the victims of, **4,** 332.
established in Barcelona and Majorca, **4,** 332.
described by Isaac Arama, **4,** 332.
in Seville, **4,** 335.
turned against the enemies of the Jews, **4,** 355.
victims of, under Torquemada, **4,** 356.
evil effects of, **4,** 356.
described by Peter Martyr, **4,** 484.
Christian victims of, **4,** 485.
executes Marranos denounced by David Reubeni, **4,** 511.
Interest, the charging of, forbidden by the Council of Narbonne, **3,** 518. *See under* Usury.
Intermarriages, between the heathen and the Israelites, **1,** 56–7.
between the Judæans and the Samaritans, **1,** 361–2, 383.
with Ammonites and Moabites prohibited, **1,** 362.
Ezra on, with the heathen, **1,** 367–9.
law against, expounded by Ezra, **1,** 380.
dissolved by Nehemiah, **1,** 386.
between Jews and Christians forbidden by Constantius, **2,** 567.
Intermarriages (*continued*), forbidden by the Council of Illiberis, **2,** 620.
in Gaul, **3,** 36.
between the Vangioni and Jewish women, **3,** 41.
in Spain in the sixth century, **3,** 44.
prohibited by the Council of Toledo and Reccared, **3,** 46.
between Jews and Arabs, **3,** 56–7.
supposed to be prevented by Jew badges, **3,** 511.
in Hungary, **3,** 521.
in southern Spain, **3,** 527.
denounced by Moses of Coucy, **3,** 546.
prohibited by the code of Alfonso X, **3,** 595.
objected to by the Remonstrants, **4,** 674.
discussed by the Assembly of Jewish Notables, **5,** 489, 491.
discussed by the French Synhedrion, **5,** 496–7.
permitted in Mecklenburg, **5,** 507.
"**Investigation** into the Evidences of Christianity against Unbelievers," by Caspar Bonnet, **5,** 309.
"**Investigation** of Religion, The," by Elias del Medigo, **4,** 293.
"**Investigation** of Van Swieden's Work in Reference to the Civil Rights of the Jews," by Friedrichsfeld, **5,** 454.
Ionians, the, buy Judæans as slaves, **1,** 227.
Ipsus, battle of, **1,** 417.
Irak, name for Babylonia among the Arabs, **3,** 89.
divided in jurisdiction between Sora and Pumbeditha, **3,** 98.

Irak (*continued*). *See* Babylonia.

Isaac, ambassador from Simon II to Nahar-Pakod, **2**, 443–4.

Isaac, father of Chasdaï Ibn-Shaprut, patron of men of letters, **3**, 216, 224.

Isaac, the Jew attached to Charlemagne's embassy to Haroun Alrashid, **3**, 143.

Isaac. *See* Mar-Isaac.

Isaac of Accho, Kabbalist, at the siege of Accho, **3**, 650.
suspicious of the authenticity of the Zohar, **4**, 20.

Isaac the Blind (1190–1210), founder of the Kabbala, doctrines and disciples of, **3**, 547–8.

Isaac the Elder. *See* Isaac ben Samuel.

Isaac de Leon, last rabbi of Toledo, disciple of, **4**, 392.

Isaac of Mayence, repentant apostate, **3**, 303.

Isaac of Salzuflen, refused the right of settlement in Hamburg, **4**, 685–6.

Isaac of Vienna, disciple of Judah Sir Leon, **3**, 409.

Isaac the Younger. *See* Isaac ben Abraham.

Isaac ben Joseph, Palestinian Amora, banished from Judæa, **2**, 567.

Isaac ben Abba-Mari, Talmudist, **3**, 399–400.

Isaac ben Abraham (Rizba, the Younger), Tossafist, **3**, 408.

Isaac ben Abraham Akrish (1489–1575), Spanish exile, wanderings of, **4**, 386.

Isaac ben Abraham Ibn-Ezra, accompanies his father on his journeys, **3**, 369, 375.
apostate to Islam, **3**, 442.

Isaac ben Abraham Ibn-Latif (1220–1290), Kabbalist, system of, **4**, 3–4.

Isaac ben Abraham Troki (1533–1596), Karaite writer, antagonizes Christianity, **4**, 648–9.

Isaac ben Asher Halevi (Riba), of Speyer, Tossafist, **3**, 345.

Isaac ben Baruch Albalia (1035–1094), descent of, **3**, 282.
at Cordova and Granada, **3**, 283.
works of, **3**, 283.
escapes the massacre of Granada, **3**, 283.
as astronomer, **3**, 283.
chief of the Jews of Seville, **3**, 283–4.
hostility of, to Alfassi, **3**, 313.
descendant of, **3**, 364.

Isaac ben Eliakim, rabbi of Würzburg, martyr, **3**, 354.

Isaac ben Jacob Alfassi (Alkalaï, 1013–1103), Talmudist, disciple of Nissim and Chananel, **3**, 282, 285.
originality of, **3**, 285–6.
death of, **3**, 309.
elegies on, **3**, 310, 323.
makes Lucena famous, **3**, 311
hostility of, to Isaac Ibn-Albalia, **3**, 313.
disciples of, distinguished, **3**, 314.
successor of, **3**, 315.
college of, attended by Jehuda Halevi, **3**, 322.
commentaries of, annotated by Serachya Halevi Gerurdi, **3**, 389.
commentary on the Talmudic work of, by Jonathan of Lünel, **3**, 397.
method of, followed by Nachmani, **3**, 532.
Talmudic decisions by, justified by Nachmani, **3**, 532.

Isaac ben Jacob Campanton (1360–1463), Talmudist, **4,** 230.
Isaac ben Jacob Halaban, Tossafist, **3,** 421.
Isaac ben Jehuda Ibn-Giat (1030–1089), poet, philosopher, Talmudist, **3,** 282, 284.
disciple of, **3,** 314.
Isaac ben Joseph of Corbeil, author of a religious manual, **3,** 587.
Isaac ben Joseph Caro, escapes from Portugal, **4,** 378.
Isaac ben Joseph Israeli II, astronomer, **4,** 51.
Isaac (I) ben Judah Abrabanel (1437–1509), descent of, **4,** 169, 337.
friend of Yechiel of Pisa, **4,** 286–7.
collects a ransom for Jewish prisoners, **4,** 287, 339.
minister of finance to Ferdinand and Isabella, **4,** 336–7, 343.
character and ability of, **4,** 337.
financier for Alfonso V of Portugal, **4,** 337–8.
noble and learned friends of, **4,** 338, 341.
instructs the Italian Jews how to receive the Portuguese embassy, **4,** 340.
family of, **4,** 340, 360, 383–4, 408–10.
flees to Toledo, **4,** 341.
as commentator, **4,** 342–3.
orthodoxy of, **4,** 342.
protects the Castilian Jews, **4,** 343–4.
tries to have the edict of banishment revoked, **4,** 348.
goes to Naples, **4,** 359.
commentary by, on the Books of Kings, **4,** 359.
Isaac (I) ben Judah Abrabanel (*continued*), employed by kings of Naples, **4,** 359, 360.
in Sicily, **4,** 383–4.
in Venice, **4,** 385.
consulted by the Venetian senate, **4,** 385–6.
old age of, **4,** 386.
censures the impure language of the German Jews, **4,** 388–9.
death of, **4,** 409.
condemns free thinkers, **4,** 479.
and Messianic expectations, **4,** 482.
Isaac ben Leon, a Granada Jew, supports Balkin, **3,** 258.
Isaac ben Meïr of Rameru, grandson of Rashi, Tossafist, **3,** 345, 375.
Isaac ben Mordecai (Maëstro Gayo), physician, **3,** 628.
Isaac ben Moses. *See* Profiat Duran.
Isaac ben Moses Ibn-Sakni, given the title Gaon at Pumbeditha, **3,** 282, 284–5.
awakens interest in Talmud studies in Bagdad, **3,** 429.
Isaac ben Reuben Albergeloni, Talmudist and liturgical poet, **3,** 284.
Isaac ben Samuel (Ri, the Elder), great-grandson of Rashi, Tossafist, completes Rashi's commentary, **3,** 403.
college of, **3,** 403–4.
collects the "old Tossafoth," **3,** 404.
son of, a martyr, **3,** 404.
forbids Jews to buy confiscated property, **3,** 406–7.
Isaac ben Sheshet Barfat (Ribash, 1310–1409), Talmudist, **4,** 145–6, 148.

Isaac ben Sheshet Barfat (*continued*), disciple of Solomon ben Adret, **4**, 147.
opposed to the study of science, **4**, 147.
rigid piety of, **4**, 147, 148, 149.
rabbi of Saragossa, **4**, 148.
opposes Chayim ben Gallipapa's innovations, **4**, 149.
authority of, **4**, 149–50.
imprisonment of, **4**, 150.
appealed to, in a dispute about the French chief rabbinate, **4**, 150, 153.
chief rabbi of Tlemçen, **4**, 198–9.
protects Marrano fugitives, **4**, 199.
attacked by Simon Duran, **4**, 199.
Isaac ben Simeon, a Spanish Jew, has the Jewish prayers compiled, **3**, 178.
Isaac ben Suleiman Israeli I (845–940), physician, medical author, and philosopher, **3**, 180–1.
admiration of, for Saadiah, **3**, 192.
influence of, on Jewish science in the Fatimide Caliphate, **3**, 211.
Isaac ben Todros, Kabbalist, disciple of, **4**, 74.
Isaac Ibn-Albalia. *See* Isaac ben Baruch Albalia.
Isaac Ibn-G'ikatilia, disciple of Menachem ben Saruk, defends him, **3**, 227.
poet, **3**, 237.
teacher of Ibn-Janach, **3**, 261.
Isaac Ibn-Sahal, teacher of Ibn-Janach, **3**, 261.
Isaac (Zag) Ibn-Said, compiler of the Alfonsine Tables, **4**, 367.
Isaac Ibn-Sakni. *See* Isaac ben Moses Ibn-Sakni.
Isaac Ibn-Zachin, commits suicide to avoid baptism, **4**, 376.
Isaac (I) Abrabanel. *See* Isaac (I) ben Judah Abrabanel.
Isaac (II) Abrabanel, son of Isaac ben Judah, physician, **4**, 340, 385.
Isaac (III) Abrabanel, son of Judah Leon, baptized, **4**, 361.
Isaac Albalag, philosopher, mysticism of, **4**, 24.
accused of heresy, **4**, 342.
Isaac Arama, on the Inquisition, **4**, 332.
Isaac Benveniste, physician, tries to prevent anti-Jewish legislation, **3**, 508.
has delegates sent to the Fourth Lateran Council, **3**, 509.
tries to have the decree on Jew badges repealed, **3**, 513.
honored by Honorius III, **3**, 515.
Isaac Bonastruc, has a tax imposed on Marrano fugitives, **4**, 199.
Isaac Cohen Shalal, Nagid of Egypt, wealth and learning of, **4**, 392.
in Jerusalem, **4**, 398.
Isaac Halevi, of Worms, on Rashi, **3**, 287.
Isaac Hamon. *See* Hamon, Isaac.
Isaac Israeli I. *See* Isaac ben Suleiman Israeli I.
Isaac Israeli II. *See* Isaac ben Joseph Israeli II.
Isaac Lurya Levi (1534–1572), descent and youth of, **4**, 618.
under the influence of the Zohar, **4**, 618–19.

Isaac Lurya Levi (*continued*), evolves a system from the Zohar, **4**, 619–22.
considers himself the Messiah of the branch of Joseph, **4**, 622, 624.
goes to Safet, **4**, 622.
glorified by Chayim Vital Calabrese, **4**, 623–4.
disciples of, **4**, 624.
glorified after death, **4**, 624–5.
principles of, taught in Italy, **4**, 625.
harm done by, **4**, 625–7; **5**, 559.
lays stress on devotion in prayer, **4**, 626.
the Sabbath in the system of, **4**, 626.
introduces a second Day of Atonement, **4**, 626.
influence of, on the Judaism of the seventeenth century, **5**, 51–2.
disciples of, spread his Kabbala, **5**, 52.
manuscripts by, **5**, 53–4.
Kabbala of, accepted by Sabbataï Zevi, **5**, 118, 119.
Messianic speculations in the works of, **5**, 120–1.
works of, studied by Chelebi, **5**, 125.
Jerusalem Jews adherents of, **5**, 125.
writings of, influence Luzzatto, **5**, 236.
prayer book of, used by the Chassidim, **5**, 386–7.
Isaac Nathan ben Kalonymos, polemic works by, **4**, 234.
Bible concordance by, **4**, 234–5.
Isaac Pulgar, refutes the charges of Alfonso Burgensis, **4**, 82.
philosopher, **4**, 91.
Isaac Sanjari, converts Bulan to Judaism, **3**, 140.
Isaac Triest, Jewish advocate before Maximilian I, **4**, 436–7.
Isaac Tyrnau, compiles the customs of various communities, **4**, 134.
orthodoxy of, **4**, 227.
Isaac Zarfati, urges the German Jews to emigrate to Turkey, **4**, 271–3.
Isaacs, the five, **3**, 282.
Isabella I, the Catholic, of Castile, candidate for the throne, **4**, 279.
marriage of, **4**, 280.
accession of, **4**, 284.
superstition of, **4**, 310.
hesitates to sanction the Inquisition for Marranos, **4**, 311.
attitude of, towards the Marranos, **4**, 311–12.
annoyed by opposition to the Inquisition, **4**, 320.
See also Ferdinand and Isabella.
Isabella II, of Castile, daughter of the preceding, to marry Manoel of Portugal, **4**, 373.
hostile to the Jews, **4**, 373, 379–80.
demands the banishment of the Jews, **4**, 374.
cruelty of, **4**, 376.
death of, **4**, 381.
Isabelle, countess of Chartres, persecutes the Jews of Blois, **3**, 379.
Isaiah, the Babylonian, prophet, describes the suffering of the exiles, **1**, 344.
oratory of, **1**, 344–5.
consolation given by, **1**, 345–6.
describes Israel as the apostle to the nations, **1**, 346–7.
prophesies the fall of Babylon, **1**, 347–8.

Isaiah, son of Amoz, prophet, prophecies of, **1,** 251–3.
wife of, **1,** 251.
disciples of, **1,** 253–4, 279. *See* Anavim, the.
warns Ahaz against the Assyrian alliance, **1,** 258–9.
advises neutrality between Egypt and Assyria, **1,** 270.
reproves Shebna, **1,** 271.
predicts the doom of Assyria, **1,** 272–3.
predicts Sennacherib's failure, **1,** 273, 276.
exhorts Hezekiah not to surrender, **1,** 275.
reproves Hezekiah for his reception of Merodach-baladan's embassy, **1,** 279.
in Immanuel Romi's work, **4,** 67.
Isaiah, the Book of, reading of, forbidden by Justinian I, **3,** 15.
commentary on, by Abraham Ibn-Ezra, **3,** 373.
Isaiah ben Abba-Mari, authorized to ordain disciples in France, **4,** 152.
relieves Jochanan of his office as chief rabbi, **4,** 152, 162.
appoints his relations to the French rabbinates, **4,** 153.
Isaiah Chassid, Sabbatian leader, **5,** 213, 229.
Isambert, French deputy, charges Ratti Menton with cruelty, **5,** 650.
Isavites, adherents of Obaiah Abu-Isa ben Ishak, **3,** 125.
Iscion, Jewish printing house in, **4,** 289.
Isebab, teacher of the Law, clerk of the Jamnia Synhedrion, **2,** 357.
charitably inclined, **2,** 405.
martyr, **2,** 429.
Ishbi of Gath, Philistine champion, **1,** 117.
Ishbosheth, son of Saul, made king of the Ten Tribes by Abner, **1,** 108.
peaceable disposition of, **1,** 109.
deserted by Abner, **1,** 110.
mourns Abner, **1,** 112.
death of, **1,** 112.
Ishmael, ancestor of the northern Arabs, **3,** 60.
Ishmael II, high priest, appointed by Agrippa II, **2,** 246.
envoy to Nero, **2,** 248.
Ishmael of Akbara, founds a Karaite sect, **3,** 157.
Ishmael ben Elisha, teacher of the Law, opponent of Akiba's system, **2,** 355–6.
martyr, **2,** 356, 427–8.
praises Simon ben Nanos, **2,** 358.
nephew of, **2,** 370.
deprecates Minæan influence on Judaism, **2,** 378.
emigrates to Usha, **2,** 405.
at Lydda, **2,** 423.
counsels religious laxness as a measure of self-preservation, **2,** 424.
Meïr disciple of, **2,** 436.
method of, in southern Judæa, **2,** 442.
Ishmael ben José (ben Chalafta), teacher of the Law, ill-treated by the Samaritans, **2,** 457–8.
denounces Jewish freebooters to the Romans, **2,** 464–5.
denounced, **2,** 465.
Ishmael Ibn-Nagrela. *See* Samuel Halevi Ibn-Nagrela.
Ishmael, son of Nethaniah, protected by Baalis of Ammon, **1,** 317–18.

Ishmael, son of Nethaniah (*continued*), treacherous to Gedaliah, **1,** 321–2.
kills Gedaliah, **1,** 322.
takes refuge with the Ammonites, **1,** 322–3.
end of, unknown, **1,** 325.
Ishmael Almansur Ibnul' Kaim, Fatimide caliph, patron of Dunash ben Tamim, **3,** 211.
Ishmael Chanina, rabbi of Bologna, steadfastness of, **4,** 591.
Ishmaelites, the northern Arabians, **3,** 61.
Isidore, archbishop of Seville, presides over the Council of Toledo, **3,** 49.
writes two books against the Jews, **3,** 50.
Isidorus, an Alexandrian actuary, hostile to the Judæans, **2,** 181.
envoy of the Greek Alexandrians to Caligula, **2,** 186.
Isis, Egyptian goddess, **1,** 9.
Islam, the faith of Mahomet, **3,** 71.
intolerance of, **3,** 87–8.
divided on the election of the fourth caliph, **3,** 90.
among the Chazars, **3,** 139.
champion of, tries to convert Bulan, **3,** 139–40.
philosophy of, called Kalâm, **3,** 146–9.
theology affects the Jews of the East, **3,** 148.
objections of, to Judaism, answered by Saadiah, **3,** 198.
conversion to, decreed by Hakim, **3,** 247.
contest of, with Christianity, **3,** 297.
characterized by Jehuda Halevi, **3,** 329, 330.
Islam (*continued*), characterized as idolatry by a Jewish writer, **3,** 453.
See also Conversions, forced, of Jews to Islam.
Isle de France, the inheritance of the kings of France, **3,** 401.
Jews banished from, by Philip Augustus, **3,** 402–3.
the Jews of, not permitted to move to Champagne, **3,** 406.
Isny, Hebrew printing house at, **4,** 474.
Ispahan, Armenian Jews colonized in, **2,** 591.
called Jehudia, **2,** 591.
Ispahan, the Jews of, persecuted by Firuz, **2,** 629.
adherents of Obaiah Abu-Isa ben Ishak, **3,** 124.
in the twelfth century, **3,** 434.
Ispahanites, adherents of Obaiah Abu-Isa ben Ishak, **3,** 125.
Israel (Ten Tribes), the house of, renounces allegiance to David, **1,** 140.
revolts from David, **1,** 148–50.
dislike of, to Judah under Solomon, **1,** 174.
Israel (Ten Tribes), the kingdom of, first indications of, **1,** 109.
founded by Jeroboam, **1,** 183.
subjects of, worship at Jerusalem, **1,** 185.
idolatry introduced into, by Jeroboam, **1,** 185–7.
loyalty to monotheism in, under Ahab, **1,** 198–9.
luxury in, **1,** 232.
immorality in, under Jeroboam II, **1,** 233.
idolatry in, under Menahem, **1,** 244, 247.
invaded by Pul, **1,** 246–7.

Israel (Ten Tribes), the kingdom of (*continued*), power of, under Menahem, **1**, 247.
invaded by Tiglath-Pileser II, **1**, 259–60.
inhabitants of, carried to Assyria, **1**, 260.
debauchery of the nobles of, under Hoshea, **1**, 262–3.
end of, **1**, 264–5.
See also Samaria, etc.

Israel (Ten Tribes), the kings of, list of:

Ahab,
Ahaziah,
Baasha,
Elah,
Hoshea,
Jehoahaz,
Jehoash,
Jehoram (Joram),
Jehu,
Jeroboam I,
Jeroboam II,
Menahem,
Nadab,
Omri,
Pekah,
Pekahiah,
Shallum,
Tibni,
Zechariah,
Zimri.

Israel (whole nation), history of, by Baruch, **1**, 336–7.
See under Israelites, the.
Israel, Young, under Hegel's influence, **5**, 585.
Israel of Enns, charged with host desecration, **4**, 223.
Israel of Kozieniza, leader of the Chassidim, **5**, 393.
Israel of Miedziboz (Baal Shem, Besht, 1698–1759), founder of the new Chassidism, **5**, 375.
early life of, **5**, 376.
intense devoutness of, **5**, 376–7.
visions of, **5**, 377.
occupation of, **5**, 378.
miracles done by, **5**, 378.
followers of, **5**, 378–9.
successor of, **5**, 379.
introduces pilgrimages, **5**, 380.
sayings by, **5**, 393.
Israel Bruna (1400–1480), rabbi of Ratisbon, **4**, 300, 302.
calumniated by an apostate, **4**, 302, 303.
Israel Bruna (*continued*), misfortunes of, **4**, 302.
opposition to, in Ratisbon, **4**, 302–3.
imprisoned, **4**, 303.
protected by Frederick III, **4**, 303–4.
released, **4**, 304.
Israel Isserlein, defends Israel Bruna, **4**, 302.
death of, **4**, 303.
Israel Najara, Damascus poet, **4**, 609.
Israel Saruk, teaches Lurya's principles in Italy, **4**, 625.
Israel Zamosc, teaches Mendelssohn, **5**, 295.
Israel, Abraham. *See* Abraham Israel.
Israeli I. *See* Isaac ben Suleiman Israeli I.
Israeli II. *See* Isaac ben Joseph Israeli II.
Israelites, the (whole nation), entry of, into the Holy Land, **1**, 1, 32.
claim Canaan, **1**, 4–5.
in Egypt, **1**, 7–18.
influenced by the Egyptians, **1**, 8–9, 10.
Egyptian bondmen, **1**, 11.
degenerate in slavery, **1**, 11–12.
liberation of, **1**, 16–18.
pass through the Red Sea, **1**, 18–19.
at Mount Sinai, **1**, 20–1.
influence of the Sinaitic revelation on, **1**, 22.
worship idols in the desert, **1**, 23–4.
wanderings of, in the desert, **1**, 25–31.
elect judges in the desert, **1**, 26.
wars of, in the desert, **1**, 26–9.
opposed by the Idumæans, **1**, 27.

Israelites, the (whole nation) (*continued*), defeat Sihon, **1**, 27.
practice idolatry at Baal-Peor, **1**, 28.
cross the Jordan, **1**, 31.
defeated at Ai, **1**, 33.
defeat the five kings of Canaan, **1**, 34–5.
conquest of Canaan by, **1**, 39–40.
and the heathen practices of the Canaanites, **1**, 51, 57–9.
relation of, to the neighboring nations, **1**, 53–9.
intermarriages of, with the heathen, **1**, 56–7.
oppressed by the Moabites, **1**, 60.
oppressed by the Philistines, **1**, 61.
oppressed by Jabin, **1**, 61.
oppressed by the Midianites, **1**, 61–3.
attacked by the Philistines, **1**, 70–2.
idolatry of, under Samuel, **1**, 75.
warfare of, with the Philistines and Ammonites, **1**, 80.
demand a king, **1**, 80.
choose a king, **1**, 82–3.
condition of, at the beginning of Saul's reign, **1**, 84.
defeat the Philistines at Michmash, **1**, 86–9.
defeat the Amalekites, **1**, 91–2.
wage war with Achish, **1**, 102–4.
divided into two kingdoms, **1**, 109.
David king of, **1**, 112.
wage war with the Philistines, **1**, 115–18.
champions of, in the Philistine war, **1**, 117.
at war with Moabites, Ammonites, etc., **1**, 125–9.

Israelites, the (whole nation) (*continued*), enlargement of the territory of, **1**, 129–30.
See also Jews, the; Judæans, the.

Israelites, the (whole nation), the kings of, list of:

David, Saul,
Rehoboam, Solomon.

"Israelitische Allianz," founders and object of, **5**, 703.

"Israel's Hope," by Manasseh ben Israel, **5**, 31–2, 33.

Issachar, the tribe of, acquires pasture land in the north, **1**, 36–7.
relation of, to the Phœnicians, **1**, 53.

Isserlein, Israel. *See* Israel Isserlein.

Isserles. *See* Moses ben Israel Isserles.

Issor, a proselyte of Machuza, **2**, 587–8.

Italy, loses its importance, **2**, 560.
a province of the Byzantine Empire, **3**, 32.
under the Lombards, **3**, 33.
Talmud scholars of, in the tenth century, **3**, 212.
French exiles settle in, **4**, 177.
Austrian exiles settle in, **4**, 224.
tolerance in, in the fifteenth century, **4**, 285.
German rabbis in, hostile to philosophy, **4**, 293.
Marranos flee to, **4**, 318, 485.
Spanish exiles go to, **4**, 352, 407–10.
ships of, carry Spanish exiles, **4**, 358.
Spanish spoken in, by the exiles, **4**, 387.
Spanish exiles leaders in, **4**, 389.

Italy (*continued*), professorships for Hebrew instituted in, **4**, 471.
Jewish fugitives in, gather in national groups, **4**, 478.
the Kabbala in, **4**, 481; **5**, 488.
liberty of, defended by Clement VII, **4**, 492.
Polish Jewish fugitives in, **5**, 16.
rabbis of, Poles, **5**, 206.
the Sabbatian movement in, **5**, 209.
congregations of, present addresses to the Synhedrion, **5**, 496.
rabbis of, oppose the Reform movement, **5**, 571.
attitude of, towards the Damascus affair, **5**, 650.
See also under Rome.

Italy, the Jews of, in the fifth and sixth centuries, **3**, 27–34.
governed by the decrees of Theodosius I, **3**, 29–30.
and Pope Gelasius, **3**, 29.
under Theodoric, **3**, 29–30.
Cassiodorus on, **3**, 31.
support Theodatus, **3**, 31–2.
under the Byzantine rule, **3**, 32.
under the Lombards, **3**, 33.
under Pope Gregory I, **3**, 33–4.
devoted to the Agada in the ninth century, **3**, 160.
banishment of, decreed by Louis II, **3**, 174.
yield precedence to the Jews of Spain, **3**, 236.
uncultured in the eleventh century, **3**, 290.
political position of, favorable, **3**, 290.
culture of, before Abraham Ibn-Ezra, **3**, 369.
taught the importance of Hebrew grammar, **3**, 371.

Italy, the Jews of (*continued*), in the twelfth century, **3**, 421–4.
not interested in Talmud study, **3**, 421.
favorable condition of, under Alexander III, **3**, 421.
speak four languages, **3**, 423.
influence of Abraham Ibn-Ezra on, **3**, 423.
address Solomon ben Adret for religious decisions, **3**, 620.
in the Maimunist controversy, **3**, 624.
refuse to support Solomon Petit, **3**, 627–8.
political condition of, in the thirteenth century, **3**, 628.
influenced by Maimonides' philosophical works, **3**, 629–30.
culture of, in the fourteenth century, **4**, 59.
Maimonides' works translated for, **4**, 60.
distress of, during Vincent Ferrer's crusade, **4**, 218.
delegates of, wait on Martin V, **4**, 219.
poetry of, in the fifteenth century, **4**, 230.
Eugenius IV's bull against, **4**, 251.
Nicholas V's bull against, **4**, 253.
Nicholas V abolishes the privileges of, **4**, 254.
privileges of, as financiers, **4**, 286.
as physicians, **4**, 287.
on friendly terms with Christians, **4**, 287–8.
culture of, in the fifteenth century, **4**, 289.
as printers, **4**, 289.
participate in the renaissance, **4**, 289, 290.

Italy, the Jews of (*continued*), influence of German immigrants on, **4,** 294.
the clergy arouses ill-will against, **4,** 295–6.
Bernardinus of Feltre preaches against, **4,** 296.
instructed how to receive the Portuguese embassy, **4,** 340.
popes friendly to, **4,** 407.
joined by numerous exiles, **4,** 408.
ruled over by the immigrants, **4,** 408.
adherents of Asher Lämmlein, **4,** 485.
submit questions to the Polish Talmudists, **4,** 639.
suffer from the Catholic reaction, **4,** 653–5.
under the jurisdiction of the Inquisition, **4,** 654.
conversion of, planned by Gregory XIII, **4,** 654–5.
bribe the censors, **4,** 659.
poor, **5,** 205.
emancipated by the French, **5,** 459.
send deputies to the Assembly of Notables, **5,** 482, 488.
emancipation of, nullified by Pius VII, **5,** 518.
address the Congress of Aix-la-Chapelle, **5,** 527.
influenced by the moderate Reform movement, **5,** 582–3.
See also under Franks, the, the empire of, the Jews of; Rome, the Jews of.

Italy, Lower, the Jews of, protected by Gregory I, **3,** 33.

Italy, northern, the Jews of, number of, **3,** 423–4.

Italy, southern, the Jews of, in the twelfth century, **3,** 421–4.
Italy, southern, the Jews of (*continued*), driven away by the Catholic reaction, **4,** 653.

Itil (Atel). *See* Volga, the.

Itil (Atel), capital of the Chazars, captured, **3,** 222.

Ittai, commander of mercenary troops under David, **1,** 137.
faithful to David in the war with Absalom, **1,** 141.
commander at Mahanaim, **1,** 144.

Ittur, Talmudic work by Isaac ben Abba-Mari, **3,** 400.

Ituræa, conquest of, planned by John Hyrcanus, **2,** 13.

Ituræans, the, converted by Aristobulus I, **2,** 37.

Itzig, Daniel, connected by marriage with Friedländer, **5,** 397.
daughter of, **5,** 413.
representative of the Berlin Jewish community, **5,** 415.

Itzig, Fanny, holds a salon in Vienna, **5,** 413–14.

Itzig, Itzig Daniel, director of the Berlin Free School, **5,** 416.

Ivan IV, of Russia, candidate for the Polish throne, **4,** 603.
refuses to permit Jews to trade in Russia, **4,** 633.

Izates, prince of Adiabene, converted to Judaism, **2,** 216.
accession of, **2,** 216–17.
arbitrator in Parthia, **2,** 217.
war of, with Abia of Arabia, **2,** 217–18.
sons of, study Hebrew, **2,** 218.
death of, **2,** 218–19.
relatives of, aid Judæa against Rome, **2,** 264.

J

Jaabez, Joseph. *See* Joseph Jaabez.
Jaazer, fortress taken by Judas Maccabæus, **1,** 474.
Jabbok, the, river, description of, **1,** 46.
Jabesh-Gilead, besieged by the Ammonites, **1,** 89–90.
the inhabitants of, bury Saul and Jonathan, **1,** 104, 107.
Jabez. *See* Emden, Jacob.
Jabin, Canaanite king, oppresses the Israelites, **1,** 61.
Jabin, king of Hazor, defeated by Joshua, **1,** 37.
Jabne. *See* Jamnia.
Jabustrissa, the Jews of, in the twelfth century, **3,** 424.
Jacob, another name for the tribe of Judah, **1,** 76.
Jacob, brother of Jesus. *See* James.
Jacob, the patriarch, buys land near Shechem, **1,** 4.
Jacob, Syrian priest, incites a crusade against the Damascus Jews, **2,** 662.
Jacob of Belzyce, controversialist, **4,** 648.
Jacob of Kephar Samia, a Jewish Christian, **2,** 370.
Jacob of London, Talmudist, chief rabbi of England, **3,** 504.
Jacob the Minæan, physician, defends the dogma of the Ascension, **2,** 539.
Jacob of Navarre, shelters a Marrano, **4,** 357–8.
Jacob of Orleans, Tossafist, founds a school in London, **3,** 409.
commits suicide, **3,** 411.
Jacob de Perpignan, permitted to remain in Bordeaux, **5,** 344.
Jacob of Segovia, Kabbalist, **4,** 2.
Jacob ben Abba Mari ben Simon Anatoli (1200–1250), Maimunist, at the court of Frederick II, **3,** 566.
as a translator, **3,** 566, 567.
public discourses of, **3,** 566.
influences Italian Jewish culture, **3,** 629.
attacked by the anti-Maimunists, **4,** 32, 39, 40, 41.
Jacob ben Asheri (Baal ha-Turim, 1280–1340), Talmudist, piety of, **4,** 87–8.
poverty and disinterestedness of, **4,** 88.
religious code of, **4,** 88–90, 537, 539.
See also Turim.
Jacob ben Eleazar, messenger to the Chazars, **3,** 220.
Jacob ben Machir Tibbon (Profiat, 1236–1312), scientist, attainments of, **4,** 30–1.
chief of the enlightened party, **4,** 31.
appeals to Solomon ben Adret, **4,** 33.
excommunicates the opponents of science, **4,** 40–2.
Jacob ben Meshullam, the Nazarite, first promoter of the Kabbala, **3,** 396.
Jacob ben Moses Mölin Halevi (Maharil, 1365–1427), compiles the customs of various communities, **4,** 135.
orders a fast during the Hussite wars, **4,** 225–6.
rigid orthodoxy of, **4,** 227.
Jacob ben Nathaniel Ibn-Alfayumi, Talmudist of Yemen, **3,** 436.
appeals to Maimonides, **3,** 462, 464.

Jacob ben Natronaï, Gaon of Sora, **3**, 184, 185, 186.
Jacob ben Nissim Ibn-Shahin, disciple of Chushiel, Talmudist, **3**, 211.
elicits Sherira's "Letter," **3**, 233.
disciple of, **3**, 252.
Jacob ben Samuel, disciple of Saadiah, defends him, **3**, 204.
Karaite reply to, **3**, 204–5, 206.
Jacob ben Sheshet Gerundi (1243–1246), Kabbalist, **3**, 556.
Jacob ben Sosa, Idumæan leader, helps the Zealots, **2**, 295, 301.
Jacob ben Yechiel Loans, physician to Emperor Frederick III, **4**, 413.
favored by Maximilian I, **4**, 414.
teacher of Reuchlin, **4**, 433.
Jacob Ibn-Chabib, scholar, **4**, 405.
Jacob Ibn-Ezra, father of the poet Moses, official under Habus, **3**, 319.
Jacob Ibn-Jau, supports Joseph Ibn-Abitur, **3**, 238, 240.
chief judge of the Andalusian Jews, **3**, 239.
loses his power, **3**, 240–1.
death of, **3**, 241.
Jacob Ibn-Nuñez, physician to Henry IV of Castile, **4**, 275.
Jacob, son of Judas the Galilean, insurrectionary leader, crucified, **2**, 199.
Jacob, son of Zebedee, disciple of Jesus, **2**, 153.
Jacob Abbassi, translator of Maimonides' Mishna commentary, **4**, 60.
Jacob Abi-Ayub, physician, executed on a charge of murder, **4**, 553.
Jacob Almansur, Almohade leader, at war with Alfonso VIII, **3**, 386–7.
Jacob Berab (1474–1541), Spanish exile, rabbi of Fez, **4**, 390.
in Egypt, **4**, 393.
Talmudist, **4**, 418.
tries to re-introduce the Semichah, **4**, 531–2.
and Levi ben Chabib, **4**, 533–4, 536.
reason adduced by, for the revival of ordination, **4**, 535.
forced to leave Palestine, **4**, 535.
ordains four Talmudists, **4**, 535–6.
death of, **4**, 536.
Jacob Emden. *See* Emden, Jacob.
Jacob Jehuda Leon. *See* Leon.
Jacob Joshua Falk. *See* Falk, Jacob Joshua.
Jacob Mantin. *See* Mantin, Jacob.
Jacob Pascate, supposed well poisoner, **4**, 102.
Jacob Perpignano (1170), head of the Marseilles Jewish community, **3**, 400.
Jacob Polak (1460–1530), Talmudist, alleged originator of the Pilpul, **4**, 418.
Jacob Querido, supposed son of Sabbataï Zevi, reverenced by the Sabbatians, **5**, 209.
declared the Messiah, **5**, 210.
profligacy of, **5**, 210.
accepts Islam, **5**, 211.
death of, **5**, 211.
son of, **5**, 211.
prayers addressed to, **5**, 274.
Jacob Tam of Rameru (1100–1171), Tossafist, respected by the king of France, **3**, 343.

Jacob Tam (*continued*), grandson of Rashi, **3**, 345.
attacked by crusaders, **3**, 355.
poem by, on Abraham Ibn-Ezra, **3**, 373, 376.
character and life of, **3**, 375–6.
as a grammarian, **3**, 376.
presides over rabbinical synods, **3**, 376–8.
orders mourning for the Jews of Blois, **3**, 380–1.
death of, **3**, 381.
disciples of, in England, **3**, 409.
ancestor of the Ibn-Yachya family, **4**, 609.
Jacob Tus, translates the Pentateuch into Persian, **4**, 401.
Jacob Weil. *See* Weil, Jacob.
Jacobacio, cardinal, on the commission to examine Paul III's Inquisition bull, **4**, 520.
Jacobi, accuses Lessing of Spinozism, **5**, 372.
Jacobson, Israel (1769–1828), procures the abolition of the poll-tax in Brunswick Lüneburg, **5**, 467.
character of, **5**, 500–1.
commemorates the emancipation of the Jews, **5**, 501.
effects consistorial organization in Westphalia, **5**, 501–2.
president of the consistory, **5**, 501, 502.
foolhardiness of, **5**, 502.
desires reforms, **5**, 502.
influence of Heine on, **5**, 546.
the reforms of, **5**, 561–2.
private synagogue of, in Berlin, **5**, 562–3.
delivers German sermons, **5**, 563.
party of, **5**, 568.
aids the Hamburg Temple, **5**, 568.
Jacobson, Israel (*continued*), enlists the aid of Libermann, **5**, 568, 571.
disciples of the school of, **5**, 578, 595.
and Mannheimer, **5**, 580.
advises the Society for Culture, **5**, 583.
Jacoby, Joel, author of the "Plaints of a Jew," **5**, 631, 632.
Jacopo, Flavio, poet, **4**, 610.
Jaddua, high priest, and Alexander the Great, **1**, 413.
Jael, Kenite woman, murders Sisera, **1**, 61.
Jaen, home of Chasdaï Ibn-Shaprut's ancestors, **3**, 216.
the Jews of, captives, **4**, 126.
Inquisition tribunals in, **4**, 325.
the Marranos of, flee, **4**, 351.
Jafa, Mordecai. *See* Mordecai Jafa.
Jaffa, Marcus Schlesinger, only Jew permitted in Venice, **5**, 172.
Jaffa. *See* Joppa.
Jager, Johann. *See* Rubianus, Crotus.
Jahaz, the Israelites victorious at, **1**, 27.
Jakim. *See* Alcimus.
James (Jacob), brother of Jesus, **2**, 148.
leader of the Law-abiding Nazarenes, **2**, 169, 222.
rebukes Peter, **2**, 231.
Jamnia (Jabne), conquered by Uzziah, **1**, 231.
occupied by Gorgias, **1**, 476.
revenue from, given to Salome, **2**, 120.
possession of the Roman emperors, **2**, 324.
school established at, **2**, 324–5, 334–5.
Simon II at, **2**, 434.

Jamnia, the Synhedrion of. *See* Synhedrion, the, of Jamnia.
Jampol, the blood accusation at, **5,** 279.
Jannaï, disciple of Judah I, on the relation between the Jews and Romans, **2,** 469.
permits the cultivation of the land in the Sabbatical year, **2,** 469.
adds supplements to the Mishna, **2,** 470.
Jannaï, neo-Hebraic poet, introduces rhyme, **3,** 116.
poems of, versified Agadas, **3,** 116.
disciple of, **3,** 116.
Janow, Hirsch (1750–1785), rabbi of Posen, opposes Mendelssohn's Pentateuch translation, **5,** 330.
acuteness and godliness of, **5,** 330–1.
Japha (Japhia), taken by Vespasian, **2,** 287.
Japhet ben Elia, Talmudist, **3,** 427.
Jarmuk, the, description of, **1,** 46.
Jarmuth, king of, defeated by Joshua, **1,** 34–5.
Jaroslav, Aaron, assists in Mendelssohn's Pentateuch translation, **5,** 334.
Jaroslaw, meeting place of the Polish Talmudists, **4,** 640, 644; **5,** 3.
Jason, brother and son of high priests, Hellenist, **1,** 435.
representative of Onias III, **1,** 439.
buys the high priesthood, **1,** 444.
introduces games and gymnasia into Judæa, **1,** 444–6.
sends ambassadors to Olympian games, **1,** 446.
Jason, brother and son of high priests (*continued*), deposed by Antiochus IV, **1,** 446–7.
takes refuge with Aretas, **1,** 447.
enters Jerusalem with troops, **1,** 451.
death of, **1,** 480–1.
Jason, son of Eleazar, Judæan envoy to Rome, **1,** 486.
Jatape, daughter of Samsigeramus, wife of Aristobulus, **2,** 195.
Jayme I, of Aragon, recommends Isaac Benveniste to the pope, **3,** 515.
exhorted not to employ Jews as diplomats, **3,** 515.
employs a Jewish physician, **3,** 536.
considers the Jews "servi cameræ," **3,** 596–7.
under the influence of Raymond de Penyaforte, **3,** 597; **4,** 77.
invites Nachmani to a disputation, **3,** 598.
expresses admiration for Nachmani, **3,** 601.
appoints censors for the Talmud, **3,** 602–3.
tries Nachmani on the charge of blasphemy, **3,** 604.
reprimanded by Clement IV, **3,** 605.
Jean d'Acre. *See* Accho.
Jean de Vendières. *See* John of Gorze.
Jebilé, the Jews of, in the twelfth century, **3,** 426.
Jebirol. *See* Solomon Ibn-Gebirol.
Jebus. *See* Jerusalem.
Jebusites, the, subdivision of the Canaanites, **1,** 3.
compact of, with Judah, **1,** 38.

Jebusites, the (*continued*), hold territory in the center of Palestine, **1**, 51.
barrier between Ephraim and Judah, **1**, 77.
subdued by David, **1**, 113–14.
occupy Mount Moriah, **1**, 119.
suffer under David, **1**, 131.
declared bondmen by Solomon, **1**, 163.
Jeconiah. *See* Jehoiachin.
Jedidiah, name of Solomon, **1**, 133.
Jeduthun, psalmist, **1**, 79, 120–1.
Jehoahaz, son of Jehu, king of Israel, at war with Syria, **1**, 221.
Jehoahaz (Shallum), son of Josiah, king of Judah, deposed by Necho, **1**, 298–9.
Jehoash, king of Judah. *See* Joash.
Jehoash (Joash), son of Jehoahaz, king of Israel, defeats Ben-hadad III, **1**, 221–2.
shows respect for the Law, **1**, 223.
reinstates the Shunamite, **1**, 223–4.
takes Amaziah of Judah prisoner, **1**, 224–5.
ransacks Jerusalem, **1**, 225.
death of, **1**, 225.
Jehoiachin (Jeconiah, Coniah), son of Jehoiakim, king of Judah, opposes Nebuchadnezzar, **1**, 306, 307.
practices idolatry, **1**, 306.
exiled to Babylonia, **1**, 307.
distinguished by Evil-Merodach, **1**, 331.
son of, **1**, 342.
grandson of, **1**, 351.
Jehoiada, high priest, loyal to the house of David, **1**, 214, 215.
anoints Joash king, **1**, 215–16.
Jehoiada (*continued*), removes Baal-worship from Jerusalem, **1**, 216–17.
raises the position of the high priest, **1**, 219–20.
death of, **1**, 220.
Jehoiakim (Eliakim), son of Josiah, king of Judah, pays tribute to Necho, **1**, 299.
idolatry and immorality under, **1**, 299–300.
slays Uriah, the prophet, **1**, 301.
refuses allegiance to Nebuchadnezzar, **1**, 304.
orders Jeremiah to be killed, **1**, 305.
vassal of Nebuchadnezzar, **1**, 306.
rebels against Nebuchadnezzar, **1**, 306.
death of, **1**, 307.
Jehoiakim, high priest, leader of the Judæan community after the exile, **1**, 360, 362.
Jehoram (Joram), son of Ahab, king of Israel, accession of, **1**, 207.
at war with Moab, **1**, 208–9.
at war with Hazael of Damascus, **1**, 210.
killed by Jehu, **1**, 210–11.
Jehoram, son of Jehoshaphat. *See* Joram.
Jehoshaphat, king of Judah, ally of Ahab, **1**, 206.
at war with Ben-hadad II, **1**, 206.
at war with Mesa, **1**, 209.
death of, **1**, 209.
Jehoshebah, daughter of Joram of Judah, saves Joash from Athaliah, **1**, 213.
wife of Jehoiada, raises Joash in the Temple, **1**, 215–16.
Jehozabad, a noble of Judah, kills Joash, **1**, 221.

Jehu, king of Israel, anointed, **1,** 210.
kills Jehoram of Israel and Ahab's other descendants, **1,** 211–12.
homage paid to, **1,** 212.
exterminates Baal-worship in Israel, **1,** 212.
loses territory, **1,** 220–1.
favorite character with the Puritans, **5,** 26.
Jehuda bar Joseph Ibn-Alfachar, bears the title prince, **3,** 385.
physician to Ferdinand III of Castile, **3,** 537.
anti-Maimunist, **3,** 540–1.
censured, **3,** 544.
Jehuda ben Asher I (1284–1349), Talmudist, piety of, **4,** 87–8.
rabbi of Toledo, authority of, **4,** 90.
disciple and successor of, **4,** 145.
Jehuda ben Asher II, great-grandson of Asheri, martyr, **4,** 170.
Jehuda ben David Melun, at the disputation with Donin, **3,** 576, 578.
Jehuda ben Elia Hadassi, Karaite writer, **3,** 362–3.
Jehuda ben Isaac ben Sabbataï, satirist, **3,** 559–60.
Jehuda ben Isaac Ibn-Wakar, treasurer to the regent of Castile, **4,** 52.
piety and severity of, **4,** 53.
Jehuda ben Meïr (Leon, Leontin), founder of the scientific study of the Talmud, **3,** 242.
teacher of Gershom ben Jehuda, **3,** 242, 243.
Jehuda ben Moses ben Daniel (Leone Romano, 1292), Italian Jewish scholar, **4,** 60, 68–9.
Jehuda ben Moses ben Daniel (*continued*), teacher of Robert of Naples, **4,** 68.
as translator, **4,** 69.
Jehuda ben Nathan (Riban), son-in-law of Rashi, Tossafist, **3,** 345.
Jehuda ben Shamua, petitions Turnus Rufus, **2,** 432.
Jehuda ben Samuel Halevi. *See* Jehuda Halevi.
Jehuda ben Solomon Cohen Ibn-Matka (1247), Jewish scholar in correspondence with Frederick II, **3,** 565–6.
Jehuda Ibn-Abbas, poet, **3,** 318, 426.
the son of, **3,** 442.
Jehuda Ibn-Balam (1070–1100), grammarian, **3,** 290.
Jehuda Ibn-Daud (Ibn-Zachariah Yachya Chayuj), defends Menachem ben Saruk, **3,** 227.
recognizes the triliteral root in Hebrew, **3,** 237.
teacher of Samuel Ibn-Nagrela, **3,** 255.
compared with Ibn-Janach, **3,** 262.
grammatical work of, translated into Hebrew, **3,** 371.
Jehuda Ibn-Ezra, commander of Calatrava, protects the Jews against the Almohades, **3,** 361–2.
steward of the imperial palace, **3,** 362.
persecutes the Karaites, **3,** 362–3.
Jehuda Alcharisi, on Abu Ayub, **3,** 312.
on the Jews of Barcelona, **3,** 387–8.
on Samuel ben Abraham Ibn-Chasdaï Halevi, **3,** 388.

Jehuda Alcharisi (*continued*), translates Maimonides' Mishna commentary, **3**, 492; **4**, 60.
satirist, **3**, 559.
in Immanuel Romi's work, **4**, 67.
Jehuda Halevi (Abulhassan Jehuda ben Samuel Halevi, 1086–1142), writes an elegy on Isaac Alfassi, **3**, 310, 323.
elegy by, on Solomon Ibn-Farussal, **3**, 313.
eulogizes Joseph ben Meïr Ibn-Migash, **3**, 315, 322, 323.
on Moses Ibn-Ezra, **3**, 321.
importance of, as a poet, **3**, 321–2; **4**, 67; **5**, 112.
character of, **3**, 322.
student at Lucena, **3**, 322.
early poems of, **3**, 322.
friendship of, with Moses Ibn-Ezra, **3**, 323.
love poems by, **3**, 323.
attainments and occupations of, **3**, 323–4.
theory of, on poetry, **3**, 324.
nature descriptions by, **3**, 325.
religious poems by, **3**, 325.
the national poetry of, **3**, 325–6, 327–8.
religious philosophical system of, **3**, 326–7, 330–6.
philosophical work by, **3**, 327–36.
on philosophy, Islam, Christianity, and Judaism, **3**, 328–31.
characterizes Judaism in detail, **3**, 331–6.
compares Talmudic Judaism and Karaism, **3**, 334.
view of, on Israel's suffering, **3**, 335–6.
view of, on the Holy Land, **3**, 336–7.
longing of, for the Holy Land, **3**, 338.
Jehuda Halevi (*continued*), sets out for Palestine, **3**, 338–9.
journey of, through Spain, **3**, 339.
at sea, **3**, 339.
at Alexandria, **3**, 339–40.
at Cairo, **3**, 340–1.
in Jerusalem, **3**, 342.
at Tyre and Damascus, **3**, 342.
death and epitaph of, **3**, 342.
and Abraham Ibn-Ezra, **3**, 367.
philosophical work of, translated into Hebrew, **3**, 397.
in Immanuel Romi's work, **4**, 67.
compared with Luzzatto, **5**, 233–4.
glorified by Heine, **5**, 555.
time of, described by Samuel David Luzzatto, **5**, 625.
Jehuda Leb Krysa. *See* Krysa.
Jehuda. *See also under* Judah; Judas.
Jehudaï. *See* Judah the Blind.
Jehudia, Ispahan, **2**, 591.
Jelal Addaulah, caliph of Bagdad, executes the last Gaon and Exilarch, **3**, 254.
Jena, the theological faculty of, permits Jews to live in Hamburg, **4**, 687.
battle of, **5**, 495.
Jenghis-Khan, the Jews of Germany accused of aiding, **3**, 580–1.
Jephet Ibn-Ali Halevi (950–990), Karaite, controversialist, **3**, 205–6.
works, ability, and style of, **3**, 206.
poetry of, **3**, 223.
Jephthah, judge, defeats the Ammonites, **1**, 64–5.
humbles the Ephraimites, **1**, 65.
daughter of, **1**, 66.

Jeremiah, Palestinian Amora, **2**, 560.
Jeremiah (645 or 640–580 or 570), prophet, character of, **1**, 289–90.
style of the prophecies of, **1**, 290–1.
the first prophecy by, **1**, 291.
announces universal ruin, **1**, 296.
lamentation by, for Josiah, **1**, 297.
prophecies of, under Jehoiakim, **1**, 301.
danger of, **1**, 302.
saved by Ahikam, **1**, 303.
has his prophecy read in the Temple, **1**, 304–5.
ordered to be killed, **1**, 305.
protected by the princes, **1**, 306.
counsels submission to Babylonian rule, **1**, 310.
rôle of, during the siege, **1**, 311–12.
reproaches Zedekiah with perjury, **1**, 312.
imprisoned, **1**, 312–13.
taken captive by the Chaldæans, **1**, 314.
lamentations of, over Jerusalem, **1**, 316.
disciple of, **1**, 319.
considerately treated by Nebuzaradan, **1**, 319–20.
joins Gedaliah at Mizpah, **1**, 320.
taken captive by Ishmael, **1**, 322.
rescued, **1**, 323.
advises against emigration to Egypt, **1**, 324.
goes to Egypt, **1**, 325.
rebukes the Egyptian Judæans for idolatry, **1**, 326–7.
end of, **1**, 327–8.
Jeremiah (*continued*), writings of, studied by the Babylonian exiles, **1**, 336.
on the conduct of Jews in foreign lands, **2**, 520.
Jericho, taken by Joshua, **1**, 32, 33.
David passes, when fleeing from Absalom, **1**, 142.
fortified by Hiel, **1**, 201.
an association of prophets at, **1**, 205, 234.
visited by Elijah, **1**, 208.
Hyrcanus II defeated at, **2**, 58.
a Synhedrion established at, **2**, 71.
Aristobulus (III) murdered at, **2**, 92.
district of, given to Cleopatra, **2**, 93.
Herod attempts suicide in, **2**, 116.
palace at, burnt, **2**, 125.
some Benu-Nadhir settle in, **3**, 79.
Jeroboam I, employed by Solomon as superintendent of buildings, **1**, 174.
incites rebellion against Solomon, **1**, 175–6.
flees to Egypt, **1**, 176.
returns to Palestine, **1**, 180.
leader of the Shechemite rebellion, **1**, 180–2.
chosen king by the Ephraimites, **1**, 182–3.
allied with Shishak, **1**, 184.
fortifies Israelitish towns, **1**, 185.
introduces calf-worship, **1**, 185–7.
rebuked by Ahijah, **1**, 188.
death of, **1**, 189.
end of the house of, **1**, 189.
Jeroboam II, king of Israel, at war with the Aramæans, **1**, 225.

Jeroboam II (*continued*), in friendly relations with Uzziah, **1**, 231, 232.
conquests and luxuriousness of, **1**, 232.
immorality and idolatry under, **1**, 233–4.
death of, **1**, 234.
Jerome (Hieronymus, 331–420), Church Father, taught by Jewish teachers, **2**, 623–4.
translates the Scriptures into Latin, **2**, 625.
hates the Jews, **2**, 625; **4**, 552.
on the Talmud, **3**, 577.
on a supposed Jewish formula of imprecation, **4**, 83.
exegetical works of, used by Isaac Abrabanel, **4**, 342.
pattern of Reuchlin, **4**, 433, 435.
Jerome Bonaparte, king of Westphalia, and the emancipation of the Jews, **5**, 500, 501.
reprimands Jacobson, **5**, 562.
Jerubbaal. *See* Gideon.
Jerusalem, the site of, occupied by the Jebusites, **1**, 3.
king of, defeated by Joshua, **1**, 34–5.
physical features of, **1**, 114–15.
becomes the royal residence, **1**, 114.
fortified and extended, **1**, 118–19.
center of religious life, **1**, 119–20.
prosperity and importance of, under Solomon, **1**, 168–9.
religious center for the northern tribes, **1**, 185.
fortified by Rehoboam, **1**, 185.
Baal-worship at, under Athaliah, **1**, 212.
Jehoiada ends Baal-worship in, **1**, 216–17.
the first conquest of, **1**, 225.
Jerusalem (*continued*), deprived of fortifications, by Jehoash, **1**, 226.
fortified by Uzziah, **1**, 231.
fortified by Jotham, **1**, 249.
besieged by Rezin and Pekah, **1**, 258, 259.
fortified against Sennacherib, **1**, 271.
celebration of the Passover at, under Josiah, **1**, 295.
the nation gathers in, to pray for help against Nebuchadnezzar, **1**, 304.
besieged by generals of Nebuchadnezzar, **1**, 307.
fortified by Zedekiah, **1**, 311.
besieged by Nebuchadnezzar, **1**, 311–12.
siege of, raised, **1**, 312.
siege of, resumed, **1**, 313.
taken by the Chaldæans, **1**, 313–14.
destroyed by Nebuzaradan, **1**, 315.
destruction of, mourned by the Babylonian Jews, **1**, 337–8.
return of exiles to, under Zerubbabel, **1**, 354–6.
arrival of Ezra in, **1**, 366.
attacked by Sanballat, **1**, 371.
taken by Sanballat, **1**, 372.
Nehemiah rebuilds the fortifications of, **1**, 374–5.
settlers invited to, by Nehemiah, **1**, 377–8.
the Law read in, by Ezra, **1**, 378–80.
the walls of, consecrated, **1**, 381–2.
a religious school established in, **1**, 396.
suffering in, under Bagoas, **1**, 409–10.
taken by Ptolemy I, **1**, 416.

Jerusalem (*continued*), the fortifications of, destroyed by Ptolemy I, **1**, 417.
improved by Simon the Just, **1**, 421.
entered by Antiochus III, **1**, 432.
taken by Scopas, **1**, 432.
athletic contests introduced in, **1**, 435.
gymnasia introduced in, **1**, 445.
occupied by Sostrates, **1**, 447.
occupied by Jason, **1**, 451.
taken by Antiochus Epiphanes, **1**, 451.
entered by Apollonius, **1**, 453–4.
entered by Judas Maccabæus, **1**, 471.
desolate condition of, after the Syrian depredations, **1**, 471–2.
besieged by Lysias, **1**, 479–80.
occupied by Alcimus, **1**, 487.
fortified by Jonathan Haphus, **1**, 494.
fortified by the Hasmonæans, **1**, 498.
venerated by the Egyptian Judæans, **1**, 509.
celebrated by Philo the Elder, **1**, 517–18.
besieged by Antiochus Sidetes, **2**, 3–4.
taken by Aristobulus II, **2**, 58.
besieged by Aretas, **2**, 60.
siege of, raised at the order of Rome, **2**, 62.
besieged by Pompey, **2**, 64–6.
walls of, razed, **2**, 67.
taken by Alexander, son of Aristobulus II, **2**, 70.
a Synhedrion established in, **2**, 71.
entered by Crassus, **2**, 74.
walls of, rebuilt by Cæsar, **2**, 76.
Jerusalem (*continued*), besieged by the Parthians, **2**, 82.
besieged by Herod, **2**, 87–8.
Herod's buildings in, **2**, 105.
the people of, hate Herod, **2**, 107.
in charge of Quintilius Varus. **2**, 122–3.
Jesus in, **2**, 161–2.
fortified by Agrippa I, **2**, 195.
occupied by Cuspius Fadus, **2**, 197.
foreign synagogues in, **2**, 201.
visited by Helen of Adiabene, **2**, 194, 218.
famine in, **2**, 218.
mausoleum of Helen in, **2**, 219.
annual pilgrimages to, **2**, 220.
the Synhedrion removed from, **2**, 239.
rebels against Cumanus, **2**, 244.
Agrippa II resides in, **2**, 247.
the Passover celebration of 66 in, **2**, 251.
the upper city of, plundered, **2**, 254.
the insurrection against Rome begins in, **2**, 255, 261.
garrisoned with Roman troops, **2**, 255.
conciliated by Agrippa II, **2**, 257–8.
the Roman garrison of, surrenders to the Zealots, **2**, 260.
the walls of, strengthened, **2**, 268.
rallying place of the patriots, **2**, 291–2.
fortifications of, **2**, 292.
undisturbed by Vespasian for two years, **2**, 297.
parties in, **2**, 301.
besieged by Titus, **2**, 301–10.
summoned to surrender, **2**, 302.

Jerusalem (*continued*), attacked from the north, **2**, 303.
famine in, **2**, 304, 305–6.
upper city of, taken, **2**, 309.
remnant in, after the Roman siege, **2**, 311.
the religious center, **2**, 322.
replaced by Jamnia as a religious center, **2**, 325.
rebuilt by Hadrian, **2**, 407, 421–2.
in the hands of the Jews under Bar-Cochba, **2**, 411.
ploughed over, by Turnus Rufus, **2**, 421.
Jews forbidden to enter, **2**, 433, 564; **3**, 23, 87.
permission for Jews to pray at, obtained from Marcus Aurelius, **2**, 457–8.
Jews permitted by Alexander Severus to enter, **2**, 482.
a Christian city, **2**, 597; **3**, 11.
taken by Sharbarza, **3**, 19.
not given to the Jews by the Persians, **3**, 21.
entered by Heraclius, **3**, 22.
Temple vessels removed to, by Justinian I, **3**, 27.
Arabian Jews pray towards, **3**, 58.
turning towards, in prayer instituted by Mahomet, **3**, 73.
taken by Omar, **3**, 87.
conflict in, between the Karaites and the Rabbanites, **3**, 135.
asceticism of the Karaites in, **3**, 181–2.
Jehuda Halevi at, **3**, 342.
Christian kingdom of, attacked by Nureddin, **3**, 349.
Christian pilgrims permitted by Saladin to enter, **3**, 405.
Jerusalem (*continued*), return to, projected by David Alrui, **3**, 431.
Maimonides in, **3**, 457.
Jews allowed by Saladin to settle in, **3**, 474.
mourning in, for Maimonides, **3**, 492–3.
rabbis of France and England emigrate to, **3**, 505–6.
notable for its illustrious dead, **3**, 506.
devastated by the Tartars, **3**, 605–6.
Nachmani in, **3**, 606.
pilgrims to, in the fourteenth century, **4**, 73–4.
the Spanish exiles in, **4**, 396–8.
improved morally by the exiles, **4**, 397, 398.
ordinances for the government of, **4**, 398.
subordinated to Safet, **4**, 533.
rabbis of, support Jacob Berab, **4**, 534.
Sabbataï Zevi at, **5**, 126–7.
rabbis of, threaten Sabbataï Zevi with excommunication, **5**, 132.
replaced by Gaza as the Sabbatian Holy City, **5**, 132.
Chayim Malach in, **5**, 213–14.
rabbis of, excommunicate Chayon, **5**, 216.
Jerusalem, the Jews of, join an expedition against the Christians of Tyre, **3**, 20.
burnt during the first crusade, **3**, 308.
dyers in the twelfth century, **3**, 427.
banished by Baldwin IV, **3**, 427.
occupations of, **4**, 74–5.
wish to build a synagogue on Mount Zion, **4**, 273–4.

Jerusalem, the Jews of (*continued*), offended by Jacob Berab, **4,** 532.
suffer through the Cossack wars, **5,** 16, 125, 127.
Kabbalists, **5,** 125-6.
credulity of, **5,** 126.
appeal to Chelebi, **5,** 127-8.
adherents of Sabbataï Zevi, **5,** 132.
oppose Napoleon, **5,** 459-60.
Jerusalem, a Babylonian, *See* Nahardea.
Jerusalem, the, of the Occident, **4,** 136.
" Jerusalem," by Mendelssohn, on ecclesiastical power and Judaism, **5,** 364-6.
praised by Kant, **5,** 365.
effect of, on Michaelis, **5,** 365-6.
Jerusalem Talmud, the. *See* Talmud, the Jerusalem.
Jesheboam, one of David's warriors, **1,** 116.
Jeshurun, Isaac, falsely charged with child murder, **5,** 42.
Jesiba de los Pintos, Jewish school at Rotterdam, **4,** 685.
Jesirat-ul-Amar, the Jews of, well treated by Zenki, **3,** 429.
Jesse, father of David, **1,** 96.
Jesse, Henry, enthusiast for Israel's restoration, **5,** 24, 35.
Jessel, Sir George, Master of the Rolls, **5,** 699.
Jesuits, the, order of, authorized by Paul III, **4,** 524.
welcomed in Portugal, **4,** 525.
influence of, **4,** 650.
instigate persecutions of the Jews in Poland, **5,** 1.
alienate the Cossacks, **5,** 2.
hold intercourse with Eibeschütz, **5,** 250.
Jesurun, David, poet, escapes from the Inquisition to Amsterdam, **4,** 669.
Jesurun, Rohel (Paul de Pina), Marrano poet, leans towards Christianity, **4,** 669.
returns to Judaism, **4,** 670.
festival songs by, **4,** 678-9.
Jesus of Nazareth (Galilee), birthplace and family of, **2,** 148-9.
moral purity of, **2,** 149.
religiousness of, **2,** 149-50.
Hillel the model of, **2,** 149-50.
disciple of John the Baptist, **2,** 150.
doctrines of, similar to Essenism, **2,** 150-1.
addresses himself to the lowest classes, **2,** 152.
unsuccessful in Nazareth, **2,** 153.
disciples of, **2,** 153, 157-8.
teachings of, **2,** 154-5.
relation of, to Judaism, **2,** 155-6.
merit of, **2,** 156.
miracles of, **2,** 156-7.
in the towns of Galilee, **2,** 157.
declares himself the Messiah, **2,** 158.
calls himself the " son of man," **2,** 158-9.
public sentiment against, **2,** 159-60.
followers of, in Bethany, **2,** 160.
in the Temple, **2,** 161.
reception of, in Jerusalem, **2,** 161-2.
betrayed by Judas Iscariot, **2,** 163.
trial of, **2,** 163-6.
declared guilty of blasphemy by the Synhedrion, **2,** 164.
execution of, according to the Roman law, **2,** 164-5.
not mentioned by Judæan historians, **2,** 166.

Jesus of Nazareth (*continued*), followers of, after his death, **2**, 166.
resurrection of, **2**, 168.
attitude of the disciples of, to Judaism, **2**, 168.
denied by Simon Peter, **2**, 169.
disciples of, claim miraculous power, **2**, 169–70.
compared with Philo, **2**, 214.
the Messianic character of, held to have annulled the Law, **2**, 221.
followers of, who cling to the Law, not molested, **2**, 222.
the resurrection of, and the apostle Paul, **2**, 225–6.
according to Paul, sets aside the Law, **2**, 230.
appeals to the Jewish peasants, **2**, 364.
as regarded by the Jewish Christians, **2**, 366, 367.
as regarded by the Pagan Christians, **2**, 367.
gradually endowed with divine attributes by the Jewish Christians, **2**, 370.
said to have been cursed by the Jews three times daily, **2**, 380; **5**, 185–6.
denial of, demanded of Christians by Bar-Cochba, **2**, 412.
spread of the worship of, counteracted by the Synhedrion, **2**, 413.
called "Lord," **2**, 413.
Julian the Apostate's opinion of, **2**, 596.
as viewed by Anan ben David, **3**, 133–4.
in the Talmud, **3**, 574, 577, 578.
Messianic character of, confirmed by the Bible and Talmud according to Pablo Christiani, **3**, 598, 599.

Jesus of Nazareth (*continued*), in the Biblical and rabbinical writings, according to Raymund Martin, **3**, 622.
the advent of, discussed by Chasdaï Crescas, **4**, 188.
proved the Messiah from the Talmud by Joseph Lorqui, **4**, 207, 208–9, 211, 212.
dogma of the divinity of, found in the Kabbala, **4**, 292.
said to be alluded to, in the Alenu prayer, **5**, 185.
Jesus ben Sapphia, Zealot leader in Tiberias, **2**, 274.
sets fire to a palace in Bethmaon, **2**, 279.
leader of discontented Galileans, **2**, 280.
Jesus, son of Pantheras, the Jesus of the Talmud, according to Yechiel of Paris, **3**, 577.
Jesus Sirach (200–176), describes Simon the Just in Ecclesiasticus, **1**, 421–2.
the book of proverbs by, **1**, 439–41.
defends social pleasures, **1**, 439.
recommends the employment of medical skill, **1**, 439–40.
condemns the Hellenists, **1**, 440–1.
urges obedience to the Law, **1**, 440.
reviews Jewish history, **1**, 440–1.
the proverbs of, considered apocryphal, **2**, 344.
the book of, translated into Greek, **2**, 359.
Jethro, father-in-law of Moses, **1**, 26.
Jew badges, decreed by Omar I, **3**, 88.

Jew badges (*continued*), decreed by Haroun Alrashid, **3**, 145.
introduced by Al-Mutavakkil, **3**, 176–7.
ordained by Hakim, **3**, 247–8.
introduced by the Fourth Lateran Council, **3**, 511–12.
supposed to prevent intermarriages, **3**, 511.
decreed by Almohade princes, **3**, 511–12.
the use of, spreads through Europe, **3**, 512.
effect of, on the wearers, **3**, 512–13.
the Jews struggle against, **3**, 513.
enforced in Spain, **3**, 513.
not enforced in southern France and Aragon, **3**, 514–15.
worn by the Jews of England, **3**, 515.
decreed by the Council of Oxford, **3**, 516.
introduced into Naples and Sicily, **3**, 518.
enforced by the Council of Narbonne, **3**, 518.
introduced into Hungary, **3**, 521.
enforced by Frederick II in Sicily and Naples, **3**, 569.
enforced by the Council of Béziers, **3**, 582.
insisted on in England under Henry III, **3**, 590.
ordained in the code of Alfonso X, **3**, 595.
enforced by the Council of Vienna, **3**, 612.
enforced by Louis IX of France, **3**, 612.
abrogated at the instance of the Jews of southern France, **3**, 612.
Jew badges (*continued*), re-introduced into France by Philip III, **3**, 613.
decreed by the Council of Buda, **3**, 614.
not used in Portugal, **3**, 618.
decreed in England by the Statute of Judaism, **3**, 642.
insisted on in Montpellier, **4**, 54.
in France under John the Good, **4**, 131, 133.
decreed for the Jews of Castile under Henry II, **4**, 139.
not worn by the Vesoul family, **4**, 150.
insisted upon in Castile under Juan II, **4**, 203.
enjoined by Benedict XIII's bull, **4**, 216.
decreed by the Council of Basle, **4**, 245.
decreed by Eugenius IV, **4**, 250.
enforced by Nicholas de Cusa, **4**, 255.
enforced in Naples, **4**, 258.
decreed by Henry IV of Castile, **4**, 278.
worn in Morocco, **4**, 389.
for the Portuguese Marranos under João III, **4**, 519.
ordered for the Jews of Bohemia, **4**, 545.
enforced by Paul IV, **4**, 566.
enforced by Pius V, **4**, 590.
worn by the Frankfort Jews, **4**, 695.
Jews released from wearing, in Vienna, **4**, 702.
proposed by Rühs, **5**, 517.
Jew quarters. *See* Ghetto; Jew's quarter, the.
"Jew-roaster," name assumed by German families, **3**, 611.
Jew streets, in Austria, **5**, 523. *See* Jew's quarter, the.

Jewish Christians, the, antagonized by Tarphon of Lydda, **2,** 357.
condemned by Samuel the Younger, **2,** 358.
observe the Law, **2,** 365–6.
view of Jesus held by, **2,** 366.
called Ebionites, **2,** 366.
as propagandists, **2,** 366.
differ from Pagan Christians, **2,** 367.
hate Paul, **2,** 367, 368.
views of, in the evangels, **2,** 369.
hate Rome, **2,** 369.
relation of, to the Jews, **2,** 369–70.
and the Tanaites, **2,** 370.
gradually endow Jesus with divine attributes, **2,** 370.
sects of, **2,** 370.
separate from the Jews, **2,** 370–2, 431.
merge into the Pagan Christians, **2,** 373.
accused of damaging the Jews with the Roman authorities, **2,** 378.
discussed by the Synhedrion, **2,** 379–80.
inimically treated by Bar-Cochba, **2,** 412.
spy upon the Jews under Hadrian, **2,** 425.
persecuted by Hadrian, **2,** 430–1.
the Mishna not hostile to, **2,** 476.
See also Ebionites, the; Judæan Christians, the; Nazarenes, the.
Jewish Church, the German, the founding of, **5,** 682, 686.
and Sachs, **5,** 691.
Jewish converts. *See* Apostates.
"**Jewish Curiosities,**" by Schudt, **5,** 549.
Jewish history. *See under* History.
"**Jewish Letters,**" to Voltaire, by a priest, **5,** 346–7.
Jewish Literature. *See under* Literature.
Jewish state, the, restored under Bar-Cochba, **2,** 412.
the restoration of, conditioned on the appearance of the Messiah, **2,** 600.
Spinoza on, **5,** 103–7.
Jews, the, libeled by Manetho, **1,** 511.
kindly treated by Vespasian and Titus, **2,** 331.
the solidarity of, **2,** 367–8; **5,** 632–3.
relation of, to the Jewish Christians, **2,** 369–70.
breach between, and the Jewish Christians, **2,** 370–2.
apostasy among, in the early Christian centuries, **2,** 377.
said to have cursed Jesus three times daily, **2,** 380; **5,** 185–6.
tamper with the Septuagint, **2,** 386.
use Akylas' translation of Scripture, **2,** 387.
extermination of, decreed by Rome, **2,** 387.
and the Flavian house, **2,** 388.
suffering of, under Domitian, **2,** 388–9.
hate Josephus, **2,** 389, 391.
kindly treated by Nerva, **2,** 391–2.
oppose Trajan, **2,** 393–4.
in rebellion against Hadrian, **2,** 399–401.
attempt the restoration of the Temple, **2,** 401–3.
peaceable disposition of, described by Hadrian, **2,** 407

Jews, the (*continued*), outraged by the rebuilding of Jerusálem as a pagan city, 2, 407.
prepare for a revolt against Hadrian, 2, 408.
join the standard of Bar-Cochba, 2, 410.
obtain possession of Jerusalem under Bar-Cochba, 2, 411.
the Romans kindly treated by, 2, 411–12.
heavily taxed by Hadrian, 2, 420.
spied upon by renegades and Jewish Christians, 2, 425–6.
forbidden to enter Jerusalem, 2, 433, 564; 3, 23, 87.
persecuted under Antoninus Pius, 2, 446.
persecuted under Verus Commodus, 2, 447.
enmity between, and the Samaritans, 2, 457–8, 534.
unkindly treated by Marcus Aurelius, 2, 463.
cruelly treated by Commodus and Niger, 2, 463–4.
under Caracalla, 2, 468–9.
under Elegabalus, 2, 469–70.
kindly treated by Alexander Severus, 2, 481–2, 482–3.
permitted to enter Jerusalem, 2, 482.
consulted by Origen on Bible exegesis, 2, 488.
hostile to Zenobia, 2, 529–30.
Diocletian tolerant to, 2, 533.
weakened by hostility to the Samaritans, 2, 535.
included in Constantine's act of toleration, 2, 561.
dignitaries of, exempt from onerous civic duties, 2, 561.
aspersed by Church dignitaries under Constantine, 2, 562.

Jews, the (*continued*), forbidden to make converts, 2, 562, 564.
privileges of, abolished by Constantine, 2, 563.
protected by Constantine against converts, 2, 564.
hostility to, shown by Constantine, 2, 566–7.
regarded as atheists under Constantine, 2, 572.
rescued from oppression by Julian, 2, 572.
oppressed by Shabur II, 2, 591.
benevolence of, admired by Julian, 2, 596–7.
not interested in the rebuilding of the Temple by Julian, 2, 599–600.
toleration of, under Valentinian I and Valens, 2, 603.
antagonized by Ambrosius and Chrysostom, 2, 613–14.
mock at the Christians, 2, 620–1.
forbidden to teach Christians Hebrew, 2, 624.
superiority of, in Scripture studies, 2, 624.
hated by Jerome and Augustine, 2, 625.
preserved by the Talmud, 2, 635.
competent witnesses only in their own cases under Justinian I, 3, 12–13.
treated kindly by the popes, 3, 25.
well treated in Arian countries, 3, 26.
and the fall of Rome, 3, 27–8.
suffer persecution from the German tribes, 3, 28.
Isidore of Seville writes against, 3, 50.

Jews, the (*continued*), antagonized by Mahomet, **3**, 75–6.
Mahomet's revelations against, **3**, 75, 78.
hostility to, in the Koran, **3**, 84.
restrictions against, in the covenant of Omar, **3**, 87–8.
freer in Islam than in Christian lands, **3**, 88.
reverence of, for Jewish Babylonia, **3**, 100–1.
of Mahometan countries speak Arabic, **3**, 110–11.
corrupt language of, in the seventh and eighth centuries, **3**, 111.
make scientific literature accessible to the Arabs, **3**, 111.
in the eighth century control commerce, **3**, 142–3.
under the Merovingian kings, **3**, 143.
considered the wards of the emperor by Louis the Pious, **3**, 170.
persecutions of, in the eleventh century, **3**, 245–8.
not permitted to hold office in Christian countries, **3**, 293–4.
during the first crusade, **3**, 298–305.
Jehuda Halevi's view of the suffering of, **3**, 335–6.
superiority of, in the twelfth century, **3**, 347.
treatment of, in Christian and Mahometan countries, **3**, 348.
persecutions of, increase in the twelfth century, **3**, 348–9.
forbidden by a rabbinical synod to purchase Church appurtenances, **3**, 377.
Jews, the (*continued*), the morality of, described by Joseph Kimchi, **3**, 393.
forbidden to keep Christian domestics, **3**, 400.
banished from the Isle de France, **3**, 402–3.
debts owing to, repudiated during the third crusade, **3**, 405.
not allowed to live in Mecca and Medinah, **3**, 436.
allowed by Saladin to settle in Jerusalem, **3**, 474.
the position of, affected by the death of Maimonides and the ascendancy of the papacy, **3**, 494.
protected against the crusaders by Innocent III, **3**, 496–7.
denounced by Innocent III, **3**, 498–501.
decrees against, by the Fourth Lateran Council, **3**, 510–11.
isolated in speech and manners by the Jew badge, **3**, 512–13.
mission of, in the Kabbalistic system, **3**, 553.
persecutions of, after the thirteenth century, **3**, 563–4, 610–11.
scholarliness of, **3**, 565.
absorbed in the study of the Talmud in the thirteenth century, **3**, 571–2.
banished from the hereditary dominions of Louis IX, **3**, 585–6.
exonerated from the blood accusation by Innocent IV, **3**, 635.
protected against forced baptism by Gregory X, **3**, 635.
banished from England, **3**, 645.

Jews, the (*continued*), permitted in Palestine under the Egyptian Sultans, **4**, 73.
charged with causing the Black Death, **4**, 101.
desolation of, after the Black Death, **4**, 127.
indispensable to the Christians in the fourteenth century, **4**, 127–8.
restrictions laid upon, by Benedict XIII's bull, **4**, 215–16.
and the Hussite war, **4**, 222.
accused of supplying Hussites with money, **4**, 222.
appeal to Martin V, **4**, 226.
feared by the papacy in the fifteenth century, **4**, 254.
well received in Italy in the fifteenth century, **4**, 286.
jeopardized by the blood accusation against the Jews of Trent, **4**, 299.
suffering of, attributed to heresy, **4**, 343.
divided into German speaking and Spanish speaking Jews, **4**, 421.
rights of, advocated by Reuchlin, **4**, 443–4.
indictment of, proposed by Hoogstraten, **4**, 444.
intercourse with, defended by Reuchlin, **4**, 447–8.
in the "Letters of Obscurantists," **4**, 461.
Luther on, **4**, 470.
affected by the Protestant Reformation, **4**, 471.
morality of, in the Middle Ages, **4**, 477.
lack spirituality, **4**, 477–8.
split up into national groups, **4**, 478.
narrow-mindedness of, in the Middle Ages, **4**, 479.
Jews, the (*continued*), suffer through the Reformation, **4**, 540.
hatred of, fed by the Unitarian tendencies of the Reformation, **4**, 542.
attacked by Eck and Luther, **4**, 546–52.
restrictions against, under Pius V, **4**, 590.
persecution of, during the Catholic reaction, **4**, 652.
prospects of the re-settlement of, in England, **4**, 18–19. *See* England.
prejudices against, in England, **5**, 19.
favorably regarded by Christian visionaries, **5**, 23.
enthusiasts for the restoration of, **5**, 24–5.
favorably regarded by the Puritans, **5**, 27.
defended by Richard Simon, **5**, 181.
attacked by Christian Hebraists, **5**, 184.
defended by Surenhuysius, **5**, 194.
degradation of, in the seventeenth century, **5**, 199–200, 204–5.
poverty of, **5**, 205–6.
speak a jargon in the eighteenth century, **5**, 300.
artificial studies of, **5**, 300–1.
neglect the Bible, **5**, 328.
slandered by Voltaire, **5**, 340.
condition of, described by Dohm, **5**, 353.
emancipated in the wake of French victories, **5**, 459. *See* Emancipation.
prejudices of Goethe against, **5**, 461.
Fichte on, **5**, 461–3.
and Napoleon, **5**, 474, 481.

Jews, the (*continued*), maligned by Bonald, **5**, 478.
the emancipation of, dependent on that of the French Jews, **5**, 480.
in the French wars, **5**, 511.
excluded from Tyrol, **5**, 523.
Heine on, **5**, 547–8, 553–5.
debt of, to Börne and Heine, **5**, 556.
rapid advance of, **5**, 557.
historical mission of, **5**, 576, 718–19.
self-respect of, **5**, 590.
effect of the July revolution on, **5**, 596–8.
criticised by Riesser, **5**, 599–600.
contrasted with the Greeks, **5**, 706–8.
the religion of, **5**, 709.
faults of, **5**, 713–14.
literature of, **5**, 714.
See also Israelites, the; Judæans, the; *and under the various countries, cities, etc.*
"Jews, The," by Lessing, **5**, 297, 320, 360.
"Jews, The, and their Just Claims on the Christian States," by August Krämer, **5**, 522.
Jews, the, conversion of. *See under* Conversion.
Jews, the, emancipation of. *See under* Emancipation.
Jew's quarter, the, in Rome, **2**, 68.
in Constantinople, **3**, 26, 425.
in Speyer, **3**, 298.
at Palermo, **3**, 567.
in Seville, **3**, 593.
of Toledo, **4**, 118.
of Seville, mobbed, **4**, 169.
in Palma, **4**, 171.
Castilian Jews forced into, **4**, 203.
Jew's quarter, the (*continued*), decreed by the Council of Basle, **4**, 245.
decreed by Eugenius IV, **4**, 250.
decreed by Henry IV of Castile, **4**, 278.
enforced by the cortes of Toledo, **4**, 335.
first, in Italy, **4**, 408.
enforced by Paul IV, **4**, 566.
in Vienna, **4**, 702; **5**, 172.
in Alsace and Metz, **5**, 348.
of Frankfort destroyed, **5**, 503–4.
Roman Jews return to, **5**, 518.
See also Ghetto; Jew street, the; Juderia.
Jews, secret. *See* Christians, Judaizing; Marranos, the.
Jezaniah, Judæan emigrant to Egypt, **1**, 324.
Jezdijird (400–420), Sassanian king, friendly to the Jews, **2**, 609–10.
Jezdijird III (440–457), Sassanian king, persecutes the Jews, **2**, 627–8.
Jezebel, daughter of Ethbaal, marries Ahab, **1**, 194.
character of, **1**, 197.
builds a temple to Baal, **1**, 197.
persecutes Elijah's disciples, **1**, 201.
has Naboth killed, **1**, 202.
threatens Elijah, **1**, 204.
end of, **1**, 211.
Jezreel, son of Hosea, **1**, 240.
Jezreel, the plain of, in Canaan, **1**, 36.
description of, **1**, 44.
Philistines encamp in, **1**, 102.
Ahab's winter palace in, **1**, 201–2.
towns in, restored to Judæa, **2**, 76.

Jikatilla. *See* Joseph ben Abraham Jikatilla.
Joab, warrior, joins David, **1,** 100.
jealous of Abner, **1,** 109.
ends the civil war, **1,** 110.
kills Abner, **1,** 111.
receives a house at Jerusalem, **1,** 119.
field officer under David, **1,** 122.
conducts the Ammonite war, **1,** 126–7, 128–9.
captures the Water-Town of Rabbath Ammon, **1,** 128.
faith of, **1,** 130.
ordered to expose Uriah the Hittite, **1,** 132.
partisan of Absalom, **1,** 135.
employs the woman of Tekoah to plead for Absalom, **1,** 135–6.
takes up a military census, **1,** 137.
faithful to David in the civil war with Absalom, **1,** 141.
commander against Absalom at Mahanaim, **1,** 144.
reproaches David for long mourning over Absalom, **1,** 145.
replaced by Amasa, **1,** 148.
victorious over Sheba, **1,** 149–50.
supporter of Adonijah, **1,** 152.
killed by Benaiah, **1,** 160.
family of, forms a league in Babylon, **1,** 330.
favorite character of the Puritans, **5,** 26.
Joachim I, elector of Brandenburg, has thirty Jews burnt, **4,** 440.
Joachim II, elector of Brandenburg, alleged to have been poisoned by a Jew, **4,** 652; **5,** 188.
Joah, chancellor, under Josiah, **1,** 292.
Joan, pope, satire on, **3,** 169.
Joanna, daughter of Ferdinand and Isabella, proposed as wife to Manoel of Portugal, **4,** 373.
Joanna, queen of Naples, appoints John of Capistrano inquisitor of the Jews, **4,** 258.
João I, of Portugal, Grand Master of Avis, rival of Leonora, **4,** 160.
regent of Portugal, **4,** 161.
popularity of, as king, **4,** 173.
promotes conquests o the coast of Africa, **4,** 217–18.
refuses assistance to Vincent Ferrer, **4,** 218.
João II (1481–1495), of Portugal, character of, **4,** 340.
executes the Duke of Braganza, **4,** 341.
confiscates the property of Isaac Abrabanel, **4,** 341.
negotiations with, for the settlement of the Spanish Jews in Portugal, **4,** 352.
baptizes the son of Judah Leon Abrabanel, **4,** 361.
permits Spanish exiles to settle in Portugal, **4,** 365–6.
summons an astronomical congress, **4,** 367.
delivers Marranos to the Inquisition, **4,** 368.
insists upon the Spanish exiles' leaving Portugal at the appointed time, **4,** 368–9.
sells Spanish exiles as slaves, **4,** 370–1.
sends the children of Spanish exiles to San Thomas, **4,** 371.
death of, **4,** 371.

João II (*continued*), cause of the misfortunes of, **4,** 373.
João III (1522–1557), of Portugal, hostile to the Marranos, **4,** 488–90.
resolves to introduce the Inquisition, **4,** 490.
gives up the plan of establishing the Inquisition, **4,** 490–1.
receives David Reubeni, **4,** 493, 498.
treats the Marranos more kindly, **4,** 493–4.
withdraws his favor from David Reubeni, **4,** 498–9.
urged to introduce the Inquisition, **4,** 499–500.
cupidity of, censured by Pucci, **4,** 505.
chooses Duarte de Paz for a secret mission, **4,** 512.
tries to influence Paul III in favor of the Inquisition, **4,** 515.
disobeys the papal injunction to absolve the Marranos, **4,** 516.
rigor of, towards the Marranos, **4,** 518–19.
enforces the rules of the Inquisition, **4,** 521.
forbids emigration, **4,** 524.
requested by the pope to treat the Marranos mildly, **4,** 527.
tries to make good Catholics of the Marranos, **4,** 528.
Joaser, coadjutor of Josephus in Galilee, **2,** 278, 279.
Joaser, son of Simon b. Boëthus, high priest, the deposition of, demanded, **2,** 121.
deposed, **2,** 127.
again installed, **2,** 127.
defends the Roman census, **2,** 134.
Joaser (*continued*), deposed by Quirinius, **2,** 135.
Joash, king of Israel. *See* Jehoash.
Joash, king of Judah, escapes the slaughter of Athaliah, **1,** 213.
raised in the Temple, **1,** 215–16.
anointed king, **1,** 216.
repairs the Temple, **1,** 218–19.
stones the high priest Zachariah, **1,** 220.
yields to Hazael, **1,** 221.
killed, **1,** 221.
"Job," poem by Jacob Israel Belmonte, **4,** 665.
Job, the Book of, composed during the captivity, **1,** 341–2.
expounded by Simon ben Lakish, **2,** 496–7.
commentary on, by Rashi, **3,** 346.
paraphrased by Zarak Barfat, **4,** 140.
Joceus, a wealthy Jew of York, takes refuge in the citadel, **3,** 413.
end of, **3,** 415.
Joceus, chief rabbi of England, **3,** 588.
Jochai, a friend of the Romans, **2,** 440.
Jochanan, secretary to Gamaliel I, **2,** 192.
Jochanan of Alexandria, the sandal maker, disciple of Akiba, **2,** 433.
Jochanan bar Moryah, Amora, **2,** 609.
Jochanan bar Napacha (199–279), chief of the Amoraim, **2,** 479.
and Judah II, **2,** 485, 493, 494.
description of the beauty of, **2,** 492–3.
method of, **2,** 493.

Jochanan bar Napacha (*continued*), at Tiberias, 2, 493–4.
leniency of, 2, 494.
explains the prophecy of Daniel, 2, 494–5.
morality of, 2, 495.
misfortunes of, 2, 495.
opponent of, 2, 495, 497.
restores order in southern Judæa, 2, 498.
on Abba Areka, 2, 514.
decisions of, 2, 515.
and Mar-Samuel, 2, 522–3.
alarm of, on account of the Babylonian Jews, 2, 525.
feeling of, against Palmyra, 2, 529, 530.
disciples of, 2, 531.
decision of, with regard to the new-moon, 2, 532.
view of, on the Samaritans, 2, 534.
permits Jewish women to acquire Greek culture, 2, 537.
quoted by Abbahu, 2, 537.
Jochanan ben Gudgada, member of the Jamnia Synhedrion, 2, 357.
Jochanan ben Mattathiah Provenci, elected chief rabbi of France, 4, 152.
relieved of his office by Isaiah ben Abba-Mari, 4, 152, 162.
appeals to Spanish authorities, 4, 153.
Jochanan ben Nuri, member of the Jamnia Synhedrion, 2, 357.
upholds the ordinances of Gamaliel II, 2, 405.
Jochanan ben Torta, opposes Akiba's Messianic hopes, 2, 410.
Jochanan ben Zakkai, disciple of Hillel, 2, 131.
abolishes the ritual for cases of suspected adultery, 2, 238.
Jochanan ben Zakkai (*continued*), abrogates the sin offering for murders, 2, 239.
leader of the faithful Judæans, 2, 240.
vice-president of the Synhedrion, 2, 240.
importance of, 2, 322-3.
member of the Peace party, 2, 323.
takes refuge in the camp of Titus, 2, 323–4.
receives permission to establish a school at Jamnia, 2, 324.
mourns for the Temple, 2, 324.
forms a Synhedrion at Jamnia, 2, 325.
changes made by, 2, 326.
disciples of, 2, 326.
proficient in the oral Law, 2, 328.
lectures by, 2, 328–9.
on the advantages of peace, 2, 329.
intercourse of, with pagans, 2, 329, 331.
gentle character of, 2, 331–2.
description of Israel in mourning by, 2, 332.
compared with Jeremiah and Zerubbabel, 2, 333.
death of, 2, 333.
maxim of, with regard to the study of the Law, 2, 338–9.
on Eliezer ben Hyrcanus, 2, 346.
Jochanan Aleman. *See* Aleman.
Jochanan. *See also* Johanan; John; Jonathan.
Joel, prophet, exhortations of, under Uzziah, 1, 230.
under Jeroboam II, 1, 237–40.
Joel, son of Samuel, acts as judge in Beersheba, 1, 79.
Joel, Emanuel, founder of the Breslau seminary, 5, 700.

Johanan, father of Mattathias, the Hasmonæan, **1,** 459.

Johanan, son of Joiada, high priest, slays his brother in the Temple, **1,** 409.

Johanan, son of Kareah, chief of the Judæans in Palestine after the fall of Jerusalem, **1,** 318.
submits to Gedaliah, **1,** 321.
informs Gedaliah of Ishmael's treachery, **1,** 322.
pursues Ishmael, **1,** 322–3.

Johanan, son of Simon Tharsi. *See* Hyrcanus I, John.

Johanan Gadi, son of Mattathias, the Hasmonæan, **1,** 459.
leader of the Hasmonæan party, **1,** 489.
killed by the Bene Amri, **1,** 491.

Johanan. *See also* Jochanan; John; Jonathan.

Johannsen, bishop of Speyer, protects the Jews during the first crusade, **3,** 300–1.

John XXII, pope, opposes a crusade, **4,** 35.
sister of, hostile to the Jews, **4,** 61.

John XXIII, pope, vices of, **4,** 201.

John II, of Aragon. *See* Juan II, of Aragon.

John II, of Brabant, protects the Jews of Brussels, **4,** 112.

John, of England, the Jews under, **3,** 416, 504–5.
pretends friendship for the Jews, **3,** 504.
appoints Jacob of London chief rabbi, **3,** 504.
protects the Jews of London, **3,** 505.
imprisons the English Jews, **3,** 505.

John, the Good, of France, captivity of, **4,** 128–9.
permits the Jews to return to France, **4,** 129.
curtails the privileges of the Jews, **4,** 131.

John, author of the Apocalypse, hates Rome, **2,** 369.

John, the Baptist, Essene, beliefs of, **2,** 145–6.
influence of, on the Judæan poor and the aristocracy, **2,** 146–7.
imprisoned and beheaded, **2,** 147.
Jesus the disciple of, **2,** 150.
the work of, continued by Jesus, **2,** 151.
identified with Elijah, **2,** 158.

John, Judæan envoy to emperor Claudius, **2,** 197–8.

John, leader of the Idumæans, helps the Zealots, **2,** 295.

John of Capistrano, Franciscan, hostile to the Jews, **4,** 249, 258–63.
executes Nicholas V's anti-Jewish bull, **4,** 253.
characteristics of, **4,** 257.
used by the popes to restore their authority, **4,** 257–8.
inquisitor of the Jews, **4,** 258.
in Germany, **4,** 258–60.
in Bavaria, **4,** 258–9.
in Franconia, **4,** 259–60.
in Silesia, **4,** 260–3.
in Poland, **4,** 263, 265–6, 418.
preaches a crusade against the Turks, **4,** 268.
advocates the baptism of Jewish children, **4,** 277.
exalted by Bernardinus of Feltre, **4,** 296.

John of Gischala. *See* John ben Levi.

John of Gorze (Jean de Vendières), ambassador from Otho I to Abdul-Rahman III, **3,** 219.

John of Valladolid, apostate, in religious disputations with Jews, **4**, 140, 141, 209.
John ben Levi, of Gischala, leader of the insurrection in Upper Galilee, **2**, 273.
troops of, **2**, 273.
repugnant to Josephus, **2**, 279–81.
accuses Josephus before the Synhedrion, **2**, 281.
escapes to Jerusalem, **2**, 290.
helps the Zealots of Jerusalem, **2**, 295.
heroism of, **2**, 296–7.
leader of the Galilean Zealots in Jerusalem, **2**, 301.
destroys Roman works, **2**, 304.
hopefulness of, **2**, 305.
refuses to lay down arms, **2**, 309.
in Titus' triumph, **2**, 313.
in a Roman dungeon, **2**, 314.
John, son of Zebedee, disciple of Jesus, **2**, 153.
leader of the early Christians, **2**, 169, 222.
John. *See also* Jochanan; Johanan; Jonathan; Juan.
John Albert of Poland, hostile to the Jews, **4**, 419.
John Casimir, of Poland, permits forced converts to return to Judaism, **5**, 13.
guards the rights of Jews in making a treaty, **5**, 14.
John Chrysostom, bishop of Antioch, preaches against Jewish institutions, **2**, 613–14.
John George, elector of Brandenburg, accuses Lippold of poisoning Joachim II, **4**, 652.
expulsion of the Jews by, **5**, 173.
John Hyrcanus. *See* Hyrcanus I, John.
John Maurice, of Nassau, stadtholder of Brazil, assisted by Marranos, **4**, 693.
John Sobieski, of Poland, scatters the Karaites, **5**, 182.
Joiada, high priest, under Nehemiah, **1**, 386.
sons of, **1**, 409.
Joigny, represented at the first rabbinical synod, **3**, 377.
Jokthel, name of Petra changed into, **1**, 223.
Jollivet, French government commissioner, protests against the imposition of a poll-tax on French Jews in Germany, **5**, 465.
Jonadab, son of Rechab, a Nazarite, **1**, 200; **3**, 55.
helps Jehu to exterminate Baal-worship, **1**, 212.
Jonah, fisherman, sons of, disciples of Jesus, **2**, 153.
Jonah II, Palestinian Amora, **2**, 560.
member of the last Synhedrion, **2**, 567.
permits bread baking on the Sabbath for the Roman army, **2**, 568.
Jonah, prophet, encourages war with the Aramæans, **1**, 225.
Jonah, rabbi of Vienna, counsels self-destruction to escape the Black Death persecutions, **4**, 110.
Jonah ben Abraham Gerundi the Elder, excommunicates the Maimunists, **3**, 529.
excommunicated, **3**, 530, 536–7.
aided by Nachmani, **3**, 536.
refers the Maimunist controversy to the Dominicans, **3**, 542–3.
repents of his persecution of Maimonides' works, **3**, 579–80, 624.

Jonah ben Abraham Gerundi (*continued*), makes public confession, **3**, 580.
author of Talmudical works, **3**, 580.
disciple of, a Maimunist, **3**, 629.
Jonah Marinus (Abulvalid Mervan Ibn-Janach, 995–1050), grammarian, **3**, 261–4.
teachers of, **3**, 261.
as a poet, **3**, 261–2.
studies medicine, **3**, 261, 262.
hostile to Samuel Ibn-Nagrela, **3**, 262, 313.
creator of Hebrew syntax, **3**, 263.
works of, **3**, 263.
calmness and clearness of, **3**, 263–4.
and Ibn-Gebirol, **3**, 264.
adversely criticised by Abraham Ibn-Ezra, **3**, 371.
works of, translated into Hebrew, **3**, 397.
Jonathan, keeper of the lists, jailer of Jeremiah, **1**, 313.
Jonathan, nephew of David, Israelite champion, **1**, 117.
Jonathan, priest, messenger from Hushai to David, **1**, 143.
Jonathan, Sadducee leader, friend of John Hyrcanus, **2**, 31.
estranges Hyrcanus from the Pharisees, **2**, 33.
Jonathan, tax-gatherer, deputy of the Judæans of Cæsarea, **2**, 253.
Jonathan, teacher of the Law, in the south of Judæa, **2**, 442.
Jonathan, Zealot leader, accuses Josephus of disloyalty to Rome, **2**, 318.
Jonathan ben Absalom, general under Simon Tharsi, **1**, 500.
Jonathan ben Amram, disciple of Judah I, rebukes him, **2**, 451.
Jonathan ben Anan, high priest, appointed by Vitellius, **2**, 172.
former high priest, envoy to Rome, **2**, 244.
seeks the appointment of Felix as procurator of Judæa, **2**, 245.
assassinated, **2**, 246.
Jonathan ben Nachman (Archinas), teacher of the Law at the fall of Jerusalem, **2**, 330.
Jonathan ben Uziel, disciple of Hillel, **2**, 131.
Jonathan, son of Saul, qualities of, **1**, 84.
destroys the Philistine garrison at Gibeah, **1**, 85.
defeats the Philistines at Michmash, **1**, 86–8.
condemned to death by Saul, **1**, 88–9.
friendship of, with David, **1**, 97, 98.
death of, **1**, 103.
body of, dishonored, **1**, 104.
remains of, buried, **1**, 124.
Jonathan, son of Simon Tharsi. *See* Hyrcanus I, John.
Jonathan Cohen, of Lünel, writes a commentary on Alfassi's Talmudical work, **3**, 397.
advocates the study of science by Jews, **3**, 397.
reverence of, for Maimonides, **3**, 489, 526.
emigrates to Jerusalem, **3**, 505, 506.
Jonathan Eibeschütz. *See* Eibeschütz, Jonathan.
Jonathan Haphus, son of Mattathias, the Hasmonæan, **1**, 459.

Jonathan Haphus (*continued*), in command beyond the Jordan, **1**, 475.
leader of the Hasmonæan party, **1**, 489.
made the leader of the people, **1**, 490.
weakness of the forces of, **1**, 491.
strengthens his defences, **1**, 492–3.
authority of, **1**, 493.
defends Bethhagla, **1**, 493.
makes a truce with Bacchides, **1**, 493–4.
friendship of, sued for by Demetrius I and Alexander Balas, **1**, 494–5.
officiates as high priest on the Feast of Tabernacles, **1**, 495.
ally of Alexander Balas, **1**, 494, 496.
entertained by Ptolemy VI and Alexander Balas, **1**, 496.
loyal to Alexander Balas, **1**, 496.
receives Ekron, **1**, 496.
besieges the Acra, **1**, 496.
compact of, with Demetrius II, **1**, 497.
espouses the cause of Antiochus VI, **1**, 497–8, 499.
distinguished by Diodotus Tryphon, **1**, 498.
taken prisoner, **1**, 499.
executed, **1**, 501.
burial of, at Modin, **1**, 501.
achievements of, **1**, 501–2.
ancestor of Flavius Josephus, **1**, 502.
state of Judæa after the death of, **1**, 501–2, 519–20.
Jonathan Levi Zion, advocate of the Jews before Maximilian I, **4**, 436–7.
Jonathan. *See also* Jochanan; John; Jonathan.
Jonghe, Isaac de, zealous for the emancipation of the Jews, **5**, 455.
Jonghe, Lublink de, objects to the emancipation of the Jews, **5**, 455–6.
Joppa (Jaffa), fortifications of, destroyed by Ptolemy I, **1**, 417.
taken by Jonathan Haphus, **1**, 496.
Simon Tharsi sends a detachment to, **1**, 500.
taken by Simon Tharsi, **1**, 524.
claimed by Antiochus Sidetes, **1**, 529.
in the possession of Antiochus Sidetes, **2**, 4–5.
in the possession of Antiochus IX, **2**, 9.
taken by Vespasian, **2**, 288.
Joram, son of Ahab. *See* Jehoram.
Joram (Jehoram), son of Jehoshaphat, marries Athaliah, **1**, 206.
king of Judah, introduces idolatry, **1**, 209.
death of, **1**, 211.
Joram, son of Tôi, king of Hamath, congratulates David on his victories, **1**, 127.
Jordan, the, Israelites cross, **1**, 29, 32.
description of, **1**, 42, 46.
José (471–520), Amora, principal of the Pumbeditha school, completes the Babylonian Talmud, **2**, 630–1.
José, brother of Jesus, **2**, 148.
José, the Galilean, member of the Jamnia Synhedrion, **2**, 357.
at Lydda, **2**, 423.
José, Palestinian Amora, **2**, 560.
member of the last Synhedrion, **2**, 567.

José (*continued*), permits bread baking on the Sabbath for the Roman army, **2,** 568.
on the second day of the festivals, **2,** 573.
José of Phaeno, servant of Judah I, **2,** 466.
José bar José Hayathom, the first poetan, poems of, **3,** 114–15.
artificiality of the works of, **3,** 115.
founder of neo-Hebraic poetry, **4,** 67.
José ben Chalafta, disciple of Akiba, **2,** 433.
on Meïr, **2,** 437.
artisan, **2,** 442.
historian, **2,** 442.
on Meïr and Nathan, **2,** 446.
on the Romans, **2,** 448.
banished to Laodicea, **2,** 448.
son of, in Rome, **2,** 449.
José, son of Joëzer, opponent of the Hellenists, **1,** 436.
probable end of, **1,** 483.
José, son of Johanan, opponent of the Hellenists, **1,** 436.
José Barnabas of Cyprus, proselytizes among the heathen, **2,** 219.
disciple of the apostle Paul, **2,** 227.
observes the dietary laws, **2,** 231.
José. *See also under* Joseph.
Joseph I, emperor, refuses to remove the ban from "Judaism Unmasked," **5,** 193.
Joseph II, emperor, improves the condition of the Jews, **5,** 357–8.
forbids the circulation of an anti-Jewish work, **5,** 359.
hymn to, by Wessely, **5,** 368.
Joseph II (*continued*), reforms of, opposed by the pious, **5,** 369.
reforms of, welcomed by the cultured, **5,** 370.
reforms of, resisted in Galicia, **5,** 394.
abolishes the poll-tax on Jews, **5,** 415, 464.
the Jewish regulations of, disregarded by Francis I, **5,** 523.
Joseph, Jewish king of the Chazars, addressed by Chasdaï Ibn-Shaprut, **3,** 220–1, 222.
residence of, **3,** 221.
answers Chasdaï Ibn-Shaprut, **3,** 221–2.
Joseph, duke of Mantua, banishes rabbis, **4,** 295.
Joseph, the tribes of, claim the central lands of Canaan, **1,** 35–6.
Joseph, apostate under Constantine, persecutes the Palestinian Jews, **2,** 564–5.
made comes, **2,** 565.
builds churches in Galilee, **2,** 565.
defames Hillel II, **2,** 566.
possible connection of, with Constantine's persecution of the Jews, **2,** 567.
Joseph, brother of Herod, guardian of Mariamne, **2,** 83.
besieged in Masada, **2,** 87.
Joseph, brother-in-law of Herod, ordered to murder Mariamne in case of his death, **2,** 93.
calumniated by his wife, **2,** 93.
beheaded, **2,** 94.
Joseph, Karaite, permits lights on the Sabbath, **4,** 269.
Joseph, of the house of Camyth, high priest under Herod II, **2,** 198.

Joseph of Arimathea, disciple of Jesus, **2**, 160.
Joseph of Arli, Kabbalist, hopes in the Messiah as announced by Molcho, **4**, 511–12.
Joseph de Avila, discovers the Zohar to be a forgery, **4**, 20–1.
Joseph of Ecija. *See* Joseph ben Ephraim Ibn-Benveniste Halevi.
Joseph of Gamala, Zealot leader, **2**, 289.
death of, **2**, 290.
Joseph of Nazareth, father of Jesus, **2**, 148.
Joseph de Vesoul, apostate, **4**, 150.
Joseph bar Abba (814), mystic, principal of the Pumbeditha academy, **3**, 154.
Joseph ben Abraham Jikatilla, Kabbalist, **4**, 3, 6.
writings of, **4**, 10.
works of, used by Reuchlin, **4**, 466.
Joseph ben Chasdaï, a Cordova poet, eulogizes Samuel Ibn-Nagrela, **3**, 273.
son of, **3**, 274, 280.
Joseph ben Chiya (270–333), refuses the Pumbeditha principalship, **2**, 577–8.
superstition of, **2**, 578.
flees from Pumbeditha, **2**, 580.
principal of the Pumbeditha academy, **2**, 581.
characteristics of, **2**, 581.
method of, **2**, 581.
devotes himself to the Targum, **2**, 581–2.
severity of, **2**, 582.
death of, **2**, 583.
Joseph ben Chiya (828–833), principal of the Pumbeditha academy, **3**, 155.
resigns, **3**, 156.
Joseph ben Chiya (*continued*), re-installed, **3**, 156.
Joseph ben Ephraim Ibn-Benveniste Halevi, of Ecija, prominent at the court of Alfonso XI of Castile, **4**, 76, 79.
attack on, in Valladolid, **4**, 79.
jealous of Samuel Ibn-Wakar, **4**, 80, 81.
patron of Gonzalo Martinez, **4**, 83.
end of, **4**, 84.
Joseph ben Gershom Loans (Joslin, Josselman of Rosheim, 1480–1555), representative of the German Jews, **4**, 414.
warns Molcho and Reubeni against petitioning Charles V, **4**, 510.
Joseph ben Gorion, a moderate zealot, **2**, 271.
"Joseph ben Gorion." *See* Josippon.
Joseph ben Isaac Ibn-Abitur (Ibn-Satanas or Santas), candidate for the Cordova rabbinate, **3**, 229–30, 238.
liturgical poetry of, **3**, 236.
translates the Mishna into Arabic, **3**, 237.
excommunicated, **3**, 238.
appeals to Alhakem, **3**, 238.
refuses the Cordova rabbinate, **3**, 240.
Joseph ben Isaac Kimchi (1150–1170), introduces Spanish culture into southern France, **3**, 392.
polemical work by, against Christianity, **3**, 392–3.
Joseph ben Israel, father of Manasseh, Marrano, emigrates to the Netherlands, **4**, 671.

Joseph ben Jacob Ibn-Sahal (1070–1124), rabbi of Cordova, poetry of, **3**, 314.
Joseph ben Joshua Cohen (1496–1575), historian and physician, dazzled by Molcho, **4**, 511.
expelled from Genoa, **4**, 544, 555.
historical works by, **4**, 555–6, 560, 590, 608.
style of, **4**, 556, 557.
Joseph ben Kisma, member of the Jamnia Synhedrion, **2**, 357.
counsels subservience to Hadrian's decrees, **2**, 426–7.
Joseph ben Matthias (Flavius Josephus, 38–95), historian, descendant of Jonathan Haphus, **1**, 502.
does not mention Jesus in his works, **2**, 166.
a moderate Zealot, **2**, 271.
governor of Galilee, **2**, 272, 275–6.
education of, **2**, 276.
at Rome in his youth, **2**, 276–7.
secretly a Roman partisan, **2**, 277–8.
relation of, to Agrippa II, **2**, 278.
administration of, **2**, 278–9.
opposed by Jesus ben Sapphia, **2**, 279.
relation of, to John of Gischala, **2**, 279–81.
duplicity of, **2**, 280–1.
deposed by the Synhedrion, **2**, 281.
deceives the envoys of the Synhedrion, **2**, 282.
wins credulous Galileans to his side, **2**, 282–3.
re-instated, **2**, 283.
breaks the strength of Galilee, **2**, 283–4.
Joseph ben Matthias (*continued*), defeated by Vespasian, **2**, 285.
appeals to the Synhedrion for aid, **2**, 286.
at Jotapata, **2**, 287-8.
gives himself up to the Romans, **2**, 288.
execrated by the Judæans, **2**, 293, 389, 391.
made commander of Titus' body-guard, **2**, 302.
tries to persuade Jerusalem to surrender, **2**, 304.
witness of Titus' triumph in Rome, **2**, 314.
rewarded by Vespasian and Titus, **2**, 317.
given the name Flavius Josephus, **2**, 317.
as an historian, **2**, 319.
on Jewish customs observed by pagans, **2**, 384.
considers circumcision optional with proselytes, **2**, 385.
favorite of Domitian, **2**, 389.
and Flavius Clemens, **2**, 389, 391.
completes his Jewish history, **2**, 389–90.
vindicates himself against the attacks of Justus of Tiberias, **2**, 390.
vindicates his race against Apion, **2**, 390.
prosecuted by Domitian, **2**, 391.
death of, **2**, 391.
immortalizes the war of the Zealots, **2**, 415.
works of, read at the court of Louis the Pious, **3**, 162.
history of, the basis of Josippon, **3**, 180.
the work of, against Apion, translated, **4**, 608.

Joseph ben Matthias (*continued*), the works of, connected with the Talmud by Azarya deï Rossi, **4**, 614.
a work of, translated by Arias, **5**, 113.
the history of, continued by Basnage, **5**, 195.
the works of, studied by Frankel, **5**, 684.
Joseph ben Meïr Ibn-Migash Halevi (1077–1144), Talmudist, eulogized by Jehuda Halevi, **3**, 315, 322, 323.
successor to Alfassi, **3**, 315–16, 323.
respect for, **3**, 316.
condemns a traitor to be stoned, **3**, 317.
son and disciples of, **3**, 317, 447.
Joseph ben Pilat, Talmudist in Damascus, **3**, 426.
Joseph ben Sabara, satirist and physician, **3**, 559.
Joseph ben Satia, Gaon of Sora, **3**, 196.
successor to Saadiah, **3**, 202.
abandons the academy of Sora, **3**, 202.
Joseph ben Shem Tob Ibn-Shem Tob (1400–1460), philosopher and preacher, dignitary at the Castilian court, **4**, 228–9.
polemic works of, **4**, 235.
opposed to his father's views, **4**, 243.
religio-philosophical system of, **4**, 244.
Joseph ben Solomon Ibn-Shoshan (1135–1204–5), favorite of Alfonso VIII of Castile, **3**, 384.
erects a synagogue in Toledo, **3**, 384.
encourages the study of the Talmud, **3**, 384, 385–6.
Joseph ben Solomon Ibn-Shoshan (*continued*), poem on, **3**, 388.
Joseph ben Solomon Kolon (1460–1490), rabbi of Mantua, wanderings of, **4**, 294.
authority of, **4**, 294–5.
controversies of, **4**, 295.
rabbi of Pavia, **4**, 295.
Joseph ben Todros Abulafia, Kabbalist, **4**, 2.
Joseph Ibn-Aknin, disciple of Maimonides, attacked by Mar-Sacharya, **3**, 477.
"The Guide of the Perplexed" addressed to, **3**, 478.
cautioned by Maimonides against letting his book fall into the hands of the Mahometans, **3**, 486.
finds Maimonides' system inconsistent with Judaism, **3**, 487.
urges the excommunication of Daniel ben Saadiah, **3**, 526.
Joseph Ibn-Alfual, translator of Maimonides' Mishna commentary, **4**, 60.
Joseph Ibn-Jau, supports Joseph Ibn-Abitur, **3**, 238, 239.
Joseph Ibn-Migash, supports Balkin, **3**, 258.
leaves Granada, **3**, 258.
occupies a high office in Seville, **3**, 280.
Joseph Ibn-Nagrela (1031–1066), eulogized by Joseph ben Chasdaï, **3**, 273.
vizir and Nagid, **3**, 274, 275.
secretary to Balkin, **3**, 274.
wife of, **3**, 274.
protects the sons of the last Gaon, **3**, 275.
as Talmudist, **3**, 275.
accused of poisoning Balkin, **3**, 275.

Joseph Ibn-Nagrela (*continued*), opposes the massacre of the Granada Arabs, **3**, 276–7.
loses the favor of Badis, **3**, 277.
accused of treason, **3**, 278.
killed, **3**, 278.
wife and son of, flee to Lucena, **3**, 279.
library of, **3**, 279.
elegy on, **3**, 279.
patron of Isaac Ibn-Albalia, **3**, 283.
patron of Isaac Ibn-Giat, **3**, 284.

Joseph Ibn-Verga, historian, **4**, 555.
ancestors of, **4**, 556.
historical work of, **4**, 557.
style of, **4**, 557.
arraignment of the Jews by, **4**, 557.

Joseph Ibn-Yachya, at the disputation of Tortosa, **4**, 208.

Joseph Ibn-Yachya, pleads with the Portuguese Jews for the Spanish exiles, **4**, 366.

Joseph, son of Tobiah, leader of the Judæans, **1**, 423–4.
flatters the Egyptian ambassador, **1**, 424.
at the court of Ptolemy III, **1**, 424–5.
tax-gatherer of Cœlesyria and Phœnicia, **1**, 425.
favorite of Ptolemy IV, **1**, 425–6.
wealth of, enriches Judæa, **1**, 426–7.
introduces Dionysian festivals into Judæa, **1**, 428.
son of, his representative, **1**, 429–30.
death of, **1**, 431.
descendants of, called Tobiades, **1**, 432.

Joseph, son of Zachariah, general of Judas Maccabæus, **1**, 476.

Joseph Albo (1380–1444), at the disputation of Tortosa, **4**, 208, 233.
holds the Agada to be authoritative, **4**, 214.
refuses to accept baptism, **4**, 215.
writes an account of a religious controversy, **4**, 234.
physician and philosopher, **4**, 239.
on freedom of inquiry, **4**, 240.
on the articles of the creed, **4**, 240.
style of, **4**, 240.
religio-philosophical system of, **4**, 240–3.
on salvation of the soul, **4**, 240, 243.

Joseph Al-Kabri persecutes the Karaites in Spain, **3**, 362.

Joseph Amarkala Halevi, prince of the Jews about Nishabur, **3**, 433.

Joseph Barihan Alfalach, representative of the Mosul congregation, and David Alrui, **3**, 433.

Joseph Caiaphas, high priest, president of the tribunal that tried Jesus, **2**, 163, 164.
removed from office, **2**, 172.

Joseph Ezobi ben Chanan (1230–1250), poet, works of, translated, **3**, 561.
advice of, to his son, **3**, 561.

Joseph Hamon. *See* Hamon, Joseph.

Joseph Jaabez, attributes the suffering of the Jews to their heresy, **4**, 343, 479.

Joseph Kara, Bible exegete, **3**, 345–6.
writes commentaries on the Prophets and the Hagiographa, **3**, 346.

Joseph Karo (1488–1575), infected with Messianic enthusiasm by Molcho, **4**, 496–7, 537.
longing of, for martyrdom, **4**, 511.
ordained by Jacob Berab, **4**, 536, 538.
learning and wanderings of, **4**, 537.
elaborates Jacob Asheri's code, **4**, 537, 539.
visions of, **4**, 537–8.
among the Kabbalists, **4**, 538.
Messianic dreams of, **4**, 538–9.
code by, intended to bring about religious unity, **4**, 539, 612.
chief rabbi of Safet, **4**, 540.
appealed to on the question of trade with Ancona, **4**, 580.
excommunicates Daud, **4**, 599.
publishes the "Shulchan Aruch," **4**, 612.
Spanish tendencies of the code of, **4**, 613.
orders Azarya deï Rossi's works to be burned, **4**, 616.
code of, commented upon by Moses Isserles, **4**, 637.
the highest Jewish authority in the seventeenth century, **5**, 51.
See also Shulchan Aruch, the.
Joseph Kaspi, philosopher, **4**, 87, 91.
Joseph Orabuena, physician, chief rabbi of Navarre, **4**, 184–5.
Joseph Pichon, receiver general of taxes under Henry II of Castile, **4**, 138.
denounced by Jewish courtiers, **4**, 156.
condemned as a traitor, **4**, 156.
beheaded by the Jews, **4**, 156.
Joseph Pichon (*continued*), the execution of, arouses excitement against the Jews, **4**, 157–8, 167.
Joseph Rabban, leader of the Jews in India, **2**, 629–30.
special rights conferred on, **2**, 630.
Joseph Saragossi, Kabbalist, disciple of, **4**, 393.
reforms life in Safet, **4**, 399.
introduces the Kabbala into Safet, **4**, 399.
Joseph Tob-Elem, writes a commentary on Abraham Ibn-Ezra's Pentateuch commentary, **4**, 144.
Joseph Zapateiro de Lamego, traveler, employed by João II of Portugal, **4**, 368.
Joseph Zevi, brother of Sabbataï Zevi, **5**, 145.
Josephus, Flavius. *See* Joseph ben Matthias.
Josephus, pseudo-. *See* Josippon.
Joshua, father of Narboni, **4**, 94.
Joshua, leader of the Israelites, **1**, 31, 32–3.
victory of, at Gibeon, **1**, 34–5.
contest of, with the tribes of Joseph, **1**, 36.
defeats Jabin, **1**, 37.
dwells among the Ephraimites, **1**, 41.
declining years of, **1**, 50.
death of, **1**, 52.
Israelites under, settle in Arabia, **3**, 54.
Joshua, of the family of Phabi, made high priest, **2**, 107.
Joshua, of the family of Sié, made high priest, **2**, 127.
Joshua deï Cantori, defames the Talmud, **4**, 583.
Joshua ben Chananya, teacher of the Law, disciple of Jochanan ben Zakkai, **2**, 324, 326.

Joshua ben Chananya (*continued*), contemporary of Gamaliel II, **2**, 335.
opposes decisions by the Bath-Kol, **2**, 337.
dispute of, with Gamaliel II, **2**, 340-2.
on the admission of proselytes, **2**, 343, 384.
reconciled with Gamaliel II, **2**, 344-5.
artisan, **2**, 344, 348, 442.
character of, **2**, 348.
popularity and homeliness of, **2**, 349.
astronomical knowledge of, **2**, 349.
condemns Shammai's rules, **2**, 349-50.
conciliatory intercourse of, with the Roman rulers, **2**, 350.
removes the ban from Eliezer ben Hyrcanus, **2**, 350.
obtains lucrative posts for poor scholars, **2**, 345, 357.
nephew of, **2**, 370, 443.
and Akylas, **2**, 385.
journey of, to Rome, **2**, 387.
and Flavius Clemens, **2**, 387, 389, 391.
influence of, on Nerva, **2**, 392.
advises against the rebellion against Hadrian, **2**, 403-4.
leader of the people under Hadrian, **2**, 404.
mourns for Gamaliel II, **2**, 404.
president of the Synhedrion, **2**, 404.
and Hadrian, **2**, 406-7.
tries to induce Hadrian not to rebuild Jerusalem, **2**, 407-8.
death of, **2**, 408.
disciples of, discard the Jewish garb, **2**, 424.
praises the Halachic knowledge of Bruria, **2**, 436.

Joshua ben Damnai, high priest, **2**, 249.

Joshua ben Gamala, high priest, obtains his office through bribery, **2**, 249.
improves the educational system of Judæa, **2**, 249.
procures the governorship of Galilee for Josephus, **2**, 277-8.
suspected of Roman proclivities, **2**, 294.
executed by the Zealots, **2**, 296.

Joshua ben Joseph Ibn-Vives Allorqui (Geronimo de Santa Fé), epistle of, attacking Christian dogmas, **4**, 186-7.
physician to Benedict XIII, **4**, 200.
instrument for the conversion of the Jews of Spain, **4**, 206, 231-2.
champion of Christianity at the disputation of Tortosa, **4**, 207.
proves the Messiahship of Jesus from the Talmud, **4**, 208-9, 211, 212.
accuses the Talmud of blasphemy, **4**, 213-14.
end of, unknown, **4**, 217.
charges of, refuted, **4**, 232, 238.
leaves the Marranos unconvinced, **4**, 256.

Joshua ben Karcha, denounces Eleazar ben Simon, **2**, 465.

Joshua ben Levi, teacher of the Law, collects the Patriarch's tax in Rome, **2**, 486, 498.
accompanies Chanina bar Chama to Cæsarea, **2**, 491.
prays for rain, **2**, 492.
reputation of, **2**, 497.
restores order in southern Judæa, **2**, 498.
legends about, **2**, 498.
and Ulla bar Kosher, **2**, 530.

Joshua, son of Jehozedek, high priest, leader of the exiles returning under Cyrus, **1,** 352.
erects an altar on the site of the Temple, **1,** 356.
urges the completion of the second Temple, **1,** 359.
sole leader of the Judæan community, **1,** 360.
Joshua, son of Joiada, slain by his brother, **1,** 409.
Joshua, son of Perachia, Pharisee leader, maxim of, **2,** 20.
Joshua Falk Cohen. *See* Cohen, Joshua Falk.
Joshua Lorqui. *See* Joshua ben Joseph Ibn-Vives Allorqui.
Joshua Sirach. *See* Jesus Sirach.
Josiah, son of Amon (638–608), king of Judah, minority of, **1,** 286.
averts the capture of Jerusalem by the Scythians, **1,** 288.
fears to suppress idolatry, **1,** 288.
repairs the Temple, **1,** 288–9.
under the influence of Jeremiah, **1,** 289.
receives the Book of the Law found in the Temple, **1,** 292, 293.
has the Book of the Law read to the people, **1,** 294.
uproots idolatry, **1,** 294–5.
desecrates the idolatrous altar at Bethel, **1,** 295.
summons the nation to celebrate Passover at Jerusalem, **1,** 295.
social conditions under, **1,** 296.
mortally wounded at Megiddo, **1,** 297.
sons of, **1,** 298.
Josiah, teacher of the Law, in the south of Judæa, **2,** 442.
Josiah Hassan, appointed Exilarch by Saadiah, **3,** 195, 196.
banished to Khorasan, **3,** 196.
Josippon (" Joseph ben Gorion," pseudo-Josephus), history of the Jews between the destruction of the first and the second Temple, **3,** 179–80.
Joslin of Rosheim. *See* Joseph ben Gershom Loans.
Josselman Rosheim. *See* Joseph ben Gershom Loans.
Jost, Isaac Marcus (1793–1860), historian, basis of the history by, **5,** 594–5.
service rendered by, **5,** 595.
objections to the work of, **5,** 595–6.
limitations of, **5,** 609, 610.
compared with Rapoport, **5,** 619.
Jotapata, resistance of, to Vespasian, **2,** 285–6, 286–7.
fall of, **2,** 287.
Jotham, son of Uzziah, regent of Judah, **1,** 246.
king, ally of Pekah and Rezin, **1,** 248.
state of the kingdom under, **1,** 248–50.
death of, **1,** 257.
Jotham, brother of Abimelech, parable of, **1,** 63.
Jourdan, French general, frees the Jews from the Frankfort Ghetto, **5,** 503–4.
Journals, Jewish, list of:
Ha-Meassef, **5,** 399–400.
Journal for the Science of Judaism, **5,** 585.
Kerem Chemed, **5,** 621, 625.
Orient, The, **5,** 693.
Scientific Journal, The, **5,** 625.
Zion, **5,** 693.
Jovianus, emperor, concludes peace with Shabur II, **2,** 602.
religious toleration under, **2,** 602.

Jozachar, a noble of Judah, kills Joash, **1**, 221.

Juan I, of Aragon, Jews under, **4**, 145, 170.
Chasdaï Crescas at the court of, **4**, 146.

Juan II, of Aragon, the Jews under, **4**, 274, 275.

Juan I, of Castile, coronation of, **4**,
punishes Fernan Martin, **4**, 157.
deprives the Jews of criminal jurisdiction, **4**, 157.
confirms anti-Jewish restrictions, **4**, 158.
possible heir to Portugal, **4**, 158.
regent of Portugal, **4**, 160–1.
makes David Negro chief rabbi of Castile, **4**, 161.
gives up Portugal, **4**, 162.
death of, **4**, 167.

Juan II, of Castile, Jews under, during his minority, **4**, 193–4.
anti-Jewish edict issued in the name of, **4**, 203–4.
issues a second edict concerning the Jews, **4**, 205–6.
admits Jews to state affairs, **4**, 228–9.
confirms the law of Avila, **4**, 229.
refuses consent to anti-Jewish bulls, **4**, 251.
protects the Jews, **4**, 251–2.
weakness of, **4**, 252–3.
complains of the backsliding Marranos, **4**, 256.

Juan de Abadia, Marrano, tries to suppress the Inquisition, **4**, 329.
hires an assassin to kill Pedro Arbues, **4**, 329–30.
suicide of, **4**, 331.

Juan de España (the Old), apostate, Christian propagandist, **4**, 233.

Juan de Lucena, minister to Aragon, urges the expulsion of the Jews, **4**, 348–9.
brother of, persecuted by the Marranos, **4**, 355.

Juan de Sevilla. *See* Samuel Abrabanel.

Juan de Seville, intercedes for the Marranos, **4**, 322–3.
circulates Sixtus IV's bull against the Inquisition, **4**, 323.

Juan Alfonso, governor of Seville, threatened by a mob, **4**, 168.

Juan Alfonso de Albuquerque, minister to Pedro the Cruel, recommends a Jew as minister of finance, **4**, 115–16.
falls into disgrace, **4**, 117.

Juan Arias, bishop of Avila, delivers up the Jews of Sepulveda to butchery, **4**, 279.

Juan Emanuel, regent for Alfonso XI of Castile, the Jews under, **4**, 52–3.

Juba, king of Numidia, marries Glaphyra, **2**, 128.

Jubilee, the year of, ceases to exist as a year of release, **1**, 393.

Judæa, under Gedaliah, **1**, 319–23.
depopulated by Nebuchadnezzar, **1**, 325.
becomes a Persian dependency, **1**, 351.
part of Cœlesyria under Macedonian rule, **1**, 414.
conquered by Ptolemy I, **1**, 416.
falls to Ptolemy I after the battle of Ipsus, **1**, 418.
revolts from Ptolemy II, **1**, 423.

Judæa (*continued*), Dionysian festivals introduced into, **1**, 428.
at peace under Joseph, son of Tobiah, **1**, 430.
under Seleucidæan kings, **1**, 432.
ravaged by the Syrians, **1**, 433.
invaded by Gorgias, **1**, 467.
invaded by Lysias, **1**, 469.
reduced by Bacchides, **1**, 491.
the army of, under Jonathan Haphus, **1**, 498.
after the death of Jonathan Haphus, **1**, 501–2, 519–20.
independent under Simon Tharsi, **1**, 520.
independence of, acknowledged by Demetrius II, **1**, 521.
the Judæans in Egypt apprised of the independence of, **1**, 522–3.
allied with Rome, **1**, 526.
a monarchy under Simon Tharsi, **1**, 526.
under John Hyrcanus, **2**, 1, 11–12.
extent of, under Alexander Jannæus, **2**, 46.
prosperity of, under Salome Alexandra, **2**, 48.
one of the conquered provinces of Rome, **2**, 67.
divided into five provinces, **2**, 71.
burdens of, lessened by Cæsar, **2**, 76.
forced to pay a money contribution to Cassius Longinus, **2**, 80.
free from foreign soldiery under Antigonus, **2**, 83.
pays a tax to Rome, **2**, 87.
invaded by Sosius, **2**, 88.
extent of, under Herod, **2**, 103.

Judæa (*continued*), extent of, under the Herodians, **2**, 118.
towns of, adorned with Greek art, **2**, 118.
given to Archelaus by Herod's will, **2**, 119.
made an ethnarchy by Augustus, **2**, 127.
wholly subject to Rome, **2**, 128.
ruled by procurators, **2**, 137.
compared with Galilee, **2**, 148.
given to Agrippa I by Claudius, **2**, 190.
the kingdom of, at its greatest extent, **2**, 190.
prosperity of, under Agrippa I, **2**, 191.
a Roman province on Agrippa I's death, **2**, 197.
the governor of, independent of the governor of Syria, **2**, 197.
Roman dominion oppressive in, **2**, 233.
aristocracy of, immoral, **2**, 234.
severity of the Roman governors of, **2**, 241.
under Cumanus, **2**, 242.
under Felix, **2**, 245–7.
turbulent state of, under Gessius Florus, **2**, 250–1.
aroused against Rome, **2**, 262.
aided against Rome by foreign Judæans, **2**, 264.
the property of Vespasian, **2**, 312.
triumph over, celebrated at Rome, **2**, 314–15.
fortresses of, in arms, **2**, 315.
after the destruction of Jerusalem by Titus, **2**, 321.
under Roman governors, **2**, 333.
in rebellion against Trajan, **2**, 394–5.

Judæa (*continued*), in rebellion against Hadrian, **2**, 399–400, 403, 408.
visit of Hadrian to, **2**, 406.
desolate condition of, under Hadrian, **2**, 431.
revolution in, under Antoninus Pius, **2**, 447.
sanctity of, **2**, 458.
Hebrew spoken in, **2**, 461–2.
Marcus Aurelius in, **2**, 463.
under Commodus, **2**, 463.
falls into the background, **2**, 503, 531.
compared with Babylonia, **2**, 505.
educational institutions of, investigated by Judah III, **2**, 532.
youths of, go to Babylonia for study, **2**, 537.
Babylonia independent of, **2**, 548.
burials in, **2**, 548.
scene of the coming of the Messiah, **2**, 548–9.
decline of, **2**, 557, 560.
teachers of the Law banished from, **2**, 566–7.
dialectics unknown in, **2**, 591.
the head of the Jewish communities in the Roman empire, **2**, 611.
last Halachic authorities of, **2**, 612.
Biblical studies in, under Theodosius II, **2**, 623–5.
See also Canaan; Israel, the kingdom of; Judah; Palestine.

Judæa, the Roman governors of, list of:

Bassus,	Rufus, Tinnius
Quietus, Lucius	Silva.

See also Procurators, the, of Judæa; Syria, the Roman governors of.

Judæan Christians, the, the early Christians, **2**, 168.
customs of, **2**, 168.
displeased with Paul, **2**, 230, 231.
declare the Law binding, **2**, 231.
differences between, and pagan Christians, **2**, 232.
See also Ebionites, the; Jewish Christians, the; Nazarenes, the.

Judæans, the, deported to Babylonia, **1**, 307.
banished, urge war against Nebuchadnezzar, **1**, 309.
flee to Egypt, **1**, 317, 318.
fugitive, molested after the fall of Jerusalem, **1**, 318.
remain in Judah, **1**, 318–19, 321.
return to Jerusalem from the countries about, **1**, 356.
moral degeneracy of, under Zerubbabel, **1**, 358.
accused of disloyalty to Persia, **1**, 361.
intermarry with the Samaritans, **1**, 361–3.
neglect the Law, **1**, 366.
receive Ezra with respect, **1**, 367.
repudiate their heathen wives, **1**, 368–9.
in part opposed to Ezra's severity, **1**, 370.
appeal to Nehemiah for aid, **1**, 372.
intrigue with Tobiah against Nehemiah, **1**, 376.
swear not to enslave the poor, **1**, 377.
listen to Ezra's reading of the Law, **1**, 378–80.
repudiate their heathen wives, **1**, 380.
swear to observe the Law, **1**, 380–1.

Judæans, the (*continued*), consecrate the walls of Jerusalem, **1**, 381–2.
disregard Nehemiah's injunctions, **1**, 383–4.
dissensions among, **1**, 384.
reforms among, introduced by Nehemiah on his second visit, **1**, 385–8.
hostility of, to the Samaritans, **1**, 392.
influence of the Samaritan sect on, **1**, 392–3.
cultivate the Law, **1**, 393–7.
cruelly treated under Artaxerxes II and III, **1**, 408–9.
taxed by Bagoas, **1**, 409–10.
hostility of the Samaritans to, **1**, 410.
legends about, and Alexander the Great, **1**, 412–13.
taxed by the Macedonians, **1**, 413.
favored by Alexander the Great, **1**, 414–15.
refuse to help in rebuilding the temple to Bel, **1**, 415.
taken captive by Ptolemy I, **1**, 416.
pay tribute to the Egypto-Macedonian court, **1**, 418.
settle in Alexandria, **1**, 418.
settle in Antioch, **1**, 419.
colonies of, in the Græco-Macedonian countries, **1**, 418–19.
dispersed in the lands of the Ptolemies and Seleucidæ, **1**, 420–1.
choose Joseph as their leader, **1**, 424.
under Greek influence, **1**, 426, 427–9.
well treated by Antiochus III, **1**, 433.
hated by surrounding nations, **1**, 434–5.
Judæans, the (*continued*), split up into Hellenists and Chassidim, **1**, 435–6.
trained in Greek athletics, **1**, 445–6.
at the Olympian games at Tyre, **1**, 446.
dissatisfied with Menelaus as high priest, **1**, 447.
kill Lysimachus, **1**, 449.
accused of partisanship for Egypt, **1**, 449.
national party of, favored at the Egyptian court, **1**, 451.
cruelly treated by Antiochus Epiphanes, **1**, 453.
commanded to sacrifice to the Greek gods, **1**, 454–5.
persecuted by the overseers of Antiochus IV, **1**, 456–7.
extermination of, planned by Antiochus IV, **1**, 463–4.
defended by Ptolemy Macron, **1**, 476–7, 478.
granted religious freedom by Antiochus V, **1**, 480, 488.
split up into parties, **1**, 489.
alliance with, sought by Demetrius I, **1**, 495.
exempted from taxation, **1**, 497.
destroy a portion of Antioch, **1**, 497.
defeat Diodotus Tryphon, **1**, 499.
regret the existence of the Temple of Onias, **1**, 509.
object to the Greek translation of the Law, **1**, 512.
count from the date of Simon Tharsi's accession, **1**, 522.
in the army of Antiochus Sidetes celebrate the Sabbath and the holidays, **2**, 5.
permitted to ship goods duty free from their ports, **2**, 9.
development of, under John Hyrcanus, **2**, 13–15.

Judæans, the (*continued*), Greek art among, **2**, 14.
cultivate the Hebrew language, **2**, 14–15.
literature of, under the Hasmonæans, **2**, 15–16.
religion of, divided into sects, **2**, 16–31.
make the half-Shekel collections in spring, **2**, 52.
flee to Egypt during the siege of Jerusalem by Aretas, **2**, 60.
with republican views appeal to Pompey, **2**, 63–4.
oppose Cæsar, **2**, 77.
present their grievances to Archelaus, **2**, 120–1.
appeal to Augustus to make Judæa a Roman province, **2**, 126–7.
petition for the removal of obnoxious emblems from the Roman standard, **2**, 139.
influenced by John the Baptist, **2**, 146–7.
morality of the middle class of, **2**, 151.
complain of Pontius Pilate's cruelty, **2**, 172.
leniently treated under Tiberius, **2**, 172–3.
object to the images of the emperors on the Roman standards, **2**, 173.
dispersed in the Roman and Parthian empires, **2**, 200–3.
of the dispersion visit the Temple, **2**, 201.
as regarded by the heathen, **2**, 203.
view held by, of paganism, **2**, 204.
manifest proselytizing tendencies, **2**, 215–19.
in Greek cities proselytized by Nazarenes, **2**, 222.

Judæans, the (*continued*), displeased with the apostle Paul, **2**, 229, 230.
hindered by Rome, in the free exercise of religion, **2**, 234.
immorality of, under the Roman dominion, **2**, 237–8.
resent the presence of a Roman cohort in the Temple, **2**, 242.
hated by the Greek and Roman inhabitants of Judæa, **2**, 246–7.
deprived by Nero of civil rights in Cæsarea, **2**, 247.
well treated by Nero and Poppea Sabina, **2**, 248.
number of, in Jerusalem at Passover 66, **2**, 251.
quarrel with the heathen in Cæsarea, **2**, 252–3.
parties among, **2**, 256.
aroused by the treatment of the Cæsareans, **2**, 262.
loyalty of, defended before Nero, **2**, 268.
joined by the Samaritans against Rome, **2**, 268.
massacre of, by the heathen, **2**, 269.
forbidden to buy articles of food from the heathen, **2**, 270.
after the destruction of Jerusalem, **2**, 311–12, 321–2.
friendly to Rome, rewarded by Vespasian, **2**, 316–17.
See also Israelites, the; Jews, the; Judæans, the, *of various cities and countries.*
Judæo-Alexandrian school, the, of Allegorists, **2**, 208–9, 329.
combat paganism, **2**, 214–15.
Judæo-Greek literature, among the Judæans in Egypt, **1**, 515–16; **2**, 204–8.
Judæo-Greek writers, spread Judæan doctrines, **2**, 204–8.

Judah, the house of, renounces allegiance to David, **1,** 140.

Judah, the kingdom of, first indications of, **1,** 109.
dislike of, to Israel, under Solomon, **1,** 174.
founded, **1,** 183.
religious conditions in, under Rehoboam, **1,** 188–9.
subjects of, sold as slaves under Uzziah, **1,** 227.
weakness of, at the beginning of Uzziah's reign, **1,** 237.
licentiousness of the princes of, under Jotham, **1,** 249–50.
Assyrian idols introduced into, **1,** 260–1.
degradation of the nobles of, under Ahaz, **1,** 261.
freed from idolatry by Hezekiah, **1,** 268.
fortified towns of, taken by Sennacherib, **1,** 272.
golden age of, under Hezekiah, **1,** 279.
idolatry in, under Manasseh, **1,** 282–3.
ravaged by the Scythians, **1,** 287.
end of, **1,** 305.
taken by Nebuchadnezzar's army, **1,** 307.
importance of, **1,** 308.
power of the nobles of, **1,** 308–9.

Judah, the kings of, list of:
Abijam,
Ahaziah,
Amaziah,
Amon,
Asa,
Jehoahaz (Shallum),
Jehoiachin (Jeconiah),
Jehoiakim (Eliakim),
Jehoshaphat,
Joash,
Joram (Jehoram),
Josiah,
Manasseh,
Rehoboam,
Uzziah,
Zedekiah (Mattaniah).

Judah, the tribe of, successful warriors in the desert, **1,** 26.

Judah, the tribe of (*continued*),
war of, for territory, **1,** 38.
description of the land of, **1,** 45.
isolation of, **1,** 51, 76–7, 109.
delivered by Othniel, **1,** 60.
attacked by the Ammonites and Philistines, **1,** 64.
enters national life, **1,** 77.
virtues of, **1,** 77.
chooses David as king, **1,** 107.
hesitates to recall David after Absalom's revolt, **1,** 146.
sends an embassy to meet David, **1,** 146–7.
quarrels with the northern tribes, **1,** 148.
loyal to Rehoboam, **1,** 182.
members of, return under Zerubbabel, **1,** 352.

Judah, brother of Jesus, **2,** 148.

Judah, chief rabbi of Portugal and minister of finance, **3,** 618.

Judah, coadjutor of Josephus in Galilee, **2,** 278, 279.

Judah, Essene seer, **2,** 38.

Judah, father of Solomon Ibn-Gebirol, **3,** 265.

Judah, favorite of Charles the Bald, **3,** 170.

Judah I (ha-Nassi, Rabbi), Patriarch, son of Simon III, closes the activity of the Tanaites, **2,** 450.
talents of, **2,** 450–1.
teachers of, **2,** 451.
made Patriarch, **2,** 451.
generosity of, **2,** 451–2.
invests the Patriarchate with autocratic power, **2,** 452–4.
lives at Sepphoris, **2,** 452.
called Rabbi, **2,** 453.
disciples of, **2,** 454–7, 511.
severity of, towards his disciples, **2,** 454–6.
punishes Chiya, **2,** 455.

Judah I (*continued*), refuses to authorize Simon bar Kappara to teach, **2**, 456.
cured by Samuel, **2**, 456.
offended by Judah and Chiskiya, **2**, 457.
admits the testimony of a Samaritan, **2**, 457.
moderates the laws of tithes, **2**, 458–9.
contemplates the abolition of the year of release, **2**, 459–60.
completes the Mishna, **2**, 460–1.
revises his own code, **2**, 461.
prefers Hebrew, **2**, 461.
gives tradition a settled form, **2**, 462.
the last of the Tanaites, **2**, 462.
rebuked by the widow of Eleazar ben Simon, **2**, 465.
death of, **2**, 465–7.
appoints his sons to offices, **2**, 466.
dying wishes of, **2**, 466.
announcement of the death of, **2**, 466–7.
funeral of, **2**, 467.
called "the Holy," **2**, 467.
maxims of, **2**, 472.
work of, completed by Ashi, **2**, 609.
Judah II (Rabbi, Rabbenu, 228), Patriarch, son of Gamaliel III, **2**, 479.
censured for irreligiousness, **2**, 480.
in favor with Alexander Severus, **2**, 480–3.
royal authority of, **2**, 481–2.
Roman dress of, **2**, 483.
leniency of, **2**, 483–5.
permits the purchase of articles of food from the heathen, **2**, 483–4.
alleviations proposed by, **2**, 484–5.
Judah II (*continued*), attacks on, **2**, 485–6.
covetousness of, **2**, 486.
draws a revenue from the Jewish communities, **2**, 486–7.
reverence for, **2**, 487.
death of, **2**, 487.
Jochanan bar Napacha the companion of, **2**, 493.
questions Levi bar Sissi on the neo-Persians, **2**, 525.
Judah III (280–300), Patriarch, has scant knowledge of the Law, **2**, 532.
determines the new-moon, **2**, 532.
investigates the educational institutions of Judæa, **2**, 532.
accused of disloyalty, **2**, 533–4.
levies a tax for the Patriarchate, **2**, 536.
accused of Christian leanings, **2**, 565.
Judah IV, Patriarch, son of Gamaliel V, **2**, 612.
Judah, proselyte, informs against Simon ben Yochai, **2**, 448.
Judah, treasurer of Ferdinand I of Portugal, **4**, 159.
removed from office, **4**, 160.
proposed as chief rabbi of Castile, **4**, 161, 162.
imprisoned, **4**, 161.
Judah (Laudadeus) de Blanis, physician and Kabbalist, **4**, 411.
Judah the Blind (Jehudaï, 759–762), Gaon of Sora, opposed to Anan ben David, **3**, 129.
author of Halachoth Ketuoth, **3**, 136.
work of, supplemented, **3**, 179.
work of, superseded, **3**, 286.
Judah ben Baba, member of the Jamnia Synhedrion, **2**, 357.

Judah ben Baba (*continued*), ordains Akiba's disciples, **2**, 429; **4**, 536.
suffers martyrdom, **2**, 429.
Judah ben Bathyra, teacher of the Law in Nisibis, **2**, 358, 443.
effects the dissolution of the Synhedrion at Nahar-Pakod, **2**, 444.
Judah ben Chiya, offends Judah I ha-Nassi, **2**, 457.
adds supplements to the Mishna, **2**, 470.
Babylonian disciple of Judah I, **2**, 511.
Judah ben Ezekiel, Babylonian Amora, founds the academy of Pumbeditha, **2**, 545, 549.
descent of, **2**, 549.
dialectic system of, **2**, 550.
and his brother, **2**, 550–1.
severity of, with regard to purity of race, **2**, 551–2.
excommunicates a Nahardean, **2**, 551–2.
principal of the Sora Metibta, **2**, 552.
method of, used by Chasda, **2**, 553.
acuteness of the disciples of, **2**, 575.
objects to emigration, **2**, 576.
Judah ben Ilai, disciple of Akiba, returns to Judæa, **2**, 433.
receives the members of the Synhedrion of Usha, **2**, 433–4.
diplomacy of, **2**, 442.
artisan, **2**, 442.
praises Rome, **2**, 448
rewarded by Rome, **2**, 448.
Judah ben Jacob Chayyat, Kabbalist, describes the suffering of the Spanish exiles, **4**, 369–70, 481.
Judah ben Joseph Ibn-Alfachar. *See* Jehuda bar Joseph Ibn-Alfachar.
Judah ben Moses Cohen, physician to Alfonso X, **3**, 593.
Judah ben Moses Ibn-Tibbon, chief of the Tibbonide party, **4**, 32.
Judah ben Saul Ibn-Tibbon (1120–1190), physician and translator, pedantry of, **3**, 397.
works translated by, **3**, 397.
Hebrew style of, **3**, 398.
Judah ben Tabbaï, Nassi of the Great Council, re-organizes it, **2**, 49.
called "Restorer of the Law," **2**, 49.
rigorous in administering the Law, **2**, 53–4.
maxim of, **2**, 54.
disciples of, **2**, 72.
Judah ben Yechiel (Messer Leon, 1450–1490), rabbi and physician in Mantua, **4**, 289.
author of books on grammar, logic, and rhetoric, **4**, 289–90.
as a classical scholar, **4**, 289–90.
hostility to, **4**, 293.
controversy of, with Joseph Kolon, **4**, 295.
banished from Mantua, **4**, 295.
Judah ben Zippori, Pharisee, instigates an uprising against Herod, **2**, 115.
burnt alive, **2**, 115.
death of, avenged, **2**, 121.
Judah Ibn-Giat, poet, **3**, 318.
Judah Ibn-Verga, Kabbalist and astronomer, teaches Marranos, **4**, 335.
martyrdom of, **4**, 336.
as a chronicler, **4**, 556.
consulted by Basnage, **5**, 196.
Judah Ibn-Yachya-Negro, prevents the forced baptism of the Jews of Portugal, **4**, 218.

Judah, son of David ben Zaccaï, quarrels with Saadiah, **3,** 195.
appointed Exilarch, **3,** 201.
son of, **3,** 201–2.
Judah, son of Simon Tharsi, 1, 520.
general, **1,** 529.
assassinated, **1,** 530.
Judah Benveniste, leader of the Spanish exiles in Salonica, **4,** 405.
Judah Chassid, leader of a Sabbatian sect in Poland, exhorts to penance, **5,** 212.
emigrates, **5,** 212.
effect of preaching of, **5,** 212–13.
death of, **5,** 213.
nephews of, **5,** 213.
Judah Del Medigo. *See* Del Medigo.
Judah Judghan (800), of Hamadan, imparts a Mutazilistic tendency to Judaism, **3,** 149–50.
asceticism of, **3,** 150.
founder of a sect, **3,** 150.
Judah Leon Abrabanel (Hebræus, Medigo, 1470–1530), treasurer to a Portuguese prince, **4,** 337.
describes his father, **4,** 339.
referred to, **4,** 340.
property of, confiscated by Alfonso V of Portugal, **4,** 341.
forbidden to leave Toledo, **4,** 360.
flees to Naples, **4,** 360.
son of, forcibly baptized, **4,** 361.
at Genoa, **4,** 384.
pursuits of, **4,** 384.
physician to Gonsalvo de Cordova, **4,** 384–5.
in Venice, **4,** 385.
Judah Leon Abrabanel (*continued*), without influence in Italy, **4,** 409.
as philosopher, **4,** 480–1.
Italian style of, **4,** 480.
Hebrew verses of, addressed to his son, **4,** 480.
esteemed by Italians, **4,** 481.
Judah Menz (1408–1509), rabbi in Padua, Talmudist, **4,** 294.
controversy of, with Elias del Medigo, **4,** 295.
narrowness of, **4,** 295.
disciples of, **4,** 406.
as a teacher, **4,** 410.
Judah Siciliano, Italian man of letters, **4,** 60.
poet, praised by Immanuel Romi, **4,** 68.
Judah Sir Leon ben Isaac (1166–1224), Tossafist, **3,** 408.
writes the "Book of the Pious," **3,** 408–9.
disciples of, **3,** 409, 539.
Judah. *See also under* Jehuda; Judas.
"**Judah's** Rod of Correction," history by Joseph Ibn-Verga, **4,** 557.
Judaism, a religious conviction after the formation of the Samaritan sect, **1,** 393.
Magian influence on, **1,** 402–5.
incompatible with Greek games, **1,** 445.
calumniated by Menelaus, the Benjamite, **1,** 449–50.
calumniated by Antiochus Epiphanes, **1,** 452.
becomes known through the Greek version of the Pentateuch, **1,** 512–13.
misrepresented by the Greek translation of the Law, **1,** 513–14.
development of, under the Hasmonæans, **2,** 16–17.

Judaism (*continued*), sects of, 2, 16–31.
leaning of Romans towards, 2, 136.
Roman proselytes to, under Tiberius, 2, 136–7.
universality of, 2, 141.
how introduced to the heathen, 2, 142.
attitude of Jesus to, 2, 155–6.
as viewed by the heathen, 2, 203.
allegorized to suit Greek notions, 2, 208–9.
apostasy from, among the Alexandrians, 2, 209.
humanitarian laws of, as expounded by Philo, 2, 211–12, 213–14.
embraced by the heathen, 2, 215–19.
leanings towards, taken advantage of by the Nazarenes, 2, 219.
taught by Paul as an introduction to Christianity, 2, 228, 229.
relation of, to Christianity according to Paul, 2, 229–30.
hampered by Rome, 2, 234.
dangers to, after the destruction of Jerusalem, 2, 322.
dissociated from the Temple by Jochanan ben Zakkai, 2, 324–5.
reviled by the Nazarenes, 2, 371–2.
consolidation of, after the fall of the second Temple, 2, 373.
as viewed by the Gnostics, 2, 377.
influence of the Minæans on, deprecated, 2, 378.
Gnostic or semi-Christian ideas in, 2, 380–1.
saved from Gnostic influences by Akiba, 2, 382.
Judaism (*continued*), influence of, upon the pagan world, 2, 382–3.
conversions to, from paganism, 2, 383–5.
Tacitus on the conversions to, 2, 384.
mocked at by Hadrian, 2, 407–8.
laws against, decreed by Hadrian, 2, 421.
Hadrian attempts to graft paganism on, 2, 422.
persecuted by Hadrian, 2, 423–6.
independence of Christianity of, demonstrated to Hadrian, 2, 431.
laws against, promulgated by Severus, 2, 464.
legal character of, due to the Mishna, 2, 471.
admired by Alexander Severus, 2, 481.
Greek civilization equal to, according to Jochanan bar Napacha, 2, 494.
in foreign lands, 2, 520.
oppressed by Christianity, 2, 535.
placed on an equality with Christianity, 2, 561.
aspersed by Church dignitaries under Constantine, 2, 562.
conversions to, forbidden by Constantine, 2, 562, 564.
separated from Christianity at the Council of Nice, 2, 563.
interest of Julian the Apostate in, 2, 596.
protected by Theodosius the Great, 2, 614–15.
preserved by the Talmud, 2, 635.
among the Arabian Jews in the sixth century, 3, 58–9.

Judaism (*continued*), inspires Mahomet, **3**, 71–2.
taught the Chazars by fugitive Greek Jews, **3**, 139.
account of the conversion of the Chazars to, **3**, 139–40.
influence of, on the Chazars, **3**, 141.
rationalistic tendency imparted to, **3**, 149–50.
orthodox adherents of, oppose the rationalists, **3**, 152–3.
mysticism in, **3**, 153–5.
Karaite interpretation of, variable, **3**, 157.
revered by the Empress Judith, **3**, 162.
revered by the Christians of the Frankish empire, **3**, 163.
promotes science during the Middle Ages, **3**, 187.
assumes a European character in the tenth century, **3**, 188.
Christian and Islam objections to, answered by Saadiah, **3**, 199.
leadership of, lost by Asia, **3**, 207.
the center of, in Spain, **3**, 229.
gloomy character of, in Germany, **3**, 309.
as expounded by Jehuda Halevi, **3**, 330, 331–6.
as characterized by Abraham Ibn-Daud, **3**, 364–5.
in Asia in the twelfth century, **3**, 440–2.
as presented by Maimonides in his Mishne-Torah, **3**, 467.
and philosophy in Maimonides' "Guide of the Perplexed," **3**, 478–9.
loses by Maimonides' philosophical system, **3**, 487.
condition of, in the twelfth century, **3**, 446–7.

Judaism (*continued*), the creed of, drawn up by Maimonides, **3**, 459–60.
divided by the Maimunist controversy, **3**, 546–7.
as interpreted by Nachmani, **3**, 533–5.
Albo on the possibility of changing, **4**, 242.
effect of the Protestant Reformation on, **4**, 471.
influence of the Shulchan Aruch on, **4**, 613.
influence of Lurya's Kabbala on, **4**, 625–7.
attacked by Martin Czechowic, **4**, 648.
influence of the Cossack persecutions on, **5**, 16–17.
condition of, in the seventeenth century, **5**, 51–2.
reform of, proposed by Leo Modena, **5**, 73–4.
defended by Simone Luzzatto, **5**, 81–4.
antagonized by Spinoza, **5**, 97–8, 101–3.
discredited by the Kabbala, **5**, 166.
glorified by Spinoza, **5**, 167.
attracts Christians, **5**, 176.
influenced by Lessing, **5**, 298.
Mendelssohn's early attitude towards, **5**, 310.
human additions to, according to Mendelssohn, **5**, 311, 317.
binding only upon Jews, **5**, 312.
Mendelssohn's glorification of, **5**, 314–15.
as defined by Mendelssohn, **5**, 364.
consequences of the renaissance of, **5**, 374–5.
view of, taken by Schleiermacher, **5**, 426–7.
view of, held by Chateaubriand, **5**, 427.

Judaism (*continued*), view of, held by Furtado, **5,** 496.
characterized by Heine, **5,** 552.
excrescences of, **5,** 557–9.
barbarous aspect of, under Polish influence, **5,** 558.
disfigurement of, among the Portuguese, **5,** 559.
reform of, suggested, **5,** 559. *See* Reform, the, of Judaism.
reconciliation of, with culture, **5,** 560.
as viewed by Bernays, **5,** 575–6.
journal for the science of, **5,** 585.
love for, fostered by the Society for Culture, **5,** 588.
the renaissance of, **5,** 589–90, 591–2, 607.
defined by Steinheim, **5,** 604–6.
the narrowing of, by the new school of scholars, **5,** 627.
view of, held by Holdheim, **5,** 680–1.
the first to recognize the rights of man, **5,** 709–10.
the moral system of, **5,** 710–11.
free from asceticism, **5,** 712.

Judaism, the sects of, list of:

Boëthuseans,	Karaites (and their sects),
Chassidim,	Menachemists,
Donmäh,	Pharisees,
Essenes,	Sabbatians,
Frankists,	Sadducees,
Isavites,	Samaritans.
Judghanites,	

Judaism, conversions to. *See* Conversions to Judaism.

"Judaism, or the Jewish Doctrine," attack by John Miller, **4,** 692.

Judaism, Rabbinical. *See* Rabbinical Judaism.

Judaism, Talmudical. *See* Talmudical Judaism.

Judaism, the Reform of. *See* Reform, the, of Judaism.

Judaism, the Statute of, passed by the House of Commons, **3,** 642.

"Judaism Unmasked," by Eisenmenger, full title of, **5,** 188.
suppressed, **5,** 189–90.
cause of, supported by Frederick I of Prussia, **5,** 192–3.
under ban for forty years, **5,** 193.

Judaizantes, sect called forth by the Protestant Reformation, **4,** 541.

Judas the Galilean, champion against the Romans, **2,** 125.
seizes the arsenal of Sepphoris, **2,** 125.
escapes from Quintilius Varus, **2,** 126.
leader of the Zealots, **2,** 133.
resists the Roman census, **2,** 133–4.
conception of the Messiah held by the disciples of, **2,** 144.
morality of the followers of, **2,** 151.
sons of, **2,** 199.
grandsons of, **2,** 239.

Judas ben Jair, killed by the Romans, **2,** 315.

Judas Aristobulus, Judæan of priestly lineage, teacher of the Egyptian king, **1,** 519.
petitioned to introduce the Chanukah celebration into Egypt, **2,** 6–7.

Judas Iscariot, follower of Jesus, betrays him, **2,** 163.

Judas Maccabæus, son of Mattathias, the Hasmonæan, **1,** 459.
chosen to succeed his father as commander, **1,** 461.
characterization of, **1,** 461.
defeats Apollonius, **1,** 461–2.

Judas Maccabæus (*continued*),
defeats Heron, **1**, 462.
joined by the half-Hellenized, **1**, 464.
exhorts his troops at Mizpah, **1**, 467.
divides his army among his brothers, **1**, 468.
dismisses all excused from military service by the Law, **1**, 468.
defeats Gorgias, **1**, 468–9, 476.
defeats Lysias, **1**, 469–70.
consecrates the Temple, **1**, 471–3.
fortifies the Temple mount, **1**, 473.
defeats the Idumæans and Ammonites, **1**, 474.
appealed to by Judæans in the provinces, **1**, 474–5.
rescues the trans-Jordanic provinces, **1**, 476.
besieges the Acra, **1**, 478.
defeated at Beth-Zachariah, **1**, 479.
besieged in Jerusalem, **1**, 479–80.
made high priest, **1**, 481.
hated by the Hellenists, **1**, 481.
accused before Demetrius I, **1**, 482.
retreats to the mountains, **1**, 482.
gathers a new army to oppose Alcimus and Bacchides, **1**, 483.
treats with Nicanor, **1**, 484.
defeats Nicanor, **1**, 484, 485.
negotiates with Rome, **1**, 485–6.
encamps at Eleasa, **1**, 486.
falls on the battlefield of Eleasa, **1**, 487.
achievements of, compared with his brother Jonathan's, **1**, 501–2.

Judas Maccabæus (*continued*),
state of Judæa after the death of, **1**, 501, 519–20.
model of Cromwell, **5**, 26.

Judas. *See also under* Jehuda; Judah.

Judenbreter, name assumed by German families, **3**, 611.

Jüdenbühl, in Nuremberg, scene of the burning of the Jews, **4**, 110.

Judenmeister, rabbis, appointed by order of Sigismund, **4**, 227.

Judenstättigkeit, permissive residence of Jews in Frankfort, **4**, 695; **5**, 503.
indulgently interpreted, **4**, 696.
abolished by Emperor Matthias, **4**, 700.

Juderia, the, of Seville, destroyed by a mob, **4**, 169. *See* Jew's quarter, the.

Judges, Jews forbidden to act as, by the Council of Mâcon, **3**, 39, 171.

Judges, the warrior, deliver the Israelites from servitude, **1**, 59.
activity of, characterized, **1**, 68–9.
un-Jewish character of, **5**, 715.

Judges, the, list of:

Abdon,	Gideon,
Abimelech,	Ibzan,
Barak,	Jephthah,
Deborah,	Othniel,
Ehud,	Samson,
Elon,	Samuel,
Shamgar.	

Judghanites, a Jewish sect, **3**, 150.

Judgment Chamber, in the House of the Forest of Lebanon, **1**, 168–9.

Judith, the Book of, admitted into the Canon by Christians, **2**, 488.
Judith, wife of Louis the Pious, friendly to Judaism, **3**, 162.
calumniated by Bishop Agobard, **3**, 164.
rebellion incited against, **3**, 166.
conspiracy against, joined by Agobard, **3**, 168.
Juglar, Gaspard, inquisitor in Aragon, **4**, 326.
Julian the Apostate, emperor, delivers the Jews from the oppression suffered under Constantine, **2**, 572.
character of, **2**, 595.
in possession of undivided power, **2**, 595.
plans of, **2**, 595.
opposes Christianity, **2**, 596.
interest of, in Judaism, **2**, 596.
admires the benevolence of the Jews, **2**, 596–7.
predilection of, for the sacrificial cult, **2**, 597.
favors the Jews of the Roman empire, **2**, 597.
letter of, to the Jewish communities, **2**, 598.
accuses the Christians of preventing the rebuilding of the Temple, **2**, 601.
in the Persian war, **2**, 601–2.
death of, **2**, 602.
Julian, Metropolitan of Toledo, presides over an anti-Jewish Council, **3**, 107.
Julian ben Sabar, Samaritan king, **3**, 13, 16.
Julianus, leader of the rebellion against Trajan in Judæa, **2**, 395.
threatened by Lucius Quietus, **2**, 401.
Julias, built by the tetrarch Philip, **2**, 138.
Jülich, a Jew of, accused of ritual murder, **5**, 642.
Julius II, pope, friendly to the Jews, **4**, 407.
employs a Jewish physician, **4**, 408.
Julius III, pope, petitioned for absolution for the Marranos, **4**, 528.
the Talmud denounced before, **4**, 564.
signs the decree against the Talmud, **4**, 565.
protects Hebrew writings except the Talmud, **4**, 565.
death of, **4**, 566.
confirms the privileges of the Marranos of Ancona, **4**, 568.
employs a Jewish physician, **4**, 569.
Julius Archelaus, husband of Mariamne, daughter of Agrippa I, **2**, 235.
Julius Capellus, partisan of Rome in Tiberias, **2**, 274.
Jullos, name given to Hillel II by Origen, **2**, 487.
July revolution, the, effect of, on Europe, **5**, 596.
on the Jews, **5**, 596, 598, 600.
"Jumpers, the," origin of, **5**, 378.
Juno, the Argive, statue of, raised by Herod in Cæsarea, **2**, 106.
Jupiter, statue of, placed in the Temple by Antiochus Epiphanes, **1**, 455.
destroyed by Judas Maccabæus, **1**, 472.
Jupiter, temple of, adorned with a golden vine destined for the Temple at Jerusalem, **2**, 63.
on Gerizim, **2**, 422.

Jupiter Capitolinus, temple to, in Jerusalem, **2**, 422.
Jupiter, Olympian, statue of, raised by Herod in Cæsarea, **2**, 106.
Jurieu, Pierre, Huguenot, on the future of the Jews, **5**, 176.
Jurisdiction, Jewish, autonomous, withdrawn by Verus, **2**, 447–8.
restored by Alexander Severus, **2**, 482.
exercised by Raba in a criminal suit, **2**, 592.
under the Patriarchs, **2**, 613.
under Arcadius, **2**, 616.
forbidden in mixed suits, **2**, 617; **3**, 28.
in civil suits in Greece, southern Italy, etc., **3**, 27, 28, 423.
in Cologne, **3**, 41.
under the Exilarchs, **3**, 89.
in Speyer, **3**, 297.
under Henry IV, **3**, 298.
in Castile, etc., **4**, 116, 155, 157, 203.
exercised by Ar-Rabbi Mor, **4**, 159.
in Vienna, **4**, 702.
in Poland, **5**, 3.
See also Courts of Justice; Witnesses.
Jussuf Pasha, governor of Rhodes, persecutes the Jews on the blood accusation, **5**, 640–1.
dismissed from his post, **5**, 647.
Justi, court preacher, denounces Mendelssohn's review of Frederick II's poetry, **5**, 302.
Justin I, emperor of the East, enforces the anti-Jewish laws of Theodosius II, **3**, 10.
appealed to, to make war upon Zorah Nowas, **3**, 66.
Justin II, emperor of the East, oppresses the Samaritans, **3**, 17–18.
expels the Jews from their quarter in Constantinople, **3**, 26.
Justinian I (483–565), emperor, closes the schools of philosophy in Greece, **3**, 7.
interferes with the religious liberty of the Jews, **3**, 12–16.
enacts that Jews are competent witnesses only in their own cases, **3**, 12–13.
orders translations of the Law to be used by Jewish congregations, **3**, 14–15.
forbids the recital of the confession of faith, **3**, 15.
removes the Temple vessels from Constantinople to Jerusalem, **3**, 27.
rule of, feared by the Jews of Italy, **3**, 31.
made exarch of Ravenna, **3**, 32.
appealed to by Imrulkais Ibn Hojr, **3**, 69.
Justiniani, Augustin, bishop of Corsica, introduces the study of Hebrew into France, **4**, 473, 474.
has Moses Kimchi's grammar printed, **4**, 474.
has a Latin translation of the "Guide of the Perplexed" made, **4**, 474.
Justus of Tiberias, historian, does not mention Jesus, **2**, 166.
leader of the Roman insurrection in Tiberias, **2**, 274.
historian of the Roman war, **2**, 319.
ambiguous conduct of, **2**, 319–20.
attacks Josephus, **2**, 390.

K

Kaab, teacher of the Law, converts Abu-Kariba to Judaism, **3,** 62–3.
goes to Yemen to convert the people, **3,** 63.
Kaab Ibn-Asharaf, Jewish opponent of Mahomet, **3,** 74.
Kaab Ibn-Assad, chief of the Benu-Kuraiza, **3,** 80.
killed by Mahomet, **3,** 81.
Kaaba, the, the Square, the holy place of the Arabs, **3,** 60.
number of idols in, **3,** 72.
Moslem turn towards, in prayer, **3,** 75.
Kaarat Kesef, by Joseph Ezobi, **3,** 561.
Kabbala, the, Jacob ben Meshullam the first promoter of, **3,** 396.
as used by Nachmani, **3,** 535.
rise of, in the thirteenth century, **3,** 547.
earliest promoters of, **3,** 547.
reduced to a system, **3,** 548.
youth of, **3,** 548.
put into philosophical language, **3,** 549.
counterpoise to the Maimunist philosophy, **3,** 529.
compromise between faith and philosophy, **3,** 549, 623.
theosophy of, **3,** 550.
principles of, concerning God, **3,** 550–1.
theory of emanation in, **3,** 551–2.
theory of creation in, **3,** 552–3.
on the mission of Israel, **3,** 553.
mystical importance of prayer in, **3,** 553–4.
on metempsychosis, **3,** 554.
on retribution, **3,** 555.
on the soul of the Messiah, **3,** 555.
Kabbala, the (*continued*), great age fraudulently claimed for, **3,** 556.
promoted by Nachmani, **3,** 556–7.
transplanted to Palestine by Nachmani, **3,** 607.
to be taught in secret, according to Solomon ben Adret, **3,** 619.
progress of, in Spain, **4,** 1–23.
furtherance of, through the Zohar, **4,** 22.
studied in Palestine, **4,** 74–5.
in Spain in the fourteenth century, **4,** 91.
influence of, increases in Spain, **4,** 196.
studied by Pico di Mirandola, **4,** 291–2, 433, 443.
Christian dogmas in, **4,** 292.
translated into Latin, **4,** 292, 443.
denounced by Elias del Medigo, **4,** 292.
introduced into Safet by Joseph Saragossi, **4,** 399.
in Salonica, **4,** 405.
defended by Reuchlin, **4,** 442–3, 466–7.
admired by Egidio de Viterbo, **4,** 457.
carried to Italy and Turkey by Spanish exiles, **4,** 481.
Christian scholars interested in, **4,** 481.
affects the liturgy, **4,** 481.
expectation of the Messiah the center of, **4,** 482, 483.
Safet center of, **4,** 538.
esteemed by the Church, **4,** 583.
influence of, in Palestine in the sixteenth century, **4,** 617.
spread of, **4,** 617.
induces a Jewish "dark age," **4,** 617.

Kabbala, the (*continued*), influence of, on Judaism, **4,** 625–7.
corrupting influence of, **4,** 626–7.
influence of, on seventeenth century Judaism, **5,** 51–2.
as taught by Vital Calabrese, **5,** 52–3.
spread by Israel Saruk, **5,** 54.
spread by Abraham de Herrera, **5,** 54.
identified with Neo-platonism, **5,** 54.
beginnings of the criticism of, **5,** 55.
attacked by Leo Modena, **5,** 67, 74.
ridiculed by Joseph Delmedigo, **5,** 77.
defended by Joseph Delmedigo, **5,** 78–9.
Simone Luzzatto on, **5,** 84.
studied by Spinoza, **5,** 88.
influence of, on Sabbataï Zevi, **5,** 118–19.
taught by Sabbataï Zevi, **5,** 119.
Messianic speculation in, **5,** 120–1.
at variance with Rabbinical Judaism, **5,** 144, 277.
brings discredit on Judaism, **5,** 166.
opposed by Jehuda Leon Brieli, **5,** 200.
supposed to teach the Trinity, **5,** 216.
unhealthy influences of, **5,** 232–3.
Moses Chayim Luzzatto under the influence of, **5,** 236.
study of, forbidden to young men, **5,** 241, 277.
generally opposed by the rabbis, **5,** 245.
sways the minds of Polish Jews, **5,** 382.

Kabbala, the (*continued*), views of, held by Elijah Wilna, **5,** 390–1.
supporters of, in Italy, **5,** 488.
disfigures Judaism, **5,** 539.
See also Zohar, the.

Kabbala, the higher, of Abraham Abulafia, **4,** 5–6.

Kabbalistic terms:
Adam Kadmon,
Diokna Kadisha,
En-Sof,
Gematria,
Ibbur,
Kartiel,
Kelifa (Kelifoth),
Kewanoth,
King,
Malka Kadisha,
Matronita,
Nizuz (Nizuzoth),
Notaricon,
Olam ha-Tikkun,
Parsophin (Parzufim),
Sefiroth,
Shechina,
Tsiruf.

Kabbalistic writings, on the Index expurgatorius, **4,** 584.

Kabbalists, the, opposed to the Maimunists in the interpretation of ceremonies, **3,** 554.
distort the Scriptures, **3,** 556.
opposed to Maimunists and Talmudists, **3,** 558.
of Accho, in the Maimunist controversy, **3,** 631–3.
and Solomon Molcho, **4,** 496–7.
at Safet, **4,** 622–3.
divorces frequent among, **4,** 627; **5,** 210.

Kabbalists, list of:
Abraham of Granada,
Abraham ben David,
Abraham ben Samuel Abulafia,
Abraham Levi,
Abraham Saba,
Aleman, Jochanan
Azriel,
Baruch of Benevento,
Chananel Ibn-Askara,
Chayim Vital Calabrese,
Cohen, Naphtali
David Ibn-Abi Zimra,
Eleazar ben Jehuda,
Ergas, Joseph
Ezra,
Frankfurter, Naphthali
Herrera, Abraham de
Hurwitz, Isaiah
Isaac of Accho,
Isaac the Blind,
Isaac ben Abraham Ibn-Latif,
Isaac Cohen Shalal,

Kabbalists, list of (*continued*):

Isaac Lurya Levi,
Israel Saruk,
Jacob of Segovia,
Jacob ben Meshullam,
Jacob ben Sheshet Gerundi,
Joseph of Arli,
Joseph ben Abraham Jikatilla,
Joseph ben Todros Abulafia,
Joseph Karo,
Joseph Saragossi,
Judah de Blanis,
Judah ben Jacob Chayyat,
Judah Ibn-Verga,
Levi ben Todros Abulafia,
Luzzatto, Moses Chayim
Meïr ben Gabbai,
Molcho, Solomon
Moses de Leon,
Moses ben Isaac Alashkar,
Moses ben Nachman,
Moses Botarel,
Moses Zacuto,
Oppenheim, David
Samuel of Medina-Celi,
Samuel Franco,
Shem-Tob ben Abraham Ibn-Gaon,
Shem-Tob ben Joseph Ibn-Shem Tob,
Solomon of Moravia,
Solomon ben Abraham b. Adret,
Solomon Petit,
Taytasak, Joseph
Todros ben Joseph Halevi Abulafia.

Kabul. *See* Cabul.

Kachtan, ancestor of the Arabs, **3,** 61, 62.

Kachtanites, the southern Arabians, **3,** 61.

Kadish, the Exilarch mentioned in, **3,** 95.

Kaffa (Theodosia), a Karaite community in, **3,** 182.

Kafnaï, Exilarch, **3,** 10.

Kahal Kados, congregation in Pernambuco, **4,** 693.

Kahana. *See* Mar-Kahana.

Kahana, Jacob, rabbi of Frankfort, exposes Kamenker, **5,** 229.
exacts a promise from Luzzatto, **5,** 241.

Kahir, Caliph of the East, deposes Saadiah, **3,** 196, 200.

Kahira. *See* Cairo.

Kahiya, political representative of the Turkish Jews, **4,** 404.

Kahtz, Christian, apostate, tries to create prejudice against the Jews, **5,** 191.

Kaila, Arab tribe, relations of, to the Jews, **3,** 55.

Kailan race, the. *See* Benu-Aus, the; Chazraj, the.

Kailil, brother of Rabba bar Nachmani, **2,** 575–6, 583.

Kaimakam, deputy vizir, **5,** 147.

Kairuan (Maghreb), the Jewish community of, **3,** 137.
center of science in the ninth century, **3,** 146, 180.
the Exilarch Mar-Ukba at, **3,** 185, 210.
new school founded in, by Chushiel, **3,** 208, 210.
chief town of the Fatimide Caliphate, **3,** 210.
study of the Talmud at, **3,** 210–11.
the Jews of, confer the title Rosh on Chushiel, **3,** 211.
Joseph Ibn-Abitur in, **3,** 238.
school at, presided over by Chananel and Nissim bar Jacob, **3,** 248.
the Jerusalem Talmud studied at the school of, **3,** 249.
decay of the school at, **3,** 249.
the Jews of, false Mahometans, **3,** 360.

Kala-Ibn-Hammad, birthplace of Alfassi, **3,** 285.

Kalâm, Arabic philosophy of religion, **3,** 146–7.

Kalba-Sabua, father-in-law of Akiba, **2,** 351, 355.

Kaliri. *See* Eleazar ben Kalir.

Kalish, the Jews of, massacred on the charge of well poisoning, **4,** 111.

Kallahs, public lectures at the Babylonian academies, **2,** 515; **3,** 5–6, 97.

Kaller, Alexander, promotes education among the Galician Jews, **5,** 394.

Kalmann, German immigrant in Turkey, **4,** 271.

Kalmann of Ratisbon, repentant apostate, condemned to the stake, **4,** 288.

Kalonymos, Italian Jew, attendant of Otto the Great, **3,** 243.

Kalonymos, the Prince, head of the Jewish community of Beaucaire, **3,** 400.

Kalonymos, scholar brought to Mayence by Charlemagne, **3,** 143.

Kalonymos, Talmudist, rabbi of Worms, **3,** 290.

Kalonymos ben Kalonymos (1287–1337), scholar at the court of Robert of Naples, **4,** 61–2.
writer on ethics and satirist, **4,** 62–3.
praised by Immanuel Romi, **4,** 68.

Kalonymos ben Todros, head of the community of Narbonne, **3,** 392.
sides with Abba-Mari, **4,** 34.
asked to prepare the ban against the study of science, **4,** 38.
draws up the ban, **4,** 39.

Kama, friend of Samuel, meets Abba-Areka, **2,** 512.
appointed judge, **2,** 512.
rebukes the Exilarch, **2,** 513.

Kanaim. *See* Zealots, the.

Kamenker, Moses Meir. *See* Moses Meïr Kamenker.

Kameoth (Kamea), amulets, **3,** 153.
used by rabbis, **5,** 201–2.
distributed by Eibeschütz, **5,** 257

Kamerau, the, a noble family, claim the Jews of Ratisbon, **4,** 300.

Kamieniec, disputation at, between Frankists and Talmudists, **5,** 280, 281.
the Talmud burnt at, **5,** 282.

Kamus, fortress of the Chaibar Jews, **3,** 55.
holds out against Mahomet, **3,** 82.
fall of, **3,** 83.

Kandy. *See* Ceylon.

Kant, Immanuel, unsuccessful candidate for the prize of the Berlin Academy, **5,** 303, 304.
on Mendelssohn's "Jerusalem," **5,** 365.
meeting of, with Mendelssohn, **5,** 398.
distinguishes Marcus Herz, **5,** 405–6.
Herz lectures on the philosophy of, **5,** 406.
philosophy of, admired by Ben-David, **5,** 409.
Ben-David lectures on the philosophy of, **5,** 410.
philosophy of, studied by Krochmal, **5,** 608.

Kapsali. *See* Elias ben Elkanah; Eliezer; Elkanah; Moses Kapsali.

Kara. *See* Avigedor Kara; Joseph Kara; Simon Kara.

Karaim. *See* Karaites.

Karaism, the religion of the sect founded by Anan ben David, **3,** 130.
original character of, obscure, **3,** 131.
rigidity of, **3,** 131–3.
unsettled character of, **3,** 133.
causes dissension among the Rabbanites, **3,** 156–7.

Karaism (*continued*), freedom in exegesis the principal dogma of, **3**, 157.
sects of, **3**, 157–8.
lack of union in, **3**, 158.
first signs of the decay of, **3**, 181.
ascetic character of, in Jerusalem, **3**, 181–2.
propaganda for, **3**, 182.
expounded by Solomon ben Yerucham, **3**, 203.
propaganda for, by Abulsari Sahal ben Mazliach Kohen, **3**, 203–5.
spread by Jephet Ibn-Ali Halevi, **3**, 205–6.
spreads during the tenth century, **3**, 206–7.
attacked by Samuel ben Chofni, **3**, 253.
inferiority of, to Talmudical Judaism proved by Jehuda Halevi, **3**, 334.
criticised by Shemarya Ikriti, **4**, 69–70.
in the fourteenth century, **4**, 70.
centers of, **4**, 71.
liturgy of, fixed, **4**, 71.
petrifaction of, illustrated, **4**, 269–70.
not attractive to Richard Simon, **5**, 180, 181.
inquired into by Charles XI of Sweden, **5**, 182.
account of the origin of, by Samuel ben Aaron, **5**, 183.
account of, by Mordecai ben Nissan, **5**, 183–4.
inquired into by Charles XII of Sweden, **5**, 184.

Karaite sects, the, list of:
Abu-Amranites (Tiflisites),
Akbarites,
Makaryites,
Moses of Baalbek, followers of

Karaite writers, the, list of:
Aaron ben Elia Nicomedi,
Aaron ben Joseph the Elder,
Abulsari Sahal ben Mazliach Kohen
Anan ben David,
Benjamin ben Moses of Nahavend,
Ibn-Sakviyah,
Isaac ben Abraham Troki,
Jehuda ben Elia Hadassi,
Jephet Ibn-Ali Halevi,
Mordecai ben Nissan,
Samuel ben Aaron,
Solomon ben Yerucham.

Karaites (Ananites), the, followers of Anan ben David, **3**, 134.
excommunicated by the heads of the academies, **3**, 134.
renounce connection with the Rabbanites, **3**, 134.
acknowledge Anan ben David as the legitimate Exilarch, **3**, 135.
hold a memorial service for Anan ben David, **3**, 135.
study the Bible, **3**, 136, 189.
of Mutazilist tendency, **3**, 149, 150–1.
adopt the ban, **3**, 151.
tradition among, **3**, 159.
marriage laws of, **3**, 159.
opposed by Natronaï II, **3**, 178.
opposed by Simon of Cairo, **3**, 179.
scientific pursuits of, **3**, 180.
shun the Rabbanites, **3**, 182.
spread of, in the East, **3**, 182.
attacked by Saadiah, **3**, 189.
calendar of, attacked by Saadiah, **3**, 190–1.
defended by Solomon ben Yerucham, **3**, 191.
later works of Saadiah against, **3**, 192.
fond of philosophical disputations, **3**, 197.
lexicographical work of, superseded by Menachem ben Saruk's, **3**, 225.

Karaites, the (*continued*), expect the Messiah in the eleventh century, **3**, 247.
views of, occasionally endorsed by Samuel ben Meïr, **3**, 346.
persecuted in Spain in the eleventh century, **3**, 362.
humbled by Jehuda Ibn-Ezra, **3**, 362–3.
rise of, after the fall of Jehuda Ibn-Ezra, **3**, 366.
and Abraham Ibn-Ezra, **3**, 366.
regarded as idolaters by Samson ben Abraham, **3**, 408.
in Constantinople in the twelfth century, **3**, 425.
in Damascus, **3**, 427.
in Askalon, **3**, 427.
degeneracy of, in Asia in the twelfth century, **3**, 443.
of Cairo, governed by a Nassi, **3**, 444.
of Alexandria, **3**, 444.
treatment of, by Maimonides, **3**, 465.
disciples of Nachmani, **3**, 607.
the way for, paved by the religious philosophers, **3**, 625.
inclined to a reconciliation with Rabbanites, **4**, 71–2.
institute pilgrim prayers, **4**, 73–4.
in Poland under Casimir IV, **4**, 265.
emigrate to Turkey, **4**, 269.
ignorance of, **4**, 269.
taught by Rabbanite teachers, **4**, 269.
celebration of the Sabbath by, **4**, 269–70.
efforts to reconcile, to Talmudic Judaism, **4**, 270.
protected by Elias Mizrachi in Constantinople, **4**, 403–4.
and Joseph Delmedigo, **5**, 76–7.

Karaites, the (*continued*), Polish and Lithuanian, degradation of, **5**, 182–3.
scattered by order of John Sobieski, **5**, 182.
invited to go to Sweden, **5**, 183.
accused of conspiring with Krochmal against the Talmud, **5**, 608.
treated of in the Scientific Journal, **5**, 626.
in Cairo reconciled with the Rabbanites by Munk, **5**, 664.
history of, cleared up by Munk, **5**, 666.
rise of, **5**, 727.
Karben, Victor von (1442–1515), apostate, employed to write anti-Jewish pamphlets, **4**, 424–5.
suggested as Pfefferkorn's coadjutor, **4**, 432.
directs the confiscation of Hebrew books, **4**, 437, 441.
decides that the Talmud ought to be burnt, **4**, 444.
Karl Ludwig, count-palatine, offers Spinoza a professorship, **5**, 108.
Karlinians, a branch of the Chassidim, **5**, 388, 391.
Karmisin, the Exilarch Mar-Ukba banished to, **3**, 184.
Karo. *See* Joseph Karo.
Kartiel, name of a Sefira, **4**, 17.
Kaspi. *See* Joseph Kaspi.
Kasser ben Aaron, reconciles Aaron Ibn-Sarjadu with Saadiah, **3**, 200–1.
Kasr, home of David ben Zaccaï, **3**, 186.
Katzenellenbogen, Ezekiel, rabbi of the "three communities," excommunicates Kamenker, **5**, 238.
forbids the study of Kabbala to young men, **5**, 241.

Kazimierz, the Jews of, number of, **4**, 632.
Kedeshim, the holy men of the Canaanites, **1**, 54.
Kedeshoth, Canaanite priestesses, **1**, 54.
in Samaria, **1**, 198.
maintained in Jerusalem under Manasseh, **1**, 283.
Kedoshim (saints), martyrs of the first crusade, **3**, 302.
graves of, visited, **3**, 309.
Keeper of the lists (rolls), under David, **1**, 122.
manager of war, **1**, 305, 313.
beheaded by Nebuchadnezzar, **1**, 314.
Kefar Nahum. *See* Capernaum.
Kelifa (Kelifoth), Kabbalistic term for sin in the Zohar, **4**, 17, 620; **5**, 120.
Kenas. *See* Census.
Kendites, the, an Arab tribe, adopt Judaism, **3**, 63.
chief of, protected by Samuel Ibn-Adiya, **3**, 68–9.
Keneseth ha-Gedolah. *See* Great Assembly, the.
Kenites, the, Moses with, **1**, 13–14.
aid the Israelites in the desert, **1**, 26.
aid Judah, **1**, 38.
allies of the Israelites, **1**, 61.
Kephar Lekitaja, military station established by Hadrian, **2**, 419.
Kephas. *See* Peter.
Kepler, and David Gans, **4**, 638.
Kerbella, the battle of, the Ommiyyades defeated at, **3**, 125.
Kerek. *See* Kir-Moab.
Kerem Chemed, Hebrew journal devoted to Jewish science, **5**, 621, 693.
contributors to, **5**, 621–2.
Kermanshah. *See* Karmisin.
Kertch, Jews of the Byzantine empire settle in, **3**, 123.
Karaites in, in the ninth century, **3**, 182.
capital of the Crimea, **3**, 222.
Kether Malchuth, philosophical poem by Ibn-Gebirol, **3**, 270.
Kewanoth, Kabbalistic term, devotion, **5**, 121.
Khataib, Sephardic synagogue at Damascus, **4**, 400.
Khemarim, idolatrous priests, under Manasseh, **1**, 283.
Khiva, the Jews of, in the twelfth century, **3**, 435.
Khorasan, under the jurisdiction of the Pumbeditha academy, **3**, 98, 184.
the Exilarch banished to, **3**, 196.
ambassadors from, bring news to Spain of the Jewish Chazar kingdom, **3**, 220.
under the jurisdiction of the Exilarch, **3**, 428.
Khorasan, the Jews of, believe themselves descendants of the Ten Tribes, **3**, 433.
occupations of, **3**, 433.
allied with the Ghuzz, **3**, 434.
aid Jenghis-Khan, **3**, 581.
Khozars, the. *See* Chazars, the.
Kiddush, the, blessing over wine at the beginning of the Sabbath, instituted, **1**, 398.
Kiera, Esther, court Jewess in Turkey, patroness of Jewish literature, **4**, 608, 629.
influence of, under Murad III, **4**, 629.
death of, **4**, 629–30.
Kiev, tributary to the Chazars, **3**, 138.
the Jews banished from the district of, **5**, 12.
Kilavun, sultan of Egypt, and David Maimuni, **3**, 620.

Kilavun (*continued*), the Jewish subjects of, under the Damascus Exilarch, **3,** 627.
Kimchi family, the, at Narbonne, **3,** 392; **4,** 442.
See David; Joseph ben Isaac; Moses Kimchi.
Kinanah Ibn-ol-Rabia, incites Arabian tribes to war against Mahomet, **3,** 79.
leader of the Jews of Chaibar, **3,** 82.
death of, **3,** 82–3.
King, Kabbalistic term, **4,** 18.
Kingdom of God, the, predicted by a Judæan poet in Egypt, **2,** 143.
Kingdom of Heaven, the, hastening of, the object of Essene asceticism, **2,** 145.
brought by the second advent of Jesus, **2,** 167.
according to Paul, **2,** 226.
Kings, the Books of, commentary on, by Isaac Abrabanel, **4,** 359.
Kinnereth. *See* Tiberias, lake.
Kir-Haraseth. *See* Kir-Moab.
Kir-Moab (Kerek, Kir-Haraseth), Moabite fortress, **1,** 209.
Kiryath-Jearim, the Ark of the Covenant at, **1,** 72.
the Ark removed from, **1,** 119.
Kiryath-Sepher (Debir), taken by the tribe of Judah, **1,** 38.
Kish, father of Saul, **1,** 83.
"Kitab Al-Assval," lexicon by Ibn-Janach, **3,** 263.
Klausner. *See* Abraham Klausner.
Kley transplants the Reform movement to Hamburg, **5,** 563–4.
inefficiency of, **5,** 564.
Heine on, **5,** 577.
Klonowicz, Polish poet, assails the Jews, **4,** 643.
Kobad, king of the neo-Persians, tool of Mazdak, **3,** 1.
disciple of Mazdak, **3,** 2.
dethroned by the nobles, **3,** 2.
persecutes Jews and Christians, **3,** 3–4.
death of, **3,** 5.
Koberger, Antonius, opponent of the Jews in Nuremberg, **4,** 415.
Kodesh ha-Kodashim, by Ibn-Labi Ferrer, **4,** 234.
Kofrim, unbelievers, antagonists of the Sabbatians, **5,** 144.
Sabbataï Zevi proposes capital punishment for, **5,** 150.
Kohen. *See* Abulsari Sahal; Nathan ben Isaac; Solomon Kohen.
Kohen-Zedek II ben Joseph (917–936), Gaon of Pumbeditha, character of, **3,** 183.
causes dissension between Sora and Pumbeditha, **3,** 184.
forces the Exilarch Mar-Ukba to remove, **3,** 184.
has Mar-Ukba banished a second time, **3,** 185.
deposed by David ben Zaccaï, **3,** 186.
recognized as Gaon by the Exilarch, **3,** 186.
proposes the closing of the Sora academy, **3,** 192.
jealous of Saadiah, **3,** 194.
espouses the side of David ben Zaccaï against Saadiah, **3,** 195.
death of, **3,** 200.
son of, **3,** 208.
"Kol Sachal," by Leo Modena, **5,** 73.
Kölbele, John Balthasar, writes a pamphlet against Mendelssohn, **5,** 316–17.

Kolon, Joseph. *See* Joseph ben Solomon Kolon.
Kompse bar Kompse, partisan of Rome in Tiberias, **2,** 274.
Koniecpolski, house of, controls Cossack colonization, **5,** 3.
employs Bogdan Chmielnicki, **5,** 7.
Königsberg, a Jewish cemetery at, **5,** 190.
the University of, admits Jews, **5,** 398-405.
the Hamburg reforms adopted in, **5,** 573.
Konigsberg, the Jews of, burnt, **5,** 110-11.
in Mendelssohn's time, **5,** 397-8.
join the "Society of Friends," **5,** 418.
apostasy of, **5,** 420.
Konstantinov, the synod of, excommunicates Frankists, **5,** 277.
Koom, defeat of Judghanites at, **3,** 150.
Korachites. *See* Korah, the sons of.
Korah, Samuel descended from, **1,** 73.
honored by the Cainites, **2,** 375.
Korah, the sons of, Samuel ancestor of, **1,** 79.
psalmists, **1,** 120.
compose psalms on Sennacherib's failure, **1,** 278.
compose a love-song in honor of Hezekiah's marriage, **1,** 279.
Korahites. *See* Korah, the sons of.
Koraishites, the, defeated by the Mahometans at Bedr, **3,** 76.
induced to make war upon Mahomet, **3,** 79.
Koraishites, the (*continued*), distrustful of their allies, **3,** 80.
Koran, the, and Jewish sources, **3,** 72.
spread by the Jewish disciples of Mahomet, **3,** 73.
revelations against the Jews in, **3,** 75, 78.
war with the Nadhirites justified in, **3,** 79.
on the slaughter of the Benu Kuraiza, **3,** 81.
accepted by the Moslem as the word of God, **3,** 84.
on the position of woman, **3,** 92.
rationalistic expounders of, **3,** 147.
violence done to the text of, **3,** 148.
consulted by Haï Gaon for the explanation of Biblical words, **3,** 251.
Korban Mussaph, special Sabbath and festival sacrifice, **1,** 401.
Kosmann, defender of the Jews, **5,** 470.
Kotzebue, assassination of, **5,** 528, 533.
Kovad. *See* Kobad.
Krämer, August, favors the emancipation of the Jews, **5,** 521-2.
Krems, the Jews of, perish during the Black Death persecutions, **4,** 110.
Krochmal, Nachman Cohen (1785-1840), founder of the Galician school, **5,** 607.
Jewish and philosophical studies of, **5,** 608.
partially hostile to Talmudism, **5,** 608.
accused of conspiring with Karaites against the Talmud, **5,** 608-9.

Krochmal, Nachman Cohen (*continued*), method of instruction of, **5**, 609.
uses the Talmud in historical researches, **5**, 609–10.
admiration for, **5**, 610.
Rapoport disciple of, **5**, 610, 614, 617.
influence of, on young Galicians, **5**, 614.
style of, **5**, 617.
influence of Rapoport on, **5**, 617–18.
devotes himself to encyclopædic studies, **5**, 618.
the father of Jewish science, **5**, 619.
contributor to the Kerem Chemed, **5**, 622.
as exegete, **5**, 695, 699.

Krysa, Jehuda Leb, Frankist rabbi, **5**, 275.
makes a Catholic confession of faith, **5**, 285.

Kryvonoss, Haidamak leader, **5**, 9.

Kufa, given to Jewish exiles by Omar, **3**, 85.
residence of Ali, **3**, 90.
capital of eastern Islam, **3**, 93.
the Jews of, in the twelfth century, **3**, 437.
Ezekiel's grave near, **3**, 440–1.

Kunigunde, sister of Maximilian I, marries her father's enemy, **4**, 428.
becomes abbess of a Franciscan convent, **4**, 428.
gives Pfefferkorn a letter to Maximilian, **4**, 428–9.
influences Maximilian to issue mandates against the Jews, **4**, 437, 440–1.

Kuraiza Place, the market place of Medina, **3**, 81.

Kuranda, Ignatz, founder of the " Israelitische Allianz," **5**, 703.

Kuru-Gismu, Hebrew printing press at, **4**, 628.

Kusari. *See* Chozari.

Kussiel. *See* Yekutiel.

Kypros. *See* Cypros.

L

La Asumção, Diogo de, Franciscan, professes Judaism, **4**, 668.
martyr, **4**, 669.
influences Rohel Jesurun, **4**, 669, 670.

Labienus, persuades the Parthians to invade Syria, **2**, 82.

Lachish, king of, defeated by Joshua, **1**, 34–5.
Amaziah killed in, **1**, 226.
headquarters of Sennacherib, **1**, 273.
offers opposition to Nebuchadnezzar, **1**, 311.

Ladislaus II, of Bohemia and Hungary, appealed to by the Jews of Ratisbon, **4**, 303.
and the Jews of Bohemia, **4**, 417.

Ladislaus IV, of Hungary, confirms the anti-Jewish decrees of the Council of Buda, **3**, 615.

Ladislaus V (Posthumus), of Hungary, and Capistrano, **4**, 262.
sanctions the expulsion of Jews from Silesia, **4**, 262–3.

Lænas, Popillius, Roman deputy to Antiochus Epiphanes, **1**, 453.

La Fare, bishop of Nancy, opposes the emancipation of the Jews, **5**, 441, 462.

La Fuente, Juan de, inquisitor, cruelty of, **4**, 484.

Lagarto, Jacob, first Talmudical author in South America, **4**, 693.

Lagrange, lauds a mathematical work by Ensheim, **5**, 401.

La Guardia, the Jews of, charged with the blood accusation, **4**, 343.

Laguna, Lopez (Daniel Israel, 1660–1720), Marrano poet in Jamaica, **5**, 203.

Lahmi, brother of Goliath, Philistine champion, **1**, 117.

Lamartine, and the Turkish Jews, **5**, 649.

Lamentations, the, of Jeremiah, **1**, 316, 319.

Lämmlein, Asher. *See* Asher Lämmlein.

Lampo, an Alexandrian hostile to the Judæans, **2**, 181.

Landau, Ezekiel (1720–1793), rabbi of Jampol, declares the Eibeschütz amulets Sabbatian, **5**, 265–6.
  distrusts Eibeschütz, **5**, 289.
  opposes Mendelssohn's Pentateuch translation, **5**, 330.
  objects to the study of the sciences, **5**, 402.
  opponent of the Berlin movement, **5**, 417.
  death of, **5**, 566.

Landfried, ambassador from Charlemagne to Haroun Alrashid, **3**, 143.

Landsberg, Jews settle in, **5**, 174.

Landtag, the Prussian, Jews in, **5**, 697.

Langton, Stephen, archbishop of Canterbury, hostile to the Jews, **3**, 504.
  convenes a Church Council at Oxford, **3**, 516.

"Language of Truth, The," pamphlet in the Eibeschütz controversy, **5**, 266.

Languedoc, the Jews of, in the tenth century, **3**, 242.
  in the twelfth century, **3**, 389–91.
  and the ban against science, **4**, 40.
  protected by the governor, **4**, 132.

Laniado, Joseph, accused of ritual murder, **5**, 636.
  tortured, **5**, 636–7.
  dies under the torture, **5**, 638.

Lansac, de, French ambassador, **4**, 577.

Laodicea (Leda), treasure house in, for the half-Shekel contributions to the Temple, **2**, 53.
  Herod at, **2**, 93.
  Verus Commodus at, **2**, 447.
  place of exile of José ben Chalafta, **2**, 448.
  the Jews of, in the twelfth century, **3**, 426.

La Papa, Aaron de. *See* Papa, Aaron de la.

La Peyrère, Isaac, on Israel's restoration, **5**, 24–5.
  in intercourse with Manasseh ben Israel, **5**, 25.

Laplace, lauds a mathematical work by Ensheim, **5**, 401.

Lara, de, noble Castilian family, **3**, 363.

Lara, David Coen de (1610–1674), preacher and philologist, **5**, 115.
  unaffected by Spinoza's attack upon Judaism, **5**, 117.

Larta. *See* Arta.
Laskorun, Frankists surprised at, **5,** 275.
Lateran Council, the third, forbids Jews to keep Christian nurses or domestics, **3,** 400, 418, 421–2.
forbids forcible baptism, **3,** 421.
the decrees of, disregarded by Philip Augustus, **3,** 498–9.
Lateran Council, the fourth, convoked by Innocent III, **3,** 508–9.
purposes of, **3,** 509.
Jewish delegates to, **3,** 509.
results of, **3,** 509.
Lateran Council, the fourth, anti-Jewish decrees of, 3, 509–11.
confirmed by the Council of Narbonne, **3,** 518.
re-enacted by the Councils of Rouen and Tours, **3,** 520.
enforced in Hungary, **3,** 521.
executed by Frederick II, **3,** 569.
Lateran Council, the fifth, the Reuchlin case submitted to, **4,** 464.
declares for Reuchlin, **4,** 465.
Lathier, opponent of the Jews of Alsace, **5,** 524–5.
Latin translations of the Scriptures, ordered to be read in Jewish congregations, **3,** 14–15. *See also* Vulgate, the.
Latin words, in the Mishna, **2,** 461.
Laurilla, Dutch consul, protects the Jews of Beyrout, **5,** 641.
Laurin, Austrian consul-general in Turkey, interferes in the Damascus affair, **5,** 647.
thanked by the London meeting, **5,** 653.
thanked by the Jews of Alexandria, **5,** 660.
Lavater, John Caspar, attracted by Mendelssohn's physiognomy, **5,** 308–9.
determines to convert Mendelssohn, **5,** 309–10.
letter addressed to, by Mendelssohn, **5,** 311–13.
unpopularity of, **5,** 313.
apologizes to Mendelssohn, **5,** 314.
anecdotes concerning, **5,** 315.
La Vega, de. *See* Penso, Joseph.
Law (Torah, Pentateuch), the, carried to Babylon by the priests, **1,** 334.
observed by the Babylonians, **1,** 364.
studied by Ezra, **1,** 365.
read to the people by Ezra, **1,** 378–80.
the Judæans swear to observe, **1,** 380–1.
displaces prophecy, **1,** 385.
strict observance of, **1,** 387.
held sacred by the Samaritans, **1,** 392.
the fundamental law of the commonwealth, **1,** 393–4.
study of, **1,** 396.
the "fence" about, **1,** 397–8.
unspiritual tendency of the laws of clean and unclean in, **1,** 401–2.
studied and observed by the Chassidim, **1,** 436.
the observance of, urged by Jesus Sirach, **1,** 440–1.
aspersed by Menelaus, **1,** 449–50.
translated into Greek, **1,** 510–14. *See* Septuagint, the.
study and observance of, under Salome Alexandra, **2,** 51.
knowledge of, spread by the schools of Hillel and Shammai, **2,** 149.

Law, the (*continued*), transgressors of, addressed by Jesus, **2**, 152.
desertion from, among the Alexandrians, **2**, 209.
observance of, urged by Philo, **2**, 210–14.
attempts to harmonize, with philosophy, **2**, 212–13.
attacked by Greek Judæans, **2**, 221–2.
upheld by the apostle Paul, **2**, 221.
to be abrogated for the conversion of the heathen, **2**, 225.
abrogated, according to Paul, by the appearance of Jesus, **2**, 226, 229–30.
declared binding by certain apostles, **2**, 231.
adhered to, by Judæan Christians, **2**, 232.
enforced by the Jamnia Synhedrion, **2**, 363–4.
declared unnecessary by Paul, **2**, 365.
observed by the Jewish Christians, **2**, 365–6.
disregarded by the Pagan Christians, **2**, 367.
the observance of, forbidden by Hadrian, **2**, 422.
said to have been altered by the Samaritans, **2**, 457.
the instruction of women in, **2**, 474.
classification of the commands in, **2**, 499.
observance of, in Samaria, **2**, 534.
Chaldaic and Syriac translations of, **2**, 581–2.
said to contain references to Mahomet, **3**, 76.
knowledge of, esteemed, **3**, 113.

Law, the (*continued*), held to be binding by Anan ben David, **3**, 134.
Tossafoth in explanation of, **3**, 345.
analyzed in the "Guide of the Perplexed," **3**, 484–5.
abrogated according to Raymund Martin, **3**, 622.
Persian translation of, **4**, 401.
significance of, **5**, 716–17, 721.
Halachic development of, **5**, 723–4.
See also Mishna, the; Scriptures, the; Talmud, the.

Law, the, the Book of (Deuteronomy), found in the Temple, **1**, 292–3.
read to the people in Jerusalem, **1**, 294.
read by Ezra in Jerusalem, **1**, 378–80.

Law, the, commentary on, by Philo, **2**, 212.
by Solomon ben Yerucham, **3**, 206.
by Chananel ben Chushiel and Nissim bar Jacob, **3**, 249.
by Samuel ben Chofni, **3**, 253.
by Samuel ben Meïr, **3**, 346.
by Abraham Ibn-Ezra, **3**, 371–2.
by Moses of Coucy, **3**, 586.
by Nachmani, **3**, 607–8.
See also Scriptures, the, commentary on.

Law, the, the disciples of, meaning of, **2**, 357.

Law, the, the reading of, instituted, **1**, 396.
at divine service in the Sopheric age, **1**, 399.
the Exilarch the first called to, **3**, 95.

Law, the, the scroll of, burnt by Antiochus Epiphanes, **1**, 455.

Law, the, the scroll of (*continued*), burnt by the overseers of Antiochus Epiphanes, **1,** 457.
carried with the Judæan army under Judas Maccabæus, **1,** 467.
profaned by a Roman soldier, **2,** 243.
burnt by Ursicinus, **2,** 569.
burnt in Nancy, **5,** 451.

Law, the, the teachers of, called Rabbis, **2,** 335.
disunited, **2,** 335.
forbid the study of Greek under Hadrian, **2,** 400.
meet at Lydda, **2,** 423–4.
artisans, **2,** 441, 442, 575.
demands upon, in the time of Judah I, **2,** 453–4.
displeased with Judah II, **2,** 485–6.
severity of, to each other, **2,** 547.
banished from Judæa under Constantine, **2,** 566–7.
superstition of, **2,** 578.
luxurious habits of, **2,** 588–9.
a privileged class, **2,** 589.
scorned, **2,** 589–90.
as compilers, **2,** 605.
persecuted by Kobad, **3,** 4.
persecuted by Hormisdas, **3,** 8.
averse from the use of Latin and Greek in the synagogue, **3,** 14.
attack the Byzantine empire, **3,** 16.
among the Arabian Jews, **3,** 59, 62.
See also Amoraim; Geonim; Sabureans; Sopherim; Tanaites.

Law, the, translations of. *See under* Pentateuch, the; Translation.

Law, the oral (Tradition), early origin of, **1,** 396–7.

Law, the oral (Tradition) (*continued*), study of, under Salome Alexandra, **2,** 51.
Pharisee study of, begins, **2,** 72.
justified by Hillel, **2,** 98–9.
knowledge of, spread by the schools of Hillel and Shammai, **2,** 149.
the study of, encouraged by Jochanan ben Zakkai, **2,** 326.
systematized by Hillel, **2,** 327–8.
committed to memory, **2,** 328.
methods of establishing, **2,** 328.
taught outside of Jamnia, **2,** 335.
disinterested study of, **2,** 338–9.
the earliest code of, **2,** 343.
as deduced by Akiba, **2,** 352–3.
Akiba's code of, **2,** 353–4.
as deduced by Ishmael ben Elisha, **2,** 355–6.
the study of, outside of Judæa, **2,** 358–9.
unity of, established, **2,** 405.
the study of, forbidden by Hadrian, **2,** 426.
importance of the study of, **2,** 427, 473–4, 544.
knowledge of, transplanted from Asia to Europe, **2,** 443.
codification of, completed, **2,** 460, 462.
new development of, in Babylonia, **2,** 511.
neglected in Babylonia, **2,** 513–14.
the study of, flourishes in Babylonia, **2,** 574–5.
the distinguishing feature of Judaism, **2,** 608.
See also Halacha, the; Mishna, the; Talmud, the; Tanaites.

La-Yesharim Tehilla, drama by Luzzatto, **5,** 242–4.

Lazarus, disciple of Jesus, **2,** 160.
Leather-arms. *See* Armleder.
Leb Herz, Sabbatian, **5,** 152.
Lebanon, mountain range, description of, **1,** 42, 44.
wood from, used for Solomon's Temple, **1,** 164.
Leblin, chamberlain of the Duke of Austria, **3,** 567.
Lecha Dodi, Sabbath song, **4,** 538.
"**Lectures** upon the Modern History of the Jews," by Löwisohn, **5,** 594.
Leda. *See* Laodicea.
Lee, Johanna, founder of the Shakers, **5,** 378.
Lefrank, satirist, Jewish champion, **5,** 471-2.
Leghorn, Elias Montalto at, **4,** 673.
the Sabbatian movement in, **5,** 149.
Nathan Ghazati at, **5,** 161.
the Portuguese Jews of, wealthy, **5,** 205.
rabbis of, espouse the cause of Eibeschütz, **5,** 264.
rabbi of, opposes the Reform movement, **5,** 571.
Leghorn, the Jews of, care for the Polish Jewish fugitives, **5,** 16.
excepted from Napoleon's restrictive laws, **5,** 499.
show honor to the Jewish envoys to Egypt, **5,** 658.
Lehren, Hirsch, interested in the Damascus affair, **5,** 649.
appeal to, from Damascus, **5,** 651.
protests against the Brunswick rabbinical conference, **5,** 682.
Leibzoll. *See* Poll-tax.
Leipsic, Jews permitted to live in, **5,** 509.
a Reform synagogue in, **5,** 573.
Leipsic, the battle of, celebrated by Jewish preachers, **5,** 528.
consecration of the Hamburg Temple on the anniversary of, **5,** 564.
Lejbovicz. *See* Frank, Jacob.
Lemberg, meeting place of the Polish Talmudists, **4,** 640.
the German population of, **5,** 3.
the Jews of, suffer through the Cossacks, **5,** 11.
Sabbatianism in, **5,** 228.
disputation at, between Frankists and Talmudists, **5,** 285-7.
Frankists baptized at, **5,** 288.
beginnings of culture among the Jews of, **5,** 612.
Lemberg (district), Jacob Frank the leader of the Sabbatians in, **5,** 273-4.
Lemon, Herz de, member of the Felix Libertate, **5,** 453.
zealous for the emancipation of the Dutch Jews, **5,** 455.
deputy to the National Assembly, **5,** 458.
Lemos, Henrietta de. *See* Herz, Henrietta.
Lenæus, guardian of Ptolemy V's sons, **1,** 450.
Leo X, pope, friendly to the Jews, **4,** 407, 592.
employs a Jewish physician, **4,** 408.
appealed to by Reuchlin, **4,** 453, 454.
worldly character of, **4,** 453-4.
orders the examination of Hoogstraten and Reuchlin, **4,** 454.
appealed to by Hoogstraten, **4,** 455.

Leo X, pope (*continued*), appoints Cardinal Grimani judge in Reuchlin's cause, **4**, 458.
yields to Hoogstraten, **4**, 464.
submits the Reuchlin affair to the fifth Lateran Council, **4**, 464.
suspends the Reuchlin suit, **4**, 465.
Reuchlin's work on the Kabbala dedicated to, **4**, 466.
encourages the printing of the Talmud, **4**, 468, 565.
Leo of Crema, a wealthy Italian Jew, **4**, 287.
Leo Hebræus. *See* Judah Leon Abrabanel.
Leo the Hebrew. *See* Levi ben Gerson.
Leo the Isaurian, emperor, forces baptism upon the Jews of the Byzantine empire, **3**, 122–3.
forces Jews to emigrate, **3**, 139.
oppresses the Jews, **3**, 175.
Leo Medigo. *See* Judah Leon Abrabanel.
Leo the Philosopher, emperor of the Byzantine empire, punishes backsliding Jewish converts, **3**, 176.
Leo (Judah) ben Isaac Modena (1571–1649), sceptic, **5**, 56.
ancestry of, **5**, 65.
precocity of, **5**, 65.
varied attainments of, **5**, 65–6.
lacks genius and character, **5**, 66.
scepticism of, **5**, 66–7.
on card playing, **5**, 67.
on the transmigration of souls, **5**, 67.
member of the Venice rabbinate, **5**, 67.
and Sarah Sullam, **5**, 70.
teacher of Christians, **5**, 71.
Leo (Judah) ben Isaac Modena (*continued*), publishes a work on Jewish customs, **5**, 71–2, 81.
attacks the Kabbala, **5**, 74.
death of, **5**, 74.
teacher of Joseph Delmedigo, **5**, 75.
fickleness of, **5**, 84.
criticism of the Kabbala by, attacked by Luzzatto, **5**, 240.
Leon, the **Jews** of, in the twelfth century, **3**, 384.
suffer from the forces of Castile and Aragon, **3**, 387.
not compelled to wear Jew badges, **3**, 513.
letter to, denouncing Solomon of Montpellier, **3**, 544.
taxed under Sancho, **3**, 617.
accept baptism under Vincent Ferrer, **4**, 205.
Leon. *See* Jehuda ben Meïr; Judah ben Yechiel.
Leon de Bagnols. *See* Levi ben Gerson.
Leon of Filneck, character in "Nathan the Wise," **5**, 324.
Leon, Jacob Jehuda (Templo, 1603–1671), supposed author of "Colloquium Middelburgense," **4**, 691.
work of, on the Temple, **5**, 114–15.
work of, translated, **5**, 115.
translator of the Psalms, **5**, 115.
unaffected by Spinoza's attack on Judaism, **5**, 117.
Leone Romano. *See* Jehuda ben Moses ben Daniel.
Leonora, duchess of Tuscany, friend of Benvenida Abrabanel, **4**, 410, 553, 544.
Leonora, widow of Ferdinand I, regent of Portugal, **4**, 160.
removes Jews from office, **4**, 160.

Leonora (*continued*), renounces the regency, **4**, 160–1.
quarrels with Juan I of Castile, **4**, 161.
Leonora de Guzman, mistress of Alfonso XI of Castile, arouses his suspicions against Gonzalo Martinez, **4**, 85.
sons of, oppose Pedro the Cruel, **4**, 113.
causes the ill-treatment of Alfonso's wife, **4**, 114.
Leonore d'Este, attachment of the Jews to, **4**, 660.
Leontin. *See* Jehuda ben Meïr.
Leontopolis, the Temple of Onias built at, **1**, 508.
Leopold I, emperor, decrees the banishment of the Jews, **5**, 170.
refuses to revoke the decree of banishment, **5**, 171–2.
re-admits Jews into Vienna, **5**, 189.
decrees the suppression of "Judaism Unmasked," **5**, 190.
appealed to, in behalf of Eisenmenger's book, **5**, 192–3.
Leopold II, of Austria, imposes new restrictions on the Jews, **5**, 508.
Leopold, duke of Austria, Jewish treasurer of, **3**, 418.
Leopoldstadt, assigned to the Jews of Vienna, **4**, 702; **5**, 172.
Lepanto, the Jews of, in the twelfth century, **3**, 424.
Lepers, the, at Bethany, **2**, 160.
treatment of, in the Middle Ages, **4**, 57.
Lepidus, member of the second triumvirate, **2**, 81.
Lerida, resists the introduction of the Inquisition, **4**, 332.
Lerida, the Jews of, excommunicate the anti-Maimunists, **3**, 537.
persecuted in 1391, **4**, 172.
converted by Vincent Ferrer, **4**, 214.
Lerin, count of, receives the Spanish exiles, **4**, 358.
Lessing, Gotthold Ephraim, liberality of, **5**, 296.
becomes acquainted with Mendelssohn, **5**, 297.
attitude of, towards Jews, **5**, 297, 336.
admiration of, for Mendelssohn, **5**, 298, 302.
has Mendelssohn's first work printed, **5**, 299.
on the Lavater controversy, **5**, 319.
becomes acquainted with the Reimarus family, **5**, 319–20.
publishes the "Fragments of an Unknown," **5**, 320–1.
attacked on account of the "Fragments," **5**, 322–3.
writes his "Nathan the Wise," **5**, 323–7.
aided by Moses Wessely, **5**, 326.
loses caste through "Nathan the Wise," **5**, 326.
death of, **5**, 326, 327.
accused of Spinozism, **5**, 372.
influence of, on German Jews, **5**, 412.
"**Letter of Aristas**," translated by Azarya deï Rossi, **4**, 615.
"**Letter**" of Gaon Sherira, on Jewish history, **3**, 232–3.
"**Letter of Warning, The**," by Solomon Alami, quoted, **4**, 154–5.
"**Letter of Zeal**," by Eibeschütz, **5**, 261.
Letters, the carrying of, regulated by Gershom ben Jehuda, **3**, 244–5.

"**Letters of Obscurantists,** The," by Crotus Rubianus, a Reuchlinist work, **4,** 461-2.
on the Jews and the Talmud, **4,** 461.
effect of, **4,** 462.
attributed to various authors, **4,** 462.
compared with Perl's attacks on Chassidism, **5,** 612.

Levelers, the, Jewish spirit among, **5,** 28. *See* Puritans, the.

Léven, Narcisse, founder of the Alliance Israélite Universelle, **5,** 701.

Levi, the tribe of, learns from the Egyptians how to write, **1,** 8.
free from Egyptian idolatrous practices, **1,** 12.
faithful to Moses, **1,** 18.
See Levites, the; Priests, the.

Levi (Matthew), publican, follower of Jesus, **2,** 153.

Levi bar Sissi, teacher of the Law in Simonias, **2,** 454.
adds supplements to the Mishna, **2,** 470.
son of, **2,** 497.
on the neo-Persians, **2,** 525.

Levi ben Abraham ben Chayim, of Villefranche (1240-1315), allegorist, system of, **4,** 24-5.
at Perpignan, **4,** 25.
opposed by Abba-Mari, **4,** 28.
forced to leave Samuel Sulami's house, **4,** 29.
ancestor of Gersonides, **4,** 91.

Levi ben Gerson (Ralbag, Gersonides, Leon de Bagnols, Leo the Hebrew, 1288-1345), philosopher, **4,** 87, 91.
scientific education of, **4,** 91.
as astronomer, **4,** 91-2.
life of, **4,** 92.

Levi ben Gerson (*continued*), religious philosophy of, **4,** 92-3.
fearlessness of, **4,** 92.
denounced as a heretic, **4,** 93.
astronomical treatise of, translated into Latin, **4,** 93, 103.
predicts the beginning of the Messianic period, **4,** 120.
authority of, questioned by Chasdaï Crescas, **4,** 146.
Isaac ben Sheshet's view of, **4,** 147.
accused of heresy by Shem Tob ben Joseph, **4,** 197.
adversely criticised by Isaac Abrabanel, **4,** 342.
exegesis of, praised by Reuchlin, **4,** 442.
commentary of, published in the Bomberg Bible, **4,** 476.

Levi ben Jacob Chabib, rabbi of Jerusalem, Talmudist, forced baptism of, **4,** 378, 532-3.
attainments of, **4,** 533.
relation of, to Jacob Berab, **4,** 533-4.
ordained by Jacob Berab, **4,** 534.
antagonizes Jacob Berab, **4,** 534, 535, 536.
confesses his forced baptism, **4,** 536.

Levi ben Shem Tob, apostate, advises the baptism of Jewish children, **4,** 375.

Levi ben Todros Abulafia, Kabbalist, **4,** 2.

Levi, Aaron. *See* Montezinos, Antonio de.

Levi, Abraham. *See* Abraham Levi.

Levi, Astruc. *See* Astruc Levi.

Levi, David (Ture Zahab), Talmudist, **5,** 152.

Levi, Elisha, Palestinian emissary, father of Nathan Ghazati, **5,** 130.

Levi, Gedaliah. *See* Gedaliah Levi.

Levi, Isaac Lurya. *See* Isaac Lurya Levi.

Levi, Isaiah, Sabbatian, **5,** 152.

Levi, Nathan Benjamin. *See* Nathan Benjamin Levi.

Levi, Raphael, charged with the blood accusation, **5,** 175–6.
guilt of, believed in by Eisenmenger, **5,** 188.

Levi, Solomon. *See* Solomon Levi.

Levi, Wolf, apostate, **5,** 213.

Levin (Varnhagen), Rachel, characteristics of, **5,** 413.
on the "hep, hep!" persecution, **5,** 534.
influence of the salon of, on Heine, **5,** 546.

Levirate marriage, the, regulated by the synod of Mayence, **3,** 518.

Levita, Elias. *See* Elias Levita.

Levite, a, author of the books of Chronicles, **1,** 411.

Levites, the, punish the idolatrous Israelites in the desert, **1,** 24.
left without territory, **1,** 40.
reside at Shiloh, **1,** 41, 69.
opposed to intermarriages with the heathen, **1,** 56.
dispersed among the tribes, **1,** 57.
reprove the people for idolatry, **1,** 58.
scattered from Shiloh, **1,** 72.
join Samuel in a guild, **1,** 76.
assist Samuel, **1,** 78.
faithful to David in the civil war with Absalom, **1,** 141.
service of, in the Temple, **1,** 167–8.
settle in Judah to escape idol worship, **1,** 187.

Levites, the (*continued*), recalled to the Temple under Josiah, **1,** 289.
carry the Psalms into the Babylonian exile, **1,** 334.
return from the Captivity under Zerubbabel, **1,** 352.
leave Jerusalem, **1,** 372.
lack of, in Jerusalem under Nehemiah, **1,** 377.
explain the Law as read by Ezra, **1,** 378–9.
at the consecration of the walls of Jerusalem, **1,** 381–2.
tithes for, collected under Ezra, **1,** 382.
lose their income, **1,** 383.
return to the Temple, **1,** 386.
abandon the Temple under Apollonius, **1,** 454.
re-instated by the Maccabees, **1,** 473.
officiate in the Temple of Onias, **1,** 508.
See also Levi, the tribe of; Priests, the.

Levy, Maurice, acquaints Napoleon with the anti-Jewish agitation, **5,** 498.

Lewin, Hirschel, rabbi of Berlin, and Mendelssohn, **5,** 317.

Lexicon, Hebrew (Aruch, Dictionary, Iggaron, Machbereth), by Saadiah, **3,** 190.
by Menachem ben Saruk, **3,** 225, 226.
by Ibn-Janach, **3,** 263.
by Solomon ben Abraham Parchon, **3,** 423.

Lexicon, Talmudical, by Mar-Zemach I ben Paltoi, **3,** 179.
by Nachshon ben Zadok, **3,** 179.
by Nathan ben Yechiel, **3,** 290.
by David de Pomis, **4,** 657.
See also Aruch.

Lexicons, Talmudical, revised, **5,** 115.
Libanius, teacher of Julian the Apostate, **2,** 595.
Libermann, Eleazar, aids the Reform movement, **5,** 568, 569, 571.
Libertini, the, synagogues of, **2,** 103, 201.
Libertinus, prefect of Sicily, razes a synagogue to the ground, **3,** 34.
"**Library** of the Fine Arts, The," Mendelssohn contributes to, **5,** 300.
Liebmann, Jost, court jeweler, favorite of Frederick I of Prussia, **5,** 190.
wife of, **5,** 190, 219.
permitted to have a private synagogue, **5,** 191.
son-in-law of, **5,** 219.
Liegnitz, the Jews of, charged with host desecration, **4,** 261.
"**Light** of the Exile, The," Gershom ben Jehuda, **3,** 243.
"**Light** of the Eyes," by Azarya deï Rossi, **4,** 615.
declared heretical, **4,** 616.
fate of, among Jews and Christians, **4,** 616–17.
Lima, David de, builds the third synagogue at Hamburg, **4,** 691.
Limpo, Balthasar, bishop, abuses Paul III before the Council of Trent, **4,** 525–6.
Lincoln, the Jews of, protected against the crusaders, **3,** 413.
Lindau, the Jews of, charged with well poisoning, **4,** 105.
burnt on the blood accusation, **4,** 227.
Lipmann (Tab-Yomi) of Mühlhausen, defends the Alenu prayer, **4,** 178.
Lipmann, Solomon, temporary chairman of the Assembly of Jewish Notables, **5,** 487.
Lippe, Jews tolerated in, **4,** 686.
Lippe-Schaumburg, the Prince of, honors Mendelssohn, **5,** 308.
Lippold, physician, accused of poisoning Elector Joachim II, **4,** 652.
Lisbon, the Jews of, agitation against, **4,** 160.
ransom Jewish captives, **4,** 339.
port open to the Jews on their banishment from Portugal, **4,** 374, 376–7.
exiles from, form a congregation in Constantinople, **4,** 402.
earthquake at, **4,** 505.
tribunal of the Inquisition in, **5,** 508.
autos-da-fé in, **5,** 32, 91.
Lisbon, the Marranos of, worship at a synagogue, **4,** 485.
massacre of, **4,** 487.
life of, inquired into, **4,** 489.
spied upon by Henrique Nunes, **4,** 490.
Lisbona, Samuel, father-in-law of Nathan Ghazati, **5,** 130.
Lissa, Jacob, leader of the orthodox party, **5,** 567.
Lissa, Mendelssohn's Pentateuch translation forbidden in, **5,** 332.
the Jews of, burn Wessely's letter, **5,** 370.
the rabbi of, opposes the Reform movement, **5,** 571.
Literature, Jewish, in Hasmonæan times, **2,** 15–16.
becomes known to the heathen, **2,** 502.
Reuchlin on, **4,** 441–3.
attractive to Christians, **5,** 178, 179.

Literature, Jewish (*continued*). *See under* Hebrew literature; Judæo-Greek literature; Rabbinical literature; Poetry.
Literature, Jewish mediæval, treated by Sachs, **5,** 693–4.
by Zunz, **5,** 694.
Lithuania, a refuge for exiled Jews, **4,** 418–19.
rabbinical schools established in, **4,** 420.
united with Poland, **4,** 631.
the Protestant Reformation in, **4,** 646–7.
Karaites in, **5,** 182–3.
the Chassidim in, **5,** 388.
Lithuania, the Jews of, the blood accusation launched against, **4,** 642.
represented in the Synod of the Four Countries, **4,** 644.
suffer from the Cossacks, **5,** 14.
"**Little Book** about the Jews, The," disproves the blood accusation, **4,** 545–6.
Liturgical poetry, introduced, **3,** 113–14, 117–18.
cultivated by the Jewish Andalusian school, **3,** 224.
by minor poets, **3,** 236, 259–60, 367, 376, 419.
by Simon ben Abun, **3,** 245.
by Moses Ibn-Ezra, **3,** 320.
See under Neo-Hebraic poetry; Piyutim; Poetanim; Poetry; Poets.
Liturgy, the, arranged by the Sopherim, **1,** 398–400.
Gamaliel II introduces the Berachoth into, **2,** 363.
amplification of, by poetanic compositions, **3,** 113–14, 117–18.
of the Karaites, **3,** 132; **4,** 71, 73–4.
Liturgy, the (*continued*), of the European Jews, compiled by Mar Amram ben Sheshna, **3,** 178.
arranged by Saadiah, **3,** 196.
Sephardic, adopted in northern Africa, **4,** 198.
German, compiled by Maharil, **4,** 225.
affected by the Kabbala, **4,** 481.
of the Chassidim, **5,** 386–7.
Liturgy, the changes in, made by Maimonides, **3,** 466.
made by Abi Zimra, **4,** 395.
in Amsterdam, **5,** 457.
made by Jacobson, **5,** 562.
made by Kley, **5,** 564.
approved by some authorities, **5,** 569.
in Vienna, **5,** 580, 581–2.
made by the Hamburg Temple Reform Union, **5,** 673.
in Mecklenburg-Schwerin, **5,** 679.
Livia, empress, heiress of Salome, sister of Herod, **2,** 128.
Livia. *See* Beth-Ramatha.
Livorno. *See* Leghorn.
Loans. *See* Jacob ben Yechiel; Joseph ben Gershom.
Lobato, Diego Gomez, and Paul de Pina, **4,** 669–70.
Löbele Prossnitz, Sabbatian, supporter of Chayon, **5,** 219.
denounced, **5,** 229.
in intercourse with Eibeschütz, **5,** 248, 249.
Lodi, the Jews of, number of, in the sixteenth century, **4,** 653.
expelled, **4,** 660.
Lodomeria, the Jews of, proscribed by the Council of Buda, **3,** 614.
Logos, the, in Philo's philosophy, **2,** 213.
in the Church, **2,** 500, 501.

Logrono, the Jews of, persecuted, **4**, 170.
Lombards, the, usury practiced by, **3**, 510.
Lombardy, German Jewish immigrants held up in, **3**, 638.
London, Abraham Ibn-Ezra in, **3**, 373–4.
Jews secretly domiciled in, **5**, 38.
excitement in, about the admission of Jews, **5**, 44.
Jewish burial ground in, **5**, 49.
first synagogue in, **5**, 50.
the Sabbatian movement in, **5**, 141.
the Mansion House meeting in, **5**, 655–7.
celebration of Montefiore's return to, **5**, 670.
rabbinical college at, **5**, 700.
London, the Jews of, prosperous under Henry II, **3**, 409.
attacked by a mob at Richard I's coronation, **3**, 410–11.
protected by John, **3**, 505.
attacked, **3**, 591–2, 643.
protected by Henry III, **3**, 592.
hold a meeting on the Damascus affair, **5**, 653–4.
London, the Portuguese Jews of, wealthy, **5**, 205.
hold aloof from the Eibeschütz controversy, **5**, 264.
Longinus, rhetorician, at the court of Zenobia, **2**, 529.
Longobard code, the, no mention of Jews in, **3**, 33.
Lope de Vega, dramatist, **5**, 112.
Lopes de Almeida, Portuguese ambassador to Rome, **4**, 340.
Lopes-Dubec, member of Malesherbes' commission, **5**, 432.
deputy of the French Jews, **5**, 438.
Lopez, Portuguese Marrano, protected by Sixtus V, **4**, 655.
Lopez, Balthasar, Marrano, burnt at the stake, **5**, 91–2.
Lopez, Juan, del Barco, inquisitor appointed by Sixtus IV, **4**, 312.
Lopez, Pedro, de Ayala, poet, on the Jews of Castile, **4**, 121, 122.
Lorch, the Jews of, the murderers of, punished, **3**, 635.
Lord Mayor, office of, held by Jews, **5**, 698.
Lord's Supper. the. *See* Transubstantiation.
Lorqui. *See* Joshua ben Joseph Ibn-Vives.
Lorraine, rabbis from, at the first rabbinical synod, **3**, 377.
Lorraine, the Jews of, petition for alleviation, **5**, 431.
representatives of, in Malesherbes' commission, **5**, 431.
number of, **5**, 435.
complain to the National Assembly, **5**, 436.
send a delegate to the National Assembly, **5**, 438.
emancipation of, opposed by the Duc de Broglie, **5**, 447.
"**Los Rumbos peligrosos**," novels by Joseph Penso, **5**, 113.
Lost Islands, the. *See* San Thomas.
Louis the Pious (814–840), emperor, the Jews under, **3**, 161–70.
wife of, **3**, 162.
refuses to countenance Agobard's anti-Jewish proceedings, **3**, 165–6.
sons of, excited against his wife, **3**, 166, 168.
heresy of, in protecting the Jews, **3**, 167.
letter addressed to, by the bishops assembled at Lyons, **3**, 167–8.

Louis the Pious (*continued*), and the conversion of Bishop Bodo, **3,** 168–70.
originates the theory that the Jews are the emperor's wards, **3,** 170.
Louis II (855), emperor, decrees the banishment of the Italian Jews, **3,** 174.
Louis the German, king of Germany, Bible commentary dedicated to, **3,** 163.
Louis IV, the Bavarian, emperor, imposes a tax on the Jews, **4,** 96–7.
tries to protect the Jews during the Armleder persecutions, **4,** 98.
sons of, deliver the Jews to the mob, **4,** 110.
Louis VI, of France, the Jews prosperous under, **3,** 343.
Louis VII, of France, the Jews prosperous under, **3,** 343.
joins the second crusade, **3,** 349.
roused against the Jews by Peter the Venerable, **3,** 349–50.
permits the repudiation of debts owing to Jews, **3,** 351.
friendly to Jews, **3,** 400–1.
resists the anti-Jewish decrees of the third Lateran Council, **3,** 508.
Louis IX, of France, has the Talmud burnt, **4,** 460, 578–9.
hostile to the Jews, **3,** 519.
encourages the conversion of Jews, **3,** 570.
fixes the rate of interest, **3,** 571.
orders a disputation on the Talmud, **3,** 576.
brother of, **3,** 583.
confiscates the property of Jews to organize a crusade, **3,** 585.
Louis IX, of France (*continued*), taken prisoner, **3,** 585.
banishes the Jews from his hereditary dominions, **3,** 585–6.
insists upon the Jew badge, **3,** 612.
Louis X, of France, recalls the Jews, **4,** 53–4.
Louis XII, of France, influenced against Reuchlin, **4,** 459, 464.
confessor of, patron of Hebrew literature, **4,** 473.
Louis XIV, of France, celebrated by Enriquez de Paz, **5,** 110.
renews the privileges of the Jews of Metz, **5,** 174.
orders criminal charges against the Jews to be tried by the royal council, **5,** 176.
presents the Jews of Metz to the house of Brancas, **5,** 348, 446.
Louis XV, of France, confirms the right of the Portuguese to expel German Jews from Bordeaux, **5,** 342, 343.
Louis XVI, of France, implored to expel the Jews from Alsace, **5,** 350.
orders lawsuits against usurers to be decided by the state councilor, **5,** 350–1.
abolishes the poll-tax on Jews, **5,** 415, 432.
government of, helped by Cerf Berr, **5,** 430.
grants privileges to Cerf Berr, **5,** 431.
disposed to ameliorate the condition of the Jews, **5,** 431.
approves of the emancipation of the Portuguese Jews, **5,** 442.

Louis XVI, of France (*continued*), grants special protection to Alsatian Jews, **5**, 446.
removes taxes from the Jews of Alsace, **5**, 446.
ratifies the Constitution, **5**, 447.
confirms the emancipation of the Jews, **5**, 448.

Louis XVIII, of France, reactionary court of, **5**, 512.
government of, does not renew the anti-Jewish restrictions, **5**, 524–5.
the emancipation of the Jews under, **5**, 596.

Louis I, of Hungary and Poland, banishes the Jews, **4**, 111.

Louis, duke of Anjou, regent of France, confirms the privileges of the French Jews, **4**, 150.
protects the Jews of Paris, **4**, 151, 152.

Louis the Rich, duke of Bavaria, plunders and expels the Jews, **4**, 253–4.
under the influence of John of Capistrano, **4**, 258.

Louis, duke of Bavaria-Landshut, claims the Jews of Ratisbon, **4**, 300.
attempts to convert the Jews, **4**, 301.

Louis of Brandenburg, orders the Jews of Königsberg to be burnt, **4**, 110–11.

Louis, count of Darmstadt, protects the Jewish exiles from Worms, **4**, 699.

Louis Philippe, of France, the emancipation of the Jews under, **5**, 596–7.
ratifies the law making rabbis state officers, **5**, 597.

Louis Philippe, of France (*continued*), supports Mehmet Ali, **5**, 633, 634.
appealed to on the Damascus affair, **5**, 645.
struggle of, with Thiers, **5**, 648.
deceives the hopes of the French Jews, **5**, 651, 658.
ambiguous attitude of, **5**, 668.
receives Montefiore, **5**, 668.

Louise, of Prussia, death of, mourned by the Berlin Jews, **5**, 508.

Louvain, the university of, sanctions the burning of the "Augenspiegel," **4**, 452.

Löwe, Joel, editor of the Meassef, **5**, 400.
mediocrity of, **5**, 417.

Löwisohn, Solomon (1789–1822), Jewish historian, **5**, 594.

Löwy, Albert, founder of the "Anglo-Jewish Association," **5**, 703.

Loyola, Ignatius, power of, over Paul III, **4**, 525.
efforts of, to re-establish the supremacy of the papacy, **4**, 562.

Lübeck, objects to Jewish inhabitants, **5**, 506.
Jews admitted into, **5**, 506.

Lübeck, the Jews of, threatened with banishment, **5**, 512.
banished, **5**, 520.

Lubienski, Wratislaw, archbishop of Lemberg, Frankist petition to, **5**, 284–5.

Lublin, meeting place of the Polish Talmudists, **4**, 640.
meeting place of the Synod of the Four countries, **4**, 644, 645; **5**, 3.
the German population of, **5**, 3.
synod of, relaxes the Jewish marriage laws, **5**, 13.

Lucca, home of the Kalonymos family, 3, 143.
Abraham Ibn-Ezra in, 3, 371–3.
the Jews of, in the twelfth century, 3, 424.
Lucena (city), the Talmud school of, famous, 3, 236.
refuge of the Jews of Granada, 3, 279.
a Jew of, threatens to betray his coreligionists, 3, 317.
Jehuda Halevi studies at, 3, 322, 323.
the school of, closed by the Almohades, 3, 361, 384.
Jews disappear from, 4, 354.
Lucena, the Jews of, correspond in Arabic with the Gaon of Sora, 3, 178.
famous through Alfassi, 3, 311.
Islam forced on, 3, 311–12.
pretend to accept Islam, 3, 361.
Lucena (district), early settlement of Jews in, 3, 43.
Lucero, Diego Rodriguez, hangman in Cordova, cruelty of, 4, 484.
disciple of, 4, 489.
Lucilla, daughter of Marcus Aurelius, cured by Simon ben Yochaï, 2, 449.
Lucuas (Andreias), leader of the Jews of Cyrene against Trajan, 2, 395.
Lucullus, Roman commander, attacks Tigranes, of Armenia, 2, 56.
Luna, Alvaro de, favorite of Juan II of Castile, invites the aid of Jews, 4, 228.
protects the Jews, 4, 251–2.
complains of the backsliding of the Marranos, 4, 256.
confessor of, 4, 277.
Luna, Pedro de. *See* Benedict XIII.
Lünel, Serachya Halevi Gerundi at, 3, 389.
letter to the wise men of, by Meïr Abulafia, 3, 524.
synagogue of, sold, 4, 48.
Lünel, the Jews of, in the twelfth century, 3, 396–8.
learning of, 3, 396.
scientific tendency of, 3, 397.
letter to, from Maimonides, 3, 489.
ask Maimonides to translate his "Guide of the Perplexed" into Hebrew, 3, 491–2.
exhorted by Maimonides to study the Talmud scientifically, 3, 492.
excommunicate Solomon of Montpellier, 3, 530.
oppose the study of science, 4, 33.
accused of outraging the image of Jesus, 4, 55.
Luneville, deputies from, to the National Assembly, and Isaac Berr, 5, 438.
the peace of, 5, 464, 465.
Lupus, governor of Alexandria, executes fugitive Zealots, 2, 318.
Lupus, Trajan's general in Egypt, 2, 395.
Lurya. *See* Isaac Lurya Levi; Solomon.
Lusitano. *See* Abraham Zacuto Lusitano.
Lusitanus, Amatus. *See* Amatus Lusitanus.
Luther, Martin, character of, 4, 467.
in the pantomime on the Protestant Reformation, 4, 468.
at the diet of Worms, 4, 469.
on the Wartburg, 4, 469.

Luther, Martin (*continued*), translates the Bible, **4,** 469.
on the Jews, **4,** 470–1, 547–52.
learns Hebrew, **4,** 473, 475.
encourages the study of the Bible, **4,** 474.
pamphlet by, **4,** 548.
proves the Messiahship of Jesus, **4,** 548.
reviews the suffering of the Jews, **4,** 549.
attacks the Talmud, **4,** 549–50.
treatment of Jews proposed by, **4,** 550–1.
advises the expulsion of the Jews, **4,** 551–2.
Lutherans, the, in Spain, persecuted by the Inquisition, **4,** 485.
the meetings of, in Poland, the model of the Synod of the Four Countries, **4,** 645.
Luzk, the Karaites of, **4,** 265; **5,** 182.
Luzzatto, Moses Chayim (1707–1747), dramatic poet, **5,** 203–4.
a prey to Kabbalistic influences, **5,** 233.
ancestry and early education of, **5,** 233.
poetic gifts of, **5,** 233–4.
studies in Hebrew meter by, **5,** 234.
composes a drama on Samson, **5,** 234.
style of, **5,** 234.
imitation of the psalter by, **5,** 234.
a second drama by, **5,** 235.
imitates the style of the Zohar, **5,** 235.
devoted to the Kabbala, **5,** 236.
writes a second Zohar, **5,** 237.
communicates his Kabbala to disciples, **5,** 237–8.
Luzzatto, Moses Chayim (*continued*), opposed by Moses Chages, **5,** 238.
refuses to justify himself, **5,** 238.
promises not to teach Kabbala in Europe, **5,** 239.
surrenders his writings to Bassan, **5,** 239.
publishes Kabbalistic writings, **5,** 239.
offends the Venetian rabbinate, **5,** 239–40.
accusations against, **5,** 240.
excommunicated by the Venetian rabbinate, **5,** 240, 242.
promises to give up Kabbala, **5,** 241.
received kindly at Amsterdam, **5,** 242.
supports himself by polishing lenses, **5,** 242.
publishes a drama, **5,** 242–4.
influence of, on the modern time, **5,** 244.
goes to Safet, **5,** 244.
death of, **5,** 244–5.
model of Bresselau, **5,** 398.
disciple of, **5,** 401.
Luzzatto, Samuel David (1800–1865), scholar, disinterestedness and enthusiasm of, **5,** 622–23.
gifts of, **5,** 623.
poetry of, **5,** 623.
devotes himself to Biblical exegesis, **5,** 623.
view held by, of the Massora, **5,** 624.
historical studies of, **5,** 624–5.
as exegete, **5,** 695, 699.
Luzzatto, Simone (Simcha, 1590–1663), on usury, **5,** 41.
sceptic, **5,** 56.
member of the Venice rabbinate, **5,** 67.
attainments of, **5,** 80.

Luzzatto, Simone (*continued*), on the relation of faith to science, **5**, 80–1.
sobriety of, **5**, 81.
on Jewish rites, **5**, 81.
defends Judaism and the Jews, **5**, 81–4.
on the Talmud and Kabbala, **5**, 84.
moderation of, **5**, 84.
Lybia, the Jews of, rebel against Trajan, **2**, 394, 396.
Lydda (Diospolis), taken by the Samaritans, **1**, 410.
besieged by Alexander Jannæus, **2**, 45.
center for the teaching of the Law under Gamaliel II, **2**, 335, 346.
restored to Judæa by Cæsar, **2**, 76.
meeting place of the teachers of the Law after the fall of Bethar, **2**, 423.
the inhabitants of, praised by Chanina bar Chama, **2**, 492.
seat of Joshua ben Levi's academy, **2**, 497.
birthplace of Simlaï, **2**, 498.
refuge of Ulla bar Kosher, **2**, 530.
seat of a Jewish revolt against Rome, **2**, 570.
partially destroyed, **2**, 570.
the original text of the Bible studied at, **2**, 623.
Lydia. *See* Croesus.
Lynn, the Jews of, massacre of, **3**, 411–12.
Lyons, the Council of, to humble the Jews, **3**, 167–8.
rabbi of, at the first rabbinical synod, **3**, 377.
Lyons (*continued*), Innocent IV at, **3**, 584.
Lyons, the Jews of, ill-treated by Agobard, **3**, 164–5.
under the protection of Louis the Pious, **3**, 165–6.
Lysanias, son of Ptolemy of Chalcis, incites the Parthians against Herod and Phasael, **2**, 82.
Lysias, Syrian commander, lieutenant of the country between Egypt and the Euphrates, **1**, 463.
commissioned to march against Judæa, **1**, 464.
chooses his subaltern officers, **1**, 466–7.
defeated by Judas Maccabæus, **1**, 469–70.
guardian of Antiochus V, **1**, 477.
invades Judæa, **1**, 478–80.
takes Bethzur, **1**, 479.
forces Judas Maccabæus to retreat, **1**, 479.
besieges the Temple, **1**, 479.
razes the fortifications of the Temple, **1**, 480.
executes Menelaus, **1**, 480.
disobeys Rome, **1**, 481.
death of, **1**, 482.
Lysimachus, ally of Ptolemy I, at the battle of Ipsus, **1**, 417.
Lysimachus, the Benjamite, Hellenist, opposed to Onias III, **1**, 437.
Jerusalem left in charge of, **1**, 448.
spoils the Temple, **1**, 448.
killed, **1**, 449.
Lysimachus, Alexander. *See* Alexander Lysimachus.

M

Maachah, wife of Rehoboam, worships Astarte, **1,** 188–9.
regent for Asa, **1,** 189.
idolatry of, hateful to the people of Judah, **1,** 190.
Maamad, public sittings of the rabbis of Amsterdam, **4,** 684.
Maasé Efod, Hebrew grammar by Profiat Duran, **4,** 191.
Maasseiah, governor of Jerusalem, appointed over the Temple funds, **1,** 292.
Maccabæus. *See* Judas Maccabæus.
Maccabean time, the, characterized, **5,** 722–3.
"**Maccabee,** The," by Miguel Silveyra, **5,** 111.
Maccabees, the, father and five sons, **1,** 458–9.
re-consecrate the Temple, **1,** 472–3.
See Hasmonæans, the.
Maccabees, the first Book of, originally written in Hebrew, **2,** 16.
considered apocryphal, **2,** 344.
"**Maccabees,** the, History of," *See* Josippon.
Macedonia, dissolution of the kingdom of, **1,** 416.
Paul establishes Greek-Christian communities in, **2,** 227.
Macedonia, the Jews of, autonomy of, **3,** 27.
in the twelfth century, **3,** 424.
Machærus, Judæan fortress, built by Alexander Jannæus, **2,** 46.
surrenders to the Romans, **2,** 73.
surrenders to Bassus, **2,** 315.
Machault, Denys, apostate, disappearance of, **4,** 175.
Machbereth, Hebrew dictionary by Menachem ben Saruk, **3,** 225.
criticised by Dunash Ibn-Labrat, **3,** 226.
"**Machbi,**" device on Molcho's banner, **4,** 510.
Machir, assists David in the war with Absalom, **1,** 144.
Machir, a learned Jew, head of the Narbonne congregation, **3,** 143.
ancestor of Kálonymos ben Todros, **3,** 392.
Machpelah, cave of, acquired by Abraham, **1,** 4.
Machuza (Maoga-Malka), a city of Babylonia, description of, **2,** 506–8.
inhabited by Jews, **2,** 507.
the Persian army stationed at, **2,** 591.
destroyed by Julian the Apostate, **2,** 602.
capital of a Jewish state, **3,** 4.
Machuza, the academy of, under Raba bar Joseph bar Chama, **2,** 571, 584–5, 590.
produces the Talmud, **2,** 591.
decline of, **2,** 593.
Machuza, the Jews of, descended from proselytes, **2,** 507, 586.
luxurious habits of, **2,** 507.
peculiarities of, **2,** 586.
marriages of, **2,** 586–7.
made captives by Kobad, **3,** 4.
put to death by Mebodes, **3,** 9.
Machuza, a district of Jewish Babylonia, **2,** 505.
Mâcon, the Council of, passes anti-Jewish resolutions, **3,** 39.
Madaba. *See* Medaba.
Madain, the Jews of, silence a Mahometan crier, **3,** 428.

Madrid, the Jews of, under Sancho, **3,** 617.
Madrid, the cortes of, petition Alfonso XI concerning usury, **4,** 80.
ask for anti-Jewish laws, **4,** 80.
Maella, the Jews of, converted by Vincent Ferrer, **4,** 214.
Mæsa, grandmother of Elegabalus, **2,** 469.
Maëstro Gayo. *See* Isaac ben Mordecai.
Magdala (Tarichæa), Judæan troops surrender to the Romans at, **2,** 75.
Jesus in, **2,** 154, 157.
rebels against Josephus, **2,** 280.
Jewish stronghold in the Bar-Cochba revolt, **2,** 414.
fall of, **2,** 416.
dissatisfied with a decision by Simon ben Yochaï, **2,** 449.
Magdeburg, Jews in, in the ninth century, **3,** 144.
a church at, granted the revenue derived from Jews, **3,** 243.
Magdeburg, the Jews of, persecuted in the thirteenth century, **3,** 611.
banished, **4,** 416.
suffer during the Black Death persecution, **4,** 111.
Maggid, the dream-interpreter, of Solomon Molcho, **4,** 496.
of Joseph Karo, **4,** 497, 537–8.
of Moses Chayim Luzzatto, **5,** 236, 237.
Maghariyites, a Karaite sect, **3,** 151.
Maghreb. *See* Kairuan.
Magi, the, practices of, forbidden by Rab, **2,** 521.
recover credit under Ardashir, **2,** 524.
Magi, the (*continued*), persecute the Christians, **2,** 524.
molest the Jews of Babylonia, **2,** 524–5.
fanaticism of, diminishes, **2,** 525–6.
and Ashi, **2,** 605.
and Jezdijird, **2,** 609–10.
influence of, over the Sassanian monarchs, **2,** 627.
and the Jews of Ispahan, **2,** 629.
religion of, reformed by Mazdak, **3,** 1–2.
cause a persecution of the Jews, **3,** 8.
Magian influence on Judaism, **1,** 402–5.
Magister Judæorum, officer in the Frankish empire, **3,** 161.
Magisterial offices, certain classes of Jews exempt from, under Constantine, **2,** 561, 563, 616.
Jewish exemption from, abolished by Theodosius I, **2,** 615.
Jews exempt from, under Arcadius, **2,** 616.
Jews forced to assume, by Justinian, **3,** 13.
Jews excluded from, by the Council of Paris, **3,** 40.
Jews exempt from, in Cologne, **3,** 41.
See Civil offices.
Magnus, Marcus, court Jew of Frederick William I, **5,** 219.
Magona, the Jews of, forced into Christianity, **2,** 619–20.
Magyars, the, made intolerant by the papacy, **3,** 614.
Mahadia. *See* Kairuan.
Mahanaim, seat of Saul's family after his death, **1,** 108, 110.
battle of, in the war with Absalom, **1,** 144.

Mahanaim (*continued*), David welcomed at, **1**, 144.
Maharil. *See* Jacob ben Moses Mölin Halevi.
Mahdi, the founder of the Fatimide dynasty, **3**, 212.
Maher-Shalal-Chash-Baz, son of Isaiah, **1**, 259.
Mahomet, inspired by Judaism, **3**, 71-2.
revelations to, from Gabriel, **3**, 71.
declaims against idolatry and immorality, **3**, 72.
tries to win over the Jews of Yathrib, **3**, 73.
character of, **3**, 74.
Jewish opponents of, **3**, 74-5.
gives up Jewish ceremonies, **3**, 75-6.
antagonism of, to Jews, **3**, 76.
victorious at Bedr, **3**, 76.
drives the Benu-Kainukaa from Arabia, **3**, 76-8.
victorious over the Benu-Nadhir, **3**, 78-80.
exterminates the Benu-Kuraiza, **3**, 80-1.
victorious over the Jews of Chaibar, **3**, 81-3.
attempt to poison, **3**, 83-4.
the Jews of Medina intrigue against, **3**, 84.
death of, **3**, 84.
acknowledged as the prophet by conquered nations, **3**, 86.
as viewed by Anan ben David, **3**, 134.
Mahomet II, Turkish conqueror of the Byzantine empire, threatens Christendom, **4**, 267.
friendly to the Jews, **4**, 268.
Mahomet IV, sultan, influence of Jewish women under, **4**, 629.
Mahomet IV, sultan (*continued*), considers the case of Sabbataï Zevi, **5**, 153.
receives Sabbataï into Islam, **5**, 154.
Mahomet Alemin, son of Haroun-Alrashid, war of, with his brother, **3**, 145.
death of, **3**, 146.
Mahomet Almansur, Hajib of Hisham, and Jacob Ibn-Jau, **3**, 239, 240-1.
Mahomet Almuktafi, Abbasside Caliph, revives the Exilarchate, **3**, 428.
Mahomet Bey, vizir, attacks Achmed Shaitan, **4**, 396.
Mahomet Sokolli, vizir, antagonizes Joseph Nassi, **4**, 596, 599, 602.
favorable to Venice, **4**, 600.
employs a Jewish agent, **4**, 603, 605.
supplants Joseph Nassi, **4**, 627.
advises the confiscation of Joseph Nassi's property, **4**, 628.
Mahometan (pseudo) Jews, despair of, **3**, 452.
exhorted to remain true to Judaism, **3**, 452.
condemned as apostates and idolaters, **3**, 453-4.
defended by Maimonides, **3**, 454-6.
Mahometans, the, looked upon by the Jews as liberators from the Christian yoke, **3**, 88-9.
conspire with the Jews to overthrow the Visigothic-Spanish empire, **3**, 108.
conquer Visigothic Spain, **3**, 109.
culture of, in Spain under the Ommiyyade caliphs, **3**, 214.

Mahometans, the (*continued*),
traditions of, used by Haï Gaon, **3,** 251.
in Spain, crusade against, **3,** 507.
condition of, in Hungary, **3,** 520–1.
proscribed in Hungary, **3,** 615.
distrusted by Argun, khan of Persia, **3,** 647.
intrigue against Saad-Addaula, **3,** 648–9.
usurers in Castile, **4,** 80.
the crusades against, begin with massacres of Jews, **4,** 222.
placed under restrictions by Eugenius IV, **4,** 250.
persecuted, **4,** 251.
protected by Juan II of Castile, **4,** 252.
the Jews under, **5,** 726–7.

Mahon. *See* Magona.

Maillotins, the, attack the Jews of France, **4,** 152.

Maimaran, Joseph, adviser of Muley Ismail, **5,** 168.

Maimi, Simon. *See* Simon Maimi.

Maimon, Solomon (1753–1800), on Hirsch Janow, **5,** 331.
philosophical thinker, **5,** 405, 407–9.
character and studies of, **5,** 407, 408.
goes to Germany, **5,** 407–8.
wanderings of, **5,** 408.
autobiography of, **5,** 409.
fame of, **5,** 409.

Maimonides, Moses. *See* Moses ben Maimun.

Maimun ben Joseph, father of Maimonides, Talmudist and scientist, disciple of Joseph Ibn-Migash, **3,** 317, 447.
influence of, on his son, **3,** 447.

Maimun ben Joseph (*continued*),
a fugitive from the Almohades, **3,** 448.
teacher of his son, **3,** 448.
emigrates to Fez, **3,** 451.
family of, assumes Islam, **3,** 451.
exhorts the pseudo-Mahometan Jews to remain true to Judaism, **3,** 452.
emigrates to Palestine and Egypt, **3,** 456–7.
death of, **3,** 457.

Maimun Asha, Arabic poet, protected by Shoraich, **3,** 70.

Maimuni. *See* Abraham (Almeni) Maimuni; Abraham Maimuni II; David ben Maimun; David Maimuni; Moses ben Maimun.

Maimunist controversy, the, **3,** 530.
in verses, **3,** 538, 544.
compromise in, proposed by Nachmani, **3,** 539–40.
taken up by the Dominicans, **3,** 542–3.
causes a division in Judaism, **3,** 546–7.
causes the neglect of poetry, **3,** 558–9.
allayed by the burning of the Talmud, **3,** 579–80.
breaks out anew in the time of Solomon ben Adret, **3,** 623–4.
in Germany, Italy, and Palestine, **3,** 624–34.
in Accho, **3,** 631, 632–3.
solution of, proposed by Hillel of Verona, **3,** 631–2.
revived by the Tibbonide party in Montpellier, **4,** 32–3, 42.
See also Anti-Maimunists, the; Maimunists, the.

Maimunists, the, partisans of Moses ben Maimun, **3,** 523; **5,** 728.
war declared against, by Solomon ben Abraham, **3,** 527.
excommunicated by Solomon ben Abraham, **3,** 528–9.
excommunicate Solomon of Montpellier, **3,** 530.
try to alienate the French rabbis from Solomon of Montpellier, **3,** 539.
denounce Solomon of Montpellier, **3,** 543–4.
opposed to the Kabbalists in the explanation of ceremonies, **3,** 554.
break away from the Talmud, **3,** 557–8.
in Perpignan, **4,** 25.
in Montpellier, **4,** 32–3.
See also Anti-Maimunists, the; Maimunist controversy, the.

Maimunists, list of:
Aaron ben Meshullam,
Abraham ben Chasdaï,
Bachiel Ibn-Alkonstantini,
David ben Daniel,
David Kimchi,
Hillel ben Samuel of Verona,
Jacob ben Abba-Mari ben Simon Anatoli,
Jonathan Cohen of Lünel,
Levi ben Abraham ben Chayim,
Moses ben Isaac Alashkar,
Moses ben Jehuda Cohen,
Samuel ben Abraham Saporta,
Samuel Cohen ben Daniel,
Yishaï ben Chiskiya.

Main(e) district, the, the Jews of, under Henry II, **3,** 409.
emigrate, **3,** 638.
find a refuge in Poland, **4,** 420.

Maiora, martyr, **4,** 570.

Majorca, French Jews emigrate to, **4,** 49.
quarrel about the chief rabbinate of, **4,** 162.
Majorca (*continued*), forced converts in, relapse into Judaism, **4,** 180.
Marranos from, in Algiers, **4,** 199.
the Inquisition established on, **4,** 332.

Majorca, the Jews of, persecuted, **4,** 77, 171.
take refuge in northern Africa, **4,** 198.
converted by Vincent Ferrer, **4,** 206.
extermination of, **4,** 246–7.

Makariyites, a Karaite sect, **3,** 151.

Maksen, leader of the Sinhajas, **3,** 256.

Malabar, the coast of, Jews emigrate to, **2,** 630.

Malach, Chayim. *See* Chayim Malach.

Malach ham-Maveth, angel of death, **1,** 403.

Malache Chabalah, evil spirits, introduced into Judaism from Magianism, **1,** 403.

Malachi, last of prophets, **1,** 384–5.

Malaga, Jews masters of, **3,** 109.
Samuel Ibn-Nagrela at, **3,** 255.
Berber city, **3,** 256.
family of Ibn-Gabirol emigrate to, **3,** 268.
suffering of the Spanish exiles in, **4,** 369–70.

Malchishua, son of Saul, death of, **1,** 103.

Malchus. *See* Porphyry.

Malchuth Shamayim. *See* Kingdom of Heaven, the.

Malcom. *See* Milcom.

Malesherbes, institutes a Jewish commission to ameliorate the condition of the Jews, **5,** 431.

Malich, king of the Nabathæans, at war with Herod, **2**, 94–5.
vassal of Herod, **2**, 95.
Malich, counselor of Hyrcanus II, poisons Antipater, **2**, 80.
assassinated by Herod, **2**, 80.
Malka bar Acha (771–773), principal of the Pumbeditha academy, **3**, 37.
Malka Kadisha, Kabbalistic term, the Messiah, **5**, 143.
Mallo, Portuguese inquisitor, **4**, 521.
Malmed, collection of sermons by Jacob Anatoli, **3**, 566.
attacked by the party of Abba-Mari, **4**, 32.
read by the Tibbonides, **4**, 30.
falls under the ban, **4**, 40.
Malshim (Malsin), traitors, **4**, 156.
Malta, Marranos transported to, **4**, 570.
Malta, the Knights of, attack Jewish exiles, **4**, 592.
forbidden to make slaves of Jews, **4**, 656.
Malthace, the Samaritan, wife of Herod, **2**, 119.
Mamal (Mamala), city of Galilee, inhabitants of, of the family of Eli, **2**, 575.
Mammæa, mother of Alexander Severus, admires Christianity, **2**, 481.
Mammon, scorn of, taught by the Essenes, **2**, 145.
taught by Jesus, **2**, 150.
Mamson, suspected of well poisoning, **4**, 104.
Manasseh, king of Judah, son of Hezekiah, **1**, 280.
state of the kingdom under, **1**, 281–4.
idolatry introduced under, **1**, 282–3.
Manasseh, king of Judah (*continued*), taken prisoner by Esarhaddon, **1**, 285.
death of, **1**, 285.
Manasseh, the tribe of, claims the central lands of Canaan, **1**, 35–6.
holds assemblies at Shiloh, **1**, 41.
opposed to intermarriage with the heathen, **1**, 56.
members of, join Gideon, **1**, 62.
in conflict with Ephraim, **1**, 63.
appeals to Samuel for help against Ammon, **1**, 80.
territory of, taken by Hazael, **1**, 220.
descendants of, in Chaibar, **3**, 437.
Manasseh, member of Eliashib's household, marries a daughter of Sanballat, **1**, 383.
banished by Nehemiah, **1**, 386.
Manasseh, relative of Simon the Just, acts as high priest, **1**, 423.
Manasseh ben Israel (1604–1657), emigrates to the Netherlands, **4**, 671.
member of the Amsterdam rabbinical college, **4**, 682.
characterized by Antonio Vieira, **4**, 683.
education of, **4**, 683.
characterization of, **4**, 683–4.
qualifications of, for effecting the re-settlement of Jews in England, **5**, 19–20.
attainments of, **5**, 20.
as a preacher, **5**, 20.
esteemed by Jews and Christians, **5**, 20.
treatises of, welcomed by Christian scholars, **5**, 22.
consulted by Christian scholars, **5**, 22–3.

Manasseh ben Israel (*continued*),
sought by Christian visionaries, **5**, 23–5.
and Messianic expectations, **5**, 24.
reasons adduced by, for the re-settlement of Jews in England, **5**, 28, 39–42.
encouraged by English writings, **5**, 28–30.
on the fortunes of the Ten Tribes, **5**, 30–3.
publishes "Israel's Hope," **5**, 31–2.
describes the terrors of the Inquisition, **5**, 31–2.
submits "Israel's Hope" to Parliament, **5**, 33.
negotiations of, interrupted, **5**, 34.
receives a safe-conduct to London from the Short Parliament, **5**, 34–5.
war delays the departure of, **5**, 35.
petitions Parliament to permit Jews to settle in England, **5**, 35.
the Messianic work by Felgenhauer dedicated to, **5**, 36–7.
expounds Jewish Messianic ideas, **5**, 37–8.
invited to England by Cromwell, **5**, 38.
petition presented by, to Cromwell, **5**, 38–9.
acts as the representative of European Jews, **5**, 39.
on the trade of the Jews, **5**, 40–1.
defends the Jews against three charges. **5**, 41–2.
proposal by, for the admission of Jews into England, **5**, 44.

Manasseh ben Israel (*continued*)
refutes theological objections to the admission of Jews, **5**, 45.
defends his course before the Dutch government, **5**, 46.
disappointment of, **5**, 46–7.
defends the Jews against the blood accusation, **5**, 47–9.
honorably dismissed by Cromwell, **5**, 49.
death of, **5**, 50.
devotee of the Kabbala, **5**, 55.
teacher of Spinoza, **5**, 86, 87.
outlines a history of the Jews, **5**, 202.
work by, translated by Marcus Herz, **5**, 362.
oath of, concerning the blood accusation taken by the London rabbis, **5**, 655.
Manchester, the Jews of, hold meetings for the Damascus affair, **5**, 654, 657.
Manessier de Vesoul, negotiates the return of the Jews to France, **4**, 129.
appointed receiver-general, **4**, 130–1, 132, 133.
active in behalf of the Jews, **4**, 132.
death of, **4**, 150.
sons of, **4**, 150, 151, 152.
Manetho, an Egyptian priest, libels the Jews, **1**, 511.
Manichæans, persecuted by Jezdijird III, **2**, 627.
Manna, description of, **1**, 20.
Mannheim, Moses Meïr Kamenker in, **5**, 229.
Mannheimer, Isaac Noah (1793–1864), intellectual qualities of, **5**, 578.
attractiveness of, **5**, 578.
dignity of, **5**, 579.
fitted for his work in Vienna, **5**, 580.

Mannheimer, Isaac Noah (*continued*), attitude of, towards Reform Judaism, **5**, 580.
changes sanctioned by, **5**, 580.
as a pulpit orator, **5**, 581.
personality of, **5**, 582.
influence of, in Germany, **5**, 582.
compared with Sachs, **5**, 690.
helps to reorganize Austria, **5**, 697.
Manoel the Great, of Portugal, releases the Spanish exiles, **4**, 372.
employs Abraham Zacuto, **4**, 372.
kindly disposed towards the Jews, **4**, 372.
sues for the hand of Isabella II of Castile, **4**, 372–3.
banishes the Jews, **4**, 374.
orders Jewish children to be baptized, **4**, 375–6.
cruelty of, **4**, 376.
limits the Jews to one port of departure, **4**, 376.
tries to force the Jews into Christianity, **4**, 377.
adopts milder measures towards the Portuguese Marranos, **4**, 379.
delivers Spanish Marranos to the Inquisition, **4**, 379–80.
permits the last Jews to leave Portugal, **4**, 380–1.
grants freedom from molestation to the Jews for a term, **4**, 485.
checks the emigration of Marranos, **4**, 485–6.
forbids the use of insulting names for Marranos, **4**, 486.
orders of, concerning Marranos, **4**, 488.
counselors of, protect the Marranos, **4**, 488.
Manrique, Inigo, chief judge of appeals for Marrano cases, **4**, 320.
Mansfeld, general, plunders the Jews, **4**, 701.
Mantin, Jacob (1490–1549), physician and scholar, ambition of, **4**, 411.
instructs Christians in Hebrew, **4**, 473.
persecutes Molcho, **4**, 506–7.
physician to Paul III, **4**, 515.
Mantua, Abraham Ibn-Ezra in, **3**, 371.
the Talmud burnt in, **4**, 565.
refuge of the Jewish exiles from the Papal States, **4**, 592.
rabbis of, forbid young men to read Azarya deï Rossi's works, **4**, 616.
Jews beg for shelter in, **4**, 660.
the rabbi of, opposes the Reform movement, **5**, 571.
Mantua, the Jews of, in the twelfth century, **3**, 424.
in the seventeenth century, **4**, 653.
appeal for permission to own the Talmud, **4**, 658.
Maoga-Malka. *See* Machuza.
Maonites, the, subjugated by Uzziah, **1**, 230.
Maor, Talmudical work by Serachya Halevi Gerundi, **3**, 389.
"Mappa," Moses Isserles' commentary on Karo's code, **4**, 637.
Mar-Aaron ben Samuel, candidate for the principalship of the Pumbeditha academy, **3**, 154.
Mar-Abraham ben Sherira (816–828), mystic, principal of the Pumbeditha academy, **3**, 154–5.

Mar-Abraham ben Sherira (*continued*), deposed, **3**, 155.
re-instated, **3**, 156.
death of, **3**, 156.

Mar-Amram ben Sheshna (869–881), Gaon of Sora, compiler of the liturgy of European Jews, **3**, 178.

Mar bar Ashi (Tabyome), Amora, principal of the Sora academy, **2**, 626–7.
finishes the compilation of the Talmud, **2**, 628.
conscientiousness of, **2**, 628.
death of, **2**, 628.

Mar bar Huna (609–620), principal of the Sora academy, **3**, 10.

Marburg, the university of, appealed to in the contest between the Senate and the Jews of Frankfort, **5**, 520.

Marcellus II, pope, reactionary, **4**, 566.

Mar-Chanina, effects Mar-Zutra II's investiture as Exilarch, **3**, 3.
executed, **3**, 4.

Marcus Aurelius Antoninus, emperor, war with Parthia under, **2**, 447.
and Simon ben Yochaï, **2**, 449.
appealed to by Jews and Christians, **2**, 449.
famine and plague under, **2**, 451.
permission of, required to pray at Jerusalem, **2**, 458.
hostility of, to the Jews, **2**, 463.

Mardeliar, chief of the Jews of India, **2**, 630.

Mardochai, Francis, Egyptian tax farmer, **4**, 618.

Mar-Elia I, Patriarch of the Eastern Christians, consulted by Haï Gaon, **3**, 250.

Mareshah (Marissa), scene of Asa's victory over an Ethiopian army, **1**, 190.
Idumæan fortress, demolished, **2**, 8.

Margalita, Aaron, apostate, reviles the Agada, **5**, 194.

Margaret, empress, has the Jews of Vienna banished, **5**, 170.

Margaritha, Anton, apostate, writes against the Jews, **4**, 551.

Marhab, a Himyarite, hero in the Chaibar war, **3**, 82.
beaten and killed by Ali, **3**, 82.
sister of, tries to poison Mahomet, **3**, 83–4.

Mar-Huna, Exilarch. *See* Huna.

Mari bar Mar, founds an academy at Firuz-Shabur, **3**, 8, 9.

Maria of the Netherlands, patroness of Joseph Nassi, **4**, 572.

Maria, Infanta of Spain, empress, Marrano confessor of, **5**, 109.

Maria, wife of Alfonso XI, ill-treated by her husband, **4**, 114.

Maria de Molina, queen of Castile, employs a Jewish physician, **4**, 2.
dowager queen, antagonizes the Jewish treasurer, **4**, 51–2.
protects the Jews of Castile, **4**, 52.

Maria de Medici, employs a Jewish physician, **4**, 673.

Maria de Padilla, supposed wife of Pedro the Cruel, **4**, 116.
party of, **4**, 117.
acknowledged as the wife of Pedro, **4**, 122.
said to be a Jewess, **4**, 123.

Maria Anna, of Austria, banishes the last remnant of Jews from the Spanish provinces, **5**, 169.
Maria Juliana, queen of Denmark, interested in Eibeschütz, **5**, 267–8.
Maria Theresa, empress, at war with Prussia, **5**, 251.
revokes the decree against the Jews of Moravia, **5**, 252.
banishes the Moravian and Bohemian Jews, **5**, 252.
revokes the decree of banishment, **5**, 253.
Mariamne, daughter of Agrippa I, immorality of, **2**, 235.
Mariamne, granddaughter of Hyrcanus II, betrothed to Herod, **2**, 81.
under the guardianship of Herod's brother, **2**, 83.
married to Herod at Samaria, **2**, 87.
under the guardianship of Herod's brother-in-law, **2**, 93.
calumniated by Salome, **2**, 93–4.
confined in Alexandrion, **2**, 96.
murder of, **2**, 104–5.
sons and daughters of, **2**, 112–13.
Mariamne, Herod's second wife of that name, **2**, 107.
son of, disinherited, **2**, 119.
Mariamne, tower of, retreat of the Roman garrison of Jerusalem, **2**, 260.
left undemolished by Titus, **2**, 309.
Mariba, trading station under the kings of Judah, **3**, 54.
Marini, Israel, disciple of Moses Chayim Luzzatto, **5**, 237.
Mar-Isaac, head of a college at Firuz-Shabur, does homage to Ali, **3**, 90.
Mar-Isaac (*continued*), Gaon of Sora, **3**, 90, 92.
Mar-Isaac, Jew of Cologne, martyr, **3**, 304.
Mar-Isaac, principal of a Babylonian academy, the murder of, **3**, 3.
Marissa. *See* Mareshah.
Mar-Kahana, Exilarch, subordinates himself to Ashi, **2**, 606.
"Mar Mar Jesu," anti-Christian work forbidden by Benedict XIII, **4**, 215.
Mar-Raba (670–680), principal of the Pumbeditha academy, reforms the divorce laws, **3**, 92.
Marranos, the, or new-Christians, origin of, **4**, 179–80; **5**, 729.
meaning of, **4**, 180.
secretly Jews, **4**, 180.
in Sicily, protected by the people, **4**, 319–20.
protected in Tudela, **4**, 357.
permitted to settle in Ancona, **4**, 408.
flee from Spain and Portugal, **4**, 529.
return of, to Judaism, reason for the revival of a Synhedrion, **4**, 535.
of Naples threatened with the Inquisition, **4**, 543.
of Marseilles aid the Neapolitan Jews, **4**, 544.
of Ferrara consoled by Samuel Usque, **4**, 558, 560.
of Ancona protected by the popes, **4**, 568.
of Ancona, persecuted by Paul IV, **4**, 568–9, 570–1.
at Pesaro and Ferrara, **4**, 569, 578–81.
persecuted by Paul IV, **4**, 581–2.

Marranos, the (*continued*), victims of the Italian Inquisition, **4,** 654.
deprived of Ferrara as a refuge, **4,** 661.
England designed as an asylum for, **5,** 46.
condemned to the stake in the seventeenth century, **5,** 91-2.
See also Spanish exiles; Inquisition, the.

Marranos, the Portuguese, buy the favor of Alexander VI, **4,** 378-9.
milder measures towards, adopted by Manoel, **4,** 379.
Samuel Usque on, **4,** 380.
descendants of, in Africa, **4,** 381.
the Inquisition established for, at Benevento, **4,** 385.
manufacture fire-arms and ammunition in Turkey, **4,** 401.
suffering of, **4,** 483.
follow Jewish observances openly, **4,** 485.
instruct their children in Judaism, **4,** 485.
emigration of, checked by Manoel, **4,** 485-6.
hated by the Christians, **4,** 486.
accused of causing scarcity of grain, **4,** 486.
ruin of, determined by the Dominicans, **4,** 486-7.
Manoel's orders concerning, **4,** 488.
protected by Manoel's counselors, **4,** 488.
usefulness of, **4,** 488.
life of, inquired into by João III, **4,** 489.
observe Jewish and Christian rites, **4,** 489.
spied upon by Henrique Nunes, **4,** 489.

Marranos, the Portuguese (*continued*), treatment of, improves with Reubeni's appearance, **4,** 493-4.
consider Reubeni the forerunner of the Messiah, **4,** 494, 497-8.
not encouraged by Reubeni to acknowledge Judaism, **4,** 495.
burnt by the Bishop of Ceuta, **4,** 499.
defended by the Bishop of Algarve, **4,** 500.
defended by Lorenzo Pucci, **4,** 505.
suffering of, at the introduction of the Inquisition, **4,** 508-9.
complain of the inhumanity of the Inquisition, **4,** 509.
represented at Rome by Duarte de Paz, **4,** 512.
absolved for defection from the Church, **4,** 513-14.
protected by Clement VII, **4,** 514.
absolution of, enforced by Paul III, **4,** 516.
protected by a bull of Paul III, **4,** 516, 517.
unable to pay the bribes promised by Duarte de Paz, **4,** 518.
gentle measures towards, recommended by Paul III, **4,** 518.
steadfastness of, **4,** 519, 528.
try to have the Inquisition revoked, **4,** 519.
complain to Paul III of the cruelty of the Inquisition, **4,** 519-20.
protected by Paul III, **4,** 520.
endangered by Emanuel da Costa, **4,** 521.
granted the right of appeal to the pope, **4,** 521.

Marranos, the Portuguese (*continued*), suffering of, from the Inquisition, **4**, 522–3.
delinquencies of, reported to the pope, **4**, 523.
draw up a memorial to the pope, **4**, 524.
forbidden to emigrate, **4**, 524.
right of, to emigrate defended before the Council of Trent, **4**, 526.
liberated from the Inquisition prisons, **4**, 527.
forced to abjure their Judaizing tendencies, **4**, 527.
mild treatment of, requested by Paul III, **4**, 527.
a profitable population to Portugal, **4**, 527–8.
absolution granted to, by popes, **4**, 528.
look to the Netherlands as a refuge, **4**, 662–3.
admission of, into Zealand opposed, **4**, 663.
first to emigrate to the Netherlands, **4**, 664–5.
in Amsterdam, **4**, 665.
taken to Holland by the Earl of Essex, **4**, 665.
capital of, acceptable to the Netherlands, **4**, 667–8.
revert to Judaism, **4**, 669.
suffering of, from the Inquisition, **4**, 670.
Philip III debtor of, **4**, 670.
granted absolution by Clement VIII, **4**, 671.
emigrate to the Netherlands, **4**, 671.
invited by Christian princes to settle in their countries, **4**, 675.
devotion of, to Judaism, **4**, 678–9.
Catholic tendencies of, **4**, 679–80.

Marranos, the Portuguese (*continued*), in Hamburg as "traders," **4**, 686–7.
objected to by Lutherans, **4**, 686, 687.
admitted into Hamburg as Jews, **4**, 688.
importance of, for trade, **4**, 689.
transported to Brazil, **4**, 693.
refused permission to settle in Frankfort-on-the-Main, **4**, 695.
culture of, **5**, 109–18.
in Bordeaux, **5**, 341–2.
See also under Amsterdam; Inquisition, the.

Marranos, the Spanish, hated by the populace, **4**, 180.
endanger the existence of the Spanish Jews, **4**, 180–1.
propagandists for Christianity, **4**, 181–2.
take refuge in northern Africa, **4**, 197.
protected by Saul Astruc Cohen and Isaac ben Sheshet, **4**, 199.
the Christian confession extorted from, by Vincent Ferrer, **4**, 202.
troublesome to the Church, **4**, 255–6.
true to Judaism in secret, **4**, 256.
inquisitors appointed for, **4**, 256.
equal rights denied to, **4**, 256–7.
plundered under Henry IV of Castile, **4**, 274.
return to Judaism under Henry IV, **4**, 276.
promoted to the highest offices in Castile, **4**, 280.
attacked at Valladolid, **4**, 280–1.

Marranos, the Spanish (*continued*), accused of Judaizing, **4**, 281.
attacks upon, grow frequent, **4**, 281–3.
high positions and character of, **4**, 309.
Judaizing tendencies of, **4**, 309.
the Inquisition for, proposed, **4**, 310.
catechism for, **4**, 311.
lose favor with Isabella, **4**, 311–12.
the Inquisition for, established in Seville, **4**, 312.
adopt measures of defense against the Inquisition, **4**, 313.
fugitive, burnt by the Inquisition, **4**, 314.
the Edict of Grace issued for, **4**, 315.
asked to denounce Judaizing Marranos, **4**, 315.
victims of the Inquisition, **4**, 317–18.
flee from the Inquisition, **4**, 318.
complain of the Inquisition to Sixtus IV, **4**, 318.
a chief judge of appeals appointed for cases against, **4**, 320.
excluded from the office of heresy judges, **4**, 321.
appeal to Sixtus IV to modify the rigors of the Inquisition, **4**, 322.
Torquemada's code for, **4**, 326–8.
try to suppress the Inquisition in Aragon, **4**, 329.
plot against Pedro Arbues, **4**, 329–30.
slaughter of, in Saragossa, **4**, 331–2.
origin of the persecution of, **4**, 333.

Marranos, the Spanish (*continued*), intimate relations of, with the Jews, **4**, 334–5.
helped by the Jews of Castile, **4**, 344.
of Granada, protected by the secret treaty of Boabdil, **4**, 345.
flee to Granada, **4**, 351.
help the exiled Jews, **4**, 354.
deliver up enemies of the Jews to the Inquisition, **4**, 355.
care exercised by, after the expulsion of the Jews, **4**, 355.
concerned in the murder of Arbues protected in Tudela, **4**, 357.
delivered up to the Inquisition in Portugal, **4**, 368, 379–80.
the Inquisition established for, at Benevento, **4**, 385.
manufacture fire-arms and ammunition in Turkey, **4**, 401.
suffering of, **4**, 483.
oppressed by Ximenes de Cisneros, **4**, 484.
try to escape to Portugal, **4**, 486.
Messianic expectations of, **4**, 494.
flee to Portugal, **4**, 494.
take David Reubeni to be the forerunner of the Messiah, **4**, 497–8.
attack Badajoz, **4**, 498.
denounced by David Reubeni, **4**, 511.
See also Spanish exiles, the; Inquisition, the.

Marriage, unlawful degrees of relationship for, established by Sopherim, **1**, 397.

Marriage laws, the, revised by Abba-Areka, **2**, 516.

Marriage laws, the (*continued*), among the Karaites, **3,** 132, 158, 159.
regulated by the Mayence rabbinical synod, **4,** 135.
changed by Menachem of Merseburg, **4,** 228.
modified by the synod of Lublin, **5,** 13.
abolition of, advocated by Holdheim, **5,** 680.
Marriages, civil, discussed by the Assembly of Notables, **5,** 491.
by the Synhedrion, **5,** 496, 497.
Marriages, Jewish, in Austria, restricted, **5,** 509.
Marriages, mixed. *See* Intermarriages.
Mar-Sacharya, of Haleb, attacks Maimonides, **3,** 477.
Mar-Samuel. *See* Samuel, son of Abba.
Marseilles, Jews in, in the sixth century, **3,** 35.
the Jews of Clermont flee to, **3,** 39.
Jewish physicians at, **3,** 582.
Jews remain in, after the banishment by Charles VI, **4,** 177.
Neapolitan Jews carried to, **4,** 544.
Marseilles, the Jews of, in the twelfth century, **3,** 400.
order a Hebrew translation of Maimonides' Mishna commentary, **3,** 492.
show honor to the Jewish envoys to Egypt, **5,** 658.
Marshall, Lord Mayor of London, calls a meeting of protest against the Damascus affair, **5,** 655-6, 657.
Mar-Sheshet, a Babylonian Amora, **2,** 545.
memory of, **2,** 553.
Mar-Sheshet (*continued*), and Chasda, **2,** 553-4.
opposed to Judah ben Ezekiel's dialectics, **2,** 554.
rebukes the Exilarch, **2,** 554.
founds a school at Silhi, **2,** 554.
Marsus, Vibius, governor of Syria, prevents Agrippa I from fortifying Jerusalem, **2,** 195.
disperses the conference of princes summoned by Agrippa I, **2,** 196.
hostile to the Judæans, **2,** 197.
soldiery of, banished to Pontus, **2,** 197.
Marten, Harry, employed by Cromwell to dispose the English in favor of the Jews, **5,** 43.
Martha. *See* Domna, Julia.
Martha, sister of Lazarus, follower of Jesus, **2,** 160.
Martha, wife of Joshua ben Gamala, obtains the high priesthood for her husband, **2,** 249.
suffering of, during the siege of Jerusalem, **2,** 306.
Martin V, pope, elected by the Council of Constance, **4,** 219.
discourteous to the Jews of Constance, **4,** 219.
confirms the privileges of the Jews of Germany and Savoy, **4,** 219.
waited on by Jewish delegates from Italy and Spain, **4,** 219.
issues a bull against forced conversions, **4,** 219-20.
issues a bull protecting the Jews from Dominican denunciations, **4,** 226-7.
privileges granted by, to Jews confirmed by Eugenius IV, **4,** 249.

Martin, Fernan, chief of police, assists the Jews against Joseph Pichon, **4**, 156.
punished by Juan I of Castile, **4**, 157.
Martin, Raymund, Dominican, rescues the Talmud from the flames in Aragon, **3**, 603.
anti-Jewish writings of, **3**, 622.
influence of, **3**, 622–3.
refuted by Solomon ben Adret, **3**, 623.
Martinet, Adam, admiration of, for neo-Hebraic poetry, **5**, 628, 629.
Martinez, Ferdinand (Ferran), agitates against the Jews in Seville, **4**, 167.
stirs up Seville a second time, **4**, 168–9.
punished by Henry III of Castile, **4**, 193.
Martinez, Gonzalo, de Oviedo, favorite of Alfonso XI of Castile, **4**, 83–4.
causes the death of Joseph of Ecija and Samuel Ibn-Wakar, **4**, 84.
proposes to deprive the Jews of their wealth, **4**, 84–5.
wins a battle over the Moors, **4**, 85.
accused of treason by Leonora de Guzman, **4**, 85.
allies himself with the enemies of Alfonso XI, **4**, 85–6.
deserted by his Order, **4**, 86.
executed, **4**, 86.
Martyrdom, when compulsory, **2**, 423–4.
Martyrology, by Ephraim ben Jacob of Bonn, **3**, 419.
Mar-Ukba (918), Exilarch, forced to remove from Bagdad, **2**, 184.
the Arabic poetry of, pleases the Caliph, **3**, 184–5.
Mar-Ukba (*continued*), restored to his office, **3**, 185.
banished to Kairuan, **3**, 185, 210.
Mar-Ukba, judge in Cafri, **2**, 512.
Mar-Ukban, grandson of Abba-Areka, Exilarch, **2**, 544, 579–80.
Maruni, priest, incites a crusade against the Damascus Jews, **5**, 662.
Mary, sister of Lazarus, follower of Jesus, **2**, 160.
Mary Magdalene, follower of Jesus, **2**, 154.
Mar-Yanka. *See* Natronaï ben Nehemiah.
Mar-Zemach I ben Paltoi (872–890), Gaon of Pumbeditha, arranges the "Aruch," **3**, 178–9.
Mar-Zutra, Amora, subordinates himself to Ashi, **2**, 606.
at the court of Jezdijird, **2**, 610.
Mar-Zutra I, Exilarch, subordinates himself to Ashi, **2**, 606.
Mar-Zutra II (496–520), Exilarch, leader of the Babylonian Jews against the Zendik, **3**, 3–4.
kept out of his office by Pachda, **3**, 3.
executed, **3**, 4.
son of, **3**, 4.
Mar-Zutra III, a distinguished scholar in Judæa, **3**, 4.
president of the Tiberias academy, **3**, 12.
Masada, fortress, refuge of Mariamne, wife of Herod, **2**, 83.
besieged by Antigonus, **2**, 87.
refuge of Herod from Cleopatra, **2**, 94.

Masada, fortress (*continued*),
taken by the Sicarii, **2,** 258.
refuge of the Sicarii, **2,** 261.
a hot-bed of insurgents, **2,** 292–3.
holds out against the Romans, **2,** 315.
under Eleazar ben Jair, **2,** 316.
garrison of, commits suicide, **2,** 316.

Mascarenhas, John Rodrigo, Portuguese Marrano, brings hatred upon the Marranos, **4,** 486.

Masechet-Gerim, tractate in the Law, on proselytes, **2,** 384.

Masechta, one of the six divisions of the Mishnic code, **2,** 354.

Mashal, an allegory, **1,** 158.

Mashal ha-Kadmoni, by Ibn-Sahula, **3,** 560.

Maskhir, recorder under David, **1,** 122.

Masserano. *See* Bezalel Masserano.

Massora, the, and the vowel points, **3,** 112.
studied by Gershom ben Jehuda, **3,** 244.
the division of the Scriptures into verses by, criticised, **3,** 290.
importance of, according to Abraham Ibn-Ezra, **3,** 371.
studied by Wolf Heidenheim, **5,** 400.
as viewed by Samuel David Luzzatto, **5,** 624.

Massorets, the, list of:
Aaron ben Asher, Ben-Naphtali, Moses ben Asher.

Masuel, Eugene, founder of the "Alliance Israélite Universelle," **5,** 701.

Mata-Mechasia. *See* **Sora.**

Matatoron, name of an angel, **1,** 403.

Mathematical knowledge, the, of the teachers of the Law, **2,** 357.

Mathematicians, Jewish. *See* Astronomers.

Mathematics, studied in Portugal, **4,** 367.

Matiah ben Charash, teacher of the Law in Rome, **2,** 443.

Matnita boraïta, supplements to the Mishna, **2,** 470.

Matri, a family of the tribe of Benjamin, **1,** 83.

Matronita, Kabbalistic term in the Zohar, **4,** 18.

Mattachery, Jews' town, **2,** 630.

Mattan, high priest of Baal, under Athaliah, **1,** 214.

Mattara, court in the palace at Jerusalem, **1,** 314.

Mattathiah ben Joseph Provenci, Talmudist, re-establishes a college at Paris, **4,** 133.
exempt from wearing the Jew badge, **4,** 133.
chief rabbi of France, **4,** 133.
death of, **4,** 152.

Mattathias, envoy of Nicanor to Judas Maccabæus, **1,** 484.

Mattathias, the **Hasmonæan,** father of the Maccabees, resists Apelles, **1,** 459.
leader of the Chassidim, **1,** 459–60.
decides to fight on the Sabbath, **1,** 460.
petty warfare of, against the Syrians, **1,** 460–1.
chooses Simon as counselor and Judas as commander, **1,** 461.
death of the sons of, **1,** 531.

Mattathias ben Simon Psellus, father of Josephus, **1,** 502.

Mattathias, son of Simon Tharsi, **1**, 520.
assassinated, **1**, 530.
Mattathias Yizhari, at the disputation of Tortosa, **4**, 208.
Matthai of Arbela, Pharisee leader, **2**, 20.
Matthew (Levi), publican, follower of Jesus, **2**, 153.
Matthew Paris, historian, charges the Franciscans with venality, **3**, 591.
Matthias, emperor, unable to punish Fettmilch, **4**, 698.
punishes Frankfort, **4**, 700.
Matthias ben Margalot, Pharisee, instigates an uprising against Herod, **2**, 115.
burnt alive, **2**, 115.
death of, avenged, **2**, 121.
Matthias ben Matthias, brother of Josephus, **2**, 276.
Matthias ben Theophilus, high priest, last of those appointed under the Herodians, **2**, 249.
summons all Judæans to Jerusalem for the Passover of 66, **2**, 251.
persuades Jerusalem to receive Roman troops amicably, **2**, 254–5.
deposed by the Zealots, **2**, 294.
Matthias Boëthus, of priestly family, executed, **2**, 304.
Maurice of Orange, well disposed towards the Jews, **4**, 674, 678.
Mauritania, rebels against Hadrian, **2**, 399.
Mauritius, emperor of the East, protects Chosru II, **3**, 9.
the Jews under, **3**, 18.
supplanted by Phocas, **3**, 18–19.
Maury, Abbé, opposed to the emancipation of the Jews, **5**, 441–2, 446, 462.
Maxarquivir, the Jews of, banished by order of Maria Anna, **5**, 169.
Maximilian I, emperor, the Jews recommended to the protection of, **4**, 413.
favors Jacob Loans, **4**, 414.
appoints Joseph Loans representative of the German Jews, **4**, 414.
indecision of, **4**, 414–15.
permits Nuremberg to expel the Jews, **4**, 415–16.
expels the Jews from Austria, Styria and Carinthia, **4**, 427.
urged to deliver the Jews to the Dominicans of Cologne, **4**, 428.
issues his first mandate giving Pfefferkorn power over the Jews, **4**, 429.
letter to, from Uriel von Gemmingen, **4**, 431.
appoints Reuchlin counselor of the Suabian League, **4**, 435.
applied to, for a second mandate, **4**, 436.
the Jewish cause pleaded before, **4**, 436–7.
appears to favor the Jewish side, **4**, 437.
issues a second mandate, **4**, 437.
homage paid to, by Pfefferkorn, **4**, 439.
directs the Frankfort Senate to restore the Hebrew books, **4**, 439.
promises to investigate Pfefferkorn's attack on Reuchlin, **4**, 446.
espouses Reuchlin's cause, **4**, 459, 464.
abused by the Dominicans, **4**, 459.

Maximilian I, emperor (*continued*), protects the Jews of Frankfort, Worms, and Ratisbon, **4**, 463–4.
death of, **4**, 467.
Maximilian II, emperor, protects the Jews of Prague, **4**, 587.
urges his son for the Polish crown, **4**, 603.
Maximus, emperor, orders the Senate to rebuild a synagogue, **2**, 614.
Maximus, teacher of Julian the Apostate, **2**, 595.
Maximus, Trajan's general in the Euphrates district, **2**, 397.
Mayence, founders of the Jewish community of, **3**, 41.
Charlemagne brings the Kalonymos family to, **3**, 143.
a Talmud school founded at, **3**, 243, 247.
Rashi studies Talmud at, **3**, 286.
represented at the first rabbinical synod, **3**, 377.
a rabbinical synod meets at, **3**, 517–18.
the congregation of, one of the three oldest of Germany, **3**, 518.
rabbinical synod at, to regulate marriage laws, **4**, 135.
exiles from, in Poland and Italy, **4**, 294.
Reuchlin tried for heresy at, **4**, 450–2.
the rabbi of, opposes the Reform movement, **5**, 571.
honor paid to Crémieux at, **5**, 668.
Mayence, the Jews of, banished by Henry II, **3**, 245–6.
perpetuate the memory of Simon ben Isaac and Gershom ben Jehuda, **3**, 247.
Mayence, the Jews of (*continued*), massacred in the first crusade, **3**, 303.
accuse their persecutors before Henry IV, **3**, 307.
charged with the blood accusation, **3**, 636.
possessions of, confiscated, **3**, 636.
emigrate to Syria, **3**, 637.
burn themselves to escape persecution, **4**, 109.
banished, **4**, 413.
well treated during the Thirty Years' War, **4**, 707.
Mayence, the university of, to counsel regarding the confiscation of Hebrew books, **4**, 437, 441.
attacks the Hebrew Bible, **4**, 444–5.
students of, object to Reuchlin's heresy trial, **4**, 451.
Mayo, Moses, excommunicated by Chayim of Lublin, **5**, 261.
Mazaca-Cæsarea (Cappadocia), study of the Law in, **2**, 358.
the Jews of, lose life in the assault of Shabur I, **2**, 520, 526.
Mazdak, reformer of Magianism, **3**, 1.
communistic principles of, **3**, 1–2.
Mazikim, evil spirits, introduced into Judaism from Magianism, **1**, 403.
Measfim, the, contributors to "The Gatherer," in Germany, **5**, 399–400.
in Holland, **5**, 400–1.
in France, **5**, 401.
in Italy, **5**, 402.
influence of, **5**, 402–3, 403–5.
consider themselves the disciples of Mendelssohn, **5**, 403.
the best production by, **5**, 404.

Measfim, the (*continued*), mediocrity of, **5**, 417.
effect of the revival of Hebrew by, **5**, 420–1.
consulted by Jacobson, **5**, 502.
Measfim, the, list of:

Ben-Zeeb,
Bresselau, Mendel J.
Ensheim, Moses
Euchel, Isaac Abraham
Friedrichsfeld, David
Heidenheim, Wolf
Homberg, Herz
Löwe, Joel
Morpurgo, Elijah
Satanow, Isaac
Wessely, Naphtali Hartwig
Wolfssohn, Aaron.

Meaux, the council of, re-enacts anti-Jewish restrictions, **3**, 171–2.
Mebarsapes, king of Adiabene, conquered by Trajan, **2**, 393–4.
Mebodes, Persian general, puts to death the Jews of Machuza, **3**, 9.
Mebo-ha-Talmud, methodology of the Talmud, by Samuel Ibn-Nagrela, **3**, 259.
Mecca (Alcharam), Jews in, in the sixth century, **3**, 56.
holy city of the Arabs, **3**, 60.
a proselyte to Judaism governor of, **3**, 63.
Mahomet's flight from, **3**, 72–3.
the praying Moslem turns to, **3**, 75.
Jews not allowed to live in, **3**, 436.
Mecklenburg, the Jews of, emancipated, **5**, 507.
Mecklenburg - Schwerin, the Jews of, forbidden the early interment of the dead, **5**, 318.
apply to Mendelssohn, **5**, 318.
interfered with by the government, **5**, 679.
Medaba, center of the Bene-Amri, **1**, 491.
Medaba (*continued*), taken by John Hyrcanus, **2**, 7.
Medeïros, Francisco (Isaac), Mendes, Portuguese Marrano in Holland, **4**, 667.
builds the second synagogue at Amsterdam, **4**, 671.
Medelsheim. *See* Berr, Cerf.
Medes, the, defeated by the Assyrians, **1**, 287.
Media, the Ten Tribes colonized in, **1**, 265.
invaded by the Scythians, **1**, 287.
half-Shekel contribution to the Temple from, **2**, 52.
visited by Petachya, **3**, 421.
Medici, the, the renascence under, participated in by Jews, **4**, 289, 290.
Medicine, prepared by Jews prohibited, in the code of Alfonso X, **3**, 596.
by Eugenius IV, **4**, 250, 252.
by Henry IV of Castile, **4**, 278.
Medicine, the study of, permitted by the opponents of science, **4**, 40.
among Polish Jews, **4**, 633.
See Physicians, Jewish.
Medina, Jewish capitalist, involves Voltaire in financial losses, **5**, 339.
Medina (Yathrib); Israelites under Joshua settle in, **3**, 54.
center of the Jewish Arabic tribes, **3**, 55.
besieged, **3**, 62.
a proselyte the governor of, **3**, 63.
Mahomet in, **3**, 72–3.
the center of Islam, **3**, 86.
Jews not allowed to live in, **3**, 436.
Medina, the Jews of, defend the city, **3**, 62.

Medina, the Jews of (*continued*), hated by the Kailan race, **3,** 67.
conquered by the Arabs, **3,** 67–8.
regain importance, **3,** 70–1.
and Mahomet, **3,** 73.
repelled by Mahomet, **3,** 74.
intrigue against Mahomet, **3,** 84.
Medina del Campo, the Jews of, burnt and plundered, **4,** 278.
the cortes of, propose an Inquisition for Marranos, **4,** 310, 313.
Medina-Celi, Kabbalistic center, **4,** 6.
the duke of, employs a Jewish physician, **5,** 116.
Medina-Sidonia, Marranos flee to, **4,** 313.
Megabyzus, satrap of Syria, revolts from Persia, **1,** 371.
Megadef, sobriquet of Joshua Lorqui, **4,** 217.
Megerlin, David Frederick, explains Eibeschütz's amulets in a Christian way, **5,** 270.
calls on the Danish king to protect Eibeschütz, **5,** 271.
Megiddo, the battle of, Josiah defeated at, **1,** 297.
Megilloth, the Five, commentary on, by Samuel ben Meïr, **3,** 346.
by Abraham Ibn-Ezra, **3,** 370.
"Mehemenuta de Cola," by Chayon, **5,** 219–20.
Mehmed Effendi, Sabbataï Zevi's Mahometan name, **5,** 154.
Mehmet Ali, Pasha of Egypt, conquers Syria, **5,** 633.
supported by Louis Philippe, **5,** 633, 634.
assents to the execution of the Damascus Jews, **5,** 640.
Mehmet Ali (*continued*), influenced by the French consul-general, **5,** 647.
appealed to by the Jews of Alexandria, **5,** 647.
letter to, from Metternich, **5,** 647.
forms a court of justice for the Damascus affair, **5,** 648.
breaks up the consular court, **5,** 649.
grants Montefiore audience, **5,** 659.
in awe of the European powers, **5,** 659.
orders the release of the Damascus prisoners, **5,** 660.
thanked by the Jews of Alexandria, **5,** 660.
subterfuge of, discovered by Munk, **5,** 660.
changes his firman, **5,** 660.
officially states the groundlessness of the blood accusation, **5,** 661.
surrenders territory to Turkey, **5,** 661.
Meïl Zedek. *See* Menachem of Merseburg.
Meinhard of Görz, captor of Meïr of Rothenburg, **3,** 639.
Meiningen, the "hep, hep!" persecutions in, **5,** 530.
Meïr, disciple of Akiba, returns to Judæa, **2,** 433.
originality of, **2,** 435.
said to be a convert, **2,** 435.
copyist of Holy Writ, **2,** 435–6.
wife of, **2,** 436.
disciple of Ishmael ben Elisha, **2,** 436.
writer of fables, **2,** 436.
death of the sons of, **2,** 436.
modesty and wisdom of, **2,** 437.
and Elisha ben Abuya, **2,** 437.
and Euonymus of Gadara, **2,** 437–8.

Meïr (*continued*), and the Stoic philosophy, **2,** 438.
dialectics of, **2,** 438–40.
completes the collection of the Mishnas, **2,** 439–40, 460.
an Agadist, **2,** 440.
and Simon II, **2,** 440.
Chacham of the Usha Synhedrion, **2,** 434, 445.
conspires to deprive Simon II of the Patriarchate, **2,** 445.
proposed for the vice-presidency of the Synhedrion, **2,** 445.
expelled from the Synhedrion, **2,** 445.
excommunicated, **2,** 446.
death of, **2,** 446.
a casuist, **2,** 476.
decision of, concerning the Samaritans, **2,** 534.
Meïr, son-in-law of Abraham Senior, accepts baptism, **4,** 351.
Meïr, teacher of the Mishna, quoted by Maimonides, **3,** 454.
Meïr de Malea, Almoxarif under Alfonso X, **3,** 593.
Meïr ben Baruch of Rothenburg (1220–1293), Talmudist, elegy of, on the burning of the Talmud, **3,** 579.
piety of, **3,** 625.
heads the emigration of German Jews to Syria, **3,** 637.
taken prisoner, **3,** 638–9.
refuses to be ransomed, **3,** 639–40.
death of, **3,** 640.
body of, ransomed, **3,** 640.
disciple of, **4,** 34, 74.
ransom of, demanded from Asheri, **4,** 37.
Meïr ben Baruch Halevi (Segal, 1370–1390), rabbi of Vienna, enforces the Morenu, **4,** 134.
Meïr ben Baruch Halevi (*continued*), compiles the customs of various communities, **4,** 134.
assumes authority over the French communities, **4,** 152–3.
Meïr ben Gabbai, Spanish exile, Kabbalist, **4,** 481.
Meïr ben Joseph Ibn-Migash, Talmudist, **3,** 317.
emigrates to Toledo, **3,** 361.
opens a Talmud academy in Toledo, **3,** 362.
Meïr ben Samuel of Rameru, son-in-law of Rashi, Tossafist, **3,** 289, 345.
sons of, **3,** 345.
Meïr ben Simon, denounces the Bahir as a forgery, **3,** 556.
Meïr ben Todros Halevi Abulafia (1180–1244), attacks Maimonides' doctrine of immortality, **3,** 524.
friends and opponents of, **3,** 524–5.
and Nachmani, **3,** 535.
assures Nachmani of his opposition to the Maimunists, **3,** 537–8.
deplores Dominican interference in the Maimunist controversy, **3,** 544.
nephew of, **4,** 2.
Meïr Alguades, physician, chief rabbi of Castile, and Solomon Levi, **4,** 185.
and Profiat Duran, **4,** 190.
influences the king favorably towards the Jews, **4,** 190.
as philosopher, **4,** 193.
tortured on the accusation of host desecration, **4,** 195.
forced confessions by, **4,** 196.
death of, **4,** 196.
Meïr Eisenstadt, teacher and confidant of Eibeschütz, **5,** 250.

Meïri. *See* Vidal Menachem ben Solomon.
Meïron, grave of Simon ben Yochaï at, **4,** 623.
Meisels, rabbi, helps to reorganize Austria, **5,** 697.
Meissen, adopts the Jewish statute of Frederick the Valiant, **3,** 569.
Mekor Chayim, philosophical work by Ibn-Gebirol, **3,** 270–1.
Meldola, David, rabbi of London, repeats Manasseh ben Israel's oath denying the blood accusation, **5,** 654–5.
Melo, Francisco, millionaire in Amsterdam, **5,** 205.
Memnon, governor of Cœlesyria, **1,** 414.
Memra, the, decisions of the Amoraim, **2,** 515.
expounded by Rabba bar Nachmani, **2,** 578.
" **Men of Faith,**" a sect of Jewish mystics, **3,** 153–4.
Menachem of Merseburg (Meïl Zedek), Talmudist, changes the Talmudic marriage law, **4,** 227–8.
Menachem ben Aaron ben Zerach (1310–1385), rabbi of Toledo, early trials of, **4,** 78, 144.
studies of, **4,** 144–5.
mediocrity of, **4,** 145.
work by, **4,** 145.
Menachem ben Perez, of Joigny, at the first rabbinical synod, **3,** 377.
Menachem ben Saruk (910–970), grammarian, founder of Judæo-Spanish culture, **3,** 215.
writes the introductory verses of a letter to the king of the Chazars, **3,** 220.
makes Hebrew the object of research, **3,** 223.
Menachem ben Saruk (*continued*), patrons of, **3,** 224.
lexicographical work by, **3,** 224–5.
verse of, awkward, **3,** 225.
traduced to Chasdaï Ibn-Shaprut, **3,** 226–7.
defended by his disciples, **3,** 227.
disciples of, **3,** 237.
grammar of, known to Rashi, **3,** 289.
unhappiness of, **3,** 313.
Menachem Bashyasi, Karaite, permits lights on the Sabbath, **4,** 269.
Menachem Maroli, Karaite, permits lights on the Sabbath, **4,** 269.
Menachemists, followers of David Alrui, **3,** 433.
Menahem (768–758), king of Israel, murders Shallum, **1,** 244.
abolishes Baal worship, **1,** 244.
submits to Pul, **1,** 246–7.
power of the kingdom under, **1,** 247.
introduces the worship of Mylitta, **1,** 247.
death of, **1,** 248.
Menahem, an Essene, Hillel's deputy in the Synhedrion, **2,** 100.
Menahem ben Jair, grandson of Judas of Galilee, leader of the Sicarii, **2,** 239.
takes Masada, **2,** 258.
kills the Roman garrison at Jerusalem, **2,** 260.
cruelty of, **2,** 260–1.
disagrees with the Zealot leader, **2,** 261.
executed, **2,** 261.
Menahem ben Solomon. *See* David Alrui.

Mendelssohn, Dorothea, culture of, **5**, 413.
marriage of, to Simon Veit, **5**, 424.
and Frederick Schlegel, **5**, 424.
apostasy of, **5**, 424.
Mendelssohn, Henrietta, accepts Catholicism, **5**, 424.
Mendelssohn, Joseph, approves of the "Society of Friends," **5**, 418.
Mendelssohn, Moses (1728–1786), causes the renaissance of the Jewish race, **5**, 292–3.
youth of, **5**, 293.
arrival of, in Berlin, **5**, 293.
under the influence of David Fränkel, **5**, 293–4.
poverty of, **5**, 294.
under the influence of Maimonides, **5**, 295.
secular studies of, **5**, 295.
self-mastery of, **5**, 295.
Hebrew style of, **5**, 295–6.
as tutor, **5**, 296.
becomes acquainted with Lessing, **5**, 297.
admiration of, for Lessing, **5**, 297–8.
acquires a German style, **5**, 298.
writes the "Philosophical Conversations," **5**, 298–9.
introduced to the learned circles of Berlin, **5**, 299.
contributes to the "Library of the Fine Arts," **5**, 300.
appreciation of the Bible by, **5**, 301.
delicacy and modesty of, **5**, 301.
lacks appreciation of history, **5**, 301.
criticises Frederick the Great's poetry, **5**, 302.
justifies himself before the king, **5**, 302–3.
Mendelssohn, Moses (*continued*), as bookkeeper. **5**, 303.
wins the prize of the Berlin Academy, **5**, 303–4.
made a "Schutzjude," **5**, 304.
writes the "Phædon," **5**, 304–8.
honors paid to, **5**, 308.
physiognomy of, analyzed by Lavater, **5**, 308–9.
letter from, to Lavater, **5**, 311–13.
reconciled with Lavater, **5**, 314.
criticises Bonnet's "Palingénésie," **5**, 314–15.
pamphlets on, and Lavater, **5**, 315–16.
attacked by Kölbele, **5**, 316–17.
offends pious Jews, **5**, 317.
intercourse of, with Polish Jews, **5**, 317–18.
opposed to hasty burial, **5**, 318.
opinion of, on the "Fragments of an Unknown," **5**, 320.
the "Fragments of an Unknown" attributed to, **5**, 322.
the hero of "Nathan the Wise," **5**, 323.
mourning of, for Lessing, **5**, 327.
translates the Pentateuch for his children, **5**, 328.
publishes his Pentateuch translation, **5**, 328–9.
mildness of, in the face of opposition, **5**, 332.
appeals to the Danish royal house, **5**, 333–4.
assistants of, **5**, 334.
inspires the young, **5**, 334–5.
helps the Jews of Switzerland and Dresden, **5**, 344.

Mendelssohn, Moses (*continued*), requested by the Alsatian Jews to draw up a memorial, **5**, 351.
and Dohm, **5**, 351–2.
attractive to Christians, **5**, 352.
inspires Dohm, **5**, 356, 361, 366.
on Dohm's "Apology," **5**, 361–2.
objects to excommunication, **5**, 362–3.
writes "The Salvation of the Jews," **5**, 362–3.
charged with apostasy, **5**, 363.
publishes "Jerusalem," **5**, 364–6.
adherence of, to Judaism, **5**, 364.
on the ceremonial law, **5**, 365.
inspires Wessely, **5**, 366.
compared with Wessely, **5**, 367.
addressed by the Jews of Trieste, **5**, 369.
death of, **5**, 371–2.
objections of, to Spinozism, **5**, 372.
defends Lessing, **5**, 372.
mourning for, **5**, 372.
statue of, **5**, 372–3.
reception of, at Königsberg, **5**, 398.
contributes to Ha-Meassef, **5**, 399.
and Herz Homberg, **5**, 401–2.
recommends the study of the sciences, **5**, 402.
glorified by the Measfim, **5**, 403.
daughters of, cultured, **5**, 412, 413.
house of, the center of culture, **5**, 412.
misunderstood by his family and his disciples, **5**, 417.
daughters of, **5**, 423, 424, 425.
influences Mirabeau, **5**, 432.

Mendelssohn, Moses (*continued*), resemblance between and Börne, **5**, 538.
criticised by Bernays, **5**, 575.
the ideal of Krochmal, **5**, 608.
influence of, on Erter, **5**, 613.
repeats Manasseh ben Israel's oath denying the blood accusation, **5**, 655.

Mendelssohnians, the, in opposition to Rabbinical Judaism, **5**, 375.
oppose Chassidism, **5**, 394.

Mendes, David Franco (1713–1792), dramatic poet, influenced by Luzzatto, **5**, 244.
devoted to Hebrew, **5**, 401.

Mendes, Franco, Portuguese Marrano, family of, in Holland, **4**, 667.

Mendes, Manuel, Portuguese Marrano leader, **4**, 516.

Mendes-Nassi, Diogo, Marrano banker at Antwerp, **4**, 572.
death of, **4**, 572.
accused of Judaizing, **4**, 573.

Mendes-Nassi, Francisco, husband of Gracia Mendesia, banker at Antwerp, **4**, 571–2.

Mendes-Nassi, Gracia, the younger, daughter of Diogo, **4**, 572.
married to Samuel Nassi, **4**, 577.

Mendes-Nassi family, the, debt owing to, repudiated by Henry II of France, **4**, 596, 597.

Mendesia (Nassi) Gracia (Beatrice, 1510–1568), Marrano philanthropist, marriage of, **4**, 571.
at Antwerp, **4**, 572.
head of a banking house, **4**, 572–3.
property of, confiscated by Charles V, **4**, 573.

Mendesia (Nassi) Gracia (*continued*), at Venice, **4,** 574.
informed against by her sister, **4,** 574.
property of, in France confiscated, **4,** 574.
cause of, espoused by the sultan, **4,** 574–5.
protected by Hercules d'Este II, **4,** 575.
described by Samuel Usque, **4,** 575–6.
the Ferrara Spanish Bible dedicated to, **4,** 577.
reconciled with her sister, **4,** 577.
goes to Constantinople, **4,** 577.
beneficence of, **4,** 577.
enlists the sultan's aid in behalf of Turkish Jews at Ancona, **4,** 579–80.
influences rabbis against trade with Ancona, **4,** 580.
Mendoza, cardinal, archbishop of Seville, prepares a catechism for Marranos, **4,** 311.
Menelaus (Onias), the Benjamite, Hellenist, opposed to Onias III, **1,** 437.
made high priest by Antiochus Epiphanes, **1,** 447.
despoils the Temple, **1,** 448.
instigates the murder of Onias III, **1,** 448.
exonerated from the charge of Temple desecration, **1,** 449.
maligns the Law, **1,** 449–50.
takes refuge in the Acra, **1,** 451.
desecrates the Temple, **1,** 451.
tries to abolish Judaism, **1,** 454–5.
executed, **1,** 480.
Meni, Chaldæan goddess, worshiped by Judæans in Babylon, **1,** 340.
Menz. *See* Abraham; Judah; Moses.
Meonenim, Philistine soothsayers, **1,** 55.
Mephibosheth, son of Jonathan, lamed, **1,** 104.
protected by David, **1,** 123.
at Jerusalem with David, **1,** 124.
Merab, daughter of Saul, offered to David as wife, **1,** 99.
son of, killed by the Gibeonites, **1,** 123.
Merari, Moses Menachem, rabbi of Venice, exacts a promise from Luzzatto not to teach the Kabbala, **5,** 239.
Merbal, a Phœnician, rules his own country, **1,** 342.
Merida, early settlement of Jews in, **3,** 43.
home of Samuel Ibn-Nagrela's father, **3,** 255.
Mérilhou, French minister of education, proposes the complete emancipation of the Jews, **5,** 597.
Merinos, the, a powerful family of Fez, **4,** 390.
Merkel, Christian, member of the Westphalian Jewish consistory, **5,** 502.
Merlato, Austrian consul at Damascus, protects Picciotto, **5,** 639.
abused, **5,** 639, 646.
issues a report on the Damascus affair, **5,** 646.
thanked by the London meeting, **5,** 653.
thanked by the Jews of Alexandria, **5,** 660.
Merlo, Diego de, commissioner to frame the statute of the Inquisition, **4,** 312.
Merodach-baladan, king of Babylon, embassy of, to Hezekiah, **1,** 278–9.

Merom, lake, battle of, **1**, 57.
Merovingians, the, the Jews under, **3**, 36–40, 143.
Merseburg, Jews in, in the ninth century, **3**, 144.
the Jews of, presented to the bishop, **3**, 243.
Merv, a scientific center in the ninth century, **3**, 146.
Mervan II, last of the Ommiyyade caliphs, rebellion against, **3**, 125.
Merwan, father of the poetess Asma, **3**, 76.
Mesa (Mesha), king of Moab, defeated, **1**, 208–9.
Meshershaya bar Pacod, Amora, executed by Firuz, **2**, 629.
Meshullam of Béziers, denounces the Bahir as a forgery, **3**, 556.
Meshullam of Rome, announces Innocent VII's opposition to the expulsion of the Jews, **4**, 346–7.
Meshullam ben Jacob (1170), patron of Jewish learning in Lünel, **3**, 396.
sons of, **3**, 396–7.
encourages Judah Ibn-Tibbon to make translations into Hebrew, **3**, 397.
encourages Abraham ben David to write a Mishna commentary, **3**, 399.
descendant of, **4**, 30.
Meshullam, son of Berechiah, marries his daughter to an Ammonite, **1**, 362.
Meshullam En-Vidas Dafiera, poet, on Nachmani, **3**, 557.
Mesopotamia, Judæans own large tracts in, **2**, 202.
laid waste by Severus, **2**, 464.
Mesopotamia, northern, a synagogue in, burnt by monks, **2**, 614.
Mesopotamia, southern, Jewish Babylonia, **2**, 504.
Mesquito, David Bueno de, millionaire in Amsterdam, **5**, 205.
Messer-Jawaih, of Bassora, physician, translates a medical work into Arabic, **3**, 111.
Messer Leon. *See* Judah ben Yechiel.
Messiah, the, a descendant of David, **1**, 528.
the coming of, foretold by a Judæo-Greek writer, **2**, 95, 143.
longing for, in the post-exilic period, **2**, 142–3.
as conceived by various parties in Judæa, **2**, 144–5.
Jesus declares himself, **2**, 158.
necessity of a precursor to, **2**, 158.
expected to come from Bethlehem, **2**, 161.
suffering, objections to, **2**, 166.
warrants in Holy Writ for Jesus as, **2**, 166–7.
expectation of, after the death of Jesus, **2**, 167–8.
Jesus believed by the apostle Paul to be, **2**, 225–6.
expectation of, in the Roman period, **2**, 240–1.
belief in Bar-Cochba as, **2**, 409, 412.
the advent of, dependent on the extinction of the Patriarchate and the Exilarchate, **2**, 457.
to appear in Rome, **2**, 498.
Mar-Samuel's view on, **2**, 519.
appearance of, a condition of the restoration of the Jewish state, **2**, 600.
hope of, suppressed by Ashi, **2**, 610.

Messiah, the (*continued*), expectation of, among the Arabian Jews, **3**, 58.
expected by the Jews of the Caliphate of the East, **3**, 145.
expected by the Chazars, **3**, 222.
expected by the Karaites, **3**, 247.
expectation of, in Germany and France in the eleventh century, **3**, 298.
the appearance of, calculated by Abraham Albargeloni, **3**, 313.
hoped for by the Jews of northern Africa under Abdulmumen, **3**, 360.
forerunner of, among the Yemen Jews, **3**, 462, 464.
doctrine of the soul of, in the Kabbala, **3**, 555.
David Alrui poses as, **3**, 431, 432.
characterized by Nachmani, **3**, 600.
the coming of, supposed to be heralded by Hulagu's devastation of Jerusalem, **3**, 606.
abrogates the Law according to Raymund Martin, **3**, 622.
the appearance of, rumored in Syria, **3**, 637.
speculations on, in the Zohar, **4**, 18.
belief in, set aside by Chayim ben Gallipapa, **4**, 149.
the expectation of, the center of the Kabbala, **4**, 482.
the advent of, predicted by Isaac Abrabanel and Asher Lämmlein, **4**, 482-3.
hope in, aroused by the Kabbalists, **4**, 483.
expectation of, aroused by David Reubeni, **4**, 494, 497-8.

Messiah, the (*continued*), expectation of, nursed by Solomon Molcho, **4**, 495-7, 529-30.
hope of, cherished by Joseph Karo, **4**, 538-9.
hope of, aroused by Isaac Lurya, **4**, 622.
references to, expunged from the Talmud by the censors, **4**, 660.
hope of, awakened by the Thirty Years' War, **5**, 23.
of the Jews, as defined by the Fifth Monarchy believers, **5**, 23.
hopes of, entertained by Manasseh ben Israel, **5**, 24, 28, 31, 33.
the advent of, connected with the re-settlement of the Jews in England, **5**, 28, 40.
hoped for, by Felgenhauer, **5**, 35-6.
hopes of, entertained by Christians, **5**, 37.
the hopes of, entertained by Jews, expounded by Manasseh ben Israel, **5**, 37-8.
Cromwell said to be, **5**, 45.
speculations on, in the Kabbala, **5**, 120-1.
Sabbataï Zevi reveals himself as, **5**, 122.
connected with the idea of suffering, **5**, 122-3.
Nathan Ghazati on, **5**, 131-2.
according to Sabbatian conceptions, **5**, 142-3.
announced by Nehemiah Cohen, **5**, 152.
Mordecai of Eisenstadt proclaims himself, **5**, 209.
Jacob Querido reverenced as, **5**, 210.
Berachya regarded as, **5**, 211.

Messiah, the (*continued*), doctrine of, by Chayon, **5**, 219–20.
Moses Meïr Kamenker regarded as, **5**, 230.
Luzzatto proclaimed as, **5**, 245.
Jacob Frank the incarnation of, **5**, 273, 274.
expectation of, in Poland, **5**, 377.
belief in, abandoned by the Hamburg Reform Temple Union, **5**, 565.
doctrine of, given up by the "Friends of Reform," **5**, 675, 676.
Holdheim on, **5**, 680.
attitude of the Berlin Reform Association towards, **5**, 683.
Messiah, the, of the branch of Joseph, Isaac Lurya considers himself, **4**, 622, 624.
Chayim Vital considers himself, **4**, 625; **5**, 52.
discussed by Sabbataï Zevi and Nehemiah Cohen, **5**, 153.
Cardoso declares himself, **5**, 207.
Messiahs, numbers of, appear during Roman sovereignty in Judæa, **2**, 144.
Messiahs, the, list of:
Abraham ben Samuel Abulafia,
Avila, the Messiah of
Ayllon, the Messiah of
Bar-Cochba,
Berachya,
Frank, Jacob
Jacob Querido,
Jesus,
Luzzatto, Moses Chayim
Mordecai of Eisenstadt,
Moses of Crete,
Moses Botarel,
Moses Meïr Kamenker,
Obaiah Abu-Isa ben Ishak,
Sabbataï Zevi,
Serene,
Theudas.
Messianic age, the, as conceived by the educated classes, **2**, 144–5.
Messianic age, the (*continued*), believed to be dawning under Vespasian, **2**, 291–2.
tokens of, according to Abraham of Granada, **4**, 197.
preparation for, according to Maimonides, **4**, 530.
as described by Isaac Lurya, **4**, 620.
Messianic year, the, set for 1358, **4**, 120.
fixed at 1648 by the Zohar, **5**, 6, 121–2.
fixed by the Fifth Monarchy believers at 1666, **5**, 120.
Messina, the Jewish community in, in the sixth century, **3**, 28.
the clerk at the mint of, a Jew, **3**, 567.
Jews from, form a congregation in Constantinople, **4**, 402.
Messina, the Jews of, enjoy equal rights with the Christians, **3**, 423.
in the twelfth century, **3**, 424.
Mesvi. *See* Moses of Baalbek; Musa of Akbar.
Metempsychosis. *See* Transmigration of souls, the.
Meter, introduced into Hebrew by Dunash ben Labrat, **3**, 223, 226.
Metibta, a session of the schools in Babylonia, **2**, 547.
Metilius, commander of the Roman garrison in Jerusalem, **2**, 255.
spared by the Zealots, **2**, 261.
Metternich, reactionary leader, **5**, 512.
disapproves of the oppression of the Jews in the Hanse Towns, **5**, 514.
accepts Humboldt's constitution as a basis for discussion, **5**, 514.

Metternich (*continued*), carelessness of, **5**, 519–20.
the Jews of Austria under, **5**, 523.
on the emancipation of the Jews, **5**, 527.
intolerant of Jews, **5**, 579.
intervention of, in the Damascus affair, **5**, 646, 647.
writes to Mehmet Ali, **5**, 647.
thanked by the London meeting, **5**, 653.
thanked by the Jews of Alexandria, **5**, 660.
Meturgeman, the, duty of, in the Synhedrion, **2**, 361.
office of, in the time of the Amoraim, **2**, 541.
employed by Samuel ben Ali, **3**, 438.
Metz, rabbis of, Poles, **5**, 17.
the Royal Society of, offers a prize on the Jewish question, **5**, 434–5.
the Talmud school of, closed, **5**, 567.
a rabbinical college at, **5**, 700.
Metz, the Jews of, privileges of, renewed by Louis XIV, **5**, 174.
the blood accusation against, **5**, 174–5.
elect Eibeschütz rabbi, **5**, 251.
limited in number, **5**, 347–8.
income from, given away by Louis XIV, **5**, 348, 446.
restrictions against, **5**, 348–9.
number of, **5**, 435.
petition for the removal of oppressive taxes, **5**, 438.
relieved of taxes, **5**, 446.
hindered in the celebration of the Passover, **5**, 452.
suffering of, **5**, 452.
Metz, Moses. *See* **Ensheim, Moses.**
Metz, Moses, follower of Joseph Delmedigo, **5**, 77.
Meyer, a Jew of Breslau, charged with host desecration, **4**, 261.
Meyer, Edward, opponent of the Jews, **5**, 602.
Meyer, Peter, pastor in Frankfort, permits Pfefferkorn to preach, **4**, 449.
Meyerbeer, father of, **5**, 563.
composes songs for the Leipsic Reform service, **5**, 573.
Meyuchas, Mordecai Joseph, rabbi of Jerusalem, encourages opposition to Napoleon, **5**, 459.
Mezuzzoth, the use of, prohibited under Hadrian, **2**, 424.
Miasa. *See* Meïr.
Micah (I), prophet. *See* Michaiah.
Micah (II), prophet, prophecies of, **1**, 261–2.
encourages the people of Judah under Hezekiah, **1**, 273.
Michael, name of an angel, **1**, 403.
Michael of Frankfort, merchant, the ruin of, urged by Luther, **4**, 551.
Michael the Old, Karaite, permits lights on the Sabbath, **4**, 269.
Michael ben Kaleb, Jewish poet in Thebes, **3**, 426.
Michael Scotus, friend of Jacob Anatoli, **3**, 566.
translator of philosophical works, **3**, 567.
Michaelis, John David, professor at Göttingen, hostility of, to the Jews, **5**, 359–60.
criticised by Mendelssohn, **5**, 361.
on "Jerusalem," **5**, 365–6.
on "The Gatherer," **5**, 404.

Michaelis, John David (*continued*), on the Jews, **5**, 414.
refuted by Mirabeau, **5**, 433.
Michaelis, John Henry, exonerates the Alenu prayer, **5**, 191.
Michaiah, son of Gemariah, reports Baruch's reading of Jeremiah's scroll, **1**, 305.
Michaiah (Micah I), son of Imlah, prophet, hostile to Ahab, **1**, 205.
Michal, daughter of Saul, devoted to David, **1**, 98.
marries David, **1**, 100.
returns to David, **1**, 110.
rebukes David, **1**, 120.
Michlol, grammatical work by David Kimchi, **3**, 394.
Michmash, Philistine camp at, **1**, 86–8.
Jonathan Haphus invests the fortress of, **1**, 494.
Microcosmos, religio-philosophical work by Abu-Amr Joseph Ibn-Zadik, **3**, 314–15.
Middelburg, admission of Jews into, proposed, **4**, 663.
Middlesex, Lord, and Manasseh ben Israel, **5**, 33.
Middoth, the seven, of Hillel, for testing the oral Law, **2**, 98.
Midian, Moses in, **1**, 14.
Midianites, the, seduce the Israelites to idolatry, **1**, 28.
routed by Gideon, **1**, 61–3.
Midoth, Mishna of Rabbi Akiba, **2**, 354.
Midras, academy among the Arabian Jews, **3**, 59.
Midrash, method of deducing the oral Law from Scripture, **2**, 328, 329.
Midrash of Simon bar Yochaï. *See* Zohar, the.
Midrash Rabba, the, laid under the ban, **5**, 195.
"**Migdal Oz,**" Sabbataï Zevi's prison at Abydos, **5**, 148.
Migration, the, of the nations, **2**, 604–5.
Mikulski, de, Canon, favors the conversion of Frankists, **5**, 285.
arranges for a disputation between Frankists and Talmudists, **5**, 285.
Milan, the Jewish community in, under the Ostrogoths, **3**, 28.
refuge of the exiles from the Papal States, **4**, 592.
Milan, the Jews of, letter to, from Theodoric, **3**, 30.
appeal for permission to own the Talmud, **4**, 658.
Milan district, the, the Jews of, expelled, **4**, 660.
Milchamoth, work by Abraham Maimuni, **3**, 545.
Milchamoth Adonaï, work by Levi ben Gerson, **4**, 92.
Milcom, Baal of the Ammonites, **1**, 55.
worshiped on the Mount of Olives, **1**, 175.
Military service, Jews admitted to, **3**, 36, 293, 384, 592.
Military service, Jews excluded from, by Honorius, **2**, 617.
by Theodosius, **3**, 28.
under Clotaire II, **3**, 40.
in the Byzantine empire, **3**, 425.
Miller, John, describes the Hamburg Jews, **4**, 690.
objections of. to the Jews, **4**, 691.
attacks Judaism, **4**, 692.
Millionaires, Jewish, at Amsterdam, **5**, 205.
in Berlin, **5**, 397, 414.
Millo, the northern elevation of Jerusalem, **1**, 118.

Millo, the (*continued*), Solomon's palace in, **1**, 168.
Milo, papal legate, humbles Raymund VI of Toulouse, **3**, 501-2.
presides over the Council of Avignon, **3**, 503.
Milo, Joseph Nassi made duke of, **4**, 596.
Minæans (Minim), the, sectaries, **2**, 369.
the writings of, influence Elisha ben Abuya, **2**, 377.
influence of, on Judaism deprecated by Tarphon, **2**, 378.
term for informers, **2**, 379.
curse of, attributed to Gamaliel II, **2**, 379-80.
curse of, subject of a charge before Alfonso XI of Castile, **4**, 83.
Minden, Jews tolerated in, **4**, 686.
Minhagim, compiled by the Austrian school of rabbis, **4**, 134-5.
Minim. *See* Minæans, the.
Minna of Speyer, tortured during the second crusade, **3**, 352.
Minorca. *See* Magona.
Minorites, the. *See* Franciscans, the.
Minui. *See* Ordination.
Minyan Yavanim (Shetaroth), the Seleucidæan era, abolished, **4**, 394-5.
Miques, João. *See* Nassi, Joseph.
Mirabeau, count (1749-1791), sympathy of, enlisted for the Jews by Dohm, **5**, 366.
in intercourse with Henrietta Herz, **5**, 413.
on Prussia under Frederick William II, **5**, 419.
influenced by Mendelssohn, **5**, 432.
Mirabeau, count (*continued*), on the Jews, **5**, 432-3.
favors the emancipation of the Jews, **5**, 433-4, 441.
protests against a dominant religion, **5**, 439.
Miracles, the nature of, as explained in "The Guide of the Perplexed," **3**, 483, 523.
theory of, by Nachmani, **3**, 533.
Mirandola. *See* Pico di Mirandola.
Miriam, mother of Jesus, **2**, 148.
Miriam, prophetess, member of the tribe of Levi, **1**, 12.
Miriam of Peræa, suffering of, during the siege of Jerusalem, **2**, 306.
"Mirror for Admonition, A," anti-Jewish pamphlet by Ortuin de Graes, **4**, 425.
"Mirror of Morals, The," by Solomon Alami, quotation from, **4**, 154-5.
"Mirror of the Jews, The," anti-Jewish pamphlet by Hundt, **5**, 532.
Mises, Jehuda Löb, patron of Jewish students in Lemberg, **5**, 612.
exempt from excommunication, **5**, 614.
Mishlé Shualim, by Berachya ben Natronaï, **3**, 560.
Mishna, the, code of the oral Law, the first, **2**, 343, 354.
of Akiba, **2**, 354.
treatise of, on proselytes, **2**, 384.
of Meïr, **2**, 439-40.
completed by Judah I, **2**, 460.
divisions of, **2**, 460.
style of, **2**, 460.
authority of, **2**, 461, 462.
not committed to writing, **2**, 461, 608.

Mishna, the (*continued*), language of, **2**, 461–2.
history of the compilation of, **2**, 462.
supplements to, **2**, 470.
impresses a legal character upon Judaism, **2**, 471.
asserts the equivalence of all religious commands, **2**, 472.
reward and punishment according to, **2**, 472–3.
on the study of the Law, **2**, 473–4.
spirituality of, **2**, 474–5.
casuistry in, **2**, 475–6.
not hostile to Christianity, **2**, 476.
contains laws against intercourse with the heathen, **2**, 476–8.
permits the heathen to glean, **2**, 478.
completion of, ends the work of the Tanaites, **2**, 478.
study of, pursued by the Palestinian Amoraim, **2**, 489–90.
not of equal legal force throughout, **2**, 493.
expounded by Rabba bar Nachmani, **2**, 578.
as studied by Raba bar Joseph bar Chama, **2**, 590–1.
amplifications and explanations of, arranged by Ashi, **2**, 607–9. *See* Talmud, the.
translated into Arabic, **3**, 237.
explained by Maimonides, **3**, 451.
methodology of, by Gersonides, **4**, 392.
translated into Latin, **5**, 193.
See also Law, the oral; Talmud, the; Tanaites, the.
Mishna, the, commentary on, by Maimonides, **3**, 458–60, 492; **4**, 60.
by Abraham ben David, **3**, 399.
Mishna, the, commentary on (*continued*), by Lipmann Heller, **4**, 704.
by Obadiah di Bertinoro, **4**, 704.
Mishna, Acharona, Akiba's code, **2**, 354.
Mishna di Rabbi Judah, the final code, **2**, 461. *See* Mishna, the.
Mishna Rishona, the earliest code, **2**, 343, 354.
"Mishne Torah," the, religious code, by Maimonides, **3**, 466–72.
clears the maze of the Talmud, **3**, 466, 467, 468–9.
place given to philosophy in, **3**, 467–8.
language of, **3**, 469.
deviates occasionally from the Talmudic decisions, **3**, 469.
on Talmudical Judaism, **3**, 470.
helps to ossify Judaism, **3**, 470.
spread of, **3**, 471.
attacked by Talmudists, **3**, 472.
criticised by Abraham ben David, **3**, 490.
the basis of Moses of Coucy's work, **3**, 586.
adhered to in Spain, **4**, 86.
Turim based on, **4**, 88.
compared with Turim, **4**, 89.
superseded by Turim, **4**, 89–90.
Mishnic rules of interpretation used by Anan ben David, **3**, 131.
Misr, and Misr, New. *See* Cairo.
Mithnagdim, opponents of the Chassidim, **5**, 392.
Mithridates, king of Pergamus, aided by Antipater, **2**, 75.
Mithridates, king of Pontus, Pompey's campaign against, **2**, 62.
suicide of, **2**, 65.
Mixed marriages. *See* Intermarriages.

Mizpah, Samuel holds popular assemblies at, **1**, 78.
fortified by Asa, **1**, 191.
seat of Gedaliah, **1**, 320, 321.
sanctuary at, **1**, 321.
Gedaliah murdered at, **1**, 322.
the inhabitants of, taken captive, **1**, 322.
Judas Maccabæus exhorts his troops at, **1**, 467.
Mizpeh, mountain, description of, **1**, 45.
Mizrachi. *See* Elias Mizrachi.
Mizriczians, a branch of the Chassidim, **5**, 388.
"**Mizvoth**," a compendium of religious duties, by Abulsari Sahal ben Mazliach Kohen, **3**, 204.
Mnevis, white bull, worshiped by the Egyptians, **1**, 9.
Moabites, the, hostile to the Israelites in the desert, **1**, 28.
idolatry of, **1**, 55.
relations of, to the Israelites, **1**, 56–9.
routed by Ehud, **1**, 60–1.
subdued by David, **1**, 125–6.
attracted to Palestine under Solomon, **1**, 173.
regain independence, **1**, 185.
tributary to Omri, **1**, 194–5.
defeated by Jehoram and Jehoshaphat, **1**, 208–9.
conquered by Jeroboam II, **1**, 226.
urge revolt from Nebuchadnezzar upon Zedekiah, **1**, 300.
allies of Nebuchadnezzar, **1**, 314.
desirous of friendly relations with the Judæans, **1**, 362.
as proselytes, **2**, 343, 384.
Moabitis, invaded by Alexander Jannæus, **2**, 44.
Moawiyah, Ommiyyade Caliph, rival of Ali, **3**, 90.
tolerance of, **3**, 110.
Moawiyah, Ommiyyade Caliph (*continued*), patron of learning, **3**, 110.
Mocenigo, Luis, doge of Venice, proposes the expulsion of the Jews, **4**, 600–1.
banishes the Jews, **4**, 606.
Mocenigo, Pietro, doge of Venice, defends the Jews from the charge of child-murder, **4**, 299.
Mochinger, John, mystic, addresses Manasseh ben Israel, **5**, 24.
Mocho, John, Dominican, incites the mob against the Portuguese Marranos, **4**, 487.
Modena. *See* Leo ben Isaac Modena.
Modena, Jews beg for shelter in, **4**, 660.
Mordecai of Eisenstadt in, **5**, 209.
rabbi of, opposes the Reform movement, **5**, 571.
Modestus, Patriarch at Jerusalem, demands the annihilation of the Jews of Palestine, **3**, 22–3.
Modin, the home of the Maccabees, **1**, 459.
Hasmonæan family mausoleum at, **2**, 14.
Mohammed, sultan of Turkey, death of, **5**, 634.
Mohammed El-Telli, opponent of the Damascus Jews, **5**, 633.
employed as a spy by Ratti Menton, **5**, 635, 636, 637–8.
Moise. *See* Meïr.
Moisling, the Jews of, trade in Lübeck, **5**, 506.
move to Lübeck, **5**, 506.
Molcho, Solomon (Diogo Pires, 1501–1532), Marrano, royal secretary, Hebrew education of, **4**, 495.

Molcho, Solomon (*continued*), Messianic mysticism of, **4,** 495–6.
undergoes circumcision, **4,** 496, 499.
goes to Turkey, **4,** 496.
among the Kabbalists, **4,** 496–7.
longs for martyrdom, **4,** 497.
as a preacher, **4,** 497.
persecuted at Ancona, **4,** 501.
at Pesaro, **4,** 501.
appears in Rome in Messianic equipment, **4,** 502.
vision of, concerning Rome, **4,** 502.
in intercourse with Clement VII and Church dignitaries, **4,** 503.
preaches at Rome, **4,** 503–4.
announces an earthquake and a flood, **4,** 504.
goes to Venice, **4,** 504.
severs his relation with Reubeni, **4,** 504.
poisoned, **4,** 505.
influence of, against the Inquisition feared by Portugal, **4,** 506.
denounced by Jacob Mantin, **4,** 506–7.
sentenced to be burnt, **4,** 507.
saved by Clement VII, **4,** 507.
leaves Rome, **4,** 507.
petitions Charles V to permit the Marranos to arm themselves against the Turks, **4,** 509–10.
burnt at Mantua, **4,** 510–11.
personality of, **4,** 511.
enthusiasm for, **4,** 511–12.
influence of, in Palestine, **4,** 529–30.
influence of, on Joseph Karo, **4,** 537.
a prey to Kabbalistic influences, **5,** 233.

Mole, count, advises exceptional laws for the French Jews, **5,** 479.
report of, not kindly received by Napoleon's council, **5,** 479.
imperial commissioner to the Assembly of Jewish Notables, **5,** 485, 489.
announces Napoleon's satisfaction with the Notables, **5,** 492.
probably frames Napoleon's Jewish law, **5,** 498.

Moloch worship, under Manasseh, **1,** 283.
under Jehoiakim, **1,** 300.

Moloch Chammon, god of fire, altar to, in Samaria, **1,** 197.

Moncado, Abraham de, Marrano in Pernambuco, **4,** 693.

Moncalvo, French exiles settle in, **4,** 177.

Moncilla, the Jews of, attacked at the instigation of Pedro Olligoyen, **4,** 78.

Mongols (Tartars), the, devastate Jerusalem, **3,** 605–6.
of Hungary, crusade against, **3,** 614.
kingdom of, in Persia, **3,** 637–8.
of the Persian khanate, conspire against Saad-Addaula, **3,** 649.

"Moniteur," the, publishes a history of the Jews, **5,** 485–6.

Monobaz I, king of Adiabene, domestic relations of, **2,** 216.

Monobaz II, regent of Adiabene, circumcised, **2,** 217.
king, presents golden vessels to the Temple, **2,** 219.
relatives of, aid Judæa against Rome, **2,** 264.

Monopoli (Apulia), Isaac Abrabanel at, **4,** 384.

Monotheism, belief held by Abraham, **1**, 5.

Mons Judaicus, near Narbonne, **3**, 35.

Montalto, Elias. *See* Elias Montalto.

Montanists, the, persecuted by Leo the Isaurian, **3**, 122–3.

Montefiore, Judith, accompanies her husband to Egypt, **5**, 654.

Montefiore, Moses, acts in the Damascus affair, **5**, 645.
- appeal to, from Damascus, **5**, 651.
- sent to Egypt on the Damascus affair, **5**, 651–2, 653.
- dignity of, **5**, 653.
- sets out for Egypt, **5**, 654, 657–8.
- honors shown to, **5**, 658–9.
- supported by the English consul-general in Egypt, **5**, 659.
- audience of, with Mehmet Ali, **5**, 659.
- obtains a firman securing Turkish Jews against the blood accusation, **5**, 662.
- honors shown to, on his return from the East, **5**, 667, 668.
- obtains the removal of Tomaso's tombstone, **5**, 668.
- received by Louis Philippe, **5**, 668.
- congratulated by Queen Victoria, **5**, 669.
- acknowledgment of the services of, **5**, 669–72.
- celebration of the return of, in London, **5**, 670.

Montemar, marquis of, friend of Isaac Abrabanel, **4**, 338.

Montesquieu, denounces the barbarous treatment of the Jews, **5**, 336.

Montezinos, Antonio de (Aaron Levi), traveler, on the whereabouts of the Ten Tribes, **5**, 30.

Monte-Zion street, occupied by the Jews of Palma, **4**, 171.

Montiel, the battle of, Henry de Trastamare victorious at, **4**, 126.

Montpellier, the Council of, omits all mention of Jews, **3**, 508.
- the Inquisition at, **3**, 542.
- Maimonides' works burnt at, **3**, 543.
- Jewish physicians at, **3**, 582, 583.
- bigotry of Jewish scholars of, **4**, 27.
- synagogue of, sold, **4**, 48.

Montpellier, the Jews of, prosperous in the twelfth century, **3**, 395.
- learning of, **3**, 395.
- influenced to oppose the study of science, **4**, 29–30, 31–2.
- refuse support to Abba-Mari, **4**, 39, 40–1.
- forced to wear badges, **4**, 54.

Monzon, the Jews of, excommunicate the anti-Maimunists, **3**, 537.

Moore, Dorothea, student of Hebrew literature, **5**, 21.

Moravia, John of Capistrano in, **4**, 258.
- Polish fugitives in, **5**, 16.
- rabbis of, Poles, **5**, 17.
- the Sabbatian movement in, **5**, 150, 208, 228.
- exiles from Vienna settle in, **5**, 172.
- Jews under restrictions in, **5**, 523.
- rabbis of, oppose the Reform movement, **5**, 571.

Moravia (*continued*), rabbis of, protest against the Brunswick rabbinical conference, **5,** 682.
Moravia, the Jews of, suffer during the persecution instigated by Hartmann von Deggenburg, **4,** 98.
urged to emigrate to Turkey, **4,** 271.
submit questions to the Polish Talmudists, **4,** 639.
outbursts against, during the Austrian War of Succession, **5,** 251–2.
suspected of treason, **5,** 252.
banished, **5,** 252.
heavily taxed, **5,** 508.
Mordecai of Eisenstadt, Sabbatian, preaching of, **5,** 208.
gives himself out as the Messiah, **5,** 208–9.
in Italy and Poland, **5,** 209.
founds a Sabbatian sect, **5,** 212.
Mordecai ben Hillel, Talmudist, martyrdom of, **4,** 36.
Mordecai ben Joseph, of Avignon, obtains the abrogation of the law on Jew badges, **3,** 612.
imprisoned for refusing to wear the badge, **3,** 613.
Mordecai ben Nissan, writes on the history of Karaism, **4,** 183–4.
Mordecai Ibn-Alcharbiya. *See* Saad-Addaula.
Mordecai Jafa (1532–1612), supposed organizer of the Synod of the Four Countries, **4,** 645.
draws up a religious code, **4,** 645.
as rabbi in Poland, **4,** 645.
Mordecai Zemach ben Gershon (Soncin), appeals to Pius IV for the return of the Jews to Prague, **4,** 586–7.
Mordecai Zevi, father of Sabbataï, prosperous, **5,** 119–20.
interested in Messianic speculations, **5,** 120.
Morea, the, the Jews of, consider trading with Pesaro, **4,** 579.
Sabbataï Zevi in, **5,** 124.
Moreh, mountain, description of, **1,** 44.
Moréh Nebuchim. *See* "Guide of the Perplexed, The."
Morenu, ordination of rabbis, enforced in Germany, **4,** 134.
rabbi, title bestowed on Crémieux, **5,** 668.
Moriah, Mount, the Jebusites settle on, **1,** 114.
situated on the east side of Jerusalem, **1,** 115, 119.
David sacrifices on, **1,** 138.
site of the Temple, **1,** 162.
Morillo, Miguel, inquisitor appointed by Sixtus IV, **4,** 312, 314, 323.
censured by the pope, **4,** 318.
Moriscos, the original Jewish inhabitants of Palestine, **4,** 399.
"Morning Baptists," name given to the Essenes, **2,** 26.
Moro, Joseph (Philip), apostate, denounces the Talmud, **4,** 564.
employed by Paul IV to annoy the Jews, **4,** 581.
Morocco, taken by Abdulmumen, **3,** 358.
the Jews of, emigrate or accept Islam, **3,** 358–9.
embassy to, under Abraham Ibn-Alfachar, **3,** 385.
forced converts emigrate to, **4,** 179.
Spanish exiles in, **4,** 389–90.
fortunes of the Jews of, **5,** 168.

Morpurgo, Elijah, one of the Measfim, **5**, 402.

Mortara case, the, **5**, 701.

Morteira, Saul Levi (1596–1660), disciple of Elias Montalto, **4**, 673.
instructor in the Talmud Torah of Amsterdam, **4**, 681.
member of the first rabbinical college, **4**, 682.
mediocrity of, **4**, 682.
eulogizes Isaac de Castro-Tartas, **5**, 32.
relations of, to Manasseh ben Israel strained, **5**, 34.
imposes penance upon Uriel da Costa, **5**, 63.
teacher of Spinoza, **5**, 87, 88.
sits in judgment on Spinoza, **5**, 92.

"**Mosaic Law, The**," by John David Michaelis, **5**, 359.

"**Mosaic religion**," the, possibility of the development of, **5**, 675, 676.

Moselle district, the, the Jews of, during the first crusade, **3**, 300.

Moser, Moses, friend of Heine, informed of his conversion, **5**, 551.
advises against the publication of the "Rabbi of Bacharach," **5**, 552.
founder of the Society for Culture, **5**, 583.
staunchness of, **5**, 587–8.

Moses, legislator and prophet, member of the tribe of Levi, **1**, 12.
at the court of Pharaoh, **1**, 13.
opposes injustice, **1**, 13.
in Midian, **1**, 14.
met by Aaron on Horeb, **1**, 15.
the leader of Israel, **1**, 17.

Moses, legislator and prophet, (*continued*), orders the punishment of the idolatrous Israelites in the desert, **1**, 24.
teaches the Israelites, **1**, 25.
forms the Council of Elders, **1**, 25–6.
death of, **1**, 30–1.
characterization of, **1**, 30–1.
how regarded by the Essenes, **2**, 28.
synagogue in Egypt attributed to, **3**, 445.
prophetic faculty of, analyzed by Maimonides, **3**, 483–4.
prophetic character of, denied by the philosophers, **4**, 24.
the Sons of, Baruch Gad's reports about, **5**, 126.
characterized by Heine, **5**, 553–5.

Moses, rabbi of Saxony, accused of using human blood, **4**, 298.

Moses (Mesvi) of Baalbek, founder of a Karaite sect, **3**, 158.

Moses de Cavarite, sheriff of Béziers, **3**, 395.

Moses of Coucy (1200–1260), Tossafist, disciple of Judah Sir Leon, **3**, 409.
alienates the French rabbis from Solomon of Montpellier, **3**, 539.
exhorts the Jews of southern France and Spain, **3**, 545–6.
ritual and ethical sermons by, **3**, 546.
at the disputation with Donin, **3**, 576, 578.
Bible commentary by, **3**, 586.

Moses of Crete, a false Messiah, **2**, 610–11.

Moses de Leon. *See* Moses ben Shem Tob; Zohar, the.

Moses de Trani, disciple of Jacob Berab, rival of Joseph Karo, **4**, 540.
appealed to on the question of trade with Ancona, **4**, 580.
Moses of Trent, refuses to confess to ritual murder, **4**, 298.
Moses ben Asher, Massoret, corrects copies of the Bible, **3**, 207.
works of, criticised by Saadiah, **3**, 207.
Moses ben Chanoch, emissary from Sora, taken captive, **3**, 208.
wife of, drowned, **3**, 208–9.
ransomed by the Cordova Jews, **3**, 209.
reveals himself as a Talmudist, **3**, 209.
chosen as rabbinical chief by the Cordova community, **3**, 209.
founder of Judæo-Spanish culture, **3**, 215.
protected by Chasdaï Ibn-Shaprut, **3**, 228.
deference paid to, **3**, 228.
title of, **3**, 229.
functions of, **3**, 229.
death of, **3**, 229.
son of, **3**, 229–30.
Moses ben Chasdaï Taku (1250–1290), Talmudist and anti-Maimunist, **3**, 624–5, 626.
Moses ben Guthiel, head of the Speyer community, and forced converts, **3**, 306.
Moses ben Isaac Alashkar, Spanish exile at Tunis, **4**, 391.
Talmudist, Kabbalist, and Maimunist, **5**, 392.
flees to Egypt, **4**, 392, 393.
Moses ben Isaac (Gajo) da Rieti (1388–1451), physician and poet, versification of, **4**, 230–1.
Moses ben Isaac (Gajo) da Rieti (*continued*), poems by, in the Italian liturgy, **4**, 231.
mediocrity of, **5**, 112.
Moses ben Israel Isserles (1520–1572), Talmudist, ancestry and attainments of, **4**, 637.
commentator upon Karo's code, **4**, 637–8.
as an astronomer, **4**, 638.
as a philosopher, **4**, 638.
teacher of David Gans, **4**, 638.
authority of, **4**, 639.
disciples of, **4**, 639.
Talmudist, **5**, 4.
highest authority in Judaism in the seventeenth century, **5**, 51.
Moses ben Jehuda Cohen, excommunicates the Anti-Maimunists, **3**, 633.
Moses ben Joshua Narboni (Maëstro Vidal, 1300–1362), philosopher, **4**, 87, 93–5.
writes commentaries on Maimonides and Averroes, **4**, 94.
persecuted, **4**, 94, 103.
religious philosophy of, **4**, 94–5.
accused of heresy, **4**, 342.
Moses ben Kalonymos (787), scholar, brought by Charlemagne to Mayence, **3**, 143.
Moses ben Maimun (Abu-Amrun Musa ben Maimun Obaid Allah, Maimonides, 1135–1204), youth of, **3**, 447.
a fugitive from the Almohades, **3**, 447–8.
studies of, **3**, 448–9.
character of, **3**, 449–50.
purpose of, to expound Judaism, **3**, 450–1.
work of, on the Jewish calendar, **3**, 451.
explains the Mishna, **3**, 451.

Moses ben Maimun (*continued*),
emigrates to Fez, **3**, 451.
assumes Islam, **3**, 451.
defends the pseudo-Mahometan Jews, **3**, 454-6.
emigrates to Palestine, **3**, 456.
brother of, dies, **3**, 457.
as a physician, **3**, 458.
completes his Mishna commentary, **3**, 458; **4**, 704.
on the science of the Mishna, **3**, 458-9.
on tradition, **3**, 459.
on the Sayings of the Fathers, **3**, 459.
draws up a creed of thirteen articles, **3**, 459-60.
reputation of, spread abroad by his disciples, **3**, 460-1.
consoles the Yemen Jews for their forced conversion to Islam, **3**, 462-4.
as rabbi of Cairo, **3**, 465.
views of, on the Karaites, **3**, 465.
abolishes the silent prayer, **3**, 465-6.
completes the "Mishne-Torah," **3**, 466, 472.
physician to Saladin's court, **3**, 472-3.
as a medical writer, **3**, 473.
refuses to become Richard I's physician, **3**, 474.
accused and acquitted of apostasy from Islam, **3**, 474.
head of the Egyptian congregations, **3**, 474.
rescues the Yemen Jews from persecution, **3**, 474.
traduced by Samuel ben Ali, **3**, 475.
on the doctrine of resurrection, **3**, 475-6, 488.
correspondence of, with Samuel ben Ali, **3**, 476-7.
attacked by Mar-Sacharya, **3**, 477.

Moses ben Maimun (*continued*),
writes the "Guide of the Perplexed," **3**, 477-85.
philosophical work of, intended only for Jews, **3**, 486.
weakness of the philosophy of, **3**, 486-7.
reverence for, in southern France, **3**, 488-9.
illness of, **3**, 489.
attacked by Abraham ben David, **3**, 490.
advises Samuel Ibn-Tibbon on the translation of the "Guide of the Perplexed," **3**, 490-1.
activity of, **3**, 491.
describes the state of Talmud studies in the twelfth century, **3**, 492.
opinion held by, of the Jews of Provence, **3**, 492.
death of, **3**, 492.
mourning for, **3**, 492-3.
son of, **3**, 493.
epitaph of, **3**, 493.
effects of the death of, **3**, 494-5.
no successor to, **3**, 495-6.
philosophy of, non-Jewish, **3**, 522.
rationalism of, **3**, 523.
on the Agada, **3**, 523.
attacked by Meïr ben Todros Abulafia, **3**, 524-5.
attacked by Daniel ben Saadiah, **3**, 525-6.
reverence for, in the East, **3**, 526.
theories of, in France and Spain, **3**, 526-7.
vilified by Solomon of Montpellier, **3**, 528-9.
desires to bring Talmudic reasoning to a conclusion, **3**, 532-3.

Moses ben Maimun (*continued*),
system of, opposed by Nachmani, **3**, 533–4, 608.
works of, burnt in Montpellier, **3**, 543.
defended by his son, **3**, 545.
causes division in Judaism, **3**, 546–7.
grandson of, **3**, 620.
works of, used by Raymund Martin, **3**, 622.
reverence for, in France and Spain, **3**, 624.
denounced as a heretic by Moses Taku, **3**, 624.
agitation against, by Solomon Petit, **3**, 626–34.
philosophical writings of, influence the Italian Jews, **3**, 629–30.
works of, excommunicated by Accho Kabbalists, **3**, 631.
epitaph of, desecrated, **3**, 631.
defended by his grandson, **3**, 632–3.
censured by Todros Abulafia, **4**, 2.
the religious philosophy of, induces the allegorization of the Scriptures, **4**, 23.
works of, fall under the ban against science, **4**, 40.
admired by Yedaya Bedaresi, **4**, 43.
translation of the works of, for the Italian Jews, **4**, 60.
described as a Kabbalist, **4**, 74.
certain views of, opposed by Gersonides, **4**, 93.
admired by Narboni, **4**, 94.
authority of, questioned by Chasdaï Crescas, **4**, 146, 192.
Isaac ben Sheshet's view of, **4**, 147.
the Messianic belief formulated by, **4**, 149.

Moses ben Maimun (*continued*),
philosophy of, expounded by Profiat Duran, **4**, 191.
accused of heresy by Shem Tob ben Joseph, **4**, 197.
condemned by Kabbalists, **4**, 239.
system of, expounded by Elias del Medigo, **4**, 290.
defended by Moses ben Isaac Alashkar, **4**, 392.
synagogue reform by, nullified, **4**, 395.
philosophical writings of, condemned by Isaac Abrabanel, **4**, 479.
on the preparation for the Messianic time, **4**, 530.
on ordination in Palestine, **4**, 531.
writings of, studied by Polish Jews in the sixteenth century, **4**, 633.
studied by Spinoza, **5**, 88.
influence of, on Mendelssohn, **5**, 295.
deficient in historical sense, **5**, 302.
influence of, on Erter, **5**, 613.
philosophy of, explained by Munk, **5**, 655.
See also Anti-Maimunists, the; Guide of the Perplexed, the; Maimunists, the; Maimunist controversy, the; "Mishne-Torah."

Moses ben Nachman (Nachmani Gerundi, Ramban, Bonastruc de Porta, 1195–1270), devotion of, to the Talmud, **3**, 531–2.
Talmudical commentaries of, **3**, 532, 607–8.
opposition of, to Maimonides' Talmudic and philosophic views, **3**, 532–4.

Moses ben Nachman (*continued*),
inveighs against Abraham Ibn-Ezra, **3**, 534.
denounces Aristotle, **3**, 534.
not an opponent of philosophy, **3**, 534–5.
view of, on the Agada, **3**, 535, 599–600.
aided by the Kabbala, **3**, 535.
aids the anti-Maimunists, **3**, 536.
letter to, from Meïr Abulafia, **3**, 537–8.
proposes a reconciliation between Maimunists and their opponents, **3**, 539–40.
deplores Dominican interference in the Maimunist controversy, **3**, 544.
a Kabbalist, **3**, 556–7.
as an exegete, **3**, 562.
invited to enter into a disputation with Pablo Christiani, **3**, 598.
demands freedom of speech, **3**, 598.
suggests three topics for discussion, **3**, 599.
refutes the assertion that Jesus is the Messiah of the Talmud, **3**, 599.
characterizes the true Messiah, **3**, 600.
victorious over Pablo Christiani, **3**, 601.
refutes the doctrine of the Trinity, **3**, 601.
publishes a report of the Barcelona disputation, **3**, 603–4.
charged with blasphemy against Christianity, **3**, 603–4.
exiled, **3**, 604.
protected by the king against the Dominicans, **3**, 604–5.
goes to Jerusalem, **3**, 605.
grief of, over Jerusalem, **3**, 606–7.

Moses ben Nachman (*continued*),
transplants Jewish science to Palestine, **3**, 607.
disciples of, **3**, 607, 609, 626; **4**, 28.
in correspondence with Spain, **3**, 608.
death of, **3**, 608.
influence of, **3**, 609.
the discovery of the Zohar attributed to, **4**, 20.
commentary of, used by Aaron ben Joseph, **4**, 71.
introduces the Kabbala into Palestine, **4**, 75.
predicts the beginning of the Messianic period, **4**, 120.
ancestor of Solomon Duran, **4**, 238.
views of, endorsed by Isaac Abrabanel, **4**, 342.
exegesis of, praised by Reuchlin, **4**, 442.

Moses ben Samuel Ibn-G'ikatilia, Biblical exegesis of, **3**, 290, 393.

Moses ben Shem Tob (Moses de Leon, 1250–1305), Kabbalist, **4**, 3, 10–11.
character of, **4**, 11.
wanderings of, **4**, 11.
forgery by, **4**, 11–12.
attributes the Zohar to Simon ben Yochaï, **4**, 12–14.
on the Messiah, **4**, 18.
said to have obtained the Zohar through Nachmani, **4**, 20.
death of, **4**, 20.
wife of, reveals his forgery, **4**, 20–1.

Moses Ibn-Ezra (Abu-Harun, 1070–1139), poet, elegy by, on Alfassi, **3**, 310.
and Joseph Ibn-Sahal, **3**, 314.
parentage of, **3**, 318–19.
early history of, **3**, 319.

Moses Ibn-Ezra (*continued*), compared with Solomon Ibn-Gebirol, **3**, 319.
style of, **3**, 319–20.
song cycle by, **3**, 320.
liturgical poems by, **3**, 320.
on the poetic art, **3**, 320.
as a philosopher, **3**, 320.
contemporary fame of, **3**, 321.
elegy by, on his lady-love, **3**, 321.
tribute to, by Jehuda Halevi, **3**, 321.
friendship of, with Jehuda Halevi, **3**, 323.
and Abraham Ibn-Ezra, **3**, 367.

Moses Ibn-Tibbon (1250–1285), physician in Montpellier, **3**, 582.

Moses Ibn-Yachya, philanthropist, **4**, 609.

Moses Abudiel, prominent at the court of Alfonso XI of Castile, **4**, 84, 86.
institutes a fast, **4**, 85.

Moses Almosnino, scientist in Salonica, **4**, 405.
preacher, as historian of Turkey, **4**, 607–8.

Moses Bashyasi, Karaite, permits lights on the Sabbath, **4**, 269.

Moses Basula, elegy on, by Leo Modena, **5**, 65.

Moses Botarel, Kabbalist, announces himself as the Messiah, **4**, 197.

Moses Cohen de Tordesillas, Jewish champion at the disputation of Avila, **4**, 141.
debates with a disciple of Alfonso Burgensis, **4**, 141–2.

Moses Gerundensis. *See* Moses ben Nachman.

Moses Hamon. *See* Hamon, Moses.

Moses Iskafat Meles, opponent of science, **4**, 44–5.

Moses Kapsali (1420–1495), chief rabbi of Turkey, dignities and functions of, **4**, 268–9.
opinion of, on the study of the Talmud by Karaites, **4**, 270–1.
raises money for the relief of the Spanish exiles, **4**, 364.
death of, **4**, 402.

Moses Kimchi (1170–1190), grammarian and exegete, **3**, 393.
grammar of, printed by Justiniani, **4**, 474.

Moses Meïr Kamenker, Sabbatian, spreads Sabbatianism, **5**, 228–9.
doctrines of, **5**, 229.
regarded as the Messiah, **5**, 230.
sentence pronounced on, **5**, 230.

Moses Menz, Talmudist, in Posen, **4**, 294.

Moses Navarro, chief rabbi of Portugal, **4**, 173.

Moses Uri Halevi (1544–1620), advises the Portuguese Marranos to go to Amsterdam, **4**, 665.
teacher and rabbi of the Marranos, **4**, 665.
imprisoned, **4**, 666.
activity of, **4**, 671.

Moses Vital, sells Isaac Lurya's manuscripts, **5**, 53.

Moses Zacuto (1630–1697), Kabbalist, pupil of the Amsterdam Talmud Torah, **4**, 682.
mysticism of, **5**, 87–8.
encourages the Sabbatian movement in Venice, **5**, 138.
superstition of, **5**, 201–2.

Moses Weil. *See* Weil, Moses.

Moses Zarzel, physician to Henry III of Castile, Spanish poet, **4**, 190.

Moslems, disciples of Mahomet, **3**, 73. *See* Mahometans, the.

Mostarabi, the, the original Jewish community in Egypt, ruled by the Spanish exiles, **4**, 395.

Mosul (New Nineveh), the Jews of, in the twelfth century, **3**, 429–30.

ignorance of, **3**, 430.

invited by Alrui to join him, **3**, 431.

"Mourners of Zion," the, **1**, 338; **3**, 182, 362, 437.

Mourning, signs of, decreed under Hadrian, **2**, 400, 420.

Mourning customs, regulated by Gamaliel II, **2**, 404.

abolished in the time of Judah II, **2**, 484–5.

Mozarabs, the, Christians living among Mahometans, lose their identity, **3**, 215.

conspire against the Mahometans of Granada, **3**, 316.

Moznaim, grammatical work by Abraham Ibn-Ezra, **3**, 371.

Mucate, Jacob, Marrano in Pernambuco, **4**, 693.

Mucianus, Licinius, governor of Syria, under Nero, **2**, 284.

won over to Vespasian's side, **2**, 300.

Mujahid, prince of Denia, patron of Yizchaki, **3**, 273.

Muley Abu-Abdallah (Boabdil), last king of Granada, secret treaty of, with Ferdinand and Isabella, **4**, 345.

goes to Africa, **4**, 345.

Muley Arshid, sultan of Morocco, oppresses the Jews, **5**, 168.

Muley Ismail, sultan of Morocco, patron of the Jews, **5**, 168.

Müller, Adam, reactionary leader, **5**, 477.

representative of the romantic school, **5**, 516.

Müller, Johannes von, Swiss historian, on the emancipation of the Jews, **5**, 359.

assists in framing the Westphalian constitution, **5**, 500.

Mulot, Abbé, president of the Assembly of the Paris Commune, on the emancipation of the Jews, **5**, 443–4, 445.

Munich, the Jews of, charged with the blood accusation, **3**, 636–7.

perish during the Black Death persecutions, **4**, 110.

Munk, Solomon (1802–1867), scholar, accompanies Crémieux to Egypt, **5**, 658.

discovers Mehmet Ali's subterfuge, **5**, 660.

exhorts the Egyptian Jews to establish schools, **5**, 663.

establishes schools in Cairo, **5**, 664.

reconciles Karaites with Rabbanites, **5**, 664.

character and learning of, **5**, 664–5.

Arabic attainments of, **5**, 665.

blindness of, **5**, 665.

studies of, on the Jewish Middle Ages, **5**, 665–6.

Karaite studies of, **5**, 666.

scientific results of the Eastern trip of, **5**, 666.

on the Damascus affair, **5**, 671–2.

expounds Jewish religious philosophy, **5**, 699.

Münster, Sebastian, prosecutes Hebrew studies, **4**, 434.

translates Elias Levita's Hebrew grammar, **4**, 472.

Murad III, son of Selim II, becomes sultan, **3,** 627.
gives Joseph Nassi land near the Sea of Tiberias, **4,** 596.
confiscates Joseph Nassi's property, **4,** 628.
influence of Jewish women under, **4,** 629.
Murad el Fallat, Turkish servant of a Damascus Jew, tortured, **5,** 637, 638.
Murcia, embassy to, under Solomon Ibn-Farussal, **3,** 312.
the Jews of, taxed under Sancho, **3,** 617.
Murder, laws against, inviolate under all circumstances, **2,** 424.
Murex, a dye, **1,** 3.
Murviedro, the Jews of, spared in the persecution of 1391, **4,** 171.
Musa (Mesvi) of Akbara, founds a Karaite sect, **3,** 157.
Musaphia, Benjamin (Dionysius, 1616–1676), physician to Christian IV of Denmark, **4,** 692.
philologist and rabbi, **5,** 115.
unaffected by Spinoza's attack upon Judaism, **5,** 117.
Sabbatian, **5,** 139.
sends a letter of homage to Sabbataï Zevi, **5,** 155.
Musaphia, Benjamin (*continued*), clings to Sabbataï after his apostasy, **5,** 161.
Mushka, a Judghanite, tries to force rationalistic doctrines upon the Jews, **3,** 150.
Mustapha Pasha, deputy vizir, cross-examines Sabbataï Zevi, **5,** 147.
Sabbataï betrayed to, **5,** 153.
Mutafarrica, the, Turkish life guard, Joseph Nassi a member of, **4,** 595.
Mutazilists, (heretics), the, the theology of, **3,** 147.
method of, borrowed by Saadiah, **3,** 197.
teachings of, foster unbelief, **3,** 199.
Muza Ibn-Nosair, governor of Africa, aided by the Jews of Spain, **3,** 109.
Mylitta, Assyrian goddess of love, worshiped in Israel, **1,** 247.
image of, in the Temple under Manasseh, **1,** 282.
temple of, in Philistia, burnt, **1,** 287.
Mysticism, in Judaism, **3,** 152–4.
denounced by Haï Gaon, **3,** 251–2.
See Kabbala, the.
Mytilene, the Jews of, in the twelfth century, **3,** 424.

N

Naamah, first wife of Solomon, **1,** 161.
Naaman, Syrian general, confesses the God of Israel, **1,** 224.
Naar, Isaac, mystic, companion of Spinoza, **5,** 88.
induces Spinoza to betray his unbelief, **5,** 92.
Sabbatian, **5,** 139.
Naar, Isaac, mystic (*continued*), prepares to join Sabbataï Zevi, **5,** 150.
encourages the Sabbatian movement in Italy, **5,** 160.
Naarda. *See* Nahardea.
Naasites, a Gnostic sect, **2,** 375.
Nabathæans (Nabatæans), the, contributions levied on, by Hyrcanus, **1,** 437.

Nabathæans (Nabatæans), the (*continued*), dispossess the Idumæans, **1**, 474; **2**, 8.
friendly to the Hasmonæans, **1**, 491.
See also Aretas; Malich; Obeda.
Nabonad, a Babylonian noble, usurps the throne, **1**, 342.
permits native kings to rule Phœnicia, **1**, 342.
entreated to permit the return to Palestine, **1**, 342-3.
ally of Lydia and Egypt, **1**, 343.
persecutes the Judæans, **1**, 343-4.
indifferent about the war with Cyrus, **1**, 349.
Nabopolassar, of Babylon, independent of Assyria, **1**, 296.
puts an end to Assyria, **1**, 303.
Naboth, killed at the instigation of Jezebel, **1**, 202.
avenged, **1**, 211.
Nachman ben Isaac (280-356), Amora, principal of the Pumbeditha academy, **2**, 593.
Nachman ben Jacob (235-324), Amora, **2**, 545.
summons Judah ben Ezekiel to justify his conduct, **2**, 552.
haughtiness of, **2**, 554-5.
treats his slaves inhumanly, **2**, 555.
introduces the oath of purgation, **2**, 556.
establishes a school at Shekan-Zib, **2**, 557.
Nachman ben Samuel Levi, Frankist rabbi, **5**, 275.
Nachmani. *See* Moses ben Nachman.
Nachshon ben Zadok (881-889), Gaon of Sora, explains difficult Talmudical words, **3**, 179.
Nachshon ben Zadok (*continued*), discovers the key to the calendar, **3**, 179.
Nachum of Gimso, teacher of the Law, supplements Hillel's rules of interpretation, **2**, 330-1.
teacher of Akiba, **2**, 351.
Nachum the Mede, teacher of the Law at the fall of Jerusalem, **2**, 330.
Nadab, king of Israel, at war with the Philistines, **1**, 189.
death of, **1**, 189.
Nagid, title of Samuel Ibn-Nagrela, **3**, 259.
of Joseph Ibn-Nagrela, **3**, 274.
of Abu Mansur Samuel ben Chananya, **3**, 340.
See also Nassi.
Nagid (Reïs), chief of the Egyptian Jews, authority of, **3**, 443; **4**, 392.
functions and privileges of, **4**, 393-4.
office of, abolished, **4**, 394.
See also Nassi.
Nahardea, a district of Jewish Babylonia, **2**, 505.
Nahardea (city), treasure house in, for the half-Shekel contribution to the Temple, **2**, 53.
Judæan center for Mesopotamia, **2**, 202.
center for the study of the Law, **2**, 358.
boundary of Babylonia in the most limited sense, **2**, 504.
a Babylonian Jerusalem, **2**, 505.
destroyed by Odenathus, **2**, 527.
the Amoraim of, flee, **2**, 527-8.
homage paid at, to the Exilarchs, **2**, 607.

Nahardea, the academy of, beginning of, **2,** 498-9.
the principal of, **2,** 512.
eclipsed by that of Sora, **2,** 522.
re-opened, **2,** 606.
Nahardea, the academy of, principals of, list of:
Amemar,
Samuel,
Shila.
Nahar Malka, a canal in Babylonia, **2,** 507.
Naharowan, the Exilarch's income from, **3,** 96.
Nahar-Pakod, a Synhedrion established at, **2,** 443-4.
a district of Jewish Babylonia, **2,** 505.
Nahar-Samara, Ezra's supposed grave at, **3,** 441.
Nahash, king of Ammon, invades the territories of Gad and Manasseh, **1,** 80.
besieges Jabesh-Gilead, **1,** 89-90.
in friendly relations with David, **1,** 100.
death of, **1,** 126.
Nahavendi, Benjamin. *See* Benjamin ben Moses of Nahavend.
Najara, prince of, converted to Christianity, **3,** 56.
Najaran, in Yemen, inhabited by Christians, **3,** 64.
besieged by Zorah Yussuf, **3,** 65.
heavy tribute laid on, **3,** 65.
Christians of, driven away, **3,** 85.
Nancy, the Jews of, threatened with pillage, **5,** 440.
compelled to attend the National Temple, **5,** 451.
Naphtali (mountain), description of, **1,** 44.
Naphtali (town), returned to Ahab, **1,** 205.
Naphtali, the tribe of, acquires land in the north, **1,** 37.
members of, join Gideon, **1,** 62.
mountainous lands of, subjugated, **1,** 191.
descendants of, near Nishabur, **3,** 433.
Naples, Jews in, in the sixth century, **3,** 28.
Jewish printing house in, **4,** 289.
the Spanish exiles in, **4,** 358-61.
the plague in, **4,** 359-60.
conquered by Charles VIII of France, **4,** 360.
occupied by the French, **4,** 384.
the Inquisition established at, **4,** 385.
Samuel II Abrabanel at, **4,** 409, 410.
the Marranos of, threatened with the Inquisition, **4,** 543.
Naples, the Jews of, support Theodatus, **3,** 31-2.
defend the city, **3,** 32.
bravery of, described by Procopius, **3,** 32.
in the twelfth century, **3,** 422, 424.
wear Jew badges, **3,** 518; **4,** 258.
help the Spanish exiles, **4,** 359.
banishment of, opposed by Gonsalvo de Cordova, **4,** 385.
annihilated, **4,** 408.
leave the city, **4,** 543-4.
Napoleon Bonaparte, victories of, in the East, **5,** 459-60.
at the summit of his power, **5,** 474.
dislikes the Jews, **5,** 474, 476-7.
lays the Jewish question before his council, **5,** 479.

Napoleon Bonaparte (*continued*), opposes the Jews in his council, **5,** 480.
modifies his views on the Jews, **5,** 481.
conceives the idea of convening Jewish notables, **5,** 481–2.
expresses satisfaction with the Jewish Notables, **5,** 490, 492.
proposes the convening of a Synhedrion, **5,** 493.
unmindful of the Synhedrion, **5,** 496.
resolutions of the Synhedrion submitted to, **5,** 498.
Jewish legislation by, **5,** 498–9.
creates new states, **5,** 500.
the Russian campaign of, **5,** 510.
fall of, **5,** 510–11.
return of, from Elba, **5,** 518.
Napoleon III, emperor, protests in the Mortara case, **5,** 701.
Napoleonic wars, the, awaken a desire for culture in Galicia, **5,** 611, 612.
Naraga, canal near Nahardea, **2,** 505.
Narbata, the Judæans of Cæsarea flee to, **2,** 253.
Narboni. *See* Moses ben Joshua Narboni.
Narbonne (city), the Jews of, expelled by Wamba, **3,** 105.
Machir founds a Talmud school at, **3,** 143.
Talmud study in, encouraged by Nathan ben Isaac Kohen, **3,** 208.
the Talmud school of, **3,** 242.
Abraham Ibn-Ezra at, **3,** 374.
principal Jewish community of southern France in, **3,** 392.
home of the Kimchi family, **3,** 392.
Narbonne (city) (*continued*), the Jews of, excommunicate Solomon of Montpellier, **3,** 530.
the archbishop of, presides over the Council of Béziers, **3,** 581.
Narbonne, the Council of, forbids Psalm singing at Jewish funeral services, **3,** 47.
confirms the decrees of the Fourth Lateran Council, **3,** 518.
Narbonne (province), Jews in, in the sixth century, **3,** 35.
Narbonne (province), **the Jews of**, enjoy equality under the early Visigoths, **3,** 45.
punished for conspiring against Egica, **3,** 108.
the possessions of, presented to the Church, **3,** 175.
Narcissus, favorite of Claudius, opposes Agrippa II, **2,** 196.
Nares, a district of Jewish Babylonia, **2,** 505.
an academy founded in, **2,** 593.
Narol, the Jews of, massacred by the Cossacks, **5,** 11.
Nasas, Jewish family name in Palermo, **3,** 28.
synagogue erected by, razed, **3,** 33–4.
Nassi, the family of, traces descent from David, **3,** 43.
See Mendes, Diogo; Francisco; Gracia; and Nassi, Joseph; Reyna; Samuel.
Nassi, Joseph (João Miques), nephew of Gracia Mendesia, favorite of Maria of the Netherlands, **4,** 572.
reported to have fled to Venice, **4,** 573.
intercedes with the sultan for Gracia Mendesia, **4,** 574.

Nassi, Joseph (*continued*), brings Gracia Mendesia to Constantinople, **4**, 577.
marries Reyna Nassi, **4**, 577.
in favor with Sultan Solyman, **4**, 577, 594.
beneficence of, **4**, 577.
gives up the trade with Ancona, **4**, 579–80.
power of, **4**, 594.
partisan of Selim, **4**, 595.
member of the Mutafarrica, **4**, 595.
denounced by the European ambassadors, **4**, 595.
given a tract of land near the Sea of Tiberias, **4**, 596, 610.
antagonized by Mahomet Sokolli, **4**, 596.
made duke of Naxos, **4**, 596.
titles of, **4**, 596.
negotiates with Ferdinand I, **4**, 597.
seizes French merchant vessels, **4**, 597.
traduced by Daud, **4**, 598.
clears himself of the charges made by Daud, **4**, 599.
incites a war with Venice, **4**, 600.
appealed to, by European sovereigns, **4**, 601–2.
head of a Turkish party, **4**, 602.
hopes to found a Jewish state, **4**, 610–11.
rebuilds Tiberias, **4**, 610–11.
influence of, not permanent, **4**, 611.
supplanted by Mahomet Sokolli, **4**, 627.
death of, **4**, 627.
property of, confiscated, **4**, 628.

Nassi, Reyna, reported to have fled to Venice, **4**, 573.
the son of Moses Hamon sues for, **4**, 575.

Nassi, Reyna (*continued*), betrothed to Joseph Nassi, **4**, 577.
sets up a Hebrew printing press, **4**, 628.

Nassi, Samuel, nephew of Gracia Mendesia, **4**, 577.
moves to Constantinople, **4**, 581.

Nassi, the, of the Great Council, a Pharisee, **2**, 49.

Nassi, name of the intercalary month in a lunar leap year, **3**, 59.

Nassi, prince, title of the president of the Synhedrion, **2**, 334.
of Isaac Ibn-Albalia, **3**, 283.
of Jehuda Ibn-Ezra, **3**, 361.
(Reïs), of the chief rabbi of the Cairo Karaites, **3**, 444.
See also Nagid.

Nassir Mahomet (1299–1341), Mameluke sultan, the Jews of Palestine under, **4**, 73.

Naszi-Beth-Ab, the head of the oldest family of a tribe, **1**, 122.

Nathan, the house of, junior branch of the house of David, power of, **1**, 249.

Nathan, president of the school of Cordova, corrected by Moses ben Chanoch, **3**, 209, 217.

Nathan, prophet, and David, **1**, 113.
rebukes David, **1**, 132–3.
parable by, **1**, 133.
forbids David to build a temple, **1**, 150–1.
opposed to Adonijah, **1**, 153.
anoints Solomon, **1**, 153.

Nathan, sheriff of Béziers, **3**, 395.

Nathan, son-in-law of Abba-Areka, Exilarch, **2**, 544.

Nathan the Babylonian, vice-president of the Synhedrion at Usha, **2**, 434, 445.
teacher of the Law in Judæa, **2**, 442–3.
ambassador from Simon II, **2**, 443–4.
conspires against Simon II, **2**, 445.
proposed for the Patriarchate, **2**, 445.
expelled from the Synhedrion, **2**, 445.
at peace with Simon II, **2**, 446.
the last of the Tanaites, **2**, 462.

"**Nathan the Wise**," by Lessing, Mendelssohn the hero of, **5**, 323.
story and characters of, **5**, 323–5.
effect produced by, **5**, 326–7.

Nathan bar Assa, disciple of Joseph ben Chiya, **2**, 582.

Nathan ben Isaac Kohen, emissary from Sora, settles at Narbonne, **3**, 208.
founder of true Talmud study in Narbonne, **3**, 242.

Nathan ben Yechiel, of Rome, compiler of a Talmudic lexicon, **3**, 290, 421.

Nathan ben Yehudaï, titular Gaon of Sora, **3**, 192.

Nathan Benjamin Levi (Ghazati, 1644–1680), studies of, **5**, 130.
marriage of, **5**, 130.
follower of Sabbataï Zevi, **5**, 130–1.
professes to be Elijah, **5**, 131.
Messianic speculations of, **5**, 131–2.
proclaims Gaza the Holy City, **5**, 132.
spreads abroad the Messiah's fame, **5**, 137.

Nathan Benjamin Levi (*continued*), addresses circulars to Amsterdam and Hamburg, **5**, 138–9.
continues to proclaim Sabbataï as the Messiah after his apostasy, **5**, 157.
excommunicated, **5**, 157, 159.
joins Sabbataï Zevi at Adrianople, **5**, 158–9.
in Salonica, the Greek Islands, and Italy, **5**, 160, 161.
death of, **5**, 161–2.

Nathan Nata, father of Jonathan Eibeschütz, **5**, 246.

Nathaniel (Abul Barkat Hibat-Allah ben Malka), physician in Bagdad, apostate, **3**, 442.
writes a commentary on Ecclesiastes, **3**, 442.

Nathaniel (Hibat-Allah Ibn-Aljami), physician, Nagid of the Egyptian Jews, **3**, 443.

Nathaniel Ibn-Almali, physician, translator of Maimonides' Mishna commentary, **4**, 60.

National Assembly, the Batavian, Jews keep aloof from, **5**, 454.
petitioned to emancipate the Jews, **5**, 455.
deputies to, oppose the emancipation of the Jews, **5**, 455–6.
establishes the emancipation of the Jews, **5**, 456.
Jewish deputies to, **5**, 458.
agrees to protect Dutch Jews in Germany, **5**, 458.

National Assembly, the French, champions of the Jews in, **5**, 435.
deputies to, instructed to attack the Jews, **5**, 436.
addressed on the subject of outrages upon Jews, **5**, 437.
Jewish deputies to, **5**, 438.

National Assembly, the French (*continued*), religious freedom discussed in, **5,** 439.
the Jewish question before, **5,** 439–441.
passes an equivocal resolution on the Jewish question, **5,** 442.
action of, objected to by the Bordeaux Jews, **5,** 442.
the emancipation of the Paris Jews demanded of, **5,** 445.
discusses finances, **5,** 446.
emancipates the Jews of France, **5,** 448.
National Guard, the French, joined by Jews, **5,** 438.
Jewish members of, petition the Paris Commune, **5,** 443.
Natkes, Galician scholar, excommunicated, **5,** 614.
style of, **5,** 617.
Natronaï ben Chabibaï, pretender to the Exilarchate, **3,** 137.
Natronaï ben Nehemiah (Mar-Yanka, 719–730), principal of the Pumbeditha academy, on Serene's adherents, **3,** 121-2.
Natronaï II, son of Hillaï (859–869), Gaon of Sora, corresponds in Arabic, **3,** 178.
opposes the Karaites, **3,** 178.
Naturalization Act, the, for the Jews of England, **5,** 337–8.
Navarre, the Spanish exiles in, **4,** 352, 357–8.
Navarre, the Jews of, in the twelfth century, **3,** 384.
take part in the Maimunist controversy, **3,** 536.
letter to, denouncing Solomon of Montpellier, **3,** 544.
hated in the fourteenth century, **4,** 76.
Navarre, the Jews of (*continued*), feeling against, aroused by Pedro Olligoyen, **4,** 77–8.
under Philip III, **4,** 78.
settle in Aragon, **4,** 142.
Navigation, pursued by the Burgundian Jews, **3,** 35.
by the Jews of Tyre, **3,** 426.
Naxos, to be given to Joseph Nassi, **4,** 596.
Joseph Nassi made duke of, **4,** 596.
as a Jewish state, **4,** 611.
Nazarenes, the, a sect of the early Christians, **2,** 168, 370.
take advantage of the leaning towards Judaism, **2,** 219.
increased by Essenes and Greek Judæans, **2,** 219.
persecuted by Paul, **2,** 222.
proselytize the Judæans in the Greek cities, **2,** 222.
in Antioch and Damascus, **2,** 222–3.
joined by Paul, **2,** 226.
displeased with Paul, **2,** 230.
separate wholly from the Jews, **2,** 371–2.
revile Judaism, **2,** 371–2.
disappearance of, **2,** 373.
merged into the Catholic Church, **2,** 500.
imprecation of, in the Jewish prayer book, **4,** 83.
See also Jewish Christians, the; Judæan Christians, the.
Nazareth, birthplace of Jesus, **2,** 148, 149.
Jesus successful in, **2,** 153.
first church at, **2,** 565.
inhabited by Jews in the sixth century, **3,** 12.
the Jews of, join Sharbarza, **3,** 19.
Nazarite practices, under Simon the Just, **1,** 422.

Neander, Augustus, church historian, declares the groundlessness of the blood accusation, **5**, 650.

Neapolis. *See* Shechem.

Neapolitanus, deputy of Cestius Gallus in Jerusalem, **2**, 257.

Nebuchadnezzar, king of Babylonia, beginning of the career of, **1**, 303–4.
Jehoiakim the vassal of, **1**, 306.
besieges Tyre, **1**, 306, 307.
ravages Judah, **1**, 306.
takes Judah, **1**, 307.
generals of, besiege Jerusalem, **1**, 307.
banishes Jehoiakim, **1**, 307.
makes Zedekiah king, **1**, 308.
subdues Judah, **1**, 311.
besieges Jerusalem, **1**, 311–14.
defeats Apries, **1**, 313.
generals of, take Jerusalem, **1**, 313–14.
beheads the dignitaries of Jerusalem at Riblah, **1**, 314.
blinds and exiles Zedekiah, **1**, 315.
appoints Gedaliah over the Palestinian Judæans, **1**, 319.
punishes the murder of Gedaliah, **1**, 325.
treats the Babylonian Judæans kindly, **1**, 329–30.
death of, **1**, 331.

Nebuzaradan, chief of Nebuchadnezzar's guard, charged to destroy Jerusalem, **1**, 315.
entrusts Zedekiah's daughters to Gedaliah, **1**, 319.
exiles the last remnant of Judah, **1**, 325.

Necho, king of Egypt, defeats Josiah, **1**, 296–7.
makes Jehoiakim king, **1**, 299.
exacts tribute from Judah, **1**, 299.

Nechunya, abettor of Chananya at Nahar-Pakod, **2**, 443, 444.

Nechunya ben Hakana, teacher of the Law, adherent of Hillel's methods, **2**, 331.
reputed author of a Kabbalistic manuscript, **3**, 556.

Neglib-Eddin, supposed assassin of Mongols, **3**, 649.

Negro. *See* Ibn-Yachya.

Negropont, the Jews of, in the twelfth century, **3**, 424.
the Spanish exiles in, **4**, 406.

Nehemiah, cup-bearer of Artaxerxes, appealed to by the Judæans, **1**, 372.
national enthusiasm of, **1**, 373.
governor of Judæa, **1**, 373.
journeys to Jerusalem, **1**, 374.
rebuilds the fortifications of Jerusalem, **1**, 374-5.
disturbed by Sanballat and Tobiah, **1**, 375–6.
rebukes the Judæans for the enslavement of the poor, **1**, 376–7.
unselfishness of, **1**, 377.
invites settlers to Jerusalem, **1**, 377–8.
exacts observance of the Law from the Judæans, **1**, 380–1.
consecrates the walls of Jerusalem, **1**, 381–2.
internal improvements by, **1**, 382–3.
returns to Persia, **1**, 383.
returns to Jerusalem, **1**, 385.
reforms the Judæan community, **1**, 385–8.
memoir of, **1**, 387–8.
formation of a Jewish sect under, **1**, 387.

Nehemiah, disciple of Akiba, returns to Judæa, **2**, 433.

Nehemiah (960–968), Gaon of Pumbeditha, position of, contested, **3**, 208.

Nehemiah, grandson of Abba-Areka, Exilarch, **2**, 544.
Nehemiah, teacher of the Law in Beth-Deli, **2**, 358.
Nehemiah Ashkafa, a Granada Jew, supports Balkim, **3**, 258.
Nehushta, mother of Jehoiachin, opposes Nebuchadnezzar, **1**, 306.
exiled, **1**, 307.
Neidhard, inquisitor-general, **5**, 169.
Neïth, queen of heaven, worshiped in Judæa, **1**, 300.
worshiped by Judæans in Egypt, **1**, 326–7.
Nekelo, chamberlain of the Duke of Austria, **3**, 567.
Nemirov, the Jews of, massacred by the Cossacks, **5**, 8–9.
the massacre of, commemorated, **5**, 13.
Neo-Hebraic poetry, the rise of, under Arabic influences, **3**, 112-13.
subjects of, **3**, 113.
liturgical character of, **3**, 113.
form subservient to the subject-matter in, **3**, 115.
rhyme introduced into, **3**, 116.
suffers by the Maimunist controversy, **3**, 558–9.
the decay of, **3**, 560.
in the Persian khanate, **3**, 648.
as developed by Immanuel Romi, **4**, 63–4, 65, 67.
in Spain in the fifteenth century, **4**, 230, 231.
in Italy, **4**, 230–1.
See also Poetry; Hebrew literature.
Neo-Persians, the, described by Levi bar Sissi, **2**, 525.
campaign of Gallus against, **2**, 568.
Neo-Persians, the (*continued*). *See also* Sassanides, the; Magi, the.
Neo-Platonism, as presented by Jehuda Halevi, **3**, 328.
identified with the Kabbala, **5**, 54.
Neo-Platonist view, a, of the book of Daniel, **2**, 502.
Nepi, Graziadio (1760–1836), deputy to the Assembly of Jewish Notables, **5**, 488.
Nergal-Sharezer, son of Sennacherib, murders him, **1**, 280.
Neriglissar murders Evil-merodach, **1**, 331.
death of, **1**, 342.
Nero, emperor, favorably inclined to the Herodians, **2**, 245–6.
deprives the Judæans of Cæsarea of civil rights, **2**, 247.
kindly inclined to the Judæans, **2**, 248.
informed of the turbulent state of Judæa, **2**, 250–1.
informed of the number of Judæans, **2**, 252.
allegiance to, renounced by the Judæans, **2**, 259.
loyalty of Judæans defended before, **2**, 268.
apprised of the Judæan revolt, **2**, 284.
appoints Vespasian general in Judæa, **2**, 284.
death of, **2**, 297, 299.
kindly disposed towards the Jews, **2**, 391–2.
coins of, **2**, 392.
successor of, **2**, 393.
Meïr said to be the descendant of, **2**, 435.
Nesselrode, Russian plenipotentiary, and the emancipation of the Jews, **5**, 527.

Netherlands, the, rebellion of, against Spain, **4,** 601.
united with Spain, **4,** 661.
the Inquisition in, **4,** 662.
refuge of the Portuguese Marranos, **4,** 662–3.
thwart Philip II's plans, **4,** 667–8.
second large emigration of Marranos to, **4,** 671.
settlement of the Jewish quarter in, **4,** 674.

Netherlands, the, the Jews of, suffering of, **4,** 661.
expelled by Charles V, **4,** 661–2.
intolerant treatment of, **4,** 673–4.

Nethinim, Temple slaves, live together in Babylon, **1,** 330.

Netira, the sons of, espouse Saadiah's cause, **3,** 195.

Neto, Bras, Portuguese ambassador at Rome, and the establishment of the Inquisition, **4,** 500, 505.
Molcho announces the Lisbon earthquake to, **4,** 504.
honors Molcho, **4,** 505.
fears Molcho's influence against the Inquisition, **4,** 506.
refuses to countenance the denunciation of Molcho, **4,** 506.

Netter, Charles, founder of the "Alliance Israélite Universelle," **5,** 701.

Neuburg, the Jews of, charged with the blood accusation, **4,** 545–6.

Neumann, Andrew, invites Jewish exiles to settle in Brandenburg, **5,** 173.

Neus, a city of refuge for Cologne Jews, **3,** 304.

Neuwied, the Jews of, present an address to the French Synhedrion, **5,** 496.

Neve, teachers of the Law in, permit leavened bread on Passover for the Roman army, **2,** 568.

Neve Shalom, second Jewish synagogue in Amsterdam, **4,** 671.

Nevers, count, threatened by Innocent III, for favoring the Jews, **3,** 500.

New Christians, the. *See* Marranos, the.

New Moon, the, announcement of, **2,** 362–3.
two days celebrated as, **2,** 363.
announced at Ain-tab, **2,** 458.
announced in Tiberias, **2,** 480.
as determined by Judah III, **2,** 532.
observance of, renewed by Anan ben David, **3,** 131.

New Nineveh. *See* Mosul.

Newport, early Jewish immigrants in, **5,** 702.

New Testament, the, relation of, to the Old, examined by Chasdaï Crescas, **4,** 188.
translated into German, **4,** 475.

New Year's day, celebrated two days in Palestine, **3,** 428.

New York, early Jewish immigrants in, **5,** 702.

Nibridius, bishop of Narbonne, letter to, concerning the Jews, **3,** 166–7.

Nicanor, gate of, entrance to the second Temple, **2,** 111.

Nicanor, son of Patroclus, Syrian general, **1,** 467.

Nicanor, Syrian general, sent to Judæa by Demetrius I, **1,** 484.

Nicanor, Syrian general (*continued*), sends envoys to Judas Maccabæus, **1**, 484.
admires Judas Maccabæus, **1**, 484.
defeated, **1**, 484.
demands the surrender of Judas Maccabæus, **1**, 484–5.
killed in battle, **1**, 485.
Nicaso, daughter of Sanballat, married to a Jew, **1**, 383, 386.
Nice, Jews invited to settle in, **4**, 675.
Nice, the Council of, completes the separation of Judaism and Christianity, **2**, 563–4.
incorporates apocryphal books in the Holy Canon, **2**, 624.
intolerance of, **3**, 25.
Nicholas. *See* Donin.
Nicholas III, pope, reproaches Alfonso X for employing Jews, **3**, 594, 615.
Nicholas V, pope, issues anti-Jewish bulls, **4**, 253, 254.
establishes the Inquisition for Marranos, **4**, 256.
orders the Marranos to be treated as equals, **4**, 256–7.
appoints John of Capistrano inquisitor of the Jews, **4**, 257, 258.
preaches a crusade against the Turks, **4**, 267–8.
bull of, against Jewish physicians unheeded, **4**, 287.
Nicholas I, of Russia, on the Damascus affair, **5**, 633, 657.
Nicholas, interpreter sent by Constantine VIII to Abdul-Rahman III, **3**, 218.
Nicholas de Cusa, scholastic philosopher, advocates a union of all religions, **4**, 255.
action of, in the Jewish question, **4**, 255.
Nicholas de Lyra, Franciscan, praises Rashi, **4**, 185.
charges of, against the Jews renewed, **4**, 232.
charges of, refuted by Chayim Ibn-Musa, **4**, 237.
exegetical works by, used by Isaac Abrabanel, **4**, 342.
exegesis of, dependent on Rashi's, **4**, 442.
Nicholas, Edward, secretary to Parliament, apologist for the Jews, **5**, 28–9.
Nicodemus, envoy of Aristobulus II to Pompey, **2**, 63.
Nicolai, friend of Mendelssohn, **5**, 300.
proposes to erect a statue to Mendelssohn, **5**, 372.
Nicolaus of Damascus, historian, friend of Herod, **2**, 90.
accuses Antipater of attempted parricide, **2**, 114.
brother of, **2**, 119.
friendly to the Judæans, **2**, 179.
Nicopolis, the Spanish exiles in, **4**, 405.
Joseph Karo at, **4**, 537.
Nicosia, taken by the Turks, **4**, 600.
Nidui. *See* Excommunication.
Niemerz, son of Casimir III, **4**, 112.
Nieto, David (1654–1728), rabbi of London, culture of, **5**, 200.
denounces Chayon, **5**, 227.
Niger, emperor, cruelty of, to the Jews, **2**, 463–4.
defeated by Severus, **2**, 464.
Niger, a Judæan hero in the Roman rebellion, **2**, 264.
executed, **2**, 296.
Nikolsburg, the Sabbatian movement in, **5**, 150.
rabbis of, Poles, **5**, 206.

Nikolsburg (*continued*), Chayon at, **5**, 218.
the rabbi of, opposes the Reform movement, **5**, 571.
Nile, the harbors of, under the control of the Judæan Alabarch, **2**, 102.
Nilus the Younger, refuses to be treated by a Jewish physician, **3**, 213–14.
"Nineteen Letters on Judaism," by Ben Usiel, **5**, 627.
Nineveh, Israelites colonized in, **1**, 265.
besieged by Cyaxares, **1**, 287.
fall of, **1**, 303.
Nishabur. *See* Khorasan.
Nisibis, treasure house in, for the half-Shekel contribution to the Temple, **2**, 53.
Judæan center for Mesopotamia, **2**, 202.
destroyed by Lucius Quietus, **2**, 298.
center for the study of the Law, **2**, 358.
the Jews of, oppose Trajan, **2**, 393.
the Christians of, persecuted by the Magi, **2**, 524.
Nîsmes, the Jews of, show honor to the Jewish envoys to Egypt, **5**, 658.
Nissim bar Jacob Ibn-Shahin (1015–1055), Talmudic authority of northern Africa, **3**, 248.
busies himself with the Jerusalem Talmud, **3**, 249.
consults Haï Gaon, **3**, 252.
son-in-law of, **3**, 274.
disciple of, **3**, 285.
Nissim Gerundi ben Reuben (1340–1380), Talmudist, opposed to Messianic speculations, **4**, 120.
attainments of, **4**, 144.
Nissim Gerundi ben Reuben (*continued*), disciple of, **4**, 146.
appealed to by Isaac ben Sheshet, **4**, 148.
death of, **4**, 149.
imprisonment of, **4**, 150.
Nissi Naharvani, effects a reconciliation between Kohen-Zedek and David ben Zaccaï, **3**, 186.
consulted upon the appointment of a Gaon of Sora, **3**, 192–3.
Nitra (mountain), the monks of, stone the prefect of Alexandria, **2**, 619.
Nizuz, divine spark, Kabbalistic term, **4**, 620.
Nizuzoth, the original soul, **5**, 120.
Nob, made a sacerdotal town, **1**, 79.
Noel, French ambassador to the Batavian Republic, and the emancipation of the Jews, **5**, 456.
interferes in the internal affairs of the Amsterdam Jewish community, **5**, 457.
Nófeth Zufim, Hebrew rhetoric by Judah ben Yechiel, **4**, 289.
Nomologia, by Immanuel Aboab, **5**, 55.
Nomology, Jewish, first developed by Hillel, **2**, 327.
Norden, Jews tolerated in, **4**, 686.
Nördlingen, the Jews of, murdered, **4**, 163.
banished, **4**, 416.
Normandy, rabbis of, at the first rabbinical synod, **3**, 377.
the Jews of, under Henry II, **3**, 409.

Northampton, the Jews of, charged with the blood accusation, **3,** 643.
Northmen, the, invade France, **3,** 172.
Norwich, the Jews of, massacre of, **3,** 412.
Notables, Jewish, the **Assembly** of, planned by Napoleon, **5,** 481–2.
deputies to, **5,** 482–4.
to hold its first session on a Sabbath, **5,** 484.
imperial commissioners to, **5,** 485.
deputies to, hold a caucus, **5,** 486.
first meeting of, **5,** 487.
president of, **5,** 487.
Italian deputies to, **5,** 488.
questions propounded to, **5,** 489.
appoints a commission to answer the questions, **5,** 489.
parliamentary tact of, appreciated by Napoleon, **5,** 490, 492.
discusses the report of the commission, **5,** 491–2.
answers of, to be made Synhedrial decisions, **5,** 493.
approves of the Synhedrion, **5,** 493.
members of, to become members of the Synhedrion, **5,** 493.
proclamation of, concerning the Synhedrion, **5,** 494.
dissolution of, **5,** 495.
re-convened, **5,** 498.
Notaricon, transposition of letters, Kabbalistic term, **4,** 5, 512.
Novak, Peter, bishop of Breslau, invites John of Capistrano to Silesia, **4,** 260.
Novi, refuge of Marranos, **4,** 553–4.
Nubia, Christians of, at war with the Jews of Aden, **3,** 436.
Numenius, delegate to Rome sent by Simon Tharsi, **1,** 526.
Numeo, character in Samuel Usque's work, **4,** 558, 560, 575.
Nunes, Henrique (Firme-Fé), apostate, spies upon the Portuguese Marranos, **4,** 489–90.
accuses the Marranos, **4,** 490.
murdered, **4,** 490.
Nuñes, Maria, Portuguese Marrano, taken to England, **4,** 664.
goes to Holland, **4,** 664.
in Holland, **4,** 667.
Nuñez, Alvar, removed from office by Alfonso XI, of Castile, **4,** 79.
Nureddin, Turkish chieftain, attacks the Christian kingdom of Jerusalem, **3,** 349.
makes Aleppo the second capital of the Eastern caliphate, **3,** 426.
power of, **3,** 431.
adherents of, at war with Saladin, **3,** 472.
Nuremberg, a refuge for the Jews, **3,** 351.
diet of, issues the "Golden Bull," **4,** 128.
rabbinical synod at, **4,** 305.
honor shown to Crémieux at, **5,** 668.
Nuremberg, the Jews of, massacred during the Rindfleisch persecutions, **4,** 36.
perish during the Black Death persecutions, **4,** 110.
charges against, **4,** 415.
banished, **4,** 415–16.
Nurses. *See* Christian nurses.

O

Oath, required of Jewish witnesses by Charlemagne, **3**, 144.
Jewish form of, **4**, 159.
concerning the blood accusation, **5**, 49, 655.
"on the true faith of a Christian" abolished, **5**, 698.
Oath of allegiance, to Herod, opposition to, **2**, 108.
Oath of purgation, introduced by Nachman ben Jacob, **2**, 556.
Obadiah, king of the Chazars, has his people taught Judaism, **3**, 140.
successors of, **3**, 141.
Obadiah, palace superintendent under Ahab, protects the prophets, **1**, 201.
Obadiah, prophet, prophesies against Edom, **1**, 326.
Obadiah (Obadya) di Bertinoro (1470–1520), rabbi of Jerusalem, improves Jerusalem morally, **4**, 397, 399.
characterization of, **4**, 398.
ordinances by, **4**, 398.
Mishna commentary by, **4**, 704.
Obadiah (Servadeus) de Sforno (1470–1550), physician and writer, **4**, 411.
Reuchlin's teacher, **4**, 434, 473.
Obaiah Abu-Isa ben Ishak, precursor of the Messiah, **3**, 124.
peculiar system of Judaism taught by, **3**, 124–5.
leader of a rebellion, **3**, 125.
adherents of, **3**, 125.
Obeda, Nabathæan king, opposes Alexander Jannæus, **2**, 44.
Oberwesel, the Jews of, murdered, **3**, 637.
murderers of, fined, **3**, 639.
"**Observations** of an Alsatian upon the Present Quarrels of the Jews of Alsace," **5**, 350.
Ocaña, the Jews of, persecuted, **4**, 170.
the cortes of, demand anti-Jewish legislation, **4**, 279.
O'Connell, urges the emancipation of the English Jews, **5**, 653.
on the Damascus affair, **5**, 657.
Octavius, Caius. *See* Augustus.
Octavius, Cneius, Roman ambassador to Syria, **1**, 481.
death of, **1**, 482.
Odenathus, predatory incursions of, **2**, 527.
destroys Nahardea, **2**, 527.
takes Mar-Samuel's daughters prisoners, **2**, 528.
prince of Palmyra, **2**, 528.
wife of, **2**, 529.
Odo, bishop of Paris, forbids Christians to have intercourse with Jews, **3**, 407.
Odo, legate of Innocent IV, enemy of the Talmud, **3**, 579.
Odura, the family of, in the Hellenist party, **1**, 489.
Offices. *See under* Civil; Magisterial; Religious.
Og, king of Bashan, **1**, 29.
Ojeda, Alfonso de, urges the Inquisition for Marranos, **4**, 310.
commissioner to frame the Inquisition statute, **4**, 312.
preaches the sermon at the first auto-da-fé, **4**, 317.
Okaz, fair of the Arabs at, **3**, 60.
Olam ha-Ba, the future world, **1**, 405-6.
Olam ha-Tikkun, divine order of the world, Kabbalistic term, **4**, 619; **5**, 121, 142.

Old Testament, the, connected with the New, **2**, 488.
Christian doctrines found in, **2**, 499, 501, 502; **4**, 141–2.
contrasted with the New, **4**, 540–1.
system of, adopted by an English political party, **4**, 541–2.
slandered, **4**, 547.
inspires the Puritans, **5**, 26, 27.
See Scriptures, the.
Oldenburg, Heinrich, on the Sabbatian movement, **5**, 139.
Olesnicki, Zbigniev, bishop of Cracow, hostile to the Jews, **4**, 265.
invites Capistrano into Poland, **4**, 265.
induces the king to revoke the privileges of the Jews, **4**, 266.
Olianow, Elijah, follower of Luzzatto, **5**, 245.
testifies in favor of Eibeschütz, **5**, 262.
Olivença, the Marranos of, burnt, **5**, 499.
Oliver y Fullana, Nicolas de (Daniel Jehuda), cartographer, **5**, 113.
wife of, **5**, 114.
unaffected by Spinoza's attack upon Judaism, **5**, 117.
Olives (Olivet), Mount of, description of, **1**, 45, 115.
David on, on his flight from Jerusalem, **1**, 141.
altars raised on, to idols, **1**, 175.
camp of the Tenth Legion on, **2**, 303.
fire-signals on, **2**, 362.
Nachmani on, **3**, 606–7.
Olligoyen, Pedro, arouses the hatred of the Navarrese against the Jews, **4**, 77.
imprisoned, **4**, 78.
Olmutz, the Jews of, banished at the instigation of Capistrano, **4**, 263.
Jews under restrictions in, **5**, 523.
Olympian games, the, introduced into Palestine and Phœnicia, **1**, 445.
celebrated at Tyre, **1**, 446.
Omar I, second Caliph, repulsed at Kamus, **3**, 82.
drives away the Jews of Chaibar, **3**, 85.
takes Jerusalem, **3**, 87.
covenant of, **3**, 87–8.
rewards the Jews of Babylonia, **3**, 89.
death of, **3**, 90.
anti-Jewish enactments of, revived, **3**, 120, 145, 176–7, 247.
Omar II (717–720), caliph, reenacts the anti-Jewish laws of Omar I, **3**, 120.
Ommiyyah, the caliphate of, extent of, **3**, 100.
Ommiyyades, the, tolerance of, **3**, 110.
overthrow of, in the East, **3**, 125.
prosperity of, **3**, 214.
overthrown by civil wars, **3**, 255.
Omri, chosen king of Israel, **1**, 192.
war of, with Tibni, **1**, 192.
removes to Samaria, **1**, 193.
character of, **1**, 193.
friendly relations of, with Judah, **1**, 194.
allied with Phœnicia, **1**, 194.
wars of, **1**, 194–5.
introduces Phœnician idolatry, **1**, 195–6.
"On the Errors of the Trinity," by Michael Servetus, **4**, 646.
"On the Speedy Glory of Judah and Israel," by Henry Jesse, **5**, 35.

Onias (Menelaus), the Benjamite. *See* Menelaus.

Onias I, high priest, does homage to Alexander the Great, **1**, 413.

Onias II, high priest, son of Simon the Just, minority of, **1**, 423.
 partisan of Seleucus II Callinicos, **1**, 423.
 authorizes Joseph to treat with Ptolemy II, **1**, 424.

Onias III, high priest, head of the Chassidim, enemies of, **1**, 437.
 allied with Hyrcanus, son of Joseph, **1**, 437.
 banishes Hellenists, **1**, 438.
 refuses to surrender the Temple treasures, **1**, 438.
 appeals to Seleucus II against the Hellenists, **1**, 438–9.
 accused of partisanship with the Ptolemies, **1**, 444.
 murdered, **1**, 448.
 son of, **1**, 504, 505.

Onias IV, son of Onias III, kindly received by Ptolemy Philometor, **1**, 506.
 commander of Ptolemy VI's troops, **1**, 506, 507.
 builds a Temple at Leontopolis, **1**, 508–10.
 fortifies his Temple, **1**, 510.
 offices and titles of, **1**, 510.
 receives a province, **1**, 519.
 assists Cleopatra, **1**, 519.
 informed of the independence of Judæa, **1**, 522–3.
 sons of, **2**, 10, 12, 40–1.

Onias, a pious man, killed by the soldiers of Hyrcanus II, **2**, 60–1.

Onias, the Temple of, origin of, **1**, 508–10.
 closed, **2**, 318.

Onias, the Temple of (*continued*), effect of closing, on the Alexandrian Judæans, **2**, 322.

Onion, a district of Heliopolis, containing the Temple of Onias, **1**, 508.

Onkelos. *See* Targum Onkelos.

Ophel, offshoot from Mount Moriah, **1**, 115.
 outside of Jerusalem, **1**, 119.

Ophir (Scinde, India), Solomon sends his fleet to, **1**, 171.
 trade with, under Uzziah, **1**, 230.
 under the jurisdiction of the Sora academy, **3**, 98.

Ophites, a Gnostic sect, **2**, 375.

Ophla, a quarter of Jerusalem, **2**, 219.
 retreat of Menahem, the leader of the Sicarii, **2**, 261.
 burnt by Titus, **2**, 308.

Ophrah, seat of Baal worship, **1**, 62.
 center for pilgrims, **1**, 63.

Oporto, Isaac Aboab dies at, **4**, 366.
 port open to the exiled Portuguese Jews, **4**, 374.

Oppenheim, painting by, presented to Riesser, **5**, 601.

Oppenheim, David, chief rabbi of Prague, library of, **5**, 217.
 opposes the Eibeschütz edition of the Talmud, **5**, 251.

Oppenheim, Joseph, patron of Chayon, **5**, 217.

Oppenheim, Samuel, settles in Vienna, **5**, 189.
 Christians assault the house of, **5**, 189–90.
 obtains the suppression of "Judaism Unmasked," **5**, 190.
 supports the Chassidim, **5**, 213.
 heir of, **5**, 217.

Oppenheim, the Jews of, emigrate to Syria, **3,** 637.
during the Black Death persecutions, **4,** 109.
Oppenheimer, Amshel, creditor of Rudolph of Habsburg, **3,** 634.
Orabuena, Joseph. *See* Joseph Orabuena.
Oral Law. *See* Law, the oral.
Oran, a refuge for persecuted Spanish Jews, **4,** 197.
suffering of the Spanish exiles in, **4,** 361.
the Jews of, banished, **5,** 169.
Ordenaçoens de Alfonso V, Portuguese code containing anti-Jewish ordinances, **4,** 338, 339.
"Order of Tradition, The," historical work by Abraham Ibn-Daud, **3,** 366.
Ordinances of Usha, **2,** 405.
Ordination (Semichah), meaning of, **2,** 356.
by the teachers of the Law, **2,** 361.
forbidden by Hadrian, **2,** 426.
of Akiba's disciples, **2,** 429.
by Moses ben Chanoch, **3,** 229.
necessity for re-introducing, **4,** 530, 535.
efforts to revive, made by Jacob Berab, **4,** 531.
revival of, antagonized, **4,** 534–5.
abandoned, **4,** 536.
Orenstein, Jacob, excommunicates young Galician scholars, **5,** 614.
compelled to withdraw his ban, **5,** 614.
satirized by Erter, **5,** 615.
Orestes, prefect of Alexandria, stoned, **2,** 619.
Oria, Talmudical scholars in, **3,** 212.
Oria (*continued*), plundered by the Mahometans, **3,** 212.
Orient, the, German-Jewish journal, **5,** 693.
Origen, Church Father, protected by Mammæa, **2,** 481.
consults Hillel II, **2,** 487.
learns Hebrew, **2,** 488.
taught Bible exegesis by the Jews, **2,** 488.
attempts the revision of the Septuagint, **2,** 488–9.
discussion of, with Simlaï, **2,** 501–2.
Original Sin, dogma of, expounded by Astruc Raimuch, **4,** 182.
refuted by Solomon Bonfed, **4,** 182.
attacked by Chasdaï Crescas, **4,** 187.
criticised by Joseph Ibn-Shem Tob, **4,** 235.
found in the Kabbala, **4,** 292.
Organ, the, in Jewish divine service, **5,** 569, 571.
Orleans, Jews in, in the sixth century, **3,** 35.
councils of, pass anti-Jewish decrees, **3,** 37.
the college of, sold, **4,** 48.
Ormuzd. *See* Ahura-Mazda.
Ornah, the Jebusite, offers Moriah to David, **1,** 138.
Orpheus, in Judæo-Greek writings, **2,** 204.
Orthodox party, the, opposes the efforts of the Mendelssohnians, **5,** 417.
opposed by the "Society of Friends," **5,** 418.
in Berlin complains of the Reform movement, **5,** 563.
not a well defined party, **5,** 566.
without leaders, **5,** 567–8.

Orthodox party, the (*continued*),
inactivity of, **5,** 569–70, 571.
formulates its objections to the Hamburg innovations, **5,** 571.
scourged by Bresselau, **5,** 572.
denies the justification of Reform, **5,** 627.
fails to support Bernays, **5,** 673–4.
protests against the Brunswick rabbinical conference, **5,** 682.
represented at the Frankfort rabbinical conference, **5,** 684.

Osius, bishop of Cordova, forbids Christians to trade with Jews, **2,** 620.
presides over the Council of Illiberis, **3,** 44.

Osorio, David, forms a third congregation in Amsterdam, **4,** 680.

Osorius, bishop, on King Manoel's relation to the Jews, **4,** 372.

Osorkon. *See* Zerah.

Ostrog, the Jews of, slaughtered by the Cossacks, **5,** 12.

Ostrogoths, the, empire of, founded, **3,** 27.
hated in Italy, **3,** 32.

Othman, the third Caliph, killed, **3,** 90.

Othniel, Caleb's brother, takes Kiryath-Sepher, **1,** 38.

Othniel, judge, delivers the southern tribes from the Idumæans, **1,** 60.

Otho, emperor, struggle of, with Vitellius, **2,** 299.

Otranto, the Jews of, in the twelfth century, **3,** 424.

Otto I, emperor, offended by Abdul-Rahman III, **3,** 219.
grants the revenue derived from Jews to a church, **3,** 243.
attended by an Italian Jew, **3,** 243.

Otto II, emperor, presents the Jews of Merseburg to the bishop, **3,** 243.

Ottolenghi, Joseph, Talmudist, opens a school at Cremona, **4,** 582.

Ottos, the, emperors, rule of, not favorable to the Jews, **3,** 243.

Ouderkerk, burial ground of the Dutch Jews at, **4,** 672.

Ouvidor, Jewish-Portuguese judge, **4,** 159.

Oxford, the Council of, anti-Jewish decrees of, **3,** 516.

Oxford, the University of, pays honor to Samuel ben Israel, **5,** 38.
the library of, Jews said to intend to buy, **5,** 45.

Ozaïr, Arabic name for Ezra, **3,** 76.

P

Paalzow, opposes the emancipation of the Jews, **5,** 468, 472.

Pablo Christiani, apostate, tries to convert Jews, **3,** 597–8.
enters into a disputation with Nachmani, **3,** 598.

Pablo Christiani (*continued*),
proves Jesus the Messiah of the Talmud, **3,** 599.
defeated by Nachmani, **3,** 601.
sent on missionary journeys, **3,** 602.
denounces the Talmud, **3,** 602.

Pablo Christiani (*continued*), authorized to exercise censorship over the Talmud, **3**, 603.
charges Nachmani with blasphemy of Christianity, **3**, 603-4.
induces Louis IX to insist upon the Jew badge, **3**, 612.
policy of, adopted by the Council of Basle, **4**, 246.

Pachda, brother-in-law of Mar-Zutra II, Exilarch during his minority, **3**, 3.

Pacheco, marquis of Villena, adviser of Henry IV of Castile, kindles a civil war, **4**, 278.
instigates an assault upon the Marranos, **4**, 283.

Pacorus, prince of the Parthians, makes Antigonus king of Judæa, **2**, 82-3.

Padua, lawyers from, attacked by an anti-Jewish mob in Trent, **4**, 299.
exiled Jews settle in, **4**, 408.
Italian center of Talmudic studies, **4**, 410.
the Talmud burnt in, **4**, 565.
Jews beg for shelter in, **4**, 660.
the rabbi of, opposes the Reform movement, **5**, 571.
a rabbinical college at, **5**, 624, 700.

Padua, the Jews of, protected, **4**, 299.
threatened with excommunication, **5**, 238.
abandon Luzzatto, **5**, 241.

Padua, the University of, appoints Elias del Medigo umpire, **4**, 291.
Elias del Medigo lectures at, **4**, 291.
Joseph Delmedigo at, **5**, 75.

Pagan Christians, the, **2**, 365, 366.

Pagan Christians, the (*continued*), differences between, and Jewish Christians, **2**, 367.
chief seat of, **2**, 367.
views of, in the evangels, **2**, 369.
submission of, to the Romans, **2**, 369.
absorb the Jewish Christians, **2**, 373.

Paganism, conversions to, in Alexandria, **2**, 184.
as viewed by the Judæans, **2**, 204.
futility of, set forth by Judæo-Greek writers, **2**, 205-8.
combated by Philo, **2**, 213, 214-15.
disintegration of, **2**, 373.
in the view of the Gnostics, **2**, 377.
influenced by Judaism, **2**, 382-3.
conversions from, to Judaism, **2**, 383-5.
Tacitus on the conversions from, **2**, 384.
attempt to graft, on Judaism, **2**, 422.
end of, **2**, 559.
See also Heathen, the.

Pahath-Moab, the family of, forms a league in Babylon, **1**, 330.

Pakotia, Sabbatians in, **5**, 272.

Palæologus family, the, dynasty of the Byzantine empire, **4**, 267.

Palæstina Secunda, capital of, **3**, 12.

Palermo, the Jews in, in the sixth century, **3**, 28.
Jewish captives transported to, **3**, 213.
the Jews of, in the twelfth century, **3**, 424.
a Ghetto established at, **3**, 567.

Palermo (*continued*), Abraham Abulafia in, **4**, 7–8.

Palestine, name for Canaan, **1**, 1.
regarded as the Holy Land, **1**, 41–2.
physical features of, **1**, 42–8.
products of, **1**, 46–8.
climate of, **1**, 45, 47–8.
picturesqueness of, **1**, 48–9.
land of the Philistines, **1**, 55.
colonization of, after the captivity, **1**, 355–6.
Joseph the governor of, **1**, 425.
the Olympian games introduced into, **1**, 445.
the Greek inhabitants of, rejoice over the death of Agrippa I, **2**, 196.
Lucius Quietus governor of, **2**, 399.
laws hostile to, promulgated by Severus, **2**, 464.
depredations in, by Odenathus, **2**, 527.
the schools of, in good repute with Babylonians, **2**, 531.
poverty of, **2**, 535.
Babylonian Jews emigrate to, **3**, 4.
succumbs to the Arabs, **3**, 86.
subordinates itself to Jewish Babylonia, **3**, 100.
Anan ben David settles in, **3**, 130.
mystical doctrines flourish in, **3**, 154.
part of the Fatimide Caliphate, **3**, 248, 249.
as viewed by Jehuda Halevi, **3**, 336–7.
longed for by Jehuda Halevi, **3**, 338.
under Christian rule, **3**, 341.
Abraham Ibn-Ezra in, **3**, 369.
visited by Petachya, **3**, 421.

Palestine (*continued*), Yechiel of Paris emigrates to, **3**, 587.
Karaites of, inclined to Rabbanism, **4**, 72.
accessible to Jews, under the Egyptian Sultans, **4**, 73.
emigration to, **4**, 74.
Karaites of, use a calendar of their own, **4**, 270.
emigration of Jews to, forbidden by the pope, **4**, 273–4.
Spanish spoken in, by the exiles, **4**, 387.
the Spanish exiles in, **4**, 396–9.
Marranos in, **4**, 529–30.
influence of the Kabbala in, in the sixteenth century, **4**, 617.
the mountains of, in Rëuel Jesurun's religious poem, **4**, 678–9.
the Kabbala in, **5**, 52.
Napoleon in, **5**, 459.
wrested from Turkey, **5**, 633.
the Christians of, under French protection, **5**, 634.
hope of the return to, given up by the "Friends of Reform," **5**, 675, 676.
See also Canaan; Judæa, etc.

Palestine, the Jews of, persecuted by Verus Commodus, **2**, 447.
deprived of their own courts of justice, **2**, 447.
injured by Odenathus, **2**, 527.
oppressed by Ursicinus, **2**, 568–9.
burdened with taxes, **2**, 569.
revolt against Rome under Constantius, **2**, 569–70.
sober Bible exegesis of, **2**, 624–5.
condition of, in the sixth century, **3**, 10–13.
educational system of, **3**, 12.

Palestine, the Jews of (*continued*), enjoy religious liberty until Justinian, **3**, 12.
under Justinian I, **3**, 13-17.
fined for celebrating the Passover before Easter, **3**, 13.
oppressed by Stephanus, **3**, 16.
aid the Samaritans in an anti-Christian riot, **3**, 17.
under Justin II, Tiberius, and Mauritius, **3**, 17-18.
join Sharbarza, **3**, 19.
destroy Christian sanctuaries, **3**, 19-20.
banished to Persia, **3**, 21.
allied with Heraclius, **3**, 21-2.
extirpation of, asked by Modestus, **3**, 22.
persecuted by Heraclius, **3**, 22-3.
help the Arabs, **3**, 87.
persecuted under the sons of Haroun Alrashid, **3**, 145.
influenced by European immigrants, **3**, 427-8.
ritual of, changed by Maimonides, **3**, 466.
participate in the Maimunist controversy, **3**, 624, 626, 631-3.
occupations of, **4**, 74-5.
"**Palingénesie**," by Caspar Bonnet, **5**, 314.
Pallache, Samuel, consul, tries to have Portuguese Marranos received into Zealand, **4**, 663.
zeal of, **4**, 665.
Pallas, favorite of Claudius, opposes Agrippa II, **2**, 196.
brother of, **2**, 242, 245.
Pallas, wife of Herod, **2**, 119.
Palm Sunday. *See* Eastertide.
Palma, Marrano fugitives in, ask for Gibraltar, **4**, 282-3.
Palma, the Jews of, persecuted, **4**, 171.
Palma, the Jews of (*continued*), charged with the blood accusation, **4**, 246.
flee, **4**, 247.
converted, **4**, 247.
Palmerston, English minister, appealed to in the Damascus affair, **5**, 645.
promises to check the cruelties in the East, **5**, 645-6.
on the Damascus affair, **5**, 652.
supports Montefiore, **5**, 659.
congratulates Montefiore, **5**, 669.
Palmyra (Tadmor), proselytes from, discussed, **2**, 384.
kingdom of, **2**, 528-30.
the Jews of, in the twelfth century, **3**, 426.
Paloma, Spanish exile, drowns herself to escape disgrace, **4**, 362.
Paltoi ben Abayi (842-858), Gaon of Pumbeditha, noted for frequent use of excommunication, **3**, 177.
Pamier, the Jews of, under the protection of the Count de Foix, **4**, 176.
Pampeluna, the Jews of, escape massacre, **4**, 78.
a religious disputation at, **4**, 142.
Panegyric, the favorite subject of Jewish Andalusian poetry, **3**, 224.
Panias, given to Philip by Herod's will, **2**, 119.
given to Agrippa II by Claudius, **2**, 245.
Diocletian summons Judah III to, **2**, 533.
Panion, Scopas defeated near **1**, 433.
Pantæus, Church Father, critical spirit of **2**, 488.

Papa bar Chanan (300–375), Amora, founds an academy at Nares, **2,** 593–4.
confused discourses of, **2,** 594.
method of, **2,** 594.
Papa bar Nazar, Jewish name of Odenathus, **2,** 527.
Papa, Aaron de la, rabbi of Smyrna, banished by the Sabbatians, **5,** 136, 144.
Papacy, the, ascendancy of, affects the position of the Jews, **3,** 494.
power of, established, **3,** 503.
viciousness of, at Avignon, **4,** 162.
attacked by Huss, **4,** 221–2.
efforts to re-establish the supremacy of, **4,** 562.
See also Bulls; Popes, the.
Papal States, the, Ferrara incorporated into, **4,** 660.
Papal States, the, the Jews of, taxed for the benefit of the catechumens, **4,** 566.
shut up in Ghettos, **4,** 566.
restrictions against, **4,** 566–7.
annoyed by apostates, **4,** 581.
persecuted by Pius V, **4,** 590.
expelled by Pius V, **4,** 591–2.
under Sixtus V, **4,** 655–6.
expelled by Clement VIII, **4,** 659.
received in Pisa, **4,** 659.
Pappos ben Judah, teacher of the Law, in prison with Akiba, **2,** 428.
Pappus, leader of the rebellion against Trajan in Judæa, **2,** 395.
life of, threatened, **2,** 401.
Paradise, the belief in, introduced into Judaism, **1,** 404.
Paran, table-land of, **1,** 45.
Parchi. *See* Estori.
Parchon. *See* Solomon ben Abraham.
Pardes, a book of morals, by Yedaya Penini, **4,** 43.
Pardo, David, rabbi of the third Amsterdam synagogue, **4,** 680.
member of the first Amsterdam rabbinical college, **4,** 682.
mediocrity of, **4,** 682.
Pardo, Joseph, rabbi of the Amsterdam Marranos, **4,** 671.
indulgent towards the weaknesses of the Amsterdam Jews, **4,** 680.
threatens Uriel da Costa with excommunication, **5,** 58.
Pardo, Josiah, rabbi of Rotterdam, **4,** 685.
Paris, Jews in, in the sixth century, **3,** 35.
half of, owned by Jews in the twelfth century, **3,** 343.
the rabbi of, at the first rabbinical synod, **3,** 377.
Maimonides' works burnt at, **3,** 543.
a seat of Talmud study, **3,** 575.
the Talmud burnt at, **3,** 579.
receives Crémieux coolly, **5,** 668.
Paris, the Commune of, discusses the emancipation of the Jews, **5,** 443–5.
requests the emancipation of the Paris Jews of the National Assembly, **5,** 445.
Paris, the Council of (615), forbids the Jews to hold magisterial power or enter military service, **3,** 40.
(846), summoned by Charles the Bald, **3,** 172.
forbids the employment of Christian midwives by Jews, **3,** 508.

Paris, the Jews of, attacked by a mob, **4,** 150–1.
attacked by the Maillotins, **4,** 152.
prosecuted for the disappearance of an apostate, **4,** 175.
number of, **5,** 435.
in the National Guard, **5,** 438.
send deputies to the National Assembly, **5,** 438.
commended by the Carmelite district, **5,** 444–5.
emancipation of, demanded by the Paris Commune, **5,** 445.
compelled to worship in the Temple of Reason, **5,** 452.
excepted from Napoleon's restrictive laws, **5,** 499.

Paris, the Talmudical college of, closed, **3,** 403.
sold, **4,** 48.
re-established, **4,** 133.

Paris, the University of, directed to banish philosophical writings from its curriculum, **3,** 528.
appealed to by Hoogstraten, **4,** 458.
appealed to by the Dominicans, **4,** 459–60.
gives judgment against Reuchlin, **4,** 460, 473.
satirized in the "Letters of Obscurantists," **4,** 461.
teaches and prints Hebrew, **4,** 473.

Parliament, three petitions to, in favor of the re-settlement of Jews in England, **5,** 35.
admission of Jews to, **5,** 698.
See also House of Commons, the.

Parliament, the Jewish, summoned by Henry III, **3,** 589–90.

Parliament, the Long, and the cause of religious liberty, **5,** 25.
the dissolution of, **5,** 34.

Parliament, the Short, the convening of, **5,** 34.
the Jewish character of, **5,** 34.
entertains the re-settlement of the Jews in England, **5,** 34.
the dissolution of, **5,** 35.

Parnesé ha-Keneset, the commission entrusted with public interests in Jewish Babylonia, **3,** 99.

Paro, Joseph Nassi duke of, **4,** 596.

Parosh, the family of, forms a league in Babylon, **1,** 330.

Parsophin (Parzufin), Kabbalistic term, **4,** 619; **5,** 217.

Parthia, the number of Judæans in, **2,** 202.
the Jewish communities of, in sympathy with the Zealots, **2,** 256.
conquered by Trajan, **2,** 393.
the Jews of, resist Trajan, **2,** 393–4.
escapes being made a Roman province, **2,** 399.
rebels against Trajan, **2,** 399.
war of, with the Romans, **2,** 447.
laid waste by Severus, **2,** 464.
the dynasty of, overthrown, **2,** 523.

Parthians, the, defeat the Syrians, **2,** 5.
defeated by Antiochus Sidetes, **2,** 5.
the campaign of Crassus against, **2,** 74.
dethrone Hyrcanus, **2,** 82–3.
characterized by Levi bar Sissi, **2,** 525.
invade the Roman empire, **2,** 527.

Parties, in Judæa after the death of Judas Maccabæus, **1,** 489–90.
Paruta, disciple of Michael Servetus in Poland, **4,** 647.
Parzufin. *See* Parsophin.
Pascal, pope, convenes a Church Council in France, **3,** 376.
Paschal lamb, the, offered at Jerusalem by order of Hezekiah, **1,** 268.
a substitute for, introduced in Rome, **2,** 68.
Paschal sacrifice, the, supersedes the Sabbath, **2,** 99.
Pasquier, imperial commissioner to the Assembly of Jewish Notables, **5,** 485.
Passau, the Jews of, charged with host desecration, **4,** 306.
Passion Week. *See* Eastertide.
Passover, celebrated under Hezekiah, **1,** 268.
celebrated under Josiah, **1,** 295.
under Zerubbabel, **1,** 359.
in the Sopheric age, **1,** 398.
the celebration of, forbidden by Archelaus, **2,** 121–2.
of the Crushing in 66, **2,** 251.
the celebration of, before Easter forbidden by Justinian I, **3,** 13.
observed by the Marranos of Lisbon, **4,** 489.
as celebrated by Sabbataï Zevi, **5,** 148–9.
the celebration of, hindered during the Reign of Terror, **5,** 452.
Pastor, a Galician scholar, excommunicated, **5,** 614.
Pastor, a lawyer of Naples, opposes the progress of Belisarius, **3,** 32.
murdered, **3,** 32.
"**Pastor Fido,**" translated by Isabel Correa, **5,** 114.
Pastoureaux (Pastorelli, Roïm), the, massacre of the French Jews by, **4,** 55–7.
Patras, the Spanish exiles in, **4,** 406.
Patriarch, title of the president of the Synhedrion, **2,** 334.
Patriarchate, the, invested with autocratic power under Judah I, **2,** 452–4.
on a level with the Exilarchate, **2,** 454.
extinction of, a condition of the advent of the Messiah, **2,** 457.
royal authority of, under Judah II, **2,** 485.
decline of the authority of, **2,** 535.
decline of, **2,** 560.
power of, over non-Palestinian communities ends with the adoption of a fixed calendar, **2,** 573.
constitutes Judæa the head of the Jewish communities of the Roman empire, **2,** 611.
fall of, **2,** 612, 617–18.
Patriarchs, the, levy a tax from the time of Judah II, **2,** 487.
support of, **2,** 535–6.
titles of, **2,** 560–1, 612.
regarded as the chief of the Jews in the Roman empire, **2,** 561.
compelled to go to Sora, **2,** 607.
exclude apostates from the Jewish community, **2,** 612–13.
exempt from civil duties, **2,** 616.
enjoy civil jurisdiction, **2,** 616.
tax of, forbidden to be collected, **2,** 617.
dignities bestowed on, **2,** 617–18.

Patriarchs, the (*continued*), number of, **2**, 618.
tax of, collected by imperial officials, **2**, 622.
the Jews under, **5**, 725.
See also Synhedrion, the, presidents of.

Patriarchs, the, list of:

Gamaliel II,	Hillel II,
Gamaliel III,	Judah I,
Gamaliel IV,	Judah II,
Gamaliel V,	Judah III,
Gamaliel VI,	Judah IV,
Simon III.	

See also Synhedrion, the, presidents of.

Patricius (Patrick Netira), leader of the Jews in a revolt against Rome, **2**, 570.

Patriotism, towards France discussed in the Assembly of Jewish Notables, **5**, 489, 492.
in the Synhedrion, **5**, 497.

Paul III (Farnese), pope, well disposed to Jews, **4**, 515.
worked upon by João III and Duarte de Paz, **4**, 515.
orders a reconsideration of the Portuguese Inquisition, **4**, 516.
protects the Portuguese Marranos, **4**, 516, 520, 521-2.
deprecates the assault on Duarte de Paz, **4**, 517.
objects to forcible conversions, **4**, 517–18.
sanctions the Portuguese Inquisition, **4**, 518, 527.
recommends gentle measures for the Marranos, **4**, 518, 527.
Marranos complain to, of the cruelty of the Inquisition, **4**, 519-20.
submits his Inquisition bull to a commission, **4**, 520.
cripples the Portuguese Inquisition, **4**, 522.

Paul III (Farnese), pope (*continued*), authorizes the order of Jesuits and the Inquisition at Rome, **4**, 524–5.
under obligations to Spain and Portugal, **4**, 525.
abused at the Council of Trent, **4**, 525–6.
defends the Marranos' right of emigration, **4**, 526.
hostile to Charles V, **4**, 526.
death of, **4**, 528.
grants privileges to the Marranos of Ancona, **4**, 568.

Paul IV (Pietro Caraffa), pope, proposes the Inquisition at Rome, **4**, 525.
efforts of, to re-establish papal supremacy, **4**, 562.
introduces the censorship of the press, **4**, 563.
decrees the burning of the Talmud, **4**, 565.
issues two bulls against the Jews, **4**, 566–7.
ill-treats the Jews of Rome, **4**, 567.
persecutes the Marranos of Ancona, **4**, 568, 571.
compelled to set free the Turkish Jews in Ancona, **4**, 578.
employs apostates to annoy Jews, **4**, 581, 584.
persecutes the Marranos, **4**, 581–2.
has the Talmud burnt at Cremona, **4**, 582–3.
death of, **4**, 586, 587.

Paul (Saul of Tarsus), apostle, proselytizes the heathen, **2**, 219.
defends the integrity of the Law, **2**, 221.
chief promoter of Christianity, **2**, 223, 365.
characterization of, **2**, 223.

Paul (Saul of Tarsus) (*continued*), opponent of the Greek Nazarenes, **2**, 224.
and the conversion of the heathen world, **2**, 224–5.
conversion of, to Christianity, **2**, 225.
vision of, **2**, 225.
and the doctrine of resurrection, **2**, 225–6.
joins the Nazarenes of Damascus, **2**, 226.
flees to Arabia, **2**, 226.
second visit of, to Damascus, **2**, 227.
at Jerusalem, **2**, 227.
establishes Greek Christian communities, **2**, 227–8.
teaches Judaism as an introduction to Christianity, **2**, 228.
inveighs against the Law, **2**, 229–30.
causes a schism in Christianity, **2**, 230.
quarrel of, with Peter, **2**, 231.
anathematizes his opponents, **2**, 231.
hated by the Jewish Christians, **2**, 367, 368.
followers of, submit to Roman domination, **2**, 369.
teaching of, becomes true Christianity, **2**, 373.
Paul, bishop of Constantinople, asperses Judaism, **2**, 562.
Paul Burgensis. *See* Solomon Levi.
Paul of Samosata, bishop of Antioch, at the court of Zenobia, **2**, 529.
Paul de Santa Maria. *See* Solomon Levi.
Pauli, Oliger, an enthusiast for the Jews, **5**, 177.
Paulus, opponent of the Jews, **5**, 601.
Pauw, Reinier, burgomaster of Amsterdam, and intermarriages between Jews and Christians, **4**, 674.
Pavia, a Jewess of, apostatizes and returns to Judaism, **4**, 288.
the Jews of, expelled, **4**, 660.
Paz, Duarte de, advocate of the Portuguese Marranos at Rome, **4**, 512.
betrays the confidence of João III, **4**, 512.
influences Clement VII against the Portuguese Inquisition, **4**, 513.
obtains a papal brief protecting Marranos, **4**, 513–14.
influences Paul III, **4**, 515.
bribes church officials, **4**, 516.
assaulted by order of the Portuguese court, **4**, 517.
misappropriates funds, **4**, 518.
tries to have the Inquisition bull revoked, **4**, 519.
Paz, Enrique Enriquez de (Antonio Enriquez de Gomez, 1600–1660), playwright, as soldier, **5**, 110.
tried by the Inquisition, **5**, 110.
in France, **5**, 110.
burnt in effigy at Seville, **5**, 111.
Jewish poem by, **5**, 111.
unaffected by Spinoza's attack upon Judaism, **5**, 117.
Peace Congress, the. *See* Rastadt.
Peace party, the, in Jerusalem, supporters of, **2**, 256.
justifies the revolt of the people, **2**, 257.
declares the refusal of heathen sacrifices unlawful, **2**, 259.
asks the authorities for troops, **2**, 259.

Peace party, the (*continued*), kept out of the Temple by the Zealots, **2,** 260.
loses its influence, **2,** 268.
Peasants, Jewish, influence of Christianity on, **2,** 364-5.
Pechah, a Persian governor of Judæa, **1,** 352, 361.
Pecht, an Egyptian goddess, **1,** 9.
Pedro II, of Aragon, the Jews under, **3,** 497-8.
Pedro IV, of Aragon, the Jews under, **4,** 145.
Pedro IV, the Cruel (1350-1369), of Castile, revolt against, **4,** 102.
character of, **4,** 113.
family relations of, **4,** 113-14.
neglected by his father, **4,** 114.
Jews attached to, **4,** 114.
the Jews under, **4,** 115-26.
refuses to curtail the privileges of the Jews, **4,** 116.
wives of, **4,** 116-17.
decoyed into the fortress of Toro, **4,** 118.
mentioned on the inscriptions in the Toledo synagogue, **4,** 120.
deposes and tortures Samuel Abulafia, **4,** 121.
determines to kill his wife, **4,** 121.
acknowledges Maria de Padilla his wife, **4,** 122.
alliance against, **4,** 122.
maligned by his brother, **4,** 122-3.
compelled to leave Burgos, **4,** 123.
loses Toledo and Seville, **4,** 124.
aided by the Black Prince, **4,** 124.
calls in the Mahometan king of Granada, **4,** 125.
Pedro IV, the Cruel (*continued*), death of, **4,** 126.
the Jews hated on account of the civil war under, **4,** 167.
Pedro de la Caballeria, apostate, Christian propagandist, **4,** 231-2.
Pedro de Herrera, Marrano, asks for Gibraltar as a refuge for Marranos, **4,** 282-3.
Pedro de Luna, cardinal. *See* Benedict XIII, pope.
Pedro de Toledo, viceroy of Naples, employs Samuel II Abrabanel, **4,** 409.
daughter of, **4,** 410.
Peel, Sir Robert, introduces the Damascus affair in Parliament, **5,** 652.
Pekah, king of Israel, characterization of, **1,** 248.
allies of, **1,** 248.
licentiousness of the nobles under, **1,** 250.
allies himself with Rezin of Damascus, **1,** 258, 259.
submits to Tiglath-Pileser, **1,** 260.
murdered, **1,** 260.
Pekahiah, king of Israel, murdered, **1,** 248.
Pelethites, the, mercenary troops under David, **1,** 122.
in the Ammonite war, **1,** 126.
faithful to David in the civil war with Absalom, **1,** 141.
in the war against Sheba, **1,** 149.
attend Solomon, **1,** 153.
Pelham, English minister, favors the emancipation of the Jews, **5,** 337.
Pelka, son of Casimir III, **4,** 112.
Pella, destroyed by Alexander Jannæus, **2,** 46.

Pelusium, besieged by Sennacherib, **1**, 276, 277.
the Egyptians defeated at, **1**, 450.
Penal law, the, of Judaism, **2**, 473.
Penini. *See* Yedaya En-Bonet.
Peñiscola, Benedict XIII holds papal court at, **4**, 217.
Penitential hymns, by Gershom ben Jehuda, **3**, 246.
Penitential prayers. *See* Prayers.
Penso, Isaac, Marrano banker, philanthropist, **5**, 111–12.
Penso, Joseph (Felice de la Vega, 1650–1703), Marrano poet, Hebrew dramas by, **5**, 112–13.
novels by, **5**, 113.
celebrated by Isaac Gomez de Sosa, **5**, 113.
unaffected by Spinoza's attack upon Judaism, **5**, 117.
compared with Luzzatto, **5**, 234.
Pentapolis, five Philistine cities, **1**, 54.
Pentateuch, the. *See* Law, the; Scriptures, the; Septuagint, the; Translation.
Pentateuch, the, Mendelssohn's translation of, for his children, published, **5**, 328–9.
commentary for, by Solomon Dubno, **5**, 329.
subscribers to, **5**, 329, 334.
arouses the opposition of pious Jews, **5**, 330–2.
interdict against, **5**, 332.
forbidden in Polish towns, **5**, 332.
interdicted by Raphael Cohen, **5**, 333.
co-workers in, **5**, 334.
appeals to the young, **5**, 334–5.
influence of, on German Jews, **5**, 395–6.
Pentateuch, the, Mendelssohn's translation of (*continued*), disseminated in Alsace, **5**, 430.
Pentecost, the Feast of, as fixed by Anan ben David, **3**, 131.
Pentekaka, prays for rain, **2**, 541–2.
Penuel (Peniel), fortified by Jeroboam, **1**, 185.
Penya, Chayim, opponent of Sabbataï Zevi, ill-treated, **5**, 136.
daughters of, Sabbatians, **5**, 136.
turns Sabbatian, **5**, 136.
rewarded by Sabbataï Zevi, **5**, 145.
Penyaforte, Raymond de, Dominican-General, devotes himself to the conversion of Mahometans and Jews, **3**, 519–20, 597.
arranges a disputation between Pablo Christiani and Nachmani, **3**, 598.
cautions Nachmani against blaspheming Christianity, **3**, 598.
continues the disputation in the Barcelona synagogue, **3**, 601.
on the Trinity, **3**, 601.
sends Pablo Christiani on missionary journeys, **3**, 602.
appointed censor of the Talmud, **3**, 603.
accuses Nachmani of blasphemy, **3**, 604.
monks trained by, act as conversionists, **3**, 621.
has Hebrew taught for conversion purposes, **3**, 640–1.
arouses the persecuting spirit against the Jews of Aragon, **4**, 77.
policy of, adopted by the Council of Basle, **4**, 245.

Peor, Mount, idolatry at, **1**, 28.
scene of the death of Moses, **1**, 31.
Peræa, land east of the Jordan, **1**, 30.
given to Herod Antipas by Herod's will, **2**, 119.
under Herod Antipas, **2**, 137.
given to Agrippa I by Caligula, **2**, 177.
Pereira, Abraham, Sabbatian, **5**, 139.
prepares to journey to Sabbataï Zevi, **5**, 150.
encourages the Sabbatian movement in Italy, **5**, 160.
Pereira, Emile and Isaac, grandfather of, **5**, 342.
Pereira, Jacob Rodrigues (1715-1780), inventor of the sign language, **5**, 342-3.
partial to Portuguese Jews, **5**, 343.
has the statute against foreign Jews in Bordeaux ratified, **5**, 343-4.
Perez, Alvar, de Guzman, mayor of Seville, protects the Jews, **4**, 168.
Pergamus, treasure house in, for the half-Shekel contributions to the Temple, **2**, 53.
Peringer, Gustavus, inquires into Karaism, **5**, 182-3.
Perizzites, the, a subdivision of the Canaanites, **1**, 3.
declared bondmen by Solomon, **1**, 163.
Perl, Joseph (1773-1839), founds a high school in Tarnopol, **5**, 612.
attacks the Chassidim, **5**, 612.
member of the Society for Culture, **5**, 612.
Pernambuco, Amsterdam Jews settle in, **4**, 693.
congregation of, **4**, 693.
Perpignan, French Jews expelled by Philip IV settle in, **4**, 50.
Perpignan, the Jews of, in the thirteenth century, **4**, 25.
protect Levi of Villefranche, **4**, 29.
agitation among, in behalf of Abba-Mari's cause, **1**, 33-4.
Persia, revolt against, **1**, 407-9.
the goddess of love, worshipped in, **1**, 408.
conquered by Alexander the Great, **1**, 412.
Alexander Severus' campaign in, **2**, 482.
succumbs to the Arabs, **3**, 86.
visited by Petachya, **3**, 421.
under the jurisdiction of the Exilarch, **3**, 428.
the khanate of, under Argun, **3**, 637-8, 646, 650.
Persia (Sassanian empire), the Jews of, persecuted by Firuz, **2**, 628-30.
under Kobad, **3**, 4.
well treated by Bahram Tshubin, **3**, 8-9.
in the twelfth century, **3**, 434-5.
Persian influence on Judaism, **1**, 402-5.
Perushim. *See* Pharisees.
Pesakim, practical application of the legal enactments of the Talmud, **3**, 345.
Pesaro, Molcho at, **4**, 501.
a refuge for Marranos, **4**, 569.
the Jews of, invite Turkish trade, **4**, 578-9.
the Marranos banished from, **4**, 580-1.
refuge of Jewish exiles from the Papal States, **4**, 592.
Pescennius, Niger. *See* Niger.
Peshat, simple text explanation, **3**, 288, 345.

Peshito, the Syriac translation of the Law, **2**, 582.
Pessach-Peter, apostate, brings charges against the Jews of Germany, **4**, 177-8.
Pesth, the Jews of, modify their divine service, **5**, 582.
See also Buda; Buda-Pesth.
Petachya of Ratisbon (1175-1190), traveler in the East, **3**, 421.
on the Jews of Susa, **3**, 435.
on the Jews of India, **3**, 435-6.
on the conversion of Armenians to Judaism, **3**, 440.
Peter (Simon, Kephas, Petrus), apostle, disciple of Jesus in Capernaum, **2**, 153.
calls Jesus the Christ, **2**, 158.
loyal to Jesus, **2**, 163.
leader of the early Christians, **2**, 169.
leader of the Law-abiding Nazarenes at Jerusalem, **2**, 222.
teachings of, opposed to those of Paul, **2**, 230.
quarrel of, with Paul, **2**, 231.
on the solidarity of the Jews, **2**, 367-8.
Peter, Tossafist, martyr, **3**, 355.
Peter of Amiens, preaches the crusades, **3**, 297.
the army of, leaves the Jews unmolested, **3**, 298.
Peter of Benevento, papal legate, convenes the synod of Montpellier, **3**, 508.
Peter Martyr, describes the terrors of the Inquisition, **4**, 484.
Peter the Venerable, abbot of Clugny, rouses the crusaders against the Jews, **3**, 349-50.
Peters, Hugh, secretary to Cromwell, employed to dispose the English in favor of the Jews, **5**, 43.
on the commission for the admission of Jews, **5**, 45.
Petit, Guillaume Haquinet, confessor of Louis XII, influences him against Reuchlin, **4**, 459.
patron of Hebrew literature, **4**, 473.
Petit, Solomon. *See* Solomon Petit.
Petra, capital of Edom, **1**, 222.
refuge of Hyrcanus II, **2**, 59.
Petronius, governor of Syria, ordered to turn the sanctuary into a pagan temple, **2**, 188.
ordered to set up Caligula's image in the Temple, **2**, 189.
ordered to prevent the desecration of synagogues, **2**, 193.
Petrus. *See* Peter, apostle.
Peyret, rabbi, supposed manufacturer of the poison for wells, **4**, 102.
Pfefferkorn, Joseph, immorality of, **4**, 423-4.
becomes an apostate, **4**, 424.
puts his name to Ortuin de Graes' "Mirror for Admonition," **4**, 425.
advises the burning of the Talmud, **4**, 425-6.
lends his name to Dominican writings, **4**, 426.
thwarted by Jewish physicians, **4**, 427.
not trusted by Christians, **4**, 427.
publishes "The Enemy of the Jews," **4**, 427-8.
obtains a letter to Maximilian I from Kunigunde, **4**, 428-9.

Pfefferkorn, Joseph (*continued*),
obtains an imperial mandate, 4, 429.
orders the Frankfort Jews to surrender their books, 4, 429.
forbids the Frankfort Jews to attend the synagogue on Tabernacles, 4, 430.
opposed by Uriel von Gemmingen, 4, 430, 431.
coadjutors of, suggested, 4, 432.
tries to make Reuchlin his confederate, 4, 436.
applies for a second mandate, 4, 436, 437.
a second time confiscates Hebrew books in Frankfort, 4, 438.
censured by the public, 4, 438.
publishes "In Honor and Praise of Emperor Maximilian," 4, 439.
directed to report the decision of his commission to Maximilian, 4, 441.
motives of, suspected by Reuchlin, 4, 442.
breaks the seal of Reuchlin's "Opinion," 4, 445.
publishes the "Handspiegel," 4, 446.
attacked by Reuchlin, 4, 446-48.
preaches in Frankfort, 4, 449.
tool of Hoogstraten, 4, 450.
tears down the notice of Reuchlin's exoneration, 4, 455.
suggests the expulsion of the Jews from Frankfort, Worms, and Ratisbon, 4, 463.
anti-Jewish charges of, repeated by Luther, 4, 548-9.

Pfizer, governor of Heidelberg, permits an assault upon the Jews, 5, 531, 602.

Phabi, family of high priests, 2, 237.

"**Phædon**, or the Immortality of the Soul," by Mendelssohn, popularity of, 5, 304-5.
object of, 5, 306.
dialogue form of, 5, 306.
argument of, 5, 306-7.
popularity of, 5, 307-8.

Phalles, king of Tyre, murdered, 1, 194.

Phaltiel, Michal's husband, 1, 110.

Phanagoria (Taman), Jews of the Byzantine empire settle in, 3, 123.

Pharaoh, in the Zohar, 4, 23.

Pharaohs, the, the Egyptian kings, 1, 8.
worshiped, 1, 10.

Pharisees, the, a national party, offshoot from the Assidæans, 2, 17.
aims of, 2, 17.
explanation of the name of, 2, 18.
principles of, 2, 18.
wherein opposed to the Essenes and Sadducees, 2, 18–19.
defenders of tradition, 2, 19-20, 22.
morality of, 2, 20.
charge of hypocrisy against, unfounded, 2, 20.
position of, with regard to Pentateuchal laws, 2, 22–3.
contrasted with the Essenes, 2, 30.
employed as civil functionaries, 2, 31.
lose their state offices, 2, 32-3.
favored by Alexander Jannæus, 2, 39.
actively oppose the Sadducees, 2, 42-3.

Pharisees, the (*continued*), hated by Alexander Jannæus, 2, 43.
instigate revolts against Alexander Jannæus, 2, 44.
take refuge in the fortress of Bethome, 2, 45.
crucified, 2, 45.
flee from Judæa, 2, 45.
rejoice over the death of Alexander Jannæus, 2, 47.
favored by Salome Alexandra, 2, 48.
obtain the chief post in the Great Council, 2, 48-9.
the interpretations of, in the Synhedrion, 2, 50.
introduce the Water Libation and the Wood festival, 2, 52.
institute the half-Shekel contributions, 2, 52.
persecute the Sadducees, 2, 53.
support Hyrcanus II, 2, 58.
reconciliation of, with the Sadducees begun by Hillel, 2, 98.
divided on the subject of swearing allegiance to Herod, 2, 108.
hate Herod, 2, 114–15.
urge revenge against Herod, 2, 121.
not in opposition to John the Baptist, 2, 147.
disapprove of Jesus, 2, 162.
aid Christianity by their methods of interpretation, 2, 166.
neglect the lower classes, 2, 220.
object to the Sadducee high priest Anan, 2, 248.
laws introduced by, justified, 2, 327.
as described by the Nazarenes, 2, 372.
accept tradition, 2, 462.

Pharos, the island of, Judæans celebrate the completion of the Septuagint on, 1, 511-12.

Phasael, brother of Herod, governor of Judæa, 2, 77.
urges mild measures upon Herod, 2, 79.
made tetrarch in Judæa, 2, 81.
opposed by the Parthians, 2, 82.
commits suicide, 2, 82.

Phasael, son of Pallas and Herod, disinherited, 2, 119.

Phasael, tower of, retreat of the Roman garrison of Jerusalem, 2, 260.
left undemolished by Titus, 2, 309.

Phasaelis, revenue from, left to Salome, 2, 120.

Phasiron, the sons of, members of the Hellenist party, 1, 489.

Pheroras, brother of Herod, wife of, a Pharisee, 2, 108.
Herod suspicious of, 2, 112.
conspires against the sons of Mariamne, 2, 112-13.
conspires against Herod, 2, 113.

Philadelphia. *See* Rabbath-Ammon.

Philanthropin, school at Frankfort, hearth of the Reform movement, 5, 674.

Philibert, Dr., a German writer, offers to defend the Damascus Jews, 5, 655.

Philip, Arab emperor of Rome, 2, 526.

Philip II Augustus, of France, leniency of, in the execution of anti-Jewish decrees, 3, 401, 508.
expresses money from the Jews, 3, 401-2.

Philip II Augustus, of France, (*continued*), banishes the Jews from the Isle de France, **3**, 402–3.
executes the Jews of Bray, **3**, 404.
in the third crusade, **3**, 404.
receives exiled Jews, **3**, 405-6.
agrees to surrender Jews from Champagne, **3**, 406.
charged with disregarding anti-Jewish decrees, **3**, 498-9.
Philip III, of France, re-introduces Jew badges, **3**, 613.
Philip IV, of France, meets Sancho IV of Castile, **4**, 2.
in strife with Boniface VIII, **4**, 44.
expels the Jews, **4**, 46.
avarice of, **4**, 47.
Philip V, the Long, of France, extends the privileges of the Jews, **4**, 54.
conceives the idea of a crusade, **4**, 55.
charges the Jews with poisoning wells, **4**, 57, 58.
Philip VI, of France, first of the House of Valois, **4**, 77.
Philip II, of Macedon, contemplates war with Persia, **1**, 411-12.
murdered, **1**, 412.
Philip V, of Macedon, takes Egypt, **1**, 432.
Philip III, of Navarre, punishes the ringleaders in the massacre of the Jews, **4**, 78.
Philip II, of Spain, hated by Paul IV, **4**, 566.
tries to introduce the Inquisition into the Netherlands, **4**, 601.
obtains peace with Turkey through Jewish mediators, **4**, 607.
pays for the polyglot Bible, **4**, 651.
Philip II, of Spain (*continued*), Jews under, in the Netherlands, **4**, 661, 667-8.
hated by the Portuguese Marranos, **4**, 663.
death of, **4**, 668.
Philip III, of Spain, condition of Spain at the accession of, **4**, 668.
debtor to the Marranos, **4**, 670-1.
Philip IV, of Spain, makes a Jew count palatine, **4**, 692.
praises the Jews of Oran, **5**, 169.
Philip, tetrarch, son of Cleopatra of Jerusalem, in Herod's will, **2**, 119.
builds Cæsarea Philippi and Julias, **2**, 138.
character of, **2**, 138.
tetrarchy of, given to Agrippa I, **2**, 177.
tetrarchy of, given to Agrippa II, **2**, 245.
Philip, favorite of Antiochus Epiphanes, regent of Syria, **1**, 477.
in Antioch, **1**, 480.
Philip, papal legate, presides over the Council of Buda, **3**, 614.
Philip, Syrian commander, kills the Chassidim in the caves, **1**, 458.
Philip of Bathyrene, leader of Agrippa II's troops against the Zealots, **2**, 259, 274.
leaves Jerusalem, **2**, 260.
escapes the machinations of Varus, **2**, 274-5.
Philippi, the republican army of Rome, defeated at the battle of, **2**, 81.
Judæans in, **2**, 203.
Paul establishes a Greek-Christian community in, **2**, 227.

Philippi, Francis Lothair. *See* Wolf Levi.

Philippion, prince of Chalcis, husband of Alexandra, daughter of Aristobulus II, **2,** 75.

Philistia, overrun by Scythians, **1,** 287.

Philistines, the, characteristics of, **1,** 54-5.
relations of, to the Israelites, **1,** 56-59.
oppress the Israelites, **1,** 61.
attack Israelite tribes, **1,** 64.
harass the Israelites, **1,** 66.
have possession of the Ark of the Covenant, **1,** 70-2.
defeated at Eben-ha-Ezer, **1,** 78.
choose a king, **1,** 80.
warfare of, with the Israelites, **1,** 80.
lay waste Sidon, **1,** 80.
oppress Israel at the beginning of Saul's reign, **1,** 84.
garrison of, at Gibeah, killed by Jonathan, **1,** 85.
encamp at Michmash against Saul, **1,** 85-6.
defeated at Michmash, **1,** 86-8.
champion of, killed by David, **1,** 95, 97.
defeated by David, **1,** 98-9.
under Achish, wage war with the Israelites, **1,** 102-4.
wage war with David, **1,** 115-118.
defeated at Mount Baal-Perazim, **1,** 116.
surrender Gath to the Israelites, **1,** 117.
champions of, in the war with David, **1,** 117.
routed by David, **1,** 118.
at war with Nadab, **1,** 189.
at war with Elah, **1,** 192.

Philistines, the (*continued*), sell Judæan captives as slaves, **1,** 227, 231.
attack Judah, **1,** 258.
subdued by Sennacherib, **1,** 270.
allied with Nebuchadnezzar, **1,** 314.
molest Judæan fugitives, **1,** 318.
in possession of Judæan territory under the Seleucidæ, **1,** 435.
join Gorgias in his invasion of Judæa, **1,** 467.
hostile to the Judæans during the Syrian invasions, **1,** 473.

Philo the Elder, Egypto-Judæan poet, extols Jerusalem, **1,** 517-18.

Philo Judæus, conception of the Messianic age held by, **2,** 144-5.
brother of the Alabarch Alexander Lysimachus, **2,** 176.
gives an account of Jewish renegades, **2,** 184.
characterization of, **2,** 184-5.
relation of, to Judaism, **2,** 185.
wife of, **2,** 186.
style of, **2,** 186.
representative of the Alexandrian Judæans before Caligula, **2,** 186.
contrasted with Apion, **2,** 186-7.
as a writer, **2,** 191.
visit of, to Jerusalem, **2,** 194.
an allegorist, **2,** 210.
reconciles the Law and his philosophy, **2,** 210.
emphasizes obedience to the Law, **2,** 210-11.
shows the beauty of the Jewish laws of humanity, **2,** 211-12.
writes a philosophic commentary on the Pentateuch, **2,** 212.

Philo Judæus (*continued*), compared with Hillel and Jesus, **2**, 214.
describes heathen proselytes of his day, **2**, 215.
system of, aids Christianity, **2**, 373.
the works of, read at the court of Louis the Pious, **3**, 162.
the works of, connected with the Talmud, **4**, 614.
studied by Frankel, **5**, 684.

Philologists, Hebrew. *See* Grammarians, Hebrew.

Philology, Hebrew, a special study of the Karaites, **3**, 180.

Philosoph, Joseph, father-in-law of Sabbataï Zevi, **5**, 166, 209.
supports the Messianic claims of Jacob Querido, **5**, 210.

Philosophers, the Arabic, the sayings of, used by Solomon Ibn-Gebirol, **3**, 267, 270.

Philosophers, Jewish, list of:
Aaron ben Elia Nicomedi,
Aaron ben Meshullam,
Abraham ben Meïr Ibn-Ezra,
Abraham Ibn-Daud Halevi,
Abraham Maimuni,
Abu-Amr Joseph ben Zadik Ibn-Zadik,
Alkuti (Chepez),
Bachya ben Joseph Ibn-Pakuda,
Chasdaï Crescas,
David Ibn-Albilla,
Elias del Medigo,
Isaac ben Suleiman Israeli,
Isaac Albalag,
Isaac Pulgar,
Jehuda Halevi,
Joseph ben Shem Tob Ibn-Shem Tob,
Joseph Albo,
Joseph Kaspi,
Kalonymos ben Kalonymos,
Leon Judah Abrabanel,
Levi ben Abraham ben Chayim,
Levi ben Gerson,

Philosophers, Jewish, list of (*continued*):
Mantin, Jacob
Meïr Alguades,
Moses ben Maimun,
Moses ben Joshua Narboni,
Moses Ibn-Ezra,
Philo,
Saadiah ben Joseph,
Samuel Ibn-Abbas,
Samuel Halevi Ibn-Nagrela,
Shem-Tob Falaquera,
Sheshet Benveniste,
Solomon Ibn-Gebirol,
Spinoza, Baruch
Steinheim, Solomon Ludwig.

"Philosophical Conversations, The," by Mendelssohn, **5**, 298-9.

Philosophy, Philo's attempt to reconcile, with the Law, **2**, 210, 212–13.
cultivated by the Spanish Jews in the tenth and eleventh centuries, **3**, 235.
characterized by Jehuda Halevi, **3**, 328, 330, 331.
connected with Judaism by Maimonides, **3**, 478-9.
in disrepute in Spain in the fourteenth century, **4**, 91.

Phineas, high priest, punishes immoral practices, **1**, 29.
seat of, at Shiloh, **1**, 41.

Phineas, leader of the Idumæans, helps the Zealots, **2**, 295.

Phineas, rabbi of Breslau, hangs himself, **4**, 262.

Phineas ben Meshullam, rabbi of Alexandria, **3**, 444.

Phineas ben Samuel, made high priest by the Zealots, **2**, 294.

Phineas, son of Eli, character of, **1**, 70.
death of, **1**, 70.

Phocas, usurps the throne of Mauritius, **3**, 18.
chastisement of, **3**, 19.

Phœnicia, subdued by Shalmaneser, **1**, 263, 264.
subdued by Sennacherib, **1**, 270.
conquered by Nebuchadnezzar, **1**, 304.
Nabonad permits native kings to rule over, **1**, 342.
conquered by Alexander the Great, **1**, 412.
Joseph made tax gatherer of, **1**, 425.
Olympian games introduced into, **1**, 445.
the towns of, revolt from Antiochus Epiphanes, **1**, 463.
Phœnician merchants settle in Jerusalem, **1**, 169.
Phœnicians, the, early culture of, **1**, 53-4.
relations of, to the Israelites, **1**, 56–8.
defeated by the Philistines, **1**, 80.
weakened by civil wars, **1**, 232.
hostile to the Judæans during the Syrian invasions, **1**, 474.
See also Canaanites, the.
Phraortes, king of Media, defeated by the Assyrians, **1**, 287.
Phylacteries (Tephillin), the, the use of, prohibited under Hadrian, **2**, 424.
abolished by Anan ben David, **3**, 132.
Physicians, Jewish, popular with the clergy of the Frankish and Burgundian kingdoms, **3**, 35.
in Taberistan, **3**, 146.
employed by Christian rulers, **3**, 170, 213, 242, 292, 425, 536, 537, 583, 628; **4**, 2, 80, 184, 185, 190, 275, 287, 367, 411, 413, 555, 584–5, 673, 692; **5**, 76, 115.
Physicians, Jewish (*continued*), employed by Mahometan rulers, **3**, 211, 312, 443, 495, 638; **4**, 401.
sought by the Christians in Palestine, **3**, 341.
in Lynn, **3**, 412.
popular with Christians, **3**, 581.
prevented by the Council of Béziers from attending Christians, **3**, 582.
indispensableness of, **3**, 583.
employed by the popes, **3**, 628; **4**, 200, 407–8, 411, 515, 569.
not permitted to practice under Juan II, **4**, 203.
forbidden to practice by Benedict XIII, **4**, 216.
employment of, forbidden by the council of Basle, **4**, 245.
proscribed by Eugenius IV, **4**, 250.
protected by Juan II of Castile, **4**, 252.
proscribed by Nicholas V, **4**, 253, 287.
employed by the nobles and the clergy, **4**, 275.
esteemed in Italy in the fifteenth century, **4**, 287.
missed after the expulsion from Spain, **4**, 353-4.
preferred in Turkey, **4**, 401.
accused of quackery by Pfefferkorn, **4**, 427.
the only ones in Portugal, **4**, 488.
forbidden by Paul IV to attend Christians, **4**, 567.
employment of, forbidden by Gregory XIII, **4**, 653.
permitted by Sixtus V to practice, **4**, 656.
defended by David de Pomis, **4**, 656-7.
envied in Hamburg, **4**, 690.

Physicians, Jewish (*continued*), forbidden to practice among Christians in Hamburg, **4**, 692.

of Berlin, not included in the list of physicians, **5**, 461.

Physicians, Jewish, list of:

Aaron ben Zion Ibn-Alamâni,
Abraham de Balmes,
Abraham of Aragon (oculist),
Abraham ben Joseph the Elder,
Abraham Ibn-Daud Halevi,
Abraham Ibn-Zarzal,
Abraham Maimuni,
Abraham Zacuto Lusitano,
Abu Ayub,
Abu Ibraham Isaac Ibn-Kastan,
Abu Sahal Ali,
Abulhassan Abraham ben Meïr Ibn-Kamnial,
Amatus Lusitanus,
Amram ben Isaac Ibn-Shalbib,
Bachya Ibn-Alkonstantini,
Benjamin Assia,
Bonet de Lates,
Cardosa, Abraham Michael
Cardoso, Fernando (Isaac)
Castro, Balthasar Orobio de
Castro, Bendito de
Castro, Rodrigo de
Chamiz, Joseph
Chasdaï Ibn-Shaprut,
Cohen, Perachya
David de Pomis,
Della Volta, Samuel Vita
Delmedigo, Joseph Solomon
Dunash ben Tamim,
Elias Montalto,
Farraj Ibn-Solomon,
Gamaliel VI,
Guglielmo di Portaleone,
Hamon, Isaac
Hamon, Joseph
Hamon, Moses
Herz, Marcus
Hillel ben Samuel,
Isaac ben Mordecai,
Isaac ben Suleiman Israeli,
Isaac II Abrabanel,
Isaac Benveniste,
Jacob ben Machir Tibbon,
Jacob ben Yechiel Loans,
Jacob Ibn-Nuñez,
Jacob Abi-Ayub,
Jehuda bar Joseph Ibn-Alfachar,
Jehuda Halevi,

Physicians, Jewish, list of (*continued*):

Joseph ben Joshua Cohen,
Joseph ben Sabara,
Joseph Albo,
Joseph Orabuena,
Joshua ben Joseph Ibn-Vives Allorqui,
Judah de Blanis,
Judah ben Moses Cohen,
Judah ben Saul Ibn-Tibbon,
Judah ben Yechiel,
Judah Leon Abrabanel,
Levi ben Gerson,
Lippold,
Mantin, Jacob
Meïr Alguades,
Messer-Jawaih,
Moses ben Isaac da Rieti,
Moses ben Maimun,
Moses ben Nachman,
Moses Ibn-Tibbon,
Moses Zarzel,
Musaphia, Benjamin
Nathaniel of Bagdad,
Nathaniel of Egypt,
Nathaniel Ibn-Almali,
Nepi, Graziadio
Nieto, David
Obadiah de Sforno,
Profiat Duran,
Raimuch, Astruc
Saad-Addaula,
Sabbataï Donnolo,
Sahal Rabban,
Samuel,
Samuel Ibn-Wakar,
Samuel Shulam,
Saul Astruc Cohen,
Serachya ben Isaac,
Shem Tob ben Isaac,
Sheshet ben Benveniste,
Silva, Samuel da
Simon ben Zemach Duran,
Simon Zarfati,
Solomon, the Egyptian,
Solomon ben Jacob,
Steinheim, Solomon Ludwig
Tobias of Trent,
Vecinho, Joseph
Vidal ben Benveniste Ibn-Labi,
Zedekiah,
Zemach, Jacob.

Physicians, Samaritan and Saracen, in favor with the Christians in Palestine, **3**, 341.

Picard, the family of, culture of, **5**, 476.

Picciotto, Isaac Levi, accused of ritual murder, **5**, 638.
upbraids the accusers with their inhumanity, **5**, 639.
protected by the Austrian consul, **5**, 639, 646.

Pichon, Joseph. *See* Joseph Pichon.

Pico di Mirandola, disciple and friend of Elias del Medigo, **4**, 290.
erudition of, **4**, 290–1.
student of the Kabbala, **4**, 291–2.
translates Kabbalistic writings, **4**, 292.
friend of Judah Leon Abrabanel, **4**, 384.
inspires Reuchlin with love of Hebrew learning, **4**, 433.
admirer of the Kabbala, **4**, 443, 583.

Piedmont, French exiles settle in, **4**, 177.

Pieva di Sacco. Jewish printing house in, **4**, 289.

Pilate, Pontius, fifth procurator of Judæa, administration of, **2**, 138–9.
uses the Temple treasures for an aqueduct, **2**, 139–40.
permits the execution of Jesus, **2**, 164.
declares Jesus guilty of treason, **2**, 164.
hated, **2**, 171.
cruelty of, to Samaritans, **2**, 171–2.
summoned to Rome, **2**, 172.

Pilgrimages among Asiatic Jews, **3**, 440–1.
of the Egyptian Jews, **3**, 445.
to Jerusalem in the fourteenth century, **4**, 73–4.

Pilpul, method of Talmud study attributed to Jacob Polak, **4**, 418.

Pimentel, Manuel. *See* Abenacar, Isaac.

Pina, Paul de. *See* Jesurun, Rohel.

Pinchas ben Jaïr, opposes the abolition of the year of release, **2**, 459–60.

Pinchas Ibn-Azura, Jewish opponent of Mahomet, **3**, 74.
one of the Benu-Kainukaa, **3**, 76.

Pinczovinians, the, Unitarians in Poland, **4**, 647.

Pinedo, Isaac (Thomas) de (1614–1679), Marrano scholar, **5**, 114.
unaffected by Spinoza's attack upon Judaism, **5**, 117.
Sachs compared with, **5**, 688.

Pinheiro, Diogo, bishop, opposes the establishment of the Portuguese Inquisition, **4**, 500.

Pinheiro, Moses, follower of Sabbataï Zevi, **5**, 123.
encourages the Sabbatian movement in Italy, **5**, 160.
teaches the Kabbala, **5**, 164.

Pinto, Aaron de, supports Chayon's cause, **5**, 223.
refuses reconciliation with Chacham Zevi, **5**, 224.
forbids opposition to Chayon, **5**, 224.
summons Chacham Zevi before the Council, **5**, 226.

Pinto, Abraham, founder of the Rotterdam Jewish community, **4**, 685.

Pinto, David, founder of the Rotterdam Jewish community, **4**, 685.

Pinto, David, espouses Eibeschütz's cause, **5**, 264.

Pinto, Diogo Rodrigues, advocate of the Portuguese Marranos at Rome, **4,** 515, 516.
Pinto, Isaac (1715–1787), Marrano, disinterestedness of, **5,** 340.
devoted to the Portuguese Jews, **5,** 341, 344.
wins the Duc de Richelieu to his side, **5,** 343.
answers Voltaire's defamation of Judaism, **5,** 345, 346.
distinguishes the Portuguese Jews, **5,** 345–6.
the work by, quoted in the Batavian National Assembly, **5,** 456.
Pintos, the, millionaires in Amsterdam, **5,** 205.
Pires, Diogo. *See* Molcho, Solomon.
Pirke Aboth, a treatise of the Mishna, **2,** 478.
Pirkheimer, Willibald, humanist, and the expulsion of the Jews, **4,** 416.
Pisa, the Jews of, in the twelfth century, **3,** 424.
the commerce of, in the fifteenth century, **4,** 285.
the Spanish exiles well treated in, **4,** 360.
exiles from the Papal States in, **4,** 659.
Pisidia, mercenaries from, hired by Alexander Jannæus, **2,** 39.
Pitholaus, general of Hyrcanus II, joins Aristobulus II, **2,** 73.
sentenced to death, **2,** 74.
Pius IV, pope, appealed to in behalf of the Jews of Prague, **4,** 586–7.
character of, **4,** 588.
appealed to by the Jews of Rome, **4,** 588.
Pius IV, pope (*continued*), permits the appearance of the Talmud, **4,** 589.
recommends censorship to be exercised over the Talmud, **4,** 658.
Pius V, pope, severity of, **4,** 589.
places the old canonical restrictions on the Jews, **4,** 590.
persecutes the Jews of the Papal States, **4,** 590.
expels the Jews from the Papal States, **4,** 591–2.
tries to organize a crusade against Turkey, **4,** 601.
hostility of, to the Jews, **4,** 653.
Pius VII, pope, opposed to the emancipation of the Jews, **5,** 518.
Pius IX, pope, action of, in the Mortara case, **5,** 701.
reactionary policy of, **5,** 701.
Piyutim, the productions of the poetans, introduced into the liturgy, **3,** 117–18.
objected to by the Chassidim, **5,** 386–7.
See also Liturgical poetry; Neo-Hebraic poetry; Poetry; Poetanim.
Place of the sellers of Ointment in Jerusalem, **1,** 140.
Placidus, Roman general under Titus, **2,** 290.
Plague, the, under Marcus Aurelius, **2,** 451.
attacks the Spanish exiles in Naples, **4,** 359–60.
keeps the Spanish exiles out of Italy, **4,** 363.
in Portugal attributed to the Jews, **4,** 368.
attributed to the Marranos, **4,** 486–7.

"**Plaints of a Jew, The,**" by Joel Jacoby, **5,** 630–1.
Plantavicius, Jacob, bishop, taught by Leo Modena, **5,** 71.
Plato, read by the Alexandrian Judæans, **1,** 505.
style of, and Philo's, **2,** 186.
the sayings of, used by Solomon Ibn-Gebirol, **3,** 267.
theories of, in the prophetical writings and the Agada, **3,** 479.
in Immanuel Romi's work, **4,** 66.
quoted by Jewish preachers, **4,** 232.
Plotina, wife of Trajan, counsels the punishment of the Jews, **2,** 395.
names Hadrian as Trajan's successor, **2,** 399.
Pneumatics. *See* Gnosticism.
Podolia, Haidamaks in, **5,** 11.
Jews banished from a part of, **5,** 12.
immorality of the Sabbatians of, **5,** 228.
Sabbatians in, **5,** 272.
leader of the Sabbatians of, **5,** 273–4.
devastated by the Cossacks, **5,** 388.
Poetanim, the, earliest works of, **3,** 114.
introduce rhyme into Neo-Hebraic poetry, **3,** 116.
liturgical compositions of, forbidden by Anan ben David, **3,** 132.
See Liturgical poetry; Neo-Hebraic poetry; Poetry; Piyutim; Poets.
Poetry, early Hebrew, **1,** 29.
on the destruction of Jerusalem, **1,** 316.
cultivated by the Arabic Jews, **3,** 57–8.
Poetry (*continued*), cultivated by the Spanish Jews in the tenth and eleventh centuries, **3,** 235.
as viewed by Maimonides, **3,** 449–50.
the Jews in, **4,** 164.
See Hebrew literature; Literature, Jewish; Liturgical poetry; Neo-Hebraic poetry.
Poetry, Jewish mediæval, treated of by Sachs, **5,** 693–4.
by Zunz, **5,** 694.
Poetry, Spanish-Jewish, in the twelfth century, **3,** 317–18.
history of, by Moses Ibn-Ezra, **3,** 320.
Poets, Jewish, list of:
Aaron ben Zion Ibn-Alamâni,
Abraham ben Chasdaï,
Abraham ben Meïr Ibn-Ezra,
Abraham Bedaresi,
Abu-Afak,
Abu-Amr ben Joseph Ibn-Zadik,
Abu Ayub,
Abu Fadhl Chasdaï,
Almeida, Manuella Nuñez da
Ascarelli, Deborah
Asma,
Belmonte, Bienvenida Coēn
Belmonte, Jacob Israel
Belmonte, Manuel
Ben Asher, Aaron and Moses
Berachya ben Natronaï Nakdan,
Dunash ben Labrat,
Eleazar ben Kalir,
Ensheim, Moses
Ephraim ben Jacob of Bonn,
Erter, Isaac
Fonseca Pinto y Pimentel, Sarah de
Gomez, Isaac, de Sosa,
Halevi, Elia
Ibn-Sahula,
Immanuel ben Solomon Romi,
Isaac ben Jehuda Ibn-Giat,
Isaac ben Reuben Albergeloni,
Isaac Ibn-Ezra,
Isaac Ibn-G'ikatilia,
Israel Najara,
Jannaï,
Jehuda ben Isaac ben Sabbataï,
Jehuda Alcharisi,
Jehuda Halevi,

Poets, Jewish, list of (*continued*):
Jehuda Zarko,
Jephet Ibn-Ali Halevi,
Jesurun, David
Jesurun, Rohel
José bar José Hayathom,
Joseph ben Chasdaï,
Joseph ben Isaac Ibn-Abitur,
Joseph ben Sabara,
Joseph Ezobi,
Judah Ibn-Abbas,
Judah Ibn-Giat,
Judah Siciliano,
Kalonymos ben Kalonymos,
Laguna, Lopez
Luzzatto, Moses Chayim
Luzzatto, Samuel David
Mar-Ukba,
Menachem ben Saruk,
Mendes, David Franco
Meshullam En-Vidas Dafiera,
Michael ben Kaleb,
Moses ben Isaac da Rieti,
Moses Ibn-Ezra,
Moses Zarzel,
Paz, Enrique Enriquez de
Penso, Joseph
Saadio Longo,
Sabbataï Donnolo,
Samuel Ibn-Abbas,
Samuel Ibn-Adiya,
Samuel Halevi Ibn-Nagrela,
Santob de Carrion,
Shem Tob Falaquera,
Sibyl, the
Silveyra, Miguel
Simon bar Kappara,
Simon ben Caipha,
Simon ben Isaac ben Abun,
Solomon ben Reuben Bonfed,
Solomon ben Yerucham,
Solomon Ibn-Gebirol,
Solomon Ibn-Sakbel,
Solomon Alkabez,
Solomon Dafiera,
Sullam, Sarah Copia
Süsskind of Trimberg,
Usque, Samuel
Usque, Solomon
Vidal ben Benveniste Ibn-Labi,
Wessely, Naphtali Hartwig
Yedaya En-Bonet,
Zarak Barfat.

Poitou, rabbis from, at the first rabbinical synod, **3,** 377.

Poitou, the Jews of, under Henry II, **3,** 409.
maltreated by crusaders, **3,** 570.
persecution of, **3,** 573.

Polak, Jacob. *See* Jacob Polak.

Poland, Jews in, in the ninth century, **3,** 144.
Jewish exiles from Austria settle in, **4,** 224.
a refuge for persecuted Jews, **4,** 263, 418–19, 420, 631–2.
clergy of, hostile to the Jews, **4,** 265.
at war with the Teutonic knights, **4,** 266.
the rabbis of, important to the crown, **4,** 420.
rabbinical schools established in, **4,** 420.
the Protestant Reformation in, **4,** 469.
professorships for Hebrew instituted in, **4,** 471.
Messianic hopes in, connected with Solomon Molcho, **4,** 497.
refuge of the Bohemian Jews, **4,** 544.
election of a king of, **4,** 603–5.
a party in, hostile to the Jews, **4,** 632.
number of Jews in, **4,** 632.
influence of the Reformation in, **4,** 633, 646–7.
Talmudical schools in, **4,** 634, 639–40.
refuge for the Jewish victims of the Thirty Years' War, **5,** 2.
value of Jews to, **5,** 2.
Joseph Delmedigo in, **5,** 76–7.
exiles from Vienna settle in, **5,** 173.
Karaites in, **5,** 182–3.
the Sabbatian movement in, **5,** 209, 212.

Poland (*continued*), spread of Sabbatianism in, **5**, 228.
the rabbis of, express willingness to excommunicate Luzzatto, **5**, 241.
the rabbis of, excommunicate Eibeschütz's opponents, **5**, 261.
the Eibeschütz-Emden controversy transplanted to, **5**, 262-3.
subscribers to Mendelssohn's Pentateuch translation in, **5**, 329.
feverish Messianic expectations in, **5**, 377.
power of the Kabbala in, **5**, 382.
dismembered, **5**, 392.
second partition of, **5**, 394.
the rabbis of, oppose the Reform movement, **5**, 571.
Poland, the Jews of, begin the study of the Talmud, **3**, 421.
indispensable to the country, **3**, 613; **4**, 263.
proscribed by the Council of Buda, **3**, 614.
privileges of, extended by Casimir III, **4**, 111.
protected by Casimir III during the Black Death persecutions, **4**, 111, 112.
the liturgy of, compiled by Maharil, **4**, 225.
privileges granted to, by Casimir IV, **4**, 263-5.
privileges of, revoked, **4**, 266.
occupations of, **4**, 418-19.
under Casimir IV, John Albert, Alexander, and Sigismund I, **4**, 419.
supported by the Polish nobility, **4**, 419-20.
culture of, in the sixteenth century, **4**, 633-4.
Poland, the Jews of (*continued*), influenced by Talmud study, **4**, 634.
Talmudic attainments of, **4**, 639-41.
language of, **4**, 641; **5**, 206.
privileges of, **4**, 642-3.
profit by the elective monarchy, **4**, 642.
well treated by Stephen Bathori, **4**, 642-3.
assailed by Klonowicz, **4**, 643.
under Sigismund III, **4**, 643.
organize regular conferences, **4**, 643-5.
influence of the Reformation on, **4**, 647-8.
helped by those of Germany, **4**, 707-8.
persecuted at the instigation of the Jesuits, **5**, 1.
made tax farmers in Cossack districts, **5**, 3.
form a state within the state, **5**, 3-4.
devoted to the study of the Talmud, **5**, 4-6.
help to enslave the Cossacks, **5**, 6.
slain by the Cossacks, **5**, 6.
plundered and murdered by Tartars and Cossacks, **5**, 7-8.
sufferings of, from the Haidamaks, **5**, 8-10, 11-12.
protected by Vishnioviecki, **5**, 10.
banishment of, from Cossack provinces, stipulated by Chmielnicki, **5**, 12.
banished from the Cossack provinces, **5**, 12.
attacked by the Cossacks, **5**, 14.
rights of, guarded in the second treaty with Chmielnicki, **5**, 14.

Poland, the Jews of (*continued*), suffering of, from Russians and Cossacks, **5,** 14–15.
suffering of, in the Swedish war, **5,** 15.
ill-used by Czarnicki, **5,** 15.
ill-used by Ragoczi, **5,** 15.
losses of, during the Cossack wars, **5,** 15.
as fugitives in Europe, **5,** 15–16.
spread their method of Talmud study throughout Europe, **5,** 16–17.
poverty of, **5,** 205–6.
fill the rabbinates of Europe, **5,** 206.
suffer during the Confederation War, **5,** 387–8.

Poland, the Sabbatians of, encouraged by the Eibeschütz controversy, **5,** 272.
Jacob Frank the leader of, **5,** 273.
scoff at Rabbinical Judaism, **5,** 276.
See Frankists, the.

Poland, Greater, adopts the Jewish statute of Frederick the Valiant, **3,** 569.
the Jews of, represented in the Synod of the Four Countries, **4,** 644.

Poland, Little, the Jews of, represented in the Synod of the Four Countries, **4,** 644.

Poland, Southern, the Karaites emigrate from, **4,** 269.

Polemical works against Christianity, by Jews in Spain in the seventh century, **3,** 50–1.
under Wamba, **3,** 105.
by Joseph Kimchi, **3,** 392–3.
by Solomon ben Adret, **3,** 623.
by Shem-Tob ben Isaac Shaprut, **4,** 142.
by Solomon Bonfed, **4,** 182.

Polemical works against Christianity (*continued*), by Joshua Vives, **4,** 187.
by Profiat Duran, **4,** 188–90.
by Isaac ben Kalonymos, **4,** 234.
by Joseph Ibn-Shem Tob, **4,** 235.
by Chayim Ibn-Musa, **4,** 237.
by Simon and Solomon Duran, **4,** 237–8.
by Abraham Farissol, **4,** 413.
by Isaac Troki, **4,** 648.
by Jacob Jehuda Leon (?), **4,** 691–2.

Polemon, prince of Cilicia, allied with Agrippa I, **2,** 196.
husband of Berenice, **2,** 235.

Polish Jews in intercourse with Mendelssohn, **5,** 317–18.

Polish translation of the Bible, **4,** 647.

Poll-tax (Leibzoll), the, on Jews, levied by Domitian, **2,** 388–9.
reduced by Nerva, **2,** 391–2.
paid by the Babylonian Jews, **2,** 508; **3,** 5.
imposed by Wenceslaus, **4,** 166.
removed by Joseph II, **5,** 357.
the abolition of, agitated in Prussia, **5,** 414.
partially abolished in Prussia, **5,** 415.
abolished in France and Austria, **5,** 415.
abrogated by Louis XVI in France, **5,** 432.
objected to by the Dutch Jews in Germany, **5,** 458.
abrogated by Austria and Prussia, **5,** 464.
imposed upon foreign Jews in Germany, **5,** 464.
objected to by the French government, **5,** 465.
removed in several small German states, **5,** 465.

Poll-tax (Leibzoll), the (*continued*), the removal of, agitated before the Congress of Ratisbon, **5,** 466.
the agitation against, led by Jacobson and Breidenbach, **5,** 466–7.
abolished in Brunswick Lüneburg, **5,** 467.
the agitation against by Breidenbach, **5,** 467–8.
abolished in some districts, **5,** 468.
not completely abolished, **5,** 472.
paid by Jews in Lübeck, **5,** 506.
in Bremen, **5,** 507.
retained in Saxony, **5,** 509.
See also Tax.
Polonnoie, the Jews of, massacred by the Cossacks, **5,** 11.
Polygamy, forbidden by Gershom ben Jehuda, **3,** 244.
the abrogation of Gershom ben Jehuda's ordinance on, **3,** 378.
discussed by the Assembly of Jewish Notables, **5,** 489, 491.
discussed by the Synhedrion, **5,** 497.
Polytheism, effects of, **5,** 709.
Pompey, legate of, in Judæa, **2,** 61–2.
bribed by Aristobulus II, **2,** 62–3.
summons Hyrcanus II and Aristobulus II to Damascus, **2,** 63.
favors Hyrcanus II, **2,** 64.
takes the field against Aristobulus II, **2,** 64.
besieges Jerusalem, **2,** 64–6.
enters the Holy of Holies, **2,** 66.
makes Hyrcanus II ethnarch, **2,** 66.
Pompey (*continued*), treats Judæa as a conquered province, **2,** 67.
a member of the first triumvirate, **2,** 73.
partisans of, poison Aristobulus II, **2,** 75.
Pons Judæorum in Rome, **2,** 68.
Pontus, the soldiery of Vibius Marsus banished to, **2,** 197.
Popes, the, tolerant of the Jews, **3,** 25, 33.
denounced by Arnold of Brescia, **3,** 370.
fugitive, convene Church Councils in France, **3,** 376–7.
employ Jewish physicians, **3,** 628; **4,** 200, 407–8, 411, 515, 569.
in Avignon, tolerate the Jews after their banishment by Charles VI, **4,** 177.
See also Bulls; Papacy, the.
Porcelain, forced on the Berlin Jews, **5,** 415.
Porobischa, the Jews of, surrender to the Tartars, **5,** 8.
Portugal, Jews in, in the twelfth century, **3,** 384.
union of, with Castile, **4,** 161.
Marranos escape to, from the Inquisition, **4,** 318.
Jewish exiles from Spain go to, **4,** 352.
the Spanish exiles in, **4,** 365–81.
fever for discoveries in, **4,** 368.
the Spanish exiles leave, **4,** 369.
Spanish exiles sold as slaves in, **4,** 371.
exiles from, form a congregation in Constantinople, **4,** 402.
considered a refuge for Marranos, **4,** 486.

Portugal (*continued*), the plague in, attributed to the Marranos, **4**, 486, 487.
Marranos a profitable population to, **4**, 527–8.
autos-da-fé in, **5**, 91.
discusses the re-admission of Jews, **5**, 532.
Portugal, the Jews of, in the thirteenth century, **3**, 617–18.
under Ferdinand I, **4**, 158–9.
under João I, **4**, 173.
spared Vincent Ferrer's propaganda, **4**, 218.
prosperity of, under Alfonso V, **4**, 338–9.
oppose the settlement of the Spanish exiles, **4**, 366.
kindly treated by Manoel, **4**, 372.
banished, **4**, 374.
delay departure, **4**, 374–5.
children of, baptized, **4**, 375–6.
urged to accept Christianity, **4**, 377–8.
depart, **4**, 380–1.
in the Netherlands, **4**, 662.
See also Marranos, the Portuguese.
Porphyry (Malchus), philosopher, writes a commentary on Daniel, **2**, 502.
Portaleone, Guglielmo. *See* Guglielmo di Portaleone.
Portalis, imperial commissioner to the Assembly of Jewish Notables, **5**, 485.
Porteiro jurado, Jewish-Portuguese sheriff, **4**, 159.
Porto, Jewish center in Portugal, **4**, 159.
Posen, the Jewish charter burnt at, **4**, 263.
number of the Jews of, **4**, 632.
the Jews of, protected by Stephen Bathori, **4**, 642.
Posen (*continued*), the German population of, **5**, 3.
Mendelssohn's Pentateuch translation forbidden in, **5**, 332.
the rabbi of, opposes the Reform movement, **5**, 571.
Posidonius, Nicanor's envoy to Judas Maccabæus, **1**, 484.
Posidonius, Stoic philosopher, maligns Judaism, **2**, 178.
Posquières, the Jews of, in the twelfth century, **3**, 399.
Potocki, Polish general, delivered to the Tartars by the Cossacks, **5**, 7.
Potocki, the house of, controls Cossack colonization, **5**, 3.
Prague, Joseph Delmedigo at, **5**, 80.
rabbis of, Poles, **5**, 206.
refuses to admit Chayon, **5**, 231.
Eibeschütz as teacher in, **5**, 249.
occupied by Charles VII, **5**, 251.
appoints no rabbi, **5**, 566.
the Talmud school of, closed, **5**, 567.
Prague, the Jews of, suffering of, during the first crusade, **3**, 305.
charged with host desecration, **4**, 164–6.
massacred, **4**, 165.
attacked on account of the Alenu prayer, **4**, 178.
plundered, **4**, 417.
lack of rabbinical learning among, **4**, 418.
exiled by Ferdinand I, **4**, 544, 586.
deprived of their prayer books, **4**, 584.
suffer from fire, **4**, 585.
in bad repute, **4**, 585–6.

Prague, the Jews of (*continued*), appeal to Pius IV, **4,** 586.
recalled, **4,** 587.
submit disputes to the Polish Talmudists, **4,** 639.
number of, in the seventeenth century, **4,** 694.
accuse Lipmann Heller, **4,** 704–5.
participation of, in the Thirty Years' War, **4,** 707.
suffering of, on being banished, **5,** 252.
restrictions against, **5,** 253.
welcome Joseph II's reforms, **5,** 370.
establish a secular school, **5,** 371.
modify their divine service, **5,** 582.
Prayer, the order of, introduced by the Sopherim, **1,** 401.
mystical importance of, in the Kabbala, **3,** 553–4.
book, Karaite, **4,** 71.
devotion in, emphasized in Lurya's Kabbala, **4,** 626.
See also Liturgy, the.
"**Prayer Book** for Israelites," compiled by the Reform Temple Union in Hamburg, **5,** 673.
the use of, forbidden by Chacham Bernays, **5,** 673.
Prayer books. *See under* Confiscation; Liturgy.
Prayers, penitential, commemorating the Cossack massacres, **5,** 13.
Prayers for rain, **2,** 492, 541–2, 579.
Prayers, set, introduced by Gamaliel II, **2,** 363.
See also Liturgy, the.
Press, the, censorship of, introduced by Caraffa, **4,** 563.
Prester John, alluded to, **4,** 368.
Preteau, president of the National Assembly, on the emancipation of the Jews, **5,** 440–1.
Priesthood, the, defended by Jesus Sirach, **1,** 440–1.
Priests, the, at Shiloh, **1,** 57.
under Samuel, **1,** 79.
under Ahaz abet licentiousness and idolatry, **1,** 261.
recalled to the Temple under Josiah, **1,** 289.
instigate an attack on Jeremiah, **1,** 302–3.
carry the Pentateuch into captivity with them, **1,** 334.
abandon the Temple after the sack of Jerusalem by Apollonius, **1,** 454.
re-instated by the Maccabees, **1,** 473.
members of the Hellenist party, **1,** 489.
fugitive, officiate in the Temple of Onias, **1,** 508.
See also Aaronides, the; High priests, the; Levites, the.
Primates, heads of the Jewish communities of Palestine, **2,** 612, 613.
Primo, Samuel, private secretary of Sabbataï Zevi, accompanies him to Smyrna, **5,** 133.
spreads abroad the Messiah's fame, **5,** 137.
wishes to modify the Rabbinical system, **5,** 142.
abolishes the Fast of Tebeth, **5,** 143.
accompanies Sabbataï to Constantinople, **5,** 146.
spreads reports of Sabbataï's reception at Constantinople, **5,** 147–8.
accompanies Sabbataï to his Abydos prison, **5,** 148.

Primo, Samuel (*continued*), proposes capital punishment for the Kofrim, **5**, 150.
abolishes the Fast of Tammuz, **5**, 151.
clings to Sabbataï after his apostasy, **5**, 156.
proves Sabbataï the true Messiah through his conversion, **5**, 157–8.
and Chayim Malach, **5**, 213.
and Nehemiah Chayon, **5**, 216.

Prince, title of the president of the Synhedrion, **2**, 334.

"Prince and the Dervish, The," moral romance by Abraham Ibn-Chasdaï, **3**, 388, 560.

Princes of the Captivity, the. *See* Exilarchate, the; Exilarchs, the.

Printing, the art of, among the Jews of Italy in the fifteenth century, **4**, 289.

Printing presses, Hebrew, in Italy, **4**, 289.
in Prague, **4**, 418.
at Isny, **4**, 474.
at Ferrara closed, **4**, 580.
of the Soncin family, **4**, 586.
established by Reyna Nassi, **4**, 628.
in Amsterdam, **4**, 675.
in Altona, **5**, 255.
in Berlin, **5**, 416.

Priscus, name borne by Gallic Jews, **3**, 36.

Procopius, historian, on the bravery of the Jews of Naples, **3**, 32.

Procurator, the, title of the representative of Imperial Rome in Judæa, **2**, 128.
duties of, **2**, 129.
installs the high priests, **2**, 129.

Procurators of Judæa, the, list of:

Ambivius, Marcus	Festus,
Albinus,	Florus, Gessius
Coponius,	Gratus, Valerius
Cumanus,	Pilate, Pontius
Fadus, Cuspius	Rufus, Annius
Felix,	Tiberius Julius Alexander.

See also Judæa, the Roman governors of; Syria, the Roman governors of.

Profiat (Profatius). *See* Jacob ben Machir Tibbon.

Profiat Duran (Isaac ben Moses, Efodi), Marrano, scholar, returns to Judaism, **4**, 188.
attacks Christianity, **4**, 188–90, 235.
commentaries, mathematical work, and grammar by, **4**, 191.

Prophecies, the, before the exile, summed up, **1**, 335.

Prophecy, meaning of, **1**, 14–15.
displaced by the written law, **1**, 385.
as explained in the "Guide of the Perplexed," **3**, 482–3.
in Maimonides' system, **3**, 523.

"Prophet of Samaria," Elisha, **1**, 218.

Prophet, the, of the Captivity, Isaiah the Babylonian, **1**, 345.

Prophets, the, activity of, under Jehoiakim, **1**, 301.
characteristics of, **5**, 719.

Prophets, the associations of, **1**, 205.
development of, under Jeroboam II, **1**, 234.

Prophets, the, the writings of, carried into the Babylonian exile, **1**, 334.
collected by the Sopherim, **1**, 400.

Prophets, the, the writings of (*continued*), rejected by the Samaritans, **1,** 400.
Chaldaic translation of, **2,** 131.
translated into Chaldaic by Joseph ben Chiya, **2,** 581–2.
commentaries on, by Joseph Kara, **3,** 346.
contain philosophical doctrines, **3,** 479.

Prophets, the, list of:

Ahijah of Shilo,
Amos,
Deborah,
Elijah,
Elisha,
Ezekiel,
Gad,
Habakkuk,
Haggai,
Hosea (I),
Hosea (II),
Huldah,
Isaiah, son of Amoz,
Isaiah the Babylonian,
Jeremiah,
Joel,
Jonah,
Malachi,
Micah (II),
Michaiah (Micah I),
Moses,
Nathan,
Obadiah,
Shemaiah,
Uriah,
Zechariah I,
Zechariah II,
Zephaniah.

"**Prophets** of the Old Testament, The," by Ewald, **5,** 696.

Prophets, the Earlier, four historical books in the Scriptures, **1,** 400.
commentary on, by Isaac Abrabanel, **4,** 342–3.

Prophets, the false, under Ahaz, **1,** 262.
under Manasseh, **1,** 283.
under Jehoiakim, **1,** 300.
instigate an attack upon Jeremiah, **1,** 302–3.
urge Zedekiah to revolt, **1,** 310.

Prophets, the Later, fifteen prophetical books in the Scriptures, **1,** 400.

Prophets, the Twelve, commentary on, by Abraham Ibn-Ezra, **3,** 373.

"**Proposals** in Favor of the Jews," pamphlet by Grégoire, **5,** 437.

Prosbol, the statute concerning debts, enacted under Hillel, **2,** 100.

Proselytes, standing of, according to Ezra, **1,** 367.
various authorities on the admission of, **2,** 384–5.
true, in the daily prayers, **2,** 384.
severely treated by Domitian, **2,** 388–9.
under Nerva, **2,** 391–2.
See also Circumcision; Conversions to Judaism.

Proselytes, list of:
Fulvia, Roman patrician, **2,** 136, 215.
the royal house of Adiabene, **2,** 194, 216–19.
Polemon of Cilicia, **2,** 235.
Aziz of Emesa, **2,** 235.
Akylas, **2,** 385.
Clemens, Flavius, **2,** 387.
the inhabitants of Machuza, **2,** 507, 586–8.
Issor, **2,** 587–8.
Abraham, a monk, **3,** 21.
the kings of the Jewish-Himyarite empire, **3,** 51.
Arab tribes before the sixth century, **3,** 61.
Abu-Kariba, **3,** 62–3.
Harith Ibn-Amru, **3,** 63.
the Kendites, **3,** 63.
Waraka Ibn-Naufal, **3,** 71.
the Chazars, **3,** 139–41.
Bodo, bishop, **3,** 168–70.
Wecelinus, chaplain, **3,** 245.
the inhabitants of the Moshic hills in Armenia, **3,** 439–40.
a dignitary of the Church in England, **3,** 516.
Redingge, Robert de, **3,** 640–1.

Proselytes, list of (*continued*),
La Asumçao, Diogo de, **4**, 668–70.
Speeth, John Peter, **5**, 177–8.
See also Circumcision; Conversions to Judaism.
Proselytism, Manasseh ben Israel exonerates the Jews from, **5**, 42.
Prosnitz, Chayon at, **5**, 218.
Protection-Jews (Schutz-Juden), in Hamburg, **4**, 688.
Mendelssohn one of the, **5**, 304.
an insulting epithet in Westphalia, **5**, 500.
in Lübeck, **5**, 506.
abolished in Prussia, **5**, 507.
Protestant Reformation, the. *See* Reformation, the Protestant.
Protestantism hostile to the Jews, **4**, 552.
Provence, the Talmudists of, use the works of Maimonides, **3**, 624.
French Jews expelled by Philip IV, settle in, **4**, 49.
Marranos flee to, from the Inquisition, **4**, 318.
Provence, the Jews of, dependent on vassal princes, **3**, 242.
culture of, in the twelfth century, **3**, 373, 389–91.
use Jacob Anatoli's Malmed, **3**, 566.
neglect Jewish studies, **4**, 133.
persecuted in 1392, **4**, 173.
presented to the Church, **4**, 175.
Proverbs, the, collected and amplified under Hezekiah, **1**, 279.
carried into the Babylonian exile, **1**, 335.
produced during the exile, **1**, 341.
Provost, title of the chief Jewish officer in France in the twelfth century, **3**, 343.
Prussia, the Protestant Reformation in, **4**, 469.
at war with Austria, **5**, 251.
willing to grant citizenship to the Jews, **5**, 518.
protects the Frankfort Jews, **5**, 520.
hatred of Jews in, **5**, 524–5.
in the Quadruple Alliance, **5**, 658.
Prussia, the Jews of, under Frederick I, **5**, 190–1.
prejudice aroused against, **5**, 191.
the "general privilege" issued for, **5**, 304.
make efforts to obtain political rights, **5**, 414–16.
restrictions against, **5**, 415.
decay of morality among, **5**, 419–20, 422.
apostasy among, **5**, 420.
continued abasement of, **5**, 461.
freed from the poll-tax, **5**, 464.
mourn over the national defeats, **5**, 495.
patriotism of, **5**, 507.
partial emancipation of, **5**, 507.
in the French wars, **5**, 511, 518.
the emancipation of, a dead letter, **5**, 524.
laws for, **5**, 524.
restricted in commerce, **5**, 524–5.
forbidden to bear Christian names, **5**, 630.
Prynne, William, publishes an anti-Jewish pamphlet, **5**, 45–6.
Psalm, at the celebration of Passover in Jerusalem, **1**, 295–6.

Psalm (*continued*), of the return from the Captivity, **1**, 352.
LXXII, commentary on, by Juan de España, **4**, 233.
Psalms, composed in celebration of Sennacherib's failure, **1**, 278.
in honor of Hezekiah, **1**, 279.
penitential, originate among the Babylonian exiles, **1**, 337.
produced during the Captivity, **1**, 340.
Psalms, the, carried into the Babylonian exile, **1**, 335.
introduced into the Temple service, **1**, 401.
homiletic exposition of, by Cassiodorus, **3**, 31.
the singing of, at Jewish funerals forbidden, **3**, 47.
certain of, attributed to a late period by Moses Ibn-G'ikatilia, **3**, 290.
commentary on, by Abraham Ibn-Ezra, **3**, 373.
translated into Spanish by Templo, **5**, 115.
translated into Spanish by Lopez Laguna, **5**, 203.
imitated by Moses Chayim Luzzatto, **5**, 234.
Mendelssohn's translation of, **5**, 335.
translated by Sachs, **5**, 693.
Psammetich, king of Egypt, propitiates the Scythians, **1**, 287.
Psusennes, king of Egypt, Solomon marries the daughter of, **1**, 161.
Psychics. *See* Gnosticism.
Ptolemais. *See* Accho.
Ptolemy, of Chalcis, protects Aristobulus II's family, **2**, 75.
Ptolemy, of Chalcis (*continued*), son-in-law of Aristobulus II, **2**, 75.
conspires against Herod and Phasael, **2**, 80–1.
Ptolemy I Soter, of Egypt, conquers Cœlesyria, **1**, 416.
opposed by Antigonus, **1**, 417.
defeats Antigonus, **1**, 417–18.
protects the Judæans, **1**, 418.
Ptolemy II Philadelphus, of Egypt, threatens to divide Judæa among foreign colonists, **1**, 423.
and the Septuagint, **1**, 514.
Ptolemy III Euergetes, of Egypt, makes Joseph tax-gatherer, **1**, 425.
Ptolemy IV Philopator, of Egypt, retains Joseph, son of Tobiah, in office, **1**, 425.
defeats Antiochus the Great, **1**, 426.
introduces bacchanalian revelries, **1**, 428.
son of, **1**, 429.
favors Hyrcanus, **1**, 430.
death of, **1**, 432.
Ptolemy V Epiphanes, of Egypt, Cœlesyria re-conquered for, **1**, 433.
makes Hyrcanus governor of trans-Jordanic territory, **1**, 437.
Ptolemy VI Philometor, of Egypt, treaty of, with Antiochus Epiphanes, **1**, 450.
proclaimed king, **1**, 452.
daughter of, marries Alexander Balas, **1**, 496.
receives Onias IV kindly, **1**, 506.
ally of Demetrius I, **1**, 506.
struggle of, with Ptolemy Physcon, **1**, 506–7.
assisted by the Judæans, **1**, 507.

Ptolemy VI Philometor (*continued*), presents Onias IV with land for a Temple, **1,** 508.
permits Onias IV to fortify his Temple, **1,** 510.
entrusts the Egyptian ports to Onias IV, **1,** 510.
causes a Greek translation of the Law to be made, **1,** 510–11.
appoints a conference between the Judæans and the Samaritans, **1,** 517.
death of, **1,** 518.
heir of, slain, **1,** 518.
Ptolemy VII Physcon, of Egypt, proclaimed king, **1,** 450.
reconciled with his brother, **1,** 452.
conspires against Ptolemy VI, **1,** 506, 507.
Cyrene given to, **1,** 507.
marries Cleopatra, his brother's widow, **1,** 518.
cruelty of, **1,** 518–19.
revenge of, on the Judæans, **1,** 519.
as author, **1,** 519.
supports Alexander Zabina, **2,** 6.
Ptolemy VIII Lathurus, of Egypt, aids Antiochus IX, **2,** 10–11.
flees from Alexandria, **2,** 12.
defeats Alexander Jannæus, **2,** 40.
ravages Judæa, **2,** 40.
retreats to Cyprus, **2,** 41.
Ptolemy, astronomer, work of, translated into Arabic, **3,** 146.
Ptolemy, brother of Nicolaus of Damascus, and Herod's will, **2,** 119.
Ptolemy ben Habub, son-in-law of Simon Tharsi, governor of Jericho, **1,** 530.
assassinates Simon Tharsi at Dok, **1,** 530.
meditates treachery against John Hyrcanus, **1,** 530–1.
shuts himself up in Dok, **1,** 531.
besieged by John Hyrcanus, **2,** 2–3.
Ptolemy, son of **Dorymenes,** general under Lysias, **1,** 466.
Ptolemy Macron, advocate of the Judæans at the Syrian court, **1,** 476–7, 478.
Publicans, the, addressed by Jesus, **2,** 152.
Pucci, Antonio, cardinal of Santiquatro, grand penitentiary of the pope, instrumental in the establishment of the Portuguese Inquisition, **4,** 507.
on the commission on the Portuguese Inquisition, **4,** 514.
opposed to the Marranos, **4,** 516.
Pucci, Lorenzo, grand penitentiary of the pope, attached to Molcho, **4,** 503.
opposes the establishment of the Portuguese Inquisition, **4,** 505.
death of, **4,** 507.
Puffendorf, John, interested in the Karaites, **5,** 183.
Pul, king of Assyria, invades the kingdom of Israel, **1,** 246–7.
Menahem of Israel submits to, **1,** 247.
Pulcelina, innocently causes a persecution of the Jews of Blois, **3,** 379.
saved by Theobald of Chartres, **3,** 379.

Pulcelina (*continued*), death of, **3,** 380.
Pumbeditha, a district of Jewish Babylonia, **2,** 505.
Pumbeditha, capital of Jewish Babylonia, description of, **2,** 506.
cunning of the inhabitants of, **2,** 506.
homage paid at, to the Exilarchs, **2,** 607.
Pumbeditha, the academy of, superior to the Palestinian academies, **2,** 532.
founded by Judah ben Ezekiel, **2,** 545, 549.
pre-eminence of, **2,** 549–50.
method pursued at, **2,** 574–5.
numerical strength of, **2,** 576–7.
prosperity of, under Rabba bar Nachmani, **2,** 578.
fund established for, **2,** 580.
generosity of Ifra-Ormuzd to, **2,** 581.
under Abayi Nachmani, **2,** 584–5.
produces the Talmud, **2,** 591.
rise of, **2,** 593.
during Ashi's time, **2,** 606.
closed under Hormisdas IV, **3,** 8.
re-opened under Bahram Tshubin, **3,** 9.
prosperity of, under Chosru II, **3,** 9.
districts under the jurisdiction of, **3,** 98.
quarrels in, about the principalship, **3,** 155–6.
gains by the decline of the Exilarchate, **3,** 177, 183.
independent of the Exilarch, **3,** 177.
claims an increase of revenue, **3,** 184.
inferior to Sora, **3,** 193.
Pumbeditha, the academy of (*continued*), importance of, under Aaron Ibn-Sarjadu, **3,** 202, 207.
decay of, under Sherira, **3,** 233.
place of, taken by the Spanish schools, **3,** 236.
dissolution of, **3,** 253.
Isaac Ibn-Sakni teacher at, **3,** 285.
See also Academies, the Babylonian.
Pumbeditha, the academy of, principals of, poor, **2,** 580.
office of, religious, **3,** 93.
bear the title of Gaon by courtesy, **3,** 93, 177.
elected from among the members of Sora, **3,** 94.
at the installation of an Exilarch, **3,** 94–5.
rank of, **3,** 96.
appoint the judges of their district, **3,** 98.
Pumbeditha, the academy of, the principals of (Geonim), list of:
Aaron Ibn-Sarjadu,
Abayi Nachmani,
Chama of Nahardea,
Chanan of Iskia,
Chaninaï,
Chiskiya,
Dudaï ben Nachman,
Haï ben David,
Haï ben Sherira,
Huna ben Chiya,
José,
Joseph bar Abba,
Joseph ben Chiya,
Kohen Zedek II ben Joseph,
Malka bar Acha,
Mar-Abraham ben Sherira,
Mari bar Mar,
Mar-Raba,
Mar-Zemach I ben Paltoi,
Nachman ben Isaac,
Natronaï ben Nehemiah,
Nehemiah,
Paltoi ben Abayi,
Raba bar Joseph bar Chama,

Pumbeditha, the academy of, the principals of (Geonim), list of (*continued*):
Rabba bar Nachmani,
Rabba ben Ami,
Semuna,
Sherira ben Chanina,
Zemach ben Kafnaï.
Puoto. *See* Bodo.
Purgation, the oath of, introduced by Nachman ben Jacob, **2,** 556.
Purgatory, the dogma of, in the Kabbala, **4,** 292.
Purim, pleasantry on, punished by Theodosius II, **2,** 620–1.
treatise on, by Kalonymos ben Kalonymos, **4,** 63.
Purim (*continued*), the feast of, ridiculed by Solomon Levi, **4,** 185.
Purim of Cairo, 4, 396.
Purim-Vincent celebrated in Frankfort, **4,** 700.
Puritans, the, obtain religious liberty for England, **5,** 26.
inspired by the Old Testament, **5,** 26.
regard the Jews kindly, **5,** 27.
Jewish spirit among, **5,** 27–8.
Pyrenees, the, Jews defend the passes of, **3,** 45.
Pyrenees, the **Lower,** the department of, the Jews of, excepted from Napoleon's restrictive laws, **5,** 499.

Q

Quadratus, Church teacher, demonstrates the independence of Christianity from Judaism, **2,** 431.
Quadratus, Umidius, governor of Syria, arbiter between Judæans and Samaritans, **2,** 244.
Quadruple Alliance, the, against France, **5,** 658.
Quemadero, place of burning, in Seville, **4,** 317.
Querido, Jacob. *See* Jacob Querido.
Quietus, Lucius, Trajan's commander in the district of the Euphrates, **2,** 397.
lays waste Babylonian towns, **2,** 398.
Quietus, Lucius (*continued*), governor of Palestine, **2,** 399.
desired by Trajan as his successor, **2,** 399.
war of, in Judæa, **2,** 400–1.
destroys the Synhedrion in Jamnia, **2,** 400.
removal of, asked by the Jews, **2,** 400–1.
execution of, **2,** 401.
Quinon, Denis, receiver-general of taxes in Languedoc, **4,** 132.
Quirinius, governor of Syria, instructions of, with regard to Judæa, **2,** 129.
deposes the high priest, **2,** 135.

R

Rab. *See* Abba Areka.
Raba. *See* Mar-Raba.
Raba bar Joseph bar Chama (299–352), Babylonian Amora, **2,** 560.
Raba bar Joseph bar Chama (*continued*), informed of calendar changes, **2,** 571.
disciple of Rabba bar Nachmani, **2,** 575, 580.

Raba bar Joseph bar Chama (*continued*), proposed as principal of the Pumbeditha academy, **2**, 583.
precocity of, **2**, 584.
rival of Abayi Nachmani, **2**, 584–5.
dialectics of, **2**, 585, 591.
principal of the Pumbeditha academy, **2**, 585.
characteristics of, **2**, 585–6.
rebukes Zeïra II, **2**, 586.
and the Machuzan marriages, **2**, 587.
covetousness of, **2**, 587–8.
heartlessness of, **2**, 588.
partiality of, in applying the Law, **2**, 588–9, 628.
and Benjamin Assia, **2**, 590.
discourses of, popular, **2**, 590.
method of, **2**, 590–1.
authority of, **2**, 591.
prevents persecutions, **2**, 591–2.
punished by Shabur II for exercising criminal jurisdiction, **2**, 592.
assisted by Ifra-Ormuzd, **2**, 592.
death of, **2**, 593, 602.
Rab Abba. *See* Rabba bar Huna.
Rabaï of Rob, a Saburean, **3**, 5.
Rabba bar Abbahu, a Babylonian Amora, **2**, 545.
Rabba bar Chana, authorized by Judah I to teach, **2**, 454.
Rabba bar Huna (Rab Abba, 309–320), principal of the Sora academy, **2**, 548, 583.
modesty of, **2**, 585.
Rabba bar Matana, Amora, proposed as principal of the Pumbeditha academy, **2**, 583.
Rabba bar Nachmani (270–330), Babylonian Amora, **2**, 560.
dialectics of, **2**, 575, 576.
Raba bar Nachmani (*continued*), a member of the family of Eli, **2**, 575.
brothers of, **2**, 575–6.
emigrates to Judæa, **2**, 576.
returns to Babylonia, **2**, 576.
proposed as the principal of the academy of Pumbeditha, **2**, 576.
and Joseph ben Chiya, **2**, 577.
principal of Pumbeditha, **2**, 578.
subjects treated by, **2**, 578.
method of, **2**, 578–9.
position of, among students of the Law, **2**, 579.
rebukes the immorality of the Jews, **2**, 579.
and Mar-Ukban, **2**, 579.
death of, **2**, 580–1.
foster-father of Abayi Nachmani, **2**, 583.
Rabba ben Ami (869–872), Gaon of Pumbeditha, **3**, 178.
Rabban, title of the president of the Synhedrion in his capacity as teacher of the Law, **2**, 335.
Rabbana, title of honor in Babylonia, **2**, 544.
title given to Ashi, **2**, 606.
Rabbanism, certain features of, adopted by Benjamin Nahavendi, **3**, 151.
Rabbanites, the, partisans of authority, opponents of the Karaites, **3**, 134.
denounce the Karaites as heretics, **3**, 134.
literary unfruitfulness of, in the eighth century, **3**, 136.
antagonistic to science, **3**, 149.
adopt Karaite teachings, **3**, 157.
begin scientific work in the ninth century, **3**, 180.
shunned by the Karaites, **3**, 182.

Rabbanites, the (*continued*), neglect the Scriptures, **3**, 189.
endeavor to effect a reconciliation with the Karaites, **4**, 69–70, 71–2, 270.
in Jerusalem in the fourteenth century, **4**, 74–5.
teach Karaites, **4**, 269–70.
bigotry of, **4**, 403.
See also Rabbinical Judaism; Talmudical Judaism, etc.
Rabbath Ammon (Philadelphia), capital of the Ammonites, **1**, 126.
taken by David, **1**, 128.
taken by Judas Maccabæus, **1**, 474.
refuge of Ptolemy ben Habub, **2**, 3.
Aretas defeated at, **2**, 62.
Rabbenu, title given to Judah II, **2**, 480.
Rabbi. *See* Judah I ha-Nassi.
Rabbi, title of a teacher of the Law, **2**, 335.
introduction of the title, **2**, 357.
title given to Judah II, **2**, 480.
Rabbi, chief, of England, functions of, **3**, 588.
"**Rabbi of Bacharach**," by Heine, **5**, 549–50, 552.
Rabbinical conference, the, at Brunswick, composition of, **5**, 677–8.
dominated by Holdheim, **5**, 678, 681.
spirit of, **5**, 682.
protests against, **5**, 682.
Rabbinical conference, the, at Frankfort, to ratify the programme of the Berlin Reform Association, **5**, 683.
excitement aroused by, **5**, 683–4.
the orthodox party represented at, **5**, 684, 685.
discusses the abolition of the Hebrew language, **5**, 685.
Rabbinical conference, the, at Frankfort (*continued*), attitude of, towards the Berlin Reform Association, **5**, 685–6.
Rabbinical Judaism proved to rest on unbroken tradition, **3**, 366.
originates in Jacob Asheri's code, **4**, 89.
practical, **4**, 534.
beginnings of the criticism of, **5**, 55.
defended by Immanuel Aboab, **5**, 55.
attacked and defended by Leo Modena, **5**, 72–4.
attacked by Joseph Delmedigo, **5**, 77.
as viewed by Sabbatians, **5**, 142, 143–4.
guarded by the Kofrim, **5**, 144.
at variance with the Kabbala, **5**, 144.
set at defiance by Sabbataï Zevi, **5**, 148–9, 152, 159.
exalted by Richard Simon, **5**, 180.
attacked by Mordecai ben Nissan, **5**, 184.
destruction of, aimed at by Chayim Malach, **5**, 214.
opposed by the Frankists, **5**, 274–5.
scoffed at in Poland, **5**, 276.
opposed by the Kabbala, **5**, 277.
attacked by Mendelssohn's followers, **5**, 371, 375, 379.
attacked by the Chassidim, **5**, 375, 379.
inadequacy of, **5**, 385.
undermined by Holdheim, **5**, 680–1.
See also Talmudical Judaism.
Rabbinical literature, studied by Christians, **5**, 21–2, 179.

Rabbinical schools, established in Poland by German exiles, **4**, 420. *See under* Colleges.

Rabbinical synod, the, of Konstantinov, appeals to Jacob Emden, **5**, 277.
of Lublin, decision of, on cases of supposed death, **5**, 13.
of Mayence, decision of, on commercial honesty, **3**, 517.
of Mayence, on the marriage law, **4**, 135.
of Nuremberg, taxes the Bavarian Jews, **4**, 305.
of Weissenfels, **4**, 163.
of Worms, rejoices over the Dominican defeat, **4**, 452-3.

Rabbinical synod, the first, under the presidency of Jacob Tam, **3**, 376-7.
members of, **3**, 377.
resolutions of, **3**, 377.

Rabbinical synods, instituted, **3**, 376-7.
the Italian, **4**, 218.
See also under Rabbinical conference.

Rabbis, the, disinterestedness of, in the Middle Ages, **3**, 287.
superior to other religious leaders in the twelfth century, **3**, 347.
high morality of, in the fourteenth century, **4**, 162.
compared with the Christian clergy, **4**, 162.
characteristics of, in the seventeenth century, **5**, 200-1.
of Europe, recruited from Poland, **5**, 206.
lack of culture among, **5**, 559.
not respected, **5**, 566.

Rabbis, lists of:
of Alexandria:
Aaron ben Zion Ibn-Alamâni,
Phineas ben Meshullam.

Rabbis, lists of (*continued*):
of Algiers:
Isaac ben Sheshet Barfat
Simon ben Zemach Duran,
Simon Duran II,
Solomon Duran.

of Alkolea de Cinca:
En-Zag Vidal de Tolosa.

of Amsterdam:
Aboab, Isaac, de Fonseca,
Ayllon, Solomon
Manasseh ben Israel,
Morteira, Saul Levi
Musaphia, Benjamin
Pardo, David
Pardo, Joseph
Pardo, Josiah
Uziel, Isaac
Vega, Judah
Weil, Moses
Zevi Ashkenazi.

of Arad:
Chorin, Aaron.

of Barcelona:
Solomon ben Abraham ben Adret
Nissim Gerundi ben Reuben.

of Berlin:
Fränkel, David
Hirschel, Lewin
Sachs, Michael
Wolf, Aaron Benjamin.

of Béziers:
Meshullam.

of Bologna:
Ishmael Chanina.

of Breslau:
Phineas.

of Brunswick:
Eger, Samuel.

of Cairo:
Algazi, Moses Joseph
David Ibn-Abi Zimra,
Moses ben Maimun.

of Canea:
Delmedigo, Judah
Elias ben Elkanah Kapsali

of Castile:
Abraham Senior,
Meïr Alguades.

Rabbis, lists of (*continued*):
of Casale:
Baki, Simon.
of Château-Thierry:
Samuel ben Solomon.
of Cuito:
Nepi, Graziadio.
of Cologne:
Eleazer ben Samson.
of Constantinople:
Elias Mizrachi,
Fresco, Moses
Moses Kapsali.
of Cordova:
Abu-Amr Joseph ben Zadik Ibn-Zadik,
Joseph ben Jacob Ibn-Sahal.
of Damascus:
Anteri, Jacob
Halfen, Azaria
Halfen, Solomon.
of Fez:
Jacob Berab.
of France:
Johanan ben Mattathiah Provenci,
Matthiah ben Joseph Provenci.
of Frankfort:
Falk, Jacob Joshua
Hurwitz, Phineas Levi
Kahana, Jacob.
of Germany:
Meïr ben Baruch Halevi.
of Gerona:
Moses ben Nachman.
of Hamburg:
Athias, Isaac
Bernays, Isaac
Salomon, Gotthold.
of Jampol:
Landau, Ezekiel.
of Jerusalem:
Levi ben Jacob Chabib,
Obadiah di Bertinoro.
of Joigny:
Menachem ben Perez.

Rabbis, lists of (*continued*):
of Leghorn:
Cohen, Malachi
Samun.
of Lemberg:
Orenstein, Jacob.
of London:
Abendana, Jacob
Ayllon, Solomon
Herschel, Solomon
Jacob,
Meldola, David
Nieto, David
Sasportas, Jacob.
of Lucena:
Isaac ben Jacob Alfassi,
Joseph ben Meïr Ibn-Migash Halevi.
of Mantua:
Brieli, Jehuda Leon
Joseph ben Solomon Kolon,
Judah ben Yechiel,
Vita, Abraham, di Cologna.
of Mayence:
Eleazer ben Nathan,
Jacob ben Moses Mölin Halevi.
of Mecklenburg-Schwerin:
Holdheim, Samuel.
of Melun:
Jehuda ben David.
of Metz:
Eibeschütz, Jonathan
Falk, Jacob Joshua.
of Minsk:
Heilprin, Jechiel.
of Naples:
David Ibn-Yachya.
of Navarre:
Orabuena, Joseph.
of Neustadt:
Shalom.
of Nikolsburg:
Benet, Mordecai.
of Nuremberg:
Sprinz, David.

Rabbis, lists of (*continued*):
of Padua:
Ghirondi,
Judah Menz.
of Palma:
En-Vidal Ephraim Gerundi.
of Pampeluna:
Chayim ben Gallipapa.
of Paris:
Yechiel.
of Perpignan:
Vidal Menachem ben Solomon Meïri.
of Persia:
Sar Shalom.
of Portugal:
Moses Navarro,
Simon Maimi.
of Posen:
Janow, Hirsch.
of Prague:
Avigedor Kara,
Heller, Lipmann
Landau, Ezekiel
Oppenheim, David
Rapoport, Solomon Jehuda.
of Presburg:
Sofer, Moses.
of Ratisbon:
Bruna, Israel.
of Safet:
Moses ben Jehuda Cohen.
of Saint Esprit:
Andrade, Abraham.
of Saragossa:
Isaac ben Sheshet Barfat.
of Sepulveda:
Solomon Picho.
of Smyrna:
Benveniste, Chayim
Papa, Aaron de la.
of Strasburg:
Sinzheim, Joseph David.
of Tamarica:
Lagarto, Jacob.

Rabbis, lists of (*continued*):
of Tarnopol:
Rapoport, Solomon Jehuda.
of the Three Communities:
Cohen, Raphael
Eibeschütz, Jonathan
Katzenellenbogen, Ezekiel.
of Toledo:
Aboab, Isaac
Asher ben Yechiel,
Isaac de Leon,
Jehuda Asheri,
Meïr ben Todros Halevi Abulafia,
Menachem ben Aaron ben Zerach.
of Trieste:
Galaïgo, Joseph Chayim.
of Tudela:
Chasdaï ben Solomon.
of Venice:
Aboab, Samuel
Belillos, Jacob
Cohen, Nehemiah Vital
Merari, Moses Menachem.
of Vercelli:
Segre, Joshua Benzion.
of Vienna:
Eskeles, Issachar Berush
Heller, Lipmann
Jonah,
Mannheimer, Isaac Noah
Meïr ben Baruch Halevi
of Worms:
Kalonymos of Rome.
of Würzburg:
Isaac ben Eliakim.

Rabbis, itinerant:
Conforte, David
Moses of Coucy

Rabbis, the German, insignificance of, in the fourteenth century, **4,** 134-5.
appointed by order of Sigismund, **4,** 227.

Rabbis, the Spanish, hostile to science, **4,** 143.
slight attainments of, **4,** 144.

Rabed II. *See* Abraham ben David.
Rabina (488–499), Amora, principal of the Sora academy, **2**, 630.
completes the Babylonian Talmud, **2**, 630–1.
death of **2**, 631.
Rab-shakeh, Assyrian official sent to Hezekiah, **1**, 274–5.
Rachel, wife of Akiba, **2**, 351, 355.
Rachel Formosa, mistress of Alfonso the Noble, **3**, 386.
Radziwill, prince, employs Joseph Delmedigo as physician, **5**, 76.
Ragesh (Razis), demanded as hostage by Nicanor, **1**, 485.
Ragoczi, Prince of Transylvania, ill-uses the Jews of Poland, **5**, 15.
Raimuch, Astruc. *See* Astruc Raimuch.
Ralbag. *See* Levi ben Gerson.
Ramadhan, the fast of, instituted by Mahomet, **3**, 75.
Ramah, home of Samuel, **1**, 73.
meeting of elders at, **1**, 78.
David at, **1**, 96–7.
taken and fortified by Baasha, **1**, 191.
re-conquered by Asa, **1**, 191.
Jeremiah released at, **1**, 320.
Ramathaim, taken by the Samaritans, **1**, 410.
Rambam. *See* Moses ben Maimun.
Ramban. *See* Moses ben Nachman.
Rameru, the Jews of, attacked during the second crusade, **3**, 355–6.
center of Talmud study, **3**, 403.
Rameses, rallying place of the Israelites on leaving Egypt, **1**, 17.
Rami, brother of Judah ben Ezekiel, his critic and opponent, **2**, 550–1.
Ramon Berengar IV, unites Aragon and Catalonia, **3**, 387.
Ramoth-Gilead taken by Benhadad II, **1**, 205, 206.
Jehu made king of Israel at, **1**, 210.
Ramson, defender of the Jews, **5**, 470.
Raphael, the healer, name of an angel, **1**, 403.
Raphia, Antiochus the Great defeated at, **1**, 426.
south-western limit of Judæa under Alexander Jannæus, **2**, 46.
Rapoport, Solomon Jehuda (1790–1867), founder of the Galician school, **5**, 607.
disciple of Krochmal, **5**, 610.
descent of, **5**, 610.
learning of, **5**, 610–11.
and Erter, **5**, 614.
makes pilgrimages to Krochmal, **5**, 614, 617.
excommunicated, **5**, 614.
rabbinical appointments of, **5**, 615, 619.
style of, **5**, 617.
influence of Krochmal on, **5**, 617–18.
devotes himself to biographical research, **5**, 618–19.
the father of Jewish science, **5**, 619.
system of, used by Zunz, **5**, 620.
contributor to the Kerem Chemed, **5**, 621–2.
inspires Luzzatto, **5**, 624.
influence of, on Sachs, **5**, 690.
Rashba. *See* Solomon ben Abraham ben Adret.
Rashbam. *See* Samuel ben Meïr.
Rashi. *See* Solomon Yizchaki.

Rastadt, the Peace Congress at, to abolish the poll-tax on Dutch Jews in Germany, **5,** 458.
"Summons" addressed to, by Michael Berr, **5,** 460.
addressed by Christians on the subject of Jewish emancipation, **5,** 463.

Rationalists, Mahometan. *See* Mutazilist.

Ratisbon, Jews in, in the ninth century, **3,** 144.
council of, protects the Jews during the Black Death persecutions, **4,** 110.
under the ban of the empire, **4,** 305.
fined by the emperor, **4,** 306.
Molcho and Reubeni at, **4,** 510.

Ratisbon, the diet at, refuses to form a crusade against the Turks, **4,** 267–8.
petitioned in behalf of the emancipation of the Jews, **5,** 465.
petition to, supported by the Austrian representative, **5,** 466.

Ratisbon, the Jews of, suffer during the first crusade, **3,** 305.
privileges granted to, **3,** 635.
not permitted to appear on the street at Easter, **3,** 635.
saved from the Rindfleisch persecution, **4,** 36.
protected from persecution, **4,** 99.
contributions exacted from, **4,** 254.
brutal treatment of, **4,** 258–9.
held in high esteem, **4,** 300.
morality of, **4,** 300.
claimed by various parties, **4,** 300.

Ratisbon, the Jews of (*continued*), appeal to the Hussites for protection, **4,** 301.
slandered by apostates, **4,** 301–2.
imprisoned on the blood accusation, **4,** 304.
assisted by the Bavarian Jews, **4,** 305.
protected by Frederick III, **4,** 305–6.
released, **4,** 306.
refuse to pay unjust fines, **4,** 306–7.
strained relations between, and the Christians, **4,** 416–17.
threatened with expulsion, **4,** 417.
send a defender of their cause to Maximilian I, **4,** 436–7.
the extermination of, suggested by Pfefferkorn, **4,** 463.

Ratisbonne family, the, culture of, **5,** 476.

Ratti Menton, French consul in Damascus, opponent of the Jews, **5,** 633.
appealed to, to search for the murderer of Tomaso, **5,** 635.
suspects the Damascus Jews of Tomaso's murder, **5,** 635.
employs a spy against the Jews, **5,** 635.
cross-examines Jewish suspects, **5,** 636.
orders the Jewish suspects to be tortured, **5,** 637–8.
hushes up evidence in favor of the Jews, **5,** 637.
abetted by the European consuls, **5,** 639.
has an anti-Jewish book circulated, **5,** 639.
pronounces the Jews guilty of Tomaso's murder, **5,** 640.

Ratti Menton (*continued*), publishes the Damascus affair in French journals, **5**, 643.
deceives the vice-consul of France, **5**, 645.
conduct of, described in the Austrian report, **5**, 646.
excluded from the consular court of justice, **5**, 649.
defended by Thiers, **5**, 650, 659.
accused by Isambert, **5**, 650.
shielded by Cochelet, **5**, 660.
Ravenna, a Jewish community in, under the Ostrogoths, **3**, 28.
asks for Jewish bankers, **4**, 286.
Ravensburg, the Jews of, burnt on the blood accusation, **4**, 227.
Rawitz, the rabbi of, opposes the Reform movement, **5**, 571.
Raymond V, of Toulouse, the Jews of Bourg de St. Gilles under, **3**, 399.
Raymond VI, of Toulouse, persecuted by Innocent III, **3**, 400.
reproached with employing Jews, **3**, 501.
forced to promise not to employ Jews, **3**, 501–2, 503.
laid under the ban, **3**, 503.
deposition of, **3**, 508, 509.
Raymond VII, of Toulouse, victorious over the crusaders, **3**, 513.
promotes Jews to offices, **3**, 514.
Raymund Roger, of Béziers, during the Albigensian crusade, **3**, 502, 503.
Raymund Trencaval, count of Béziers, the Jews under, **3**, 394.
assassination of, **3**, 394–5.
"Raza di Yechuda," by Nehemiah Chayon, **5**, 217.
Razi, Arabic medical authority, taught by a Jew, **3**, 146.
Razio. *See* Ragesh.
Reaction, the, in France under the Bourbons, **5**, 596.
Reactionary movement, the, in Germany, **5**, 508–9.
after Napoleon's fall, **5**, 512–13.
Real estate, Jews of Visigothic Spain forbidden by Egica to hold, **3**, 107–8.
owned by Jews in France in the tenth century, **3**, 242.
German Jews under the Saxon emperors forbidden to own, **3**, 242.
owned by German and French Jews in the eleventh century, **3**, 281, 297.
owned by French Jews in the twelfth century, **3**, 343.
owned by Silesian Jews in the twelfth century, **3**, 418.
owned by the Jews of Tyre, **3**, 426.
Jews forbidden to buy, from Christians, **3**, 592.
acquired by Jews in Castile, **4**, 193.
Silesian Jews forbidden to own, **4**, 260.
owned by Jews in Poland, **4**, 419.
Jews forbidden to own in Hamburg, **4**, 688.
Jews forbidden by Paul IV to own, **4**, 566–7.
Reason, the religion of, established in France, **5**, 450–1.
and the Jews, **5**, 451–2.
Rebbe, leader of a Chassidistic group, **5**, 392, 393.
subordinate to the Zaddik, **5**, 393.

Recanate, the Jews of, annoyed by apostates, **4,** 581.

Reccared, Visigothic king, hostile to the Jews, **3,** 34, 46–7.
commended by Pope Gregory I, **3,** 46.
laws of, fall into desuetude, **3,** 47.

Receiver-general of taxes for the Jews of France, **4,** 130, 132.
See also Taxes, farmers of.

Receswinth, Visigothic king, forces Christianity upon the Jews, **3,** 102–4.
forbids Christians to befriend Jews, **3,** 104.

Recha, character in "Nathan the Wise," **5,** 324.

Rechabites, the, Nazarites, **1,** 200.
descendants of, in Chaibar, **3,** 55.

Recife, Jews settle in, **4,** 693.
siege of, **4,** 694.

Red Sea, the, passage of the Israelites through, **1,** 18–19.

Redemption, the dogma of, expounded by Astruc Raimuch, **4,** 182.
attacked by Chasdaï Crescas, **4,** 187.

Redingge, Robert de, Dominican, converted to Judaism, **3,** 640–1.

"**Reflections,**" by Isaac Pinto, **5,** 344–5.

Reform Association, the, of Berlin, founded by Stern, **5,** 683.
programme of, **5,** 683.
and the Frankfort rabbinical conference, **5,** 683–4.
partially condemned by the conference, **5,** 685–6.
forms itself into a congregation, **5,** 686.
innovations of, **5,** 686–7.

Reform Association, the (*continued*), antagonized by Michael Sachs, **5,** 687.

Reform of Judaism, the, difficulties in the way of, **5,** 559–60.
begins in Germany, **5,** 560.
objections to, by the orthodox, **5,** 561, 571.
undertaken by Jacobson, **5,** 561–2.
protests against, **5,** 562.
encouraged in Berlin, **5,** 563.
interfered with by Frederick William III, **5,** 563.
Hamburg made the center of, **5,** 563–5.
in Leipsic, **5,** 573.
in various places, **5,** 573.
in Vienna, **5,** 580.
advocated by Zunz, **5,** 621.
Geiger devoted to, **5,** 626.
opposition to, **5,** 627.
forced upon German Jews, **5,** 628.
attitude of the school of, **5,** 629–30.
progress of, in Hamburg, **5,** 672–4.
causes a rupture among German Jews, **5,** 674.
in Frankfort, **5,** 674–7.
discussed at rabbinical conferences, **5,** 677.
in Mecklenburg-Schwerin, **5,** 679.
in Breslau, **5,** 682–3.
in Berlin, **5,** 682–3, 686–7.
Frankel's attitude towards, **5,** 684–5.
attitude of Sachs to, **5,** 689.
in the United States, **5,** 702.

Reform of Judaism, the moderate, Bernays exponent of, **5,** 574–8.
Mannheimer exponent of, **5,** 578–82.

Reform of Judaism, the moderate (*continued*), in Germany, France, and Italy, **5,** 582.
Reform party, the, in Judaism, beginning of, **5,** 563.
leaders of, **5,** 568.
cause of, advanced by Jacobson and Libermann, **5,** 568–9.
joined by Aaron Chorin, **5,** 569.
Reform Temple Union, the, in Hamburg, origin of, **5,** 564.
principles of, **5,** 565.
achievements of, **5,** 565.
produces a split in Judaism, **5,** 565–6.
aided by Jacobson, **5,** 568.
liturgy of, approved by some authorities, **5,** 569.
action of the Hamburg Dayanim against, **5,** 570.
supported by Lazarus Riesser, **5,** 570.
innovations of, declared heterodox, **5,** 571.
branches of, **5,** 573.
members of, belong to the Society for Culture, **5,** 584.
precipitates a quarrel, **5,** 672.
compiles a new prayer book, **5,** 672–3.
charges of, against Bernays, **5,** 673.
Reformation, the Protestant, in Germany, **4,** 422.
affected by the Talmud, **4,** 423.
affected by the study of Hebrew, **4,** 434.
beginnings of, **4,** 467.
pantomime on, **4,** 468.
spread of, **4,** 469.
effect of, on the Jews, **4,** 470–1.
effect of, on Judaism, **4,** 471.
results of, **4,** 540–3.
influence of, in Poland, **4,** 633.
in Poland and Lithuania, **4,** 646–7.
Reformation, the Protestant (*continued*), effect of, on the Jews of Poland, **4,** 647–8.
Reggio, Italian Jewish scholar, **5,** 622.
Reggio, Jewish printing house in, **4,** 289.
Isaac (II) Abrabanel, physician at, **4,** 385.
Jews beg for shelter in, **4,** 660.
Jews invited to settle in, **4,** 675.
Mordecai of Eisenstadt in, **5,** 209.
Regnault, French state councilor, advocates Jewish emancipation, **5,** 480–1.
Rehoboam, son of Solomon, **1,** 177.
undisputed succession of, **1,** 179.
lacks ability, **1,** 179–80.
and the rebellious Shechemites, **1,** 180–1.
flees from Shechem, **1,** 182.
makes a treaty with the king of Damascus, **1,** 183.
fortifies Jerusalem, **1,** 184.
defeated by Shishak, **1,** 184–5.
indifference of, **1,** 188.
permits Astarte worship, **1,** 188–9.
end of the reign of, **1,** 189.
Reign of Terror, the, suffering of the Jews under, **5,** 450.
end of, **5,** 452.
Reimarus, Eliza, friend of Lessing, **5,** 320.
collects subscriptions for Mendelssohn's Pentateuch translation, **5,** 329.
brother-in-law of, **5,** 333.
Reimarus, Hermann Samuel, predecessor of, **5,** 179.
rejects revealed religion, **5,** 319–20.

Reimarus, Hermann Samuel (*continued*), work by, published by Lessing, **5,** 320–3.
Reïs, Arabic word for Nagid, **5,** 443.
Reischer, Nehemiah, excommunicated by Chayim of Lublin, **5,** 261.
Release, the year of. *See* Sabbatical year, the.
Relics, the miracle working power of, discussed by the Jews of France, **3,** 343.
Religious offices, not to be accepted from Christians, **3,** 518.
" **Religious Poetry** of the Jews in Spain," by Sachs, **5,** 693–4.
Rembrandt, supplies engravings for a work by Manasseh ben Israel, **5,** 38.
Remonstrants, the, a religious party in Holland, **4,** 673.
complain of the Jews, **4,** 673, 674.
Renaissance, the, of the Jewish race, **5,** 291–2.
Renaissance of Judaism, the, consequences of, **5,** 374–5.
description of, **5,** 589–90, 591–2.
shaped by Poland, **5,** 607.
Rephaim, the original inhabitants of Canaan, **1,** 2.
Rephidim, station of the Israelites on their journey through the desert, **1,** 21.
Resettlement, the, of the Jews in England. *See under* England.
Resh-Galutha. *See* Exilarch.
Resh-Kalla, title of the professors in Babylonia, **2,** 547.
title of the chief of the Kairuan community, **3,** 210.
title given to Chasdaï Ibn-Shaprut, **3,** 217.
Resh-Lakish. *See* Simon ben Lakish.
Resh-Metibta, director of the school sessions in Babylonia, **2,** 547.
Resh-Sidra, principal of a school, **2,** 512.
" **Restorers** of the Law," Simon ben Shetach and Judah ben Tabbaï, **2,** 49.
Resurrection of the dead, the, a foreign element in the divine service, **1,** 401, 405–6.
and the apostle Paul, **2,** 225–6.
bodily, denied by the Tiflisites, **3,** 158.
as taught by Maimonides and his disciples, **3,** 475–6, 487–8.
treatise on, by Samuel ben Ali, **3,** 476.
treatise on, by Maimonides, **3,** 488.
Retribution, the doctrine of, among the Pharisees, **2,** 18.
among the Sadducees, **2,** 21.
according to the Mishna, **2,** 472–3.
in the Kabbala, **3,** 555.
Return from the Captivity, the, **1,** 351–6.
" **Return** of the Jewish Warrior, The," painting by Oppenheim, **5,** 601.
" **Return** of the Jews, The," by Isaac La Peyrère, **5,** 25.
Reubell, opposes the emancipation of the Jews, **5,** 441, 448.
Reuben, the tribe of, asks for land east of the Jordan, **1,** 29–30.
harassed by the Moabites, **1,** 125.
district of, taken by Hazael, **1,** 220.
descendants of, in Chaibar, **3,** 437.

Reubeni, David. *See* David Reubeni.

Reuchlin, John (Capnion, 1455–1522), suggested as Pfefferkorn's coadjutor, **4,** 431–2.
rôle of, in the Protestant Reformation, **4,** 432.
as a humanist, **4,** 432.
studies Hebrew, **4,** 433.
writes a panegyric on the Hebrew language, **4,** 433–4.
taught by Obadiah di Sforno, **4,** 434, 473.
compiles a Hebrew grammar, **4,** 434.
disciples of, **4,** 434.
prejudice of, against Jews, **4,** 435.
charges the Jews with blasphemy, **4,** 435.
honors conferred upon, **4,** 435.
discredited with the Dominicans, **4,** 435–6.
invited to join Pfefferkorn, **4,** 436.
appointed to direct the confiscation of Hebrew books, **4,** 437, 441.
issues an opinion favorable to Jewish literature, **4,** 441–3.
advises the teaching of Hebrew at German universities, **4,** 443.
declares the Jews entitled to the privileges of the Holy Roman empire, **4,** 443.
defends the Jews from the charge of heresy, **4,** 443–4.
opinion of, on Jewish literature opened by Pfefferkorn, **4,** 445.
complains to Maximilian I of Pfefferkorn, **4,** 446.
publishes the "Augenspiegel," **4,** 446–8.

Reuchlin, John (*continued*), charged with having been bribed to defend the Talmud, **4,** 447.
summoned to answer the charge of heresy, **4,** 450.
charges against, **4,** 450–1.
appears in Mayence, **4,** 451.
execution of the judgment against, delayed, **4,** 452.
appeals to Leo X, **4,** 453, 454.
examination of, ordered by Leo X, **4,** 454
appears in Speyer, **4,** 454.
exonerated, **4,** 455.
enemies of, **4,** 456.
adherents of, **4,** 456–7.
excused from appearing at Rome, **4,** 458.
Maximilian I intercedes for, **4,** 458–9.
cause of, in Paris, **4,** 459–60.
supposed author of the "Letters of Obscurantists," **4,** 462.
cause of, submitted to the fifth Lateran Council, **4,** 464.
cause of, favorably decided, **4,** 465.
on the Kabbala, **4,** 466–7, 481, 583.
in the pantomime on the Reformation, **4,** 468.
publishes a work on Hebrew accents, **4,** 471.
encourages the study of the Bible, **4,** 474.
cause of, espoused by Lorenzo Pucci, **4,** 503.
introduces Rabbinical literature to Christians, **5,** 179.

Reuchlinists, the, composed of Young Germany, **4,** 456–7.
motto of, **4,** 457.
friends of the Jews, **4,** 457.
conspire against Hoogstraten, **4,** 465.

Reuel, father-in-law of Moses, **1**, 14.
Revelation, the belief in, shaken in the time of Saadiah, **3**, 198.
the belief in, **5**, 715–16.
"**Revelation according to the System of the Synagogue**," by Steinheim, **5**, 604–6.
Revolution. *See* February revolution, the; French revolution, the; July revolution, the.
Rezin, becomes king of Damascus, **1**, 177.
allies himself with the kings of Israel and Judah, **1**, 248.
ally of Pekah against Judah, **1**, 258.
slain, **1**, 259.
Rhabanus Maurus, abbot of Fulda, dedicates his works to the empress Judith, **3**, 162.
indebtedness of, to Jews, **3**, 163.
Rheims, rabbinical synods meet at, **3**, 377.
rabbi of, at the first rabbinical synod, **3**, 377.
study of Hebrew at the university of, **4**, 474.
Rheingau, the, the Jews of, molested, **4**, 543.
Rhenish Confederation, the, Prince Primate of, **5**, 504.
dissolution of, **5**, 505.
Rhine district, the, the Jews of, origin of, **3**, 40–1.
during the first crusade, **3**, 300, 305.
devoted to the study of the Talmud, **3**, 345.
during the second crusade, **3**, 352.
protected by Bernard of Clairvaux, **3**, 353.
Rhine district, the, the Jews of (*continued*), observe a fast for the Jews of Blois, **3**, 380.
emigrate, **3**, 638.
assaulted by the imperial army, **4**, 225.
find a refuge in Poland, **4**, 420.
Rhine district, the Lower. *See* Alsace; Lorraine.
Rhine district, the Upper, the Jews of, banished, **4**, 107.
propose a distinction for Crémieux, **5**, 670.
Rhineland, the, the Jews of, during the Armleder persecutions, **4**, 97.
urged to emigrate to Turkey, **4**, 271–2.
the poll-tax abolished in, **5**, 468.
present addresses to the Synhedrion, **5**, 496.
Rhinokolura, the river of Egypt, boundary of Israel under David, **1**, 129.
south-western limit of Judæa under Alexander Jannæus, **2**, 46.
Rhodes, Herod presents himself before Octavius at, **2**, 101.
criminal colony of Turkey, **4**, 599.
prophets at, silenced by Sabbataï's apostasy, **5**, 157.
Rhodes, the Jews of, in the twelfth century, **3**, 424.
the blood accusation brought against, **5**, 640–1.
tortured, **5**, 640, 641.
revision of the trial of, **5**, 647.
acquitted, **5**, 647.
Rhodez, Abraham Ibn-Ezra in, **3**, 373, 374.
Rhodosto, the Jews of, in the twelfth century, **3**, 424.
Cardoso at, **5**, 207.

Rhyme, introduced into neo-Hebraic poetry under Arab influences, **3,** 116.
Rhynsburg, Spinoza at, **5,** 95.
Rhynsburgians, a Dutch sect, **5,** 94.
Ri. *See* Isaac ben Samuel.
Riba. *See* Isaac ben Asher Halevi.
Riban. *See* Jehuda ben Nathan.
Ribash. *See* Isaac ben Sheshet Barfat.
Riblah, Necho at, **1,** 299.
Nebuchadnezzar at, **1,** 313.
dignitaries of Jerusalem beheaded at, **1,** 314.
Riccio, Paul, apostate, translates the Kabbalistic writings of Joseph Jikatilla, **4,** 466.
Richard I, of England, concludes a truce with Saladin, **3,** 405.
first persecution of English Jews at the coronation of, **3,** 409–10.
protects the Jews, **3,** 411.
joins the third crusade, **3,** 411.
orders those guilty of the massacre of the Jews to be punished, **3,** 416.
capture of, **3,** 418.
wishes to appoint Maimonides his physician, **3,** 474.
Richard, brother of Henry III, the Jews of England pledged to, **3,** 590.
Richelieu, celebrated by Enriquez de Paz, **5,** 111.
Richelieu, duc de, expels the German Jews from Bordeaux, **5,** 343–4.
Richter, Friedrich (Jean Paul), attitude of, towards the Jews, **5,** 533.
Riess, David, permitted to have a private synagogue in Prussia, **5,** 191.
Riesser, Gabriel (1806–1860), grandfather of, **5,** 330.
father of, **5,** 570–1.
character of, **5,** 598.
attitude of, towards Judaism, **5,** 599.
unable to procure a position as jurist, **5,** 599.
works for the emancipation of the German Jews, **5,** 599.
criticises the Germans and the Jews, **5,** 599–600.
advocates the formation of societies for the emancipation of the Jews, **5,** 600.
influence of, **5,** 600–1, 602.
honored by the Jews of Baden, **5,** 601.
contest of, with Judæophobists, **5,** 601–2.
puts the Jewish question on the liberal programme, **5,** 602.
friend of, **5,** 602.
proposes means of commemorating the services of Montefiore and Crémieux, **5,** 669–70.
secretary of the Hamburg Reform Temple Union, **5,** 672.
and the proscription of the new prayer book, **5,** 673.
asked to join the "Friends of Reform," **5,** 675–6.
in the Prussian Landtag, **5,** 697.
Riesser, Lazarus, supports the Hamburg Reform Temple Union, **5,** 570–1.
Rieti. *See* Moses ben Isaac da Rieti.
Rigle, the, festival lectures at Sora, **2,** 515.
of the Exilarch, **2,** 607.

Rihana, a woman of the Benu-Kuraiza, taken captive by Mahomet, **3**, 81.
Rimmon, the plain of, battle on, in the Bar-Cochba revolt, **2**, 416.
Rindfleisch persecution, the, of the German Jews, **4**, 35–7.
"**Rites**, The," by Leo Modena, translated by Richard Simon, **5**, 180.
Ritual, the, work on, by Samuel ben Chofni, **3**, 253.
Ritual murder. *See* Blood accusation, the.
Rivarola, cardinal, promises to remove Tomaso's tombstone, **5**, 668.
Rizba. *See* Isaac ben Abraham.
Rizpah, wife of Saul, **1**, 95.
coveted by Abner, **1**, 110.
sons of, killed, **1**, 123.
devotion of, **1**, 123–4.
"**Roaring** of the Lion, The," by Leo Modena, **5**, 73.
Robert, archbishop, ordered to enforce the decrees of the Fourth Lateran Council in Hungary, **3**, 521.
Robert of Anjou, king of Naples, protector of the Jews, **4**, 59.
appealed to by the Jews of Rome, **4**, 61.
patron of Kalonymos ben Kalonymos, **4**, 61, 63.
taught by Leone Romano, **4**, 68.
patron of Shemarya Ikriti, **4**, 69, 70.
Robert, Ludwig, brother of Rachel Levin, **5**, 534.
Robert, Rachel. *See* Levin, Rachel.
Robespierre, favors the emancipation of the Jews, **5**, 441.
fall of, **5**, 452.
Robles, Antonio, Marrano, indicted as a Papist, **5**, 49.
Rocamora, Vincent (Isaac) de (1601–1684), Marrano monk, poet and physician, returns to Judaism, **5**, 109–10.
judge of poetry, **5**, 113.
Roderic, the last of the Visigothic kings of Spain, **3**, 109.
Rodosto. *See* Rhodosto.
Rodrigo, physician of, at the congress summoned by João II, **4**, 367.
Rodrigo, João, de Castel-Branco. *See* Amatus Lusitanus.
Rodrigues, Isaac, member of Malesherbes' commission, **5**, 432.
deputy of the French Jews, **5**, 438.
Roger, count of Béziers, Jews under, **3**, 395.
Roger II, of Sicily, permits the Jews to have their own jurisdiction, **3**, 422–3.
brings Jews from Greece, **3**, 424.
Rohrer, Joseph, writes against the Jews, **5**, 472.
Roïm. *See* Pastoureaux.
Rokeach. *See* Eleazar ben Jehuda.
Rolls, the, contain a register of the property of English Jews, **3**, 588.
Romagna, the, the Talmud burnt in, under Julius III, **4**, 565.
Roman, distinction between, and non-Roman disappears, **2**, 468.
Roman eagle, the, torn down by Judæans, **2**, 115, 121.
Roman era, the, used in public documents, **2**, 134.
Roman exile, the, **2**, 321.
Roman garrison of Jerusalem, the, under Metilius, **2**, 255.

Roman garrison of Jerusalem, the (*continued*), capitulates to the Zealots, **2,** 260.
retreats to the towers of the wall, **2,** 260.
destroyed by the Zealots, **2,** 261.

Roman governors of Judæa, the, severity of, **2,** 241. *See* Judæa, the Roman governors of.

Roman provinces, the, rebel against Hadrian, **2,** 399.
the Jews of. *See under* Jews, the.

Roman Senate, the, acknowledges the rights of Ptolemy VI, **1,** 506.
gives Cyrene to Ptolemy VII, **1,** 507.
defied by Ptolemy VI, **1,** 507.
promulgates a law against Judaism in Rome, **2,** 136.

Roman standard, the, obnoxious emblems on, **2,** 139.

Romano, Solomon. *See* Baptista, John.

Romans, the, defeat Antiochus the Great, **1,** 434.
in the second century before the common era, **1,** 443.
favor Antiochus IV, **1,** 443.
espouse the cause of Egypt against Antiochus IV, **1,** 453.
order Lysias to give up elephants in the army, **1,** 481–2.
Judas Maccabæus negotiates with, **1,** 485–6.
allies of Judæa under Simon Tharsi, **1,** 525–6.
embassy sent to, by John Hyrcanus, **2,** 4–5.
forbid Antiochus IX to molest the Judæans, **2,** 9.
besiege the Temple, **2,** 123.
take of the Temple treasures, **2, 124.**

Romans, the (*continued*), end the revolt against Sabinus, **2,** 126.
leaning of, towards Judaism, **2,** 136–7.
in Judæa despise the Judæans, **2,** 246–7.
of Judæa receive Hadrian with servility, **2,** 406.
kindly treated by the Jews under Bar-Cochba, **2,** 411–12.
under Antoninus Pius, persecute the Jews, **2,** 446.
See also Rome.

Romantic movement, the, in Germany, **5,** 515–16.

Romanus, teacher of Alexander Severus in Jewish customs, **2,** 482.

Rome (city), Judæans in, before Pompey's time, **2,** 67.
Judæan quarter in, **2,** 68.
struggle of parties in, after Cæsar's death, **2,** 79–80.
conversions to Judaism in, **2,** 383–5.
the bishops of, bring about the Catholic Church, **2,** 500.
a synagogue in, burnt by Christians, **2,** 614.
the fall of, and the Jews, **3,** 27–8.
the Jewish community in, under the Ostrogoths, **3,** 28.
riot in, against Jewish slaveowners, **3,** 30–1.
immorality of, in the ninth century, **3,** 169.
Council of, decrees against Jews' holding offices, **3,** 293-4.
Abraham Ibn-Ezra in, **3,** 369–71.
declared a republic, **3,** 370.
exiled Jews settle in, **4,** 408.
David Reubeni at, **4,** 492, 493.
sack of, confirms Messianic hopes, **4, 497.**

Rome (city) (*continued*), Marranos of, permitted to profess Judaism, **4**, 500.
Solomon Molcho at, **4**, 502–4, 505–7.
flood in, **4**, 505.
the Inquisition at, authorized, **4**, 525.
Marranos well treated at, **4**, 525.
the Talmud burnt at, **4**, 565.
Nathan Ghazati at, **5**, 161.

Rome (city), **the Jews of**, protected by Gregory I, **3**, 33.
do honor to Alexander III, **3**, 421.
in the twelfth century, **3**, 424.
live secure until the fourteenth century, **4**, 58.
prosperity and culture of, **4**, 58–9.
order a translation of Maimonides' works, **4**, 60.
threatened with banishment, **4**, 61.
oppose the influx of Spanish exiles, **4**, 363.
ill-treated by Paul IV, **4**, 567.
do homage to Pius IV, **4**, 588.
obtain privileges from Pius IV, **4**, 588.
permitted to remain on the expulsion of Jews from the Papal States, **4**, 591, 659.
number of, in the sixteenth century, **4**, 653.
under Sixtus V, **4**, 655–6.
intercede for the Jews of Vienna, **5**, 171.
return to the Ghetto under Pius VII, **5**, 518.

Rome (city), **the Judæans of**, power of, **2**, 68.
banished to Sardinia, **2**, 136–7.
first religious persecutions of, **2**, 137.
number of, **2**, 202.

Rome (city), **the Judæans of** (*continued*), in part banished by Claudius, **2**, 202.
avoid the arch of Titus, **2**, 314–15.

Rome (empire), Herod's submission to, **2**, 105.
the Temple placed under the protection of, **2**, 111.
Judæa wholly in the possession of, **2**, 128.
subdued by Christianity, **2**, 174, 559.
Agrippa I makes plans against, **2**, 195–6.
the yoke of, on Judæa, **2**, 233–4.
the Judæan insurrection against, begun, **2**, 255.
taxes of, not paid in Judæa, **2**, 258.
allegiance to, renounced in Judæa, **2**, 259.
in the estimation of the Jewish and the Pagan Christians, **2**, 369.
the last emperors of, **2**, 526.
weakness of, at home, **2**, 526–7.
invaded by Parthians and Goths, **2**, 527.
loses its importance, **2**, 560.
revolt of the Jews against, under Constantius, **2**, 570.
dissolution of, **2**, 604–5.
See also East, the, empire of; Romans, the; West, the, empire of.

Rome (empire), **the Jews of**, appeal to Marcus Aurelius for the abolition of anti-Jewish laws, **2**, 449.
favored by Julian the Apostate, **2**, 597.
under Theodosius the Great, **2**, 614–15.
See also Jews, the.

Rome (empire), the Judæans of, favored by Cæsar, **2,** 76.
mourn the murder of Cæsar, **2,** 79.
favored by Octavius, **2,** 103.
See also Judæans, the.
Rome, Little, name of Cæsarea, **2,** 106.
Ronda, Berber ruler of, slain by the Arabs, **3,** 276.
Rosales, a Jewish author, made count palatine, **4,** 692.
Rosh, title of the chief of the Kairuan community, **3,** 210, 211.
Rostock, the theological faculty of, forbids the employment of Jewish physicians, **4,** 692.
Rothenburg on the Tauber, the Jews of, indifferent to the confiscation of Hebrew books, **4,** 438.
Rothschild, James de, entertains the diplomatic corps at Paris, **5,** 529.
action of, in the Damascus affair, **5,** 653.
Rothschild, Lionel de, refused his seat in Parliament, **5,** 698.
Rothschild, Mayer Amschel, obtains the emancipation of the Frankfort Jews, **5,** 505.
civic honors of, **5,** 514.
the son of, before the Congress of Vienna, **5,** 514.
Rothschild, Nathaniel M. de, acts in the Damascus affair, **5,** 645, 651.
obtains a revision of the trial of the Jews of Rhodes, **5,** 647.
dignity of, **5,** 653.
an English Peer, **5,** 698.
Rothschilds, the, the house of, a power, **5,** 513.
the residence of, mobbed, **5,** 529.
Rothschilds, the, the house of (*continued*), awe of, **5,** 530.
zealous in the Damascus affair, **5,** 646.
hostile to Thiers, **5,** 649.
appeal to, from Damascus, **5,** 651.
attempt to extort money from, **5,** 655.
Rotterdam, the second Jewish colony of Holland, **4,** 685.
Röttingen, the Jews of, burnt by Rindfleisch, **4,** 35.
Rouelle, the, a Jew badge introduced into France in the fourteenth century, **4,** 131.
Rouen, the Jews of, persecuted, **3,** 299.
Rouen, the Council of, forbids Jews to keep Christian slaves or nurses, **3,** 294.
re-enacts the decrees of the fourth Lateran Council, **3,** 520.
Roundheads. *See* **Puritans.**
Rousseau praises Pereira's sign language, **5,** 343.
Roussillon, French exiles emigrate to, **4,** 49.
Rubianus, Crotus (Johann Jäger), espouses Reuchlin's cause, **4,** 456.
writes the "Letters of Obscurantists," **4,** 461-2.
Rubio, Abraham, Sabbatian, 5, 145.
Ruchaïm. *See* Solomon ben Yerucham.
Rückert, inspires Sachs, **5,** 692.
Rüdiger, Huozmann, bishop of Speyer, grants privileges to the Jews, **3,** 297-8.
Rudolph (I) of Habsburg, emperor, Jews persecuted before the crowning of, **3,** 611.
extorts money from the Jews of Germany, **3,** 634.

Rudolph (I) of Habsburg (*continued*), grants privileges to the Jews of Ratisbon, **3,** 635.
confirms the Jewish statute of Frederick the Valiant, **3,** 635.
ratifies papal bulls protecting the Jews, **3,** 635.
blood accusations under, **3,** 635–7.
confiscates the property of the Jews of Mayence, **3,** 636.
imprisons Meïr of Rothenburg, **3,** 639.
Rudolph II, emperor, attitude of, towards the Jews, **4,** 652.
Rudolph, a French monk, preaches the second crusade in Germany, **3,** 351.
arouses the people against the Jews, **3,** 351.
denounced by the clergy, **3,** 352–3.
disappears, **3,** 353–4.
Ruez, Juan, inquisitor appointed by Sixtus IV, **4,** 312.
Rufinus, chamberlain of Arcadius, favorably disposed to the Jews, **2,** 615–16.
Rufus, commander of the Tenth Legion, takes Simon bar Giora prisoner, **2,** 313.
Rufus, Annius, third procurator of Judæa, **2,** 135.
Rufus, Tinnius, governor of Judæa, retreats before Bar-Cochba, **2,** 411.
Rufus, Turnus, general, sent to Judæa by Hadrian, **2,** 421.
draws the plow over Jerusalem, **2,** 421.
severity of, towards Akiba, **2,** 428.
cruelty of, to the dead, **2,** 430.
wife of, and the Jews, **2,** 432.
Rühs, Friedrich, opposes the emancipation of the Jews, **5,** 517.
Rupert of the Palatinate, emperor, accession of, **4,** 178.
privileges granted by, to Jews, confirmed, **4,** 219.
Russia, Jews not allowed in, under Ivan IV, **4,** 633.
allied with the Cossacks, **5,** 14.
inflicts suffering upon the Polish Jews, **5,** 14–15.
supports Turkey, **5,** 634.
in the Quadruple Alliance, **5,** 658.
Russia, the Jews of, begin to study the Talmud, **3,** 421.
represented in the Synod of the Four Countries, **4,** 644.
condition of, inquired into by Alexander I, **5,** 472–3.
certain classes of, exempt from exceptional laws, **5,** 473.
forced to attend schools, **5,** 473.
forced into the cities, **5,** 473.
Russia, Little, the Cossacks enjoy independence in, **5,** 2.
the Jews of, massacred, **5,** 10.
Russia, West, the Haidamaks in, **5,** 11.
the Jews banished from, **5,** 12.
Russians, the, wage war with the Chazars, **3,** 221.
Ruta al Jahud, a fortress near Saragossa, **3,** 42.
Ruth, the Book of, composed to counteract Ezra's views on intermarriage, **1,** 370–1.
Ruthard, archbishop of Mayence, permits the massacre of Jews by crusaders, **3,** 303, 306.
accused before Henry IV, **3,** 307.
flees to Erfurt, **3,** 307.
Ruthenia, rabbinical schools established in, **4,** 420.
Ruy Capron, ancestor of the Jew hater Pacheco, **4,** 278.

S

Saad-Addaula (Mordecai Ibn-Alcharbiya), physician to Argun, **3**, 638.
regulates the finances of Argun, **3**, 646.
advises diplomatic connections with Europe, **3**, 647.
administration of, **3**, 647–8.
patron of learning, **3**, 648.
intrigue against, by the Mahometans, **3**, 648–9.
Mongol enemies of, **3**, 649.
execution of, **3**, 649.
Saadiah ben Joseph (892–942), makes science a principle of Judaism, **3**, 187, 188.
last important exponent of Eastern Judaism, **3**, 188.
wide knowledge of, **3**, 188.
decided character of, **3**, 188.
attacks the Karaites, **3**, 189.
translates the Bible into Arabic, **3**, 189–90.
Hebrew grammar and lexicon by, **3**, 190.
attacks the Karaite calendar, **3**, 190–1.
later works of, against Karaism, **3**, 192.
appointed Gaon of Sora, **3**, 193.
dissatisfaction of, with Babylonian-Jewish communal life, **3**, 193–4.
refuses to abet the injustice of the Exilarch, **3**, 195–6.
deprived of his office, **3**, 195.
names Josiah Hassan Exilarch, **3**, 195.
deposed by Caliph Kahir, **3**, 196.
at Bagdad, **3**, 196.
arranges a prayer book, **3**, 196.
collects the rules of the calendar, **3**, 196.
writes against Aaron ben Asher, **3**, 196–7, 207.
Saadiah ben Joseph (*continued*), philosophical works of, **3**, 197–8.
skepticism of the time of, **3**, 198–9.
combats the opinions of Chivi Albalchi, **3**, 199.
in favor with the caliph Abradhir, **3**, 200.
reconciled with David ben Zaccaï, **3**, 200–1.
restored to the Gaonate of Sora, **3**, 201.
responses of, **3**, 201.
son of, **3**, 202.
attacked by Karaites, **3**, 203, 204.
defended by Jacob ben Samuel, **3**, 204.
objects to meter in Hebrew, **3**, 223.
lexicographical work of, supplanted by Menachem ben Saruk's, **3**, 225.
works of, criticised by Dunash ben Labrat, **3**, 226.
compared with Haï Gaon, **3**, 250.
philosophical work of, translated into Hebrew, **3**, 397.
denounced as a heretic, **3**, 624.
Saadio Longo, poet, patronized by Gedalya Ibn-Yachya II, **4**, 609.
Saatz, Hussite victory at, **4**, 226.
Saba, Abraham. *See* Abraham Saba.
Sabako, king of Egypt, designs of, on Palestine, **1**, 257.
Sabbaï, champion of the Samaritan religion, **1**, 517.
Sabbataï ben Solomon, Italian scholar, **3**, 630.
Sabbataï Donnolo (913–970), taken prisoner by the Mahometans, **3**, 212.

Sabbataï Donnolo (*continued*), ransomed in Trani, 3, 213.
physician to the Byzantine viceroy of Calabria, 3, 213.
offers to treat Nilus the Younger, 3, 213.
poetry of, 3, 223.
Sabbataï Raphael, emissary of Sabbataï Zevi, 5, 133.
spreads abroad the Messiah's fame, 5, 137.
clings to the Messiah after his apostasy, 5, 157.
encourages the Sabbatian movement in Italy, Germany, and Amsterdam, 5, 160–1.
Sabbataï Zevi (1626–1676), compared with Spinoza, 5, 118.
attractive appearance of, 5, 118.
boyhood and studies of, 5, 119.
early marriage of, 5, 119.
teaches the Kabbala, 5, 119.
father of, 5, 119–20.
interested in Messianic speculations, 5, 120–1.
reveals himself as the Messiah, 5, 122.
excommunicated and banished from Smyrna, 5, 122.
gains followers, 5, 123.
the Messiahship of, confirmed by an old document, 5, 123.
celebrates his marriage with the Torah, 5, 124.
banished from Salonica, 5, 124.
meets opposition at Athens, 5, 124.
introduced to Raphael Joseph Chelebi, 5, 125, 127.
attracts the Jews of Jerusalem, 5, 127.
sent as a messenger to Chelebi, 5, 127–8.
journey of, to Cairo, 5, 128.
second marriage of, 5, 128–9.
Sabbataï Zevi (*continued*), beginning of public career of, 5, 129.
becomes acquainted with Nathan Ghazati, 5, 131.
threatened with excommunication in Jerusalem, 5, 132.
preparations for the arrival of, in Smyrna, 5, 133.
reception of, in Aleppo and Smyrna, 5, 133.
declares himself the Messiah in Smyrna, 5, 134.
enthusiasm for, in Smyrna, 5, 134–5.
sole ruler at Smyrna, 5, 136.
attracts wide attention, 5, 137.
honors paid to, 5, 141–2.
divides the world among his adherents, 5, 145.
goes to Constantinople, 5, 145–6.
arrested on his arrival, 5, 146.
reception of, in Constantinople, 5, 146–7.
imprisoned with debtors, 5, 147.
enthusiasm aroused by, in Constantinople, 5, 147–8.
imprisoned at Abydos, 5, 148.
celebrates the Passover illegally, 5, 148–9.
visitors crowd to, 5, 149.
homage paid to, 5, 149–50.
abolishes the fast of Tammuz, 5, 151–2.
summons Nehemiah Cohen, 5, 152.
betrayed by Nehemiah Cohen, 5, 153.
conversion of, to Islam resolved on, 5, 153.
taken to Adrianople, 5, 154.
converted to Islam, 5, 154.
third marriage of, 5, 154.
letters of homage to, from Amsterdam, 5, 155.

Sabbataï Zevi (*continued*), Messianic claims of, acknowledged after his apostasy, **5**, 156-7.
proved the true Messiah by his apostasy, **5**, 157-8.
joined by Nathan Ghazati, **5**, 158.
begins his Messianic doings anew, **5**, 162.
preaches before Jews at Adrianople, **5**, 162-3.
lives as a Jew and a Mahometan, **5**, 165-6.
banished to Constantinople, **5**, 166.
fourth marriage of, **5**, 166.
banished to Dulcigno, **5**, 166.
death of, **5**, 166.
Cardoso declares himself the successor of, **5**, 207.
cause of the failure of, **5**, 209.
supposed son of, **5**, 209.
immorality of the widow of, **5**, 209-10.
successors of, **5**, 211, 230, 274.
biography of, **5**, 212, 266.
See also Sabbatian movement, the; Sabbatians, the.
Sabbataï Zevi, the followers of, list of:
Aboab, Isaac, de Fonseca
Abudiente, Abraham Gideon
Aguilar, Raphael Moses d'
Ashkenazi, Jacob
Ayllon, Solomon
Benveniste, Chayim
Berachya,
Bloch, Mattathias
Bonafoux, Daniel Israel
Cardoso, Abraham Michael
Castro, Bendito de
Chayim Malach,
Chayon, Nehemiah Chiya
Chelebi, Raphael Joseph
Cuenqui, Abraham
Duchan, Jacob Israel
Eibeschütz, Jonathan
Faliachi, Jacob
Galante, Moses
Sabbataï Zevi, the followers of, list of (*continued*):
Isaiah Chassid,
Jacob Querido,
Judah Chassid,
Leb Herz,
Levi, Isaiah
Löbele Prosnitz,
Mordecai of Eisenstadt,
Moses Meïr Kamenker,
Naar, Isaac
Nathan Benjamin Levi (Ghazati),
Penya, Chayim
Pereira, Abraham
Pinheiro, Moses
Primo, Samuel
Rubio, Abraham
Sabbataï Raphael,
Salvador, Jonah
Silveira, Isaac
Sofino, Raphael
Texeira, Manoel
Wolf, Levi
Yachini, Abraham
Zacut, Moses.

Sabbath, the, the observance of, by Babylonian proselytes, **1**, 339.
by Babylonian Judæans, **1**, 364.
as ordered by Nehemiah, **1**, 386-7.
after Nehemiah, **1**, 397-8.
forbidden by Antiochus Epiphanes, **1**, 456.
according to the school of Shammai, **2**, 131, 132.
by the disciples of Jesus, **2**, 155.
forbidden in Alexandria, **2**, 184.
by Pagans, **2**, 384.
forbidden by Hadrian, **2**, 422.
respected by Honorius, **2**, 617.
forbidden by Jezdijird III, **2**, 627, 628.
as ordained by Anan ben David, **3**, 132.
among the Karaites, **3**, 132, 157, 158, 435; **4**, 269-70.
on Cyprus, **3**, 425.

Sabbath, the, the observance of (*continued*), a sign of heresy, **4,** 316.
by the Marranos of Lisbon, **4,** 489.
song for, **4,** 538.
the center of Lurya's mystic system, **4,** 626.
Jews of France compelled to violate, **5,** 451.
national according to Holdheim, **5,** 680.
on Sunday, **5,** 687, 702.
"Sabbath Epistle, The," by Abraham Ibn-Ezra, **3,** 374.
Sabbatian movement, the spread of, from Smyrna over Europe, **5,** 135–41.
and Rabbinical Judaism, **5,** 142, 143–4.
the Messiah in, **5,** 142–3.
opposed by the Kofrim, **5,** 144.
strengthened by the Messiah's imprisonment, **5,** 149–51.
causes stagnation of trade, **5,** 149.
in Italy, **5,** 160–1.
after Sabbataï Zevi's death, **5,** 207–14.
profligacy sanctioned in, **5,** 210.
growth of, **5,** 211–13, 228–9.
in Poland, **5,** 212, 228.
in Podolia, **5,** 228.
generally opposed by the rabbis, **5,** 245.
history of, **5,** 266.
Sabbatians, the, accept Islam, **5,** 154, 211.
ridiculed on Sabbataï's conversion to Islam, **5,** 155.
threatened with persecution in Turkey, **5,** 156.
refuse to believe Sabbataï's apostasy, **5,** 156–7.
excommunicated, **5,** 157.
at Adrianople, **5,** 159.
abrogate fasts. **5.** 159.
Sabbatians, the (*continued*), in Italy, **5,** 160–1.
adhere to Sabbataï, **5,** 163.
character of, unknown, **5,** 259.
existence of, denied, **5,** 271.
encouraged by the Eibeschütz controversy, **5,** 273.
Jacob Frank the leader of, **5,** 273.
Sabbatical year, the, kept after Ezra and Nehemiah, **1,** 393.
Alexander the Great remits the tax in, **1,** 415.
abolition of, contemplated by Judah I, **2,** 459–60.
tax during, exacted by Caracalla, **2,** 469.
Jannaï permits the cultivation of the land during, **2,** 469.
Sabea, a province of southern Arabia, **3,** 54.
Sabina, Poppea, wife of Nero, preference of, for Judaism, **2,** 248.
favorable to Judaism, **2,** 248.
appoints Gessius Florus procurator of Judæa, **2,** 249.
th of, **2,** 251.
releases Pharisees at the instance of Josephus, **2,** 276.
Sabinus, treasurer of Augustus, sent to seize Herod's treasures, **2,** 123.
instigates a siege of the Temple by the Romans, **2,** 123–4.
appropriates treasures from the Temple, **2,** 124.
urges Quintilius Varus against the Judæan insurgents, **2,** 125.
Sabureans (Saboraim), the, post-Amoraic teachers of the Law, render the Talmud available for practical use, **3,** 6.
commit the Talmud to writing, **3**, 6–7.

Sabureans (Saboraim), the (*continued*), chronicle of, by Sherira, **3**, 233.
See under Law, the, the teachers of.

Sabureans, the, list of:

Ahunai,	Mar bar Huna,
Chanan of Iskia,	Mari bar Mar,
Chananya,	Mar-Zutra III,
Chaninaï,	Rabaï of Rob,
Giza,	Semuna.

Sacharya. *See* Mar-Sacharya.

Sachs, Michael (1808–1864), author of the "Religious Poetry of the Jews in Spain," **5**, 555, 693–4.
contributor to the "Kerem Chemed," **5**, 622.
antagonizes the Berlin Reform Association, **5**, 687.
compared with Holdheim, **5**, 687–8, 692.
compared with the Marranos, **5**, 688.
Hebrew and Greek studies of, **5**, 688.
characteristics of, **5**, 688–9.
attitude of, to the Reform movement, **5**, 689.
dislikes organized action, **5**, 689.
as a preacher, **5**, 689–90, 692.
friendship of, with Rapoport, **5**, 690.
as a Talmudist, **5**, 690, 691.
appointed rabbi in Berlin, **5**, 691.
scorn of, for the German Jewish church, **5**, 691–2.
scientific activity of, **5**, 692–4.
exegetical work of, **5**, 692–3, 695, 699.

Sacrifices, the, place of, in the Sinaitic teaching, **1**, 24–5.
in Israel's early history, **1**, 57.
Samuel's view of, **1**, 74.
diminished importance of, **1**, 79.
how replaced by the synagogue services, **1**, 401.
to Jupiter, **1**, 455, 456.
daily, paid for by the half-Shekel contributions, **2**, 52.
during the siege of Jerusalem by Aretas, **2**, 60.
offered to the Cæsars, **2**, 103.
offered by Vitellius, **2**, 173.
not opposed by Jesus, **2**, 155.
Jochanan ben Zakkai on, **2**, 209, 324, 325.
offered by heathens, **2**, 258–9.
system of, admired by Julian the Apostate, **2**, 597.

Sadducæism, revived by the high priest Anan, **2**, 248.

Sadducees, the, the sect opposed in religion and politics to the Pharisees, **2**, 17.
wherein opposed to the Pharisees, **2**, 18.
pay a tribute to the purity of the Pharisees, **2**, 20.
the kernel of the Hasmonæan following, **2**, 21.
derivation of the name of, **2**, 21.
patriotism of, **2**, 21.
political and religious principles of, **2**, 21–2.
position of, with regard to the Pentateuchal laws, **2**, 22–3.
unpopularity of, **2**, 23.
employed as diplomatists by John Hyrcanus, **2**, 31.
replace the Pharisees in state offices, **2**, 33.
actively opposed by the Pharisees under Alexander Jannæus, **2**, 42–3.
compose the Great Council, **2**, 42.
favored by Alexander Jannæus, **2**, 42–3.

Sadducees, the (*continued*), deprived of their seats in the Synhedrion, **2**, 50.
make the sacrifices depend on voluntary contributions, **2**, 52.
persecuted by the Pharisees, **2**, 53, 55.
protected by Salome Alexandra, **2**, 55.
support Aristobulus, **2**, 58.
reconciliation of, with the Pharisees, begun by Hillel, **2**, 98.
a sect of, **2**, 108.
opposed to the oral or traditional law, **2**, 327, 462.
the opposition of, accentuates the legal character of Judaism, **2**, 471.

Sadolet, bishop of Carpentras, on Paul III's friendliness to the Jews, **4**, 515.

Safa Berurah, grammatical work by Abraham Ibn-Ezra, **3**, 374.

Safet, the Jews of, excommunicate the Anti-Maimunists, **3**, 633.
Kabbalistic center, **4**, 74, 399, 405, 622–3.
importance of, **4**, 399, 531.
Spanish exiles in, **4**, 399.
influence of Solomon Molcho in, **4**, 529–30.
Joseph Karo at, **4**, 538.
Azarya deï Rossi's works declared heretical at, **4**, 616.
Chayim Vital in, **5**, 52.
Luzzatto at, **5**, 244.

Safi (Assafi), Spanish exiles in, **4**, 389.

Safia, daughter of Hujej Ibn-Achtab, taken captive by Mahomet, **3**, 83.

Safran, Karaite center, **3**, 158.

Sagan. *See* Segan.

Sahaduta di Mehemnuta, Sabbatian work, **5**, 162.

Sahal Rabban (800), physician and mathematician, translates the Almagest, **3**, 146.

Said. *See* Saadiah ben Joseph.

Saida. *See* Sidon.

Saif-Eddin Ghasi, friendly to the Jews of Mosul, **3**, 429.

St. Bartholomew, the massacre of, influences the election of the Polish king, **4**, 604.

Saint Etienne, Rabaud, deputy to the National Assembly, speaks in behalf of the Jews, **5**, 439.

St. Gall, the Jews of, charged with well poisoning, **4**, 105.

St. Gilles, the Jews of, in the twelfth century, **3**, 399–400.
Jewish deputies meet at, **3**, 509.

St. Jean d'Acre. *See* Accho.

St. John, Lord Oliver, English ambassador to Holland, visits a synagogue, **5**, 33–4.

St. Paul's cathedral, Jews reported to have bought, **5**, 45.

Saints, the worship of, discussed by French Jews, **3**, 343.

Sais, center of the worship of Neïth, **1**, 300.

Saladin, sultan of Turkey, maintains his hold upon Jerusalem, **3**, 405.
power of, **3**, 431.
has a Jewish physician, **3**, 443.
succeeds the Fatimide Caliphs, **3**, 461.
the Jews under, **3**, 461.
at war with Nureddin's adherents, **3**, 472.
allows Jews to settle in Jerusalem, **3**, 474.
patron of Abdel-latif, **3**, 488.
in "Nathan the Wise," **5**, 324.

Salamanca, the Jews of, accept baptism, **4**, 205.
charged with child murder, **4**, 276.
Salamis, capital of Cyprus, destroyed by Jewish rebels against Trajan, **2**, 397.
Salee, the Sabbatians of, persecuted, **5**, 151.
Salerno, the Jews of, in the twelfth century, **3**, 424.
Salins, François, enemy of the Damascus Jews, **5**, 661.
Sallam Ibn-Mishkam, a prominent Nadhirite, urges war against Mahomet, **3**, 79.
Salman of Lemberg, spies upon Luzzatto, **5**, 240.
Salman of Liadi, leader of the Chassidim, **5**, 393.
imprisoned, **5**, 394.
Salome, sister of Herod, calumniates Mariamne, **2**, 93, 104.
Herod's suspicions of, **2**, 112.
daughter of, **2**, 112.
conspires against Mariamne's sons, **2**, 112-13.
ordered to execute prominent Judæans on the day of Herod's death, **2**, 116.
bequest to, from Herod, **2**, 119.
disputes the succession of Archelaus, **2**, 120.
towns belonging to, bequeathed to Empress Livia, **2**, 128, 132.
Salome Alexandra, wife of Aristobulus I, accused of instigating her brother-in-law's murder, **2**, 38.
said to have released Alexander Jannæus from prison, **2**, 39.
partisan of the Pharisees, **2**, 42, 48.
made regent, **2**, 47.
gentle character of, **2**, 47-8.
Salome Alexandra, wife of Aristobulus I (*continued*), coins of, **2**, 48.
proclaims Hyrcanus high priest, **2**, 48.
protects the Sadducees, **2**, 55.
treats with the king of Armenia, **2**, 55-6.
end of, **2**, 56.
Salomon, Gotthold, preacher of the Hamburg Reform Temple, **5**, 564-5.
Heine on, **5**, 577.
Salomons, David, in the Damascus affair, **5**, 645, 653.
fined for taking his seat in Parliament, **5**, 698.
Salonica (Saloniki, Thessalonica), the Jews of, in the twelfth century, **3**, 424.
Samuel II Abrabanel studies at, **4**, 385.
Spanish spoken in, by the exiles, **4**, 388.
the Spanish exiles at, **4**, 404-5.
becomes a Jewish town, **4**, 404-5.
a Kabbalistic center, **4**, 405, 538.
the Jews of, split up into national groups, **4**, 478.
the Kabbalists of, and Solomon Molcho, **4**, 496-7.
the Jews of, consider trading with Pesaro, **4**, 579.
Amatus Lusitanus in, **4**, 580.
Sabbataï Zevi in, **5**, 124.
the Sabbatian enthusiasm in, **5**, 135.
Nathan Ghazati at, **5**, 160.
the Sabbatians of, devoted to Sabbataï, **5**, 163.
profligacy of the Sabbatians in, **5**, 210.
the Donmäh in, **5**, 211.
growth of the Sabbatian movement in, **5**, 211.
Nehemiah Chayon at, **5**, 216.

Salonica (Saloniki, Thessalonica) (*continued*), Jacob Frank in, **5**, 272.
See also Thessalonica.
Saloniki. *See* Salonica.
Saloniki, Moses, accused of ritual murder, **5**, 636.
tortured, **5**, 636–7.
Salt mines, owned by Jews, **3**, 242.
farmed by Jews, **3**, 521.
Salt Sea, the, description of, **1**, 43.
Salvador, Jonah, defends the Jews of Metz from the blood accusation, **5**, 176.
Salvatierra, the Jewish community of, destroyed by the Almohades, **3**, 506–7.
"**Salvation of the Jews, The**," by Mendelssohn, **5**, 362–3.
Salvation, the dogma of, criticised by Joseph Ibn-Shem Tob, **4**, 235.
according to Joseph Albo, **4**, 240–1.
Salzring, in Breslau, scene of the burning of Jews by John of Capistrano, **4**, 262.
Samach, wife of Izates, convert to Judaism, **2**, 216.
Samael, chief of demons, introduced into Judaism from Magianism, **1**, 403.
name of a Sefirah, **4**, 17.
Samaria (city) (Sebaste), made the capital of Israel, **1**, 193.
center of Phœnician idol-worship, **1**, 197–8.
Elisha in, **1**, 218.
besieged by Ben-hadad III, **1**, 221–2.
taken by Shalmaneser, **1**, 264.
subdued by Sennacherib, **1**, 270.
gubernatorial seat of Cœlesyria under Macedonian rule, **1**, 414.
a colony of Idumæans near, **2**, 9.
besieged by Hyrcanus, **2**, 10.
Samaria (city) (Sebaste), *continued*), capitulates, **2**, 211.
Mariamne married to Herod at, **2**, 87.
incorporated with Judæa under Herod, **2**, 103.
called Sebaste and ornamented by Herod, **2**, 106.
the sons of Mariamne executed at, **2**, 113.
given to Archelaus by Herod's will, **2**, 119.
ruled by procurators, **2**, 137.
given to Agrippa I, **2**, 190.
Greek citizens of, and Agrippa I, **2**, 194, 196.
Cumanus procurator of, **2**, 242.
a Christian city, **3**, 12.
Samaritans in, in the twelfth century, **3**, 427.
Samaria, the kingdom of. *See* Israel, the kingdom of.
Samaritan, a, brings about the fall of Bethar, **2**, 417–18.
the, account of the fall of Bethar, **2**, 418.
Samaritans (Cuthæans), the, a mixed population colonized in Samaria by Esarhaddon, **1**, 285.
worship at Mizpah, **1**, 321.
settled to the north of Judæa, **1**, 355.
and the second Temple, **1**, 357.
hostility of, to the Judæans, **1**, 358.
accuse the Judæans of disloyalty to Persia, **1**, 361.
intermarry with the Judæans, **1**, 361–2.
attack Jerusalem, **1**, 371.
take Jerusalem, **1**, 372.
build a Temple on Gerizim, **1**, 390.
declare themselves a remnant of the Ten Tribes, **1**, 390–1.

Samaritans (Cuthæans), the (*continued*), characteristics of, **1**, 391-2.
the first Jewish sect, **1**, 392.
hostility of, to the Judæans, **1**, 392, 410, 435.
retain the old Hebrew characters, **1**, 396.
reject the prophetical writings, **1**, 400.
reject the dogma of resurrection, **1**, 406.
Andromachos governor of, **1**, 414.
taken captive by Ptolemy I, **1**, 416.
money-lenders among, equip Joseph for court, **1**, 424.
join Gorgias in his invasion of Judæa, **1**, 467.
hostility of, to the Judæans, re-awakened in Egypt, **1**, 515-16.
forced to renounce Judaism by Antiochus IV, **1**, 516.
emigrate to Egypt, **1**, 516.
objection of, to the Septuagint, **1**, 516.
dispute with the Judæans in Egypt, **1**, 516-17.
Greek literature of, **1**, 517.
hostile to Judæa under John Hyrcanus, **2**, 7.
Temple of, destroyed, **2**, 7-8.
pollute the Temple, **2**, 135.
cruelly treated by Pontius Pilate, **2**, 171-2.
murder Galilean pilgrims, **2**, 243.
of Acrabatene, exterminated, **2**, 243.
join the Judæans against Rome, **2**, 268.
influence Hadrian against the Jews, **2**, 403.
receive Hadrian with servility, **2**, 406.
Samaritans (Cuthæans), the (*continued*), religion of, mocked at by Hadrian, **2**, 407-8.
participate in the revolt of Bar-Cochba, **2**, 410.
testimony of, declared valid, **2**, 457.
enmity of, to the Jews, **2**, 457-8, 534.
compelled to idolatry by Diocletian, **2**, 533.
declared heathens by the Synhedrion, **2**, 534.
weakened by their hostility to the Jews, **2**, 535.
in Babylonia and Abayi Nachmani, **2**, 584.
forbidden to enter military service under Honorius, **2**, 617.
evidence of, declared invalid by Justinian I, **3**, 13.
obliged to assume the decurionate, **3**, 13.
forced into Christianity, **3**, 16-17.
massacre the Christians of Cæsarea, **3**, 17.
oppressed by Justin II, **3**, 17-18.
help the Arabs in Palestine, **3**, 87.
in the twelfth century, **3**, 427.
Samarkand, the Jews of, in the twelfth century, **3**, 435.
Samega, John Hyrcanus at, **2**, 7.
Samiel. *See* Samael.
Samogitia, Karaites in, **5**, 182.
Samos, the Jews of, in the twelfth century, **3**, 424.
Sampsigeramus, king of Emesa, allied with Agrippa I, **2**, 195.
Samson, judge, fights with the Philistines, **1**, 64, 66.
hero of a poem by Enriquez de Paz, **5**, 111.

Samson, judge (*continued*), subject of Luzzatto's drama, **5**, 234.
the Syrian Hercules, **5**, 715.
Samson ben Abraham of Sens, Tossafist, regards Karaites as idolaters, **3**, 408; **4**, 72.
emigrates to Jerusalem, **3**, 505.
anti-Maimunist, **3**, 524, 527.
party of, defeated, **3**, 526.
brother-in-law of, **3**, 539.
Samson ben Meïr, collects twenty signatures against the study of science, **4**, 38.
Samuel, candidate for the Exilarchate, **3**, 439.
Samuel, disciple of Jochanan bar Napacha, defends a political offender before Zenobia, **2**, 529–30.
Samuel, Jewish treasurer of Ferdinand IV of Castile, **4**, 51–2.
Samuel, Kabbalist, disciple of Abraham Abulafia, **4**, 6.
Samuel, prophet, characterization of, **1**, 72–3.
descent of, **1**, 73.
at Shiloh, **1**, 73.
prophetic inspiration of, **1**, 73, 75.
on sacrifices, **1**, 74.
versed in the Law of Moses, **1**, 74.
reclaims the nation from idolatry, **1**, 75–6.
as a preacher, **1**, 75.
unites the northern and the southern tribes, **1**, 77–8.
holds popular assemblies, **1**, 78.
introduces music into the divine service, **1**, 78–9.
sons of, **1**, 79, 80.
and the demand for a king, **1**, 80.
chooses Saul as king, **1**, 82–3.
abandons Saul at Gilgal, **1**, 86.
Samuel, prophet (*continued*), accompanies Saul against Nahash, **1**, 90.
anoints Saul, **1**, 90.
reproves Saul for disobedience in the Amalekite wars, **1**, 92–3.
kills Agag, **1**, 93.
anoints David, **1**, 95–6.
influences David, **1**, 96–7.
regulations for pilgrims to the grave of, **4**, 398.
Samuel the Younger (Hakaton), condemns the Jewish Christians, **2**, 357–8.
prophecy of, **2**, 358.
supposed author of the Birchath ha-Minim, **2**, 379.
Samuel bar Bun, Amora, contemporary of Ashi, **2**, 609.
Samuel bar Judah, Amòra, emigrates from Judæa, **2**, 567.
Samuel ben Aaron, Karaite, gives an account of Karaism, **5**, 183.
Samuel ben Abraham Ibn-Chasdaï Halevi (1165–1216), prominent in Barcelona, **3**, 388.
Samuel ben Abraham Saporta, Maimunist, addresses the rabbis of France, **3**, 539.
denounces Solomon of Montpellier, **3**, 543.
Samuel ben Ali Halevi, Talmudist, Gaon of Bagdad, **3**, 438–9.
as a philosopher, **3**, 438.
as a teacher, **3**, 438–9.
judge of appeals, **3**, 439.
functions and authority of, **3**, 439–40.
daughter of, **3**, 439.
opposes Maimonides, **3**, 472.
traduces Maimonides, **3**, 475, 477.

Samuel ben Ali Halevi, Talmudist (*continued*), treatise by, on the resurrection, **3**, 476.
correspondence of, with Maimonides, **3**, 476–7.
disciple of, **3**, 525.
Samuel ben Asher, murdered in Cologne during the first crusade, **3**, 304.
Samuel ben Chofni, last Gaon of Sora, exegetical works of, **3**, 253.
attacks Karaism, **3**, 253.
Samuel ben Israel, son of Manasseh, academic honors paid to, in England, **5**, 38.
Samuel ben Judah Ibn-Tibbon (1160–1239), translator, character of, **3**, 398.
corresponds with Maimonides, **3**, 491.
trains Jacob Anatoli as a translator, **3**, 566.
not in favor with the obscurantists, **4**, 32.
Samuel ben Meïr (Rashbam, 1100–1160), grandson of Rashi, Tossafist, **3**, 288, 345.
converts Rashi to a rational exegesis, **3**, 288, 346.
Bible exegete, **3**, 345–6.
commentaries by, **3**, 346.
maintains that the Biblical day begins in the morning, **3**, 374.
compared with Jacob Tam, **3**, 375.
at the first rabbinical synod, **3**, 377.
Samuel ben Meïr Allavi (Abulafia), minister of finance to Pedro the Cruel, **4**, 115–16, 117–18.
rectitude of, **4**, 116.
espouses the cause of Maria de Padilla, **4**, 117.
Samuel ben Meïr Allavi (Abulafia) (*continued*), shares the king's imprisonment, **4**, 118.
protector of the Jews, **4**, 119.
builds a synagogue at Toledo, **4**, 119–20.
agitation against, **4**, 120–1.
fall and death of, **4**, 121.
synagogue of, turned into a church, **4**, 354.
Samuel ben Solomon at the disputation with Donin, **3**, 576, 578.
Samuel ben Solomon Sir Morel, Tossafist, **3**, 586.
Samuel ben Yechiel, martyr of the first crusade, **3**, 305.
Samuel Ibn-Abbas, apostate to Islam, writes against the Jews, **3**, 442.
Samuel Ibn-Adiya (500–560), Jewish Arabic poet, chief of an Arabic tribe, **3**, 68.
protects Imrulkais Ibn-Hojr, **3**, 68–9.
son of, **3**, 69, 70.
defense of, **3**, 70.
death of, **3**, 70.
Samuel Ibn-Nagdela. *See* Samuel Halevi Ibn-Nagrela.
Samuel Ibn-Wakar (Abenhuacar), at the court of Alfonso XI of Castile, **4**, 76, 79.
physician to Alfonso XI, **4**, 80.
jealous of Joseph Ecija, **4**, 80.
made farmer of revenues, **4**, 80–1.
accused of depreciating the coinage, **4**, 81.
end of, **4**, 84.
Samuel, son of Abba (Arioch, Mar-Samuel, Yarchinai, 180–257), cures Judah I, **2**, 456.
an Amora, **2**, 479, 518.
enforces the authority of the Patriarch in Babylonia, **2**, 484.

Samuel, son of Abba (*continued*), returns to Babylonia, **2**, 511, 519.
principal of the Nahardea academy, **2**, 512, 519.
decisions of, **2**, 515.
view held by, on the Messiah, **2**, 519.
establishes the principle of the sanctity of the law of the land, **2**, 519–20.
and Shabur I, **2**, 520, 526.
Persian leanings of, **2**, 520–1.
as astronomer, **2**, 521.
draws up a calendar, **2**, 521–2.
as a physician, **2**, 522.
subordination of, to Rab, **2**, 522.
recognized as the religious chief of Babylon, **2**, 522.
and Jochanan bar Napacha, **2**, 522–3.
daughters of, taken captive by Odenathus, **2**, 528.
superiority of, acknowledged in Palestine, **2**, 531.
influence of, on Jewish Babylonia, **2**, 544.
on Judah ben Ezekiel, **2**, 550.
humanity of, towards his slaves, **2**, 555.
calendar of, used by Hillel II, **2**, 574.
Samuel, son of Joseph Ezobi, advice to, **3**, 561.
Samuel I Abrabanel (Juan de Sevilla), Almoxarif to Henry II de Trastamare, **4**, 138, 169.
exerts himself in behalf of the Jews, **4**, 139–40.
patron of Menachem ben Aaron, **4**, 145.
accepts baptism, **4**, 169.
delegate of the Spanish Jews to Martin V, **4**, 219.
grandfather of Isaac Abrabanel, **4**, 337.
Samuel II Abrabanel (1473–1550), son of Isaac, student at Salonica, **4**, 340, 385.
eminence of, **4**, 409.
as financier, **4**, 409.
beneficence of, **4**, 409.
wife of, **4**, 409–10.
patron of Jewish learning, **4**, 410.
advises the Jews to leave Naples, **4**, 543.
settles in Ferrara, **4**, 544.
Samuel Alvalensi, Spanish exile, prominent in Fez, **4**, 390.
disciple of, **4**, 392.
Samuel Çarça, on the condition of the Jews of Castile, **4**, 137.
comments on Abraham Ibn-Ezra's Pentateuch commentary, **4**, 144.
Samuel Cohen ben Daniel, head of the Bagdad academy, Maimunist, **3**, 633.
Samuel Franco, Kabbalist in Salonica, **4**, 405.
Samuel Halevi, delegate of the Spanish Jews to Martin V, **4**, 219.
Samuel Halevi, invents a water-clock, **3**, 594.
Samuel (Ishmael) Halevi Ibn-Nagrela (Nagid, 993–1055), consults Haï Gaon, **3**, 252, 260.
accomplishments of, **3**, 254–5.
taught by Chanoch and Chayuj, **3**, 255.
leaves Cordova and settles in Malaga, **3**, 255.
linguistic attainments of, **3**, 255.
master of Arabic calligraphy, **3**, 255.
private secretary to the vizir, **3**, 256.
minister to Habus, **3**, 256–7.

Samuel (Ishmael) Halevi Ibn-Nagrela (*continued*), poem by, addressed to Habus, **3**, 257.
gentleness of, **3**, 257.
plots to depose, **3**, 258.
partisan of Badis, **3**, 258.
vizir under Badis, **3**, 258.
formulas of Moslem rulers used by, **3**, 259.
exercises authority over the Granada congregations, **3**, 259.
writes a methodology of the Talmud, **3**, 259.
writes a commentary on the Talmud, **3**, 259.
as poet, **3**, 259–60.
as patron of learning, **3**, 260.
as grammarian, **3**, 261.
hostile to Ibn-Janach, **3**, 262, 313.
patron of Ibn-Gebirol, **3**, 268.
eulogized by Joseph ben Chasdaï, **3**, 273.
poem by, in praise of Joseph ben Chasdaï, **3**, 274.
death of, **3**, 274.
son of, **3**, 274.
patron of Isaac ben Baruch Albalia, **3**, 283.
patron of Isaac Ibn-Giat, **3**, 284.
unique figure in Spanish Jewish history, **3**, 313.
employs the father of Moses Ibn-Ezra, **3**, 319.
research of, furnishes material for Abraham Ibn-Daud's history, **3**, 366.

Samuel Lisbona. *See* Lisbona, Samuel.

Samuel Nagid. *See* Samuel Halevi Ibn-Nagrela.

Samuel Shulam, physician, historical works by, **4**, 608.

Samuel Sidillo, scholar, Spanish exile at Cairo, **4**, 392.

Samuel Sulami, patron of Jewish learning, **4**, 25–6.
in correspondence with Solomon ben Adret, **4**, 26.
censured for harboring Levi of Villefranche, **4**, 29.

Samuel Vital, publishes his father's Kabbalistic visions, **5**, 53.
superintends Chelebi's penances, **5**, 125.

Samuel Zacuto, son of Abraham, escapes from Portugal, **4**, 378.

Samuges, king of Assyria, defection of the nations from, **1**, 287.

Samun, rabbi of Leghorn, recalls his approval of the Reform movement, **5**, 571.

Sanaa (Usal), Israelitish trading station at, **3**, 54.
prince of the Jews of Talmas in, **3**, 437.

Sanballat, leader of the Samaritans, qualities of, **1**, 362.
hostility of, to the Judæans under Ezra, **1**, 369–70.
attacks Jerusalem, **1**, 371.
chagrined at Nehemiah's appointment, **1**, 374.
disturbs Nehemiah's work, **1**, 375.
intrigues against Nehemiah, **1**, 375–6.
daughter of, **1**, 383, 386.
projects a Temple on Mount Gerizim, **1**, 389–90.
invites settlers to Samaria, **1**, 391.

San Benito, the garment of the victims of the Inquisition, **4**, 317, 327.

Sanchez, Juan Perez, Marrano, tries to suppress the Inquisition in Aragon, **4**, 329.

Sanchez, Juan Perez, Marrano (*continued*), plots against Pedro Arbues, **4,** 329.
Sancho IV, son of Alfonso X, rebels against his father, **3,** 616.
Jews of Castile under, **3,** 616–17.
regulates the taxation of the Jews, **3,** 617.
Todros Abulafia at the court of, **4,** 2.
Sancho Ramirez, king of Leon, concludes a treaty with Abdul-Rahman III, **3,** 216.
Sancta Anastasia, cardinal de, favorably inclined towards the Portuguese Marranos, **4,** 379.
Sand, Karl, assassin of Kotzebue, **5,** 528, 530, 533.
Sangisa, sister of Pope John XXII, hostile to the Jews, **4,** 61.
San Martin, Juan de, inquisitor appointed by Sixtus IV, **4,** 312, 323.
censured by Sixtus IV, **4,** 318.
San Miguel, the order of, awarded to Enriquez de Paz, **5,** 110.
Sans-Souci, Mendelssohn at, **5,** 302.
Santa-Cruz, Gaspard de, Marrano, dishonored after his death, **4,** 331–2.
Santarem, Jewish center in Portugal, **4,** 159.
refuge of Leonora of Portugal, **4,** 160.
Santas. *See* Joseph ben Isaac Ibn-Abitur.
Sante-Fé, Francisco de, Marrano, martyrdom of, **4,** 331.
San Thomas, children of Spanish exiles sent to, **4,** 371.
Santiago de Compostela, autos-da-fé in, **5,** 91.
Santob de Carrion (1300–1350), Spanish Jewish poet, **4,** 87, 114–15.
style of, **4,** 115.
rebukes the king and wealthy Jews, **4,** 115.
Saporta. *See* Enoch Saporta; Samuel ben Abraham Saporta.
Saragossa, early traces of Jews near, **3,** 42.
Cordova Jews emigrate to, **3,** 255.
Ibn-Janach settles at, **3,** 262.
Ibn-Gebirol banished from, **3,** 268.
a Jewish vizir at, **3,** 280.
Ibn-Kamnial at, **3,** 312.
conquered by Alfonso I of Aragon, **3,** 316.
capital of Aragon, **3,** 387.
first victims of the Inquisition in Aragon fall in, **4,** 329.
Jews disappear from, **4,** 354.
Saragossa, the Jews of, censured by Ibn-Gebirol for neglecting Hebrew, **3,** 267.
try to prevent the execution of the decree concerning Jew badges, **3,** 513.
Maimunists, **3,** 536–7.
converted by Vincent Ferrer, **4,** 206, 214.
Saragossa, the Marranos of, plot against Arbues, **4,** 330.
protected by Alfonso of Aragon, **4,** 330.
slaughtered, **4,** 331–2.
Saragossi. *See* Joseph Saragossi.
Sarah, wife of Abraham, buried in Machpelah, **1,** 4.
in the Zohar, **4,** 23.
Sarah Zevi, suffering of, during the Chmielnicki massacres, **5,** 128–9.

Sarah Zevi (*continued*), declares herself to be the destined wife of the Messiah, **5**, 129.
brought from Leghorn to Cairo, **5**, 129.
marries Sabbataï Zevi, **5**, 129.
immorality of, **5**, 130, 135.
at Abydos, **5**, 149.
accepts Islam, **5**, 154.
Saramalla, a rich Judæan of Antioch, assists Herod, **2**, 87.
Saraph-Bashi, Egyptian title, **5**, 124.
Sardes, the goddess of love worshiped in, **1**, 408.
Sardinia, Roman Judæans banished to, **2**, 136–7.
the Jewish community in, in the sixth century, **3**, 28.
Sardinia, the Jews of, protected by Gregory I, **3**, 33.
proclamation expelling, **4**, 347.
Sarepta (Zarephath), Elijah dwells in, **1**, 203.
Sariel, name of a Sefirah, **4**, 17.
Sarkel, Chazar fortress, taken by Sviatislav, **3**, 222.
Sarmatia, rebels against Hadrian, **2**, 399.
Sarrão, Thomé, Portuguese Marrano leader, **4**, 516.
Sarsar, meeting place of Kohen-Zedek and David ben Zaccaï, **3**, 186.
Sar Shalom, rabbi of the Persian congregations, **3**, 434.
Sartaba. *See* Alexandrion.
Saruk, Israel, introduces the Luryan Kabbala into Italy and Holland, **5**, 54.
Sason, Prussian consul, protects the Jews of Beyrout, **5**, 641.
Sasportas, the family of, distinguished in Oran, **5**, 169.
Sasportas, Jacob, scholar, accompanies Manasseh ben Israel to England, **5**, 38.
rabbi of London, **5**, 50.
opposes the Sabbatian movement, **5**, 138, 141, 150, 161.
tries to expose Sabbataï's roguery, **5**, 151.
Sasportas, Jacob, zealous for the emancipation of the Dutch Jews, **5**, 455.
Sassanides, the, dynasty of, established by Ardashir, **2**, 523.
Satan, beginning of the belief in, **2**, 170.
Satanov, Sabbatians before the council of rabbis at, **5**, 276.
Satanow, Isaac, one of the Measfim, **5**, 400.
Satire, the favorite burden of Jewish Andalusian poetry, **3**, 224.
Satirical romance, the, in Hebrew poetry, **3**, 559.
Saturnalia, the, Jews have no intercourse with the heathen before, **2**, 477.
Saubert, John, translator of Templo's work, **5**, 115.
Saul, choice of, as king, **1**, 83.
qualities of, **1**, 83.
discontent with, **1**, 83.
son of. *See* Jonathan.
offends Samuel at Gilgal, **1**, 86.
condemns Jonathan to death, **1**, 88–9.
at Gibeah, **1**, 89–90.
defeats the Ammonites, **1**, 89–90.
homage paid to, at Gilgal, **1**, 90.
creates new offices, **1**, 91.
defeats Agag, **1**, 91–2.
beginning of the madness of, **1**, 93–4.
orders a massacre of the Gibeonites, **1**, 94.

Saul (*continued*), royal ostentation of, **1,** 94–5.
permits David to fight with Goliath, **1,** 97.
invites David to his court, **1,** 98.
fears David as a rival, **1,** 99.
attempts David's life, **1,** 99.
murders the descendants of Eli, **1,** 100.
consults the witch of Endor, **1,** 103.
death of the sons of, **1,** 103.
death of, **1,** 103.
body of, dishonored by the Philistines, **1,** 104.
remains of, buried, **1,** 124.
Israelites under, settle in the Hejas, **3,** 54.
favorite character of the Puritans, **5,** 26.
Saul, member of the Herodian family, wickedness of, **2,** 236.
accuses Gessius Florus before Nero, **2,** 268.
Saul of Tarsus. *See* Paul, apostle.
Saul, son of Anan ben David, succeeds him, **3,** 136.
Saul Astruc Cohen, physician in Tlemçen, **4,** 198.
protects Marrano fugitives, **4,** 199.
Saul Cohen Ashkenasi, disciple of Elias del Medigo, **4,** 293.
letter to, from Isaac Abrabanel, **4,** 386.
pure style of, **4,** 389.
Saurim, brother of Raba bar Joseph, heartlessness of, **2,** 588.
Savoy, Oran Jews settle in, **5,** 169.
Savoy, the Jews of, charged with well poisoning, **4,** 103–4.
during Vincent Ferrer's crusade, **4,** 218.
Savoy, the Jews of (*continued*), privileges of, confirmed by Martin V, **4,** 219.
Saxon emperors, the, position of the Jews under, **3,** 241, 242–3.
Saxony, the Jews of, under heavy restrictions, **5,** 509.
Sbaráz, battle of, between Cossacks and Poles, **5,** 12.
Scaliger, Joseph, philologist, tolerance of, **4,** 685.
quickens learning, **5,** 20.
devotes himself to Rabbinical literature, **5,** 21.
introduces Rabbinical literature to Christians, **5,** 179.
Scaurus, legate of Pompey in Syria, attacks Aretas, **2,** 70.
called upon to arbitrate between Hyrcanus II and Aristobulus II, **2,** 61–2.
commands Aretas to raise the siege of Jerusalem, **2,** 62.
bribed to favor Hyrcanus II, **2,** 62.
Schaffhausen, the Jews of, charged with well poisoning, **4,** 105.
Schiller, expresses regard for Solomon Maimon, **5,** 409.
Schimmelpennik, Grand Pensioner of the Batavian Republic, appoints Jews to public offices, **5,** 458.
Schlegel, Frederick, character of, **5,** 423–4.
union of, with Dorothea Mendelssohn, **5,** 424.
representative of the romantic school, **5,** 515, 516.
Schleiermacher, intimacy of, with Henrietta Herz, **5,** 423.
hostile to Judaism, **5,** 426–7, 428.
refuses to acknowledge the Jewish origin of Christianity, **5,** 426

Schleiermacher (*continued*), ill-will of, towards Jews, **5,** 462.
Schmidt, Bremen deputy to the Congress of Vienna, opposes the emancipation of the Jews, **5,** 519.
Schmidt of Hildburghausen, defends the Jews, **5,** 522.
Scholastic philosophy, the, and Ibn-Gebirol's works, **3,** 270–1.
influenced by the "Guide of the Perplexed," **3,** 486.
studied by Leone Romano, **4,** 69.
quoted by Jewish preachers in the fifteenth century, **4,** 232.
Schools, elementary, established in Judæa by Joshua ben Gamala, **2,** 249.
in Spain by the law of Avila, **4,** 229.
Schools for young men, origin of, in Palestine, **1,** 396.
reorganized by Simon ben Shetach, **2,** 50–1.
lack of, in Galilee, **2,** 148.
in Asia Minor and Egypt, **2,** 357–8.
in Judæa inspected by order of Judah III, **2,** 532.
at Sora established by Chasda, **2,** 553.
in Palestine in the sixth century, **3,** 12.
at Yathrib, **3,** 59.
founded in the West by emissaries from Sora, **3,** 208.
in Amsterdam, **4,** 681–2.
in Rotterdam, **4,** 685.
See under Education *for other headings.*
Schools, secular, founded by Jews, in Trieste, **5,** 369–70.
in Prague, **5,** 371.
in Berlin, **5,** 405, 416.
in Tarnopol, **5,** 612.
Schools, secular, founded by Jews (*continued*), in Egypt, **5,** 664.
Schools, the, of the prophets, 1, 205, 234.
Schor, Elisha, Frankist, **5,** 275.
draws up the Frankist confession of faith, **5,** 280.
Schudt, author of "Jewish Curiosities," **5,** 549.
Schurmann, Anna Maria, student of Hebrew literature, **5,** 21.
"Schutzjuden." *See* Protection-Jews.
Schwager, preacher, on the emancipation of the Jews, **5,** 358.
Schwarz, Peter, apostate, maligns the Jews, **4,** 301.
motives of, suspected by Reuchlin, **4,** 442.
Schweidnitz, the Jews of, engaged in money-lending, **4,** 260.
charged with host desecration, **4,** 261.
Science, promoted by Judaism during the Middle Ages, **3,** 146, 187.
Science, the study of, by Jews, advocated by Jonathan of Lünel, **3,** 397.
opposition to, at the end of the thirteenth century, **4,** 27–34, 37–45.
ban against, **4,** 39–40.
controversy on, continued at Perpignan, **4,** 50–1.
baneful effect of the ban against, **4,** 143.
opposition to, in the fourteenth century, **5,** 147.
See also Maimunist controversy, the.
Science of Judaism, the, subserves the Reform movement, **5,** 627.

"Scientific Journal, The," the tone of, 5, 625.
founder of, 5, 626.
inculcates self-respect, 5, 626.
recalls the Karaites, 5, 626.
Scipio, follower of Pompey, has Alexander, son of Aristobulus II, beheaded, 2, 75.
Scopas, an Ætolian, takes Jerusalem, 1, 432.
garrisons the Baris, 1, 433.
routed by the Syrians near Panion, 1, 433.
Scopus Zophim, camp of Titus, 2, 302.
Scotus. *See* Duns Scotus.
"**Scourge of the Jews**," name given to John of Capistrano, 4, 260.
Scribes, the. *See* Sopherim, the.
Scriptures, the, written with Assyrian characters, 1, 395-6.
studied in the schools of Judæa, 2, 50-1.
allegorical interpretation of, by the Judæo-Alexandrian school, 2, 208-9.
as interpreted by Paul, 2, 230.
canon of, completed, 2, 344.
translated into Greek by Akylas, 2, 385, 386-7.
Chiya bar Abba ignorant of, 2, 536.
translations of, 2, 581-2.
studied in Palestine under Theodosius II, 2, 623-5.
the Latin translation of, 2, 625.
incorrect explanation of, favored by the Talmud, 2, 633.
vowel-points and accents introduced into, 3, 7.
use of translations of, ordered by Justinian I, 3, 14-15.
knowledge of, among the Arabian Jews, 3, 59.
Scriptures, the (*continued*), love for, among the Arabs, 3, 59.
Mahomet's doctrines borrowed from, 3, 72.
study of, revived among Jews under Mahometan influence, 3, 111-12.
rendered comprehensible by the introduction of vowel points, 3, 112.
study of, stimulates poetic composition, 3, 118.
studied by the Jews of Arabia, 3, 119-20.
replaced by the Talmud, 3, 128.
a return to the letter of, advocated by Anan ben David, 3, 130.
study of, stimulated by Anan ben David, 3, 133.
ardently studied by the Karaites, 3, 136.
commentators on, among the Karaites, 3, 136.
neglected by the Rabbanites, 3, 189.
translated into Arabic by Saadiah, 3, 189-90.
trustworthiness of, doubted in Saadiah's time, 3, 198.
the Ben-Asher copies of, 3, 207.
the Massoretic text of, now in use, 3, 207.
the oldest copy of, in Spain destroyed, 3, 387.
the distortion of, by the Kabbalists, 3, 556.
verses of, happily used by the fabulists, 3, 560.
as interpreted in the Zohar, 4, 15-16.
as explained by the mystics and the philosophers, 4, 23-4.

Scriptures, the (*continued*), study of, neglected in Spain in the fourteenth century, **4**, 91.
study of, neglected in Spain in the fifteenth century, **4**, 231, 234.
concordance of, by Isaac Nathan ben Kalonymos, **4**, 234–5.
taught to Karaites by Rabbanites, **4**, 269.
in Hebrew declared heretical, **4**, 444–5.
German translation of, by Luther, **4**, 469, 475.
study of, encouraged by Luther and Reuchlin, **4**, 474–5.
translated into the European languages, **4**, 475, 540.
in Hebrew, demand for copies of, **4**, 475–6.
studied by Marranos, **4**, 485.
Ferrara Spanish edition of, dedicated to Gracia Mendesia, **4**, 576.
translated into Polish, **4**, 647.
polyglot edition of, published by Arias Montano, **4**, 651.
study of, declines under the influence of the Polish Talmudists, **5**, 17.
neglect of, among Jews, **5**, 327.
studied by German Jews, **5**, 395.
French translation of, projected, **5**, 449.
Heine's admiration for, **5**, 553–4.
translation of, by Sachs, **5**, 693.
See also Law, the; Old Testament, the; Pentateuch, the; *and under the various books.*
Scriptures, the, commentary on, by Abraham Ibn-Ezra, **3**, 370–3.
Scriptures, the, commentary on (*continued*), by Abulsari Sahal ben Mazliach Kohen, **3**, 204.
by Isaac Abrabanel, **4**, 342.
by Jephet Ibn-Ali Halevi, **3**, 206.
by Joseph ben Isaac Kimchi, **3**, 392.
by Joseph Kara, **3**, 345.
by Moses ben Nachman, **3**, 607.
by Rashi, **3**, 288.
by Saadiah, **3**, 189–90.
by Samuel ben Meïr, **3**, 345.
by Shemarya Ikriti, **4**, 70.
by Solomon ben Yerucham, **3**, 206.
by Yizchaki, **3**, 273.
See Law, the, commentary on.
Scriptures, the, exegesis of. *See* Exegesis of the Bible.
Scriptures, the, translations of. *See under* Translation.
Scrutinium Scriptuarum, polemic against Judaism by Solomon Levi, **4**, 233.
Scythians, the, invade Media, Assyria, and Philistia, **1**, 287.
bribed by Psammetich of Egypt, **1**, 287.
ravage Judæa, **1**, 287.
Scythopolis. *See* Bethshean.
"Searching the Scriptures," polemic against Judaism by Solomon Levi, **4**, 233.
Sebaste. *See* Samaria.
Sebastian, of Portugal, defeated in Africa, **4**, 381.
Sebastus, harbor of Cæsarea, built by Herod, **2**, 106.
Sebel ha-Yerusha, hereditary teaching, among the Karaites, **3**, 159.
Seche, a Christian Shylock, punished by Sixtus V, **4**, 657.
Sechel ha-Poel, term used by Maimonides, **3**, 480.

"**Secret of the Trinity,**" by Nehemiah Chayon, **5,** 217.

Sects, Jewish. *See* Judaism, the sects of.

Secundinus, bishop, and the Jew Antoninus, **3,** 29.

Seder ha-Kabbalah, historical work by Abraham Ibn-Daud, **3,** 366.

Seder Olam, historical work by José ben Chalafta, **2,** 442.

Sefer ha-Osher, grammatical work by Samuel Ibn-Nagrela, **3,** 261.

Sefer Madda, Maimonides' code, attacked by anti-Maimunists, **3,** 523.

Sefer Refuoth, attributed to king Solomon, used by the Essenes, **2,** 29.

Sefer Yezirah, commentary on, by Saadiah, **3,** 197.

Sefer Yizchaki, Biblical work, **3,** 273.

Sefer Yochasin, chronicle by Abraham Zacuto, **4,** 391.

Sefiroth, the Ten, emanations from the Deity, in the Kabbala system, **3,** 551.
- qualities of, **3,** 552.
- correspond to the Temple, **3,** 553.
- prayer addressed to, **3,** 554.
- in the Zohar, **4,** 14, 17.
- names of, **4,** 17.
- instruments of the creation, **4,** 619.
- streams of mercy flow through, **5,** 121.

Segal. *See* Meïr ben Baruch Halevi.

Segan (Sagan) ha-Cohanim, deputy of the high priest, **1,** 492; **2,** 330.

Segelmessa, the Jews of, persecuted by the Almohades, **3,** 360.

Segovia, the synagogue of, transformed into a church, **4,** 196.
- the Marranos of, slain, **4,** 283.

Segovia, the Jews of, accused of host desecration, **4,** 195-6.
- accept baptism under Vincent Ferrer, **4,** 205.
- riot against, **4,** 278-9.
- carry their tombstones into exile with them, **4,** 352.

Segre, Joshua Benzion (1720-1809), deputy to the Assembly of Jewish Notables, **5,** 488.
- on the commission to answer the twelve questions put to the Notables, **5,** 490.
- vice-president of the Synhedrion, **5,** 495.

Ségur, French state councilor, advocates Jewish emancipation, **5,** 480-1.

Seir, mount, the capital of Edom on, **1,** 222.

Sejanus, minister of Tiberius, hostile to Judaism, **2,** 136.
- sends Pontius Pilate to Judæa as procurator, **2,** 138.
- treachery of, revealed by one of the Herodians, **2,** 172.

Selden, John, student of Hebrew, **5,** 21.

Seleucia, north-eastern limit of Judæa under Alexander Jannæus, **2,** 46.

Seleucidæan era, the, used by Jews, **1,** 417.
- abolished, **4,** 394-5.

Seleucidæan kings, the, gain possession of Judæa, **1,** 432.

Seleucus I, ally of Ptolemy I at the battle of Ipsus, **1,** 417.
- the era of, **1,** 417.
- founds Antioch, **1,** 419.
- invites Judæans to Antioch, **1,** 419.

Seleucus II, orders the confiscation of the Temple treasures, **1**, 438.
appealed to by Onias III, **1**, 438–9.
Seleucus, son of Demetrius Nicator, killed by his mother, **2**, 6.
Selichoth. *See* Prayers, penitential.
Selig, Eliakim, obtains from the pope an acquittal of the Jews from the blood accusation, **5**, 282, 285.
Selim I, sultan of Turkey, conquers Egypt, **4**, 393.
employs a Jewish financier, **4**, 393.
makes the Jewish Egyptian communities autonomous, **4**, 394.
employs a Jewish physician, **4**, 401.
Jews under, **4**, 402.
Selim II, sultan of Turkey, the cause of, espoused by Joseph Nassi, **4**, 594–5.
espouses the cause of Joseph Nassi against the French ambassador, **4**, 595.
conveys land near the Sea of Tiberias to Joseph Nassi, **4**, 596.
proposes to give Naxos to Joseph Nassi, **4**, 596.
makes Joseph Nassi duke of Naxos, **4**, 596.
protects Joseph Nassi against France, **4**, 597.
banishes Daud to Rhodes, **4**, 599.
enters upon a war with Venice, **4**, 600.
favorably inclined towards Jews, **4**, 602.
death of, **4**, 627.
Selve, George de, bishop, studies Hebrew under Elias Levita, **4**, 472.
has Elias Levita invited to France, **4**, 474.
Selvia, the second ban against the Chassidim published in, **5**, 393–4.
Semak, manual of religious duties, by Isaac ben Joseph, **3**, 587.
Semender (Tarki), Jews settle in, **3**, 124.
second town of the Chazars, **3**, 222.
Semicha. *See* Ordination.
Semijudæi, sects called forth by the Protestant Reformation, **4**, 541.
Semi-Judaizantes in Poland, **4**, 647.
Semuna, principal of the Pumbeditha academy, **3**, 5.
Saburean, **3**, 6.
commits the Talmud to writing, **3**, 6–7.
successors of, not known, **3**, 7.
Senbaris, scroll of the Law burnt at, **2**, 569.
Seneca, the Persian. *See* Abuzurj-Mihir.
Sen Escalita. *See* Samuel Sulami.
Senior. *See* Abraham Benveniste Senior.
Sennacherib, king of Assyria, subdues Syria, **1**, 270.
takes the fortified towns of Judah, **1**, 272.
makes Lachish his headquarters, **1**, 273.
demands unconditional surrender from Hezekiah, **1**, 274.
besieges Pelusium, **1**, 276.
returns to Assyria, **1**, 277–8.
murdered, **1**, 280.
son of, murdered, **1**, 284.

Sens, archbishop of, anti-Jewish sentiments of, **3,** 171.
rabbi of, at the first rabbinical synod, **3,** 377.
archbishop of, banished for harsh treatment of the Jews, **3,** 401.
college of, sold, **4,** 48.
Sephardic Jews, the, looked upon as the nobility, **4,** 382-3.
distinguished by Pinto, **5,** 344-5.
See also Marranos, the; Portugal, the Jews of; Spanish exiles, the; Spain, the Jews of.
Sepharvaim, the inhabitants of, colonized in Samaria, **1,** 285.
Sepphoris (Diocæsarea), a Synhedrion established at, by Aulus Gabinius, **2,** 71.
an arsenal for Antigonus, **2,** 85.
arsenal of, seized by Judas the Galilean, **2,** 125.
burnt by Quintilius Varus, **2,** 126.
capital of the tetrarchy of Herod Antipas, **2,** 137.
school of, **2,** 148.
the only Galilean city faithful to Rome, **2,** 276.
ordered by the Synhedrion not to protect Josephus, **2,** 281.
makes overtures to Rome, **2,** 283.
seat of Agrippa II's Jewish governors of Galilee, **2,** 333.
sides with the Romans during the Bar-Cochba revolt, **2,** 414.
home of José ben Chalafta, **2,** 442.
seat of the Synhedrion, **2,** 452.
center of the Jewish community, **2,** 458.
ceases to be the seat of the Patriarch, **2,** 480.
Sepphoris (Diocæsarea) (*continued*), people of, characterized by Chanina bar Chama, **2,** 491-2.
academy of, loses prestige, **2,** 532.
the first church at, **2,** 565.
revolt of the Jews at, against Rome, **2,** 570.
razed to the ground, **2,** 570.
Septimania, the governor of, promises Jews religious freedom, **3,** 105.
the Jews of, punished for conspiracy against Egica, **3,** 108.
Septuagint, the, Greek translation of the Scriptures, made at the instigation of Ptolemy VI, **1,** 510-11.
criticism of, by Judæans, **1,** 512.
makes Judaism known, **1,** 512-13.
inaccurate, **1,** 513-14.
why so called, **1,** 514.
Samaritan objections to, **1,** 516.
tampered with, by various religious bodies, **2,** 385-6.
Origen tries to revise, **2,** 488-9.
recommended to Jewish congregations by Justinian I, **3,** 14.
declared not authoritative by Chayim Ibn-Musa, **4,** 237.
studied by Z. Frankel, **5,** 684.
Sepulveda, the Jews of, charged with child murder, **4,** 278-9.
Serach ben Nathan, and Joseph Delmedigo, **5,** 76-7, 79.
Serachya ben Isaac (Ben Shaltiel-Chen), physician and Aristotelian, **3,** 630.
influence of, on the Italian Jews, **4,** 59.

Serachya Halevi Gerundi, (1125–1186), Talmudist, annotates Alfassi's commentary, **3,** 389, 392, 399.
settles at Lünel, **3,** 389.
controversies of, with Abraham ben David, **3,** 389, 490.
on friendly terms with Judah Ibn-Tibbon, **3,** 397.
refuted by Nachmani, **3,** 532.
Serachya Halevi Saladin, at the disputation of Tortosa, **4,** 208.
sermon by, **4,** 212.
Seraiah, high priest, beheaded by Nebuchadnezzar, **1,** 314.
grandson of, **1,** 352.
ancestor of Ezra, **1,** 365.
Serene, a pseudo-Messiah leads the onslaught upon Talmudic Judaism, **3,** 120–2.
joined by the Jews of Spain, **3,** 121.
brought before Yezid, **3,** 121.
adherents of, wish to rejoin their communities, **3,** 121–2.
opposition of, to the Talmud, without result, **3,** 128.
Sergius, bishop, intercedes for the Samaritans, **3,** 16–17.
Serkes, Joel, Talmudist, **4,** 703.
grandson of, **5,** 152.
Sermons, origin of, among the Judæans in Egypt, **1,** 514–15.
Sermons for the conversion of Jews, preached by the Dominicans in England, **3,** 643.
in France in the fourteenth century, **4,** 132.
ordered by Benedict XIII, **4,** 216.
ordered by the Council of Basle, **4,** 245.
ordered by Gregory XIII, **4,** 654–5.
in Hamburg, **4,** 690.
in Vienna, **4,** 706.
Sermons for the conversion of Jews (*continued*), inefficacy of, **5,** 186.
Sermons, vernacular, under Louis the Pious, **3,** 163.
by Jews, attract Christians, **3,** 173.
by Moses of Coucy, **3,** 546.
by Jacob Anatoli, **3,** 566; **4,** 32, 39, 40.
in the Middle Ages, **4,** 478.
introduced into Germany by Jacobson, **5,** 562, 563.
the age of, pointed out by Zunz, **5,** 621.
Serra, Nicolas, papal nuncio, not favorable to the conversion of the Frankists, **5,** 285.
objects to the Lemberg disputation, **5,** 285.
believes the blood accusation, **5,** 285–6.
Serrarius, Peter, Messianic visionary, **5,** 24, 36.
Servants. *See* Christian servants.
Servetus, Michael, anti-Trinitarian, martyr, **4,** 541.
disciples of, in Poland, **4,** 646–7.
"Servi Cameræ," Jews become, after the second crusade, **3,** 356–7.
Jews considered, by Frederick I, **3,** 416–17.
why Jews were considered, **3,** 417.
name given to the Jews of Germany, **3,** 516.
Jews called, by Frederick II, **3,** 569.
Jews of Aragon considered, by Jayme I, **3,** 597.
possession of, granted to the electors, **4,** 128.
Sesonchosis. *See* Shishak.
Seth, family of high priests, **2,** 237.

Seth, the Pneumatic type of the Gnostics, **2**, 377.

Setubal, port open to Jews on their banishment from Portugal, **4**, 374.

Severus, emperor with Niger, **2**, 463.
  victorious over Niger, **2**, 464.
  promulgates laws against Judaism, **2**, 464.
  death of, **2**, 468.
  wife of, **2**, 468

Severus, bishop of Magona, burns the synagogues, **2**, 619.

Severus, Alexander. *See* Alexander Severus.

Severus, Julius, sent to quell the Bar-Cochba revolt, **2**, 414.
  military tactics of, **2**, 415.
  takes the Jewish strongholds in the north, **2**, 416.
  helped by a Samaritan at Bethar, **2**, 418.
  returned to Britain, **2**, 421.

Seville, early Jewish settlements in the environs of, **3**, 43.
  Jewish political fugitives from Granada settle in, **3**, 258, 279–80.
  the Arab ruler of, organizes a revolt against the Berbers, **3**, 276
  the center of Jewish Spain, **3**, 284.
  the Mahometan court of, cultured, **3**, 291.
  Abu-Ayub in, **3**, 312.
  the Ibn-Migash family in, **3**, 315.
  the Jewish academy of, closed by the Almohades, **3**, 361, 384.
  lost by Pedro the Cruel, **4**, 124.
  the persecution of the Spanish Jews arises in **4**, 167–8.

Seville (*continued*), outbreak against the Marranos in, **4**, 282–3.
  first seat of the Inquisition for Marranos, **4**, 312.
  citizens of, opposed to the Inquisition, **4**, 313.
  victims of the Inquisition in, **4**, 317
  the Inquisition in, **4**, 335.
  expulsion of the Jews from, proposed, **4**, 336.
  Jews disappear from, **4**, 354.

Seville, the Jews of, well treated by Alfonso X, **3**, 592–3.
  ravages of the Black Death among, **4**, 113.
  fury against, **4**, 157.
  attacked, **4**, 168–9.

Seville, the Marranos of, and the Inquisition, **4**, 313.
  taught by the Jews, **4**, 334–5.
  tortured, **4**, 350.
  flee to Granada, **4**, 351.

Sèze, de, deputy to the National Assembly, speaks in behalf of the Bordeaux Jews, **5**, 442.

Sezira, John, scholar, friend of Isaac Abrabanel, **4**, 338.
  pleads with Sixtus IV for the Jews, **4**, 340.

Sforza, Galeazzo, duke of Milan, employs a Jewish physician, **4**, 287
  stops the preaching of Bernardinus of Feltre, **4**, 296–7.

"Shaagath Aryeh," by Leo Modena, **5**, 73.

"Shaashuim," satire by Joseph ben Sabara, 3, 559.

Shäbs, the. *See* **Frankists, the: Sabbatians, the.**

Shabur I, king of the neo-Persians, and Mar-Samuel, **2**, 520, 526.

Shabur II, king of the neo-Persians, and the Jews, **2,** 580.
oppresses the Jews, **2,** 591–2.
punishes Raba bar Joseph for exercising criminal jurisdiction, **2,** 592.
and Chama of Nahardea, **2,** 594–5.
at war with Julian the Apostate, **2,** 601.
concludes peace with Jovianus, **2,** 602.

Shach. *See* Cohen, Sabbataï.

Shachna. *See* Shalom Shachna.

Shakers, the, origin of, **5,** 378.

Shakespeare, defended from the charge of Jew baiting, **5,** 552–3.

Shalal. *See* Isaac Cohen Shalal.

Shaliach Zion, messengers of the Synhedrion, **2,** 535.

Shallum, conspires against the king of Israel, **1,** 243.
made king of Israel, **1,** 244.
murdered, **1,** 244.

Shallum, uncle of Jeremiah, **1,** 290.

Shalmaneser, king of Assyria, subdues Tyre and Phœnicia, **1,** 263.
propitiated by Hoshea, **1,** 263.
conquers Phœnicia a second time, **1,** 264.
ends the kingdom of Israel, **1,** 264–5.

Shalom of Neustadt, compiles the customs of various communities, **4,** 134.

Shalom Shachna, Talmudist in Poland, **4,** 634, 639; **5,** 4.

Shaltiel-Chen, famous Jewish family, **3,** 630.

Shamgar, judge, chastises the Philistines, **1,** 61.

Shammah, one of David's warriors, **1,** 116.

Shammai, president of the Synhedrion, with Hillel, **2,** 100.
character of, **2,** 100–1.
maxims of, **2,** 101.
spreads the knowledge of the law in Judæa, **2,** 149.
the rules of, condemned by Joshua ben Chananya, **2,** 349–50.

Shammai, the disciples of, conception of the Messiah held by, **2,** 144.
morality of, **2,** 151.

Shammai, the followers of, refuse to take the oath of allegiance to Herod, **2,** 108.
hostile to Herod, **2,** 114–15.
constitute the Zealots, **2,** 133.
support the revolutionary party, **2,** 256.
prohibit the purchase of certain articles from the heathen, **2,** 270.

Shammai, the school of, 2, 101.
rigor of, **2,** 131–2.
Pharisee principles of, **2,** 132.
displeased with Jesus, **2,** 162.
disputes with the school of Hillel under Gamaliel II, **2,** 335, 336.
estimation of, by the Nazarenes, **2,** 372.
limits the application of tradition, **2,** 462.

Shaphan, scribe, the family of, joins Jeremiah, **1,** 292.
receives Deuteronomy for Josiah, **1,** 292.

Sharbarza, Persian general, takes Jerusalem, **3,** 19.

Sharon (Shefelah), plain, description of, **1,** 45.

Shealtiel, son of Jehoiachin, entreats for the return of the Judæans to Palestine, **1,** 342.

Shear-Jashub, son of Isaiah, accompanies him to Ahaz, **1**, 258.
Sheba, the Bichrite, leads the revolt of the northern tribes from David, **1**, 148–50.
Sheba, the Queen of, visits Solomon, **1**, 173.
Shebet Jehuda, historical work by Joseph Ibn-Verga, **4**, 557.
Shebna, brother of Hillel, supports him, **2**, 96.
Shebna, Sochen under Hezekiah, power of, **1**, 268.
wrests power from Hezekiah, **1**, 268–9.
prepares Jerusalem for Sennacherib's attack, **1**, 271.
reproved by Isaiah, **1**, 271.
displaced by Eliakim, **1**, 272.
Shebuot hesset, oath of purgation, introduced by Nachman ben Jacob, **2**, 556.
Shechaniah, suggests the repudiation of heathen wives by the Judæans, **1**, 368.
Shechem (Neapolis), taken by Jacob, **1**, 4.
chief city of Canaan, **1**, 36.
unfitness of, to be David's capital, **1**, 114.
the inhabitants of, rebel under Jeroboam, **1**, 180–1.
fortified by Jeroboam, **1**, 185.
called Blessing by the Samaritans, **1**, 390.
a Samaritan center, **1**, 391.
celebrated by Theodotus, **1**, 517.
destroyed by John Hyrcanus, **2**, 7–8.
battle at, between Alexander Jannæus and Eucærus, **2**, 44.
hostility in, to Jews, **2**, 457.
sparsely inhabited by Christians, **3**, 12.
Samaritans in, in the twelfth century, **3**, 427.
Shechina, the, Kabbalistic term, the female person in the Godhead, **5**, 217.
Shedim, evil spirits, introduced into Judaism from Magianism, **1**, 403.
Shefaram, temporary seat of the Synhedrion, **2**, 452.
Shefelah. *See* Sharon.
Shekan-Zib, academy at, established by Nachman ben Jacob, **2**, 545, 557.
Shekel, the half-, contributions to the Temple, **2**, 52–3.
Sheloh. *See* Hurwitz, Isaiah.
Shema, the, integral part of the morning service, **1**, 399.
recitation of, punishable under Hadrian, **2**, 424.
forbidden by the Portuguese Inquisition, **5**, 32.
Shem-Addaula. *See* Saad-Addaula.
Shemaiah, prophet, prevents war between Judah and Israel, **1**, 184.
Shemaria ben Elchanan, emissary from Sŏra, settles in Cairo, **3**, 208, 210.
Shemarya Ikriti (1290–1320), tries to reconcile Rabbanism and Karaism, **4**, 69, 71.
writes a commentary on the Bible, **4**, 70.
Shemaya (Sameas), successor to Simon ben Shetach in the Synhedrion, **2**, 71–2.
maxims of, **2**, 72.
disciples of, **2**, 72, 96.
reproves Herod and Hyrcanus II, **2**, 79.
opposed to Antigonus, **2**, 85–6.
counsels submission to Herod, **2**, 88.
spared by Herod, **2**, 89.
death of, **2**, 90.

Shemer, owner of the plateau of Samaria, **1**, 193.
Shem-Tob. *See* Levi ben Shem-Tob.
Shem-Tob de Carrion. *See* Santob de Carrion.
Shem-Tob ben Abraham Ibn-Gaon (1283–1330), Kabbalist, **4**, 74.
Shem-Tob ben Isaac of Tortosa (1206–1264), medical writer, lectures at Marseilles, **3**, 582.
history of, **3**, 582–3.
Shem-Tob ben Isaac Shaprut, polemic writer, debates with Pedro de Luna, **4**, 142.
works of, **4**, 142–3, 144.
Shem-Tob ben Joseph Ibn-Shem Tob, Kabbalist, work of, **4**, 197.
opponent to philosophy, **4**, 239.
opposed in views to his son, **4**. 243.
Shem-Tob Falaquera, poet and philosopher, defends the "Guide of the Perplexed," **3**, 634.
mysticism of, **4**, 24.
Sherif-Pasha, governor of Damascus, permits the persecution of the Jews, **5**, 635.
orders the bastinado for a Jewish suspect, **5**, 636.
tortures children. **5**, 637.
destroys the houses of Jews, **5**, 637.
circulates an anti-Jewish book, **5**, 639.
orders the translation of suspicious Talmud passages, **5**, 640.
obtains assent for the execution of the Jews, **5**, 640.
ordered to discontinue the torture, **5**, 648.
releases the prisoners, **5**, 661.
executed, **5**, 661.
Sherira ben Chananya (Chanina, 920–1000), judge of Pumbeditha, opposes the Gaon Nehemiah, **3**, 208.
Gaon of Pumbeditha, **3**, 231, 232.
descent of, **3**, 232.
devoted to the Talmud, **3**, 232.
"Letter" of, **3**, 232–3.
arraigned before the Caliph, **3**, 233–4.
abdication and death of, **3**, 234.
Sheshbazzar, Babylonian name of Zerubbabel, **1**, 351.
Sheshenk. *See* Sheshet.
Sheshet. *See* Mar-Sheshet.
Sheshet Benveniste (1131–1210), head of the Barcelona community, patron of Jewish learning, **3**, 388.
poem by, **3**, 388.
epigram by, **3**, 524–5.
Shibli Ajub, opponent of the Damascus Jews, **5**, 633.
"**Shield and Sword**," polemic by Chayim Ibn-Musa, **4**, 237.
Shila, principal of the school at Nahardea, **2**, 512.
acknowledges the authority of Abba-Areka, **2**, 512.
precedence of the family of, **2**, 522.
Shiloh (Salem), the seat of the sanctuary, **1**, 41.
not sufficiently centrally located for the sanctuary, **1**, 57.
the rallying point under the later judges, **1**, 69, 70.
destroyed by the Philistines, **1**, 71.
Shimei, the Benjamite, reviles David, **1**, 142.
welcomes David on his return to Jerusalem, **1**, 147.
executed, **1**, 160–1.
Shiraz, the Jews of, in the twelfth century, **3**, 434.

Shir-ha-shirim. *See* "Song of Songs, the."
Shishak, of Egypt, protects Solomon's enemies, **1,** 176.
protects Jeroboam, **1,** 180.
in alliance with Jeroboam, **1,** 184.
defeats Rehoboam, **1,** 184–5.
Shobach, Aramæan general, killed at the battle of Helam, **1,** 127.
Shobi, made king of the Ammonites by David, **1,** 129.
aids David against Absalom, **1,** 144.
Shofetim. *See* Judges, the.
Shoraich, son of Samuel Ibn-Adiya, bravery and nobility of, **3,** 70.
"Short and Established Practice," work by Judah the Blind, **3,** 136.
"Short Demurrer, A," by William Prynne, **5,** 45–6.
refuted, **5,** 46.
Shulam, Samuel. *See* Samuel Shulam.
Shulamit, daughter of Aminadab, heroine of the "Song of Songs," **1,** 431.
Shulchan Aruch, the, code by Joseph Karo, **4,** 612–13.
expected to unite Judaism, **4,** 612.
partiality of, **4,** 613.
authority of, **4,** 613.
influence of, on Judaism, **4,** 613.
commentary on, by Moses Isserles, **4,** 637.
not binding in the Messianic time, **5,** 142.
Shunamite woman, the, and Jehoash, **1,** 233.
Shunem, Philistine camp against Saul, **1,** 102.
"Shylock," Heine on, **5,** 552–3.
Sibbechai of Hushah, Israelite champion in the Philistine war, **1,** 117.
Sibili, Astruc. *See* Astruc Sibili.
Sibyl, the, used to spread Judæan doctrines, **2,** 204–5, 402.
Sicarii, the, a band of Zealots, lawlessness of, **2,** 239.
rob a servant of Claudius, **2,** 242.
employed by Felix, **2,** 246.
punished by Albinus, **2,** 249.
favored by Gessius Florus, **2,** 250.
leader of, **2,** 258.
take the fortress of Masada, **2,** 258.
join the Zealots in the Temple, **2,** 260.
kill the Roman garrison in Jerusalem, **2,** 260.
cruelty of, **2,** 260–1.
escape to Masada, **2,** 261.
one of the factions in Jerusalem, **2,** 301.
Sichin (Asochis), the Judæans defeated at, **2,** 40.
stronghold in the Bar-Cochba revolt, **2,** 414.
fall of, **2,** 416.
Sicily, the Jewish community in, in the sixth century, **3,** 28.
subjugated by Belisarius, **3,** 31.
a synagogue in, razed, **3,** 34.
a refuge for Jewish fugitives, **3,** 569.
Abraham Abulafia in, **4,** 7–8.
opposition to the Inquisition in, **4,** 319–20.
Sicily, the Jews of, protected by Gregory I, **3,** 33.
in the twelfth century, **3,** 422–3, 424.
wear Jew badges, **3,** 518.
excluded from offices under Frederick II, **3,** 567.

Sicily, the Jews of (*continued*), persecuted in the fourteenth century, **4**, 77.
proclamation expelling, **4**, 347-8.
Siddur Rab Amram, the liturgy of the European Jews, **3**, 178.
Siderius, name borne by Gallic Jews, **3**, 36.
Sidillo. *See* Samuel Sidillo.
Sidon (Saida), built by the Canaanites, **1**, 3.
center of Phœnician culture, **1**, 53.
laid waste by the Philistines, **1**, 80.
surrenders to Shalmaneser, **1**, 264.
urges revolt from Nebuchadnezzar, **1**, 310.
the inhabitants of, threaten the Galilean Judæans, **1**, 475.
the Jews of, in the twelfth century, **3**, 426.
Sidra, academy, **2**, 514.
Sigismund, emperor, advises Benedict XIII to abdicate, **4**, 216.
the Jews under, **4**, 218, 219.
has the privileges of the Jews confirmed by Martin V, **4**, 219.
in the Hussite war, **4**, 225.
protection of, ineffectual, **4**, 227.
appoints three Judenmeister, **4**, 227.
death of, **4**, 248.
Sigismund, of Burgundy, raises a barrier between Jews and Christians in Burgundy, **3**, 37.
Sigismund I, of Poland, kindly disposed towards Jews, **4**, 419.
Sigismund III, of Poland, confirms the privileges of the Jews, **4**, 643.
alienates the Cossacks, **5**, 2.
Sigismund, ambassador from Charlemagne to Haroun Alrashid, **3**, 143.
Sigismund Augustus, of Poland, appeals to Joseph Nassi, **4**, 601.
death of, **4**, 603, 642.
protects the Jews, **4**, 633.
Sihon, king of the Emorites, defeated by the Israelites, **1**, 27.
Silas, the Babylonian, Judæan hero in the Roman rebellion, **2**, 264.
Silesia, adopts the Jewish statute of Frederick the Valiant, **3**, 569.
John of Capistrano in, **4**, 258.
Silesia, the Jews of, own real estate in the twelfth century, **3**, 418.
suffering of, through John of Capistrano, **4**, 260-3.
restricted to money-lending, **4**, 260.
charged with host-desecration, **4**, 261.
charged with the blood accusation, **4**, 261-2.
burnt at Breslau, **4**, 262.
improvement of the condition of, **5**, 416.
heavily taxed, **5**, 508.
Silhi, academy founded at, by Mar-Sheshet, **2**, 554.
Silk spinning, by the Jews of Greece, **3**, 175, 425.
Silk worms, the breeding of, carried on by Jews in Palermo, **3**, 424.
Siloah, spring south of Jerusalem, **1**, 114.

Siloah, spring south of Jerusalem (*continued*), supplies the water for the Water Libation during Tabernacles, **2**, 51.
Silva, governor of Judæa, takes Masada, **2**, 316.
Silva, Diogo de, inquisitor-general of Portugal, **4**, 508.
resigns, **4**, 513.
Silva, Miguel de, Portuguese ambassador to the pope, effects Reubeni's disgrace, **4**, 498–9.
Silva, Samuel da, physician, publishes a work against Uriel da Costa, **5**, 59.
answered by Uriel da Costa, **5**, 60.
Silvani family, the, support Chiya bar Abba, **2**, 536.
Silveira, Isaac, follower of Sabbataï Zevi, **5**, 144.
"**Silver Dish, The**," by Joseph Ezobi, **3**, 561.
Silveyra, Miguel, Marrano poet, **5**, 111.
Simaï bar Ashi, father of Ashi, disciple of Papa bar Chanan, **2**, 594.
Simcha ben Samuel, Talmudist, member of the synod at Mayence, **3**, 517.
Simcha Cohen, martyr during the first crusade, **3**, 302.
Simeon, the tribe of, successful warriors in the desert, **1**, 26.
allied with Judah, **1**, 38–9.
delivered by Othniel, **1**, 60.
enters national life, **1**, 77.
loyal to Rehoboam, **1**, 183.
Simeon, Syrian bishop, enemy of Zorah Yussuf, **3**, 65–6.
Simeon. *See also* Simon.
Simlaï, assessor of Judah II, **2**, 484.
versed in the Scriptures, **2**, 488, 499.
Simlaï (*continued*), Agadist, **2**, 498, 499.
settle at Nahardea, **2**, 498.
relations of, to Judah II, **2**, 499.
on the commands of the Law, **2**, 499.
discusses Bible exegesis with the Church Fathers, **2**, 499.
defends the doctrine of the unity of God, **2**, 501–2.
Simon, brother of Jesus, **2**, 148.
Simon, brother of John of Gischala, accuses Josephus, **2**, 281.
Simon, companion of Ishmael ben Elisha, **2**, 427–8.
Simon I, high priest (the Just, 300–270), said to have appeared to Alexander the Great, **1**, 413.
improves Jerusalem and the Temple, **1**, 421.
described by Sirach, **1**, 422.
as teacher, **1**, 422.
objects to Nazarite practices, **1**, 422.
daughter of, **1**, 423.
Simon II, high priest, hostile to Hyrcanus, son of Joseph, **1**, 432.
son of, **1**, 437.
Simon III, high priest. *See* Simon Tharsi.
Simon IV, high priest. *See* Simon, son of Boëthus.
Simon, leader of the Idumæans, helps the Zealots, **2**, 295.
Simon I, president of the Synhedrion, son of Hillel, **2**, 130.
Simon II, president of the Synhedrion, son of Gamaliel I, **2**, 240.
member of the war party, **2**, 269.
coins in honor of, **2**, 269.
power of, **2**, 271.
head of the Pharisees, **2**, 271.

Simon II, president of the Synhedrion (*continued*), decrees the deposition of Josephus, **2**, 281.
Simon III, president of the Synhedrion, son of Gamaliel II, minority of, **2**, 404.
escapes from Bethar, **2**, 434.
Patriarch, resides at Jamnia, **2**, 434.
joins the Galilean synod, **2**, 434.
teachings of, **2**, 435.
relation of, to Meïr, **2**, 440.
dissolves the Synhedrion at Nahor-Pakod, **2**, 443–4.
seeks increase of dignity, **2**, 444–5.
conspiracy against, **2**, 445.
expels Meïr and Nathan from the Synhedrion, **2**, 445.
at peace with Nathan, **2**, 446.
excommunicates Meïr, **2**, 446.
on the Roman persecution of the Jews, **2**, 446.
death of **2**, 451.
Simon, slave of Herod, proclaimed king, **2**, 124–5.
Simon the Benjamite, Hellenist, opponent of Onias III, **1**, 437.
banished, **1**, 438.
gives information about the Temple treasures, **1**, 438.
hires assassins to murder Onias III, **1**, 438.
Simon of Cairo, author of the "Great Halachas," **3**, 179.
Simon the Hasmonæan. *See* Simon Hasmonai.
Simon de Montfort, leads the crusade against the Albigenses, **3**, 502.
receives the estates of Raymond VI of Toulouse, **3**, 508, 509.
opposed by Raymond VII of Toulouse, **3**, 514.
protects the Jews, **3**, 514.
Simon the Parthian, servant of Judah I, **2**, 466.
Simon the Pious, murdered, **3**, 352.
Simon of Trent, martyr, the Jews charged with the death of, **4**, 298.
pilgrimages to the remains of, **4**, 298–9.
Sixtus IV refuses to canonize, **4**, 299.
Eisenmenger believes in the martyrdom of, **5**, 188.
Simon bar Abba, Amora, urged to marry Mar-Samuel's daughter, **2**, 528.
austerity of, **2**, 537.
misfortunes of, **2**, 543.
Simon bar Giora, Judæan hero in the Roman rebellion, **2**, 264, 273.
leader of the Sicarii, **2**, 293.
life of, in Acrabattine, **2**, 293.
war of, with the Idumæans, **2**, 293.
wife of, taken prisoner, **2**, 297–8.
allies himself with the aristocratic party in Jerusalem, **2**, 298.
in Jerusalem, **2**, 298.
revengeful feeling of, towards the Zealots, **2**, 301.
followers of, executed, **2**, 304.
refuses to lay down arms, **2**, 309.
graces the triumph of Titus, **2**, 313–14.
hurled from the Tarpeian rock, **2**, 314.
Simon bar Kappara, propounds a riddle, **2**, 455–6.
authorization to teach refused to, **2**, 456.
announces the death of Judah I, **2**, 466–7.

Simon bar Kappara (*continued*), adds supplements to the Mishna, 2, 470.
Simon bar Yochaï. *See* Simon ben Jochai.
Simon ben Anatolio, head of the Talmudic college of Marseilles, 3, 400.
Simon ben Asai (Azai), theosophist teacher of the Law, 2, 358, 381.
favors the instruction of women in the Law, 2, 474.
Simon ben Caipha, neo-Hebraic poet, author of an Abodah, 3, 115.
Simon ben Ezron, leader of the Jerusalem Zealots, 2, 301.
Simon ben Isaac ben Abun, commentator on the Talmud and poet, 3, 245.
dirge by, 3, 246.
stays the persecution of the Jews of Mayence, 3, 246.
memory of, perpetuated by the Mayence community, 3, 247.
related to Rashi, 3, 286.
Simon ben Jochai (bar Yochaï), disciple of Akiba, returns to Judæa, 2, 433.
reputed a Kabbalist, 2, 440.
at the Synhedrion of Usha, 2, 440.
an enemy of Rome, 2, 440–1, 447.
method of, 2, 441.
pursues the Law exclusively, 2, 441.
rejoices in the deprivation of judicial rights, 2, 447–8.
accuses the Romans of selfishness, 2, 448.
condemned to death, 2, 448.
lives in a cave, 2, 448.
declares Tiberias clean, 2, 448–9.
Simon ben Jochai (*continued*), at Rome, 2, 449.
teacher of Judah I, 2, 451.
son of, 2, 457.
son-in-law of, 2, 459–60.
said to have foretold the rise of Islam, 3, 88–9.
supposed revelation to, 3, 606.
authorship of the Zohar attributed to, 4, 12.
glorified in the Zohar, 4, 12–14, 16.
Midrash of, 4, 19.
declared not to be the author of the Zohar, 4, 292.
Isaac Lurya pretends to hold intercourse with, 4, 622.
grave of, visited by Kabbalists, 4, 623.
homage paid to, by the Frankists, 5, 274.
Simon ben Kathla, Idumæan leader in Jerusalem, 2, 301.
Simon ben Lakish (Resh Lakish), Amora, 2, 479.
opposes the leveling policy of Judah II, 2, 485.
rebukes Judah II for covetousness, 2, 485–6.
brother-in-law of Jochanan bar Napacha, 2, 495.
strength of, 2, 496.
gloom of, 2, 496.
Agadist, 2, 496–7.
opponent of Jochanan bar Napacha, 2, 497.
disciples of, 2, 531.
Simon ben Nanos, disciple of the Law, 2, 358.
Simon ben Saul, Judæan hero of Bethshean, 2, 262–3.
Simon ben Shetach, brother of Salome Alexandra, Pharisee leader, 2, 39.
mediator between the Pharisees and the Sadducees, 2, 42.

Simon ben Shetach (*continued*), member of the Great Council, **2**, 42.
counselor of Salome Alexandra, **2**, 48.
proposed as Nassi of the Great Council, **2**, 49.
called "Restorer of the Law," **2**, 49.
promotes the establishment of schools, **2**, 50–1.
rebukes Judah ben Tabbaï, **2**, 53.
president of the Synhedrion, **2**, 54.
severity of, **2**, 54.
condemns his son to death on a false charge, **2**, 54–5.
successors of, **2**, 71–2.
Simon ben Zemach Duran I (1361–1444), chief rabbi of Algiers, attacks Isaac ben Sheshet, **4**, 199.
first Spanish-Jewish rabbi to take pay, **4**, 199–200.
polemics by, **4**, 238.
and the conversion of the Jews of Palma, **4**, 247.
Simon ben Zoma, theosophist teacher of the Law, **2**, 358, 381.
Simon, son of Boëthus, father-in-law of Herod, high priest, **2**, 107.
founder of the Boëthusans, **2**, 108.
Simon, son of Dositheus, ambassador to Rome, **2**, 4–5.
Simon, son of Judah I, Chacham, **2**, 466.
Simon, son of Judas the Galilean, leader of an insurrection, **2**, 199.
crucified, **2**, 199.
Simon Duran I. *See* Simon ben Zemach Duran.
Simon Duran II (1439–1510), rabbi of Algiers, protector of the Spanish exiles, **4**, 390–1.
Simon Episcopius, chief of the Arminians, and Manasseh ben Israel, **5**, 22.
Simon Hasmonai, grandfather of Mattathias the Hasmonæan, **1**, 459.
Simon Kara, compiler of the Yalkut, **3**, 346.
Simon Kephas. *See* Peter, apostle.
Simon Maimi, chief rabbi of Portugal, martyrdom of, **4**, 380.
family of, martyrs, **4**, 380, 381.
Simon Stylites, ascetic, rebukes Theodosius II, **2**, 621–2.
Simon Tharsi, son of Mattathias, the Hasmonæan, **1**, 459.
chosen as counselor to succeed his father, **1**, 461.
rescues the Galilean Judæans, **1**, 475.
leader of the Hasmonæan party, **1**, 489.
strengthens the defenses of Judæa, **1**, 492–3.
forces Bacchides to raise the siege of Bethhagla, **1**, 493.
commander of the Syrian forces on the Mediterranean shores, **1**, 498.
chosen leader of the people, **1**, 500.
prepares to oppose Diodotus Tryphon, **1**, 500.
pays tribute to Tryphon to save his brother's life, **1**, 501.
sons of, **1**, 520.
makes Judæa independent, **1**, 520.
high priest, **1**, 521.
negotiates with Demetrius II, **1**, 521.

Simon Tharsi (*continued*), dates the independence of Judæa from the year of first coining money, **1**, 522.
drives the Hellenists from their strongholds, **1**, 523–4.
takes down the towers of the Acra, **1**, 524–5.
sues for an alliance with Rome, **1**, 525–6.
supreme sovereignty conferred upon, **1**, 526–7.
title of, **1**, 527.
coins money, **1**, 528.
attacked by Antiochus Sidetes, **1**, 528–9.
names his sons as his generals, **1**, 529.
assassination of, **1**, 530.
wife of, imprisoned, **1**, 531.
temporary character of his descendants' rule, **2**, 143.
Simon Zarfati, physician to Pope Julius II, **4**, 408.
Simon. *See also* Simeon.
Simon, Richard, Father of the Oratory, clears the Jews of the charge of child murder, **5**, 175–6.
lays the foundations of Bible exegesis, **5**, 178–9.
attractive style of, **5**, 179.
introduces Rabbinical literature to Christians, **5**, 179.
taught by Jonah Salvador, **5**, 175, 180.
exalts Rabbinical Judaism, **4**, 180.
translates Leo Modena's "Rites," **5**, 180.
shows Christianity to be based on Judaism, **5**, 180.
defends the Jews and the Talmud, **5**, 180–1.
recants his praise of the Jews, **5**, 181–2.
Simon, Richard (*continued*), ridicules superstitious usages, **5**, 202.
Simoneta, cardinal, opposes the Portuguese Inquisition, **4**, 516.
on the commission to examine Paul III's Inquisition bull, **4**, 520.
Simonias, the Jews of, ask Judah I for a teacher of the Law, **2**, 453–4.
Simonists, the, followers of Simon bar Giora, **2**, 301.
Sin, Original. *See* Original Sin.
Sin, the theory of, in the Zohar, **4**, 17.
Sin-offering, the, for murders, abrogated by Jochanan ben Zakkai, **2**, 239.
Sinai, desert of, Moses in, **1**, 15.
Israelites in, **1**, 20.
Sinai, mount, the Israelites at, **1**, 20–1.
Sinaï, title of Joseph ben Chiya, **2**, 581.
Sinaitic revelation, the, characterized, **1**, 23.
place of sacrifices in, **1**, 24–5.
Sinhajas, the, a Berber race, found a kingdom in the south of Spain, **3**, 256.
unfriendly to the Arabs, **3**, 261.
Sinjar Shahin-Shah, Seljuk Sultan, expedition of, against the Ghuzz, **3**, 434.
assigns a final resting place to the supposed remains of Daniel, **3**, 435.
Sinzheim, Joseph David (1745–1812), compelled to flee from Strasburg, **5**, 452.
deputy to the Assembly of Jewish Notables, **5**, 483–4.
character of, **5**, 484.
attainments of, **5**, 484.

Sinzheim, Joseph David (*continued*), rabbi of Strasburg, **5**, 484.
on the commission to answer the twelve questions to the Notables, **5**, 490.
works out the report of the commission, **5**, 490.
president of the Synhedrion, **5**, 495.
opens the first session of the Synhedrion, **5**, 495.
delivers the closing speech of the Synhedrion, **5**, 497.
member of the French consistory, **5**, 502.
not gifted with the temper of a reformer, **5**, 559.
Sinzig, the Jews of, burnt in the thirteenth century, **3**, 611.
Sippai of Gath, Philistine champion, **1**, 117.
Sirach. *See* Jesus Sirach.
Sirach, grandson of Jesus Sirach, translates Ecclesiasticus into Greek, **2**, 359.
"Siraj," Maimonides' Mishna commentary, **3**, 458.
Sisebut, Visigothic king, fanaticism of, **3**, 40, 47.
renews Reccared's anti-Jewish laws, **3**, 48.
orders the Jews to be baptized or banished, **3**, 48.
laws of, repealed by Swintila, **3**, 49.
Sisenand, Visigothic king, the Jews under, **3**, 49–50.
Sisera, Jabin's general, defeated by Barak, **1**, 61.
Akiba said to be a descendant of, **2**, 351.
Sixtus IV, pope, has Kabbalistic writings translated into Latin, **4**, 292, 443.
refuses to canonize Simon of Trent, **4**, 299.
Sixtus IV, pope (*continued*), authorizes the Inquisition for Marranos, **4**, 311.
appoints four inquisitors, **4**, 312.
censures the cruelty of the Inquisition, **4**, 318–19.
sanctions the Inquisition in Aragon, **4**, 319.
troubled by the opposition to the Inquisition, **4**, 320.
appoints a chief judge of appeals for Marrano cases, **4**, 320.
forbids Marranos to be judges in heresy trials, **4**, 321.
infamy of, **4**, 321.
modifies the rigors of the Inquisition, **4**, 322.
recalls his bull, **4**, 322–3.
appoints Torquemada inquisitor-general for Spain, **4**, 324.
congratulated on his accession by Alfonso V of Portugal, **4**, 340.
Sixtus V, pope, removes restrictions from the Jews, **4**, 655–6.
a Talmudic dictionary dedicated to, **4**, 657.
punishes a Christian Shylock, **4**, 657.
permits the reprinting of the Talmud, **4**, 657–8, 659.
death of, **4**, 658.
avarice of, **4**, 658–9.
Sixtus Senensis, employed by Paul IV to annoy the Jews, **4**, 581.
urges the burning of the Talmud, **4**, 582.
rescues the Zohar from burning, **4**, 584.
Skytte, Swedish royal councilor, projects a university in Brandenburg, **5**, 174.
Slave-owners, Jewish, in Rome, riot against, **3**, 30–1.

Slave-trade, the, among the Jews of Italy, **3**, 28–9.
permitted to the Jews of the Frankish empire, **3**, 34.
discussed by the Church Councils, **3**, 40.
under Charlemagne, **3**, 142.
among Spanish Jews, **3**, 229.
among Bohemian Jews, **3**, 305.
See also Christian slaves.
Slaves, Judæans sold as, **1**, 227.
enfranchised by Josiah, **1**, 296.
in the time of Ezra, **1**, 376–7.
cease to exist among Judæans, **1**, 393.
treatment of, by Nachman ben Jacob, **2**, 555.
Jews made, by Egica, **3**, 108.
owned by Jews, forbidden to be baptized under Louis the Pious, **3**, 161, 164–5.
Jewish, ransomed by Abrabanel, **4**, 339.
the Spanish exiles as, **4**, 371.
Jews as, among the Knights of Malta, **4**, 656.
See also Christian slaves.
Slavonia, the Jews of, proscribed by the Council of Buda, **3**, 614.
Slavonian countries, Jews in, in the ninth century, **3**, 144.
Smith, member of Parliament, on the Damascus affair, **5**, 656.
Smyrna, small Jewish community in, in the fifteenth century, **4**, 406.
enriched by the war between Venice and Turkey, **5**, 119.
Sabbataï Zevi banished from, **5**, 122.
return of Sabbataï Zevi to, **5**, 133–4.
enthusiasm at, for Sabbataï Zevi, **5**, 134–5.
Smyrna (*continued*), Christians at, interested in Sabbataï Zevi, **5**, 137.
Sabbataï Zevi leaves, **5**, 145.
prophets at, silenced by Sabbataï's apostasy, **5**, 157.
Sabbatians at, continue to believe in Sabbataï, **5**, 157.
rabbis of, excommunicate the Sabbatians, **5**, 157, 159.
Sabbatians of, devoted to Sabbataï, **5**, 163.
Sabbatianism at, after Sabbataï's death, **5**, 207.
Sabbatians in, **5**, 210.
Nehemiah Chayon at, **5**, 216.
the writings of Cardoso burnt at, **5**, 220.
Soares, João, Portuguese inquisitor, **4**, 521.
Sochen, manager of the court in Judah, chosen from the house of Nathan, **1**, 249.
power of, under Hezekiah, **1**, 268.
"**Society** for the Culture and Science of the Jews, The," joined by Heine, **5**, 547.
founders of, **5**, 551.
limitations of, **5**, 600.
losses caused by, **5**, 602.
members of, in Galicia, **5**, 612.
"**Society** for the Good and the Noble, The," formed by Mendelssohn's disciples, **5**, 403.
"**Society** for the Promotion of Christianity among Jews, The," publishes a history of the Jews, **5**, 593.
"**Society** of Friends, The," formed to oppose the orthodox party, **5**, 418–19.
motto and symbol of, **5**, 418.
weakness of, **5**, 419.
encourage the Reform movement, **5**, 563.

"**Society** of the Friends of Reform, The," in Frankfort, innovations of, **5**, 675.
invite Riesser to join them, **5**, 675.
declare circumcision optional, **5**, 676.
relinquish certain points in their programme, **5**, 676.
Socinus, disciple of Michael Servetus in Poland, **4**, 647.
Socrates, the sayings of, used by Solomon Ibn-Gebirol, **3**, 267.
Sodomites, the, honored by a Gnostic sect, **2**, 375.
Soem, gaoler of Mariamne, **2**, 96.
beheaded, **2**, 104.
Sofer, Moses, aggressiveness of, **5**, 567.
opposes the Reform movement, **5**, 571, 572.
Sofino, Raphael, encourages the Sabbatian movement in Italy, **5**, 160.
Sogane, taken by Alexander Jannæus, **2**, 46.
Solgat. *See* Sulchat.
Solidarity, the, of the Jewish race, **2**, 367–8; **5**, 632–3.
Solis, Pedro de, commissioner to frame the statute for the Inquisition, **4**, 312.
Solms, the princes of, remove the poll-tax, **5**, 465.
Solomon, king of Judah, son of David and Bathsheba, **1**, 133.
succession of, opposed, **1**, 135.
anointed by Nathan and Zadok, **1**, 153.
spares the life of Adonijah, **1**, 154.
characteristics and achievements of, **1**, 156–8.
vision of, at Gibeah, **1**, 158.
wisdom of, **1**, 158.
allegorical poems by, **1**, 158–9.
Solomon, king of Judah (*continued*), failings of, **1**, 159.
has Adonijah killed, **1**, 160.
deposes Abiathar, **1**, 160.
executes Shimei, **1**, 160–1.
harem of, **1**, 161.
and Hiram of Tyre, **1**, 162.
royal splendor of, **1**, 162.
division of land by, **1**, 162.
buildings of, **1**, 162–9.
Temple of, **1**, 162–8.
workmen of, **1**, 163, 164.
prayer of, at the dedication of the Temple, **1**, 167.
royal palace of, **1**, 168–9.
alliances of, **1**, 169–70.
fleet of, **1**, 170–1.
opens a route to India, **1**, 170.
has roads built, **1**, 171–2.
officers of, **1**, 172.
prosperity under, **1**, 172.
receives the Queen of Sheba, **1**, 173.
permits idolatry, **1**, 175.
and Jeroboam, **1**, 175–6.
children of, **1**, 177.
death of, **1**, 177.
"Sefer Refuoth" attributed to, **2**, 29.
in Immanuel Romi's work, **4**, 67.
Solomon, brother of Bachiel Ibn-Alkonstantini, Maimunist, **3**, 536.
Solomon (761–762), Exilarch, dies without issue, **3**, 128.
Solomon (Chasdaï?), made Exilarch by Mahomet Almustafi, **3**, 428, 438.
prevents a persecution of the Jews of the Abbasside Caliphate, **3**, 433.
Solomon I, prince of the Cairo Karaites, **3**, 444.
Solomon, prince of the Jews of Talmas, **3**, 437.

Solomon the Egyptian, physician to Emperor Emanuel, **3,** 425.
Solomon of Lithuania. *See* Maimon, Solomon.
Solomon (Shlomel) of Moravia, devotee of the Kabbala, **5,** 55.
Solomon of Rohatyn, Frankist, makes a Catholic confession of faith, **5,** 285.
Solomon of Tarascon, obtains the abrogation of the law on Jew badges, **3,** 612.
Solomon de Vesoul, receiver-general of France, **4,** 150.
robbed by a mob, **4,** 151.
Solomon ben Abraham of Montpellier, Talmudist, disciple of Judah Sir Leon, **3,** 409.
anti-Maimunist, **3,** 527.
literalness of, **3,** 527–8.
excommunicates the Maimunists, **3,** 528–9.
excommunicated, **3,** 530.
opposed by David Kimchi, **3,** 531.
aided by Nachmani, **3,** 536.
excommunicated by the Jews of Aragon, **3,** 536–7.
renounced by the French rabbis, **3,** 539, 540–1.
refers the Maimunist controversy to the Dominicans, **3,** 542–3.
denounced for inviting Dominican interference, **3,** 543–4.
partisans of, punished, **3,** 544.
imitated by Abba-Mari, **4,** 32.
Solomon ben Abraham ben Adret (Rashba, 1245–1310), disciple of Nachmani, **3,** 609.
character of, **3,** 618–19.
as Talmudist, **3,** 619–20.
as Kabbalist, **3,** 619.
authority of, **3,** 620, 621.
assists Maimonides' grandson, **3,** 620.
Solomon ben Abraham ben Adret (*continued*), refutes Raymund Martin, **3,** 623.
informed of the condemnation of the Eastern Anti-Maimunists, **3,** 634.
warns the Sicilian congregations against Abraham Abulafia, **4,** 7.
denounces the Messiah of Avila, **4,** 9.
in correspondence with Samuel Sulami, **4,** 26.
invited to oppose Levi of Villefranche, **4,** 28, 29.
appealed to by the Tibbonide party, **4,** 33.
refuses to prohibit the study of science without the co-operation of twenty congregations, **4,** 34.
pronounces the ban on science, **4,** 38, 39–40.
tries to have the ban accepted beyond his own community, **4,** 40.
attacked by Yedaya Bedaresi, **4,** 42–4.
protests admiration for Maimonides, **4,** 44–5.
in correspondence with Eleazar ben Joseph, **4,** 49.
again interferes in the controversy on the study of science, **4,** 50.
death of, **4,** 51.
has Maimonides' works translated into Hebrew, **4,** 60.
disciple of, **4,** 74, 147.
Solomon ben Abraham Parchon, disciple of Abraham Ibn-Ezra, teaches Hebrew to the Italians, **3,** 423.
Solomon ben Abraham Zarfati, French Talmudist, on the Spanish rabbis of the fourteenth century, **4.** 144, 162.

Solomon ben Asher, letter to, from Abraham Maimuni, **3**, 545.
Solomon ben Jacob, physician, translator of Maimonides' Mishna commentary, **4**, 60.
Solomon ben Joseph Ibn-Shoshan, virtues of, **3**, 384.
Solomon ben Nathan Ashkenazi, travels and learning of, **4**, 602-3.
employed as an agent by Mahomet Sokolli, **4**, 603.
brings about the election of Henry of Anjou as king of Poland, **4**, 605.
concludes peace between Turkey and Venice, **4**, 605-6, 608.
honors shown to, in Venice, **4**, 605-6.
secures the position of the Venetian Jews, **4**, 606-7.
supplants Joseph Nassi, **4**, 627.
as a diplomat, **4**, 628-9.
sons of, live in Venice, **4**, 629.
wife of, saves the sultan's wife, **4**, 630.
supports Stephen Bathori as candidate for the Polish throne, **4**, 642.
Solomon ben Reuben Bonfed, poet and satirist, **4**, 182, 230.
Solomon ben Yerucham (Ruchaïm, 885-960), defends Karaism against Saadiah, **3**, 191.
combats the opinions of Chivi Albalchi, **3**, 199.
makes propaganda for Karaism, **3**, 203.
commentaries of, **3**, 206.
hostile to philosophy, **3**, 206.
poetry of, **3**, 223.
Solomon Ibn-Almuallem. *See* Abu Ayub.
Solomon Ibn-Farussal, diplomat in the employ of a Christian prince, **3**, 312-13
Solomon Ibn-Gebirol (Abu Ayub Sulaiman Ibn-Yachya, Avicebron, 1021-1070), eulogizes Haï Gaon, **3**, 253.
protected by Samuel Ibn-Nagrela, **3**, 260, 268.
and Ibn-Janach, **3**, 264.
early life of, **3**, 265.
Hebrew style of, **3**, 266.
immortalizes Yekutiel Ibn-Hassan, **3**, 266.
writes a versified Hebrew grammar, **3**, 267.
writes a work on moral philosophy, **3**, 267-8.
banished from Saragossa, **3**, 268.
philosophy of, **3**, 269-71.
importance of, for European philosophy, **3**, 270.
philosophy of, foreign to Jewish thinkers, **3**, 270.
eulogy of, on Samuel Ibn-Nagrela, **3**, 274.
death of, **3**, 280.
legend about, **3**, 281.
unhappiness of, **3**, 313.
poetic forms developed by, **3**, 317.
compared with Moses Ibn-Ezra, **3**, 319.
works of, translated into Hebrew, **3**, 397.
works of, interdicted by the Church, **3**, 503.
philosophy of, studied by Duns Scotus, **3**, 644.
marks the zenith of neo-Hebraic poetry, **4**, 67.
lyric and didactic poet, **5**, 112.
Solomon Ibn-Sakbel, poet, satirical romance by, **3**, 318.
Solomon Ibn-Verga, chronicler, **4**, 556.
Solomon Alami, on the degeneracy of fourteenth century Jews of Spain, **4**, 154-5.

Solomon Alami (*continued*), describes the misery of Castilian Jews under Juan II, **4**, 204.
Solomon Alkabez, poet, companion of Joseph Karo, **4**, 538.
Solomon Dafiera, neo-Hebraic poet, **4**, 230.
Solomon Duran (1400–1467), rabbi of Algiers, defends the Talmud, **4**, 238.
son of, **4**, 390.
Solomon Gracian, opponent of the study of science, protests admiration for Maimonides, **4**, 45.
Solomon Kohen, disciple of Maimonides, **3**, 461.
Solomon Levi of Burgos (Paul Burgensis, or de Santa Maria, 1351–1435), apostate, attainments and character of, **4**, 182–3.
renounced by his family, **4**, 183.
ordained as a Catholic priest, **4**, 183.
in favor with Benedict XIII, **4**, 184.
ecclesiastical offices of, **4**, 184, 190.
propagandist, **4**, 184–5.
satirizes Jewish customs, **4**, 185.
caluminates the Jews, **4**, 185–6.
controversies of, with Jews, **4**, 186–8.
prevails upon David Bonet to remain a Christian, **4**, 188.
privy councilor to Henry III, **4**, 190.
executor of Henry III's will, **4**, 194.
in the council of regency for Juan II, **4**, 194, 195.
causes the death of Meïr Alguades, **4**, 195, 196.
Solomon Levi of Burgos (*continued*), issues an anti-Jewish edict, **4**, 203–4.
sons of, **4**, 216, 249–50.
propagandist for Christianity, **4**, 231–2.
writes a tract against Judaism, **4**, 233.
leaves the Marranos unconvinced, **4**, 256.
exegetical works of, used by Isaac Abrabanel, **4**, 342.
Solomon Lurya (1510–1573), Polish Talmudist, **4**, 634–7; **5**, 4.
critical ability of, **4**, 634–5.
aggressive nature of, **4**, 635–6.
admiration for, **4**, 636.
efforts of, to establish religious practice, **4**, 636.
as a grammarian, **4**, 637.
reproves Moses Isserles, **4**, 638.
authority of, **4**, 639.
disciples of, **4**, 639.
Solomon Petit, anti-Maimunist and Kabbalist, **3**, 626.
threatened with excommunication, **3**, 627.
persuades rabbis of Europe to denounce Maimonides' writings, **3**, 627.
fails in Italy, **3**, 627–8, 630.
has Maimonides' writings excommunicated, **3**, 630, 631.
excommunicated by two Exilarchs, **3**, 632.
Solomon Picho, rabbi of Sepulveda, **4**, 278.
Solomon Romano. *See* Baptista, John.
Solomon Yizchaki (Rashi, 1040–1105), parentage of, **3**, 282, 286.
studies Talmud at Mayence, Worms, and Speyer, **3**, 286.
early fame of, **3**, 286–7.
rabbi of Troyes, **3**, 287.
as teacher, **3**, 288.

Solomon Yizchaki (*continued*),
clearness of, **3**, 288.
commentaries of, on the Talmud and the Bible, **3**, 288–9.
grammatical knowledge of, **3**, 289.
family of, his disciples, **3**, 289.
daughter of, **3**, 289.
on Kalonymos of Rome, **3**, 290.
protests against the unkind treatment of repentant apostates, **3**, 308–9.
death of, **3**, 309.
legends about, **3**, 310.
influence of, **3**, 344.
supplements to the Talmud commentary by, **3**, 344.
sons and grandsons of, **3**, 345, 403.
commentary by, on Job completed, **3**, 346.
converted to rational exegesis, **3**, 288, 346.
works of, used by Raymund Martin, **3**, 622.
praised by Nicholas de Lyra, **4**, 185, 442.
exegesis of, praised by Reuchlin, **4**, 442.
commentary of, published in Bomberg's Bible, **4**, 476.
Solyman I, Turkish sultan, informed of the treachery of his Egyptian viceroy, **4**, 395.
employs a Jewish physician, **4**, 401.
the Jews under, **4**, 402.
espouses the cause of Gracia Mendesia, **4**, 574–5.
patron of Joseph Nassi, **4**, 577, 594.
intercedes in behalf of Turkish Jews in Ancona, **4**, 578.
contemplates war with Spain, **4**, 594.
jealousy among the sons of, **4**, 594–5.
Solyman I, Turkish sultan (*continued*), espouses Joseph Nassi's cause against the French ambassador, **4**, 595.
gives Joseph Nassi a tract near the Sea of Tiberias, **4**, 596.
death of, **4**, 596.
Son of God, epithet adopted by Jesus, **2**, 159, 162, 163.
Son of man, epithet adopted by Jesus, **2**, 158.
Soncin family, the, of printers, **4**, 586.
Soncino, Jewish printing house in, **4**, 289.
Soncinus. *See* Cohen, Gershon.
"Song of Deborah, The," celebrates the victory over Jabin, **1**, 61.
"Song of Songs, The," a product of Greek influences, **1**, 430–1.
rebukes the evils of the times, **1**, 432.
holiness of, discussed in the Synhedrion, **2**, 343–4.
commentary on, by Shemarya Ikriti, **4**, 70.
"Songs of Glory," by Wessely, **5**, 404.
"Songs of Obadiah ben Amos in Exile, The," by Steinheim, **5**, 603–4.
Sopher, keeper of the lists, **1**, 122, 305, 313, 314.
Sopheric age, the development of the Law in, **1**, 395–7.
the divine service in, **1**, 398–400.
Sopherim (Scribes), the, wise men, activity of, **1**, 396.
make a "fence" about the Law, **1**, 397.
new institutions of, **1**, 397–8.
divine service arranged by, **1**, 398–401.

Sopherim (Scribes), the (*continued*), prophetic writings collected by, **1**, 400.
traditional customs ascribed to, **2**, 19.
Hillel justifies the laws introduced by, **2**, 327.
as described by the Nazarenes, **2**, 372.
Sophia, Nathan Ghazati dies at, **5**, 161.
Sophocles, Judæan doctrines attributed to, **2**, 204.
Sophronius, bishop of Jerusalem, surrenders the city to Omar, **3**, 87.
Sora, a district of Jewish Babylonia, **2**, 505.
Sora (Mata-Mechassia), frontier town of Babylonia in the most limited sense, **2**, 504.
on the lake of Sora, **2**, 506.
honesty of the inhabitants of, **2**, 506.
assemblies at, **2**, 514–15.
Chasda's school in, **2**, 553.
homage paid at, to the Exilarchs, **2**, 606–7.
center of Jewish Babylonia, **2**, 607.
destroyed under Firuz, **2**, 629.
the Exilarch holds annual court at, **3**, 95.
Sora, the academy of, established by Abba-Areka, **2**, 513–14.
devotion of Rab to, **2**, 518.
superior to that of Nahardea, **2**, 522.
superior to the Palestinian academies, **2**, 532.
supremacy of, under Huna, **2**, 548.
method of, a continuation of that pursued in Judæa, **2**, 574–5.
numerical strength of, **2**, 576.
Sora, the academy of (*continued*), principals of, wealthy, **2**, 579–80.
decline of, **2**, 583.
prosperity of, under Ashi, **2**, 605.
rebuilt, **2**, 606.
closed under Hormisdas IV, **3**, 8.
re-opened under Bahram Tshubin, **3**, 9.
prosperity of, under Chosru II, **3**, 9–10.
principal of, receives the title Gaon, **3**, 90.
districts under the jurisdiction of, **3**, 98.
quarrels in, about the principalship of the Pumbeditha academy, **3**, 156.
without a Gaon, **3**, 156–7.
decline of, in the ninth century, **3**, 183.
pays homage to David ben Zaccaï, **3**, 186.
rise of, in the tenth century, **3**, 186.
decadence of, **3**, 192.
Kohen-Zedek proposes to close, **3**, 192.
restored by David ben Zaccaï, **3**, 192.
raised by Saadiah, **3**, 193, 201.
members of, side with Saadiah, **3**, 195.
questions sent to, under Saadiah, **3**, 201.
decline of, after Saadiah's death, **3**, 202.
abandoned by Joseph ben Satia, **3**, 202–3.
unsuccessful attempt to restore, **3**, 203, 208.
emissaries from, **3**, 208.
place of, taken by the Spanish schools, **3**, 236.
the last Gaon of, **3**, 253.

Sora, the academy of (*continued*). *See also* Academies, the Babylonian.
Sora, the academy of, the Gaon (principal) of, of equal rank with the Exilarch, **3**, 93.
deference paid to, **3**, 93.
privileges of, **3**, 93–4.
at the installation of a new Exilarch, **3**, 94.
pays homage to the Exilarch, **3**, 95.
rank of, **3**, 96.
appoints the judges of his district, **3**, 98.
Sora, the academy of, Geonim of, list of:
Chaninaï Kahana ben Huna,
Jacob ben Natronaï,
Joseph ben Satia,
Judah the Blind,
Mar-Amram ben Sheshna,
Nachshon ben Zadok,
Nathan ben Yehudaï (titular),
Natronaï II,
Saadiah ben Joseph,
Samuel ben Chofni,
Yom-Tob Kahana ben Jacob.
Sora, the academy of, principals of, list of:
Ashi, son of Simaï,
Chananya,
Chasda of Cafri,
Giza,
Huna,
Judah ben Ezekiel,
Mar bar Ashi,
Mar bar Huna,
Rabba bar Huna,
Rabina.
Sora, lake in the Euphrates, **2**, 506.
Soranzo, Jacopo, Venetian agent in Constantinople, procures the revocation of the banishment of the Jews from Venice, **4**, 606.
Soreg, screen between the outer and the inner court of the second Temple, **1**, 492.
Sorai, the cortes of, deprive the Jews of criminal jurisdiction, **4**, 157.
Sosius, Antony's general, sent to help Herod, **2**, 87.
invades Judæa, **2**, 88.
army of, ravages the Temple, **2**, 88.
Sostrates, officer of Antiochus Epiphanes, deposes Jason, **1**, 447.
Soul, the, theory of, in the Zohar, **4**, 16–18.
Souls, doctrine of, held by Isaac Lurya, **4**, 619–22.
transmigration of, explained by Isaac Lurya, **4**, 620.
impregnation of, **4**, 621.
sexes of, **4**, 621–2.
Spain, settlement of Jews in, **2**, 620; **3**, 42–3.
intermarriages between Jews and Christians in, **3**, 44.
Karaites spread to, in the tenth century, **3**, 207.
Talmud schools established in, **3**, 208, 210.
Moslem culture in, under the Ommiyyade Caliphs, **3**, 214.
the center of Judaism from the time of Chasdaï Ibn-Shaprut, **3**, 229.
split into parties in the twelfth century, **3**, 316.
characteristics of the rabbis of, in the age succeeding Nachmani, **3**, 609.
Talmudists of, use the works of Maimonides, **3**, 624.
entirely Christian, **4**, 346.
effect of the Inquisition on, **4**, 356.
the Protestant Reformation in, **4**, 469.
war with, contemplated by Solyman, **4**, 594.

Spain (*continued*), rebellion against, in the Netherlands, **4**, 601.
condition of, at the accession of Philip III, **4**, 668.
autos-da-fé in, **5**, 91.
the Jews in, **5**, 727–8.
Spain, the Jews of, forbidden to trade with Christians, **2**, 620.
held in high esteem in the sixth century, **3**, 43–4.
well treated by the early Visigoths, **3**, 45.
defend the passes of the Pyrenees, **3**, 45.
orthodoxy of, under the Visigoths, **3**, 45.
under the Catholic Visigoths, **3**, 46–52.
under Reccared, **3**, 46–7.
under Sisebut, **3**, 47–9.
emigrate, **3**, 48–9, 51–2.
under Swintila, **3**, 49.
under Sisenand, **3**, 49–50.
refute Isidore of Seville, **3**, 50–1.
under Chintila, **3**, 51–2.
enthusiastic for science and culture, **3**, 214–15.
cultivate their own individuality, **3**, 215.
not permitted to hold offices under the Mahometans, **3**, 216–17.
the first persecution of, **3**, 279, 281.
as diplomats at Mahometan and Christian courts, **3**, 281–2, 291.
devote themselves to the study of the Talmud, **3**, 282.
culture of, in the first half of the twelfth century, **3**, 313, 317–18.
politics of, in the twelfth century, **3**, 317.
culture of, at its zenith, **3**, 343.
Spain, the Jews of (*continued*), active in the struggle between the Christians and the Almohades, **3**, 363.
history of, in Abraham Ibn-Daud's work, **3**, 366.
struggle against Jew badges, **3**, 513.
Maimunists, **3**, 526–7, 536.
philosophical leanings of, **3**, 549.
higher culture of, in the thirteenth century, **3**, 615.
superior to the Jews of other countries, **3**, 618.
Castilians the leaders of, in the fourteenth century, **4**, 75.
neglect Jewish science, **4**, 86, 91.
charged with causing the Black Death, **4**, 101–2.
humiliated by the civil war between Pedro and Henry de Trastamare, **4**, 126.
at the beginning of Henry II's reign, **4**, 136.
intellectual decadence of, **4**, 143–4.
selfishness of, **4**, 153–5.
informers against, **4**, 155–6.
effect of persecution on, **4**, 166–7, 172–3.
persecution of, in 1391, **4**, 167–73.
existence of, endangered by the forced converts, **4**, 179, 180.
recognize Solomon Levi as their enemy, **4**, 185–6.
take refuge in northern Africa, **4**, 197–8.
crusade against, by Vincent Ferrer, **4**, 202–3.
conversion of, planned by Benedict XIII, **4**, 206–7.
take refuge in Portugal, **4**, 218.

Spain, the Jews of (*continued*),
send delegates to Martin V, **4**, 219.
intellectual decadence of, in the fifteenth century, **4**, 228, 229-30.
hatred of, increases in the fifteenth century, **4**, 248.
the object of papal hatred, **4**, 254.
privileges of, abolished by Nicholas V, **4**, 254.
charged with child murder, **4**, 276.
measures proposed against, by Alfonso de Spina, **4**, 277.
and the Inquisition, **4**, 308.
intimate relations of, with the Marranos, **4**, 334-5.
amenities of the position of, under Ferdinand and Isabella, **4**, 336.
taxed for the war with Granada, **4**, 344.
expulsion of, decided on, **4**, 346.
proclamation expelling, **4**, 347-8.
losses sustained by, on their expulsion, **4**, 349-50.
attempts to convert, after the promulgation of the edict, **4**, 350.
steadfastness of, **4**, 350-1.
solidarity of, **4**, 351.
settlement of, in Portugal, negotiated for, **4**, 352.
leave Spain, **4**, 352-3.
effect of the expulsion of, **4**, 353-4.
expulsion of, censured by European princes, **4**, 356.
last remnant of, banished, **5**, 169.
history of, by S. D. Luzzatto, **5**, 624, 625.

Spain, the Jews of (*continued*),
See also under Aragon, Castile, etc.; Inquisition, the; Marranos, the.

Spain, Andalusian, the Jews of, admitted to state offices under Moslem rule, **3**, 234-5.
characteristics of, in the tenth and eleventh centuries, **3**, 235-6.
nobility of, **3**, 235-6.
position of, in foreign communities, **3**, 236.
heirs of Judæa, Babylonia, and northern Africa, **3**, 254.

Spain, Christian, divided against itself in the twelfth century, **3**, 316.
the Jews in the kingdoms of, **3**, 383-4.

Spain, Jewish, importance of, **3**, 41-2.

Spain, Jewish, center of, at Cordova under Chasdaï Ibn-Shaprut, **3**, 217.
at Granada under Samuel Ibn-Nagrela, **3**, 259.
at Seville under Isaac Ibn-Albalia, **3**, 284.

Spain, Mahometan, the Jews of, well treated, **3**, 110.
sympathize with the false Messiah Serene, **3**, 121.

Spain, northern, lacks Talmud schools in the twelfth century, **3**, 322.
refuge of the Jews banished from England, **3**, 646.
taken by Henry de Trastamare, **4**, 124.

Spain, northern, the Jews of, exposed to persecution in the fourteenth century, **4**, 53.
suffering of, during the Pastoureaux rising, **4**, 57.

Spain, northern, the Jews of (*continued*), institute fasts to avert the Black Death persecutions, **4,** 100.
Spain, southern, Judæans in, **2,** 203.
Spain, southern, the Jews of, devoted to science and poetry in the eleventh century, **3,** 281, 289, 290.
intermarry with Christians and Mahometans, **3,** 527.
Spain, Visigothic, the Jews of, send names for mention at the memorial services of the Babylonian academies, **3,** 101.
forcibly converted under Chintila, **3,** 101.
under Chindaswinth, **3,** 101–2.
forced to profess Christianity under Receswinth, **3,** 102–4.
revolt against Wamba, **3,** 104–5.
publish anti-Christian treatises, **3,** 105.
under Erwig, **3,** 106–7.
under Egica forbidden to possess real estate, **3,** 107–8.
conspire against the Visigothic empire, **3,** 108.
enslaved, **3,** 108.
aid Tarik against Spain, **3,** 109.
aid Muza Ibn-Nosair, **3,** 109.
Spalding, approves of Mendelssohn's views on church discipline, **5,** 363.
translates Wessely's "Songs of Glory," **5,** 404.
Spanish America, laws of Alfonso V in force in, **3,** 596.
Spanish Caliphate, the. *See* Ommiyyades, the.
Spanish exiles, the, in Navarre, **4,** 357–8.
go to Italy, Africa, Turkey, **4,** 358, 383, 400.
Spanish exiles, the (*continued*), in Naples, **4,** 358–61.
suffer from the plague in Naples, **4,** 359–60.
in Pisa, **4,** 360.
in Africa, **4,** 361–2.
sufferings of, **4,** 362, 383.
in Genoa, **4,** 362–3.
on the Greek islands, **4,** 363–4.
in Turkey, **4,** 364, 400–5.
in Portugal, **4,** 365–81.
permitted to settle in Portugal, **4,** 368.
leave Portugal, **4,** 369.
suffering of, on leaving Portugal, **4,** 369–70.
in Portugal sold as slaves, **4,** 371.
children of, sent to San Thomas, **4,** 371.
accept baptism under Manoel of Portugal, **4,** 378.
looked upon as the Jewish nobility, **4,** 382–3.
distinction of manner of, **4,** 387–8.
purity of language of, **4,** 388.
love of, for the Spanish, **4,** 388, 421.
superiority of, admitted by other Jews, **4,** 389.
prominence of, **4,** 389.
of distinction in Africa, **4,** 389–96.
religious severity of, **4,** 395.
in Palestine, **4,** 396–9.
in Syria, **4,** 399–400.
in Constantinople, split up into national groups, **4,** 402.
in Salonica, **4,** 404–5.
in Asia Minor, **4,** 405–6.
in Italy, **4,** 407–10.
do not settle in Germany, **4,** 413.
narrow-mindedness of, **4,** 479.
carry the Kabbala to Italy and Turkey, **4,** 481.

Spanish language, the, spoken by Sephardic Jews after their exile, **4,** 387, 388, 421.
Spanish poetry, influenced by Judæo-Christian satirists, **4,** 181.
Spanish preachers, sermons of, pedantic, **4,** 478.
Spanish satirists, use Hebrew words, **4,** 181.
Spanish translation of the Bible, by Abraham Usque, **4,** 475.
Speeth, John Peter (Moses Germanus), becomes a Jew, **5,** 177, 178.
disproves the blood accusation, **5,** 178.
Speyer, Rashi studies Talmud at, **3,** 286.
the congregation of, one of the three oldest in Germany, **3,** 518.
decisions of, **4,** 135.
Reuchlin and Hoogstraten tried at, **4,** 454–5.
Speyer, the **Jews** of, kindly treated by Bishop Rüdiger, **3,** 297, 298.
defended by Bishop Johannsen, **3,** 300–1.
emigrate to Syria, **3,** 637.
persecuted on the charge of well poisoning, **4,** 107–8.
Spina, Alfonso de. *See* Alfonso de Spina.
Spinoza, Baruch (1632–1677), pupil of the Amsterdam Talmud Torah, **4,** 682.
fearlessness of, **5,** 86.
youth of, **5,** 87.
teachers of, **5,** 87.
companions of, **5,** 87–8.
studies the old Jewish philosophers, **5,** 88.
learns Latin, **5,** 88.
scientific pursuits of, **5,** 89.
Spinoza, Baruch (*continued*), scepticism of, **5,** 89–90.
renounces Judaism, **5,** 90.
tried by the rabbis, **5,** 92.
laid under the lesser ban, **5,** 93.
refuses the conditions of the rabbis, **5,** 93.
life of, attempted, **5,** 93–4.
leaves Amsterdam, **5,** 94.
laid under the greater ban, **5,** 94.
writes a pamphlet justifying himself, **5,** 95.
supports himself by polishing lenses, **5,** 95.
"The Theologico - Political Treatise" by, **5,** 95–107, 108.
finds the source of law in might, **5,** 96–7.
hostile to Jews and Judaism, **5,** 97–8, 101–3.
on God, **5,** 98–9.
on man, **5,** 99–100.
on knowledge, **5,** 100–1.
on Christianity, **5,** 102–3.
on the Jewish state, **5,** 103–7.
peaceableness of, **5,** 107, 109.
refuses a pension, **5,** 107.
refuses a professorship, **5,** 108.
publishes his "Treatise" anonymously, **5,** 108.
attack by, upon Judaism leaves the Amsterdam Marranos unaffected, **5,** 117.
compared with Sabbataï Zevi, **5,** 118.
on the Sabbatian movement, **5,** 138, 142.
letter to, on the Sabbatian movement, **5,** 139.
publishes his Ethics, **5,** 167.
death of, **5,** 167.
refuted by Isaac Orobio de Castro, **5,** 167.
influences Richard Simon, **5,** 178.

Spinoza, Baruch (*continued*), system of, repugnant to Mendelssohn, **5**, 299.

Spinozism, Lessing charged with, **5**, 372.

Spira, Nathan, Palestinian emissary at Reggio, **5**, 126.

"Spirit of the Laws," by Montesquieu, **5**, 336.

Sprinz, David, rabbi of Nuremberg, defends Israel Bruna, **4**, 302.

Stambuli, Aaron, of Damascus, accused of ritual murder, **5**, 638.

Stamford, the Jews of, persecution of, **3**, 412.

Stanislaus Augustus Poniatowski, of Poland, forbids the meeting of the synod of the Four Countries, **5**, 387.

Starodub, the Jews of, massacred by Haidamaks, **5**, 10.

States General, the Dutch, forbids the sale of Spinoza's "Treatise," **5**, 108.

Stättigkeit. *See* Judenstättigkeit.

Steel, Lord Chief Baron, on the commission for the Jewish question, **5**, 43.

Steinheim, Solomon Ludwig (1790–1866), physician, emphasizes the mission of the Jew, **5**, 602–3.
- first work by, **5**, 603–4.
- deplores the estrangement of the Jews, **5**, 603–4.
- second work by, **5**, 604–6.
- contrasts heathenism and Judaism, **5**, 604–5.
- keeps aloof from the Jewish community, **5**, 606.
- externally faithful to Judaism, **5**, 607.
- expounds Jewish religious philosophy, **5**, 699.

Stephanus, governor of Palæstina Prima, oppresses the Jews, **3**, 16.
- killed by the Samaritans, **3**, 17.
- widow of, reports his death at Constantinople, **3**, 17.

Stephen, of England, protects the Jews from the crusaders, **3**, 356.

Stephen, Greek Judæan, stoned for blasphemy, **2**, 221.

Stern, lecturer in Berlin, founds the Reform Association, **5**, 683.

Stoic system, the, and Meïr, **2**, 438.

Strabo, geographer, friendly to the Judæans, **2**, 179–80.

Strasburg, the Jews of, protected by the councilors during the Black Death persecutions, **4**, 106.
- the representatives of, plead the cause of the Benfelden Jews, **4**, 107.
- the Jews of, burnt, **4**, 108.
- the theological faculty of, forbids the employment of Jewish physicians, **4**, 692.
- Jews under restrictions in, **5**, 349.
- Jews not allowed to live in, **5**, 430.
- Jews drawn to, by Cerf Berr, **5**, 431.
- objects to the presence of Jews, **5**, 447, 476.
- the Jews of, compelled to violate the Sabbath, **5**, 451.
- culture of the Jews of, **5**, 476.
- citizens of, prejudice Napoleon against the Jews, **5**, 476–7.

Straton, the tower of, scene of Antigonus' murder, **2**, 38.
- beautified by Herod, **2**, 106.
- *See* Cæsarea.

Strauss, David, predecessor of, **5,** 179.
Streckfuss, opponent of the Jews, **5,** 602.
" Strengthening of Faith, The," by Isaac Troki, **4,** 648-9.
" Stübel," the Zaddik's room, **5,** 382.
Sturm, Gosse, asserts the innocence of the Jews in the charge of well poisoning, **4,** 106.
deposed, **4,** 108.
Styria, the Jews of, urged to emigrate to Turkey, **4,** 271-2.
expelled by Maximilian I, **4,** 427.
Suabia, the Jews of, suffer during the Armleder persecutions, **4,** 97.
during the Black Death persecutions, **4,** 110.
persecuted, **4,** 163.
expelled, **4,** 307, 413.
find a refuge in Poland, **4,** 420.
Suabian League, the, Reuchlin counselor of, **4,** 435.
Suasso, Isaac (Antonio), advances money to William III, of England, **5,** 205.
Suevi, the, antagonistic to the Catholics, **3,** 44.
Suger, Abbot, prevents a persecution of the Jews of France, **3,** 351.
Sulami, Samuel. *See* Samuel Sulami.
Sulchat (Solgat, Eski-Crimea), Jews of the Byzantine empire settle in, **3,** 123.
a Karaite community in, in the ninth century, **3,** 182.
Karaite center, **4,** 71.
Suleiman, Barbary chieftain, takes Cordova, **3,** 255, 262.
Suliman, Ommiyyade caliph, tolerance of, **3,** 110.
Suliman, Ommiyyade caliph (*continued*), patron of learning, **3,** 110.
Sullam, Jacob, husband of Sarah, **5,** 69.
Sullam, Sarah Copia (1600-1641), poetess, education of, **5,** 69.
addresses Ansaldo Ceba, **5,** 69.
resists attempts to convert her, **5,** 69-70.
accused of denying the immortality of the soul, **5,** 70.
honored by Leo Modena, **5,** 70.
Sully, the Jews of, attacked by crusaders, **3,** 356.
Sulzer, musician in Vienna, **5,** 581.
" Summons," addressed to the princes of Europe by Michael Berr, **5,** 460.
Sumptuary laws, against the Jews of Castile, **4,** 138-9, 203-4, 205-6, 275-6.
Sunna, Mahometan tradition, **3,** 110.
Superstitious usages, among Jews, **5,** 201-2.
Surenhuysius, William, translates the Mishna into Latin, **5,** 193-4.
enthusiasm of, for the Jews, **5,** 194.
Suriel, name of an angel, **1,** 403.
Susa, the goddess of love worshiped in, **1,** 408.
the inhabitants of, force Antiochus Epiphanes to retreat, **1,** 477.
the Jews of, in the twelfth century, **3,** 434-5.
Susannah, the Book of, translated into Greek, **2,** 359.
admitted into the canon by Christians, **2,** 488.
Susiana, Armenian Jews colonized in, by Shabur II, **2,** 591.

Suson, Diego de, Marrano, burnt at the stake, **4,** 317.
Süsskind (Süzkint) of Trimberg, minnesinger, poetry of, **3,** 420.
Suwailim, of Medina, harbors conspirators against Mahomet, **3,** 84.
Sviatislav, of Kief, drives the Chazars from their land, **3,** 222.
Swaber, Peter, asserts the innocence of the Jews in the charge of well poisoning, **4,** 106.
deposed, **4,** 108.
Sweden, the Protestant Reformation in, **4,** 469.
Swedes, the, treat the Jews of Mayence well, **4,** 707.
Swieden, van, opposes the emancipation of the Jews, **5,** 453–4.
Swintila, Visigothic king, repeals anti-Jewish laws, **3,** 49.
dethroned, **3,** 49.
Switzerland, the Black Death persecutions in, **4,** 103–5.
the Protestant Reformation in, **4,** 469.
the Jews of, assisted by Mendelssohn, **5,** 344.
Sylvester, bishop of Rome, asperses Judaism, **2,** 562.
Symmachos, translation of the Scriptures by, used by Origen, **2,** 489.
Symmachos ben Joseph, disciple of Meïr, a sophist, **2,** 440.
Synagogue poetry. *See* Liturgical poetry.
Synagogues, established in the Sopheric age, **1,** 401.
service at the, **1,** 401.
for foreigners in Jerusalem, **2,** 201.
Synagogues (*continued*), desecration of, punished by the emperors, **2,** 193, 614, 616, 621–2.
turned into churches, **3,** 26; **4,** 196, 354.
destroyed under Hakim, **3,** 248.
the desecration of, forbidden by Martin V, **4,** 220.
Synagogues, building of, forbidden by Theodosius II, **2,** 617; **3,** 28.
by Justinian I, **3,** 10.
by Theodoric, **3,** 30.
by Gregory I, **3,** 34.
by Omar I, **3,** 87.
by Omar II, **3,** 120.
in England, **3,** 516.
by Alfonso X, **3,** 595.
by Eugenius IV, **4,** 250.
in Hamburg, **4,** 688.
Synagogues, noteworthy, in Alexandria, **2,** 183.
in Cordova, **3,** 360.
in Toledo, **3,** 384; **4,** 119.
of Moses, **3,** 445.
on Mt. Zion, **4,** 273–4.
in Amsterdam, **4,** 667, 671, 678, 680; **5,** 166–7.
in Hamburg, **4,** 689, 691.
Synagogues, private, in Berlin, **5,** 191, 563.
Synhedrion, a, established in five towns of Judæa, **2,** 71.
at Nahar Pakod, **2,** 443–4.
the establishment of, a condition of the Messianic time, **4,** 530.
necessity for the establishment of, **4,** 530, 535.
importance of, **4,** 532.
the revival of, antagonized, **4,** 534–5.
Synhedrion, the French, the convening of, proposed by Napoleon, **5,** 493.

Synhedrion, the French (*continued*), constitution of, similar to that of the ancient body, **5**, 493.
approved by the Assembly of Notables, **5**, 493.
composition of, **5**, 493.
proclaimed by the Assembly of Notables, **5**, 494.
creates interest in Europe, **5**, 494.
the assembling of, **5**, 495.
officers of, **5**, 495.
second sitting of, **5**, 496.
addresses and messengers to, **5**, 496.
powers and justification of, **5**, 496.
speeches delivered before, **5**, 497.
decisions of, **5**, 497.
action of, displeases Jews in general, **5**, 497.
dissolution of, **5**, 498.

Synhedrion, the Great, reorganized, **2**, 49, 50.
the traditional code introduced into, **2**, 50.
divorce law of, **2**, 50.
institutes the half-Shekel contribution to the Temple treasury, **2**, 52.
forbids the breeding of swine, **2**, 60.
under Aulus Gabinius, **2**, 71.
summons Herod to answer for the execution of Ezekias, **2**, 78.
discusses the Paschal sacrifice on the Sabbath, **2**, 99.
tries and condemns Jesus, **2**, 163–4.
authority of, wanes under the Roman rule, **2**, 129.
under Gamaliel I, **2**, 192–3.
power of, diminished under Herod II, **2**, 198.

Synhedrion, the Great (*continued*), the legislative body for the dispersed Judæans, **2**, 201.
transferred from Jerusalem to Bethany, **2**, 239–40.
re-established after the defeat of Cestius, **2**, 268–9.
supremacy of, under Simon ben Gamaliel, **2**, 271.
decrees the deposition of Josephus, **2**, 281.
envoys of, deceived by Josephus, **2**, 282.
envoys of, sent back in chains, **2**, 283.
aid asked of, by Josephus against Vespasian, **2**, 286.
suspected of Roman proclivities, **2**, 293–4.
formed by the Zealots, **2**, 296.
ceases with the fall of Jerusalem, **2**, 322.
meetings of, interrupted after the fall of Bethar, **2**, 423.
seats of, after its dissolution at Usha, **2**, 452.
completeness of, at Sepphoris, **2**, 452.
invests Judah I with sovereign power, **2**, 452–3.
in Galilee, **2**, 458.
pronounces the Samaritans heathens, **2**, 534.
resolutions of, announced to distant communities, **2**, 535.
end of, under Constantius, **2**, 567.
members of, favor a fixed calendar, **2**, 573.
and the smaller in Babylonia, **3**, 96.
See also Council, the Great, of Seventy.

Synhedrion, the, of Jamnia, established by Jochanan ben Zakkai, **2**, 325.
called Beth-Din, **2**, 325.

Synhedrion, the, of Jamnia (*continued*), tries to reconcile the schools of Hillel and Shammai, **2,** 337-8.
revises Gamaliel II's laws, **2,** 342.
members of, **2,** 357.
supremacy of, **2,** 359, 360.
order of proceedings in, **2,** 361-2.
the unity in, admired by Peter, **2,** 367-8.
discusses the Jewish-Christians, **2,** 379-80.
destroyed by Lucius Quietus, **2,** 400.
Synhedrion, the, of Usha, ordinances of, **2,** 405.
provides against the spread of the worship of Jesus, **2,** 413.
dissension in, **2,** 444-6.
dissolved, **2,** 448.
Synhedrion, the, presidents of, the family of Bene Bathyra, **2,** 90.
the descendants of Hillel, **2,** 130.
reverence paid to, **2,** 360.
rights of, **2,** 360-1.
duties of, **2,** 361.
fix the calendar, **2,** 362-3.
See Patriarchs, the.
Synhedrion, the, presidents of, list of:

Abtalion,
Gamaliel I,
Hillel,
Joshua ben Chananya,
Judah ben Tabbaï,
Menahem,
Shammai,
Shemaya,
Simon I,
Simon II,
Simon ben Shetach.

See Patriarchs, the, list of.
Synod of the Four Countries, the. *See* Four Countries, the synod of.
Synod, the Galilean, the second assembly of teachers of the Law at Usha, **2,** 434.
Synods. *See* Rabbinical synods.
Syria, conquered by Alexander the Great, **1,** 412.
end of the Seleucidæan dynasty of, **2,** 6.
Judæans in, make the half-Shekel contribution to the Temple, **2,** 52.
Judæa part of, under Roman rule, **2,** 128.
number of Judæans in, **2,** 201.
rights of Judæans in, **2,** 202.
Judæans of, go to Jerusalem for the Passover of 66, **2,** 251.
devastated by the king of Parthia, **2,** 447.
depredations in, by Odenathus, **2,** 527.
succumbs to the Arabs, **3,** 86.
the Karaites spread to, in the ninth century, **3,** 182.
part of the Fatimide Caliphate, **3,** 248.
the Jews of, in the twelfth century, **3,** 426-7.
Spanish spoken in, by the exiles, **4,** 387.
the Spanish exiles in, **4,** 399-400.
See Damascus; the kings of Aram and of the Seleucidæan dynasty, etc.
Syria, the Roman governors (legates, prætors) of, list of:

Cæsar, Sextus
Cassius Longinus, Caius
Cassius Longinus, Caius
Cornelianus, Atidius
Crassus,
Flaccus,
Gabinius, Aulus
Gallus, Cestius
Marsus, Vibius
Mucianus, Licinius
Petronius,
Quadratus, Umidius
Quirinius,
Scaurus,
Varus, Quintilius,
Vitellius.

Syria, the Roman governors (legates, prætors) of (*continued*). *See also* Judæa, the Roman governors of; Procurators, the, of Judæa.
Syriac, despised by Judah I, **2**, 461.
Syroes, son of Chosru II, revolts against his father, **3**, 22.
makes peace with Heraclius, **3**, 22.

T

Tabæ, Antiochus IV dies at, **1**, 477.
Taberistan, home of Jewish physicians in the ninth century, **3**, 146.
David Alrui in prison in, **3**, 432.
Tabernacle, the, at Shiloh destroyed by the Philistines, **1**, 71.
Tabernacles, the Feast of, celebrated at Jerusalem under Ezra and Nehemiah, **1**, 380.
as celebrated in the Second Temple, **2**, 51.
wreath of, abolished by Anan ben David, **3**, 132.
confiscation of prayer books on, **4**, 430.
Tabi, favorite slave of Gamaliel II, **2**, 336.
"**Tables of Testimony, The**," defense by Eibeschütz, **5**, 270.
Tables of the Seven Planets, by Abraham Zacuto, **4**, 367.
Tables of the Testimony, the, **1**, 22.
Tabor, mountain, description of, **1**, 44.
considered holy by the Canaanites, **1**, 51.
Alexander, son of Aristobulus II, defeated at, **2**, 73.
fortress of, in possession of the Zealots, **2**, 289.
fortress of, taken by the Romans, **2**, 290.
fire signals on, **2**, 363.
Tabyome. *See* Mar bar Ashi.
Tab-Yomi. *See* Lipmann of Mühlhausen.
Tachkemoni, satirical romance by Solomon Ibn-Sakbel, **3**, 318.
romance by Jehuda Alcharisi, **3**, 559.
Tachos, king of Egypt, at war with Artaxerxes II, **1**, 408.
Tachpanches. *See* Taphnai.
Tacitus, historian, on the conversions to Judaism, **2**, 384.
Tadmor. *See* Palmyra.
Tafilet, the Jews of, fortunes of, **5**, 168.
Taima, castle of Shoraich, **3**, 70.
submits to Mahomet, **3**, 83.
the Jews of, in the twelfth century, **3**, 437.
Taku. *See* Moses ben Chasdaï Taku.
Talleyrand, speaks to the National Assembly in behalf of the Bordeaux Jews, **5**, 442.
reactionary leader, **5**, 512.
Talmai, of Geshur, protects Absalom, **1**, 134.
Talmas, the Jews of, in the twelfth century, **3**, 437.
Talmide Chachamim, disciples of the wise, **1**, 396.
Talmud, the, application of the oral Law to new questions, **2**, 328, 329.
the creation of Pumbeditha and Machuza, **2**, 591.
the sole object of attention of the disciples of the Amoraim, **3**, 5.

Talmud, the (*continued*), stagnation in the development of, **3**, 5–6.
made available for practical use by the Sabureans, **3**, 6.
committed to writing, **3**, 6–7.
teachings of Mahomet borrowed from, **3**, 72.
the result of the opposition of Pauline Christianity, **3**, 127.
supplants the Bible, **3**, 128.
opposition to, without result, **3**, 128.
opposed by Anan ben David, **3**, 130.
rendered popular and intelligible by the Halachoth Ketuoth, **3**, 136.
exposition of, the work of the Geonim, **3**, 178–9.
the exclusive subject of the literary activity of the Geonim, **3**, 180.
criticised in Saadiah's time, **3**, 198.
copies of, transferred from Sora to Spain, **3**, 203, 228.
studied carefully by Sherira, **3**, 232.
studied by the Jews of Spain in the tenth and eleventh centuries, **3**, 235.
scientific study of, founded by Jehuda ben Meïr, **3**, 242.
civil law of, treated by Haï Gaon, **3**, 251.
methodology of, by Samuel Ibn-Nagrela, **3**, 259.
work on the civil jurisprudence of, by Isaac Albergeloni, **3**, 284.
work on, by Alfassi, **3**, 285–6.
studied by the Jews of Maghreb while pretending to be Mahometans, **3**, 360.
work on, by Jonathan of Lünel, **3**, 397.

Talmud, the (*continued*), work on, by Isaac ben Abba-Mari, **3**, 399.
maligned by Donin before Gregory IX, **3**, 573–4.
confiscation of, by Gregory IX and in France, **3**, 575–8.
disputation on, under Louis IX, **3**, 576–8.
defended by Yechiel of Paris, **3**, 577.
defended by Jehuda of Melun, **3**, 578.
condemned to be burnt, **3**, 578.
burnt in Paris, **3**, 578–9; **4**, 460.
Jesus of Nazareth in, **3**, 599.
denounced by Pablo Christiani, **3**, 602.
confiscation of, ordered by Clement IV, **3**, 602.
subjected to censorship in Aragon, **3**, 603.
in the Zohar, **4**, 19.
burnt by order of the king of Majorca, **4**, 50.
burnt at Toulouse, **4**, 55.
guaranteed against confiscation by John of France, **4**, 130.
extermination of, planned by Benedict XIII, **4**, 209.
accused of blasphemy by Joshua Lorqui, **4**, 213–14.
Benedict XIII's bull against, **4**, 215–16.
defended by Vidal ben Benveniste Ibn-Labi, **4**, 234.
defended by Solomon Duran I, **4**, 238.
reading of, forbidden by Eugenius IV, **4**, 251.
influence of, on the Protestant Reformation, **4**, 423, 467, 468.
the Dominicans desire to confiscate, **4**, 425.

Talmud, the (*continued*), attacked by Pfefferkorn, **4,** 425–6, 427, 439.
defended by Reuchlin, **4,** 442, 466.
decision against, **4,** 444.
the watchword of the Reuchlinists, **4,** 457.
in the "Letters of Obscurantists," **4,** 461.
printing of, encouraged by Leo X, **4,** 468, 565.
attacked by Luther, **4,** 549–50.
endangered by the censor, **4,** 563.
burnt at Rome and elsewhere, **4,** 565.
persecuted by Paul IV, **4,** 582.
taught at Cremona, **4,** 582.
burnt at Cremona, **4,** 582–3.
appearance of, permitted by Pius IV, **4,** 589.
printed at Basle, **4,** 589.
connected with other ancient writings by Azarya deï Rossi, **4,** 614.
as viewed by Solomon Lurya, **4,** 635.
confiscation of, ordered by Gregory XIII, **4,** 654.
dictionary of, by David de Pomis, **4,** 657.
reprinting of, permitted by Sixtus V, **4,** 657–8.
reading of, forbidden by Clement VIII, **4,** 659.
expurgated edition of, **4,** 659.
mutilation of, **4,** 659–60.
beginnings of the criticism of, **5,** 54–5.
scoffed at by Joseph Delmedigo, **5,** 77.
Simone Luzzatto on, **5,** 84.
opposed by the Sabbatians, **5,** 142, 228.
defended by Richard Simon, **5,** 181.

Talmud, the (*continued*), studied by Polish Jews, **5,** 206.
privilege of printing, obtained through Eibeschütz, **5,** 250.
rejected by the Frankists, **5,** 274.
slandered by Frankists, **5,** 280–1.
burnt at Kamieniec, **5,** 582.
excessive study of, favors Chassidism, **5,** 383, 385–6.
neglected in Germany after Mendelssohn's death, **5,** 395.
attacked by the "Moniteur," **5,** 485–6.
an alleged Oriental form of, **5,** 651.
exonerated by Zunz, **5,** 669.
aspersions upon, permitted by Geiger, **5,** 669.
authority of, not recognized by the "Friends of Reform," **5,** 675, 676.
opposed by Holdheim, **5,** 678.
authority of, not recognized by the Brunswick rabbinical conference, **5,** 682.
rejected by the Berlin Reform Association, **5,** 683.
development of, **5,** 726.
See also Amoraim, the; Law, the oral; Mishna, the; Talmud, the Babylonian.

Talmud, the, commentary on, by Gershom ben Jehuda, **3,** 243–4.
by Samuel Ibn-Nagrela, **3,** 259.
by Isaac Ibn-Albalia, **3,** 283.
by Rashi, **3,** 288, 344, 403.
by Jacob Tam, **3,** 376.
by Serachya Halevi Gerundi, **3,** 389.
by Nachmani, **3,** 532.
See also under Talmud, the.

Talmud, the, the study of, degenerates into a matter of memory, **3,** 128.

Talmud, the, the study of (*continued*), encouraged in Spain by Chasdaï Ibn-Shaprut, **3,** 227–8.
among the French and German Jews in the eleventh century, **3,** 281.
in Spain, **3,** 282.
pursued by the German Jews after the first crusade, **3,** 309.
flourishes in Spain in the twelfth century, **3,** 317.
cultivated by the French Jews in the twelfth century, **3,** 343–5.
divided into two branches by the Tossafists, **3,** 345.
at Toledo, **3,** 386.
preserves the Jews of northern France from moral decay, **3,** 407–8.
in Germany in the twelfth century, **3,** 419.
in Bohemia, **3,** 420, 421.
facilitated by Maimonides' Mishna commentary, **3,** 458.
in the twelfth century described by Maimonides, **3,** 492.
the absorbing occupation of the Jews in the thirteenth century, **3,** 571–2.
in Spain in the fourteenth century, **4,** 86, 144.
decays in Germany in the fourteenth century, **4,** 96.
neglected in France in the fourteenth century, **4,** 132–3.
neglected in Germany in the fifteenth century, **4,** 227.
neglected in Spain in the fifteenth century, **4,** 230, 231.
by Karaites, **4,** 269, 270.
in Thebes, **4,** 406.
in Prague, **4,** 418.
in Poland, **4,** 420.
in Frankfort, **4,** 429.

Talmud, the, the study of (*continued*), in Poland in the sixteenth century, **4,** 634, 639–40, 640–1.
neglected in Germany during the Catholic reaction, **4,** 653.
in Poland in the seventeenth century, **5,** 4–6.
Polish method of, dominant in Europe, **5,** 16–17.
by Frankel, **5,** 684, 694–5.
See also under Talmud, the.

Talmud Babli. *See* Talmud, the Babylonian.

Talmud, the Babylonian, collected by Ashi, **2,** 607–9.
not committed to writing, **2,** 608.
the study of, disturbed under Theodosius II, **2,** 623.
compilation of, finished by Mar bar Ashi, **2,** 628.
completed by Rabina and José, **2,** 630–2.
uniqueness of, **2,** 632.
compared with the literature of the Church Fathers, **2,** 632.
blemishes of, **2,** 632–3.
diversified character of, **2,** 633–4.
as distinguished from the Jerusalem Talmud, **2,** 634.
intellectual character of, **2,** 634–5.
dialectics of, **2,** 635.
the preserver of the Jewish nation, **2,** 635.
the constitution of the Babylonian Jewish community, **3,** 118.
authority of, extended by the Islamic conquests, **3,** 118–19.
irksome to the Arabian Jews, **3,** 119–20.
printed by Daniel Bomberg, **4,** 468.
See also Talmud, the.

Talmud, the Jerusalem (or Palestinian), compiled, 2, 609.
compilers of, unknown, 2, 612.
compared with the Babylonian, 2, 634.
studied at Kairuan in the eleventh century, 3, 249.
commentary on, by David Fränkel, 5, 294.

Talmud, shel Erez-Israel. *See* Talmud, the Jerusalem.

Talmud, the, of the Holy Land. *See* Talmud, the Jerusalem.

Talmud Torah, graded Jewish school in Amsterdam, 4, 681–2.

Talmud Torah, synagogue at Hamburg, 4, 689–90.

Talmud Torah, the greatest virtue, according to the Mishna, 2, 473–4.

Talmud Torah schools, contrasted with the rabbinical colleges, 5, 700.

Talmudical Judaism, founded by Hillel, 2, 327.
rejected by Arabian Jews, 3, 120.
opposition to, led by Serene, 3, 120–2.
opposition to, led by Obaiah Abu-Isa ben Ishak, 3, 124.
opposed by the adherents of Anan ben David, 3, 129.
Anan ben David's opposition to, inconsistent, 3, 135.
superiority of, over Karaism proved by Jehuda Halevi, 3, 334.
as regarded by Maimonides, 3, 469–70.
undermined by Maimonides' arguments, 3, 529.
becomes Rabbinism in Jacob Asheri's code, 4, 89.
efforts to reconcile the Karaites to, 4, 270.

Talmudical Judaism (*continued*).
See also Rabbinical Judaism.

Talmudical lexicon. *See* Lexicon, Talmudical.

Talmudists, the, dialecticians, 2, 591.
ranged against the Maimunists and the Kabbalists, 3, 558.
of the sixteenth century characterized by Solomon Lurya, 4, 635–6.
disputations of, in Poland, 4, 640–1.
Polish, dominant influence of, 5, 17.
mocked at by the Chassidim, 5, 379.

Talmudists, list of:

Aaron Halevi,
Abraham ben David,
Abraham ben Isaac,
Abraham Ibn-Shoshan,
Abraham Maimuni,
Abu-Amr Joseph ben Zadik Ibn-Zadik,
Asher ben Yechiel (Asheri) (Tossafist),
Ashkenazi, Jacob
Ashkenazi, Zevi
Baruch ben Samuel,
Chages, Jacob
Chananel ben Chushiel,
Chanoch ben Moses,
Chasdaï Crescas,
Chushiel
Daniel ben Saadiah,
David ben Kalonymos (Tossafist),
David Ibn-Abi Zimra,
Edles, Samuel
Eibeschütz, Jonathan
Elchanan ben Isaac (Tossafist),
Eleazer ben Joel Halevi,
Eleazer ben Joseph (Tossafist),
Elias Mizrachi,
Elijah Wilna,
Emden, Jacob
Ephraim ben Jacob (Tossafist),
Eskapha, Joseph
Florentin, Solomon
Frankel, Zachariah
Gershom ben Jehuda,
Haï Gaon,

Talmudists, list of (*continued*):
Heller, Lipmann
Hillel ben Samuel,
Holdheim, Samuel
Isaac ben Abba-Mari,
Isaac ben Abraham (Rizba) (Tossafist),
Isaac ben Asher Halevi (Riba) (Tossafist),
Isaac ben Baruch Albalia,
Isaac ben Jacob Alfassi,
Isaac ben Jacob Campanton,
Isaac ben Jacob Halaban (Tossafist),
Isaac ben Jehuda Ibn-Giat,
Isaac ben Joseph (Tossafist),
Isaac ben Meïr (Tossafist),
Isaac ben Reuben Albergeloni,
Isaac ben Samuel (Ri) (Tossafist),
Isaac ben Sheshet Barfat,
Isaac Ibn-Sakni,
Jacob of London,
Jacob of Orleans (Tossafist),
Jacob ben Asheri,
Jacob ben Nathaniel Ibn-Alfayumi,
Jacob ben Nissim Ibn-Shahin,
Jacob Ibn-Chabib,
Jacob Berab,
Jacob Polak,
Jacob Tam,
Japhet ben Elia,
Jehuda ben Meïr (Leontin),
Jehuda ben Nathan (Riban) (Tossafist),
Jehuda Asheri,
Jehuda Halevi,
Jonah ben Abraham Gerundi (the Elder),
Jonathan Cohen of Lünel,
Joseph ben Isaac Ibn-Abitur,
Joseph ben Meïr Ibn-Migash Halevi,
Joseph ben Pilat,
Joseph Ibn-Nagrela,
Joseph Ottolenghi,
Joseph Karo,
Judah the Blind,
Judah Menz,
Judah Sir Leon ben Isaac (Tossafist),
Kalonymos of Rome,
Lagarto, Jacob
Levi ben Gerson,
Levi ben Jacob Chabib,
Levi, David
Maimun ben Joseph,
Mar-Zemach I ben Paltoi,
Mattathiah ben Joseph Provenci,
Meïr ben Baruch of Rothenburg,
Meïr ben Joseph Ibn-Migash,

Talmudists, list of (*continued*):
Meïr ben Samuel (Tossafist),
Menachem of Merseburg,
Menachem ben Aaron ben Zerach,
Mordecai ben Hillel,
Moses of Coucy (Tossafist),
Moses ben Chanoch,
Moses ben Chasdaï Taku,
Moses ben Isaac Alashkar,
Moses ben Israel Isserles,
Moses ben Maimun,
Moses ben Nachman,
Moses Menz,
Nachshon ben Zadok,
Nathan ben Isaac Kohen,
Nathan ben Yechiel,
Nissim bar Jacob Ibn-Shahin,
Nissim Gerundi ben Reuben,
Peter (Tossafist),
Philosoph, Joseph
Samson ben Abraham (Tossafist),
Samuel ben Ali Halevi,
Samuel ben Meïr (Rashbam) (Tossafist),
Samuel ben Solomon Sir Morel (Tossafist),
Samuel Alvalensi,
Samuel Cohen ben Daniel,
Samuel Halevi Ibn-Nagrela,
Samuel Sidillo,
Sasportas, Jacob
Serachya Halevi Gerundi,
Serkes, Joel
Shalom Shachna,
Shemaria ben Elchanan,
Sheshet Benveniste,
Simcha ben Samuel,
Simon of Cairo,
Simon ben Isaac ben Abun,
Sinzheim, Joseph David
Solomon ben Abraham,
Solomon ben Abraham ben Adret (Rashba),
Solomon ben Abraham Zarfati,
Solomon Lurya,
Solomon Yizchaki (Rashi),
Taytasak, Joseph
Yechiel of Paris,
Zadok.

Taman. *See* Phanagoria.

Tamar, daughter of David, seduced, **1**, 134.

Tamarah. *See* Zoar.

Tamarica, the Jewish community in, **4**, 693.

Tamarite, the Jews of, converted by Vincent Ferrer, **4**, 214.
Tamgiz, anti-Karaite work by Saadiah, **3**, 192.
Tammuz, the fast of, abolished by Sabbataï Zevi, **5**, 151–2.
abrogated by the Sabbatians, **5**, 159.
Tana. *See* Sanaa.
Tanaites, the, teachers of the Law, **2**, 356.
and the Jewish Christians, **2**, 370.
reviled by the Nazarenes, **2**, 371–2.
deprecate the influence of the Minæans on Judaism, **2**, 378.
protect Judaism from Gnostic-Christian influences, **2**, 382.
uphold Gamaliel II's ordinances, **2**, 405.
refuse subservience to Hadrian's decrees, **2**, 427.
end of the second generation of, **2**, 429.
activity of, culminates in Judah I, **2**, 450.
conclude their activity by the compilation of the Mishna, **2**, 462, 478.
half, supplement the Mishna, **2**, 470–1.
connection of, with the Amoraim, **2**, 479.
compared with the Amoraim, **2**, 490.
subordinated to the Amoraim by Raba bar Joseph bar Chama, **2**, 590.
See also Law, the, the teachers of.
Tanaites, the, list of:
Abba Saul,
Akiba ben Joseph,
Chalafta,
Tanaites, the, list of (*continued*):
Chananya (nephew of Joshua ben Chananya),
Chanina,
Chanina ben Teradion,
Dossa ben Nachman (Archinas),
Eleazar ben Arach,
Eleazar ben Azariah,
Eleazar ben Jacob,
Eleazar ben José (ben Chalafta),
Eleazar ben Shamua,
Eleazar ben Simon (ben Jochai),
Eleazar Chasma,
Eliezer of Modin,
Eliezer ben Hyrcanus,
Elisha ben Abuya,
Gamaliel I,
Gamaliel II,
Ilai,
Ishmael ben Elisha,
Ishmael ben José (ben Chalafta),
Jochanan of Alexandria (the sandal maker),
Jochanan ben Gudgada,
Jochanan ben Nuri,
Jochanan ben Zakkai,
Jonathan,
Jonathan ben Nachman (Archinas),
José the Galilean,
José ben Chalafta,
Joseph ben Kisma,
Joshua ben Chananya,
Joshua ben Karcha,
Josiah,
Judah ben Baba,
Judah ben Bathyra,
Judah ben Ilai,
Judah I ha-Nassi,
Matiah ben Charash,
Meïr,
Nachum of Gimso,
Nachum the Mede,
Nathan of Babylon,
Nechunya ben Hakana,
Nehemiah,
Pinchas ben Jaïr,
Samuel the Younger,
Simon (companion of Ishmael b. Elisha),
Simon II,
Simon III,
Simon ben Asai,
Simon ben Jochai,
Simon ben Nanos,
Simon ben Zoma,
Symmachos ben Joseph,
Tarphon of Lydda,
Zadok.

Tanchuma bar Abba, Amora, Agadist, **2,** 611-12.
Tangermünde, projected university at, **5,** 174.
Tangier, Jews taken prisoners at, by Alfonso V of Portugal, **4,** 286.
"**Tantalus** in the Lawsuit," comedy by Frederick the Great, **5,** 339.
Taphath, daughter of Solomon, **1,** 177.
Taphnai (Tachpanches), Judæans take refuge in, after Gedaliah's murder, **1,** 324.
Jeremiah summons the Egyptian Judæans to, **1,** 326-7.
Tapuach. *See* Tiphsah.
Tarazona, Jews of Navarre settle in, **4,** 142.
the cortes at, cancel the privileges of Aragon, **4,** 326.
the Marranos of, conspire against Pedro Arbues, **4,** 330.
Tarentum, the Jews of, in the twelfth century, **3,** 424.
Targum, the, declared not authoritative by Chayim Ibn-Musa, **4,** 237.
Targum Onkelos, the, Aramæan translation of Akylas' Greek version of the Scriptures, **2,** 387, 581-2.
Tarichæa. *See* Magdala.
Tarik, Mahometan conqueror of Visigothic Spain, aided by the Jews, **3,** 109.
Tarki. *See* Semender.
Tarnopol, beginnings of culture among the Jews of, **5,** 612.
school founded by Joseph Perl in, **5,** 612.
Tarphon, teacher of the Law, on Akiba, **2,** 353.
member of the Jamnia Synhedrion, **2,** 357.
Tarphon (*continued*), on the influence of the Minæans on Judaism, **2,** 378.
at Lydda, **2,** 423.
Tarragona, the city of the Jews, **3,** 42.
Tarshish, ships of, fitted out under Uzziah, **1,** 231.
Tarsus, birthplace of the apostle Paul, **2,** 223.
Tartars, the, in Armenia, converted to Judaism, **3,** 440.
devastate Jerusalem, **3,** 605-6.
kingdom of, in Persia, **3,** 637-8.
plundered by the Cossacks, **5,** 2.
allies of the Cossacks, **5,** 7.
Jews as captives of, **5,** 8.
defeat the Poles, **5,** 11.
Taska, land tax paid by the Babylonian Jews, **2,** 508.
Tavs. *See* Jacob Tus.
Taytasak, Joseph, Talmudist and Kabbalist, **4,** 405.
the circle of, and Solomon Molcho, **4,** 496.
letter to, from Molcho, **4,** 506.
Tax, the, levied on the daily sacrifice by Bagoas, **1,** 409-10.
on the Judæans levied by the Macedonians, **1,** 413.
levied by the Egypto-Macedonian dynasty on the Judæans, **1,** 418.
levied by Syria upon the Judæans removed by Demetrius II, **1,** 497.
levied on Jerusalem by Pompey, **2,** 67.
paid by Judæa to Rome, **2,** 87.
levied by Augustus in Judæa, **2,** 129-30.
Judæan, lightened by Tiberius, **2,** 135.
imposed by Albinus, **2,** 249.
Roman, not paid by Judæa, **2,** 258.

Tax, the (*continued*), paid by Judæans to the Capitoline Jupiter (fiscus Judaicus), **2**, 316.
levied on the Jews by Hadrian, **2**, 420.
imposed on Judæa under Judah I, **2**, 463.
paid by the Jews in the Sabbatical year under Caracalla, **2**, 469.
on land remitted by Gregory I in the case of converts, **3**, 33.
imposed upon Jews and Christians by Omar, **3**, 88.
levied by the Exilarchs, **3**, 96.
paid by the Jews of Spain to the Mahometan conquerors, **3**, 110.
imposed upon Jewish merchants by Charles the Bald, **3**, 172.
imposed upon the Jews by the Carlovingian and Saxon emperors, **3**, 243.
paid by the French and German Jews in the eleventh century, **3**, 281.
paid by the Jews to the emperors of Germany, **3**, 357.
levied on money transactions in northern France, **3**, 407.
imposed on the Jews of the Byzantine empire, **3**, 425.
imposed on Jews by the Fourth Lateran Council, **3**, 510.
exacted from the Jews by the Council of Oxford, **3**, 516.
upon the German Jews discussed by the synod of Mayence, **3**, 517.
imposed on Jews enforced by the Council of Narbonne, **3**, 518.

Tax, the (*continued*), levied on Jewish immigrants by Frederick II in Sicily, **3**, 569.
imposed on the Jews by the Council of Béziers, **3**, 582.
levied by Henry III upon the Jews of England, **3**, 589.
on the Jews of Castile regulated by Sancho, **3**, 617.
on the Jews of England decreed by the Statute of Judaism, **3**, 642.
imposed on the Jews by Emperor Louis IV, **4**, 96–7.
levied on the Jews of Burgos, **4**, 123, 124.
levied on the French Jews under John the Good, **4**, 130–1.
exacted from the Jews by Emperor Wenceslaus, **4**, 166.
imposed on Marranos in Algiers, **4**, 199.
imposed on the Spanish Jews for the war with Granada, **4**, 344.
imposed on the Jews of Bohemia, **4**, 545.
paid by the Jews of Amsterdam, **4**, 673.
levied on the Jews of Vienna, **5**, 170.
paid by the Jews of Brandenburg, **5**, 173.
paid by the Jews of Prussia, **5**, 191.
See Poll-tax, the; Taxes; Tithes.

Tax, the Patriarch's, levied from the time of Judah II, **2**, 486–7, 536.
forbidden by Honorius to be collected, **2**, 617.
collected by the imperial officials under Honorius, **2**, 622.

Tax-gatherers. *See* Taxes, the farmers of.

Taxes, paid by the Babylonian Jews, **2,** 508.
imposed upon the Jews under Constantius, **2,** 569, 572.
laid upon the Jews by Louis the Pious, **3,** 161.
imposed upon the German Jews burdensome, **3,** 517.
the payment of, discussed by the synod of Mayence, **3,** 517.
paid by the Jews of Poland, **4,** 632.
imposed on the Jews of Bohemia, **4,** 652, 702.
imposed on the Frankfort Jews, **4,** 700.
paid by the Jews of Metz and Alsace, **5,** 348.
discussed by the National Assembly, **5,** 446.
removed from the Jews of Metz, **5,** 446.
imposed on the Jews of Austria, **5,** 508.
See Poll-tax, the; Tax, the; Tithes.

Taxes, the farmers of (tax-gatherers, receivers-general), Jews act as, **1,** 425; **2,** 253; **4,** 80–1, 132, 138, 150, 156, 275, 618.

Taxes, the farming of, by Jews, forbidden by the Council of Mâcon, **3,** 39, 171.
in the Frankish empire, **3,** 161.
in Hungary, **3,** 521.
forbidden by the Council of Buda, **3,** 614.
objected to in Burgos, **4,** 125.
in Portugal, **4,** 160, 339.
in Poland, **5,** 3.

Teacher, title of the members of the Synhedrion in Babylonia, **3,** 96.

Teachers, the, of the Law. *See* Law, the, the teachers of.

Tebeth, the fast of, abolished by Sabbataï Zevi, **5,** 143.

Tekanoth Shum, decisions of Speyer, Worms, and Mayence, **4,** 135.

Tekanoth Usha, ordinances of the Synhedrion at Usha, **2,** 405.

Tekoah, the woman of, employed to plead for Absalom, **1,** 135–6.
home of Simon ben Jochai, **2,** 441.

Telesina, a Jew of, the friend of Pope Gelasius, **3,** 29.

Teller, consistorial councilor, approves of Mendelssohn's views on Church discipline, **5,** 363.
letter addressed to, by Jews, **5,** 421–2.

Templars. *See* Reform Temple Union, the, in Hamburg.

Temple, the first (Solomon's), the site of, **1,** 162.
materials for, **1,** 162–4.
internal decoration and arrangement of, **1,** 164–6.
transfer of the ark to, **1,** 166.
consecration of, **1,** 166–7.
service of, **1,** 167–8.
breaches of, repaired by Josiah, **1,** 218–19.
ransacked by Jehoash of Israel, **1,** 225.
the people of Israel permitted to make pilgrimages to, **1,** 232.
the ornaments of, removed, **1,** 274.
image of Mylitta in, **1,** 282.
decay of, under Josiah, **1,** 288–9.
idol-worship in, under Jehoiakim, **1,** 300.
Jeremiah's prophecies read in, **1,** 304.

Temple, the first (Solomon's) (*continued*), the treasures of, taken by Nebuchadnezzar, **1**, 307.
burnt by Nebuzaradan, **1**, 315.
the treasures of, taken to Babylon, **1**, 315.
the slaves of, live together in Babylon, **1**, 330.
the vessels of, restored by Cyrus, **1**, 351.
Temple, the second, beginnings of, under Zerubbabel, **1**, 356–7.
difficulties in the way of building, **1**, 359.
consecration of, **1**, 359.
spared by the Samaritans, **1**, 372.
the service of, neglected during Nehemiah's absence, **1**, 383–4.
the service of, restored by Nehemiah, **1**, 386.
the form of prayer used in, **1**, 399.
Joshua slain by his brother in, **1**, 409.
renovated by Simon the Just, **1**, 421.
Hyrcanus stores his wealth in, **1**, 437–8.
despoiled by Menelaus and Lysimachus, **1**, 448, 449.
desecrated by Antiochus Epiphanes, **1**, 451.
abandoned, **1**, 454.
the statue of Jupiter placed in, **1**, 455.
re-consecrated by Judas Maccabæus, **1**, 472.
fortified by Judas Maccabæus, **1**, 473.
attacked by the Hellenists, **1**, 478.
besieged by Lysias, **1**, 479.
the fortifications of, razed by Lysias, **1**, 480.
Temple, the second (*continued*), occupied by Alcimus, **1**, 487.
the sacrifices in, maintained by the half-Shekel contributions, **2**, 52.
taken by Aristobulus II, **2**, 58.
a tower of, falls on Pompey's attack, **2**, 66.
entered by Pompey, **2**, 66.
votive offerings of, taken by Flaccus, **2**, 68.
robbed by Crassus, **2**, 74.
ravaged by Sosius, **2**, 88.
remodeled by Herod, **2**, 109–11.
courts of, **2**, 110.
gates of, **2**, 111.
dedication of, **2**, 111.
placed under the protection of Rome, **2**, 111.
besieged by the Romans, at the instigation of Sabinus, **2**, 123–4.
the treasures of, taken by the Romans, **2**, 124.
polluted by the Samaritans, **2**, 135.
offerings sent to, by Roman proselytes, **2**, 136.
the treasures of, used for an aqueduct, **2**, 139–40.
Jesus in, **2**, 161.
Vitellus sacrifices in, **2**, 173.
Caligula orders, to be desecrated, **2**, 188.
the bringing of first fruits to, in the time of Agrippa I, **2**, 194.
the center of the dispersed Judæans, **2**, 201.
portal presented to, by Helen of Adiabene, **2**, 218.
golden vessels given to, by Monobaz II, **2**, 219.
despoiled by the high priests, **2**, 237.
Cumanus places a cohort in, **2**, 242.

Temple, the second (*continued*), watched by Agrippa II, **2,** 247–8.
the treasures of, demanded by Gessius Florus, **2,** 253.
attacked by Gessius Florus, **2,** 255.
occupied by the Zealot chief Eleazar ben Ananias, **2,** 259.
barred against the Peace party, **2,** 260.
besieged by Anan, **2,** 295.
the western colonnade of, destroyed, **2,** 305.
siege of, begun by Titus, **2,** 306–7.
fire-brand thrown into, **2,** 307.
burnt to the ground, **2,** 308.
the vessels of, in Titus' triumph, **2,** 314.
the vessels of, deposited in the Temple of Peace, **2,** 315.
contribution to, changed into the fiscus Judaicus, **2,** 316.
the restoration of, attempted under Hadrian, **2,** 401–3, 411.
the vessels of, seen in Rome by Eleazar ben Joseph, **2,** 449.
preparations for rebuilding, by Julian the Apostate, **2,** 597, 598, 599.
the rebuilding of, superintended by Alypius, **2,** 599.
Jews not interested in the rebuilding of, **2,** 599–600.
obstacles to the rebuilding of, **2,** 600.
the vessels of, in the possession of the Vandals, **2,** 611.
the vessels of, taken from Carthage to Constantinople, **3,** 26–7.
the vessels of, removed to Jerusalem, **3,** 27.
in the Kabbala, **3,** 553.
the model of, made by Jacob Jehuda Leon, **5,** 114–15.

Temple, the, of Onias, in Heliopolis, built by Onias IV, **1,** 508.
appearance and furnishings of, **1,** 508.
as regarded by Judæans in Egypt and Judæa, **1,** 509–10.
fortified, **1,** 510.
closed by Vespasian, **2,** 318.

Temple, the, of Peace, the spoils from the Jerusalem Temple deposited in, **2,** 315.

Temple, the, on Gerizim, built by the Samaritans, **1,** 390.
destroyed by John Hyrcanus, **2,** 8.

Templo. *See* Leon, Jacob Jehuda.

Ten Categories, the, of the Aristotelian philosophy, compared with the Ten Commandments, **3,** 197.

Ten Commandments, the, part of the morning service in the Sopheric age, **1,** 399.
commentary on, by Saadiah, **3,** 197.

Ten Tribes, the, the dispersion of, **1,** 265.
a part of, join the Judæans in Babylonia, **1,** 335–6.
the Samaritans declare themselves a remnant of, **1,** 390–1.
supposed to be in Chazaria, **3,** 141.
the descendants of, around Nishabur, **3,** 433.
in Chaibar, **3,** 437.
theory of, held by Manasseh ben Israel, **5,** 30–3.
Simone Luzzatto on, **5,** 81.

Ten Tribes, the, kingdom of, *See* Israel, the kingdom of.

Tenes, a refuge for persecuted Spanish Jews, **4,** 197.

Tenth Legion, the, defeated by the Judæans, **2,** 303.

Tephillah, the principal prayer in the morning service of the Sopheric age, **1,** 399. *See* Liturgy, the.

Tephillin. *See* Phylacteries.

Teraphim, the, the Israelites believe in, **1,** 75.

Tertullian, Church Father, prohibits intercourse between heathens and Christians, **2,** 476–7.

Teruel, opposition to the Inquisition in, **4,** 328.

"Teshuboth," by Dunash ben Labrat against Saadiah, **3,** 226.

Tetragrammaton, the, pronounced by Sabbataï Zevi, **5,** 122.

Tetrarch, title of the governors of Judæa, **2,** 81.

See also Herod I; Herod Antipas; Phasael; Philip.

Teutomania, retards the emancipation of the Jews, **5,** 516.

Texeira, a family of Marranos in Holland, **4,** 690.

Texeira, Diego, de Mattos, banker in Hamburg, **4,** 690–1; **5,** 140.

Texeira, Manoel (Isaac Señor, 1630–1695), diplomat in Hamburg, Sabbatian, **5,** 140.

intercedes for the Jews of Vienna, **5,** 171.

Texeiras, the, millionaires in Hamburg, **5,** 205.

Texel, Polish Jewish fugitives in, **5,** 16.

Thabit, a friend of the Benu-Karaiza, **3,** 81.

Thafar. *See* Zafara.

Thapsacus (Tiphsah), frontier town of Israel under David, **1,** 129.

Theatre, the, in the time of the Amoraim, **2,** 542.

Thebes, Zealots flee to, after the destruction of Jerusalem, **2,** 318.

Thebes, the Jews of, occupations of, **3,** 425.

fine Talmudists, **4,** 406.

Themudo, George, inquires into the life of the Portuguese Marranos, **4,** 489.

Theobald, count of Chartres, imprisons the Jews of Blois on the blood accusation, **3,** 379.

offers to release them for a sum of money, **3,** 379.

has them burnt at the stake, **3,** 380.

Theodatus, Ostrogoth, supported by the Jews, **3,** 31–2.

Theodebert, of Austrasia, permits Jews to own slaves, **3,** 34.

Theodora, wife of Justinian I, and her Samaritan favorite, **3,** 17.

Theodoric, of Burgundy, permits Jews to own slaves, **3,** 34.

Jews in the army of, **3,** 36.

Theodoric, founder of the Ostrogothic empire, **3,** 27.

hostile to the Jews, **3,** 29–30.

protects Jewish slave-owners, **3,** 30–1.

successors of, **3,** 31.

Theodosia. *See* Kaffa.

Theodosia, the straits of, the Jews of the Byzantine empire settle on, **3,** 123.

Theodosius I (the Great, 379–395), emperor, protects the Jews and the Patriarchs from the bishops, **2,** 612–13.

orders the rebuilding of a synagogue at Callinicus, **2,** 614.

enacts laws for and against the Jews, **2,** 615.

Theodosius I (*continued*), division of the Roman empire under, **2,** 615.
the laws of, govern the Jews of Italy, **3,** 28–9.
Theodosius II, emperor of the East, forbids the building of synagogues, **2,** 617.
bestows distinctions on Gamaliel V, **2,** 617–18.
orders the Spanish Jews to cease mockery of Christianity, **2,** 620.
rebuked by Simon Stylites, **2,** 621–2.
anti-Jewish laws of, enforced by Justin I, **3,** 10.
expels the Jews from their quarter in Constantinople, **3,** 26.
anti-Jewish decree of, revived, **3,** 171.
Theodosius, Samaritan champion in the dispute with the Egyptian Judæans, **1,** 517.
Theodotion, translation of the Scriptures by, used by Origen, **2,** 489.
Theodotus, Egypto-Samaritan poet, extols Shechem, **1,** 517.
Theodotus, envoy of Nicanor to Judas Maccabæus, **1,** 484.
Theodus, introduces a substitute for the Paschal lamb, **2,** 68.
"Theologico-Political Treatise, The," by Spinoza, an apology for freedom of thought, **5,** 95.
on the source of law, **5,** 96.
on the state, **5,** 96–7.
on freedom of thought, **5,** 97.
displays hatred of Jews and Judaism, **5,** 97–8, 100–3.
on God, **5,** 98–9.
on man, **5,** 99–100.
on knowledge, **5,** 100–1.
"Theologico-Political Treatise, The" (*continued*), on Christianity, **5,** 102–3.
on the Jewish state, **5,** 103–7.
published anonymously, **5,** 108.
produces a stir, **5,** 108.
Theology, Jewish, first developed by Hillel, **2,** 327.
"Theorica," astronomical work translated by Moses Isserles, **4,** 638.
Theosophy, in the Kabbala, **3,** 550.
Thessalonica, Judæans in, **2,** 203.
Paul establishes a Greek-Christian community in, **2,** 228.
See Salonica.
Thessaly, the Jews of, in the twelfth century, **3,** 424.
Theudas, a false Messiah, end of, **2,** 198.
Thibaut, of Champagne, agrees to surrender Jews from the Isle de France to Philip Augustus, **3,** 406.
Thibaut, professor, protects the Jews of Heidelberg, **5,** 531.
Thibet, under the jurisdiction of the Exilarch, **3,** 429.
Thiers, struggle of, with Louis Philippe, **5,** 648.
espouses the side of Ratti Menton, **5,** 648–9, 650, 658.
questioned by Fould on the Damascus affair, **5,** 649.
opposes the Jewish envoys in Egypt, **5,** 659.
Thiery, competes for the Metz prize on the Jewish question, **5,** 434.
Thirty Years' War, the, effect of, on the Jews, **4,** 701–2, 707.
Jewish victims of, seek refuge in Poland, **5,** 2.
awakens Messianic hopes, **5,** 23.

Tholuck, exegete, **5**, 695.
Thomas à Becket, rouses fanaticism, **3**, 409–10.
Thomas Aquinas. *See* Aquinas, Thomas.
Thomists, the, opposed to Reuchlin, **4**, 456.
satirized in the "Letters of Obscurantists," **4**, 461.
Thompson, chairman of the Mansion House meeting, on the Damascus affair, **5**, 656.
Thonon, the Jews of, suspected of well poisoning, **4**, 104.
Thrace, the Jews of, in the twelfth century, **3**, 424.
"**Three Communities**, The," Altona, Hamburg, Wandsbeck, **5**, 238.
Eibeschütz rabbi of, **5**, 254, 256.
espouse the cause of Eibeschütz, **5**, 260.
Throne Chamber, the, in the House of the Forest of Lebanon, **1**, 168–9.
Thuringia, adopts the Jewish statute of Frederick the Valiant, **3**, 569.
Thuringia, the Jews of, perish during the Black Death persecutions, **4**, 109.
assaulted by the imperial army against the Hussites, **4**, 225.
Tibbon. *See* Jacob ben Machir Tibbon; Judah ben Moses; Judah ben Saul; Samuel ben Judah Ibn-Tibbon.
Tibbon family, the, instructors in medicine, **3**, 582.
Tibbonide party, the, in favor of the study of science, **4**, 32, 34.
appeals to Solomon ben Adret, **4**, 33.
obtains the ascendancy in Montpellier, **4**, 39.
Tibbonide party, the (*continued*), issues a counter-ban against the opponents of science, **4**, 40–2.
appeals to the secular authorities in Montpellier, **4**, 41.
defends Maimonides, **4**, 42.
emigrates to Perpignan, **4**, 50.
Tiberias, built by Herod Antipas, capital of his tetrarchy, **2**, 137.
pious Judæans refuse to live in, **2**, 137–8.
conference at, called by Agrippa I, **2**, 195–6.
given to Agrippa II by Nero, **2**, 246.
a focus of insurrection in Galilee, **2**, 272.
population of, Zealots, **2**, 273–4.
partisans of Rome in, **2**, 274.
jealous of Sepphoris, **2**, 276.
men of, meet with Josephus at Bethmaon, **2**, 279.
ordered by the Synhedrion not to protect Josephus, **2**, 281.
rebellion in, fomented by Josephus, **2**, 283.
seat of Agrippa II's Jewish governors of Galilee, **2**, 333.
declared clean by Simon ben Jochai, **2**, 448–9.
the seat of the Patriarch, **2**, 480.
the new-moon announced in, **2**, 480.
meeting place of disciples, **2**, 493–4.
sinks into insignificance, **2**, 560.
the first church at, built by Joseph, the apostate, **2**, 565.
partially destroyed, **2**, 570.
the birthplace of the Jerusalem Talmud, **2**, 612.
the text of the Bible studied at, **2**, 623.

Tiberias (*continued*), seat of authority for the Jews in the sixth century, **3**, 12.
seat of a bishopric, **3**, 12.
Abraham Ibn-Ezra in, **3**, 369.
burial place of Maimonides, **3**, 493.
rebuilt by Joseph Nassi, **4**, 610–11.
grave of Luzzatto at, **5**, 244.
Tiberias, the Jews of, flee to escape taxation, **2**, 463.
join Sharbarza, **3**, 19.
join an expedition against the Christians of Tyre, **3**, 20.
driven out by Omar, **3**, 87.
in the twelfth century, **3**, 427.
Tiberias, the school of, **2**, 148.
loses prestige, **2**, 532, 537.
end of, under Constantius, **2**, 567.
gives religious instruction to the Arabian Jews, **3**, 59.
Tiberias, lake, description of, **1**, 42.
district about, subjugated by Ben-hadad I, **1**, 191.
tract near, given to Joseph Nassi, **4**, 596, 610.
Tiberinus, Matthias, physician, testifies to Simon of Trent's violent death, **4**, 298.
Tiberius, emperor, lightens the taxes of Judæa, **2**, 135.
antipathy of, towards Judæans, **2**, 135–6.
instrumental in banishing Judæans from Rome, **2**, 136–7.
friendly to Judæans, **2**, 172–3.
helps Herod Antipas against the Nabathæans, **2**, 173.
death of, **3**, 174.
kindness of, to Agrippa I, **2**, 176.
imprisons Agrippa I, **2**, 176.
Tiberius, emperor of the East, the Jews under, **3**, 18.
Tiberius Julius Alexander, son of the Alabarch Alexander Lysimachus, renegade from Judaism, **2**, 184, 235.
procurator of Judæa, **2**, 198.
unpopularity of, **2**, 198–9.
governor of Egypt, **2**, 199.
orders a massacre of Judæans, **2**, 263–4.
won over to Vespasian's side, **2**, 300.
aids Titus in the siege of Jerusalem, **2**, 302.
Tibni, king of Israel, chosen by the opponents of Omri, **1**, 192.
Ticini, Bernardinus of Feltre preaches against the Jews in, **4**, 296.
Tiflis, a Karaite center, **3**, 158.
Tiflisites, a Karaite sect, **3**, 158.
Tiglath-Pileser, king of Assyria, designs of, on Palestine, **1**, 258–9.
captures Damascus, **1**, 259.
invades the kingdom of Israel, **1**, 259–60.
Tigranes, king of Armenia, threatens to invade Judæa, **2**, 55–6.
attacked by Lucullus, **2**, 56.
Tigranes, son of Alexander and Glaphyra, king of Armenia, **2**, 128.
Tigris, the district of, the Jews of, in the twelfth century, **3**, 428–33.
Tikkunim, Sabbatian prayer books, **5**, 139.
Tilly, general, plunders the Jews, **4**, 701.
Timnath-Serah, seat of Joshua **1**, 41.
Timotheus, Ammonite leader, defeated by Judas Maccabæus, **1**, 474.

Timotheus, Ammonite leader (*continued*), attacks the trans-Jordanic provinces, **1**, 475, 476.
Tiphsah (Tapuach), refuses to admit Menahem, the murderer of Shallum, **1**, 244.
Tirado, Jacob, leader of the Portuguese Marranos emigrating to the Netherlands, **4**, 664, 665.
saves the Marranos of Amsterdam, **4**, 666.
builds the first synagogue in Amsterdam, **4**, 667.
Tirhakah, king of Egypt, at war with Sennacherib, **1**, 276.
Tirzah, capital of the kingdom of Israel under Jeroboam, **1**, 189.
under Baasha, **1**, 190.
revolution in, **1**, 191.
abandoned as the capital of Israel, **1**, 192–3.
Tithes, collected under Ezra and Nehemiah, **1**, 382.
the laws of, moderated by Judah I, **2**, 458–9.
Tithes, exacted from Jews, by Innocent III, **3**, 499.
by the Fourth Lateran Council, **3**, 510.
by the Council of Oxford, **3**, 516.
Titus, brings Vespasian two legions from Alexandria, **2**, 285.
captivated by Berenice, **2**, 285.
kindly disposed to Josephus, **2**, 288.
takes Gischala, **2**, 290.
goes to Rome to do homage to Galba, **2**, 299.
urges his father to proclaim himself emperor, **2**, 299.
wins Licinius Mucianus to his father's side, **2**, 300.
in Egypt, **2**, 300.
Titus (*continued*), prepares to besiege Jerusalem, **2**, 301–2.
three Judæan traitors help, **2**, 302.
summons Jerusalem to surrender, **2**, 302.
begins the siege, **2**, 303.
cruelty of, to Judæan prisoners, **2**, 304.
again summons the besieged to surrender, **2**, 305.
hesitates to destroy the Temple, **2**, 307.
enters the Holy of Holies, **2**, 308.
saluted as emperor, **2**, 308.
besieges the upper city, **2**, 309.
treatment of Judæans by, **2**, 312–13.
celebrates his triumph over Judæa, **2**, 313–15.
arch of, **2**, 314.
rewards Josephus, **2**, 317.
protects Josephus from calumny, **2**, 318.
permits the establishment of a school at Jamnia, **2**, 324.
kindly treatment of the Jews by, after the fall of Jerusalem, **2**, 331.
and Berenice, **2**, 332–3.
abandons Berenice and Agrippa II, **2**, 388.
said to have settled Jews in Spain, **3**, 43.
Titus Aurelius Antoninus Pius. *See* Antoninus Pius.
Tlemçen, a refuge for persecuted Spanish Jews, **4**, 197.
the Spanish exiles in, **4**, 390.
"To my Co-religionists in Hamburg," by Lazarus Riesser, **5**, 570–1.
"To the Confusion of the Jews," polemic work by Samuel Ibn-Abbas, **3**, 442.

"**To the Friends of Lessing**," by Jacobi, **5**, 372.
Tobba, name of the Himyarite kings, **3**, 62.
Tobiades, the, partisans of Antiochus the Great, **1**, 432.
opposed to Onias III, **1**, 437.
banished by Onias III, **1**, 438.
Tobiah, Ammonite leader, marries a Judæan, **1**, 362.
son of, marries a Judæan, **1**, 362.
hostility of, to the Judæans, **1**, 369–70.
vexed at Nehemiah's appointment, **1**, 374.
disturbs Nehemiah's work, **1**, 375.
intrigues against Nehemiah, **1**, 376.
a Temple court assigned to, **1**, 383.
expelled from the Temple, **1**, 385.
Tobiah, son-in-law of Simon the Just, son of, **1**, 423–5.
Tobias, Jewish physician in Trent, on friendly terms with Christians, **4**, 297.
Tobiene, the Judæans in, slaughtered, **1**, 475.
Tobit, the **Book** of, composed under Hadrian, **2**, 430.
admitted into the canon by the Christians, **2**, 488.
Toble Shacharith, **2**, 26. *See* Essenes, the.
Toda, queen of Navarre, concludes a treaty with Abdul-Rahman III, **3**, 216.
Todros of Beaucaire, ally of Abba-Mari, **4**, 31.
Todros ben Joseph Halevi Abulafia (1234–1304), Kabbalist, **4**, 1, 2–3.
prominent at the court of Sancho IV, **4**, 2, 52.
Todros ben Joseph Halevi Abulafia (*continued*), opponent of philosophy, **4**, 2.
Kabbalistic work dedicated to, **4**, 3.
Tôi, king of Hamath, congratulates David on his Ammonite victory, **1**, 127.
Tokat, the Spanish exiles in, **4**, 405.
the Jews of, accused of murder, **4**, 553.
Toland, John, favors the emancipation of the Jews in England, **5**, 197–8.
"**Toldoth Jesho**," a Hebrew parody of the gospels, **5**, 185–6.
Toledano, Daniel, adviser of Muley Ismail, **5**, 168.
Toledo, early settlement of Jews in the environs of, **3**, 43.
played into the hands of Tarik by the Jews, **3**, 109.
Cordova Jews emigrate to, **3**, 255.
the Mahometan court of, cultured, **3**, 291.
taken by Alfonso VI of Castile, **3**, 294.
made Alfonso VI's capital, **3**, 295.
Jehuda Halevi in, **3**, 324.
college at, presided over by Jehuda Halevi, **3**, 338.
Jews of Lucena emigrate to, **3**, 361.
center of Jewish science in the twelfth century, **3**, 361, 362.
scene of a civil war, **3**, 363.
synagogue in, erected by Joseph Ibn-Shoshan, **3**, 384.
study of the Talmud at, **3**, 386.
the center of the supposed well poisoners, **4**, 101.

Toledo (*continued*), synagogue built in, by Samuel Abulafia, **4,** 119–20.
lost by Pedro, **4,** 124.
cortes of, disapprove of the Inquisition, **4,** 313.
tribunals of the Inquisition in, **4,** 325.
cortes of, enforce Jew quarters, **4,** 335.
rabbis of, ordered to inform against Judaizing Marranos, **4,** 335.
refuge of the Abrabanels, **4,** 341.
synagogue of, turned into a church, **4,** 354.
exiles from, form a congregation in Constantinople, **4,** 402.

Toledo, the Council of (589), passes anti-Jewish decrees, **3,** 46.
(633), decrees of, against backsliding converts, **3,** 49–50, 51.
(the eighth) confirms the anti-Jewish laws of the fourth Council, **3,** 102.
cited by the Fourth Lateran Council, **3,** 511.

Toledo, the Jews of, give a written assurance of their acceptance of Christianity, **3,** 103–4.
well treated by Alfonso VI, **3,** 295.
prosperity and culture of, in the twelfth century, **3,** 384.
assist Alfonso VIII against the Almohades, **3,** 386–7.
attacked by foreign crusaders, **3,** 507.
try to prevent the enforcement of Jew badges, **3,** 513.
in the Maimunist controversy, **3,** 537–8, 540–1.
under Sancho, **3,** 617.

Toledo, the Jews of (*continued*), supposed to be opposed to the study of science, **4,** 38.
ravages of the Black Death among, **4,** 113.
suffer during the civil war between Pedro and Henry II, **4,** 118–19, 124, 126, 136–7.
efforts to reorganize, **4,** 140.
decadence of, **4,** 140, 142.
persecuted in 1391, **4,** 169–70.

Toletum. *See* Toledo.

Tomaso, Father, in Damascus, disappearance of, **5,** 634–5.
Jews suspected to be the murderers of, **5,** 635.
reward for the murderer of, **5,** 652.
inscription on the tomb of, **5,** 668.

Tongern, Arnold of, Dominican professor of theology, **4,** 424.
tool of Hoogstraten, **4,** 450.
satirized in the "Letters of Obscurantists," **4,** 461.

Torah, the. *See* Law, the; Pentateuch, the.

Toro, fortress of, Pedro decoyed into, **4,** 118.
the cortes of, petition that restrictions be laid on the Jews, **4,** 138–9.
the Jews of, accept baptism, **4,** 205.

Toron de los Caballeros, the Jews of, in the twelfth century, **3,** 427.

Torquemada, Thomas de, confessor of Isabella of Castile, **4,** 310.
refutes the work of a Marrano, **4,** 312.
appointed inquisitor, **4,** 319.
appointed inquisitor-general of Spain, **4,** 324.

Torquemada, Thomas de (*continued*), appoints Inquisition tribunals in different parts of Spain, **4**, 324.
appoints inquisitors for Aragon, **4**, 326.
publishes the "Constitutions" for inquisitors, **4**, 326–7.
has two Marrano bishops burned, **4**, 333.
bids the rabbis of Toledo inform against Judaizing Marranos, **4**, 335–6.
condemns Jews to the stake on the blood accusation, **4**, 343.
urges the expulsion of the Jews, **4**, 346, 348.
forbids intercourse between Christians and the exiled Jews, **4**, 350.
tries to convert the Jews, **4**, 350.
complains of the Marranos, **4**, 355.
victims delivered to the Inquisition by, **4**, 356.
in fear of assassination, **4**, 356.
Torre de Montcorvo, Jewish center in Portugal, **4**, 159.
Tortosa, traces of early Jewish settlements near, **3**, 42–3.
birthplace of Menachem ben Saruk, **3**, 225.
the Jews of, converted, **4**, 206.
Tortosa, the religious disputation at, **4**, 207–15.
Jewish delegates to, not firm, **4**, 208, 210.
Jewish delegates to, unfairly treated, **4**, 212.
Vincent Ferrer's converts brought to, **4**, 215.
Tossafists, the, disciples of Rashi, **3**, 344, 345.
acumen of, **3**, 344–5.
Tossafists, the (*continued*), divide the study of the Talmud into two branches, **3**, 345.
as Bible exegetes, **3**, 345.
in Champagne, **3**, 403–4.
in England, **3**, 409.
in Germany, **3**, 419.
leniency of, **3**, 470.
methods of, transplanted to the East, **3**, 506.
of northern France, anti-Maimunists, **3**, 529.
activity of, during Louis IX's persecutions, **3**, 586–7.
compilers in the thirteenth century, **3**, 587.
See in the list of Talmudists.
Tossafoth, supplements to Rashi's commentary on the Talmud, **3**, 344.
on the Pentateuch, **3**, 345.
"the Old," collected by Isaac ben Samuel, **3**, 404.
"Sens," compiled by Samson ben Abraham, **3**, 408.
new collection of, by Samuel ben Solomon Sir Morel, **3**, 586.
Tossafoth Yom-Tob, commentary on the Mishna, by Lipmann Heller, **4**, 704.
Tou. *See* Tôi.
"**Touchstone, The**," satire by Kalonymos ben Kalonymos, **4**, 63.
Toulouse, Jews remain in, after the banishment by Charles VI, **4**, 176.
the Talmud burnt at, **4**, 55.
Toulouse, the Jews of, attacked at Easter, **3**, 174.
persecuted by Alice of Montmorency, **3**, 514.
protected by Simon de Montfort, **3**, 514.

Toulouse, the Jews of (*continued*), not forced to wear the Jew badge, **3,** 514.
converted under Philip IV, **4,** 48.
during the Pastoureaux massacre, **4,** 56.
Touraine, the Jews of, under Henry II, **3,** 409.
Tours, the Council of, re-enacts the anti-Jewish decrees of the Fourth Lateran Council, **3,** 520.
Elias Montalto dies at, **4,** 673.
Tovey, on the treatment of Jews under Edward I, **3,** 642.
"Tower of Strength, The," Sabbataï Zevi's prison at Abydos, **5,** 148.
Trachonites, the, conquered and converted by Aristobulus I, **2,** 37.
Trachonitis, given to Philip, son of Cleopatra, by Herod's will **2,** 119.
under Philip, **2,** 137.
given to Agrippa II as a royal province, **2,** 245.
cavalry from, assists the Peace party, **2,** 259, 260.
Trade. *See* Commerce.
Trades, among the Jews of the Frankish and Burgundian kingdoms, **3,** 35.
pursued by the German and French Jews in the eleventh century, **3,** 281.
pursued by the Jews of Poland, **4,** 419.
forbidden to the Jews of Alsace, **5,** 348.
opened to the Jews of Austria, **5,** 357.
See also Artisans; Handicrafts.
Tradition, rejected by the Sadducees, **2,** 22.
Tradition (*continued*), among the Karaites, **3,** 159.
See also Halacha; Law, the oral; Mishna, the; Talmud, the; Rabbinical Judaism; Talmudical Judaism.
Trajan, emperor, hostility of, to the Jews, **2,** 350.
conquest of Parthia by, **2,** 393.
opposed by the Jews, **2,** 393–7.
conquers Adiabene, **2,** 393–4.
fails to make Parthia a Roman province, **2,** 399.
death of, **2,** 399.
Trani, the Jews of ransom Sabbataï Donnolo, **3,** 213.
in the twelfth century, **3,** 424.
Translation of the Pentateuch, into Chaldaic, **2,** 581–2.
into Syriac, **2,** 582.
into Persian, **4,** 401.
by Mendelssohn, **5,** 328–35.
Translation of the Scriptures, into Arabic by Saadiah, **3,** 189–90.
into German by Luther, **4,** 469, 475.
into the European languages, **4,** 475.
into Spanish by Abraham Usque, **4,** 475.
during the Reformation, **4,** 540.
into Polish by Simon Budny, **4,** 647.
by Sachs, **5,** 693.
See also Akylas; Septuagint, the; Vulgate, the.
Translations of the Scriptures, various, **2,** 489, 581–2.
ordered to be read in Jewish congregations, **3,** 14–15.
not authoritative, **4,** 237.
Transmigration of souls (Metempsychosis), the, the doctrine of, adopted by Isaac the Blind, **3,** 547–8.

Transmigration of souls (Metempsychosis), the, the doctrine of (*continued*), in the Kabbala, **3,** 554.
as explained by Isaac Lurya, **4,** 620.
Leo Modena on, **5,** 67.
Transubstantiation, the dogma of, expounded by Astruc Raimuch, **4,** 182.
refuted by Solomon Bonfed, **4,** 182.
attacked by Chasdaï Crescas, **4,** 188.
Travelers, Jewish, list of:
Abraham de Beya,
Benjamin ben Jonah of Tudela,
Joseph Zapateiro de Lamego,
Petachya of Ratisbon.
" **Treatise** on the Immortality of the Soul, A," by Samuel da Silva, **5,** 59.
" **Treatise** on the Position of the Hebrews, A," by Simone Luzzatto, **5,** 81-4.
" **Treatises** of the Righteous Brethren," adapted by Kalonymos ben Kalonymos, **4,** 62.
" **Tree of Life,** The," by Aaron (II) ben Elia Nicomedi, **4,** 95.
Trent, the Council of, to deal with the Protestants, **4,** 525.
Paul III abused at, **4,** 525-6.
the Marranos' right of emigration defended at, **4,** 526.
deals with the Talmud, **4,** 589.
Trent, the Jews of, Bernardinus of Feltre preaches against, **4,** 297.
charged with the blood accusation, **4,** 297-9.
burnt, **4,** 298.
Treves, Israel, disciple of Moses Chayim Luzzatto, **5,** 237.
Treves, pilgrimage to the holy coat of, **5,** 682.
Treves, the Jews of, kill their children in the first crusade, **3,** 300.
baptized, **3,** 300.
Tria, the Spanish exiles in, **4,** 405.
" **Trial of the World,** The," by Yedaya Bedaresi, **4,** 49.
Triana, castle in, the first house occupied by the Inquisition, **4,** 314.
Tribal government, under David, **1,** 122.
Trier, Solomon, invites opinions on the obligation of circumcision, **5,** 677.
Trieste, the rabbi of, opposes the Reform movement, **5,** 571.
honor shown to Crémieux at, **5,** 668.
Trieste, the Jews of, address Mendelssohn in behalf of their normal school, **5,** 369.
letter addressed to, by Wessely, **5,** 370-1.
Trietsch, the rabbi of, opposes the Reform movement, **5,** 571.
Trigland, Jacob, inquires into Karaism, **5,** 183-4.
Trimberg, castle in which Süsskind sang his poems, **3,** 420.
Trinity, the, the doctrine of, introduced into Christianity, **2,** 500-1.
derived from the Old Testament, **2,** 501.
attacked by Simlaï, **2,** 501-2.
supposed protests against, in Jewish literature, **3,** 15.
discussed by the French Jews in the twelfth century, **3,** 343.
refuted by Nachmani, **3,** 601.
in the Zohar, **4,** 23.
refuted by Moses Cohen de Tordesillas, **4,** 141.

Trinity, the, the doctrine of (*continued*), expounded by Astruc Raimuch, **4**, 182.
refuted by Solomon Bonfed, **4**, 182.
attacked by Chasdaï Crescas, **4**, 187.
found in the Kabbala by Pico di Mirandola, **4**, 292.
inculcated by Nehemiah Chayon, **5**, 216–17, 220.
in the Frankist confession of faith, **5**, 280, 281, 285, 287.
belief in, threatened, **5**, 682.
Tripoli, Spanish exiles in, **4**, 389.
Triumvirate, the first, divides the Roman possessions, **2**, 73–4.
Triumvirate, the second, formation of, **2**, 81.
purpose of, **2**, 143.
Trok (Troki), Karaite center, **4**, 265; **5**, 182.
Troyes, the birthplace of Rashi, **3**, 286.
Rashi the rabbi of, **3**, 287.
rabbinical synods meet at, **3**, 377, 378.
college of, sold, **4**, 48.
the Jews of, compelled to violate the Sabbath, **5**, 451.
"True Shepherd, The," translated by Isabel Correa, **5**, 114.
Tryphon. *See* Diodotus Tryphon.
Tryphon, Judæan envoy to Claudius, **2**, 197–8.
Tsiruf, Kabbalistic term, **4**, 5.
Tuch, exegete, **5**, 695.
Tucker, Josiah, favors the naturalization of the Jews in England, **5**, 338.
Tudela, protects Marranos concerned in the murder of Arbues, **4**, 357.
Tudela, the Jews of, enjoy equality with Christians and Mahometans, **3**, 388.
attacked at the instigation of Pedro Olligoyen, **4**, 78.
baptized, **4**, 358.
Tugaï Bey, Tartar chieftain, defeats the Polish troops, **5**, 11.
Tugendbund, the, founded by Berlin Jewesses, **5**, 423, 425.
Tulczyn, the Jews of, betrayed by the Poles to the Cossacks, **5**, 9–10.
Tunis, Louis IX dies at, **3**, 612.
forced converts emigrate to, **4**, 179.
Spanish exiles in, **4**, 391–2.
Turbo, Martius, Trajan's general, in Egypt, **2**, 397–8.
cruelty of, **2**, 398.
Ture Zahab. *See* Levi, David.
Turim (Tur), religious code compiled by Jacob ben Asheri, **4**, 88.
based on Maimonides' code, **4**, 88.
treats of religious practice, **4**, 88.
compared with Maimonides' code, **4**, 89.
Kabbalistic elements in, **4**, 89.
reception of, **4**, 89–90.
Turkey, the beginnings of, **4**, 267.
hospitable to Jews, **4**, 268.
the Karaites in, **4**, 269–71.
tolerance of, in the fifteenth century, **4**, 285.
Spanish exiles go to, **4**, 358.
treatment of the Spanish exiles in, **4**, 364.
the chief refuge of the Spanish exiles, **4**, 383, 400.
the Spanish exiles in, **4**, 400–5.
the Jewish fugitives in, dispose themselves in national groups, **4**, 478.

Turkey (*continued*), the Kabbala in, **4**, 481.
Portuguese Marranos emigrate to, **4**, 485.
Solomon Molcho in, **4**, 496.
Messianic enthusiasm in, **4**, 497.
Marranos in, **4**, 529.
refuge of the Neapolitan and Bohemian Jews, **4**, 544.
refuge of the exiles from the Papal States, **4**, 592.
war of, with Venice, enriches Smyrna, **5**, 119.
refuge of the Ancona Marranos, **4**, 570.
victorious over Ferdinand I, **4**, 597.
victorious over Venice, **4**, 601.
peace of, with Venice, **4**, 605–6.
supported by Russia, **5**, 634.
Turkey, the Jews of, happy condition of, **4**, 271–3.
granted liberties, **4**, 400.
occupations of, **4**, 401.
linguists, **4**, 402.
molested by the Greek Catholics, **4**, 552–3.
trade with Pesaro instead of Ancona, **4**, 578–9.
prosperity of, **4**, 593.
under Selim II, **4**, 602, 607.
interested in the choice of a king for Poland, **4**, 604.
culture of, **4**, 607–10.
mediocrity of, **4**, 611–12.
religious stagnation among, **4**, 627.
submit questions to the Polish Talmudists, **4**, 639.
ransom Polish Jews from the Tartars, **5**, 8.
free from persecution, **5**, 168.
join Jacob Frank, **5**, 273.
emancipated, **5**, 641.
hated, **5**, 641.
praised by Delaborde, **5**, 649.
Turkey, the Jews of (*continued*), secured against the blood accusation, **5**, 662.
urged to use Turkish, **5**, 664.
Tur-Simon, stronghold fortified by Bar-Cochba, **2**, 415.
fall of, **2**, 416.
Tus. *See* Jacob Tus.
Tuscany, the Jews of, protected against Bernardinus of Feltre, **4**, 297.
Tuster. *See* Susa.
Tusti, Father, suspects the Damascus Jews of Tomaso's murder, **5**, 635.
Tyre (Zor), built by the Canaanites, **1**, 3.
founded, **1**, 80.
subdued by Shalmaneser, **1**, 263.
surrenders to Shalmaneser, **1**, 264.
besieged by Nebuchadnezzar, **1**, 306, 307.
messengers from, urge Zedekiah to revolt from Nebuchadnezzar, **1**, 310.
merchants from, desecrate the Sabbath in Jerusalem, **1**, 387.
taken by Alexander the Great, **1**, 412.
Olympian games celebrated at, **1**, 446.
court held at, to try Menelaus, **1**, 449.
inhabitants of, threaten the Galilean Judæans, **1**, 475.
inhabitants of, meditate the massacre of the Christians, **3**, 20.
Jehuda Halevi at, **3**, 342.
the Jews of, in the twelfth century, **3**, 426.
Tyrol, the Jews of, persecuted, **4**, 297–9.
excludes Jews, **5**, 523.

U

Ubaid-Allah, founder of the Fatimide dynasty, patron of Isaac Israeli, **3,** 180–1.
Ubaid-Allah Ibn-Suleiman, vizir, appoints Jews to state offices, **3,** 183.
Ucles, the battle of, Mahometans victorious at, **3,** 312.
Ueberlingen, the Jews of, charged with well poisoning, **4,** 105.
burnt on the blood accusation, **4,** 227.
Ukba. *See* Mar-Ukba.
Ukban. *See* Mar-Ukban.
Ukraine, the Cossacks enjoy independence in, **5,** 2.
Jews banished from, **5,** 12.
Jews permitted to live in, **5,** 14.
devastated by the Cossacks, **5,** 388.
Ulam, an open vestibule in the Temple, **1,** 165.
Ulamma, the Jews of, in the twelfth century, **3,** 427.
Ulla, friend of Judah ben Ezekiel, on the purity of the Jewish race, **2,** 551.
insulted by Yalta, **2,** 556.
Ulla bar Kosher, political offender against Zenobia, **2,** 530.
Ulm, conference at, to transfer the claims of Jews upon Christians to Emperor Wenceslaus, **4,** 166.
the Jews of, banished, **4,** 416.
Ulpianus Trajan. *See* Trajan.
Ultramontanes. *See* Caorsini, the.
Unger, Christian Theophilus, supplements Basnage's work, **5,** 197.
"Union of American Hebrew Congregations, The," the objects of, **5,** 702.
Unitarians, the, a Christian sect of the Reformation period, **4,** 541.
meetings of, the model of the Synod of the Four Countries, **4,** 645.
influence of, in Poland, **4,** 647.
United States, the, espouse the cause of the Damascus Jews, **5,** 633, 657.
early Jewish immigrants in, **5,** 702.
Unity of God, the, ceases to be a doctrine of Christianity, **2,** 500.
defended by Simlaï, **2,** 501–2.
University degrees, Jews forbidden by the Council of Basle to take, **4,** 245.
"Upon Ecclesiastical Power and Judaism." *See* "Jerusalem."
"Upon Mendelssohn and the Political Reform of the Jews," by Mirabeau, **5,** 432.
"Upon the Aim of Jesus and his disciples," one of the "Fragments" published by Lessing, **5,** 321.
"Upon the Civil Amelioration of the Condition of the Jews," by Dohm, **5,** 352–62.
emphasizes political advantages, **5,** 352–3.
describes the condition of the Jews, **5,** 353.
reviews the history of the Jews in Europe, **5,** 354.
programme outlined in, **5,** 355–6.
effect of, **5,** 356–7.
discussion of, **5,** 358–62.
appendix to, **5,** 362.
spread in Alsace by Cerf Berr, **5,** 431.

"**Upon the Inutility of the Jews in the Kingdoms of Bohemia and Moravia,**" called forth by Dohm's apology, **5,** 359.
Uranso, Vidal de, assassin hired against Arbues, **4,** 330.
Urban V, pope, enemy of Pedro the Cruel, **4,** 122, 126.
Urbib, of Alexandria, generosity of, **3,** 23.
Urbino, Abraham Abulafia in, **4,** 6.
  refuge of Jewish exiles from the Papal States, **4,** 592.
Uriah, high priest, summoned as witness against Ahaz, **1,** 259.
Uriah, the Hittite, betrayed by David, **1,** 131–2.
Uriah of Mayence, apostate, sets fire to the synagogue, **3,** 303.
Uriah, son of Shemaiah, prophet, slain by Jehoiakim, **1,** 301.
Uriel, name of an angel, **1,** 403.
Urim and Thummim, in the Zohar, **4,** 23.
Urraca, queen of Castile, marries Alfonso I of Aragon, **3,** 316.
Ursicinus, legate of Gallus, oppresses the Jews of Judæa, **2,** 568–9.
  punishes the inhabitants of Sepphoris, **2,** 570–1.
  falls into disfavor with Constantius, **2,** 572.
Usal. *See* Sanaa.
Usha, school of, **2,** 148.
  a center for the teaching of the Law, **2,** 356.
  the Synhedrion removed to, **2,** 405.
  a second time the meeting place of the teachers of the Law, **2,** 433–4.
Usha (*continued*), home of Judah ben Ilai, **2,** 433, 442.
  See Synhedrion, the, of Usha.
Ushaya, the Elder, adds supplements to the Mishna, **2,** 470.
  compilation of, authoritative, **2,** 471.
  establishes an academy at Cæsarea, **2,** 543.
Ushaya, the Younger, brother of Rabba bar Nachmani, Agadist, **2,** 575-6.
Usque, Abraham (Duarte de Pinel), Marrano, translates the Bible into Spanish, **4,** 475.
  editor of the Ferrara Spanish Bible, **4,** 576.
  printing press of, closed, **4,** 581.
Usque, Samuel, poet, on the Inquisition, **4,** 324–5, 522.
  on the Portuguese Marranos, **4,** 380.
  on Salonica, **4,** 404–5.
  on Samuel II Abrabanel, **4,** 409.
  Jewish historical subjects of, **4,** 588.
  historico-poetical dialogue of, **4,** 558–61.
  describes Gracia Mendesia, **4,** 575–6.
Usque, Solomon (Duarte Gomez), poet and historian, **4,** 555, 558.
  tragedy by, on Esther, translated, **5,** 90.
Usques, the three, protected by Gracia Mendesia, **4,** 576.
Usury, the laws of, as enforced by Meïr, **2,** 439.
  taken by Jews from Christians, **3,** 376, 393.
  practiced in France in the twelfth century, **3,** 400.

Usury (*continued*), restrictions of, by the Fourth Lateran Council, **3,** 510.
prohibited by the Council of Narbonne, **3,** 518.
in England and France in the thirteenth century, **3,** 571.
practiced by Jews in England under Henry III, **3,** 591.
prohibited by the Statute of Judaism, **3,** 642.
among the Jews of Castile, **4,** 80.
in France in the fourteenth century, **4,** 174.
legalized in Mantua, **4,** 286.
charged against the Jews of Nuremberg, **4,** 415.
Manasseh ben Israel exonerates the Jews from the charge of, **5,** 41.
practiced by Christian capitalists, **5,** 205.
practiced by the Jews of Alsace, **5,** 349, 350–1.
charged against the Jews of France, **5,** 481, 482.
discussed in the Assembly of Jewish Notables, **5,** 489, 492.
discussed by the Synhedrion, **5,** 497.

Utrera, the Marranos of, adopt means of defense against the Inquisition, **4,** 313.

Uzza, the garden of, burial place of Manasseh, **1,** 285.

Uzzah, son of Abinadab, sudden death of, **1,** 119.

Uzziah, son of Amaziah of Judah, **1,** 226.
king of Judah, character and ability of, **1,** 228-9.
the earthquake under, **1,** 229.
drouth under, **1,** 229–30.
conquests of, **1,** 230–1.
fortifies Jerusalem, **1,** 231.
friendly relations of, with Jeroboam II, **1,** 231, 232.
models his kingdom after Solomon's, **1,** 231.
warlike spirit of, **1,** 244.
attempts to sacrifice in the Temple, **1,** 245.
attacked by leprosy, **1,** 245.
last years of, passed in solitude, **1,** 246.
death of, **1,** 248.

Uziel, Isaac, preacher at Amsterdam, influence of, **4,** 672.
scourges the immorality of the Amsterdam Jews, **4,** 680.
disciples of, **4,** 682, 683, 689.
threatens Uriel da Costa with excommunication, **5,** 58.

V

Vaad Arba Arazoth. *See* Four Countries, the, the Synod of.

Valavigny, surgeon, suspected of poisoning wells, **4,** 104.

"Vale of Weeping," by Joseph Cohen, **4,** 590, 608.

Valencia, quarrel about the chief rabbinate of, **4,** 162.
Marranos from, in Algiers, **4,** 199.

Valencia (*continued*), opposition to the Inquisition in, **4,** 328.
refuge of the last king of Toledo, **3,** 295.

Valencia, the Jews of, possess penal jurisdiction, **4,** 155.
exterminated in 1391, **4,** 170–1.
accept baptism, **4,** 205, 206.
charged with the blood accusation, **4,** 344.

Valencia, the Jews of (*continued*), possessions of, sequestrated by Ferdinand the Catholic, **4,** 350.

Valencia de Alcantara, Gonzalo Martinez besieged in, **4,** 86.

Valens, Emperor of the East, tolerance of, **2,** 603.

Valensino, Alexandrian Jew, seconds Munk's efforts to establish schools, **5,** 663.

Valentinian I, Emperor of the West, tolerance of, **2,** 603.

Valerianus, emperor, taken prisoner, **2,** 527.

Valladolid, besieged by Alfonso XI of Castile, **4,** 79.
 the Marranos of, attacked, **4,** 280–1.

Valladolid, the cortes of, petition Alfonso XI against usury, **4,** 80.
 petition for the curtailment of Jewish privileges, **4,** 116.
 pass anti-Jewish regulations, **4,** 158.

Valladolid, the Jews of, under Sancho, **3,** 617.
 deny the charges of Alfonso Burgensis, **4,** 83.
 despoiled, **4,** 125.
 accept baptism, **4,** 205.

Van den Enden, Dr. Franz, philologist, Spinoza's teacher, **5,** 88–9.

Vandals, the, the empire of, conquered by Belisarius, **3,** 26.
 antagonistic to the Catholics, **3,** 44.

Vangioni, the, marry Jewish women, **3,** 41.

Vannes, the Council of, forbids the clergy to take part in Jewish banquets, **3,** 36.

Vanni, mufti, proposes the conversion of Sabbataï Zevi, **5,** 153.
 instructs Sabbatian converts, **5,** 154.
 teaches Sabbataï Zevi Mahometan customs, **5,** 162.

Van Oven, Bernard, English Jew, interested in the Damascus affair, **5,** 653.

Van Swieden. *See* Swieden, van.

Vantabiet, Armenian bishop, incites a crusade against the Damascus Jews, **5,** 662.

Varnhagen von Ense, husband of Rachel Levin, **5,** 443.
 attitude of, towards the Jews, **5,** 533.

Varus, representative of Agrippa II, treachery of, **2,** 275.
 dismissed, **2,** 275.

Varus, Quintilius, governor of Syria, convicts Antipater of attempted parricide, **2,** 114.
 given charge of Jerusalem, **2,** 122–3.
 orders out Roman troops against the Judæan insurgents, **2,** 125–6.
 subdues the Judæan insurgents, **2,** 126.

Vayol, Hans, calumniates Israel Bruna, **4,** 302, 303.
 retracts his calumnies, **4,** 304.

Vaz, Diego, Marrano, murders Henrique Nunes, **4,** 490.

Vecinho, Joseph, physician and astronomer, at the congress summoned by João II, **4,** 367.

Vega brothers, the, found an academy at Jerusalem, **5,** 126.

Vega Enriques, Rachel de, marriage of, **5,** 242.

Vega, Judah, rabbi in Amsterdam, indulgent towards the weaknesses of the Jews, **4,** 680.

Veit, in the Prussian Landtag, **5**, 697.
Veit, Simon, husband of Dorothea Mendelssohn, **5**, 424.
Veitel, Ephraim, Voltaire's agent, **5**, 339.
school founded by, **5**, 405.
Velasquez de Tordesillas, bishop of Segovia, accuses the Jews of host desecration, **4**, 195–6.
Venaissin, Jews in, after the banishment by Charles VI, **4**, 177.
the Jews of, expelled by Pius V, **4**, 592.
Venice, commerce of, in the fifteenth century, **4**, 285.
the Abrabanel family at, **4**, 385–6.
Spanish spoken at, by the exiles, **4**, 388.
exiled Jews settle in, **4**, 408.
the Marranos of, unmolested, **4**, 500.
Molcho and Reubeni at, **4**, 504–5.
Marranos well treated at, **4**, 526.
the Talmud burnt in, **4**, 565.
the rulers of, prosecute Gracia Mendesia, **4**, 574.
ordered by Turkey to liberate Gracia Mendesia, **4**, 575.
ambassador of, denounces Joseph Nassi, **4**, 595.
hostility of, to Joseph Nassi, **4**, 600.
war of, with Turkey, **4**, 600.
imprisons the Levantine merchants, **4**, 600.
peace of, with Turkey, **4**, 605–6.
Elias Montalto in, **4**, 673.
the war of, with Turkey enriches Smyrna, **5**, 119.
the Sabbatian movement in, **5**, 138, 150.
Venice (*continued*), Nathan Ghazati in, **5**, 161.
Jewish exiles from Vienna settle in, **5**, 173.
Nehemiah Chayon at, **5**, 216–17.
honor shown to Crémieux at, **5**, 668.
Venice, the Jews of, in the twelfth century, **3**, 424.
threatened with expulsion, **4**, 600–1.
depart, **4**, 606.
position of, secured by Solomon Ashkenazi, **4**, 606–7.
number of, in the sixteenth century, **4**, 650.
in the time of Leo Modena, **5**, 68.
order Luzzatto to justify himself, **5**, 238.
Venice, the rabbis of, exact a promise from Luzzatto not to teach the Kabbala, **5**, 239.
offended by Luzzatto, **5**, 239–40.
excommunicate Luzzatto, **5**, 240, 242.
excommunicate the writer of Sabbatian amulets, **5**, 263, 264.
Venus, temple to, on Golgotha, **2**, 422.
Vera y Alarcon, Lope de, martyr, celebrated by Enriquez de Paz, **5**, 111.
Verdun, fortress of, refuge of the Jews, **4**, 56.
Verona, Jews beg for shelter in, **4**, 660.
Vesoul family, the, privileges of, **4**, 150.
extinction of, **4**, 152.
Vespasian, general of the Roman army in Judæa, **2**, 284.
met at Ptolemais by Judæan partisans of Rome, **2**, 285.

Vespasian (*continued*), army of, **2**, 285.
defeats Josephus, **2**, 285.
defeated at Jotapata, **2**, 285-6.
takes Gabara, **2**, 286.
takes Jotapata, **2**, 287.
kindly disposed to Josephus, **2**, 288.
takes Gamala, **2**, 289-90.
truce declared by, **2**, 290.
hesitates to attack Jerusalem, **2**, 297, 298.
in fear of Licinius Mucianus, **2**, 300.
fealty sworn to, in Syria and Egypt, **2**, 300.
declares Judæa his property, **2**, 312.
celebration of the birthday of, **2**, 312.
celebrates his triumph over Judæa, **2**, 314-15.
appoints Bassus governor of Judæa, **2**, 315.
institutes the fiscus Judaicus, **2**, 316.
rewards the Judæans friendly to Rome, **2**, 316-17.
closes the Temple of Onias, **2**, 318.
treats the Jews kindly after the fall of Jerusalem, **2**, 331.
gives Galilee to Agrippa II, **2**, 333.

Viana, the Jews of, attacked at the instigation of Pedro Olligoyen, **4**, 78.

Victoria, of England, congratulates Montefiore upon his success in the East, **5**, 669.
honors Montefiore, **5**, 670.
approves of the abolition of the form of oath, **5**, 698.

Vidal. *See* Bonafoux Vidal; Crescas Vidal.

Vidal, Maëstro. *See* Moses ben Joshua Narboni.

Vidal ben Benveniste Ibn-Labi (Ferrer), champion of Judaism at the Tortosa disputation, **4**, 207, 211.
holds the Agada to be authoritative, **4**, 214.
refuses to accept Christianity, **4**, 215.
relations of, become converts, **4**, 215.
neo-Hebraic poet, **4**, 230.
defends the Talmud, **4**, 233-4.

Vidal Menachem ben Solomon Meïri (1249-1306), rabbi of Perpignan, style of, **4**, 26-7.

Vieira, Antonio, Jesuit, characterizes Isaac Aboab and Manasseh ben Israel, **4**, 683.

Vienna, the Council of, confirms the anti-Jewish decrees of Innocent III, **3**, 611-12.
court Jews appointed in, **4**, 702.
Jews re-admitted into, **5**, 189.
Judah Chassid at, **5**, 213.
Chayon at, **5**, 218, 230.
Jews allowed to live in, under certain conditions, **5**, 358.
a Jewish salon in, **5**, 413-14.
intercourse with, awakens a desire for culture in Galicia, **5**, 611.
honor shown to Crémieux at, **5**, 668.

Vienna, the Congress of, and the emancipation of the Jews, **5**, 513, 518-20.
statesmen of, favor the emancipation of the Jews, **5**, 514.

Vienna, the Jews of, declared ineligible to office, **3**, 635.
protected from the Deggenburg persecution, **4**, 99.
kill themselves to escape the Black Death persecutions, **4**, 110.
number of, **4**, 694.

Vienna, the Jews of (*continued*), importance of, during the Thirty Years' War, **4**, 702.
privileges of, **4**, 702–3.
build a synagogue, **4**, 702.
tax paid by, **5**, 170.
banished at the instigation of Empress Margaret, **5**, 170.
call upon outsiders to have the decree revoked, **5**, 171.
go into exile, **5**, 171–2.
dispersion of, **5**, 172–4.
suppress "Judaism Unmasked," **5**, 189–90.
join the "Society of Friends," **5**, 418.
heterogeneous character of, **5**, 579–80.
reforms of, **5**, 580.
the Temple service of, **5**, 581.
importance of, **5**, 582.
Viennet, French deputy, proposes the abolition of a state religion, **5**, 597.
Villadiego, the Jews of, exterminated by Pedro's English allies, **4**, 125.
Villafranca, Oran Jews settle at, **5**, 169.
Villareal, tribunals of the Inquisition established in, **4**, 325.
Villaris, treasurer, insists upon the payment of taxes by the Jews of Spain, **4**, 344.
Ville-Neuve, the Jews of, suspected of well poisoning, **4**, 104.
"**Vindiciæ Judæorum**," by Manasseh ben Israel, translated by Marcus Herz, **5**, 362.
fundamental idea of, **5**, 363.
Virgin Mary, the, doctrine of, discussed by the Jews of France, **3**, 343.
refuted by Moses Cohen de Tordesillas, **4**, 141.
Viseu. *See* Vecinho.
Vishnioviecki, prince, Polish general, protects the Polish Jews against Cossack cruelty, **5**, 10.
retreats before the Cossacks, **5**, 10–11.
Vishnioviecki, the house of, controls Cossack colonization, **5**, 3.
Visigothic code, the, the Jews under, **3**, 292.
translation of, **3**, 594–5.
Visigoths, the, the kings of, dependent on the Church, **3**, 37.
antagonistic to the Catholics, **3**, 44–5.
treat the Jews kindly until Catholic times, **3**, 45–6.
the anti-Jewish decrees of, revived by the Council of Meaux, **3**, 171.
Vismes, the secretary of, shows the injustice done the Jews of Metz, **5**, 446.
Vital. *See* Chayim; Samuel.
Vitellius, proclaimed emperor in Lower Germany, **2**, 299.
drives Otho to suicide, **2**, 299.
death of, **2**, 300.
Vitellius, governor of Syria, appealed to, against Pontius Pilate, **2**, 172.
befriends the Judæans, **2**, 172–3.
offers sacrifices in the Temple, **2**, 173.
Vitoria, the Jews of, deed their cemetery to the town, **4**, 352.
left without physicians by the expulsion of the Jews, **4**, 353.
Vivo. *See* Yechiel of Paris.
Vizeu, Jewish center in Portugal, **4**, 159.
Vladislav, of Poland, death of, **5**, 8.

Volga (Itil, Atel), the, Jews settle at the mouth of, **3**, 123.
kingdom of the Chazars founded on, **3**, 138.
Volhynia, rabbinical schools established in, **4**, 420.
Haidamaks in, **5**, 11.
Vologeses, king of Parthia, and Izates of Adiabene, **2**, 218.
Vologeses, king of Parthia, defeats Atidius Cornelianus, **2**, 447.
Voltaggio, Joseph Cohen at, **4**, 555.
Voltaire, Arouet de, compared with Lessing, **5**, 296.
hostility of, to Jews, **5**, 338-9.
financial losses of, through Medina, **5**, 339.
quarrel of, with Hirsch, **5**, 339.
Frederick the Great enraged at, **5**, 339.
slanders the Jews, **5**, 340.
answered by Pinto, **5**, 345.
compliments Portuguese Jews, **5**, 345.
"Jewish Letters" addressed to, **5**, 346-7.
Voltaire, Arouet de (*continued*), admired by Jews, **5**, 411.
Von Bohlen, exegete, **5**, 695.
Von der Recke, countess, and David Friedländer, **5**, 534.
Voss, Julius von, defends the Jews, **5**, 533.
Vossius, Dionysius, translates a work by Manasseh ben Israel, **5**, 22.
Vossius, Isaac, recommends Manasseh ben Israel to Christine of Sweden, **5**, 22.
Manasseh ben Israel dedicates a work to, **5**, 37.
Vossius, John Gerard, friendly to Manasseh ben Israel, **5**, 22.
Vowel-points, added to the Hebrew consonants, **3**, 112.
Vries, Simon de, friend of Spinoza, **5**, 107.
Vulgate, the, Latin translation of the Bible by Jerome, **2**, 625.
placed above the Hebrew Bible, **4**, 444-5.

W

"**Waage, Die**," journal published by Börne, **5**, 542.
Wadil-Kora, inhabited by Jews, **3**, 55-6.
submits to Mahomet, **3**, 83.
the Jews of, driven away by Omar, **3**, 85.
the Jews of, bring love of the Arabic to Babylonia, **3**, 111.
Wagenseil, John Christopher, Hebraist, accuses the Jews of blaspheming Jesus, **5**, 185-6.
interested in the conversion of Jews, **5**, 186.
Wagenseil, John Christopher (*continued*), tolerance of, **5**, 186-7.
denounces the blood accusation, **5**, 187.
Wala, incites the sons of Louis the Pious against their stepmother, **3**, 166.
Waldenses, the, crusades against, begin with massacres of the Jews, **4**, 222.
Wales, the Jumpers in, **5**, 378.
Wallachia, the Jews of, join Frank, **5**, 273.
Wallenstein, general, plunders the Jews, **4**, 701.

Walter Cornutus, archbishop of Sens, and the burning of the Talmud, **3**, 578.
Walther von der Vogelweide, the style of, adopted by Süsskind von Trimberg, **3**, 420.
Wamba, Visigothic king, revolt against, **3**, 104-5.
expels the Jews from Narbonne, **3**, 105.
Jews enjoy religious freedom under, **3**, 105, 106.
forced by Erwig to become a monk, **3**, 106.
"War for God," defense of Maimonides by his son, **3**, 545.
"War of the Fosse," between Mahomet and an alliance of tribes, **3**, 80.
Waragi, the, wage war with the Chazars in the tenth century, **3**, 221.
Waraka Ibn-Naufal, convert to Judaism, influences Mahomet, **3**, 71.
Wars of God, the, book of, early Hebrew poetry, **1**, 29.
Warsaw, Frank's baptism at, **5**, 288.
the duchy of, created by Napoleon, **5**, 500.
Wartburg, the, Luther on, **4**, 469, 475.
Wasit, under the jurisdiction of the Sora academy, **3**, 98.
the Jews of, in the twelfth century, **3**, 437.
Water-gate, the, Ezra reads the Law near, **1**, 378.
Water libation, the, mocked at by Alexander Jannæus, **2**, 43.
re-introduced under Salome Alexandra, **2**, 51.
as celebrated on the Feast of Tabernacles, **2**, 51.
Water-Town, the. *See* Rabbath-Ammon.
Way, Lewis, addresses the Congress of Aix on the emancipation of the Jews, **5**, 525-7.
Wecelinus, chaplain, proselyte, lampoons Christianity, **3**, 245.
Weil, Jacob, teacher of Israel Bruna, defends him, **4**, 302.
death of, **4**, 303.
Weil, Moses, rabbi of the German Jews of Amsterdam, **4**, 681.
Weissenburg, the Jews of, persecuted in the thirteenth century, **3**, 611.
indifferent to the confiscation of Hebrew books, **4**, 438.
Weissenfels, rabbinical synod at, **4**, 163.
Well poisoning. *See* Black Death, the.
Wenceslaus, emperor, punishes the priests, **4**, 164.
appealed to, by the Bohemian Jews, **4**, 165-6.
exacts a poll-tax from the Jews, **4**, 166.
friend of the rabbi of Prague, **4**, 166.
deposed, **4**, 178.
Wenzel, Francis, apostate, tries to arouse prejudice against the Jews, **5**, 191.
Werner, archbishop of Mayence, protects the Jews, **3**, 636.
"Werner, the good," supposed to have been murdered for ritual purposes, **3**, 637.
Werry, English consul at Damascus, abets Ratti Menton, **5**, 639.
Wertheimer, Joseph, founder of the "Israelitische Allianz," **5**, 703.
Wessely, Moses, aids Lessing, **5**, 326.

Wessely, Naphtali Hartwig, (1725-1805), poet, assists in Mendelssohn's Pentateuch translation, **5,** 334.
inspired by Mendelssohn, **5,** 366.
youth and education of, **5,** 366–7.
interested in the Bible, **5,** 367.
piety of, **5,** 367.
poetic gifts of, **5,** 367–8.
composes a hymn to Joseph II, **5,** 368.
on general culture for the Jews, **5,** 368, 370–1.
in negotiation with the Jews of Trieste, **5,** 369.
censured by the pious, **5,** 369, 370.
encouraged by Italian rabbis, **5,** 371.
contributor to the Meassef, **5,** 399.
permits the study of the sciences, **5,** 402.
last poem by, **5,** 404.
poetry of, compared with Luzzatto's, **5,** 623.
compared with Munk, **5,** 663.
West India Company, the, Jews interested in, **4,** 677.
West, the, the empire of, the Jews of, under Honorius, **2,** 616–17, 622.
forbidden to enter military service, **2,** 617.
Westphalia, the kingdom of, created by Napoleon, **5,** 500.
constitution of, **5,** 500.
the Jews of, emancipated, **5,** 500.
Jewish consistory in, **5,** 501–2.
functions of the consistory in, **5,** 502.
added to Prussia, **5,** 525.
reforms of Judaism in, **5,** 562.
Wetterau, the, the Jews of, emigrate to Syria, **3,** 637.
"White Company," the, troops of Henry de Trastamare, **4,** 123.
Widmannstadt, prosecutes Hebrew studies, **4,** 434.
William I, of England (the Conqueror), forbids Jews to keep Christian slaves and nurses, **3,** 294.
William III, of England, addressed by Oliger Pauli on the Jews, **5,** 177.
assisted by Suasso, **5,** 205.
William VIII, of Montpellier, unfriendly to the Jews, **3,** 395.
William of Orange, appeals to Joseph Nassi, **4,** 601.
tolerance of, **4,** 663.
well disposed towards Jews, **4,** 678.
William II, of Sicily, permits the Jews to have their own jurisdiction, **3,** 422–3.
William, bishop of Béziers, discontinues the Easter persecution of the Jews, **3,** 394.
William, bishop of Paris, entrusted with the persecution of the Talmud, **3,** 575.
William the Carpenter, leader of the first crusade, and the Jews, **3,** 299–301.
Wilna, the Jews of, slaughtered by the Russians, **5,** 14.
the Chassidim in, **5,** 388, 391.
rabbis of, excommunicate the Chassidim, **5,** 391–2.
Wimpfen, Süsskind Alexander, ransoms the body of Meïr of Rothenburg, **3,** 640.
Wine, on the Sabbath and the Passover, **1,** 398.
Wintzenheim, the consistory of, rabbis of, oppose the Reform movement, **5,** 571.

"**Wisdom** and Wealth," dialogue by Jehuda ben Sabbataï, **3**, 559.
Wisdom, the Book of. *See* Ecclesiasticus.
Witiga, Visigothic king, **3**, 109.
Witnesses, Christian, against Jews recognized by the Fourth Lateran Council, **3**, 422.
Samaritan, testimony of, admissible, **2**, 457.
baptized Jews, evidence of, valid, **4**, 36–7.
Witnesses, Jewish, competent only in Jewish cases, under Justinian, **3**, 12–13.
cannot testify against Christians, **3**, 102, 520; **4**, 250.
the oath of, under Charlemagne, **3**, 144.
not recognized in the Visigothic code, **3**, 292.
See also Jurisdiction, Jewish, autonomous.
Witold, duke of Lithuania, grants privileges to the Karaites, **4**, 265.
Wittenberg, the theological faculty of, forbids the employment of Jewish physicians, **4**, 692.
Wolf, Aaron Benjamin, rabbi of Berlin, and Chayon, **5**, 219, 220.
Wolf, John Christopher, supplements Basnage's work, **5**, 197.
Wolf, Levi, apostate, Sabbatian, **5**, 213.
Wolfkan of Ratisbon, apostate, charges the Jews with the blood accusation, **4**, 298, 304.
Wolfram of Eschenbach, style of, adopted by Süsskind of Trimberg, **3**, 420.
Wolfssohn, Aaron, editor of the Meassef, **5**, 400.
founder of the "Society of Friends," **5**, 418.
Wolkenburg, the castle of, refuge of the Cologne Jews, **3**, 352.
Wolowski, Frankist family, **5**, 289.
"**Woman-Hater**, The," satire by Jehuda ben Sabbataï, **3**, 559–60.
"**Wonderful Word**, The," panegyric on the Hebrew language by Reuchlin, **4**, 433–4.
"**Wonderworker** by Means of Invocation in the Name of God." *See* Israel of Miedziboz.
Wood-festival, the, as celebrated in the second Temple, **2**, 52.
Worcester, the Jewish Parliament meets in, **3**, 590.
"**Word** to the Impartial, A," philo-Jewish pamphlet, **5**, 470.
"**Words of Peace** and Truth," by Wessely, **5**, 368–9.
Worms, founders of the Jewish community of, **3**, 41.
Rashi studies Talmud at, **3**, 286.
congregation of, one of the oldest in Germany, **3**, 518.
decisions of, **4**, 135.
rabbinical synod at, **4**, 452–3.
deputies from, consider the Jewish question, **4**, 463.
Luther at the diet of, **4**, 469.
Jews tolerated in, **4**, 686.
Joseph Delmedigo at, **5**, 80.
Worms, the Jews of, faithful to Henry IV, **3**, 293.
during the first crusade, **3**, 301–2.
defend the city, **3**, 417.

Worms, the Jews of (*continued*), emigrate to Syria, **3**, 637.
burn themselves to escape the Black Death persecutions, **4**, 108–9.
threatened with expulsion, **4**, 417.
the extermination of, suggested by Pfefferkorn, **4**, 463.
number of, **4**, 694.
antipathy to, **4**, 694–5.
the expulsion of, urged, **4**, 698.
ordered to leave, **4**, 699.
suffering of, **4**, 699.
re-admitted, **4**, 699.
restrictions upon, **4**, 700.
protected by Ferdinand II, **4**, 701.

Wratislaw II, duke of Bohemia, **3**, 305.
prevents the emigration of the Jews, **3**, 307.

Writers (Historians, Pamphleteers, Scholars, etc.), non-Jewish, on Jewish subjects, list of:

Abdel-latif,
Abu Ishak al-Elviri,
Abul-Ala,
Abul-Arab Ibn-Moïsha,
Adams, Hannah
Agobard,
Alexander Polyhistor,
Alfonso de Spina,
Alfonso Burgensis,
Alsaid Ibn-Sina Almulk,
Alvarez, Alfonso, de Villasandino
Apion,
Apollonius Malo,
Apollonius Molo,
Appian,
Aristides,
Augustine,
Bail,
Barlæus, Caspar
Basnage, Jacob
Buchholz,
Buxtorfs, the
Cassiodorus,
Ceba, Ansaldo
Chateaubriand,
Cicero,
Closener of Strasburg,
Collier, Thomas
Czechowic, Martin
Delitzsch, Franz
Diebitsch, von
Diego de Valencia,
Diez,
Dio Cassius,
Dohm, Christian William
Duns Scotus,
Dury, John
Eck, John
Erasmus,
Eusebius,
Ewald, Heinrich

Writers (Historians, Pamphleteers, Scholars, etc.), non-Jewish, on Jewish subjects, list of (*continued*):

Ewald, Johann Ludwig
Felgenhauer, Paul
Ferrajo, Lucio
Fichte,
Frankenberg, Abraham
Fries, J. F.
Gesenius,
Goethe,
Graes, Ortuin de
Grattenauer,
Grégoire,
Grund, Christian
Hartmann, Frederick Traugott
Hengstenberg,
Herder,
Holmes, Nathaniel
Holst, Ludwig
Hooghe, Romein de
Hoornbeck, John
Hosiander,
Hundt, Hartwig
Hutten, Ulrich von
Ibn-Alfara,
Isidore, archbishop of Seville,
Jerome,
Jesse, Henry
Jurieu, Pierre
Klonowicz,
Kölbele, John Balthasar
Kosmann,
Krämer, August
Lamartine,
La Peyrère, Isaac
Lavater, John Caspar
Lessing, Gotthold Ephraim
Longinus,
Lopez, Pedro, de Ayala
Luther, Martin
Manetho,
Martin, Harry
Martin, Raymund
Martinet, Adam
Matthew Paris,
Megerlin, David Frederick
Meyer, Edward
Michaelis, John David
Miller, John
Mirabeau,
Münster, Sebastian
Nicholas, Edward
Nicolaus of Damascus,
Paalzow,
Porphyry,
Posidonius,
Procopius,
Prynne, William
Ramson,
Reuchlin, John
Rhabanus Maurus,
Rohrer, Joseph
Rubianus, Crotus
Rühs, Friedrich
Scaliger, Joseph
Schleiermacher,
Schmidt of Hildburghausen,
Schudt,
Schwager,
Simon, Richard
Speeth, John Peter
Strabo,
Streckfuss,
Surenhuysius, William
Swieden, van
Tacitus,
Tovey,
Unger, Christian Theophilus
Varnhagen van Ense,
Voss, Julius von
Vossius, Dionysius
Wagenseil, John Christopher
Wülfer, John.

Wülfer, John, Hebraist, attacks the Alenu prayer, **5,** 185.
denounces the blood accusation, **5,** 185.
Würtemberg, the liturgy of, introduced into Mecklenburg-Schwerin, **5,** 679.
Würzburg, the Jews of, suffer martyrdom during the second crusade, **3,** 354.
Würzburg, the Jews of (*continued*), blotted out during the Rindfleisch persecution, **4,** 35.
perish during the Black Death persecutions, **4,** 110.
the "hep, hep!" persecution of, **5,** 528–9.
Wycliffe, denounces the Church, **4,** 202.
inspires Huss, **4,** 221.

X

Xeres, battle of, gives the Mahometans possession of Visigothic Spain, **3,** 109.
Xerifs, the, a powerful family of Fez, **4,** 390.
Xerxes (Ahasuerus), king of Persia, the Judæans under, accused of disloyalty, **1,** 361.
Ximenes de Cisneros, third inquisitor-general, forbids Charles V to tolerate the Jews, **4,** 484.
Xystum, colonnade before the Hasmonæan palace, **2,** 14.

Y

Yachini, Abraham, preacher at Constantinople, confirms Sabbataï Zevi's Messiahship, **5,** 123, 131.
rewarded by Sabbataï Zevi, **5,** 145.
Yachya Ibn-Mondhir, patron of Yekutiel Ibn-Hassan, **3,** 266.
Yachya Alkader, last Mahometan king of Toledo, **3,** 295.
Yalkut, the, a Midrash collection by Simon Kara, **3,** 346.
Yalta, wife of Nachman ben Jacob, **2,** 554–5.
pride of, **2,** 556.
Yarche Kalla, months of assembly at Sora, **2,** 514–15.
Yarchinaï. *See* Samuel, son of Abba.
Yarob, ancestor of the Arabs, **3,** 61.
Yathrib. *See* Medina.
Yazates, Persian good spirits, **1,** 403.
"Year of Flying," the, era for the Jews of Bagdad, **3,** 433.
"Year of Penitence," the, inaugurated by Asher Lämmlein, **4,** 483.
Year of Release, the. *See* Sabbatical year, the.
Year, the Jewish, character of, **2,** 362–3. *See* Calendar, the.
Yechiel (Vivo) of Paris, Talmudist, invited to defend the Talmud against Donin, **3,** 576.
refuses to answer questions, **3,** 576.
refuses to take an oath, **3,** 577.
disproves the charge of immorality and blasphemy, **3,** 577.
maintains that there are no references to Jesus in the Talmud, **3,** 577.
disciples of, **3,** 586.

Yechiel (Vivo) of Paris (*continued*), obtains supplies from Palestine, **3**, 586.
emigrates to Palestine, **3**, 587.
buried at Chaifa, **3**, 608.
Yechiel of Pisa, financier and patron of Hebrew literature, **4**, 286.
friend of Isaac Abrabanel, **4**, 286.
ransoms Jewish prisoners, **4**, 287.
on Jewish physicians in Italy, **4**, 287.
accused of protecting the Jews by means of bribery, **4**, 297.
instructed how to receive the Portuguese embassy, **4**, 340.
sons of, help the Spanish exiles, **4**, 360.
Yechiel ben Abraham, manages the finances of Pope Alexander III, **3**, 421.
Yedaya En-Bonet Bedaresi (Penini, 1280–1340), poet, bombastic style of, **4**, 26, 42–3.
works of, **4**, 43.
defends the study of science, **4**, 43–4.
on the expulsion of the French Jews, **4**, 49.
Yekum Purkan, blessing for the Exilarchs and Geonim, **3**, 95.
Yekutiel (Kussiel) of Wilna, disciple of Moses Chayim Luzzatto, **5**, 237, 245.
spreads Luzzatto's Kabbala, **5**, 238.
Yekutiel Ibn-Hassan, protector of Solomon Ibn-Gebirol, **3**, 266.
Yemen, a part of southern Arabia, **3**, 54.
king of, converted to Judaism, **3**, 62–3.
under the jurisdiction of the Exilarch, **3**, 429.
Yemen, the Jews of, numerous, **3**, 56.
prevent the spread of Christianity, **3**, 56.
in the twelfth century, **3**, 436.
benevolence of, **3**, 436.
forced into Islam, **3**, 461–2.
consoled by Maimonides, **3**, 462–4.
devoted to Maimonides, **3**, 464.
rescued from persecution by Maimonides, **3**, 474.
See also Himyarite kingdom, the.
Yezid I, Ommiyyade Caliph, tolerance of, **3**, 110.
patron of learning, **3**, 110.
cross-questions the false Messiah Serene, **3**, 121.
Yishaï ben Chiskiya, of Damascus, Exilarch, in the Maimunist controversy, **3**, 627.
excommunicates Solomon Petit, **3**, 632–3.
reports the condemnation of the Anti-Maimunists of Acho, **3**, 633.
Yizchaki. *See* Abraham; Abu Ibraham Isaac Ibn-Kastar ben Yasus; Solomon.
Yoktan, ancestor of the Himyarites, **3**, 60.
Yom har Gerizim, anniversary of the destruction of the Samaritan Temple, **2**, 8.
Yom Tob, of Joigny, counsels the Jews of York to slay one another, **3**, 414–15.
Yom-Tob Kahana ben Jacob (926–928), Gaon of Sora, **3**, 192.
Yom Trajanus, a half-holiday, **2**, 401.
York, the governor of, deposed, **3**, 416.
York, the Jews of, persecuted under Richard I, **3**, 413–15.

York, the Jews of (*continued*), take refuge in the citadel, **3**, 413.
refuse to admit the governor, **3**, 414.
besieged, **3**, 414–15.
kill each other, **3**, 415.
Yotabe, island, a Jewish free state on, **3**, 56.
"Youth," drama by Mendel Bresselau, **5**, 398.
Yussuf Ibn-Teshufin, Almoravide prince, aids the Mahometans against Alfonso VI of Castile, **3**, 296.
forces Islam upon the Jews of Lucena, **3**, 311–12.

Z

Zab, the, Antiochus Sidetes defeats the Parthians at, **2**, 5.
Zaba, tribal contingent to David's army, **1**, 122.
Zabir Ibn-Bata, survivor of the Benu-Kuraiza, **3**, 81.
Zaccaï, head of the Jewish congregation at Mosul, **3**, 429–30.
tries to influence David Alrui, **3**, 433.
Zaccaï ben Achunaï, pretender to the Exilarchate, confirmed in the office, **3**, 137.
Zachariah ben Jehoiada, high priest, stoned, **1**, 220.
Zachariah. *See also* Zechariah.
Zacharias, founder of a Judaizing sect in Poland, **4**, 633.
Zachib as-Schorta, minister of police, **3**, 313.
Zachot, grammatical work by Abraham Ibn-Ezra, **3**, 371.
Zacuto. *See* Abraham; Moses; Samuel.
Zaddik, the, in the Kabbala, **5**, 121.
Zaddik, the, Chassidean leader, requirements of, **5**, 380, 381.
importance of, magnified by Beer of Mizricz, **5**, 381–2.
pilgrimages to, **5**, 382, 384.
gifts to, **5**, 382–3, 384.
superior to the Rebbe, **5**, 393.
Zadok, high priest, at Gibeon, **1**, 120.
faithful to David, **1**, 141.
urges the recall of David, **1**, 146.
ranked above Abiathar, **1**, 152.
anoints Solomon king, **1**, 153.
of the house of Eleazar, **1**, 155.
made sole high priest, **1**, 160.
Zadok, leader of the Sadduceans, **2**, 21.
Zadok, Talmudist of Accho, **3**, 427.
Zadok, teacher of the Law, follower of Shammai, **2**, 133, 330, 338.
leader of the Zealots, **2**, 133.
resists the Roman census, **2**, 133.
maxim of, **2**, 338–9.
Zadukim. *See* Sadducees.
Zafara (Thafar), falls into the hands of the Ethiopian king, **3**, 66.
Zag. *See* Isaac Benveniste.
Zag (Isaac) ben Meïr de Malea, Almoxarif under Alfonso X, **3**, 593, 615–16.
Zag (Isaac) Ibn-Said, compiler of the Alfonsine Tables, **3**, 593–4.
Zähringen, the Jews of, accused of well poisoning, **4**, 108.
Zainab, sister of Marhab, tries to poison Mahomet, **3**, 83–4.

Zain-Eddin, commander of Amadia, patron of David Alrui, 3, 430.
brings about the death of David Alrui, 3, 433.
Zaken, title of the ordained, 2, 361.
Zalmunna, Midianite king, punished by Gideon, 1, 63.
Zamaris, founder of the colony of Babylonian Judæans in Batanæa, 2, 274.
Zamora, the Council of, renews anti-Jewish laws, 4, 52.
the Jews of, accept baptism, 4, 205.
Zamosc, Israel. *See* Israel Zamosc.
Zapateiro, Joseph. *See* Joseph Zapateiro.
Zaporogians, the. *See* Cossacks, the.
Zarak Barfat, poet, 4, 140.
Zarephath (Sarepta), Elijah lives in, 1, 203.
Zarfati. *See* Simon; Solomon ben Abraham.
Zarko, Jehuda, poet, 4, 609.
Zarzal. *See* Abraham Ibn-Zarzal.
Zarzel. *See* Moses Zarzel.
Zaslaw, the fair of, the Polish Talmudists meet at, 4, 640.
Zealand, admission of Jews into, opposed, 4, 663.
Zealots, the, republican party in Judæa, principles and leaders of, 2, 133.
resist the Roman census, 2, 133-4.
object to the use of the Roman era, 2, 134.
conception of the Messiah held by, 2, 144.
disapprove of Jesus, 2, 162.
depredations of, 2, 238-9.
a band of, called Sicarii, 2, 239.
Zealots, the (*continued*), kill the Samaritan inhabitants of Acrabatene, 2, 243.
in favor of war with Rome, 2, 256.
allied with the royal house of Adiabene, 2, 256.
leader of, 2, 256.
supported by Shammai's followers, 2, 256.
hold the Temple mount, 2, 259.
keep the Peace party out of the Temple, 2, 260.
increased by the masses of the people and the Sicarii, 2, 260.
force the Roman garrison to capitulate, 2, 260.
disagree with the Sicarii, 2, 260-1.
disinterestedness of, 2, 261.
defeat Cestius Gallus, 2, 265.
occupy the inner town, 2, 265.
force Cestius to retreat, 2, 266-7.
exaltation of, 2, 267-8.
coins of, 2, 268.
avenge the massacre of Judæans, 2, 269-70.
forbid the purchase of certain articles of food from the heathen, 2, 270.
in Galilee, 2, 272-4.
in Jerusalem after the conquest of Galilee, 2, 291, 292.
treatment by, of those suspected of Roman proclivities, 2, 294.
besieged in the Temple by Anan, 2, 295.
dissolve the aristocratic Synhedrion, 2, 296.
reign of terror under, 2, 296-7.
at war with Simon bar Giora, 2, 297-8.
split up into factions, 2, 301.
heroism of, 2, 306, 316.

Zealots, the (*continued*), massacred by the Romans, **2**, 315.
flee to Arabia, Egypt, etc., **2**, 317–18; **3**, 54.
end of the movement of, **2**, 318–19.
and Jochanan ben Zakkai, **2**, 323.
war of, immortalized by Josephus, **2**, 415.
Zebah, Midianite king, punished by Gideon, **1**, 63.
Zebaoth, Adonai, meaning of, **1**, 130–1.
Zebedee, the sons of, disciples of Jesus, **2**, 153.
suggest the necessity of a precursor to the Messiah, **2**, 158.
Zebulon, the tribe of, settles north of Mount Tabor, **1**, 37.
relation of, to the Phœnicians, **1**, 53.
extends its territory, **1**, 67.
descendants of, around Nishabur, **3**, 433.
Zebulon, tribesmen of, join Gideon, **1**, 62.
join Solomon's fleet, **1**, 170.
Zechariah, king of Israel, murder of, **1**, 243.
Zechariah (I), prophet, son of Berechiah, prophecies of, **1**, 254–6.
summoned as witness against Ahaz, **1**, 259.
Zechariah (II), prophet, urges the completion of the second Temple, **1**, 359.
extols the high priest Joshua, **1**, 360.
Zechariah. *See also* Zachariah.
"**Zeda la-Derech,**" by Menachem ben Aaron ben Zerach, **4**, 145.
Zedekiah (Mattaniah), made king of Judah by Nebuchadnezzar, **1**, 308.
Zedekiah (Mattaniah) (*continued*), swears fealty to Nebuchadnezzar, **1**, 308.
character of, **1**, 309.
urged to revolt from Nebuchadnezzar, **1**, 309–10.
refuses tribute to Nebuchadnezzar, **1**, 310–11.
flight of, **1**, 314.
blinded and taken to Babylon, **1**, 315.
Zedekiah, the daughters of, in Gedaliah's care, **1**, 319.
taken prisoners by Ishmael, **1**, 322.
rescued by Johanan, **1**, 323.
Zedekiah, Jewish physician of Charles the Bald, **3**, 170.
Zeïra I, Amora, a Babylonian, **2**, 531.
emigrates to Judæa, **2**, 557.
method of, **2**, 557–8, 590.
modesty of, **2**, 558.
death of, **2**, 558.
Zeïra II, Amora, proposed as principal of Pumbeditha, **2**, 583.
and the Machuzan marriages, **2**, 586–7.
Zeïra bar Chanina, political offender against Zenobia, **2**, 529–30.
Zekenim, elders among the Israelites, **1**, 7.
Zelah, family tomb of Saul, **1**, 124.
Zemach. *See* Mar-Zemach.
Zemach ben Kafnaï, Gaon of Pumbeditha, **3**, 200.
Zemach ben Shahin, candidate for the Sora Gaonate, **3**, 192–3.
Zemach, Jacob, Marrano physician, Kabbalist, **5**, 125–6.
Zemach David, history by David Gans, **4**, 638–9.

Zend-Avesta, Persian code, compiled by Ardashir, **2**, 524.
Zendiks, the, adherents of the Magian religion reformed by Mazdak, **3**, 2.
recruited from the lower classes, **3**, 2.
Zenki, makes Mosul a capital of the Eastern Caliphate, **3**, 429.
kindly disposed to Jews, **3**, 429.
Zeno, Emperor of the East, hostile to the Jews, **3**, 10–11.
Zeno Cotylas, governor of Philadelphia, protects Ptolemy ben Habub, **2**, 3.
Zenobia, queen of Palmyra, the court of, **2**, 529.
feeling of the Jews against, **2**, 529–30.
end of, **2**, 530.
Zephaniah, captain of the Temple, beheaded, **1**, 314.
Zephaniah, prophet, prophecy of, **1**, 286–7.
Zerah, Egyptian general, defeated by Asa, **1**, 190.
Zerubbabel, grandson of Jehoiachin, intercedes with Cyrus for the return of the Judæans, **1**, 351.
leader of the exiles returning under Cyrus, **1**, 351–2.
governor of Judæa, **1**, 352.
erects an altar on the site of the Temple, **1**, 356.
refuses the help of the Cuthæans, **1**, 357–8.
urges the completion of the Temple, **1**, 359.
returns to Babylon, **1**, 360.
great-grandson of, accompanies Ezra to Palestine, **1**, 366.
the Exilarchs descended from, **2**, 509.
Zevi. *See* Elijah; Joseph; Mordecai; Sabbataï; Sarah Zevi; Jacob Querido.
Zevi Ashkenazi, Chacham, anti-Sabbatian, **5**, 221.
as a Talmudist, **5**, 221.
rabbi of Amsterdam, **5**, 221.
and Solomon Ayllon, **5**, 221.
denounces Chayon, **5**, 221–2.
refuses to co-operate with Ayllon, **5**, 222.
excommunicates Chayon, **5**, 224.
abused by the Portuguese Jews of Amsterdam, **5**, 224.
deserted by the German community, **5**, 225.
laid under the ban, **5**, 226.
compelled to leave Amsterdam, **5**, 226.
cause of, espoused by Jews elsewhere, **5**, 227.
the son of, **5**, 254.
Ziadeth-Allah, Aghlabite prince, Isaac Israeli physician to, **3**, 180.
Ziba, slave of Saul, appointed Mephibosheth's steward, **1**, 124.
Zicareo, character in Samuel Usque's work, **4**, 558, 560.
Zidon. *See* Sidon.
Ziklag, given to David by Achish, **1**, 101.
burnt by the Amalekites, **1**, 106.
Zimra. *See* David Ibn-Abi Zimra.
Zimri, commander of the war-chariots, kills Elah, **1**, 192.
short reign of, in Israel, **1**, 192.
Zinzendorf, count, addressed by the Jews of Trieste, **5**, 369.
Zion, celebrated by Jehuda Halevi, **3**, 325–6.
Zion, Hebrew journal devoted to Jewish science, **5**, 693.

Zion, mountain, description of, **1**, 45.
taken from the Jebusites, **1**, 113.
on the west side of Jerusalem, **1**, 115.
the Ark of the Covenant transferred to, **1**, 120.
permission to build a synagogue on, **4**, 273-4.
Zion, mourners of, in Babylon, **1**, 338.
Zion, the songs of, by Jehuda Halevi, **3**, 337-8, 342.
Zion, upper city of Jerusalem, plundered by Gessius Florus, **2**, 254.
taken by Titus, **2**, 309.
Zipporah, wife of Moses, **1**, 14.
Zisca, Hussite leader, bravery of, **4**, 225, 226.
Zoar (Tamarah), city of palms, **1**, 43.
south-eastern limit of Judæa under Alexander Jannæus, **2**, 46.
Zohar, the, authorship of, **4**, 11-12.
attributed to Simon bar Yochaï, **4**, 12.
glorifies Simon bar Yochaï, **4**, 12-14.
description of, **4**, 14.
the underlying principle of, **4**, 14-15.
interpretation of the Scriptures in, **4**, 15-16.
theory of, on the soul, **3**, 16-18.
the Messiah in, **4**, 18.
on the Talmud, **4**, 19.
spread of, **4**, 19.
discovery of, attributed to Nachmani, **4**, 20.
discovered to be a forgery, **4**, 20-1.
reception of, among the Kabbalists, **4**, 21-2.
Zohar, the (*continued*), influence of, **4**, 22-3.
and Christian dogmas, **4**, 23.
the Kabbalistic authority, **4**, 196.
denounced as a forgery by Elias del Medigo, **4**, 292.
affects the liturgy, **4**, 481.
printed at Mantua, **4**, 583.
edited by Vittorio Eliano, **4**, 584.
a canonical book, **4**, 584.
influence of, on Isaac Lurya, **4**, 618-19.
a system evolved from, by Isaac Lurya, **4**, 619-22.
esteemed at Safet, **4**, 622.
placed above the Bible and the Talmud, **4**, 625.
fixes the Messianic year, **5**, 6, 24, 121-2.
the genuineness of, defended by Joseph Delmedigo, **5**, 78.
annihilates Rabbinical Judaism, **5**, 144.
opposed by Jehuda Brieli, **5**, 200.
the style of, imitated by Moses Chayim Luzzatto, **5**, 235.
accepted by the Frankists, **5**, 274-5.
exposed as a forgery by Emden, **5**, 278.
teaches the Trinity, **5**, 287.
Zohar Tinyana, by Moses Chayim Luzzatto, **5**, 237.
Zoharites. *See* Frankists.
Zoilus, governor of Gaza, **2**, 40.
Zolkiew, home of Krochmal, **5**, 608, 614.
Zollikofer, approves of Mendelssohn's views on Church discipline, **5**, 363.
Zor. *See* Tyre.
Zorah Yussuf Dhu-Nowas (520-530), Jewish king of Yemen, retaliates upon the Byzantine emperors, **3**, 64.

Zorah Yussuf Dhu-Nowas (*continued*), defeated by Aidug, **3,** 64.
takes Najaran, **3,** 65.
levies a tribute upon the Christians of Himyara, **3,** 65.
enemies of, **3,** 65-6.
war of, with the Nejus of Ethiopia, **3,** 66.
end of, **3,** 66.
Zorba-me-Rabbanan, master of the Law in Babylonia, **2,** 544.
Zoroaster, the doctrines of, restored by Ardashir, **2,** 524.
Zosina, Russian metropolitan, joins a Judaizing sect, **4,** 633.
Zuhara, castle of the Benu-Nadhir, **3,** 78.
Zunz, Leopold, founder of the Society for Culture, **5,** 583.
staunchness of, **5,** 587-8.
uses Rapoport's methods, **5,** 620.
issues his first great work, **5,** 620-1.
contributor to the "Kerem Chemed," **5,** 622.
on the blood accusation, **5,** 669.
on Jewish mediæval poetry, **5,** 694.
Zurich, the Jews of, charged with poisoning wells, **4,** 105.
Zütphen, adviser of the Duke of Alva, **4,** 662.
Zutra. *See* Mar-Zutra.
Zwingli, declares himself against the papacy, **4,** 469.